Peter Hart was born in 1955, and went to Liverpool University before joining the Sound Archive at the Imperial War Museum in January 1981. As the Museum's Oral Historian his work primarily involves him in interviewing war veterans.

By Peter Hart
Bloody April

By Peter Hart and Nigel Steel
Defeat at Gallipoli
Tumult in the Clouds
Passchendaele
Jutland 1916

THE SOMME

PETER HART

CASSELL

Cassell Military Paperbacks

Cassell
Wellington House, 125 Strand
London WC2R 0BB

5 7 9 10 8 6 4

First published in 2005
by Weidenfeld & Nicolson
This Cassell Military Paperbacks edition 2006

British Library Cataloguing-in-Publication Data.
A catalogue record for this book is available
from the British Library.

ISBN-13 978-0-3043-6735-1
ISBN-10 0-3043-6735-4

Printed and bound in Great Britain by
Clays Ltd, St Ives plc

To my favourites:
Polly, Lily and Ruby

Contents

List of Maps

Preface

The Battle of the Somme will always be controversial. By the early 1960s a stark image was firmly established in the public consciousness of long lines of men marching bravely to their futile deaths, cut down in their thousands by massed German machine guns. The casualties were beyond comprehension with 57,470 British casualties on the first day alone. Of these a staggering 19,240 were killed. The unimaginative generalship of bewhiskered idiots safe in their chateau headquarters far behind the lines was roundly pilloried on all sides. This slaughter of the innocents was deftly portrayed by the theatrical production and film *Oh! What a Lovely War*. Slowly, however, another view began to emerge that took account of the problems faced by General Sir Douglas Haig and his subordinate commanders. This more sympathetic perspective recognised the sheer complexity of modern warfare. It saw that there was a grim necessity to wear down the might of the German Empire on the battlefields of the Western Front before there could be any hope of victory. It discussed the 'learning curve' that had to be surmounted before the new legions of the British Empire could gain the skills required of the new 'all arms' tactics that would finally defeat the German Army in 1918. The controversy rages on to this day: raw emotive sentiments and folk myths vying with the academic assessments of military historians such as the great John Terraine.

There is no doubt that the Somme *was* a tragedy and the massed slaughter and endless suffering it epitomises cannot simply be brushed aside by the justification of cold-blooded military necessity. Although the British Army used the Battle of the Somme *de facto* as a primer to emerge as a stronger fighting machine, the 'learning curve' theory is not a mantra that can deflect all criticism. Yet, it is equally inane to adopt the morbid sentimentality of portraying the men who took part as helpless victims, mere stooges in a titanic battle that somehow engulfed them all unawares. On the contrary, many were actively looking forward to the moment when they could finally prove themselves as fully-fledged 'warriors'. When engulfed in the fighting many confirmed themselves as brave men in the most dreadful and terrifying of circumstances. Others, unsurprisingly, faltered. But they were not sheep-like victims: such descriptions do a considerable disservice to the memory of a large number of heavily armed soldiers, confident in their abilities, who would have killed their enemies – if only they had had the chance.

Neither was the First World War the result of the machinations of a few politicians and their 'henchmen' generals. We should never allow ordinary people to abrogate their role in the genesis of Armageddon, either then or now. War in 1914 was the near-inevitable result of the frequently expressed wishes and prevailing attitudes of the British population – it was hence a national responsibility. Popular jingoism was certainly stirred then as now, by cynical politicians and morally opaque newspaper proprietors; however, it had its wellspring deep within the dark corners of the popular consciousness. The political imperatives of defending the bloated empire, the endemic racism and all-embracing casual assumption of moral superiority of the age, the overwhelming reliance on blunt threats to achieve what might have been better achieved by subtle diplomacy – these were all part of the British heritage in 1914. All social classes in the Home Country benefited to some extent from the operation of the global British Empire. Amidst the ceaseless jockeying of the old European Continental and Imperial powers, additionally complicated by the remorseless rise of the militaristic new German Empire, conflict was inevitable and in truth no one did much to avoid a war that was easily portrayed as a crusade. War was a risk, casually accepted. When it arrived it was not as they had imagined, but by then it was too late. The remorseless rhythms of global war had already wrapped themselves around the British Empire.

In battle, for the most part their leaders had plans that, although built at times on shaky foundations, were pretty sound in themselves. The generals were not stupid; they were no 'donkeys'. Their military education had been accelerated beyond all pre-war comprehension, but they had for the most part struggled through, just as one would expect of men who stood near the peak of their chosen profession. Mistakes were frequent and there were undoubtedly some outright blunders. Yet several generals proved themselves to be rapid learners. New and old weapons were eventually slotted into their correct place in the great complex puzzle of war. Above all the primacy of the artillery was recognised. Throughout, although the exigencies of military necessity were their primary concern, the British Army commanders did stand accountable for the consequences of their decisions. The British generals held most responsible for the Battle of the Somme – Douglas Haig, Henry Rawlinson and Hubert Gough – knew full well that the men they sent into battle would pay the price for *their* actions and misjudgements. It was a grave responsibility that they did not shirk.

Even blessed with hindsight, there are still real difficulties in making a final judgement on the overall conduct of the Somme campaign. All this book can do is to try to show what the generals were attempting and chart the effects of their decisions on the men who served them. In the end it is inevitable that the interpretation of such a complicated mélange of issues is a deeply personal matter; in essence the reader must make up their own mind as to what degree the Battle of the Somme was militarily justified.

The general approach adopted in this book is to provide an outline of events within which I have layered personal accounts to help bring dry facts and complex concepts to life. The contemporary quality and vivid writing of the veterans, the raw emotions of participants in a calamity, these cannot be matched by the musings of inevitably distanced modern commentators. There is a vitality, a pathos, even a beauty in the unsullied words of those who were actually present while history was being made around them, qualities that cannot be faked. I have been led by the power of these sources to concentrate where they most eloquently reveal a general truth. Anything else would lead to an uncomfortable amount of repetition without making the salient points any clearer.

My main interest is in the insights into the human condition granted by studying the conduct of men of all ranks under conditions of incredible stress, fear and suffering. All of life is here amidst the reeking dead. The gallant young officer leading his men to death or glory: his reward in the main dull oblivion, but just occasionally, a Victoria Cross and a life marked out as a wondrous oddity. The stolid sergeant, solicitous of his men, critical of their manifold faults during the long months of training, yet willing, when needs must, to die to save them from the consequences of their foolish mistakes in action. The feckless private, drunk and brawling out of the line, good for nothing, the 'scum of the earth', yet transformed by the 'grace' of battle into a hero, battling forward when all but hope had gone, risking his life for reasons he surely could not comprehend. These clichés will be made flesh in this book. For such near-caricatures certainly did exist.

However, the unpublished memoirs, personal letters, diaries and recorded interviews that I have used also reveal their complex motivations and it is the purpose of this book to interpret these. How could men voluntarily walk into the fire of the machine guns and the crunching maelstrom of massed shell fire? Was it duty or sheer grit and determination? Was it to prove something to themselves, that they too were men, as good as any around them? Was it a hatred of 'Hunnish' Germans, a desire for revenge for relatives and friends already lost in battle? Or was it a conviction that God was on their side, perhaps even that the day of Armageddon had truly dawned and that they must stand up to be counted in the final battle? And, after all, most of their best friends were going over the top with them. Was it the comradeship engendered by the ordinary experiences of their former lives – the classroom, the Sunday school, the factory floor, the office, the pit, the merry banter of the pub, the casual crudities of barrack-room life – that carried them forward almost despite themselves? Were others simply trapped when the whistles blew, too scared to escape from the mess in which they were embroiled, left with no alternative in those final grim moments before they went over the top?

Peter Hart

2005

CHAPTER ONE

The Rocky Road

> We do not live alone in Europe but with three other powers that hate and envy us.[1]
>
> Prince Otto von Bismarck, Chancellor of Imperial Germany

The Battle of the Somme was the direct result of the British government abandoning their traditional maritime geo-political strategy. In previous European conflicts Britain had sought to stand back and minimise her involvement in Continental land campaigns. Wherever possible Britain would use her economic strength to inveigle her Allies into bearing the bulk of the fighting while addressing herself to the far more profitable agenda of preying on the overseas colonies of her enemies. Britain's strength was based on the Royal Navy and the pre-eminence of her maritime empire. Unlike the Continental powers who were forced to raise huge armies able to compete with the equally powerful countries that surrounded them, the British Isles were just that – islands – unattainable unless her enemies could first comprehensively defeat the Royal Navy.

British global strategy in the nineteenth century could be encapsulated within three simple rules of thumb. Firstly, the Royal Navy would be maintained in accordance with a 'two power standard' – it must be equal, or better still, superior to the strength of the next two naval powers. Secondly, no one country should be allowed to secure domination of Europe – in particular the coastline of Belgium and the Netherlands should not be occupied or controlled by any of the Great Powers. In essence this was perceived as buffer territory, intended to prevent any army gaining a base from which an effective invasion of the British Isles could be mounted with minimal warning. Thirdly, the British Empire was to be defended, and where possible expanded, across the globe to provide the resources and markets that fuelled the economy. These 'eternal and perpetual' policies may have seemed defensive to the British, but they were highly aggressive to other Great Powers who found themselves constantly baulked by the British in attempting to chart their own course to a global empire.

The overall dynamic of power in Europe was complicated following the rapid rise of the German Empire. Since the defeat of Napoleon in 1815 successive British governments had devoted much of their time to suspiciously monitoring and countering the real and imagined activities of France and Russia. France was an obvious cause of concern – she already had ports just across the Channel and had thus been the traditional enemy since time immemorial, and she was still considered a potent threat to British colonial ambitions in Africa and the Middle East. Russia meanwhile was seen as a looming menace to the jewel of the British Empire – India. Now, however, there was a new Continental power. Germany had not only the military might to threaten domination of the European mainland, but also the burgeoning industrial and manufacturing base to threaten British economic interests.

Germany was determined to carve out a new colonial empire in China and Africa and equally determined to build a navy fit to challenge any fleet afloat. The successive German Naval Laws commencing in 1898 specifically set out the size of the fleet they wished to achieve and their promulgation struck directly at the heart of British concerns in a manner that they could not ignore. The massive German Army had already proved itself the dominant military force in Europe by defeating the Austrians in 1866 and the French in 1870. Ever since 1882, Germany had been at the heart of the powerful Triple Alliance alongside Austria–Hungary and Italy. Now the Germans appeared to want to supplement this with a significant element of naval power. If Germany was to achieve her aims then others must surrender power and as such her rise was a direct economic, colonial and naval challenge to the hegemony exerted by the British Empire. Inevitably Germany came to be perceived as the main threat and gradually her enemies came to be viewed as putative friends.

Towards the end of the nineteenth century the French and the Russians had been driven to resolve their own multifarious differences by the threat posed by their common enemy in Imperial Germany. At first they merely pledged to assist each other in the event of a German attack, but slowly their affiliation deepened as the threat from the Triple Alliance was perceived to grow. Britain was soon determined to resolve her differences with France and Russia – differences that seemed to melt away with every battleship launched by the German shipyards. The relationship was formalised in the *Entente Cordiale* signed with France in 1904. Year by year increasing diplomatic tension and the precautionary countermeasures taken by both sides only served to create an overall mood of a Europe simmering in crisis.

But what could Britain offer the *Entente Cordiale*? The first part was obvious – the power and global reach of the Royal Navy would deliver maritime superiority at a stroke. An arrangement with the French fleet left the bulk of the Royal Navy free to concentrate its power against the German fleet across the North Sea. What they could *not* offer was a powerful standing army. The British Army was established as a force to garrison the far-flung empire and as a mobile strike force to be swiftly deployed by sea to any developing point of conflict. It was certainly not an army capable of playing a significant part in a full-scale Continental war – it was simply too small. From the German standpoint the *Entente Cordiale* offered an encircling threat – with the Russians to the east, the French to the west and the British balefully eyeing them across the North Sea, they seemed to be surrounded by enemies. German diplomacy seemed unable to resolve the conundrum and various ham-fisted attempts to break up the *Entente Cordiale* merely had the effect of pushing their putative enemies still closer together. The expensive continuation and escalation of the naval race following the genesis of HMS *Dreadnought* in 1906 provoked a significant groundswell of anti-German feeling right across Britain.

Slowly the British Army began to be drawn into the Continental equation. The hearts and minds of the Royal Navy were concentrated only on a great naval set-piece battle with the German High Seas Fleet and they inevitably spared little thought for the type of operations that had typified the British approach in previous wars. In the resulting vacuum it became accepted in joint army staff talks with the French that the British Expeditionary Force (BEF) – small though it may be – might mark the difference in the coming battle between the mighty French and German armies and ought therefore to be deployed on the mainland. Thus it was over the next few years mobilisation plans were laid for the six divisions of the BEF under the Commander-in-Chief General Sir John French to cross the Channel and enter the main Continental war alongside the mighty sixty-two divisions of the French Army.

War, when it came, was triggered by the assassination of Archduke Franz Ferdinand, the heir apparent to the Austro-Hungarian throne, in far away Sarajevo on 28 June 1914. In a sense war was inevitable: *all* the Great Powers harboured essentially selfish ambitions that could not all be achieved without thwarting the aims of other powers. No single power particularly sought war, but equally none did enough to avoid it as the crisis flared through the embassies of Europe during the next few weeks. Serbia was blamed for the assassination and threatened by Austria–Hungary: Germany supported Austria–Hungary, Russia supported Serbia; Germany threatened Russia: France supported Russia, and so the ultimatums and mobilisations began, until there was no longer any room for talking. When Austria–Hungary declared war on Serbia on 28 July 1914, Britain simply could not stand by. The German invasion of Belgium on 3 August triggered all the traditional British foreign policy concerns and if Britain abandoned her commitments to her European Allies it would inevitably lead to her utter diplomatic isolation – she would be alone in a dangerous world. Britain really had no choice and finally declared war on 4 August. To a large extent the British still saw their role as naval and although the BEF would be sent to fight alongside the French, as far as the British government was concerned this was an afterthought.

War brought massed crowds out in celebration on the streets of cities all across Europe. War was exciting, a break from the dull routine of the factory, the office, the mines and farms. It evoked strong notions of chivalry and national pride in the populations of all the belligerent nations. Underpinning this enthusiasm was the widespread conviction that the war would be relatively quick and painless; all nicely wrapped up with a crushing victory before Christmas. It is important to emphasise, however, that not everyone reacted with such jubilation and confidence: realists feared the catastrophic effect of war on society across Europe, and many socialist and workers' groups had real concerns and doubts. There were even pacifists opposed to the very idea of war on religious or moral grounds. Yet, nevertheless, the clear majority of people across Europe undoubtedly welcomed war. As such they did not act as a brake to the machinations and posturing of their governments but cheered them on even as they collectively careered towards the horror of the Great War.

The German war plan envisaged a violent thrust through Belgium to push on into northern France, swinging round behind the main French armies to seize Paris and thereby secure victory at a stroke. Meanwhile, a defensive front would be established in the East to thwart any attempted advance of the Russian 'steamroller'. The French Army had nurtured a blind faith in the powers of the offensive rather than its previous rather more pragmatic reliance on an immensely strong series of concrete forts, typified by those at Verdun, built to defend the Franco-German frontier. It would instead charge blindly forward into the 'lost' provinces of Alsace-Lorraine, forfeited in the aftermath of France's humiliating defeat in the Franco-Prussian War of 1870. The results were predictable as the French, dressed in the brightly coloured red and blue uniforms more attuned to another age of warfare, were duly slaughtered by the weapons of the twentieth century. By the end of 1914 the French had suffered an incredible 955,000 casualties.

As the French charged to their doom, the German columns were marching through Belgium and the almost undefended Franco-Belgian frontier. Here they encountered an unconsidered trifle – the BEF under the command of General Sir John French, which in accordance with mobilisation plans had moved up to Maubeuge to take its allotted place on the left of the French line. The British found themselves right in the path of the onrushing German juggernaut at the Battle of Mons on 23 August. In the succession of desperate defensive actions that followed as the British fell back into France, the quality of the British regulars seemed apparent, but their trusty Lee Enfield rifles could not stop the masses of well-trained German soldiers who were equally committed to the cause of their country. As the situation teetered in the balance the tiring Germans began to falter in their final approach to Paris, just as the French dredged up sufficient troops to launch a flanking thrust of their own and together with the BEF created the 'miracle' of the Marne. The Germans were forced back through France until they made a determined stand in swiftly dug trenches ranging along the easily defensible ridges behind the Aisne River.

The swirling, sidelong race to the sea followed as attempts were made by both sides to turn their opponents flank, bouncing and cannoning from each other in desperate encounter battles. There was much slaughter on both sides, but the battle for the key Belgian town of Ypres was fought with a particular intensity in mid-October. Ypres guarded the approach to the Channel ports, the linchpin of the BEF communications back to Britain. The German Army suffered grievous casualties at the Battle of Ypres, but at the same time the battle consumed the bulk of the original BEF. The British fought to the end and at the last gasp managed to hold back the Germans from a breakthrough that at one point seemed all but inevitable. Stalemate ensued and the trenches stretched in unbroken lines from Switzerland to the North Sea.

Trenches were not a new development. They had been used many times in warfare especially during the sieges of fortresses and cities. What made the problem so intense for the generals of both sides was the power of modern weapons acting in concert. Belts of barbed wire slowed the approach of attacking infantry to the trench and gave the defending troops ample opportunity to pour in rapid rifle and machine-gun fire from the relative safety of their own trenches. But the real difference lay in the destructive potential of massed modern artillery. Superficially it appeared to offer the opportunity to easily sweep away the barbed wire and trenches in a welter of shrapnel and high explosive. Yet both sides had artillery. If the defending batteries were not knocked out of action, then they would let loose a devastating fire of their own when the attacking infantry advanced into the open across No Man's Land. Even if the front line was captured the support and reserve lines of trenches still stood in front of the attacking troops and the defending reserves would rush to counter-attack. Any kind of breakthrough was extremely difficult to achieve.

In 1915 both sides made attempts to break free from the constraints imposed on them by the lines of trenches, but the strategic imperative was clear: the Germans had possession of a large and economically invaluable tranche of France and Belgium. As this situation could not be allowed to continue, the French and their British Allies had to drive them out. The French launched numerous offensives and fought with a savage desperation to reclaim their homeland, but were held back by the brutal realities of trench warfare. The casualty lists grew, casting a black shadow over countless families across France. The British were also flexing their muscles as the BEF slowly began to grow in size. The first real attempt at a breakthrough was made by the First Army under the command of General

Sir Douglas Haig at the Battle of Neuve Chapelle on 10 March 1915.

Douglas Haig was born on 19 June 1861. Educated at Clifton College and Brasenose College, Oxford, he entered the Royal Military College, Sandhurst as a cadet in 1884. Here he had found his vocation and applied his considerable intelligence and disciplined personality to mastering his chosen career. After service as a regimental officer with the 7th Hussars he went to the Staff College at Camberley in 1896 where he gained a theoretical understanding of war that coloured much of his subsequent career. His first real active service experience occurred in a typical colonial conflict as a staff officer in the Sudan in 1898. During the Boer War, Haig was given command of one of the many small columns trying to snuff out the Boer commandos. By this time Haig had been marked out as a very promising officer and he was soon rewarded with command of the 17th Lancers and appointment as the *aide de camp* to King Edward VII. His career then flourished. He was appointed first as Inspector General of Cavalry and then promoted major general and became Director of Military Training at the War Office. At this point Richard Haldane, the Liberal Secretary of State for War, was engaged in a thorough overhaul of the structure of the British Army. Haig was tasked with creating a new Territorial Army out of the mish-mash of part-time volunteer units that served as Britain's second line.

Haig's capacity for hard work and analytical abilities were much prized and the next mark of high approbation was his appointment as chief of staff in India. He struggled with the inherent problems in the Indian Army until he was rescued by another promotion to lieutenant general and made commander-in-chief at Aldershot in 1912 – the home of the British Army. Here he was responsible for training and preparing the two divisions under his command ready to take up their wartime role as the I Corps within the BEF. Haig had already developed a firm belief in some of the classic principles of war, which decreed that any conflict would go through several stages: the initial manoeuvring for position, the first clash of battle, then the wearing out process of indeterminate length before one side began to fold and the decisive stroke could then be struck home. This conviction would endure throughout the war but his somewhat naive early belief that the power of 'the spirit' could overcome an inferiority of numbers, arms or training would soon wither from exposure to harsh reality. Haig also believed that any decision, even if misguided, was better than indecision and that a bad plan resolutely pursued was better than a good plan that was not pushed through vigorously.

Haig took his I Corps across to France and into Belgium where it played a full part in the open warfare of the 1914 campaign. He drew a key lesson from his personal experiences in the First Battle of Ypres in October 1914, where he was convinced that the day would have been lost had the Germans only persevered in their attacks a little while longer. This was to colour much of his subsequent thinking about the merits of hammering on in battle, in the hope and expectation of finally triggering the sudden collapse of a staggering enemy and thereby capitalising on all the hard fighting and sacrifices already invested. As the BEF expanded he was promoted to full general in command of the First Army made up of the IV and Indian Corps in December 1914. Now he was charged with the overall responsibility of attempting to pinch out the German salient that jutted into the British line at the village of Neuve Chapelle. His subordinate, General Sir Henry Rawlinson as the commander of the IV Corps, was charged with the task of drawing up the actual battle plans.

Henry Rawlinson was a highly respected professional officer who had a distinguished military career. Born on 20 February 1864, he was the privileged son of a diplomat. Educated at Eton he was soon destined for the army and passed through the Royal Military College, Sandhurst before serving in India for much of his early career. As a young officer he amassed useful experience in colonial campaigns in the Myanmar expedition, chasing dacoits in Burma during 1886–7. Following these adventures he returned to Britain and passed through Staff College. As a staff officer he served under Lord Kitchener in the successful Sudan campaign of 1898. When the Boer War broke out in 1899 he was caught up in the disastrous start to the campaign and besieged in Ladysmith until it was finally relieved in the spring of 1900. Afterwards he served both on the staff and in command of independent columns of troops trying to hunt down the Boer commandos. His reputation was enhanced by these episodes and on his return once more to England he was given various prestigious appointments, including commandant of the Staff College, before being given command of an infantry brigade and then a division at Aldershot. On the outbreak of war, Rawlinson was given command first of the 4th Division operating on the Aisne in September 1914, and then of the makeshift IV Corps, which was sent to assist the Belgian Army in the doomed campaign

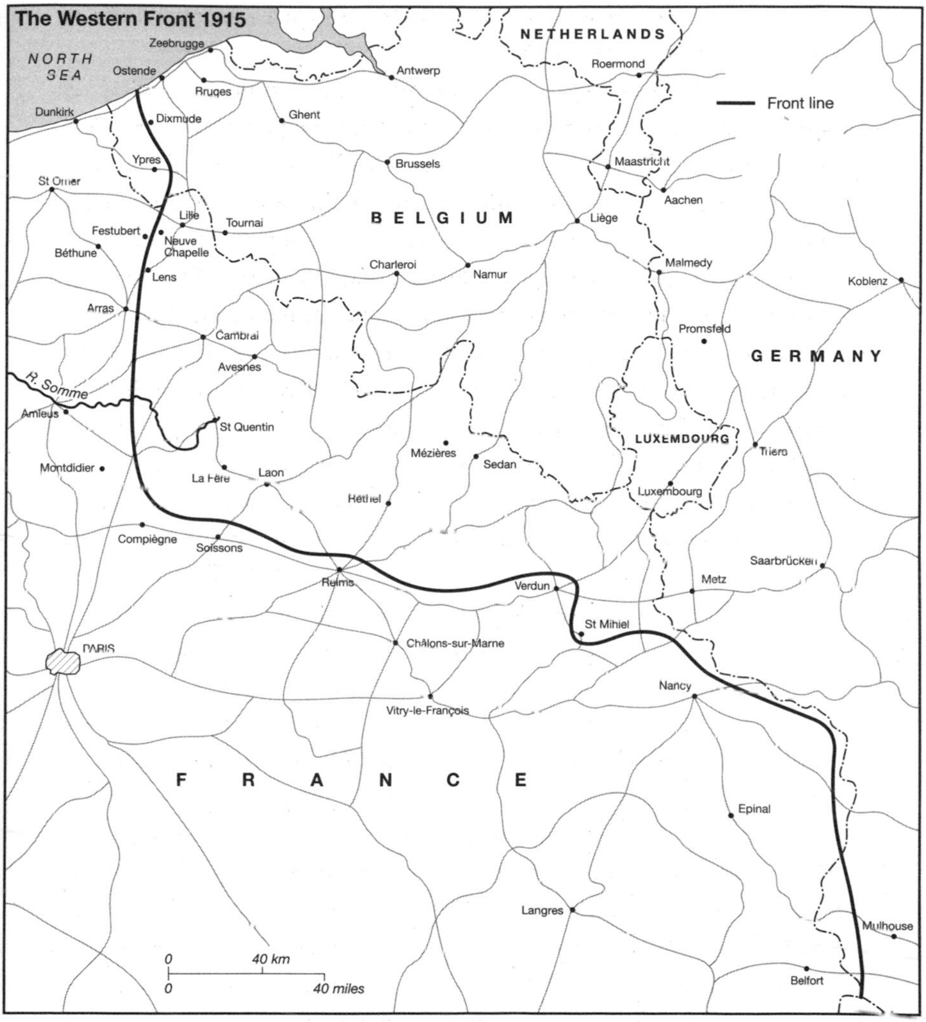
The Western Front 1915
NORTH SEA
Zeebrugge
Ostende
Dunkirk
Bruges
Ghent
Antwerp
NETHERLANDS
Roermond
Front line
Dixmude
Ypres
St Omer
Maastricht
Brussels
Aachen
Lille
Festubert
Tournai
BELGIUM
Liège
Neuve Chapelle
Béthune
Lens
Charleroi
Namur
Malmedy
Koblenz
Arras
Cambrai
Promsfeld
Avesnes
GERMANY
R. Somme
Amiens
St Quentin
LUXEMBOURG
Mézières
Trier
Montdidier
Sedan
La Fère
Laon
Rethel
Luxembourg
Compiègne
Soissons
Saarbrücken
Reims
Verdun
Metz
St Mihiel
PARIS
Châlons-sur-Marne
Nancy
Vitry-le-François
FRANCE
Epinal
Langres
Mulhouse
0
40 km
0
40 miles
Belfort

to save Antwerp in October 1914. The Corps subsequently joined the main body of the army just in time for the First Battle of Ypres.

For the battle of Neuve Chapelle, Rawlinson and his headquarters staff had under their command the 7th and 8th Divisions that together made up the IV Corps. In planning to pinch out the Neuve Chapelle salient they conceived of a revolutionary new plan to use the power of massed artillery to smash a way through for his men into the German lines. In this he was certainly ahead of many of his fellow generals of the time. He summed up his views pithily: 'It is primarily an artillery operation and if the artillery cannot crush and demoralise the enemy's infantry by their fire effect the enterprise will not succeed.' [2] It is ironic that in this, the first major British offensive against the German lines, so much was done in accordance with what would become accepted as 'best practice' in the last two years of the war. A concentration of some 340 guns along the 2,000 yards frontage of the assaulting IV and Indian Corps meant that there was a ration of one gun for every 6 yards of the front attacked. Even more impressively in view of the difficulty in moving heavy guns this was all achieved without significantly alerting the Germans. Then a crushing hurricane-style short bombardment flayed the barbed wire and smashed down the relatively weak German defences. Photographs and artillery observation carried out by the Royal Flying Corps were used to direct the power of the massed guns to maximum effect.

Yet for all the innovations the battle was still a painful experience for the British Army. Although the ruined village of Neuve Chapelle was duly captured and the line straightened, the attempts made to try and push on to the next raft of objectives proved painfully expensive against the massed German reinforcements who rushed to the scene. Rawlinson had always been of the opinion that the attack should be suspended after the capture of the immediate localised objective of Neuve Chapelle, but when ordered by Haig to try and achieve more for the massive investment of men and materials he swallowed his objections and pressed home the attacks with every appearance of enthusiasm. However, a breakthrough on such an easily plugged narrow front was impossible and in the end the First Army suffered 11,652 casualties. A pattern of behaviour had been established between Haig and Rawlinson that both would repeat time and time again on the Somme.

Rawlinson was a man of considerable intelligence who had already divined the holy grail of successful generalship on the Western Front in 1916 – don't aim too high.

> What we want to do now is what I call, 'bite and hold'. Bite off a piece of the enemy's line, like Neuve Chapelle, and hold it against counter-attack. The bite can be made without much loss, and, if we choose the right place and make every preparation to put it quickly in a state of defence, there ought to be no difficulty in holding it against the enemy's counter-attacks and inflicting on him at least twice the loss that we have suffered in making the bite.[3]
>
> Lieutenant General Sir Henry Rawlinson, Headquarters, Forth Army

Of course, this was simply not possible in 1915. There was a lack of guns and ammunition to carry out the pulverising bombardments on a sufficient scale. The other problem for Rawlinson was that this slow step-by-step process did not appeal to the prevailing mood of the British and French senior command. General Sir John French and General Joseph Joffre were determined to finish the war in 1915 and thus constitutionally disinclined to take a longer more painstaking route to success.

It is also sadly true that although Rawlinson seemed to have intuitively grasped the essence of 'bite and hold' he did not himself adhere to its principles in action if pressed forward by his seniors. At the attack on Aubers Ridge on 8 May 1915 there was not only slightly less artillery per yard of front than at Neuve Chapelle (one for every 8 yards) but the bombardment also included all three trench lines. This left the German front line receiving far fewer shells and introduced the very real possibility that the British would never get across No Man's Land. This is precisely what happened. The almost intact German garrison simply manned their machine guns and shot the advancing battalions to pieces resulting in over 11,000 casualties to no practical gain whatsoever.

By the time of the Battle of Loos in September 1915, Haig had three corps in his First Army. The opening assault would be made by Rawlinson's IV Corps fighting alongside the I Corps commanded by Lieutenant General Sir Hubert Gough, whom Haig considered an extremely promising officer. Hubert Gough was born in Ireland on 12 August 1870. He attended Eton before passing through Sandhurst and undergoing a lengthy stint as a regimental officer with the 16th Lancers in India from 1890, which culminated in an attachment to the Tirah expedition on the

North West Frontier in 1897–8. He then attended Staff College in 1899. During the Boer War he saw considerable active service and marked himself out as a thrusting young officer in command of a composite cavalry regiment acting as a mobile column. Disaster, however, claimed him when he boldly attacked a party of some 200 Boers, who turned out to be only a detachment from a much larger grouping of about 1,000 Boers in the valley of the aptly named Blood River on 17 September 1901. As a result Gough and most of his men were first surrounded and then captured. It took all his considerable initiative to conceal his identity from the naturally inquisitive Boers and then to escape. He continued to lead his mobile column until he was finally wounded in the hand and arm in a skirmish and sent home to recuperate.

Gough served from 1903 to 1906 on the directing staff of the Staff College, which was then under the command of Rawlinson. A period in command of his old regiment followed from 1907 to 1910 and he soon established close links with Haig, who was at that time also the Inspector General of Cavalry in his other capacity as Director of Military Training. In 1911 Gough was promoted to command the 3rd Cavalry Brigade based at Curragh Camp in Ireland. This nearly destabilised his entire career for the Irishman in him surfaced when he became involved in the Curragh incident in March 1914, threatening to resign rather than suppress Unionist opposition to the Liberal government's proposed Home Rule Bill. The affair burnt out quickly though his career may well have suffered but for the shortage of experienced officers on the outbreak of war a few months later. Gough was quickly promoted to command first the 2nd Cavalry Division, with whom he fought at the First Battle of Ypres, and then the 7th Division in April 1915. His next promotion to lieutenant general was startlingly quick. He was given command of the I Army Corps within Haig's First Army. The Battle of Loos would be his first great test as a corps commander.

It was a daunting prospect that faced these commanders. The British Army was still cripplingly short of guns and ammunition. Yet Sir John French had no choice but to order Haig to attack, for Joffre was adamant that the British must attack in strength on the widest possible front as part of the overall plan for a huge French autumn offensive in the Champagne and Artois regions. In their turn Rawlinson and Gough were chivvied on by Haig. A decision was made to use clouds of poisonous gas to make up for the shortfall of guns. The Germans had used a surprise gas attack earlier in the year on 22 April to launch the Second Battle of Ypres – they had nearly broken through when the arrival of British reserves managed at the last gasp to seal the line just short of Ypres itself. Rawlinson remained generally pessimistic as to the chances of any real success. There simply were not enough guns, shells or men for the scale of attack that was being undertaken. The I and IV Corps between them had just 533 guns facing an 11,200-yard front, which included two strong German trench lines covered by thick belts of barbed wire.

The preliminary bombardment was designed to last for four days prior to the release of the gas and the infantry attack. This then was no hurricane bombardment and there was no element of surprise. Despite some prevaricating over the wind direction, the attack went ahead with a final artillery bombardment and the release of the gas clouds at 0530 to presage the infantry attack at 0610 on 25 September 1915. The results were patchy in the extreme, but even so in some sectors the speed of advance by the infantry across No Man's Land occasionally allowed them to surprise the Germans before they could emerge from their deep dugouts. Yet the German second line was not taken and the British reserve formations from the IX Corps were delayed in coming forward through a frustrating confusion in command and control that was later blamed on Sir John French. As a result the German reinforcements arrived first and the offensive petered out in a welter of attacks that achieved nothing.

Even as new offensive tactics were being developed in the painful laboratory of the Western Front so defensive tactics were mutating to counter them. Barbed wire belts thickened exponentially, trenches became deeper and better sited to secure raking fields of fire, dugouts were deeper and substantially reinforced by the use of concrete, while villages and farms became fortresses, support lines were properly integrated to cover the front lines and the once sketchy reserve lines gradually became fully-fledged defensive systems in their own right.

The failure at Loos was unacceptable to the British government and people. This time a scapegoat was required. A confusion over the method and speed of deployment of the reserve troops was seized upon and, after considerable intrigue amongst the soldiers and politicians, on 19 December 1915 Field Marshal Sir John French was summarily dismissed. He was replaced as commander of the BEF by his erstwhile subordinate, General Sir Douglas Haig.

AS COMMANDER-IN-CHIEF of the BEF Douglas Haig was the dominating figure in the history of the British Army for the duration of the war on the Western Front. The responsibility on his shoulders was truly immense. It happened that Haig's birth certificate accidentally omitted his Christian name and there was indeed a slightly chilly remoteness that clung to Haig throughout his life. Hard working, with a driving sense of duty, he was self-sufficient and seemed to live only for the army. Even his devoted wife was not privy to his inner depths: 'All who knew Douglas will know of his extraordinary reserve (true to Scots type), and he had told me very little of what he had done before I married him.'[4] Cool, calm and aloof, his chiselled jaw and flinty blue eyes seem to have expressed much of the essence of the man within.

Unfailingly polite and even-tempered, he possessed an equable temperament that did not betray any trace of panic or temper no matter how grim the state of affairs at the front. Indeed, his wisest recorded words in conversation were probably, 'The situation is never so bad or so good as first reports indicate'.[5] Mere expressions of opinion were irrelevant to him and he demanded reasoned arguments based on facts before making any decision. Increasingly religious as he grew older, Haig became possessed of a firm belief in his own destiny. He had a deep and abiding confidence in his own powers of judgement and would not revisit decisions already taken unless new evidence was brought before him.

His own usual chronic inarticulacy was both explained and excused by the staff officers who knew him best – it was his very speed of thought that thereby outran his tongue and caused him to disconcertingly break off sentences or omit the verbs normally considered essential to verbal communication. They pointed to the force and clarity of thought as demonstrated in his self-written work to indicate his true level of intellect. Nevertheless, he frequently lapsed into long periods of gruff silence that could be disconcerting to those who did not know him, although his faithful staff swore it did not reflect any underlying sourness of mood. One brief quote sums it up in a nutshell: 'He was obviously in very good spirits, and kept silence merrily.'[6]

Haig's capacity for sustained hard work was formidable. His General Headquarters were soon moved into a small château located just outside the town of Montreuil. There his office was dominated by a huge map of the Western Front and an empty desk that betrayed his indomitable work ethic. Haig believed in clearing each day's work as it came. His personal routine was metronomic.

> Punctually at 8.25 each morning Haig's bedroom door opened and he walked downstairs. In the hall was a barometer, and he invariably stopped in front of the instrument to tap it, though he rarely took any particular note of the reading. He then went for a short four minutes' walk in the garden. At 8.30 precisely he came into the mess for breakfast. If he had a guest present, he always insisted on serving the guest before he helped himself. He talked very little, and generally confined himself to asking his personal staff what their plans were for the day. At nine o'clock he went into his study and worked until eleven or half past. At half past eleven he saw army commanders, the heads of departments at General Headquarters, and others whom he might desire to see. At one o'clock he had lunch, which only lasted half an hour, and then he either motored or rode to the Headquarters of some army or corps or division. Generally when returning from these visits he would arrange for his horse to meet the car so that he could travel the last 3 or 4 miles on horseback. When not motoring he always rode in the afternoon, accompanied by an ADC and his escort of 17th Lancers, without which he never went out for a ride. Always on the return journey from his ride he would stop about 3 miles from home and hand his horse over to a groom and walk back to Headquarters. On arrival there he would go straight up to his room, have a bath, do his physical exercises and then change into slacks. From then until dinner-time at eight o'clock he would sit at his desk and work, but he was always available if any of his staff or guests wished to see him. He never objected to interruptions at this hour. At eight o'clock he dined. After dinner, which lasted about an hour, he returned to his room and worked until a quarter to eleven.[7]
>
> Brigadier General John Charteris, General Headquarters, BEF

And so to bed. This routine was only rarely broken. The visitors to Haig's headquarters were courteously treated but some of them found his austere hospitality somewhat inhibiting. On one memorable visit the Prime Minister Herbert Asquith was driven almost to distraction by his puritanical host.

> D.H. has some excellent old brandy, which, however, he only sends round once at each meal; after that it stands in solitary grandeur in front of him on the table. The Prime Minister obviously appreciated it very much and wished for more, but did not feel that he could ask for another glass. His method of achieving his aim was to move his glass a little nearer the bottle and then try and catch D.H.'s eye and draw it down to his glass and then to the bottle. The glass advanced by stages as small as those of our attack, until, last of all, it was resting against the bottle; then, overcoming all his scruples, the Prime Minister, with a sweep of the arm, seized the bottle and poured himself out a glass. I was sitting opposite and the by-play was indescribably funny. D.H. did not notice it at all. When I told it to him afterwards his comment was, 'If he has not enough determination to ask for a glass of brandy when he wants it he should not be Prime Minister.'[8]
>
> Brigadier General John Charteris, General Headquarters, BEF

The passage is almost too revealing for all concerned. Asquith's anguish may have been real – he had already acquired the undesirable sobriquet of 'Squiffy' with all that this entailed; while Haig's general lack of awareness or sensitivity is equally amusing. But then, as was so often the case with Haig, it is incontrovertible that he had drawn the right lesson from the incident – once it had been brought to his notice.

Much of what Brigadier John Charteris considered admirable about Haig could be and has been, frequently turned on its head by those inclined to be critical of his beloved chief. Thus his lack of any facility or sympathy for intuitive reasoning; his stubbornness once he had made up his mind; his anal retentive mindset and habits; his easily caricatured inarticulacy and occasional social ineptness – these have been commonly held perceptions of the great man. Yet as the responsibilities of his command are almost unimaginable perhaps we should not be surprised that Haig needed hard facts before making decisions that would commit his men to battle; that he would not arbitrarily chop and change his best laid plans; that he would work hard all day and every day in the cause of his country for which the men he commanded were risking their lives. As to his restricted, almost stunted lifestyle it is certainly not surprising that anybody under such incredible pressure should need the bolster and reassurance of a set routine, especially one brought up and thoroughly indoctrinated in the ways of the British Army.

Haig, together with General Sir William Robertson who had just been appointed as Chief of the Imperial General Staff back in London, were the foremost 'Westerners': men who made it their determined business to discourage or stamp out all schemes that they considered diluted the war effort in the only place where it really mattered – the Western Front. To them it was blindingly self-evident that Germany was the beating heart of the Central Powers; that without her Austria–Hungary, Bulgaria and Turkey would soon collapse. Germany could not and would not be defeated until her main armies had been defeated in the field. That meant the Western Front. He succinctly summarised his policy in his diary.

> The principles which we must apply are:
> 1. Employ sufficient force to wear down the enemy and cause him to use up his Reserves.
> 2. Then, and not till then, throw in a mass of troops (at some point where the enemy has shown himself to be weak) to break through and win victory.[9]
>
> General Sir Douglas Haig, General Headquarters, BEF

Clearly, given the strength of the German Army, this would be a painful, exhausting process, the casualties on all sides would be dreadful, but they would just have to grit their teeth and get on with it. For Haig and Robertson there was no easy option, no magical solution to the challenge. They may have been unimaginative, they were definitely ruthless when required, but above all they were hard, practical men and they were entirely right.

The 'Easterners', who were led in the first two years of the war by the First Lord of the Admiralty Winston Churchill and subsequently by David Lloyd George, wished to avoid the full implications of engaging in a Continental war on the Western Front and therefore consistently sought another way. They were sentimentally attached to the traditional British strategy of using her omniscient naval power to strike at the periphery of her enemies, seeking to inflict maximum damage at the minimum cost and avoiding entanglement in the bloodbath of Continental warfare. They also held the fervent belief that Germany must have a soft underbelly – if only it could be located. The 'Easterners' looked to strike at Germany via the weaker Central Powers: through Turkey at Gallipoli, Palestine or Mesopotamia; through Bulgaria at Salonika; through Austria–Hungary from an attack launched by Italy.

Yet the military realities of the First World War meant that each of these 'easy' options offered only a mirage of painless success. Trenches could be quickly dug almost anywhere, barbed wire was cheap and a very substantial investment of British troops, guns and munitions would be required before there was any realistic chance of success in any of these theatres of war all of which, coincidentally, seemed to feature the worst extremes of terrain and climate. In seeking new avenues to victory, the 'Easterners' often made new enemies and gave them, too, an opportunity to fight the British and tweak the lion's tail. And of course, as Haig was well aware, every British division so engaged correspondingly weakened Britain's forces amassed on the Western Front in the decisive battle that would determine the outcome of the war. Fundamentally, the 'Easterners' were looking for a shortcut to victory; but shortcuts, as any Gallipoli veteran could have told them, can often lead to setbacks, unforeseen disaster and humiliating defeat. Yet almost every British politician seemed to be looking for an easy way out. Haig's staff endured the visits of the great and the good to General Headquarters with an amused contempt.

> Sooner or later they, one and all, bring the conversation round to the Eastern versus the Western Front problem. That is easy argument, but leaves an uneasy feeling that there is some very strong leaning at home towards easy victories in unimportant theatres, with small casualties and no real results. How on earth one can hope to beat Germany by killing Turks or Bulgars passes comprehension. It is like a prize-fighter leaving the ring to trounce his opponent's seconds.[10]
>
> Brigadier General John Charteris, General Headquarters, BEF

Haig took over command of the BEF at a point when the British Army had achieved a considerably increased stature with some thirty-eight infantry divisions deployed on the Western Front by January 1916 – a total of nearly a million men. The massive recruitment programmes of 1914 and 1915 had duly delivered their harvests of soldiers. The peoples of the empire had also put their shoulder to the wheel: Indians, Australians, New Zealanders, South Africans and Canadians all flocked to the colours. Plans were afoot to send a further batch of New Army and Territorial divisions to the front before the summer of 1916. There was even the promise of the arrival of at least some of the nine assorted divisions that were kicking their heels in the Middle East after the final evacuation of Gallipoli in January 1916. At home the collective strength of the British engineering and manufacturing industries had been fully mobilised onto a war footing, and at last guns and munitions were beginning to pour forth in the unprecedented quantities required for trench warfare. It was two years late from a French perspective, but the British had finally managed to mobilise a force commensurate in size with the inherent potential of the massive British Empire.

Yet Haig was by no means the master of his own destiny. The Minister of War Lord Kitchener had specifically ordered him to cooperate with the French Army as a united army while at the same time maintaining his independence of command.

> I am *not under* General Joffre's orders, but that would make no difference, as my intention was to do my utmost to carry out General Joffre's wishes on strategical matters, as if they were orders.[11]
>
> General Sir Douglas Haig, General Headquarters, BEF

This difficult balancing act was essential. The French Army was still clearly the dominant factor in the alliance – in the field the army numbered some ninety-five infantry divisions in early 1916. When the six Belgian divisions were added into the equation there were some 139 Allied divisions on the Western Front of which twenty-three were available for an offensive in that they were not required in a defensive capacity to hold the line. Much of the overall strategy for the Western Front in 1916 was therefore decided by the French Commander-in-Chief Joseph Joffre.

Born in 1852, Joffre was the son of a cooper and he entered the army as a cadet in 1870. His leadership potential soon became apparent when he took command of an artillery battery during the Paris uprising the same year. After a career serving in the French colonies in Indo-China and later North Africa, he became Director of Engineers in 1904. In 1911 he was made Chief of the General Staff of the French Army and had a major part in the development of the disastrous plan for the frontier offensives on the outbreak of war in August 1914. However, to counter this he was fêted as the man who had stopped the Germans on the Marne.

This then was the man with whom Haig must forge an effective working relationship from a position of *de facto* inferiority. Effective liaison was not easy, given the inevitable stresses and strains of war transmitted down fallible communication lines and interpreted by officers brought up in different social and military cultures. A degree of tolerance on both sides was absolutely essential. The situation was further complicated as Joffre had already agreed the basic programme for 1916 with Haig's predecessor.

> The general lines of the grand strategy for this oncoming year have already been settled between Joffre and Sir John French, a combined and practically simultaneous offensive on the Russian, Italian and this front. Kitchener is doubtful whether France will stand more than another year of war, and thinks unless we win this year, the war will end in stalemate, with another war in the near future, and therefore urges that we must force the issue this year. Much depends upon what reserve of fighting power the French still have. They have borne the brunt so far, but they cannot go on for ever. This next year the big effort must be ours.[12]
>
> Brigadier General John Charteris, General Headquarters, BEF

It is not surprising that the French, who had suffered so terribly in the first two years of the war, were insistent that the British should begin to finally pull their weight in 1916. At the conference held at Joffre's General Headquarters at Chantilly on 6 December 1915 it had already been decided that the Allies should try to negate the Central Powers' advantage of internal communications by launching a joint Anglo-French offensive on the Western Front in concert with simultaneous offensives from Russia and Italy. Haig was fully in agreement with this overall concept but as ever the devil was in the detail. Joffre had already decided that the main attack of the summer should be where the two armies adjoined by the River Somme in Picardy in the summer of 1916. While the French launched an attack south of the Somme the British would attack north of the river.

> The French offensive would be greatly aided by a simultaneous offensive of the British forces between the Somme and Arras. Besides the interest which this last area presents on account of its close proximity to that where the effort of the French armies will be made, I think that it will be a considerable advantage to attack the enemy on a front where for long months the reciprocal activity of the troops opposed to each other has been less than elsewhere. The ground is, besides, in many places favourable to the development of a powerful offensive.[13]
>
> General Joseph Joffre, General Headquarters, French Army

This would entail in total a combined Franco-British attack on a front stretching some 60 miles. It was a hugely ambitious plan. In fact Joffre was being slightly tendentious. His real reason for proposing a joint offensive carried out side by side was to ensure that the French could keep a tight hold of the military agenda and prevent 'postponements' and other backsliding from the British. His stated reasons are almost nonsensical: true, the Somme had been a quiet sector but the German had spent their time wisely in constructing a series of defensive fortifications almost without parallel in warfare up to that time. However, Joffre did not particularly care where the attack was made as long as the British pulled their full weight. He aimed to grind down the German reserves and thereby bring nearer the possibility of a decisive breakthrough offensive to end the war once and for all. The newly promoted Haig had little choice but to fall in with the requirements of the French. Success on the Somme would offer the British no immediate tangible strategic rewards and Haig personally favoured an offensive in Flanders where he could attain the strategic objective of clearing the Belgian coast. Yet in the end he was willing to fall in line with Joffre's plan for the sake of the alliance. Only unity of purpose amongst the Allies could ever defeat the Germans.

There was actually far more debate as to the nature of preliminary operations to be carried out before the main event, with Joffre trenchantly insisting on at least two preparatory spring offensives from the British to wear down the Germans before the main thrust. Haig was only willing to launch one such offensive and the negotiations were at times a little fraught, for he was not willing to accept tactical as opposed to strategical direction from Joffre. The debate, however, would soon be rendered irrelevant as events overtook them.

It is often forgotten that there were two sides striving to win the war on the Western Front – that the Germans, too, were more than capable of making and carrying out their own plans. General Erich von Falkenhayn was the Chief of General Staff (and therefore effective commander) of the Imperial German Army. Falkenhayn had a somewhat pessimistic view of the overall German strategic position and he developed a plan for a new offensive against the French which was designed to capitalise on the 1.43 million casualties already inflicted on the French nation and attempt to finally knock her out of the war. The Germans had around 117 divisions on the Western Front, of which twenty-five could be risked in an offensive.

Falkenhayn selected his battleground with considerable care before launching a stunning assault on the fortress of Verdun on 21 February 1916. Here a potent combination of national pride and military necessity made it almost impossible for the French to do anything but fight to the death. The original German concept for Verdun was to suck in the flower of French manhood and bleed them dry in the mincing machine established by the massed power of the German artillery. Unfortunately for Falkenhayn, in the heat of battle the local German commander, Crown Prince Wilhelm, got carried away in a desperate effort to actually capture Verdun and in doing so rashly exposed his men to losses that matched, or at times exceeded, those suffered by the French. Contrary to all Joffre's best intentions it would after all be the French and not the British who would bear the brunt of exhausting the German reserves before the offensive on the Somme.

The Battle of Verdun was an extreme trial for the French Army, forcing them to commit most of their available reserves to the battle. It became apparent that it would be grossly unrealistic for the French to play their originally intended lead role in the joint offensive on the Somme. Indeed the strain was such that Joffre came to see the Somme offensive less as a part of the main Allied assault on Germany and more as a way of relieving the pressure piling up at Verdun. The French would still make a contribution to the offensive but it was inevitably scaled down to leave the British Army bearing the brunt of the battle.

It still had to be decided exactly when the attack should be launched. Haig was rather cautious. In his opinion his men were by no means adequately trained for the shock of battle. As he bluntly put it: 'I have not got an army in France really, but a collection of divisions untrained for the field. The actual fighting army will be evolved from them.'[14] Unfortunately, they were not to be given any chance to hone their battle skills. As the German attacks rained down on the defenders of Verdun the French reached a state of sheer desperation. At a meeting called on 26 May at Montreuil to finalise the date of the Somme attack, Joffre put a forceful case for urgent British action. This was not the sort of request that could be ignored if the military alliance was to endure in good health. Haig was backed into a corner from which there was no escape.

> General Joffre explained the general situation. The French had supported for three months alone the whole weight of the German attacks at Verdun … If this went on, the French Army would be ruined! He therefore was of the opinion that 1 July was the latest date for the combined offensive of the British and French. I said that before fixing the date I would like to indicate the state of preparedness of the British Army on certain dates and compare its condition. I took 1 and 15 July, and 1 and 15 August. The moment I mentioned 15 August, Joffre at once got very excited and shouted that 'The French Army would cease to exist, if we did nothing till then'! The rest of us looked on at this outburst of excitement, and then I pointed out that, in spite of the 15th August being the most favourable date for the British Army to take action, yet, in view of what he had said regarding the unfortunate condition of the French Army, I was prepared to commence operations on the 1st July or thereabouts.[15]
>
> General Sir Douglas Haig, General Headquarters, BEF

And what were Haig's real intentions in launching the Battle of the Somme? In essence he hoped to achieve victory in 1916 but was well aware that it might prove impossible, even with the best will in the world.

> My policy is briefly to: 1. Train my divisions, and to collect as much ammunition and as many guns as possible. 2. To make arrangements to support the French attacking in order to draw off pressure from Verdun, when the French consider the military situation demands it. But while attacking to help our Allies, not to think that we can for a certainty destroy the power of Germany this year. So in our attacks we must also aim at improving our positions with a view to making sure of the result of campaign next year.[16]
>
> General Sir Douglas Haig, General Headquarters, BEF

The die was cast. The British were about to fight their first real Continental battle in modern war against the main enemy on the decisive front. They were fighting as an integral part of a Continental alliance in order to relieve the pressure on their French Allies and as part of a continuing effort to destroy the main strength of the German Army, prior to launching *the* decisive attack. And that battle would be fought in the valley and surrounding hills of the Somme.

CHAPTER TWO

Armies and Weapons

The German Army the British were about to assault on the Somme was a formidable and well-trained body of men that had been deliberately honed for war. Germany had developed a highly efficient conscription system which ensured that almost 50 per cent of all her young men had experienced two years of military training from the age of 20 to 22 before being released to the reserve forces. There they would be liable to annual military training with the Reserve Army until they were 27, followed by a further period of intermittent training with the *Landwehr* until they reached 39, at which point they passed into the *Landsturm,* which could be mobilised as a kind of home-guard force. Only at the grand old age of 45 were German men completely free of military obligations to their country. Mobilisation was a complex but thoroughly well considered process. The serving army units would be topped up with the youngest reservists, while the rest of the reservists formed their own formations, which also took their place in the line of battle. The already huge German peacetime army of some fifty-one divisions could thus be rapidly supplemented with a further thirty-one reserve divisions and multifarious ancillary formations. By such means the Germans were able to mobilise a trained field army of nearly 2.5 million in 1914.

The British Army was in sharp contrast a truly New Army. Before the war Britain had relied on a volunteer system to raise her small Regular Army. In characteristically immodest fashion the British claimed that the BEF was the best trained, best equipped army in the world, but with a total of just 160,000 men it was, nevertheless, a negligible force on the battlefields of Continental Europe. At home was a further body of partially trained voluntary soldiers known as the Territorial Army. The British

Army had been thoroughly reorganised in 1908 by the Secretary of State for War, Richard Haldane, assisted by the ubiquitous figure of Major General Douglas Haig in his earlier capacity as Director of Military Training. As a result six regular infantry divisions and one cavalry division would be available for overseas service, while fourteen territorial divisions complete with artillery and fourteen Yeomanry cavalry brigades were designated for home defence duties. The territorials were part-time soldiers organised into extra battalions raised by local voluntary associations, but based on the existing regular regiments. The soldiers were expected to indulge in weekly drill night-training sessions, with additional weekend training and an annual fortnight at summer camp. In the event of war it was expected that the existing territorial battalions would expand their recruitment activities to quickly raise second line battalions that would effectively double their numbers. When push came to shove on the declaration of war, the home service restriction on territorials was quickly abandoned as the men were 'invited' to volunteer for overseas service, which the majority duly did. Yet it soon became obvious that more troops would be needed than the existing system could supply.

In August 1914 the newly appointed Secretary of State for War, Field Marshal Lord Kitchener, was far-sighted in his immediate perception that hostilities would be long and hard fought. It was apparent to him that *millions* of soldiers would be needed if Britain was to take her proper place in the line on the Western Front. This was completely foreign to the British military tradition and there was simply no framework on which such an expansion could be easily based. Kitchener had the usual regular soldier's marked distrust of volunteers, which had been further reinforced by what he considered as their inadequate performance in the Boer War. As a natural autocrat, confident in his own judgement and constitutionally unable to delegate, it was inevitable that he would act on his personal instincts. He resolved, therefore, not to expand the Territorial Army, which was already in crisis in its attempts to 'double up' on the outbreak of war. Indeed as it still had a home defence function to perform, it clearly had enough on its plate in the short term without further pressure. Instead Kitchener would create a 'New Army', still based on the regiments, but administered and trained by the regular battalions rather than delegating that power to the territorial voluntary associations. Such battalions came to be known as 'service' battalions. Significantly his first appeal for mass volunteers referred to service for three years or until the war was over, which emphasised his belief that a war with Germany would be a prolonged trial of strength. Indeed, Kitchener would have preferred the introduction of national conscription, but reluctantly bowed to the judgement of his Cabinet colleagues that this might trigger popular unrest which would undermine the all-important spirit of national unity in the face of war.

In response to Kitchener's iconographic 'Your King and Country Need You' poster and the first appeal for recruits in August 1914 the volunteers poured in. The initial stream became a torrent, until at the height of popular enthusiasm some 30,000 men a day were flooding into the recruitment offices up and down the country. Their motivations were many and varied. A simple patriotism and a genuine desire to stand up against the foe for 'King and Country' was undoubtedly present for many. For others it was a simple zest for adventure: a change from the tedium of the office, the hard graft of the shop floor, the loneliness of the farmyard, the filth and ever-present dangers of the pit. Many went because their best pals were going. The minimum recruiting age was just a petty rule to be overcome by young lads determined not to be left out of the 'adventure of a lifetime', and the hard-pressed recruiting sergeants were often all too compliant in allowing them to enlist.

> I went down to Colston Hall with the hope of enlisting in the newly formed battalion by the City, called 'Bristol's Own', official title, 12th Battalion The Gloucestershire Regiment. I went to the recruiting table and the recruiting sergeant was there. I knew that the age of enlistment was nineteen so that it was no good me telling the truth – I would say I was nineteen instead of seventeen and a half! But I wasn't asked how old was I – I was asked, 'When were you born?' I gave the answer I'd given throughout my life – 12th February, 1897! The recruiting sergeant said, 'Well, I don't know whether we can take you at that age....' He must have seen my sad look, and he said, 'But if you go outside the Colston Hall, run round the building three times – you'll be three years older when you come back!' That was a good enough hint for me! When I came back he said, 'How old are you?' and I said, 'Twenty!' So that got me into the battalion.[1]
>
> Private Harold Hayward, 12th Battalion, Gloucestershire Regiment, 95th Brigade, 5th Division

Faced with this mass of civilians the existing regimental structures simply could not cope and civilian committees were established by prominent local dignitaries, industrialists and politicians both to promote and manage the recruitment process. The most famous development was that of 'Pals' battalions raised exclusively from a single locality, or in the cities from an identifiable strata of society.

> I saw this lot in the paper and it said it was all Leeds people, and I joined up, I didn't even know that infantry walked, to be quite truthful with you, I didn't know anything about soldiers. I ought to have joined the cavalry lot, being brought up with horses, but it appealed to me and I went and I've never regretted a moment of it really, because I never met a finer lot of fellows in my life. He looked at me and he says, 'Sallow complexion, prominent nose, mole on the right cheek'. Before he'd done with me I felt a bit like Frankenstein! Then he says, 'Initials?' I says, 'F.A.' He says, 'You're going to have some trouble with that! – F.A. in the army doesn't stand for your initials!'[2]
>
> Private (Fewster) Arthur Dalby, 15th Battalion, West Yorkshire Regiment, 93rd Brigade, 31st Division

Allowances could even be made to allow groups of friends to join up and serve together.

> Everyone rushing to get in, thinking it was a Pals army, they were all full of sportsmanship and that sort of thing. We were all footballers together, I was one of six. The height was then five foot six and a half. I was five foot six and was worried stiff, so I filled my shoes with paper and fastened big rubber heels on the soles and heels. They asked me my height and I told them; they hummed and hawed about it so he says, 'Well take your shoes off!' Well that jiggered it! Anyway I says, 'Well there's all my pals joining and there was six of us all footballers!' So he says, 'Oh, go on, let him go in!'[3]
>
> Private Morrison Fleming, 15th Battalion, West Yorkshire Regiment, 93rd Brigade, 31st Division

The Pals battalions came to represent a significant proportion of the front-line service battalions that were raised. That they were the pride and joy of their communities was demonstrable by the response of the local newspaper when the Manchester and Salford Pals were paraded in front of Kitchener in Manchester on 21 March 1915.

> Only now and then in these months of war has it been forced fully home to us that we are living history, but the dullest could not see the march of the 12,000 yesterday without knowing that of this, his children's children will be told. Nor could he see it without a deep and quickening sense of his personal relation to the facts behind it. For Manchester's army is Manchester, and the New Army is Britain, in a way no soldiers ever have been before or, it is hoped, will ever need be again. The people who cheered and the people who marched were not spectators and a spectacle. They were kin in the truest sense, and every eligible man who watched the City Battalions swing by must have felt it an incongruous thing that he was not on the other side of the barrier.[4]
>
> Reporter, Manchester Guardian

The fatal disadvantages of putting all the community's eggs in one basket had not yet become apparent.

WHEN THE DUST had died down the situation was somewhat complex. In a typical British county regiment the 1st and 2nd Battalions were regular; the 3rd was the original regular reserve battalion which remained at home; the 4th, 5th and 6th Battalions were usually territorial battalions, which each in turn often raised second-line battalions numbered the 2/4th, 2/5th and 2/6th Battalions; there would then follow a number of Kitchener service battalions, which typically would be numbered 7th, 8th, 9th, 10th, 11th and 12th Battalions. Sometimes they too would raise second-line battalions. The exact number of battalions would vary depending on the recruitment potential of the parent regiment's area. Thus, while the Dorsetshire Regiment only raised eleven battalions during the course of the war, the Royal Sussex Regiment had twenty-six battalions, the Northumberland Fusiliers had fifty-one battalions, while the all-territorial London Regiment managed a total of eighty-eight battalions.

Each battalion consisted of a headquarters company and four companies totalling about 800 men when on active service. In the Royal Artillery the typical field artillery battery would have about 200 men and six guns. The various units that together made up a typical infantry division were three infantry brigades (each of four battalions), four field artillery brigades (each of four batteries) and one heavy artillery battery. In addition there was a squadron of cavalry, ambulance units, divisional supply and ammunition trains, and engineers. The total strength was nominally 18,000 men. Broadly according to this pattern the new units were fitted into Kitchener's New Army destined for the most part for the Western Front. Thus, the Regular Army divisions were numbered 1st to 8th; the New Army divisions were numbered 9th to 26th; the anomalous 27th to 29th divisions were in fact Regular Army divisions scraped up from units on Imperial garrison service, then the 30th to 41st were more New Army divisions, before finally the 42nd through to 74th divisions were the Territorial Army divisions (with the exception of the 63rd or Royal Naval Division which was originally formed from 'spare' naval reservists).

IT WAS ONE thing to recruit soldiers, but another thing entirely to convert them into soldiers capable of meeting the relatively well-trained Germans in battle. Variously lacking officers, NCOs, uniforms, kit, modern weapons or even the most basic accommodation for the men – the situation was soon desperate. There was a shortage of specialist personnel of all kinds: clerks to record the details on recruitment, drill and weapons instructors, doctors to check and maintain the recruits' health, cooks to prepare food, armourers to set up and maintain weapons. Any kind of military experience was soon at an absolute premium and many old officers and NCOs were 'dug out' and called back to the colours to drill the ranks into some semblance of discipline. Even worse were the problems in recruiting new artillery units. There were hardly any guns left in the country to train with and the skills that accurate gunnery required were considerably more advanced than those required by the infantry.

With these quickly amassed and ramshackle legions the old British boast of the quality rather than the quantity of her army now rebounded. In contrast to the instruction received by the bulk of the German Army there is no doubt that the British training programme was rushed, lacked any depth or detail and was often irrelevant to the real needs of the troops in modern conditions of trench warfare. In an attempt to give newly arrived battalions an easy introduction to the war, they were first attached to a regular battalion serving in the line to gain practical experience under close supervision in the strange routines and lurking dangers of trench life. Then the whole division would serve in a quiet area before being 'blooded' in battle. For many soldiers the Somme would be their first real baptism of fire. The training process never really finished. When they were out of the line after a couple of days rest all units would resume a programme of individual training designed to reinforce the basic military skills and to prepare them for the imminent offensive. For the service battalions this was little more than a continuation of the training they had received before they crossed the Channel, but even the 'old sweats' in the regulars could greatly benefit from a course of refresher training.

> Our time was devoted to training for the offensive, or 'fattening up for the slaughter' as we cheerfully called it. For the first week or so we confined ourselves to platoon and company training, to smarten up the men and correct the somewhat slouching habits which there was always a tendency to contract during a long spell in the trenches. Three or four days of drill, bayonet fighting, musketry, bomb throwing and kindred pursuits had a wonderfully enlivening effect on us, and we were soon in fine fettle.[5]
>
> Lieutenant William Colyer, 2nd Battalion, Royal Dublin Fusiliers, 10th Brigade, 4th Division

The men were armed with the Short Magazine Lee-Enfield rifle, a bolt action rifle, which in the hands of the pre-war regulars could fire up to 15 aimed rounds per minute. Accurate up to a mile it was at its most effective at ranges of up to about 600 yards. The 18-in sword bayonet that clipped on to the end was not neglected and many of the older officers put great store in bayonet fighting. The usual myths were peddled, implying some racial inferiority lurking deep within the heart of the German soldier, which thereby rendered him constitutionally unable to face any attack pushed home at the point of the bayonet.

> A red-tabbed and red-faced Major gave a lecture, a gruesome lecture on the use of the bayonet. He might as well have been trying to teach his grandmother to suck eggs, talking to infantrymen who had been there in battle on the use of the bayonet. He said he'd been to examine men who had been killed by the bayonet and how unnecessarily it had been used. Because the bayonet is grooved, if you bayonet a man and try and withdraw, very often it's very hard because the flesh closes – you've got to give it a twist. If you withdraw without giving it a twist, the outside could close and it won't bleed, it will only bleed internally.

> As the bayonet's grooved, giving it a twist allows the air into it; then the blood flows freely.[6]
>
> Private Basil Farrer, 2nd Battalion, Green Howards, 21st Brigade, 30th Division

One of the most important new weapons that the pressures of war had added to the British armoury was the Lewis light machine gun. This weighed just 26 lbs and it fired drums of 47 rounds up to a range of 2,000 yards. Sustained fire was impossible and the gun was not particularly accurate, but what the Lewis gun offered was relatively high firepower that could actually accompany the attacking infantry as they moved forward. It was a complex weapon and officers and NCOs were sent on training courses to master the intricacies of the gun mechanism.

> For three days, then, I thought and talked of nothing but body-locking pins, feed actuating studs, pinion casings, pawls, racks, plungers, strikers and all the other jargon connected with the study of the Lewis gun. My great desire was to attain the record speed for changing the bolt of the gun. This operation is not at all as simple as it sounds; for instance, it would probably take you about three-quarters of an hour, at the end of which time you would be oily and angry and flushed, and moreover would probably have put in the new bolt the wrong way round, with the distressing result of the bullet shooting backwards, prematurely completing the day's work of the firer. My time for changing the bolt correctly was thirteen seconds.[7]
>
> Lieutenant William Colyer, 2nd Battalion, Royal Dublin Fusiliers, 10th Brigade, 4th Division

There were soon some sixteen Lewis guns for every battalion, one per platoon and the specialist knowledge of how to operate them was assiduously passed on to their men once the officers and NCOs returned to their units.

The Vickers machine gun was the heavy machine gun used by the British Army. By 1916 the guns had already been withdrawn from the infantry battalions and concentrated in specialist machine gun battalions of the Machine Gun Corps, whose numbering corresponded to the infantry brigade to which they were attached. The water-cooled, belt-driven Vickers heavy machine gun fired at a rate of up to 500 rounds per minute, spraying bullets across the beaten zone with a range of 4,500 yards. It was also slowly being appreciated that the Vickers could be fired as part of a barrage, using indirect firing at extreme elevation to hose bullets up into the air that would then pour down on targets behind the German lines. It was indeed a heavy weapon and needed a six-man crew to carry the 40-lb gun, 50-lb tripod, water container, condenser tubes and ammunition belts. Once in action, however, it could be operated by a team of two with the rest occupied in bringing up ammunition and extra water supplies.

One crucially important weapon that had to be mastered was the hand grenade. The lineage of this weapon was fairly ancient but it had not been considered part of modern war until the reality of trench warfare forced a rapid reassessment. Many different, makeshift 'bombs' were tried, of which the two best known were the 'hair brush', which had a slab of explosive tied to a wooden handle, and the 'jam tin' bomb – a lethal concoction of explosive and shrapnel packed into an ordinary jam tin with a spluttering fuse to complete its ramshackle appearance. By 1916 the army had settled on the mass-produced Mills bomb, which was reliable, could be thrown with a round arm cricket bowling-style action to about 30 yards and was possessed of a segmented case that fragmented to maximum lethal effect.

All in all there were many new skills for the soldier to learn as the horrors of war unfolded before them. Gas had not been considered when the war started, but now every man had to learn to put his gas mask on properly in conditions designed to simulate the kind of pressure they might face in action.

> Yesterday we had the regiment 'gassed'. All had to pass through a room and stay in it in squads for two or three minutes while gas was fired off at them. The idea is to give the men confidence in their flannel helmets and also to show them the necessity of wearing them in such a way that no outside air can get in under them. Which means the bottom end of the bags have to be tucked well into their coats which later must be buttoned up over them. One man I hear funked it, so no doubt the experience has now overcome his fears.[8]
>
> Lieutenant Colonel Frank Maxwell VC, 12th Battalion, Middlesex Regiment, 54th Brigade, 18th Division

The gas helmets described were undoubtedly of the hooded P. H. helmet pattern that had been introduced in November 1915 and would continue to be the standard gas mask in the British Army until replaced by the small box respirator in August 1916. Even such a grim item of personal protection was not immune from the slightly surrealistic perceptions of the British soldier.

> The gas mask was a grey flannelled hood, saturated in an evil smelling chemical and uncomfortably sticky. It was drawn over the head and the base was tucked under the collar of the jacket or shirt, as the case may be. The hood had two large eye-pieces of metal rimmed glass. A rubber mouthpiece within the hood was gripped tightly between the teeth, through which the heavily impregnated disinfectant air, inhaled through the nose, was expelled through a rubber 'flipper' outside the mask, which opened and closed as one breathed. After a while the excess saliva in the tube coagulated – for want of a better word – causing the 'flipper' to sound like a raspberry blower each time one exhaled. It is not difficult to imagine the cacophonous effect of thirty-odd 'flippers' performing at the same time![9]
>
> Signaller Dudley Menaud-Lissenburg, 97th Battery, 147th Brigade, Royal Field Artillery, 29th Division

BOOKS ABOUT THE war in 1916 have often deliberately downplayed the most important element of the weaponry of the British Army because it does not fit in with their neo-romantic picture of helpless suffering amongst the 'victim' infantry. Yet it was the artillery that lay at the centre of the Battle of the Somme, which was destined to be a gunners' battle right from the start. By 1916 the generals had correctly identified that artillery held the key to success on the Western Front, although they had not yet gained the experience in how best to use it to unlock the tactical conundrum that bedevilled them. The generals knew, however, that they needed ever-greater concentrations of guns and howitzers if they were to make any progress at all. Yet gunnery demanded a complex network of skills that could not quickly be imparted. The hordes of new gunners needed constant practice at gun drill to build up the kind of teamwork and fitness that was required to allow rapid fire for long periods of time.

> The No. 1 was the sergeant or NCO in charge. He'd repeat the orders that would come from the officers, say they got the order, 'Drop 50 yards!' He used to give that order. The No. 2 on the right-hand side of the gun, he worked the range drum, it was just a dial all calibrated up to about 6,800 yards that was your total range. Instead of sitting on the seat facing forward, he always used to sit swivel legged, with his left leg out and his left arm out. His right arm was on the range drum. When the gun fired with the recoil of the gun the cam lever practically came into his hand as the gun came back, he used to whip that out, the breech would open and the empty cartridge case used to fly out. The No. 3, the gunlayer got onto the aiming point, laid the gun and actually fired it, he had a handle at the side. We used to register, you couldn't see the targets you were firing at. They used to plant an aiming post out in front about four foot high, black and white and on the top was a little square, that was white. They used to lay this gun on to that post and any target was so many degrees right or left of this aiming post. The No. 4 and No. 5 worked alternately as loaders, standing there with another shell, they'd whip the shell in. The weight of the shell going in practically helped to close the breech. While No. 5 was loading No. 4 would be picking another one and setting the fuses if it was needed. No. 6 would assist in setting fuses. No. 2 would close the breech again. As soon as he'd closed the breech he used to say, 'Set!' No. 3 used to say, 'Ready!' No. 1 would say, 'Fire!' Set, ready, fire! When you've got into the style, you could fire the gun and before the gun came back at the end of its recoil, it was nearly loaded again.[10]
>
> Gunner George Cole, C Battery, 253rd Brigade, Royal Field Artillery

While their men sweated over drill, officers had to master the skills of ranging shells on to targets from observation posts and faced the problem of mastering the mathematics, and in particular the trigonometry, that had blighted so many of their young lives at school.

The 18-pounder gun was the workhorse of the British artillery. A solid, reliable weapon, firing as one might expect a shell weighing just over 18 lbs, its main fault was its limited range of just 6,500 yards, although this could be raised to 7,800 yards by digging in the gun trail. The other field artillery gun was the 4.5-in howitzer. These fired a 35-lb shell up to 6,600 yards with an entirely different looping trajectory. The heavy artillery were in short supply in 1914 but the demands for ever-heavier shells to smash down the German defences soon caused a massive expansion in the siege batteries of the Royal Garrison Artillery who operated the heavier guns and mortars. These were many and varied but the key type amongst the artillery was the 60-pounder guns that hurled their shell up to 10,500 yards. The bulk of the howitzers were 6-in or 9.2-in types although the 8-in howitzer was developed by the simple expedient of shortening the barrel of the 6-in gun. The howitzers had an obvious value in conditions of trench warfare.

> The howitzer fires upwards in a rather curved trajectory, so that when it arrives at the target it drops rather from the sky, instead of a flatter trajectory of a gun that doesn't rise so much. A gun is superb for shooting at a battleship and a howitzer is superb for shooting at targets which are behind a hill. A lot of enemy batteries were behind hills so that howitzers were ideal for that purpose, and also for dropping down on trenches where there were *minenwerfers* and machine guns. A gun couldn't touch them but a howitzer could.[11]
>
> Second Lieutenant Montague Cleeve, 36th Siege Artillery Battery, Royal Garrison Artillery

At the start of the war when the whole emphasis of the Royal Artillery had been on the necessity of providing shrapnel shell-fire support for the infantry the range was not a problem as the guns were brought into action in direct sight of the enemy. Shrapnel shells were indeed lethal weapons if they caught infantry advancing across open ground.

> Shrapnel shell is like a shotgun cartridge really. The nose of the shell is spigotted into the body of the shell and is held by either lead or little wooden rivets. In the bottom there's a bursting charge, a cast iron plate above that, a rod goes right through the shell. There's a time fuse and a percussion fuse and the flash from that goes down into the base, ignites the bursting charge, the iron plate pushes the bullets up and forces the nose of the shell off and then the bullets are all sprayed out of the shell. Well, if the shell hits the ground first, it's useless. You did have a percussion fuse, but all that happened is that the bullets are just driven into the ground. I've had a shrapnel shell burst alongside me and no damage at all – practically all gone into the ground. The shrapnel shell time fuse has to be set according to what height you want it to burst.

> The fuse has a ring marked out in tenths of a second and according to your time of flight, you try to make that shrapnel shell burst just nicely above ground level.[12]
>
> Signaller Leonard Ounsworth, 124th Heavy Battery, Royal Garrison Artillery

Once trench warfare began it was soon found that infantry in the trenches were relatively safe from the effects of shrapnel. High explosive shells with direct-action fuses that exploded only on impact were required to blast them out from their burrows, but these were initially in very short supply. Shrapnel shells came to be used mainly as a means of cutting barbed wire. This was not what they had been designed to do.

> At that time we had no really efficient means of cutting the many square miles of wire entanglements protecting the German lines. Shrapnel to be effective had to burst low, which meant that three-quarters of the shells burst on percussion. It was extremely expensive and almost useless. We did not at that time possess a high explosive shell with direct-action fuse sensitive enough to cut wire.[13]
>
> Second Lieutenant Alfred Darlington, 283rd Brigade, Royal Field Artillery, 56th Division

By this time methods had been developed by which the fire of the guns could be controlled even when the gunners at the gun positions could not see their targets. Observation posts would be set up in the front line with telephone lines leading back to the guns' positions. The forward observation officer would correct the fire of the guns up and down in range by means of a simple bracketing system.

Yet the view from the front line was restricted, particularly when the German lines ran along the higher ground which prevented any view of the German rear lines and artillery battery positions. Here the men of the Royal Flying Corps truly came into their own. At the start of the war, during the period of open warfare, aircraft had been seen as a minor addition to the armoury of war. The RFC was mainly used as an advanced reconnaissance patrol, to send a pilot out to locate the enemy and discover in which direction they were moving. As such it had performed a valuable role. But when the trench lines became established it was obvious that aircraft could perform a far greater role. The pressure cooker of war acted to speed up the technological development of aircraft and their engines, allowing more equipment to be carried aloft. It was soon realised that cameras could allow the pilots to bring back a record of what they had seen for later intensive study back on the ground. Soon cameras capable of taking pin-sharp glass negatives were being fitted to the basic army cooperation aircraft – the BE2c. Once the plates were back on the ground the emerging science of photographic interpretation allowed a large amount of valuable information to be gleaned. German gun batteries were exposed despite their best efforts at camouflage, machine-gun posts were obvious, the entrances to dugouts could be clearly seen and headquarters or communications centres were apparent by the tracks of buried telephone wires. Such information was obviously invaluable in planning the assault. The BE2cs could also take up a wireless with which the crews could guide shells right on to their targets using a simple clock-code system for range corrections. The work of the army cooperation aircraft was invaluable and the commander of the RFC, Brigadier General Sir Hugh Trenchard, had developed an aggressive aerial policy to enable them to carry out their duties free from the attentions of German scout aircraft. The British scouts waged a ceaseless offensive, pushing forward over the German lines and seeking to engage any German aircraft as soon as they appeared, keeping them well away from the crucial battlefield where the army cooperation aircraft plied their trade.

Through the hard work of the RFC, the Royal Artillery had developed the capacity to destroy targets behind the German lines that were not actually visible from the British front line. One limitation still remained. The artillery never could and never would be able to guarantee perfect accuracy even after they had been ranged on to a target. The failure of the guns recoil action to recreate the exact same firing position (especially in wet and muddy conditions), slight differences in every shell fired, the varying effects of wind, atmospheric pressure and other meteorological factors – all these resulted in shells flying slightly over the precise target, dropping slightly short or very slightly deviating to left or right, resulting in a rectangular beaten zone that could be up to 50 yards long and less than 10 yards wide, depending on the gun calibre. This made it difficult to guarantee that even after a zone had been flayed with shells any had actually landed in the trenches or gunpits that were the real target.

The emergence of trench warfare led to a demand for a simple short-range weapon that could throw a shell upwards and across the short divide of No Man's Land, to drop and explode within the opposition front line.

No great sophistication was required and the brighter engineer officers used their initiative to construct primitive mortars redolent of a much earlier style of siege warfare. The requirement for mortars had not been anticipated and the British Army did not have a single trench mortar when the war started. As ever, the press of war ensured that the design, assessment and manufacturing process was constricted into months rather than years and soon every division was equipped with a Stokes light mortar battery attached to each of the infantry brigades and three further 2-in medium mortar batteries as an integral part of the divisional artillery. Although the trench mortars were relatively simple weapons the men still had to be trained.

> I was sent to a remote village in the back areas to go on a trench mortar course to learn something about the 2-in trench mortar pudding stick toffee apple. It consisted of a bomb weighing 42 lbs on a steel rod weighing 8 lbs and about 3 feet long, the rod fitted with a long tube at the lower end of which was a rifle mechanism. There were several different lengths of charges which could be used. The maximum range was 570 yards. The platform was extremely difficult to fix steadily and was nearly always uprooted after a few rounds had been fired. There was, however, one good feature of the mortar. The bombs were provided with a sensitive direct-action fuse that made them the best weapon we had at that time for wire cutting.[14]
>
> Second Lieutenant Alfred Darlington, 283rd Brigade, Royal Field Artillery, 56th Division

As the trench mortar batteries gained in confidence they in turn would demonstrate their potential and capabilities to the infantry within the division. Sometimes these exhibitions did not go entirely according to plan. Lieutenant Edgar Lord went to one such demonstration with his best friend Lieutenant Ivan Doncaster.

> We sat down in a field near to some sandbag emplacements awaiting the arrival of the 'brass hats', who were to occupy the stalls. The personnel of the Trench Mortar Battery were preparing for the show, shortening fuses and such like, when suddenly we heard a cry, 'Run for it!' Scores of people rushed madly in all directions, so I rose to my feet and tried to move away from the emplacements, but had only gone a few yards, when I felt rather than heard a tremendous explosion. At

once I flung myself on the ground covering my head with my arms. An unbelievable roar rent the air; earth and pieces of metal flying everywhere. Everyone there was hit with either or both. Two more explosions followed, during which time I did the 'worm turn' in a useless endeavour to reach cover. When we gathered our scattered wits, I discovered a hole an inch long in the shoulder of my tunic and my right thigh felt as if it had been beaten with a heavy stick, whilst I was covered with earth. A few yards away a man lay groaning across a few strands of barbed wire, through which he had been trying to crawl, but the gust had merely blown him into it, assisted by a piece of shell in the seat of his pants. I bandaged him, but as the leg of my trousers felt warm and sticky, I had to ask Doncaster to attend to two small wounds of mine. As the pain became more severe, I found it more comfortable to lie on my stomach. It was at least an hour before ambulances arrived to take us away. Only one man was killed outright, but several died later from the seventy or eighty casualties, a number surprisingly small considering the nearness of the crowd. If it had happened ten minutes later, most of the staff and senior officers would have been involved. An officer was shortening fuses on some of the shells, when he accidentally released a striker which fired a ten-second fuse. Instead of throwing the shell into an empty emplacement or traverse, he dropped it where he was among all the bombs – and ran for it – he was not hurt at all![15]

Lieutenant Edgar Lord, 15th Battalion, Lancashire Fusiliers, 96th Brigade, 32nd Division

What would in the modern world be regarded as an absolute calamity was just another incident in the dangerous pageant of war. The infantry took an almost instant dislike to this new weapon of war. The trench mortars would descend on the front-line troops, fire a few rounds and then depart as quickly as possible. The German retaliation would be swift, but not quite swift enough to catch the trench mortar crews. The answering burst of shell fire would land squarely on the long-suffering front-line troops. However, the mortars were formidable weapons of war simply because they had the power to deliver large amounts of high explosive accurately on to a target.

AFTER IMPROVING THEIR weapons skills the soldiers were ready to commence the programme of tactical exercises that would try and get them ready for what would face them when they went over the top in a few weeks' time. Battalion parades and route marches would get them used to working en masse as a battalion. Most of the men were keen to learn, recognising perhaps that they needed all the help they could get.

> We moved back for our training for the 'Big Push', full of enthusiasm, which carries one a long way. This training business was infinitely harder work than being in the line. There was no rest all day and far into the night for a good many of us. Our headquarters were at Ailly-sur-Somme, a most charming place, and all the battalions were equally well situated round about. Our training ground was a big open bit of country which, when we came to it, was covered with beautiful crops, but these we had absolutely to ignore, and in no time there was very little left. What compensation the farmers got I cannot imagine, but certainly it would not be less than £1,000 for our piece of ground alone. It seemed wicked, but there was nothing else to be done as all this country was very closely cultivated and it was absolutely necessary to carry out this training.[16]
>
> Brigadier General F. C. Stanley, Headquarters, 89th Brigade, 30th Division

Although the training programme varied immensely according to the whims of the divisional commanders, in many cases an effort was made to layout on the ground the overall shape and course of the battlefield and particularly the relative positions of the specific German lines that would be their objectives.

> We dug, I suppose, from 6,000 to 7,000 yards of trenches; of course not to full depth, but enough to show what it looked like. Here we practised every day, getting every man to know exactly what was required of him and what the ground would look like on *the* day. They all tumbled to it fairly well, and certainly our practice improved all of us very much indeed. We practised all day and every day. First, battalions singly, and then two or more battalions together. We had a sort of dress rehearsal which the Divisional Commander attended. As regards weather, it was a beast of a day, pouring with rain and

everybody got soaked through. But things went off quite satisfactorily and he was very nice.[17]

Brigadier General F. C. Stanley, Headquarters, 89th Brigade, 30th Division

The last exercises were often seen as a chance to demonstrate what they had learnt in front of the generals and staff.

We finally made our last 'dress rehearsal' witnessed by the commander of the Army Corps, the 56th divisional general and all the brigadier generals, so there was plenty of red tape around. The smoke bombs were sent over just before the commencement, the attack was carried out quite satisfactorily and all the positions carried quite easily, but of course we had no opponents on this occasion.[18]

Lance Corporal Sidney Appleyard, 1/9th Battalion (Queen Victoria's Rifles), London Regiment, 169th Brigade, 56th Division

For the exercises were in no sense realistic: there was no live firing from fixed-line machine guns, no deafening explosive detonations to recreate the sheer shock and awe of war; such training concepts had not yet been developed and belonged to the future. The result was that an aura of unreality often permeated accounts of these training exercises.

The whole of the division was assembled and grouped as for the attack. After the usual explanations and pow-wows, beginning from the brass-hats and commanding officers and finishing with the platoon officers and section leaders, we moved across country against imaginary Boche trenches. As we went along the various bodies of men unfolded themselves into smaller groups, and eventually into extended order, as per programme, according to the amount of opposition which we were supposed to be encountering. After some time, having advanced a great distance and captured an immense tract of country (with such surprising ease that we all felt it was a pity we hadn't thought of doing it this way before) a halt would be called. Whereupon the brass-hats would ride up again and there would be criticisms, more explanations and more pow-wows. This being over we could collect ourselves together and hurry home, so as not to be late for tea. War under these conditions certainly was very enjoyable.[19]

Lieutenant William Colyer, 2nd Battalion, Royal Dublin Fusiliers, 10th Brigade, 4th Division

The British Army had been hastily assembled, if not thrown together, but it had an unshakeable confidence in its own abilities. Whether Regular, Territorial or New Army every constituent unit seemed to firmly believe that they were the finest unit in the British Army – bar none. Even a regular sapper, Major Philip Neame VC who had been attached to a territorial division soon swallowed any doubts and became a true believer in the mighty prowess of his new division.

> The best territorial divisions within a matter of a few months of getting to France were as good as a regular division – they became first class. I know that because I went from being a sapper officer with a regular division to become a brigade major in a territorial division and in the closest touch with the four battalions in my brigade. They were first class. When they were first sent to France, they were split up and a battalion attached to different regular divisions and thereby had something like six months attachment to a regular brigade. So they'd had that training and when they were collected again and made a division, their own division again, they were absolutely first class. The personnel were, taken on the whole, more intelligent than the average regular soldier. Most of them in the London territorial division were highly educated in that a great number of them were London clerks and that sort of thing. They became a first-class division and in battle they could be counted on to undertake any task.[20]
>
> Major Philip Neame VC, Headquarters, 168th Brigade, 56th Division

Major Neame was undoubtedly an intelligent man and a good judge of men, but his confidence in his division was not so much misplaced, as influenced by his own optimism and natural pride in their achievements thus far. Everything possible at the time had been done to get these men ready for war, but the chronic lack of experienced men to train the hundreds of thousands of raw youths meant that in reality there was small chance of turning this vast conglomeration of office workers, pitmen, factory workers and farm labourers into cohesive units of hard-bitten soldiers. The Territorial and New Army divisions may have been promising material, but they lacked the sheer intensity of battle experience, while the Regular divisions were regular only in name by 1916 – they, too, were filled with raw recruits, as their original ranks were for the most part either dead or still recovering from wounds. These then were the men that would meet the German Army in battle on the downlands of the Somme.

CHAPTER THREE

Moving On Up

The Somme was originally a green and pleasant land. The rolling chalk ridges were liberally dotted with small villages, farms and woods. The Germans looked on this unspoilt rural scene with the sole intention of eking out every defensive advantage they could squeeze from the configuration of the land. Having roughly sketched out their front in the hectic days of 1914, the Germans then set about digging themselves in properly – they were there for the duration.

The river Somme flowed in a generally westerly direction between Péronne and Amiens and over the centuries it had gradually eroded a mile-wide flat valley about 200 feet lower than the general level of the surrounding ground. On the northern bank the slopes were broken by several small valleys, and the larger valley of a sizeable tributary, the river Ancre, on which lay the small town of Albert. The Ancre in turn had a series of small valleys dropping down to it from the higher ground. Between the Somme and the Ancre lay a chalk ridge dotted with villages running from Morval, Guillemont, Longueval, Bazentin-le-Petit, Pozières (which marked the highest point) to Thiepval immediately above the Ancre. North of the Ancre the ridge continued through Beaucourt to Serre. Behind this first ridge lay another low ridge centred on the town of Bapaume. Communications were not extensive and the main road between Amiens and Bapaume ran through Albert, up and across the ridge passing directly through Pozières.

The German front line crossed the Somme just in front of the village of Curlu and then ran along the forward slopes of the ridge bending round to follow the contour lines of the minor valleys running down to the main rivers. It also incorporated several villages enclosing Mametz,

Fricourt, La Boisselle, Ovillers, Thiepval, crossing the Ancre below Beaucourt; then through Beaumont Hamel before running north in front of Serre. Unfortunately for the British the expression 'front line' was something of a misnomer. In fact it was a fully-realised trench system consisting in itself of three lines about 200 yards apart, linked together by communication trenches and incorporating fortress villages. The trenches were extremely well constructed with the plentiful provision of deep dugouts with multiple exits up to 40 feet deep, which could accommodate in relative comfort the whole of the trench garrison. In front of them were two belts of tangled barbed wire that were up to 30 yards wide. The houses of the villages had been fortified, largely by the use of reinforcing concrete, and the extension of existing cellars to form an underground warren. Also incorporated into the First Line, or standing just behind it, were trench-based strong points, which were independent fortresses in their own right. Perhaps typical of these was the Hawthorn Redoubt, which lay in front of Beaumont Hamel, and the Schwaben Redoubt, which lay on the ridge spur behind Thiepval. A Second Line defensive system had also been constructed between 2,000 and 5,000 yards (depending on the local tactical configuration of the ground) behind the First Line. This ran along the top of the Guillemont–Pozières Ridge before crossing the Ancre and running to the north and was very similar in its characteristics to the forward system. Finally the Germans had made considerable progress on digging a Third Line system a further 3,000 yards back. This then was the citadel that the British Army sought to crack wide open.

When the tide of battle had first washed round the Somme ridges, the pursuing French Army found it politically impossible to cede any more ground to the German invader for mere tactical reasons. Every inch of their homeland was precious to them and they therefore dug in on the lower ground facing the Germans rather than stepping back and occupying a less overlooked position. When the British took over the sector in 1915 they were equally bound by considerations that transcended mere tactics. For the British lines were in no way comparable to the trenches carved out by the Germans. The entire philosophy of the British Army was totally different. They were engaged in a strategic offensive designed to drive the German Army out of France and Belgium. Their trenches were more a jumping-off point for the next attack than a

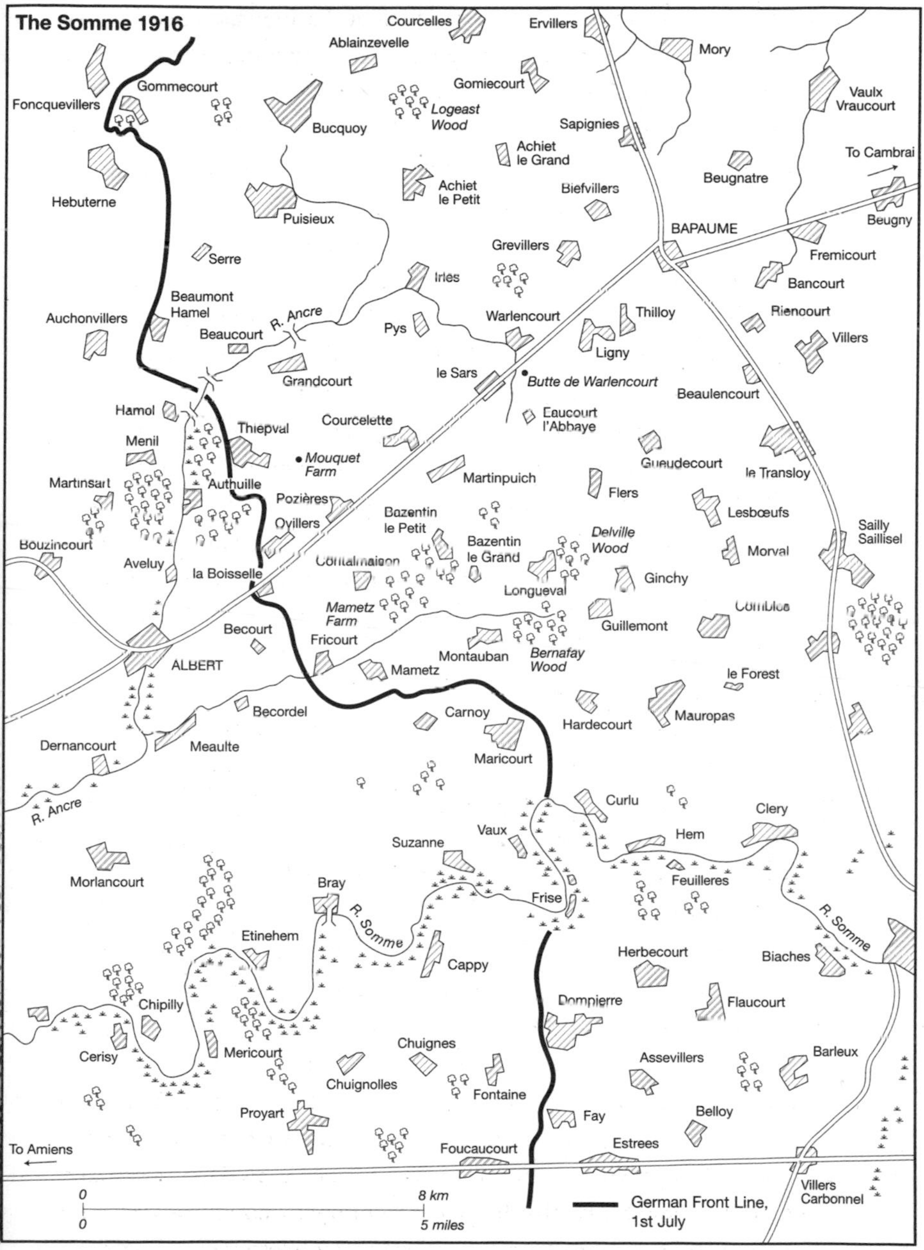
The Somme 1916
Courcelles
Ervillers
Ablainzevelle
Mory
Gommecourt
Foncquevillers
Gomiecourt
Vaulx
Vraucourt
Logeast
Wood
Bucquoy
Sapignies
Achiet
le Grand
To Cambrai
Hebuterne
Achiet
le Petit
Biefvillers
Beugnatre
Puisieux
BAPAUME
Beugny
Grevillers
Serre
Fremicourt
Irles
Bancourt
Beaumont
Hamel
R. Ancre
Pys
Warlencourt
Thilloy
Auchonvillers
Beaucourt
Riencourt
Ligny
Villers
Grandcourt
le Sars
Butte de Warlencourt
Beaulencourt
Hamel
Eaucourt
l'Abbaye
Thiepval
Courcelette
Menil
Mouquet
Farm
Gueudecourt
le Transloy
Martinsart
Authuille
Martinpuich
Flers
Pozières
Bazentin
le Petit
Lesbœufs
Ovillers
Sailly
Saillisel
Bouzincourt
Bazentin
le Grand
Delville
Wood
Morval
Aveluy
Contalmaison
la Boisselle
Ginchy
Longueval
Combles
Mametz
Farm
Becourt
Guillemont
Fricourt
Montauban
Bernafay
Wood
ALBERT
Mametz
le Forest
Becordel
Carnoy
Hardecourt
Mauropas
Dernancourt
Meaulte
Maricourt
Curlu
R. Ancre
Clery
Vaux
Hem
Suzanne
Morlancourt
Feuilleres
Bray
Frise
R. Somme
Etinehem
R. Somme
Herbecourt
Biaches
Cappy
Chipilly
Dompierre
Flaucourt
Cerisy
Mericourt
Chuignes
Assevillers
Barleux
Chuignolles
Fontaine
Proyart
Fay
Belloy
Estrees
To Amiens
Foucaucourt
Villers
Carbonnel
0
8 km
0
5 miles
German Front Line,
1st July

considered defensive system *per se.* As a result, although there was some superficial similarity in the basic front line, communication and support trenches, there were no concrete reinforced machine-gun posts, no village fortresses, no proper switch lines and above all no deep reinforced dugouts to shelter the bulk of the troops. The British soldier had no conception of the underground billets afforded their German counterparts on the Somme front. The ordinary British soldier usually had to be content with a 'cubby hole' burrowed out in the side of the trench. It provided some shelter from the pitter-patter of rain or shrapnel, but left them painfully exposed to high explosive shells.

When the British took over the line on the Somme front from the French they found that an unofficial policy of 'live and let live' had undoubtedly prevailed between the French and the German front-line troops. Such a mutually convenient and apparently sensible arrangement was anathema to the British High Command who firmly believed that their inexperienced troops needed to be blooded and given experience in the grim business of war. The overall level of artillery fire rose inexorably month by month and the battalions at the front were ordered to probe and test the Germans in every way possible. One simple method was to increase the level of sniping at German soldiers unwise enough to expose themselves for a moment of two within sight of the British lines. The better shots amongst the men were given *carte blanche* to try their luck. But this was a dangerous task for it was soon two-way traffic as German snipers responded in kind.

> If you get a little gap about as square as a matchbox, you get a good view in front of you. The least thing you see move; you let go, you'd be aiming at anything that bloody moved. Sometimes you'd strain and strain. You'd see tree trunks that had been shattered, you'd look at that and you could see it move. The more you stare the more it moves. But you've got to be very careful, because if you let go at a thing like that there might be one of their snipers watching where the shot comes from and have a go at you. But you can see things move in the dark. You take it for granted that you've aimed and you'd hope that it hit a German. You'd easily tell if you don't get any trouble after. If you get trouble with a sniper firing occasionally and you just mark and weigh up what position he comes from. Then you fire at that – if you don't

> hear no more after that you know you've done your job. Of course you can't guarantee it, you can't be certain in the dark.[1]
>
> Private Ralph Miller, 1/8th Battalion, Warwickshire Regiment, 143rd Brigade, 48th Division

At night the British sent out numerous small reconnaissance patrols to swarm all over No Man's Land in an effort to probe the German defences. Creeping out after dusk had fallen they were nakedly vulnerable to devastating bursts of fire. Sometimes German patrols were also out and it could be an extremely tense business.

> I was out on patrol one night in No Man's Land, eight of us under a young officer named Lieutenant Jones. We crawled through the mud right across to the German lines and then crept along the outside of their barbed wire entanglements. We got so far without being spotted and we could hear them talking. Our object was to gain, if possible, some idea of the strength of the enemy at that point, and any other information that might be useful. So far, so good! Then, horror of horrors, we heard shouts in German, and found that we were practically surrounded. There was one enemy patrol only about 100 yards away to our left, another a similar distance away to our right and a third patrol almost right in front of us, but on their side of the wire! We had, of course, been spotted and it seemed certain that our game was up, that we would either be taken prisoner of shot out of hand. But strangely enough, the Jerries seemed suddenly to disappear! Just as we were preparing to make a run for it, the reason for their withdrawal from the scene became obvious. Up in the sky went a number of Very lights which lit up the place brighter than daylight – and then – all Hell was let loose! They opened fire on us with rifles and machine guns and I shall always remember lying flat on the ground pressing myself and my face as deep as possible into the mud, with hundreds of machine-gun bullets zipping just inches above my head! Not content with that, they also opened up with ground shrapnel, that is, shells timed to explode a few feet above us. After about ten or fifteen minutes of this strafing, they ceased fire, evidently believing that they had successfully annihilated us. Anyway, when quietness and darkness once more returned, like 'Phoenix' we rose again, and running, slipping and sliding in and out of shell holes full of water,

> we eventually got safely back to our own front line. There we found that, by an absolute miracle, not one of us had even been wounded! Our guardian angels must have been watching over us that night – I am sure![2]
>
> Private Albert Atkins, 1/7th Battalion, Middlesex Regiment, 167th Brigade, 56th Division

As the British raised the tempo of the war the Germans were soon stung into retaliatory action with the result that what had been a fairly quiet front soon became a deeply threatening environment.

> Very lights lit the place up just like one of those Christmass cards, but death lurked there waiting for anybody who was foolish enough to admire the scenery. The long nights I spent on sentry alone in the fire bay at night straining my eyes peering at the German lines in the distance. I could even hear their transport behind the village; sounds carry a long way at night. The large black rats disturbed the empty bully beef tins out in front of the wire causing them to tinkle, made my hair stand on end. Sometimes thinking a German patrol was cutting the wire, I would fire off a round or two to scare them off. Every now and again a lone machine gun would traverse the parapet and then I would hear a soft plop from the trenches in the distance. Then I would scan the night sky and watch an object like a comet coming towards our trenches. These mortars, which we named 'flying pigs', caused havoc if they fell in one of the fire bays.[3]
>
> Private Albert Conn, 8th Battalion, Devonshire Regiment, 20th Brigade, 7th Division

Inevitably, as the level of fighting increased so did the day-to-day losses. Each and every death in those early days seemed excruciatingly painful to men forced to watch their young friends dying for the first time. Each victim was still an individual; this was not yet a crude mass slaughter. Private Davie Starrett was heartbroken when one of his best friends was badly hit and obviously dying from his wounds.

> As I went to him he opened his eyes. He was all in. He put out a weak hand and I held it, wanting to grip it and afraid too lest I hurt him more. 'Hard luck!' I managed to say, and he whispered, 'Thanks, Davie … ' Then he smiled and they took him away. I am not ashamed to say I blundered back to the dugout without seeing where I was

> going. Telling the Colonel, he said, 'Always the best who go, Starrett, always the best. The best friends, the best soldiers, the best fighters.' He added fiercely, 'And while they go west others at home grow fat in security – the cowards!'[4]
>
> Private Davie Starrett, 9th Battalion, Royal Irish Rifles, 107th Brigade, 36th (Ulster) Division

Slowly, but surely, the rolling Somme countryside surrendered to the bleak embrace of total war. One young private in the Devonshire Regiment witnessed what seemed to him a deeply significant incident.

> A small bird sang on a stunted tree in Mansell Copse. At the break of dawn we used to listen to it and wonder that amongst so much misery and death a bird could sing. One morning a corporal visiting the fire posts heard the bird singing and muttering, 'What the hell have you got to sing about?' fired and killed it. A couple of the lads told him to fuck off out of it. We missed the bird.[5]
>
> Private Albert Conn, 8th Battalion, Devonshire Regiment, 20th Brigade, 7th Division

The needless slaughter of the harmless bird was an obvious harbinger of what was to come. Soon Mansell Wood would be a place of mass death and destruction and far too many of the men of the 8th Devons would find their last resting place under its splintered trees.

DESPITE THE OVERALL failure of the Loos offensive, Haig had retained his trust in General Sir Henry Rawlinson and was impressed by the overall vigour shown by General Sir Hubert Gough. As a result he appointed Rawlinson to command the new Fourth Army formed to conduct the initial stages of the Somme offensive and decided to appoint Gough to command the not yet constituted Reserve Army (later known as the Fifth Army) charged with the important task of energetically exploiting the anticipated breakthrough. Rawlinson, who had both the greater experience and the greater responsibility, had certainly realised many of the prerequisites for success on the Western Front. After his appointment to the Fourth Army on 1 March 1916, Rawlinson began to prepare his plans. Inevitably these plans passed through many versions, but the dilemmas that he had to resolve can usefully be simplified. He had to decide where exactly to attack, what length and type of bombardment to use, how far he was to attempt to go in the first phase, what delay before the second phase, and whether he was to attempt any kind of a breakthrough or merely secure the Somme ridges by use of 'bite and hold' tactics. Having toured the front line and examined the aerial photographs that revealed the intimidating strength of the German defences, Rawlinson had no doubt that a cautious approach would be wise.

Rawlinson's first plan was put forward to Haig on 3 April 1916. It was soundly rooted in the lessons he had assimilated in the battles of 1915. He had noted that the one advantage the British had in the Somme sector was that most of the German First Line system was under observation from the British lines, lying as it did on the forward slopes of the ridge. The long white chalk scars snaking across the green hills were obvious targets for his gunners. However, he equally noted that not only was the reverse slope Second Line system only visible by use of aerial observation but it was well out of range of the British field artillery – indeed, only the longest range guns could hope to reach it. He therefore proposed an advance in the first instance of just 2,000 yards to seize the German front-line system from Serre to Maricourt. Then, after a suitable gap to allow the guns to move forward and register their targets, a second stage would attempt another 'bite' of about 1,000 yards and include a limited section of the German Second Line system from Serre via Pozières to Contalmaison before 'rolling up' the line to the south. In spirit this was pure 'bite and hold'. As to the bombardment, although he tended to the hurricane bombardment theory, he felt that he still had too few guns for such a length of front to guarantee cutting the wire and smashing the German front line. He was inclined to ignore the possibilities of gas attacks – undoubtedly chastened by his experiences at Loos. He did, however, hope to explore the potential of smoke screens to screen the passage of his infantry across the open wastes of No Man's Land.

These plans were not considered anywhere near bold enough by Haig and his General Headquarters staff.

> I studied Sir Henry Rawlinson's proposals for attack. His intention is merely to take the enemy's first and second system of trenches and 'kill Germans', He looks upon the gaining of three or four kilometres more or less of ground immaterial. I think we can

> do better than this by aiming at getting as large a combined force of French and British across the Somme and fighting the enemy in the open![6]
>
> General Sir Douglas Haig, General Headquarters, BEF

Haig proposed that the first step should be much more ambitious and incorporate within the objectives all the German Second Line system from Serre via Pozières and right down to the ridge facing the British held village of Maricourt. He wanted a short hurricane bombardment to provide an element of surprise and allow the infantry to rush forward and be on the German defenders in the First and Second Line systems before they knew what was happening. He feared that caution might cause missed opportunities if the German front showed signs of collapse. North of the Ancre they were to seize possession of the ridge as it ran from Serre to Miraumont to provide a strong defensive flank for the main attack. The second phase would then be a push forward to take the sector of the ridge stretching from Bazentin-le-Grand to Ginchy, before driving further eastwards towards Combles. Meanwhile the French would thrust forward to take from Maurepas to Hem, some 10 miles to the north of the Somme, and the Flaucourt ridge facing Péronne to the south of the river. Haig also proposed a diversionary attack on the Gommecourt salient a little further to the north to try and engender some measure of tactical surprise. This additional, almost throwaway scheme would eventually mature as the simultaneous attack carried out by the Third Army under the command of General Sir Edmund Allenby.

What Haig was proposing was emphatically not 'bite and hold'; this would be an attempt at an outright breakthrough. Haig had been seduced by the potential of massed artillery as demonstrated at least in part by the early German operations at Verdun. But questions remained: even in 1916, had the British Army sufficient guns and shells to carry out this kind of devastating bombardment on such a wide 25,000-yard front? Did they have enough heavy guns to reach deep behind the front line to destroy a complete Second Line system that could not even be seen except from the air? By including the Second Line system as a first day objective, Haig also included it in the prior bombardments. Unless the amount of artillery was increased – and it was not – it was plain that every shell fired into the German Second Line trenches and the wire that would bar their

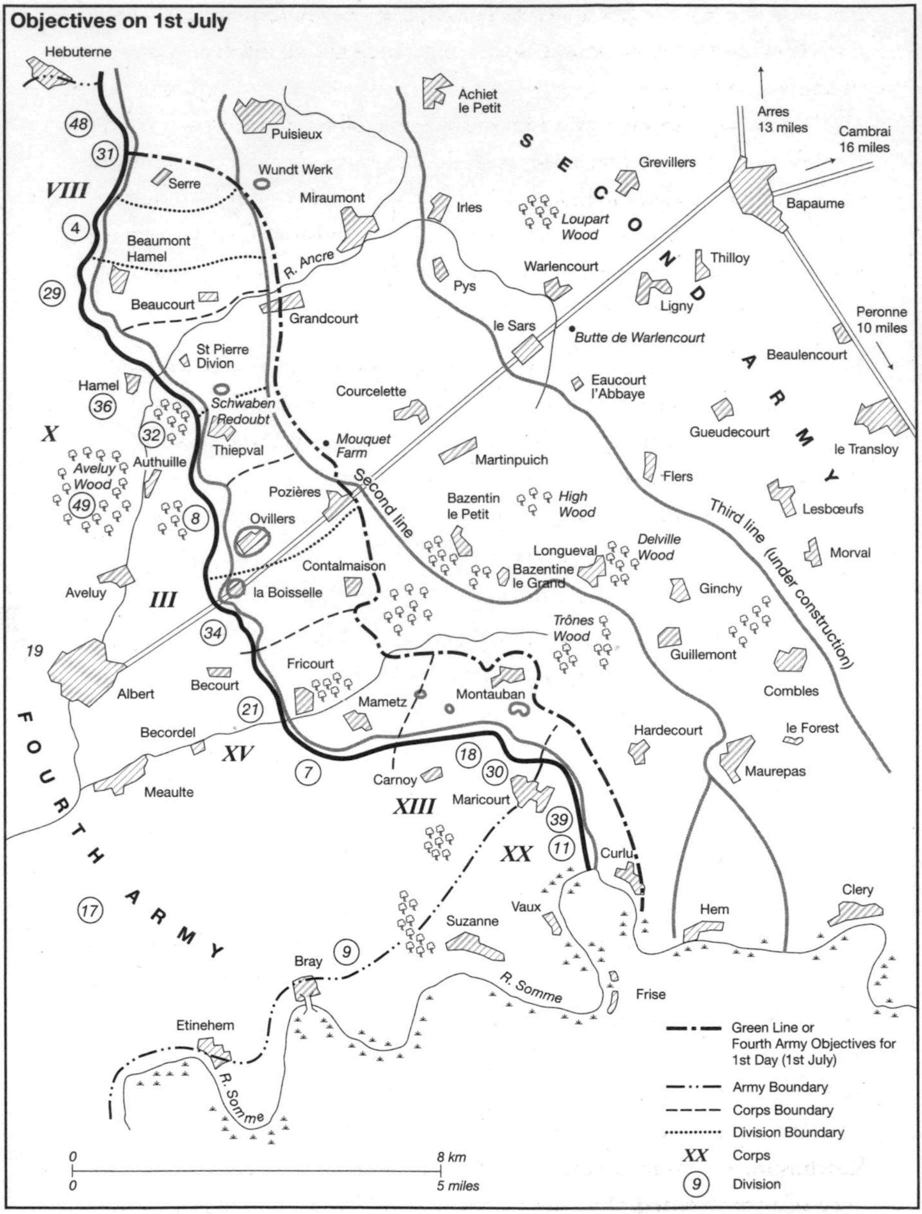

Objectives on 1st July
Hebuterne
Puisieux
Achiet le Petit
Arres 13 miles
Cambrai 16 miles
Wundt Werk
Serre
Miraumont
Irles
Grevillers
Bapaume
Loupart Wood
Beaumont Hamel
R. Ancre
Thilloy
Warlencourt
Pys
Beaucourt
Grandcourt
Ligny
le Sars
Peronne 10 miles
Butte de Warlencourt
St Pierre Divion
Beaulencourt
Hamel
Courcelette
Eaucourt l'Abbaye
Schwaben Redoubt
Gueudecourt
Mouquet Farm
Thiepval
le Transloy
Authuille
Aveluy Wood
Martinpuich
Flers
Second line
Pozières
Bazentin le Petit
High Wood
Third line (under construction)
Lesbœufs
Ovillers
Delville Wood
Longueval
Morval
Contalmaison
Bazentine le Grand
Aveluy
Ginchy
la Boisselle
Trônes Wood
Guillemont
Albert
Fricourt
Becourt
Combles
Montauban
Mametz
Becordel
Hardecourt
le Forest
Maurepas
Carnoy
Meaulte
Maricourt
Curlu
Clery
Hem
Vaux
Suzanne
Bray
R. Somme
Frise
Etinehem
SECOND ARMY
FOURTH ARMY
VIII
X
III
XV
XIII
XX
48
31
4
29
36
32
49
8
34
19
21
7
18
30
39
11
17
9
0
8 km
0
5 miles
Green Line or Fourth Army Objectives for 1st Day (1st July)
Army Boundary
Corps Boundary
Division Boundary
XX Corps
9 Division

way, was one less fired at the German First Line – which, after all, would have to be overcome before the advancing troops could make any progress at all.

Rawlinson's response was interesting – and all too redolent of his willingness the previous year to sway with the breeze during the planning process that preceded the Battle of Neuve Chapelle. Privately he remained convinced that slow and steady was best, and although he was brave enough to restate his objections, ultimately he was all too willing to kowtow to Haig's request for a redrafted plan.

> It still seems to me that an attempt to gain more distant objectives, that is to say the enemy's Second Line system … involves considerable risks. I, however, fully realise that it may be necessary to incur these risks in view of the importance of the object to be attained. This will, no doubt, be decided by the Commander in Chief, and definite instructions be sent me in due course.[7]
>
> Lieutenant General Sir Henry Rawlinson, Headquarters, Fourth Army

Indeed, Rawlinson actually won the point over the length of the preliminary bombardment, but the concluding passage exposed a weakness at the heart of Rawlinson's generalship. The importance of an objective does not have any effect on the *likelihood* of a successful attack upon that objective. It merely increased the chance that the Germans would have taken every defensive precaution and be equally willing to risk everything to hold on to the prize.

Rawlinson's instructions to attempt the German Second Line positions were finally confirmed in writing on 16 May. The fatal decision had been taken. At the same time he was informed that after he had secured the expected breakthrough then General Gough would have two corps for exploitation, either under the aegis of Rawlinson or independently under his own command as a separate Reserve Army.

Throughout the planning process Haig did not relax his pressure on Rawlinson, watching closely for signs of backsliding into an easy acceptance of more limited objectives. At least until it was proved impossible, Haig was determined that they had to be ready to exploit a major breakthrough. The fact that this would involve the use of the cavalry has often been satirised, but the cavalry was, after all, Haig's only means of rapid exploitation and pursuit in 1916.

> I told him to impress on his corps commanders the use of their Corps Cavalry and mounted troops, and if necessary supplement them with regular cavalry units. In my opinion it is better to prepare to advance beyond the enemy's last line of trenches, because we are then in a position to take advantage of any breakdown in the enemy's defense. Whereas if there is a stubborn resistance put up, the matter settles itself! On the other hand if no preparations for an advance are made till next morning, we might lose a golden opportunity.[8]
>
> General Sir Douglas Haig, General Headquarters, BEF

Haig was also greatly concerned to urge Rawlinson to strain every sinew to accelerate the training of the divisions under his command. This was a matter of increasing importance as the British Army began to realise the seriousness of sending in half-trained infantry against experienced German units occupying superbly fortified defensive positions. But before the training process could begin the exact tactics to be employed on the day of the assault had to be decided, and the men trained in their exact roles, so that they would not be overcome by nerves when they went over the top.

The basic plan developed by the Fourth Army was simple and built round the power of the guns amassed for the attack. The industrial might of the British Empire was symbolised by these guns: there were 1,010 field artillery guns and howitzers (808 18-pounder guns and 202 4.5-in howitzers), 182 medium and heavy guns (32 4.7-in guns, 128 60-pounders, 20 6-in guns, one 9.2-in gun and one 12-in gun) and 245 medium and heavy howitzers (104 6-in howitzers, 64 8-in howitzers, 60 9.2-in howitzers, 11 12-in howitzers and 6 15-in howitzers). In addition there were 100 French guns assigned to the front. This meant an unprecedented total of 1,537 guns and howitzers – in other words one field gun to every 20 yards of front and one heavy gun to every 58 yards of front. Ammunition, so often in short supply in 1915, was now plentiful with each gun having access to hundreds of rounds of ammunition in dumps close to hand, with proper resupply arrangements. The artillery plans prepared by the Fourth Army laid down the general tasks to be achieved by the guns under the subordinate corps' control during the planned six-day bombardment, but left the actual achievement of those tasks to the individual corps and divisional commanders. Simply put, the guns were to clear away the

German barbed wire defences, smash their lines of fortifications and destroy their artillery batteries.

It was clearly recognised that the German artillery would pose a severe threat if it was not dealt with before the infantry exposed themselves in No Man's Land and therefore special arrangements were made for counter-battery fire. Only the heavier guns and howitzers had the long range necessary to reach the German gun lines and each corps allotted a certain number of heavy and medium batteries to the task. Unfortunately, amidst the many other priorities that fought for their attention, it was inevitable that sometimes there were simply not enough guns to go round. One corps allocated only derisory numbers of shells – as few as six in one case – to deal with target batteries. There was no overall understanding of the absolute necessity for pinpoint accuracy in counter-battery fire and even with the help of artillery observation aircraft the task was often beyond the raw gunners.

Throughout the artillery planning process, much thought was given to the question of the manner of movement of the barrage line of exploding shells during the actual assault. In general it was considered that this should lift directly to the next German line of trenches when the British infantry emerged from their trenches and set off across No Man's Land. But there was an emerging interest in new theories introducing a much more sophisticated form of barrage which would start in No Man's Land and move up to and over the German front line, covering and carrying with it the attacking infantry who would be close behind. This would then creep forward to the next objective in the same manner. The idea was that shells would continue bursting between the attacking infantry and the Germans leaving the defenders no time to wreak their havoc on the British infantry following up. This form of barrage would become know as the 'creeping barrage' and it was to become the fulcrum of British attacks for the next two years. However, these were early days. Many of the gunners were worried by the daunting task of preparing and firing accurately such a barrage; the infantry did not really see the point and certainly many divisional and brigade commanders did not understand why the barrage had to start in front of the German lines. As the artillery plans were left to the corps and divisional commanders most preferred to stick with what they knew.

The end result was that in the majority of cases the preliminary bombardments followed the old pattern – building to a crescendo in the lead up to Zero Hour before lifting abruptly to drop on to the next identified German trench. The infantry, who were meant to have crept into No Man's Land about 100 yards from the back of the barrage line of bursting shells prior to the lift, would then move forward to seize the German front line. Then, according to a timetable, they would move into the gap between the German trenches and await the next lift to the next German line. It was intended that this process would be repeated several times in accordance with the timetable. This optimistic approach, which allowed nothing for hold-ups and the general confusion of war, was based on the belief expressed by both Haig and Rawlinson that the bombardment would sweep everything before it and that the infantry would be faced with minimal opposition.

As there was not going to be any opposition there was, therefore, no need for any haste. According to the tactical instructions issued by the Fourth Army the advance across No Man's Land would be made at a steady walking pace in long lines of men just 2 or 3 yards apart. This would ensure that the relatively untrained troops did not lose their alignment and would thereby arrive upon the German line at exactly the same time. There would only be 100 yards or so between waves: if there was some kind of a hold-up it was hoped that these closely following waves would add their weight to the assault to overcome the blockage swiftly and get them back on 'timetable'. The first wave was not intended to mop up the German front line but was to keep going to their deeper objectives, while the following waves mopped up and then pushed on behind the first wave. The men would carry with them everything that they might need on the first two days to allow them properly to consolidate their imagined gains. This, as we shall see, was a considerable undertaking in that the weight of all their kit and equipment (66 lbs) would inevitably restrict the mobility and speed of the men across any kind of broken ground.

The Fourth Army tactical instructions were for guidance and some formations developed their own subtle variations but, for the most part, there was a fair degree of uniformity in tactics all along the British line. More complex tactics of small columns, advance infiltration patrols and the use of lightly equipped parties of men to race ahead across No Man's Land to surprise the Germans right on the heels of the barrage were almost completely eschewed. Fundamentally the British Army commanders did not feel that their men were sufficiently well trained to be trusted in any form of tactic that needed either brains or skill. Yet in a sense this was a pessimistic stance as in the battles of 1915 the territorial divisions had responded well under the stimulus of battle.

As the battle approached the British began to tire of the French chopping and changing their plans and commitments on the Somme. Dismissive remarks are frequently found in letters and diaries from men who could have had no conception of the nature of the fighting at Verdun. They would soon learn for themselves just how bad war could be.

> I wonder what the French are playing at – from the little I hear I think they are at their old game, they do not want us to pull the chestnuts out of the fire. They growl when we do not attack and growl still more when they think we are going to be successful – that may be exaggerated, but certainly the date was put forward to please them and now it is delayed again.[9]
>
> Brigadier Archibald Home, Headquarters, 46th Division

There was certainly a degree of exasperation in Haig's diary account of his meeting with Joffre on 17 June. He certainly felt that the British plans were being threatened by the French dithering:

> We discussed the date for starting our offensive. He wished it to be 1 July. I pointed out that we had arranged to be ready on the 25th to please him. The 29th ought to be the latest date; in my opinion it was unwise to run the risk of the enemy discovering our area of concentration and then attacking where our lines were thin and ill provided with artillery. Finally we agreed that the attack should be fixed for 29th but Rawlinson and Foch will be given power if the day is bad to postpone the attack from day to day till the weather is fine.[10]
>
> General Sir Douglas Haig, General Headquarters, BEF

Despite his own reservation about the state of training of his troops and his oft-stated personal preference for an offensive in Flanders fields, and despite the inability of the French to play their original role, Haig was willing to risk his army for the greater good of the alliance – the Anglo-French Alliance, which offered the only feasible way of winning the war. Ready or not the British were coming.

EARLY IN 1916 the headquarters staff of the BEF and Fourth Army had begun the awesome task of achieving the deployment of some 400,000 men, over 1,000 guns and 100,000 horses ready for the battle that was at the heart of the Allied plans. They were immediately aware that the Somme area was by no means the ideal place for the concentration of such an unprecedented amount of men, horses, equipment, stores and munitions. The Somme had been chosen because that was where the British and French sectors adjoined each other and could attack together. There were no particular strategic reasons other than this contiguity and, indeed, the Somme was an agricultural province that was almost devoid of a modern road and rail network. This presented a nightmare for the planners. Before they could even begin to move the military pieces into place in the battlefield jigsaw they had to create an infrastructure almost from scratch. War in 1916 was simply not possible without a thorough grasp of the theory and practice of the science of logistics.

Overall communications were poor and the paucity of the railway network linking Albert at the heart of the Somme to the rest of the French rail network was a particularly severe problem. Only freight trains had anything like the physical capability to move the huge quantities that were required for the offensive in the given timescale. Industrious staff officers calculated that every single day the Fourth Army would need fourteen trains to carry ammunition, a further eleven trains for supplies and six trains to carry the reinforcements, horses and general stores. This meant that all in all some thirty-one trains per day were needed just to service the Fourth Army and when the offensive began it was reckoned that this might rise to seventy trains. As only two lines served the Albert area and one of those was of an inconveniently non-standard gauge, it was obvious that something drastic would have to be done if this capacity was to be met. It is a testament to the scale and importance of the operations being planned that it was decided without further ado to construct two new standard gauge lines, which would provide a much-increased number of railheads for the battlefront. Further rail spurs and sidings were built to service ammunition and supply depots, while stations were expanded and developed with more and longer platforms. Understandably, while this major construction project was going on, light railway systems to extend forward from the railheads were not considered a priority, although the tracks already installed by the French were taken over and extended as appropriate.

This was perhaps unfortunate as the inevitably rural character of the area meant that the roads were not robust enough to withstand the heavy demands that would be placed upon them by a veritable army of feet, hooves and grinding wheels. Even the few metalled main roads were not constructed to sufficiently stringent standards and were liable to break up once the surface had been cracked open to expose the chalk rubble that lay below. Side roads were essentially little more than rough tracks and soon became so muddy that they were all but indistinguishable from the neighbouring fields. Efforts were made to improve and widen the roads leading directly from the railheads and bridges were strengthened as necessary, but these efforts were insufficient to resolve the problem. A widespread programme of road construction could have been undertaken, but that in turn would have only massively increased the burden placed on the already struggling railways, as there was no local source of the huge quantities of stone necessary for road foundations. So in the end patchwork repairs, carried out only as and when the road surface collapsed, would have to suffice.

Behind the British lines small country villages and local farms that would have struggled in peacetime to provide sufficient billets for a couple of hundred men were soon swamped. Bivouacs, tents and huts were the obvious answer and imposing camps were soon erected all around the villages and woods.

> It was decided that Ville-sous-Corbie should be company headquarters on the Somme. The billets consisted of one large barn with a large and absolutely barren field. Within a fortnight Major Philpotts had made comfortable beds of timber and wire netting for everyone, cookhouses and stables. At the lower end off the yard he had improvised a band-saw, two circular saws, a drilling machine, lathe and grindstone – all driven from one shaft by two 10 hp steam engines and a small petrol engine – and at very little cost for practically all the machinery was salvaged from damaged French factories at Albert. A party of men worked in the woods which lie close to Ville in the Ancre marshes, cutting down suitable trees and lopping off branches. A pair of horses dragged the trees to the workshop, where another party of men barked them and they were then lifted by the crane, another home-made patent of the Major's, up to the band-saw, from there to the circular

> saws, cut to the required size and loaded straight on to the wagons, which were parked within a few feet, and up the line the same night.[11]
>
> Sergeant Frank Aincham, 97th Field Company, Royal Engineers, 21st Division

Water supplies that had been adequate enough for the existing population were soon overwhelmed by demand. Thirsty men also needed water to wash themselves and their uniforms, and the thousands of horses seemed to drink their own weight in water on a regular basis. Even the lorry radiators needed plentiful water. New wells had to be dug, pumping equipment installed and miles of piping laid to ensure that proper high-capacity water points were available as near as possible to the front lines. Overall the effort required from the British Empire to drag this segment of rural French countryside – the Somme valley – into the twentieth century was a truly monumental undertaking. It was deeply ironic that it was being modernised solely to facilitate the prosecution of a battle that would eventually reduce much of it to mud, splinters and rubble.

Even the deceptively simple problem of moving the infantry and guns forward was a nightmare of complexity. Roads had to be assigned for the move, signposts erected, control posts established at major crossroads and military police used to control the burgeoning traffic. Clear instructions had to be given to everyone concerned. A million mind boggling details had to be resolved by a chain of command that was at times stretched gossamer thin. The roads were packed with traffic that ranged from the huge howitzers, churning up the *pavé*, tail-to-tail convoys of motor traffic, horse transport of myriad varieties and, of course, the endless column of infantry. There was little or no margin for error.

> The whole of the roads for the 5 miles I travelled were filled with artillery, infantry, motor lorries, ration carts, ammunition wagons, etc., in one unbroken line – going up to the lines full, and being met by a similar continuous stream of empty vehicles returning, like Oliver Twist, for more. Blocks were frequent and it took me over two hours to get to Etinehem, I estimated I saw not less than 3,000 vehicles – all with six horse teams – no Lord Mayor's Show was in it at all.[12]
>
> Lieutenant William Bloor, C Battery, 149th Brigade, Royal Field Artillery, 30th Division

A traffic census[13] taken on one vital thoroughfare discovered that in just one day some 26,536 soldiers; 63 guns; 568 cars; 617 motorcycles; 5,404 riding horses; 813 lorries and a frankly incredible 3,756 horse wagons passed by. In these circumstances there were of course delays, blockages and confusion but in the main the process worked relatively smoothly.

> Everybody seemed lively on the march and we swung along to some of our favourite marching songs such as 'Blighty Land' and 'I want to go Home'. Great scenes were to be seen along the roads and long streams of ammunition columns and motor lorries were making their way to the scene of operations. The guns were now heard distinctly and the crump of our big guns encouraged us greatly, for we infantrymen always like to know that we have got good artillery behind us.[14]
>
> Lance Corporal Sidney Appleyard, 1/9th Battalion (Queen Victoria's Rifles), London Regiment, 169th Brigade, 56th Division

To the Germans, watching from their lines along the ridges, the sight of the whole strength of the British Army steadily amassing below them was ominous. No one knew for certain what was happening but they could be sure that the British meant them no good.

> The preparation of the coming great offensive had begun long ago. Day and night we heard trains roll across the valley of the Ancre and speculated what they were transporting. Three months later we should get the answer to our queries.[15]
>
> Lieutenant F. L. Cassel, 99th Infantry Reserve Regiment, 26th Reserve Division, German Army

As the day of the offensive drew ever nearer the units occupying the front line began to dig trenches in No Man's Land. This was fundamentally intended to cut down the distance across No Man's Land, to minimise the distance they would have to cross under fire when the great day finally dawned. In front of the village of Gommecourt the gap between the lines was an excessive 800 yards, which would have left any assaulting troops under fire for far too long. It was decided that it was worth running the risk of exposing thousands of men digging a new line in the middle of No Man's Land. This would have the additional benefit of clearly demonstrating an intention to attack – and, after all, the assault on Gommecourt was a diversion.

Firstly, the new trenches were marked out and then the work proper began on the night of 26 May. It was an enormous undertaking for some 2,900 yards of trenches were required, serviced by a further 1,500 yards of communication trenches. The digging men were covered by darkness, but extraordinarily vulnerable to an outbreak of German machine-gun fire or shell fire should the alarm be triggered. As a precaution every British artillery unit in the sector was placed on alert ready to plaster the German lines and batteries. Despite the risks, all went well and good progress was made as the shallow new lines began to take shape before the dawn suspended their digging. Over the next couple of nights the 1/9th London Regiment were amongst those sent forward to finish the task. With only half-dug, shallow trenches for shelter they were still considerably exposed.

> The enemy was very quiet, not a shot nor the boom of a gun, and the stillness was oppressive. From previous experience I knew that something was coming – and it did. We started to dig at ten o'clock, but we hadn't started two minutes before the enemy bombarded us like fury with shells of all sizes, they crashed and splintered all around us. The din was terrific and the flashes from bursting shells blinding. All we could do was to lay flat down in the bottom of the shallow trench. For ten minutes the shells fell thick and fast, striking the parapets and burying many with earth. One shell crashed into the top of the trench above my head, but fortunately didn't explode. All this time the enemy's machine gun spouted bullets at us, but by providence no casualties occurred. Soon the bombardment ceased and we resumed work again. During the enemy's bombardment our artillery had been very quiet, but within half an hour of our resuming work the artillery burst forth in a deafening crash on this wood and the trenches surrounding it. The crash of our shells as they fell in the wood was a sight terrible but wonderful. The wood appeared to catch on fire. Our men stood up head and shoulders above the trench to see the effects, but even that must end, and soon everything was quiet again.[16]
>
> Private Reuben Stockman, 1/9th Battalion (Queen Victoria's Rifles), London Regiment, 169th Brigade, 56th Division

Next night Stockman was assigned to the covering party sent out in front of the new trench system in No Man's Land to provide a defensive screen while the barbed wire was installed. They were there to prevent the wiring party being surprised by a German fighting patrol.

> When darkness came we were waiting in the trench and when all was ready we creep out in a single file towards the German trenches.

> Through a gap in a hedge we pushed as silently as possible, and every man ready to drop flat in the event of a machine gun being turned on us. Arriving about 80 yards in front of our trenches the first man takes up his position laying flat on his stomach with his rifle well forward and hand near the trigger. The man behind comes up on his right or left and does the same thing at an interval of 3 yards and so the whole company proceeds until a human barricade has been formed between the Germans and our trench. Behind us another company is swiftly but silently fixing up the barbed wire and it's this party that we are protecting. To try and explain one's feelings while lying there is utterly impossible. My own feelings were awful. My heart was thumping like a sledge-hammer and my whole body was on a shiver. For upwards of an hour we lay so. Then the enemy must have heard the wire party, for immediately in front of us a star shell was sent up lighting everything around for a hundred yards or so. All we could do was to lie perfectly still. Two more star shells in quick succession follow, and my heart stood still as it seemed impossible that they couldn't discover us. I think it must have been a signal to the artillery, because within fifteen seconds of the last star light burning out their artillery burst out. Those shells seemed to burst all around us, but fortunately they burst too much to our rear, and so on, till it was quiet again, except for a machine gun that tried to get us, but was aiming too high. In an hour's time the same thing was repeated and much nearer, yet still we had no casualties. Still they weren't satisfied for at half past twelve again the shells came and this time they got us. Shrapnel burst right above our heads – pieces of shells whizzed across our backs, and I thought I was for it. But no, when it was all over, I was still unhurt, but bathed in cold perspiration. I could hear several groans on my right.'[17]
>
> Private Reuben Stockman, 1/9th Battalion (Queen Victoria's Rifles), London Regiment, 169th Brigade, 56th Division

By sheer hard work they had managed to cut the distance across No Man's Land to around 400 yards. The new lines of trenches and aggressive posture of the 46th and 56th Divisions at Gommecourt were clearly visible to the Germans. The Germans reacted by bringing up another division to face the obvious threat to the salient. As Lieutenant General Sir Thomas Snow commander of the parent VII Corps, reported to Haig, 'They know we are coming all right.'[18] So far the Gommecourt diversion was working well.

As the time for the offensive grew imminent there was even more digging to be carried out all along the line: every battalion, every battery, every higher formation needed a headquarters dugout to accommodate the commanding officer, his adjutant, staff and signallers. These dugouts varied wildly in size according to whim, but for larger formations such as the infantry brigades they had to be of a considerable size just to accommodate the sheer numbers that needed shelter. But a far greater commitment was to dig assembly trenches for the attacking troops. The existing front line could not possibly contain all the men that would have to attack together and a series of extra trenches had to be dug to shelter them before they went over the top. This was back-breaking work under conditions that caused considerable resentment towards the Royal Engineers that supervised the tasks.

> The men were given tasks which could not be done in the time specified. In the Royal Engineer textbooks and manuals there were standard times for work like digging trenches – so many cubic feet dug per hour. These times were obtained in ideal conditions at Aldershot in pre-war days, by highly trained regular soldiers, and it was not reasonable to expect the same performance in the most difficult war conditions – frequently under direct hostile machine-gun fire – from our mixed collection of old and young men, strong and weak. The human element was very often quite ignored by RE authorities. If a party of men could dig a 50 yards length of trench in two hours, they did not see any reason why they should not dig 150 yards in six hours. The possibility of their becoming exhausted after the third hour of strenuous digging and of their being incapable of doing anything at all after the fourth hour didn't seem to occur to them. The work would be carried on until 2 or 3 in the morning, when we would collect ourselves together and march home, being pretty well exhausted by the time we had got there.[19]
>
> Lieutenant William Colyer, 2nd Battalion, Royal Dublin Fusiliers, 10th Brigade, 4th Division

When at last the assembly trenches were completed they were usually covered with a layer of wire netting and roughly chopped grass in the hope that they would be invisible to the Germans. In the area targeted for the real assault it was essential to conceal as much as possible of the offensive preparations.

The Royal Engineers themselves were engaged in constructing a series of 'Russian saps' out under the wire and deep into No Man's Land. These were shallow tunnels, just a couple of feet under the surface, which could be opened up as required to provide relatively safe communication across No Man's Land. In some cases the head of the tunnel could be opened and expanded to allow the insertion of a Vickers machine gun or Stokes mortar in a post threateningly close to the German front line. Several such Russian saps were constructed towards the village of Serre. Naturally, the infantry were keen to make use of the shelter offered by the tunnels.

> One day a few of us in turns went for a rest just behind the front line in a 'mine-head' which is the entrance to an underground passage running under No Man's Land to underneath the enemy trenches where explosives were packed ready to be fired when the attack began. It was dry and seemed safe enough when suddenly a German shell fell right on the entrance and we were trapped. After a search we found the only way out was to get through a small passage to the next mine-head and hope that was clear. Never shall I forget the feeling of suffocation as we crawled on our stomachs dragging our rifles and equipment after us. It couldn't have been very far, but it seemed miles.[20]
>
> Private Clifford Carter, 10th Battalion, East Yorkshire Regiment, 92nd Brigade, 31st Division

The damage was quickly repaired and the Russian sap remained ready for action.

The tunnelling companies were also frenetically but quietly busy constructing a series of nineteen mines to be detonated under the German lines at the crucial moment. These were very different in scale from the Russian saps and represented major engineering projects in their own right. In the north, the 252nd Tunnelling Company succeeded in drilling a large mine some 75 feet deep and over 1,000 feet long all the way out towards the German strong point of Hawthorn Redoubt in front of Beaumont Hamel. The chalk was rock hard, which made silent digging excessively difficult. In the end it was found that if the chalk was first soaked then it could be prised out in lumps without too much noise. Next in line, the 179th Tunnelling Company had dug two huge mines and flanking mines under the La Boisselle Salient. This sector had been the focus of virulent underground warfare and No Man's Land was a confused tangle of craters left by the explosion of mines. Here there were different problems for the sappers as the chalk had been powdered by the concussive effect of frequent explosions and as a result the men had to dig right down to 100 feet to find solid chalk. Meanwhile the 178th Tunnelling Company was responsible for three large mines feeling their way out from the Tambour Salient towards the village of Fricourt; the 174th Tunnelling Company was digging mines towards Mametz; and, finally, the 183rd Tunnelling Company was located next to the French sector in the south.

This was an area that had been the scene of underground warfare for over a year. Secrecy was crucial and as the tunnels approached the German front the digging was carried out with extreme caution to avoid tell-tale noises seeping through to the Germans working in their own tunnels not many feet away. Both sides were aware that the other was tunnelling but, of course, they did not know where. Talking was absolutely forbidden, and a thick carpet of sandbags on the floor of the tunnel allowed the men to remove their heavy boots to go barefoot. Soundless progress in the unyielding chalk was only achieved by using bayonets on spliced handles. Piece by piece was prised from the chalk face and they inched towards the Germans at a rate of about 18 inches a day. The importance of silence could be judged by the clear audibility of the Germans working close by in their own mines.

> You had to listen to what the Germans were doing; you had to outsmart them. You had listening posts deep down in the chalk, I took my turn in listening. Sitting down in the bowels of the earth listening for what was going on. You had primitive listening instruments, electrified earphones and you could easily hear people tapping away a long distance through the chalk. Then if you listened carefully if they were making a chamber to put the explosive charge in you could hear the much more hollow noise of digging. Following that you would hear the sinister sliding of bags of explosive into the chamber. Following that you got out![21]
>
> Lieutenant Norman Dillon, 178th Tunnelling Company, Royal Engineers

The sappers finished their work during the final weeks and it was left to repair parties to ensure that nothing untoward happened to the shafts.

WITHOUT DOUBT, the most important component in the British attack on the Somme was the Royal Artillery. With the Royal Flying Corps conducting aerial reconnaissance and observation for them, the artillery was the weapon of war that was intended to bring the Germans to their knees. As the guns began to move forward into their battle positions it was essential that they do so as unobtrusively as possible without drawing the attention of the Germans. If new battery-gun positions were identified they would be vulnerable to potentially devastating German counter-battery fire. Sometimes gun-pits had already been prepared to minimise the visual disturbance to the landscape and some of these were almost works of art. The 147th Brigade, RFA moved into such positions along the poplar-tree-lined road between Englebelmer and Mailly-Maillet.

> The gun emplacements, set at 20-yard intervals, closely resembled the tumuli frequently seen on Salisbury Plain and had at the 'business end' an aperture large enough to allow for elevation and a sweep of 80 degrees. Well dug in and each skilfully camouflaged and protected by an overhead half-barrel shaped roof, supported by strong beams of timber on which was heaped several layers of sandbags covered with turfs of green grass. It was difficult even at close quarters to detect that concealed here was a formidable unit of destruction. On either side of the spade of the trail, four steps led down to, on one side the sleeping quarters of the detachment and, on the other, a recess for storing ammunition. The battery staff and signallers' pit was positioned 20 yards south of No. 1 gunpit in line under the trees. It was certainly a masterpiece of engineering ingenuity – a holiday chalet in fact. Six steps led down to a spacious floor above which heavy crossbeams of timber-supported layers of sandbags and turfs similar to the gunpits. The interior was well appointed with tiered bunks along the walls, a space on the floor for the equipment and a frame holding the blanketed gas-screen for placing over the door, if necessary. The command post, which was connected to the signallers' pit by a communication trench, was a deep pit, seven foot by seven foot by seven foot, provided with a small rough table sufficient to accommodate a message pad and a D3 telephone, an empty ammunition box as a bench, and two sleeping bunks, tiered – one for the officer on duty and the other for the signaller at rest. A ladder led from the floor up to the

command post above, up which the officer would shin when alerted, to shout his orders to the guns, through a megaphone from an aperture facing the guns.[22]

Signaller Dudley Menaud-Lissenburg, 97th Battery, 147th Brigade, Royal Field Artillery, 29th Division

More and more batteries of guns flooded into the Somme and Ancre valleys. Most were the 18-pounder and 4.5-in field artillery guns but there were new heavier guns and howitzers beginning to appear at the front. Of these one of the most startling was the 8-in howitzer used by the 36th Siege Artillery Battery.

We were the first battery to arrive with guns any bigger than 6-inch and caused a great deal of attention by the higher authorities because of the sheer weight of ammunition which these 8-inch howitzers could produce. But they were improvised howitzers, because they were old 6-inch Mark Is, cut in half and the front half was thrown away. The rest was bored out to 8-inch with rifling and they were given modern breech mechanisms. They were mounted on enormous commercial tractor wheels as they were available. They were monstrous things and extremely heavy, but the machinery of the guns was very simple and that's why they did so extremely well and didn't give nearly as much trouble as some of the more complicated guns that came to appear later on. One was the very first one to be made and it was marked, 'Eight-inch Howitzer No. 1 Mark I' so we called that gun, 'The Original'. It was marvellously accurate.[23]

Second Lieutenant Montague Cleeve, 36th Siege Artillery Battery, Royal Garrison Artillery

Usually the gunners dug their own gunpits and for the crews of the 8-in howitzers this was an exhausting prospect that involved the removal of literally tons of soil and rubble. Again, there was an attempt on relative invisibility using an early type of camouflage netting.

We moved to a splendid position near Beaumetz. The guns were dug into an enormously deep bank about 10 feet deep by the side of a field. The digging we had to do to get into that gun position – 10 feet deep and about 40 feet in length – was simply gigantic. We camouflaged it extremely well by putting wire netting over it threaded with real grass. We had an awful job to manoeuvre the guns into it, because the caterpillars were useless, they could get them into the neighbourhood of the guns, but then we had to manhandle these enormous monsters – they weighed several tons. We had to push them, couldn't pull them, push them into their positions. When they were there they were very well concealed, so much so that a French farmer with his cow walked straight into the net and both fell in. We had the most appalling job getting this beastly cow out of the gun position. The man came out all right, but the cow! However it was enormous fun! It was one of those delightful moments when you all burst out laughing.[24]

Second Lieutenant Montague Cleeve, 36th Siege Artillery Battery, Royal Garrison Artillery

The huge howitzers of the siege artillery were enormously powerful, heavy monsters that needed special measures to tamp down and tame the ferocious recoil every time they were fired. Untrained teams would find that the howitzers had minds of their own and were soon firing with a complete lack of accuracy that rendered them good for nothing but harassing fire. This was the kind of training that only real firing practice, rather than 'gun drill' could give, and many artillery units went through a prolonged learning process before they made the maximum use of their guns' potential accuracy and destructive capacity.

They had to have a wooden platform put down over the rather soft earth to strengthen the surface from which they had to fire. Then they had huge wooden chocks which we put behind the wheels. After the gun was laid, the final thing was to shove these chocks up, hoping they wouldn't move, but they always did because they took half the recoil. Half the recoil was taken by the buffer and half by the movement of the gun. The wheels used to ride right up to the top of the chocks and then the curvature of the chocks made them go back forwards again by gravity. If the drill was bad and the chocks weren't put in quite the right position the gun went back and got slewed round completely off line. One of the skills we developed, purely down to the men, a splendid lot of Durham miners, was to get so good at placing the chocks that we could fire quite rapidly, knowing that the gun would recoil back only a fraction of a degree off the line to the target. It was largely that that I think got us our reputation for being so accurate.[25]

Second Lieutenant Montague Cleeve, 36th Siege Artillery Battery, Royal Garrison Artillery

When the guns' positions were established that was by no means the end of the hard work. The guns relied a great deal on range corrections from their forward observation officers located in the front line. Unfortunately, in the absence of any effective two-way wireless communication the only real alternative was the telephone, which meant that a line had to be laid from the battery signal post right forward to the observation post.

> We had great difficulty in maintaining communications between batteries and the forward observation posts at this time. Our telephone wires ran over open ground for a short distance from the battery and then entered the communication trenches. The first communication trench approached the front line head on, down a long and fairly steep gradient and was, therefore, open to enfilade, so it had a traverse every few feet. The soil here was clay and the rains made it most difficult to progress along the trench. Our telephone wires, together with those of many other units, were stapled to the side of the trench in a bunch. They were easily torn by infantrymen who, loaded with all the paraphernalia of war, could not possibly avoid doing so. The soft, sticky and slippery floor of the trench was treacherous and the poor fellows were labouring through clay at times over their ankles and up to their putteed legs, so it was not prudent to remonstrate when they were near. The wire was torn from the side of the trench, fell to the ground and was trampled into the clayey bottom by all and sundry. It was a nightmare, especially when dark, to follow the wire from the battery to break point 'A' and then, from the forward observation post to break point 'B' and find the ends did not meet.[26]
>
> Signaller Dudley Menaud-Lissenburg, 97th Battery, 147th Brigade, Royal Field Artillery, 29th Division

The infantry watched the guns coming forward with undiluted pleasure, fully aware as they were that their very survival over the next few weeks depended on the guns clearing the German wire, destroying the trenches and strong points, and suppressing the answering roar of the German artillery.

> The face of the earth is changed up there, has changed within the last seven days. It is now honeycombed with gun emplacements. Guns are everywhere. Guns of all calibres. Some 9.2s were registering on Mametz whilst we were watching. They are terrible shells and simply

knocked lumps out of the village. There are 9.2's, 8-ins, 6-ins, 4.7s, 4.5s, 18-pounders and 13-pounders, all sorts and conditions, all bristling out of the ground ready to belch forth a regular tornado of fire. As Worthy said when he saw it, 'Fritz, you're for it!' It is a sentiment I quite agree with. Ammunition is pouring up, that for the heavies by motor transport, that for the lighter fry by wagon and limber. Two convoys of the latter, each of them fully 500 yards in length passed the Bois at sundown. It was a great sight. It is marvellous, this marshalling of power. This concentrated effort of our great nation put forward to the end of destroying our foe. The greatest battle in the world is on the eve of breaking. Please God it may terminate successfully for us. Fritz I think knows all about it. At any rate a day or two ago he put the following notice on his wire opposite the 4th Division. 'When your bombardment starts we are going to bugger off back five miles. Kitchener is buggered. Asquith is buggered. You're buggered. We're buggered. Let's all bugger off home!' It is vulgar, as his humour invariably is, but the sentiments are so eminently those of 'Tommy Atkins' that it must certainly have been a man with a good knowledge of England and the English who wrote the message.[27]

Captain Charles May, 22nd Battalion, Manchester Regiment, 91st Brigade, 7th Division

The planned expenditure of ammunition was enormous and the logistical effort required to get the hundreds of thousands of rounds forward to the batteries and neighbouring ammunition dumps was simply staggering.

For our four guns we accumulated 5,000 rounds of ammunition in holes and pits and anything. It was brought up in wagons to the nearest point to the road and then we had to carry it from there by hand after dark down to whatever pits we were putting them in. You sling two shells together with a stick between the slings and slung them over your shoulder. Sometimes they came up loose and we had to carry them singly. They were very, very hard on your shoulder, a 60-pounder shell, so we used to put a folded sandbag under your braces like a shoulder pad, otherwise your shoulder was very sore by the end of the spell. The cartridge boxes, there were ten in a box, each cartridge weighed 9 lbs 7 oz, plus the metal-lined box, nearly a hundredweight altogether. There

> were wire handles towards the top in each side, of such a length that as you walked the bottom edge was catching on your ankle – devilish things! We used to get two chaps to lift it on your shoulder and you'd carry it on your shoulder, your back and then drop them off. We dug some pits, but we'd strewn them out within a radius of 100 yards behind the battery, so as not to risk too much being hit at once in case the enemy started shelling round there. And by the end of that week we'd used up all that ammunition, plus what had been brought up as well.[28]
>
> Signaller Leonard Ounsworth, 124th Heavy Battery, Royal Garrison Artillery

The days of ammunition shortages had largely disappeared as the industrial might of the British Empire was whipped into the production of munitions. Every 18-pounder gun had been allotted 200 rounds a day for the six days of the bombardment. This worked out at 1,200 rounds a gun or roughly 7,200 rounds per six-gun battery. Heavier guns with a far slower firing rate had a lesser allotment in proportion. One problem that had not yet really become apparent was that although the number of shells was adequate the quality of individual shells had not been maintained. Some of the 6-in shells varied in length by up to four inches which caused them to vary in flight enormously. The fuses in particular were often faulty, which meant that they did not go off and were hence 'duds'.

The importance of the counter-battery role in destroying or subduing the German guns was frequently demonstrated when they opened up in retaliation. Every German shell that landed was a reminder of the destructive power that any surviving German batteries would have if they had not been dealt with before the moment the infantry went over the top.

> At 11.40 p.m. a tremendous roar commenced as every Hun gun along the whole front sprang to life simultaneously in a beautifully timed opening; a moment later a man dashed into my dugout to say that No. 4 pit had blown up! Gum-boots, steel hat, gas mask and electric torch were ready to hand, and in thirty seconds Maclean and I were doing an unpleasant 1,000 yard sprint through the mud to the guns. I am not sure which was the worst, the Hun shells that were coming pretty fast all round, or the scalp-raising blast of the French 75mm guns behind us, their shells only just clearing our heads by a few feet. No. 4 pit had not as yet blown up, but I thought it would very soon do so. There were some 1,500 shells stacked in or near the pit, and it already

resembled a furnace, with flames shooting 3 feet above the roof. Anticipating the SOS signal which came through shortly after, three guns started gun fire, while Maclean organised a party to try and save the burning gun. A chain of men was formed, and they passed up shell boxes and sandbags full of mud to Maclean and two other men who stood at the entrance to the pit. The gun-charges were stacked in piles of forty all around the pit, and when the fire reached them, they exploded pile after pile and added fuel to the furnace. One man was pulled out dead, killed by the shell that had started the fire, and gradually the gun and the stacks of shell were covered with a coating of mud and slime. That done, they attacked the flames on the roof and walls. To add to their troubles, another shell entered the pit opening, actually hit the trail, knocking the gun sideways, and then by some miracle burying itself in the platform without exploding. By degrees the fire was got under control, though the shells and gun had become so hot that they could not be touched. Every leather fitting on the gun was of course destroyed.[29]

Major Neil Fraser-Tytler, D Battery, 149th Brigade, Royal Field Artillery, 30th Division

Shells rained down on the British front lines in an attempt to 'spoil' the preparations that the Germans knew would be on hand for the attack The result was an extremely tense and nerve-racking time for the British infantry as the casualties edged higher and higher. The 1/7th Middlesex were holding the line at Hébuterne facing across to Gommecourt.

Imagine yourself, standing in a trench with water well over your knees, crouching against the side of the muddy trench, while thousands of unseen shells come shrieking and whining overhead and most of them dropping with a crash on the parapet or parados, followed by a terrific explosion which temporarily blinds, deafens and strikes one dumb. Even if you are lucky enough to miss being hit by one of the thousands of pieces of red-hot shrapnel, the concussion is sufficient to knock you over. Imagine yourself, being slowly buried by the displaced earth which falls down on you like rain and half drowned by the water in the trench; and while in this predicament, the shells continue to rush over. Each one approaches swiftly with a gradually rising crescendo, nearer and nearer until it reaches a wild hissing shriek, then it seems to stop

> suddenly. There is a very slight pause – then CR-R-R-ASSH! It bursts with a tearing, rumbling blinding crash, sending tons of earth into the air to fall back on the inmates of the trench, and hurling thousands of red-hot splinters in all directions, killing or maiming all whom they happen to strike. And all around are men moaning in agony or lying still on the ground.[30]
>
> Private Albert Atkins, 7th Battalion, Middlesex Regiment, 167th Brigade, 56th Division

The infantry of the 8th East Surrey's also felt the awesome power of the German guns when a bombardment crashed down all around their trenches as the Germans attempted a localised trench raid. Captain Wilfred Nevill was truly proud of his men.

> I was just going off to bed when it started, so my beauty sleep was a bit disturbed. I simply cannot very well describe one of these night bombardments. Picture, say twenty electric railway flashes at once continuously for one and a half hours and throw in incessant overhead thunderclaps and if you think that out you'll get some idea of what it looks like. Owing to the perfectly magnificent way the men manned the parapet and the steady and deliberate fire they kept up, and also owing to the tremendous response by our artillery, no Boche ever reached our trench, or tried to. We gave 'em hell and I don't think there's a shadow of doubt that they meant to cut us out, but damned soon found it was we who were opposite and not some dud exponents of the gentle art of keeping cool. I never felt any anxiety about them getting into our trenches, though the shells were dropping like hail and how anyone lived I don't know. I had about fifty in my face I should think and so did everyone, but somehow the bits get past you, though some of us stopped some I'm afraid. It was really awfully topping to walk round and see the men, all quite happy, and yelling out, 'Come on Fritz, we're here!' and such like expressions as, 'Come right in and don't bother to knock first!' etc. etc. The men were great and it has put their tails up no end.[31]
>
> Captain Wilfred Nevill, 8th Battalion, East Surrey Regiment, 55th Brigade, 18th Division

On 24 June, the great bombardment intended to send a tremor through the German Empire finally began with a mighty roar of guns.

One of the best testaments to the awesome power of the guns can be found from an unlikely venue – in this case, a humble latrine tucked in close behind the gunpits of the 18-pounders of 97th Battery, Royal Field Artillery. Here Signaller Dudley Menaud-Lissenburg was attending to a little vital morning business.

> It was in the early morning and a miserably wet day. I was sitting on the pole in the lavatory over a deep and narrow trench, with a sand-bagged roof supported by spars of timber overhead, situated at the end of a long communication trench running parallel to and 20 yards in rear of the line of guns. I, of course, knew the barrage was to commence that day, but with other personal matters on my mind I sat on the pole in contemplation and alone. The silence was indeed eerie! Suddenly, as if struck by an earthquake, the ground shook and the roof fell in, as hundreds of guns opened fire simultaneously. I extricated myself from the debris. Seeing blood on the shoulder of my jacket from a wound somewhere on my head, which was numbed, I panicked for a moment. I heard the lads at the guns lustily cheering and hurried to the command post, hoisting my slacks the while. Here I found Gunner Roach seated at the telephone, 'What happened to you?' he enquired, as he looked at my blanched face and bleeding head. 'Is it a "Blighty"?' I asked. 'No!' he replied as he examined the wound, 'It's only a scratch on your earlobe!' I must confess I was disappointed, but relieved.[32]
>
> Signaller Dudley Menaud-Lissenburg, 97th Battery, 147th Brigade, Royal Field Artillery, 29th Division

Lieutenant William Bloor was at his battery-gun positions when the guns blazed out. Most of the 18-pounders were concentrating on cutting and blowing apart the streams of barbed wire in front of the German lines, but many batteries soon encountered severe problems in maintaining communications with the forward observation officer as their telephone lines were cut by retaliatory shells from the German guns or the routine accidents of a congested battlefield.

> The best day yet! Breakfast at 5.30 a.m., as we intended starting the bombardment early. I stayed at the guns – the Major went to the observation post. Our wires were cut in less than five minutes – did not establish communication until 10 a.m. We fired for two and a half hours

at a steady pace when, communications still being very bad, we gave up for that day. In that time we fired 398 rounds. Spent the afternoon in sponging out our guns etc., and received eight wagons of ammunition (608 rounds) to replace. At 8 p.m. received information that poisonous gas was to be used against enemy trenches at 10 p.m., and that the artillery would cooperate. Accordingly at 10 p.m. exactly, we started an intense fire and continued until 11.30 p.m. We fired 70 rounds per gun (280 rounds). For the rest of the night we fired 50 rounds per hour in order to prevent 'Fritz' from getting out to repair his entanglements or rebuild trenches. I would not be in the Hun trenches today or any other day in the next week for all the wealth of the Indies![33]

Lieutenant William Bloor, C Battery, 149th Brigade, Royal Field Artillery, 30th Division

The forward observation officers had a vision of destruction before them as they gazed through their binoculars. It was their job to use the telephone to report shells as over or short and gradually edge towards the intended targets that were, of course, entirely invisible from the guns themselves.

Armageddon started today and we are right in the thick of it. I am now living in my 'damp hedge' and there is such a row going on I absolutely can't hear my self think! Day and night and all day and all night, guns and nothing but guns – and the shattering clang of bursting high explosives. This is the great offensive, the long looked for 'Big Push', and the whole course of the war will be settled in the next ten days – *some* time to be living in. I get a wonderful view from my observing station and in front of me and right and left, as far as I can see, there is nothing but bursting shells. It's a weird sight, not a living soul or beast, but countless puffs of smoke, from the white fleecy ball of the field-gun shrapnel, to the dense greasy pall of the heavy howitzer HE. Now you will understand why life has been so strenuous – we have been working like niggers getting this show ready and of course I couldn't say a word about it. It's quite funny to think that in London life is going on just as usual and no one even knows this show has started – while out here at least seven different kinds of Hell are rampant.[34]

Captain Cuthbert Lawson, 369th Battery, 15th Brigade, Royal Horse Artillery, 29th Division

Yet there was a strange contrast between this picture of hell on earth that lay before them and the viewpoint from a rural idyll located just a few hundred yards behind the British lines.

> I am sitting out here on an old plough in a half-tilled field watching the smoke of the shells rising over the German lines. There is a very wide view from here and you can see quite a wide front. It is a pleasant rather cloudy day, after a night of heavy rain, and the light breeze blowing from the west lessens for us the sound of the guns, besides being a protection, as far as we know, against gas. There are poppies and blue flowers in the corn just by, a part of the field that is cultivated, and on the rise towards the town is a large patch of yellow stuff that might be mustard and probably isn't. On the whole the evening is 'a pleasant one for a stroll' with the larks singing.[35]
>
> Second Lieutenant Roland Ingle, 10th Battalion, Lincolnshire Regiment, 101st Brigade, 34th Division

On 25 June the barrage continued without any sign of a let up; if anything the British seemed to bring more guns into action, increasing the firing rate, concentrating on pouring in ever more shells to break down the German resistance.

> Up on the top watching the bombardment over La Boisselle, Fricourt and Mametz. The 'speeding up' has commenced. The hill sides over there are under a haze of smoke already. Shells which, bursting, throw up clouds bulkier than the 'Cecil', white puffs, black puffs. Brown puffs and grey. Puffs which start as small downy balls and spread sideways and upwards till they dwarf the woods. Darts of flame and smoke – black smoke these last which shoots high and into the air like a giant poplar tree. These are the HE. The shooting was magnificent. Time and time again the explosions occurred right in the Hun trenches. By Mametz Wood an ammunition dump must have been struck. The resultant smoke column was enormous, Mametz itself one cannot see. It is shrouded in a multi-coloured pall of smoke all its own. It must be awfully rotten for the Huns holding the line. Yet one feels no sympathy for them. Too long they have been able to strafe our devoted infantry like this and without hindrance or answer from us. What is sauce for the English goose is surely sauce for the German gander – and may his stomach relish it.[36]
>
> Captain Charles May, 22nd Battalion, Manchester Regiment, 91st Brigade, 7th Division

The British gunners were afflicted by the kind of problems that were almost inevitable in such a gigantic bombardment, fired for the most part by newly trained gunners and with ammunition of variable quality. As a result there were a distressing number of regrettable incidents.

> We started at 12 midday and fired consistently till 8.15 p.m. (598 rounds). This has been a most unfortunate day for us. Dod was up in the front-line trenches with the Major observing the fire. At about 5.15 p.m. we had two 'premature' bursts. The first killed two of our infantry (17th King's Liverpool Regiment) and the second hit Dod himself in the back. He was carried off to the dressing station at once and the Major went on by himself. After we had finished firing, I went up to the trenches and saw Dod. He has a shrapnel bullet through the kidneys and is for 'Blighty' at once. These prematures are the very devil but cannot be avoided. The barrel of the gun gets very hot with continuously firing, and this affects the charge of cordite and the shell sometimes bursts too soon. But it is a thousand pities and an extraordinary mischance that we ourselves should shoot an officer of 'ours'.[37]
>
> Lieutenant William Bloor, C Battery, 149th Brigade, Royal Field Artillery, 30th Division

There were so many guns crammed into the rear areas that they were stacked up, behind each other with the bigger guns firing literally over the very heads of the field artillery. The prevalence of misfires made this a severe trial on nerves.

> Immediately in the rear of the battery position a 60-pounder battery, 90th Heavy Royal Garrison Artillery, was positioned and proved more dangerous than anything the enemy offered. Invariably when in action and firing directly over us a number of shells burst prematurely with frightening effect. In fact, except for the occasional German 5.9-in, we had more to fear from our 60-pounder friends in the rear. Ever alert, we would rush to earth each time we heard the order 'Action!' in our rear.[38]
>
> Signaller Dudley Menaud-Lissenburg, 97th Battery, 147th Brigade, Royal Field Artillery, 29th Division

Overall, however, the view from the British front line could only engender optimism. Nobody had ever seen anything like this before and it seemed from the British perspective that the Germans were doomed.

It was a sight to see the hostile trenches. The whole countryside was just one mass of flame, smoke and earth thrown up sky high. About 5,000 shells *per diem* are pitching on a front of about 500 yards. Whilst observing I could not resist feeling sorry for the wretched atoms of humanity crouching behind their ruined parapets, and going through hell itself. Modern war is the most cruel thing I have heard of and the awful ordeal of those poor devils, even though they *are* Boches, must be impossible to describe.[39]

Lieutenant William Bloor, C Battery, 149th Brigade, Royal Field Artillery, 30th Division

For the German soldiers the commencement of the bombardment was the beginning of a living nightmare that they would need every ounce of their luck to survive. One of the men that faced the deluge of shells was Private Eversmann of the 26th Reserve Division which held the Wundtwerk Redoubt to the south of Thiepval.

They went at it left and right with heavy calibre guns and hammered us with shrapnel and light calibre pieces. Only with difficulty and distress have we obtained rations today. Two of my comrades got fatal hits while fetching dinner. The uncertainty is hard to bear. They have just found another of my comrades on his way back from ration carrying, Drummer Ollesch, of Gelschenkirchen, a dear chap, three days back from leave and there he's gone.[40]

Private Eversmann, 26th Reserve Division, German Army

The Germans did not relish the treatment they were getting. For them the sheer uncertainty was very much part of a choking mental pressure that would inexorably build up as the bombardment continued.

The barrage has now lasted thirty-six hours. How long will it go on? Nine o'clock: a short pause of which we avail ourselves to bring up coffee, each man got a portion of bread. Ten o'clock: veritable drum fire. In twelve hours shelling they estimate that 60,000 shells have fallen on our battalion sector. Every communication with the rear has been cut, only the telephone is working. When will they attack – tomorrow or the day after? Who knows?[41]

Private Eversmann, 26th Reserve Division, German Army

The Germans had dreadful problems in getting food and supplies forward as the infra-structure that fed their front lines was battered to pieces. Yet although inconvenienced and threatened they always managed to find a way to get enough forward to keep the men going.

> The second day goes on in the same way. Again no hot food comes and the order is given to break out the iron ration. Now we become aware of the usage of the special iron rations kept in the platoon commander's dugout. The bread of course was not exactly fresh and rumour had it that not all the meat rations could be found. But at least it gave something for the stomach. When the fire went on through the third day we began to look at the situation as critical. It appeared they wanted first to starve us and then to shoot us out of our positions. Luckily we could still obtain water from the wells in the position in Thiepval, the use of which had been prohibited for drinking as they were suspected to be contaminated. Now it was a help in an emergency. On the evening of the third day a message came: food will arrive. The organisation began to work. Food was brought on detours around all the villages and viable roads which were under heavy fire. First with motorcars from a distance and then on foot in large containers. Now we could watch the development for a while longer.[42]
>
> Lieutenant F. L. Cassel, 99th Infantry Reserve Regiment,
> 26th Reserve Division, German Army

There is no doubt that the conditions the German troops endured were uncomfortable in the extreme but, crucially, they were not exposed in open trenches. The vast majority were deep in the bowels of the earth. And there were simply not enough heavy high explosive shells to crack open the reinforced concrete bunkers.

> We now, to our cost, became the target for the heaviest calibre. The English were damned cautious. They wanted to be sure of overkill. Nobody should be alive when their infantry left their trenches. One afternoon, while I was lying on my wire bedstead, I heard the dull boom of a heavy gun, the awesome whizz and swish of a rising heavy missile, then the earth was quaking, and while dirt was falling through the boards, I saw the beams above me bend and slowly descend by about 10 centimetres. My heart seemed to stop, now comes the end … But the catastrophe did not come. After the momentary paralysis was gone I left my bed and

went into the trench. Rather die in the open air than be crushed between the boards. In the evening I went and inspected the rampart above my dugout and found a crater with a diameter of several metres, made by a 21-cm shell – a dud! Had it exploded whoever was in the dugout would not have seen daylight – not before the day of resurrection.[43]

Lieutenant F. L. Cassel, 99th Infantry Reserve,
26th Reserve Division Regiment, German Army

The Germans were exhausted, they were scared and anxious, but they were ready.

We were tired and slept as much as one could. The noise of the barrage was too monotonous and so prevented sleep for over-tired people. There was only one harassing question – could one rely on the sentries? They stood on the top steps of the dugout and had to watch lest the fire was changed to the rear and had to look in quieter moments across the ramparts whether the enemy was not coming across. Day-long, night-long. And not all men are heroes, so from time to time one had to go up to see whether the sentries did their duty. After five or six days, it seemed like becoming a permanent state of affairs. Won't the scoundrels ever come to the end of this terrible game of waiting? No, they did not![44]

Lieutenant F. L. Cassel, 99th Infantry Reserve Regiment,
26th Reserve Division, German Army

The German soldiers may have experienced a large number of close escapes but for the most part those in the dugouts remained relatively unscathed as a military force ready to be deployed in a matter of minutes into whatever remained of the trench strong points above.

On the whole we had very few casualties: some sentries were wounded and in one dugout that was partly squashed there were some deaths and seriously wounded. But the company on the whole, and my platoon in particular, kept its battle strength, thanks to the superior quality of our construction of the position. But how long could this last? We had been in the front line already for weeks. More than a week we had lived with the deafening noise of the battle. Dull and apathetic we were lying in our dugouts, secluded from life, but prepared to defend ourselves whatever the cost.[45]

Lieutenant F. L. Cassel, 99th Infantry Reserve Regiment,
26th Reserve Division, German Army

AS THE MOMENT approached for the attack, every corps, division and brigade had been assigned its place in the battle line and begun preparing its plans tailored to the exact local situations. There was a great deal of responsibility in their work. All were clearly aware that mistakes would cost lives. As the commanders gazed at the task that lay before them many began to wonder whether the artillery bombardment really would be the panacea that would cure all the ills that seemed to threaten. One amongst many was Brigadier Rees, in command of the 94th Brigade in the 31st Division, who found himself on the left of the main assault.

> One of my criticisms of the general plan of operations was that the time allowed for the capture of each objective was too short. I had a severe argument with Hunter Weston before I induced him to give me an extra ten minutes for the capture of an orchard, 300 yards beyond the village of Serre. I was looked upon as something of a heretic for saying that everything had been arranged for, except for the unexpected, which usually occurs in war. The short space of time allowed for the capture of each objective made it essential for the whole of my brigade, with the exception of three companies, to advance at Zero hour, otherwise they would not reach the positions assigned to them at the time laid down. In twenty minutes, I had to capture the first four lines of trenches in front of Serre. After a check of twenty minutes, I was allowed forty minutes to capture Serre, a village 800 yards deep, and twenty minutes later to capture an orchard on a knoll 300 yards beyond. My criticisms on these points are not altogether a case of being wise after the event, I did not like them at the time, but I do not profess to have foreseen the result of these arrangements should a failure occur. A great spirit of optimism prevailed in all quarters.[46]
>
> Brigadier General Hubert Rees, Headquarters, 94th Brigade, 31st Division

Gradually the orders for the assault were being passed around the infantry. Young officers desperately tried to assimilate the minutiae of detail, to commit the layout of the ground and German defences to memory and to assess the probability of success. Optimism was undoubtedly widespread. As they gazed on the masses of shells falling on the German lines there seemed to be every chance of a relatively painless success.

> No great difficulty was anticipated in the successful accomplishment of these operations, for it was calculated that Beaumont Hamel and the Hun front trench system would be practically obliterated by our artillery preparation. There was already an increasing volume of gunfire directed on to that area and this was to grow in intensity day by day until it reached a pitch quite unprecedented and almost undreamt of. This was very encouraging, especially to those of us who had gone through the dark days at Ypres, where we hadn't a shell to bless ourselves with. Now we were going to get a bit of our own back. Surely no human opposition could withstand that terrible avalanche of shell fire. The task of us infantry would be easy after this. We should simply walk over, the Boche defences would be hopelessly disorganised, the remnants of the defenders would be captured without difficulty, we should engage his reserves in the open and set them trekking back Rhinewards at the double![47]
>
> Lieutenant William Colyer, 2nd Battalion, Royal Dublin Fusiliers, 10th Brigade, 4th Division

The perils of tomorrow could be buried beneath the confidence of youth, and the ability to ignore the future that marks out those with little experience of life.

> The shadow of impending disaster certainly did not rest upon us during the last days of the preparation. We sat in our company billet and laughed and talked and smoked and sang and drank and retold evil stories and won money at bridge (and lost it again at poker) and otherwise conducted ourselves after the usual and well-established custom of high-spirited subalterns.[48]
>
> Lieutenant William Colyer, 2nd Battalion, Royal Dublin Fusiliers, 10th Brigade, 4th Division

After all they were only part of the great scheme of things and many took comfort from being a mere cog in a mighty wheel. Whatever would happen to them would happen to all of them, and whatever they had to face in No Man's Land they would not be alone. Their friends would be with them every step of the way.

> One man's part on any move nowadays is so small that he is not likely to be nervous about the effect of his work in the final result. Fortunately the habit of 'carrying on', that immortal phrase, is by this time

so ingrained in him that he will be able to do it. And no one should forget that a free throwing of yourself into a forward move gives the thing a momentum that nothing else can, beyond any mechanical discipline. If the least thoughtful could analyse his feelings, he would say, I suppose, that provided he was hitting hard he did not care what happened to him. And the men who are going to be knocked out in the push – there must be many – should not certainly be looked on with pity, because going forward with resolution and braced muscles puts a man in a mood to despise consequences; he is out to give more than he gets, he really dies fighting. A man who is used to sport, takes things, even in the great chance of life and death, as part of the game.[49]

Second Lieutenant Roland Ingle, 10th Battalion, Lincolnshire Regiment, 101st Brigade, 34th Division

As the men steeled themselves there was a definite wish to get it all over with – one way or another – to resolve the unanswerable questions that surrounded them. Only then could they attain some kind of peace.

We got so fed up – to the point that we thought, 'The quicker the bloody whistles go for us to go over the top the better!' We always said to one another, 'Well, it's a two to one chance that we either get bowled over or get wounded and go home'. One of the two – that's all we used to bother. We got so browned off with the waiting, the weather, you can't really explain what it was like. Doing your bit and hoping for the best.[50]

Private Ralph Miller, 1/8th Battalion, Warwickshire Regiment, 143rd Brigade, 48th Division

Unfortunately, as the bombardment continued the onset of poor weather severely hampered the efforts of the Royal Flying Corps to carry out their artillery observation duties and to take the vital aerial photographs needed to chart the effects of the shelling. Although the Royal Artillery increased their rate of fire to try and compensate, they could not match the accuracy of firing assisted by aerial observation. Eventually it was decided to extend the artillery bombardment by a further two days in the hope that the weather would improve. As can be imagined this postponement was not welcomed by the infantry.

We were all ready and anxious to get away, to get up and moving and done with the waiting. Waiting is rotten. I think it tries the nerves more

> than the actual moment of assault. Then one has action, movement, a hundred things to strive for and to occupy one's attention. But, in waiting, there is nothing but anxiety and fruitless speculation on every phase conceivable. But we had not moved. At the last moment came an order, 'Stand by!' And so here we are still, the artillery pounding on as ever and we left, with speculation rife, and rumours bright and rumours grave, flying about on all sides, to twiddle our thumbs and wonder.[51]
>
> Captain Charles May, 22nd Battalion, Manchester Regiment, 91st Brigade, 7th Division

So the bombardment continued into the sixth and seventh days, stretching and depleting the huge shell dumps still further.

> The bombardment still goes on. Mametz, they tell us, has ceased to be. The Hun should be getting pretty well fed up. Indeed from the statements of various prisoners and deserters it would appear certain that he is. Nearly six days of the most appalling bombardment he has had now – a thing calculated to shake the morale of the finest troops in the world. It destroys sleep and interferes with rationing. Lack of either of these always affects a soldier. If his old machine gunners have only suffered in proportion to his other ranks we should not be too seriously hurt doing our job. We are all agog with expectancy, all quietly excited and strung to a pitch, but unhesitatingly I record that our only anxiety is that we will all do our job well. That is but natural. This is the greatest thing the battalion or any of us have ever been in.[52]
>
> Captain Charles May, 22nd Battalion, Manchester Regiment, 91st Brigade, 7th Division

On 30 June the battalions began to move forward. The mood of the men was not bad on the whole. Many were understandably nervous but they jollied each other along and collectively managed to put on a good show.

> We knew that quite a lot of us would be casualties on the morrow, we knew what was going to happen and it was interesting to see the different responses of the different soldiers. One man he would go away on his own, communicate with himself somewhere and he seemed rather moody. I tried to cheer him up. Others again they put on a form of jollification. When the march started up there towards

the line it was all happy and 'Long way to Tipperary' – biscuit tins being hammered – and all jollification like that to keep up the spirits.[53]

Private James Tansley, 9th Battalion, York and Lancaster Regiment, 70th Brigade, 23rd Division

Those who were left behind found themselves in a peculiarly invidious position as they watched their comrades preparing for battle without them. Lieutenant Edgar Lord watched helplessly as his friend Lieutenant Ivan Doncaster went forward without him to face his destiny.

Handshakes were given, goodbyes were said and I turned away with a lump in my throat and tears in my eyes, as if I had a foreboding of events to come, and deploring the fact that I was not allowed to go with my friends.[54]

Lieutenant Edgar Lord, 15th Battalion, Lancashire Fusiliers, 96th Brigade, 32nd Division

Different songs stirred different emotions both within the men and those watching. Even the most banal of lyrics were given significance when sung by a company of men marching in unison to an unknown fate. Those who watched them go found themselves strangely stirred.

Our battalion was moved back a little way into reserve trenches and another battalion took our place in the front line ready to go over the top at dawn next day. As they passed us on their way to take up their positions, they were all lustily singing a sentimental song of the period, which was not only pathetic, but, as it transpired, was also prophetic. It went thus:

Break the news to Mother
Tell there is no other.
Tell her not to wait for me
For I'm not coming home.

In the case of most of them, how true that turned out to be! Since then, to hear that song again has always brought a lump to my throat.[55]

Private Albert Atkins, 1/7th Battalion, Middlesex Regiment, 167th Brigade, 56th Division

The men were heavily laden as they carried with them everything they would need next morning when they went over the top.

> As they passed through Foncquevillers the various platoons drew their supplies of bombs, grenades, barbed wire, spades, picks, sandbags, and all the various paraphernalia essential for a modern attack. After this, a short rest was allowed, in the little tree-surrounded orchards which still survived, wild and tangled, on the outskirts of the ruined village. There, sitting on the sandbags they were to carry, they rested and waited, eating enormous bacon sandwiches – the ration which caused so much amusement when issued, destined to be, for many, their last meal. Presently came the Padre, asking permission to say a few short prayers, preparatory to proceeding to the trenches. Just two simple prayers, one of which began, 'Lord God of Battles', then the Lord's Prayer, said very humbly, very earnestly, and very reverently by all, and last the voice of the Padre half-drowned by the din of the guns, 'The Blessing … Almighty … upon you … now and for evermore'.[56]
>
> Lieutenant C. W. Wood, 1/7th Battalion, Sherwood Foresters, 139th Brigade, 46th Division

THE ARMY COMMANDERS could do little at this stage to impact on what would happen in just a few short hours. What would be would be. The attack could not be cancelled, plans could no longer be changed. Mistakes could no longer be rectified without making the situation far worse. It was now down to the ordinary soldiers to go over the top and overcome whatever lay before them. Haig and his generals had fashioned their plans to the very best of their abilities but it remained an enormous responsibility that they bore alone in their beds that night. Inevitably they chose to be optimistic.

> The weather report is favourable for tomorrow. With God's help, I feel hopeful for tomorrow. The men are in splendid spirits: several have said that they have never before been so instructed and informed of the nature of the operation before them. The wire has never been so well cut, nor the artillery preparation so thorough. I have seen personally all the corps commanders and one and all are full of confidence.[57]
>
> General Sir Douglas Haig, General Headquarters, BEF

For the ordinary rank and file, the strain of that last night was almost unbearable. Many officers, relatively cosseted by superior pay and private incomes from the worst monotony of general rations, sought to mark the occasion by pushing the boat out a little. After all, they might never have the chance again.

> Taylor, one of the C Company subalterns, returned from leave with a case of wines, amongst which was a particularly good brown sherry, and a tumbler of this nectar was sent to the Colonel's dugout with C Company's compliments. Unfortunately for the Colonel, Thomson, our medical officer, arrived first, and, feeling perhaps that a little refreshment would relieve the stress of war, he gulped it down at one draught, remarking afterwards that it was, 'Dammed funny whisky!' This was poor old Thomson's last crime, however, for he was killed a few days later.[58]
>
> Lieutenant W. D. Allen, 7th Battalion, Royal Sussex Regiment, 36th Brigade, 12th Division

Often men sought solace in the safety of numbers and the warmth of comradeship. They amused themselves with feeble jokes and a general inconsequential banter that could trigger forced laughter, which somehow simultaneously belied and confirmed the desperate situation.

> Some were writing letters – perhaps their last – home; others were conversing in subdued tones; some were making a brave attempt at ribaldry. The anxiety, though brave attempts were made to hide it, was clearly discernable on the faces of those seated in silent contemplation of tomorrow and the pathos of it all overwhelmed me and I found it hard to disguise my emotions.[59]
>
> Signaller Dudley Menaud-Lissenburg, 97th Battery, 147th Brigade, Royal Field Artillery, 29th Division

Others sought a quiet spot for contemplation; a chance to muse on what had brought them to this pass and on how they might react in the moment of truth that lay before them.

> One had time to reflect on the immediate prospect. I was not very dismayed by it, in spite of my not being a brave man. There was of course the unpleasant possibility of my not living to see sunset, but somehow I felt that I should not be killed. On the other hand the contingency of surviving the show without a mishap seemed too highly satisfactory to be probable. Once more there returned to me the old

> feeling of wonderment at the perversity of mankind in making all these elaborate preparations for the sole purpose of slaughtering one another and destroying the fair face of the earth. The whole situation struck me with a curious sense of unreality. I had read books, describing the emotions of the hero on the eve of battle. It was hard to realise that tonight *I* was the hero, tonight *I* was on the eve of battle. Nor was it a romantic fancy, but a fact as cold and hard as the ground on which I should sleep and dream of home. In fact my sleep consisted of a series of dreamless dozes, separated by my waking up, swearing and turning over on my other side, all in the most prosaic manner possible.[60]
>
> Lieutenant William Colyer, 2nd Battalion, Royal Dublin Fusiliers, 10th Brigade, 4th Division

Fear was the all-pervading emotion that invisibly bound the men together that night; yet each man was alone with his thoughts. Empirically they knew that almost everyone must be afraid but it was, nevertheless, utterly taboo to admit it openly to others.

> Bravery and fear are inextricably bound up with each other. Unless a man can feel fear he can never be brave: bravery being nothing more than the successful control of fear. Fear is the protest made by the instinct of self-preservation; the most powerful instinct implanted in man, though more or less dormant in our coddled peacetime existence. Every man has intelligence. Every man has the instinct of self-preservation; therefore every man is capable of feeling fear. That fine sounding phrase, 'Brown was a man who did not know what fear was', if it were to be taken literally, would have the comparatively unflattering meaning that Brown was a congenital idiot. And if there were such a being there would be no great glory in any acts of 'bravery' he might accomplish. All men feel fear, but it is the degree with which they control the emotion which stamps them as brave or otherwise.[61]
>
> Lieutenant William Colyer, 2nd Battalion, Royal Dublin Fusiliers, 10th Brigade, 4th Division

Each had their own methods to try and keep fear at bay. One officer, Captain Wilfred Nevill of the 8th East Surreys, had brought back two footballs from his last leave, which he had given to the men of his company to kick ahead when they went over the top into No Man's Land. He has been unfairly traduced as a sporting fool who expected a 'cake-walk', but his intention was almost certainly to encourage his men forward in circumstances that he recognised would test them to the limits.

> Captain Nevill, was commanding B Company, one of our two assaulting companies. A few days before the Battle of the Somme he had come to me with a suggestion that as he and his men were all equally ignorant of what their conduct would be when they got into action he thought it might be helpful as he had 400 yards to go and knew that it would be covered by machine-gun fire, it would be helpful if he could furnish each platoon with a football and allow them to kick it forward and follow it. That was the beginning of the idea and I sanctioned that on condition that he and his officers really kept command of the unit and didn't allow it to develop into a rush after the ball, just if a man came across the football he could kick it forward but they mustn't chase after it.[62]
>
> Lieutenant Colonel Alfred Irwin, 8th Battalion, East Surrey Regiment, 55th Brigade, 18th Division

Nevill certainly had an eye on the risks he faced and his own threatened mortality, for he made distinct reference to his will in his final letter home. The possible imminence of death stalked them all. Yet, as did so many men that night, he swiftly consoled himself, 'I seem to be pretty bullet-proof.'[63] Only time would tell.

Many took the opportunity to write home to try and explain their emotions to their parents. These letters express a blend of conflicting emotions as young men vainly sought to compress their short lifetime of experience and beliefs into a few lines: undoubtedly seeking sympathy, respect and approbation; trying indeed to leave a worthy epitaph to speak for them should the worst happen, and at the same time trying to soften the blow to their loved parents by reassuring them of their absolute acceptance of their possible mortal sacrifice.

> My dearest mother and father,
> I'm writing this letter the day before the most important moment of my life – a moment which I must admit I have never prayed for, like thousands of others have, but nevertheless a moment, which, now it has come, I would not back out for all the money in the world. The day has almost dawned when I shall really do my little bit in the cause of

civilisation. Tomorrow morning I shall take my men – men whom I have got to love, and who, I think, have got to love me – over the top to do our bit in which the London Territorials have taken part as a whole unit. I'm sure you will be pleased to hear that I am going over with the 'Westminsters'. The old regiment has been given the most ticklish task in the division; and I'm very proud of my section, because it is the only section in the whole of the machine gun company that is going over the top; and my two particular guns have been given the most advanced, and therefore most important, positions of all – an honour that is coveted by many. So you can see that I have cause to be proud, inasmuch as at the moment that counts I am the officer who is entrusted with the most difficult task. I took my Communion yesterday with dozens of others who are going over tomorrow; and never have I attended a more impressive service. I placed my soul and body in God's keeping, and I am going into battle with His name on my lips, full of confidence and trusting implicitly in Him. I have a strong feeling that I shall come through this safely; but nevertheless, should it be God's holy will to call me away, I am quite prepared to go; and I could not wish for a finer death; and my dear Mother and Dad, will know that I died doing my duty to my God, my country, and my King. I ask that you should look upon it as an honour that you have given a son for the sake of King and Country. I wish I had time to write more but time presses. I fear I must close now, *au revoir*, dearest Mother and Dad. Fondest love to all those I love so dearly, especially yourselves,

Your devoted and happy son,

Jack.[64]

Second Lieutenant Jack Engall, 1/16th Battalion (Queen's Westminster Rifles), London Regiment, 169th Brigade, 56th Division

The next day he was dead: another 20-year-old corpse that would never grow old. The majority of the men were far too young to have already gathered a wife and children, but there is no doubt that those that did were under even greater pressure as they weighed the clear-cut path of duty with their responsibilities to their family.

I must not allow myself to dwell on the personal – there is no room for it here. Also it is demoralising. But I do not want to die. Not that I mind for myself. If it be that I am to go, I am ready. But the thought

> that I may never see you or our darling baby again turns my bowels to water. I cannot think of it with even the semblance of equanimity. My one consolation is the happiness that has been ours. Also my conscience is clear that I have always tried to make life a joy to you. I know at least that if I go you will not want. That is something. But it is the thought that we may be cut off from one another which is so terrible and that our babe may grow up without my knowing her and without her knowing me. It is difficult to face. And I know your life without me would be a dull blank. Yet you must never let it become wholly so. For to you will be left the greatest charge in all the world; the upbringing of our baby. God bless that child, she is the hope of life to me. My darling *au revoir*. It may well be that you will only have to read these lines as ones of passing interest. On the other hand, they may well be my last message to you. If they are, know through all your life that I loved you and baby with all my heart and soul, that you two sweet things were just all the world to me. I pray God I may do my duty, for I know, whatever that may entail, you would not have it otherwise.[65]
>
> Captain Charles May, 22nd Battalion, Manchester Regiment, 91st Brigade, 7th Division

Charles May, too, would be killed next day and is buried in Danzig Alley Cemetery at Mametz. The very few who had any poetic talent could express themselves far more concisely in verse. One such was Lieutenant Noel Hodgson, the bombing officer of the 9th Battalion, Devonshire Regiment.

> Hodgson knew quite well that the chances were that he would be killed. It wasn't, as was sometimes said, a case of premonition. The chances were all in favour of that, and he knew it. Two nights before the attack was due to start, he was billeted in a beautiful wood, Le Bois des Talles, about 3 miles behind the line. It was lovely summer weather, and even nightingales could be heard at times. In these surroundings Hodgson took up his pen and wrote. With the memory of the many wonderful sunsets he had witnessed from what is perhaps the finest view in all England – Durham Cathedral from the hill to the west where the school is situated at which he was educated.[66]
>
> Chaplain Ernest Crosse, 8th and 9th Battalions, Devonshire Regiment, 20th Brigade, 7th Division

In these circumstances Hodgson's poem has a tremendous sense of pathos ending as it does with a plain spoken plea for courage in the face of his imminent death and the loss that it would entail of all that had made his life worthwhile.

> I that on my familiar hill
> Saw with uncomprehending eyes
> A hundred of thy sunsets spill.
> Their fresh and sanguine sacrifice
> 'Ere the sun sheathes his noonday sword
> Must say goodbye to all of this.
> By all delights that I shall miss
> Help me to die, O Lord.[67]
>
> Lieutenant Noel Hodgson, 9th Battalion, Devonshire Regiment, 20th Brigade, 7th Division

Even today, to read this tragic little poem whilst sitting alone on the hill that overlooks the calm beauty of Durham Cathedral and Castle can generate uncomfortable emotions. But Hodgson did not seek the pity of others in his predicament. His inner qualms were confided only to paper and he remained his normal self towards his fellow officers, who shared his predicament.

> Such thoughts as these must have been common to many before a battle. But there are times when a man's thoughts are best left to himself, and though I lived with Hodgson at this time, he never mentioned these to me.[68]
>
> Chaplain Ernest Crosse, 8th and 9th Battalions, Devonshire Regiment, 20th Brigade, 7th Division

From the other side of the barbed wire thousands of young Germans were undergoing physical and mental agonies without even having the dubious luxury of knowing when the blow would fall. Yet the thread of common humanity crossed No Man's Land to embrace them too.

> It is still going on – ninety-six hours of it now. What will be the upshot, heaven knows! It is night, 'Thou fearsome night, what will thou bring us?' asks every man. Shall I live till morning? Haven't we had enough of this frightful horror? Five days and five nights now this Hell concert has lasted. Hell indeed seems to be let loose. One's head is a

> madman's; the tongue sticks to the roof of the mouth. Five days and five nights, a long time, to us an eternity. Almost nothing to eat and nothing to drink. No sleep, always wakened again. All contact with the outer world cut off. No sign of life from home, nor can we send any news to our loved ones. What anxiety they must feel about us. How long is this going to last? Still there is no use thinking about it. If I may not see my loved ones again, I greet them with a last farewell.[69]
>
> Private Eversmann, 26th Reserve Division, German Army

And so thousands upon thousands of young men spent their last few hours, wracked by a mingled combination of hope and fear. Daring to hope that they might survive; yet facing up to the duties of sacrifice and the horrors that lay before them. Tomorrow was the 1 July 1916.

CHAPTER FOUR

1 July 1916

Dawn breaks early in July and the short night soon gave way to the first rays of sunlight. As the darkness dissipated what was revealed to the anxious watchers was not a completely devastated region. What faced them was in the main a still recognisable sylvan scene. It was obviously no longer entirely pristine, clearly scarred as it was by the white lines of trenches, in places well worked over and battered by the artillery, but nevertheless still replete with many grassy fields and woods overgrown in the absence of the scything hands of farmers. The morning was perfect with clear skies and the more religious might have pondered that truly only the work of man was vile. As the men awoke from their disturbed sleep they could not help but dwell on what lay before them. Their eyes did not see the calm wonders of nature but looked beyond such distractions to fix on the devastated strip of land that lay between them and the menacing lines of German trenches. Here their destiny would be decided in a few short hours.

> 5.45 a.m. It is a glorious morning and is now broad daylight. We go over in two hours' time. It seems a long time to wait and I think, whatever happens, we shall all feel relieved once the line is launched. No Man's Land is a tangled desert. Unless one could see it one cannot imagine what a terrible state of disorder it is in. Our gunnery has wrecked that and his front-line trenches all right. But we do not yet seem to have stopped his machine guns. These are pooping off all along our parapet as I write. I trust they will not claim too many of our lads before the day is over.[1]
>
> Captain Charles May, 22nd Battalion, Manchester Regiment, 91st Brigade, 7th Division

In time-honoured fashion the men looked for their breakfasts to fill the empty void in their stomachs, something that the inevitable jitters emphasised to an uncomfortable degree. They would feel better with something inside them.

> At approximately 6 a.m. on Saturday 1st we had a breakfast on a beautiful summer morning and then a dozen of us had a bit of sing-song in one of the dugouts. I remember two of the songs very well, 'When you wore a tulip' and 'I love the ladies'.[2]
>
> Private Harry Baumber, 10th Battalion, Lincolnshire Regiment, 101st Brigade, 34th Division

Tea, the eternal panacea and balm of the British Army, was served out to the men as they sat on the firestep and prepared themselves for the grim ordeal that lay before them.

> Ah good! Here comes the fellow with the tea. That will cheer us up. A bite of something to eat wouldn't do any harm, either. The men are all fully awake and are variously engaged in cleaning their rifles, having breakfast, talking and smoking. I think they are pretty confident. They are stout-hearted fellows and I do not anticipate any difficulty in controlling them.[3]
>
> Lieutenant William Colyer, 2nd Battalion, Royal Dublin Fusiliers, 10th Brigade, 4th Division

Gradually a firmer purpose took over as the men busied themselves with the routine tasks that they had to carry out before the 'off'. The British wire had already been taken down during the night, ladders were set in place to allow the men to climb quickly out of the trenches, and bridges constructed by the Royal Engineers were fitted in position to allow troops coming forward to get over the front-line trench as they advanced. Some of the officers were keenly aware that their men would be looking to them for leadership. They would not have been human if they had not wondered whether they would prove worthy of that trust.

> I must be alive to the task in front of me. First, there must be no mistake about my own behaviour – a steady going forward, whatever the opposition may be. I have confidence in my own courage; it did not fail me at Ypres and there is no reason why it should fail me now. My wits must be alert, for the lives of these forty-odd men, and perhaps

many more, depend to a great extent on my leadership. I must be sure to appear calm and cheerful, whatever I may feel like.[4]

Lieutenant William Colyer, 2nd Battalion, Royal Dublin Fusiliers, 10th Brigade, 4th Division

The colonels in charge of each battalion were internally torn between a natural urge to share the risks faced by *their* men and the sheer military necessity of standing back from the fray if they were to have any chance of retaining some semblance of control during those crucial moments when the fighting hung in the balance.

One's instinct was to get on with the chaps and for one thing see what was going on. On the other hand we had been warned over and over again that officers' lives must not be thrown away in doing something that they oughtn't, in fact that commanding officers of battalions should lead from behind. When the attack had lost its impetus then was the moment to go forward. And that's what I tried to do.[5]

Lieutenant Colonel Alfred Irwin, 8th Battalion, East Surrey Regiment, 55th Brigade, 18th Division

While the officers pondered their role, the men had their personal kit to get into position. They had much to carry.

I will tell here what I carried: rifle and bayonet with a pair of wire cutters attached; a shovel fastened on my back; pack containing two days' rations, oil sheet, cardigan, jacket and mess tin; haversack containing one day's iron rations and two Mills bombs; 150 rounds of ammunition; two extra bandoliers containing 60 rounds each, one over each shoulder; a bag of ten bombs.[6]

Private Albert Andrews, 19th Battalion, Manchester Regiment, 21st Brigade, 30th Division

Although the guns had not stopped firing, many men noticed that their fire had appreciably slackened during the final night and some men even claimed to have heard the birds singing a dawn chorus. The final cannonade let rip at 0630 as almost every gun in the sector poured in a rapid fire drenching the German trenches with bursting shells.

The artillery, which had been firing in a desultory fashion, began to speed up, and within fifteen seconds there was a perfect hurricane of sound. Every gun, large or small started firing 'rapid', the trench mortars

> in the front line joining in, while above all could be heard the tearing rattle of the Vickers machine guns firing from somewhere near us.[7]
>
> Major Walter Vignoles, 10th Battalion, Lincolnshire Regiment, 101st Brigade, 34th Division

Unfortunately, in many sectors this bombardment did not go unanswered. This was the moment for which the German artillery had been waiting. Now they *knew* the attack was coming and every German battery blazed out in defiance. It was very obvious that the German artillery had not been silenced or even reduced to a relative quiescence. The British gunners had certainly failed to carry out one of their most important tasks and the infantry soon began to suffer the consequences of that failure.

> About seven o'clock, the enemy suddenly dropped a barrage on our trench, blowing it in and causing many casualties. Dazed by the perpetual crashes we crouched in the bottom of the trench, half buried under the debris which fell around us. This barrage accounted for close on forty killed and wounded in the company. I was struck by two pieces of shrapnel on the upper part of my left arm and on my shrapnel helmet, but escaped with a bruise on my arm and a dent in my helmet, plus, of course, a splitting headache.[8]
>
> Sergeant Frank Hawkings, 1/9th Battalion (Queens Victoria's Rifles), London Regiment, 169th Brigade, 56th Division

In more fortunate sectors the infantry were left in relative peace as the minutes ticked slowly by. There was a sort of confidence that merged seamlessly with wishful thinking – perhaps the Germans would not, after all, put up much of a resistance.

> We were in very good spirits; I don't know why, for we all knew that there was a good chance of many of us being killed or wounded, but we *were* in good spirits and they were not assumed either. Even those who grouse as a rule were cheerful; I think the fact that at last we hoped to get to close quarters with the Boche and defeat him accounted for it. We had an hour to wait, so lighted pipes and cigarettes while the men chatted and laughed, and wondered whether the Boche would wait for us. I had a look round but could not see much. The morning was fine and the sun shining, but the enemy's trenches were veiled in a light mist made worse no doubt by the smoke from the

> thousands of shells we were pumping into his lines. Nearby I could see our machine gunners, out in the open already, trying to get the best position from which to enfilade certain parts of the Boche line. There was a kind of suppressed excitement running through all the men as the time for the advance came nearer.[9]
>
> Major Walter Vignoles, 10th Battalion, Lincolnshire Regiment, 101st Brigade, 34th Division

Even so, the final countdown could not be anything but a grievous trial to the nerves as the minutes slowly drifted away from them.

> I was apprehensive, I wondered if I'd be alive that night, I wondered whether I was going to be killed. I accepted the fact that as a soldier, the thing was you had to be a fatalist. We often said, 'If it's got your name and address on it, it will find you – so what's the use of worrying!' So you've just got to go and you hope for the best.[10]
>
> Private Basil Farrer, 2nd Battalion, Green Howards, 21st Brigade, 30th Division

Only a few found their courage deserted them in the final analysis so that they took the desperate measure of a self-inflicted wound.

> One of my friends shot himself through the hand. He was a brave man; he was one of the last I would have thought of doing that. He just said, 'I'm not going over, where are the clean sandbags?' He put a sandbag over his rifle and shot himself. He was right by me.[11]
>
> Private Albert Hurst, 17th Battalion, Manchester Regt, 90th Brigade, 30th Division

His friend got away with it. No one in authority saw him and the men themselves had their own problems to think about. All along the line the men checked rifle bolt actions were clean one last time and fixed their bayonets. They were as ready as they ever would be.

> The orders came down: 'Half an hour to go!' 'Quarter of an hour to go!' 'Ten minutes to go!' 'Three minutes to go!' I lit a cigarette and up the ladder I went.[12]
>
> Private Albert Andrews, 19th Battalion, Manchester Regiment, 21st Brigade, 30th Division

The Battle of the Somme had finally begun.

VII Corps, Third Army: *The Gommecourt Diversion*

A FEW MILES TO the north of the main Fourth Army attack two territorial divisions of the Third Army's VII Corps began their 'diversionary' action. There was no intent here of breaking through, or of rolling up the German line. It was designed to attract the fire of German artillery and infantry that might otherwise busy itself by interfering with the northern flank of the main assault at Serre. The diversion was a standard 'pincer' attack, intended to pinch out the Gommecourt Salient and force the surrounded German garrison to surrender. Coming in from the northern flank facing Gommecourt Wood was the 46th (North Midland) Division, which was required to break into the German lines and then form a strong defensive flank to block any German counter-attack launched from the north. They were also to attack along the Fill Trench to make a rendezvous with the other pincer supplied by the 56th (London) Division in the First Switch Trench to the east of the village of Gommecourt. The 56th Division was to break through and seize the German third line, (variously named from Feud to Fame) which was to be consolidated, before a second assault swung round through the Maze and Quadrilateral fortifications to make their intended rendezvous with 46th Division. To the south of the 56th Division, just two battalions of the neighbouring 48th Division thinly held the line over the whole 2 miles that stretched down to the northern flank of the main attack launched by 31st Division of VIII Corps. These battalions were meant to simulate readiness for an imminent attack by cutting holes in the German barbed wire and releasing smoke as if about to assault. In the absence of any convincing British artillery support barrage, and the lack of assembly trenches or corresponding holes cut in the British wire, this ruse unsurprisingly failed to distract the Germans and they were left free to concentrate their fire against the 56th Division.

Taken as a whole this was an extremely ambitious plan, for the German defences around the Gommecourt Salient were amongst the strongest on the whole Somme front. A complex interlocked system of trenches and communication trenches was centred on the Maze lying to the eastern side of the village, while three further additional defensive switch lines isolated the whole salient in the event of the British successfully breaking through. Most of the garrison was preserved from the worst effects of the preliminary bombardment by a comprehensive pattern of

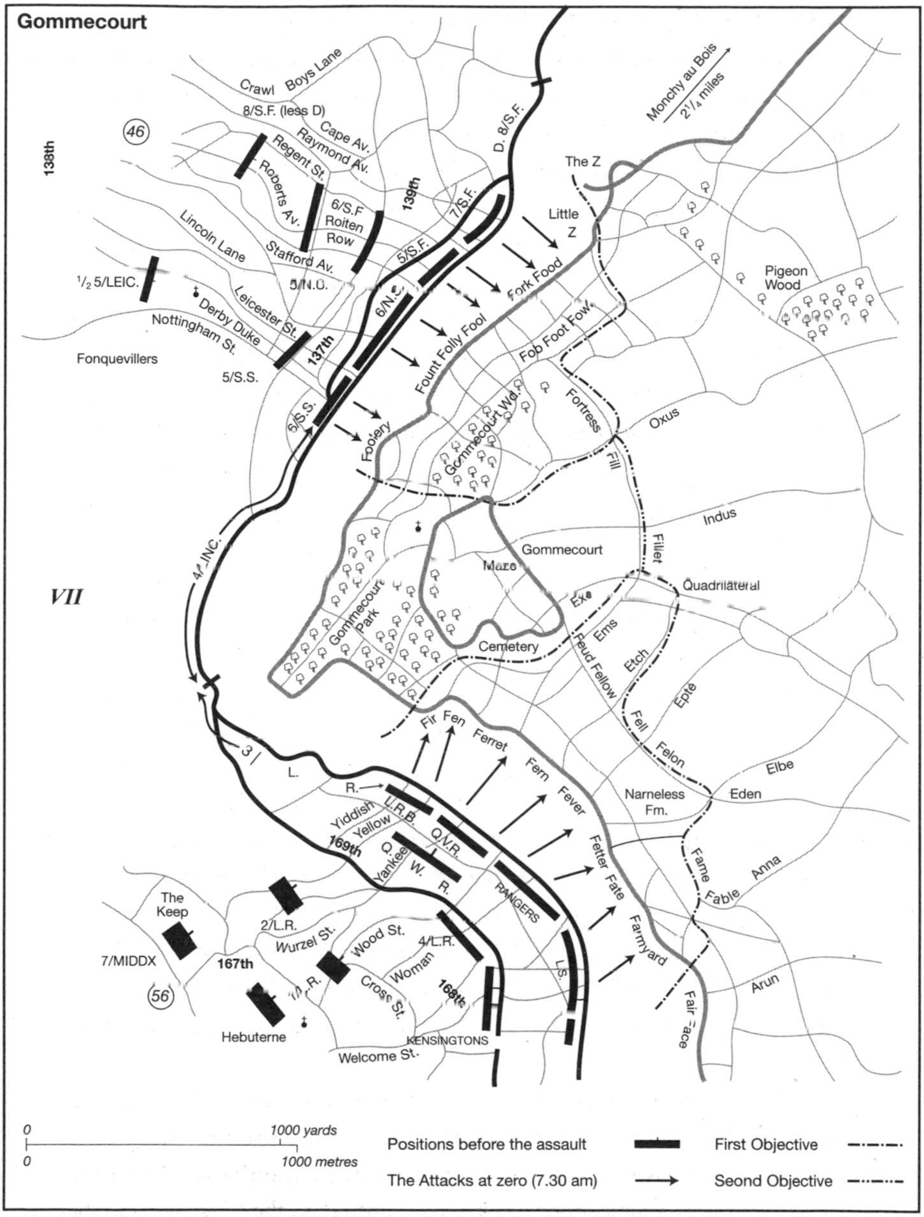
Gommecourt
Crawl
Boys Lane
8/S.F. (less D)
Cape Av.
Raymond Av.
Regent St.
Roberts Av.
46
138th
139th
D. 8/S.F.
7/S.F.
6/S.F
Roiten
Row
5/S.F.
Lincoln Lane
Stafford Av.
1/2 5/LEIC.
Leicester St.
Derby Duke
Nottingham St.
137th
Fonquevillers
5/S.S.
6/S.S.
Monchy au Bois
2 1/4 miles
The Z
Little
Z
Fork Food
Fount Folly Fool
Fob Foot Fow
Pigeon
Wood
Fortress
Oxus
Foolery
Gommecourt Wd.
Fill
Indus
Gommecourt
Maze
Fillet
Quadrilateral
VII
4/LINC.
Gommecourt
Park
Exe
Ems
Cemetery
Feud Fellow
Etch
Epte
Fell
Felon
Fir
Fen
Ferret
Fern
Fever
Elbe
Eden
Narneless
Fm.
3
L.
R.
Yiddish
L.R.B.
Yellow
169th
Q.V.R.
Q.
W.
R.
Yankee
Fetter Fate
Fame
Fable
Anna
RANGERS
Farmyard
The
Keep
2/L.R.
Wurzel St.
Wood St.
4/L.R.
7/MIDDX
167th
Woman
Cross St.
168th
L.S.
Arun
56
Hebuterne
KENSINGTONS
Welcome St.
0
1000 yards
0
1000 metres
Positions before the assault
First Objective
The Attacks at zero (7.30 am)
Seond Objective

deep dugouts. Furthermore, although a strong force of medium and heavy batteries had been theoretically devoted to counter-battery fire this was comprehensively undermined by the small allocation of ammunition to the task – just 20 rounds per gun. Even worse there was only one aircraft allocated to them for aerial observation. As a result most of the German batteries in the Gommecourt area had survived unscathed.

To their credit, the British had foreseen the risk of concentrated flanking fire from unengaged German troops and artillery lying to the east, north and south of the British attack and in an effort to counter this and conceal what was going on an attempt was made to generate a smoke screen across the front of both attacking divisions at 0720. Unfortunately, on the 46th Division front, this seems to have confused the attackers far more than the Germans. The combination of thick smoke clouds and the maze of old trenches and new assembly trenches that were littered all across No Man's Land meant that the troops found it difficult to get the correct alignment of attack. To complicate matters further the belts of barbed wire, which had been reported clear, had mostly been patched up by the Germans overnight and they once again posed a serious obstacle to rapid progress.

Once the assault began at 0730 the German troops were very soon out of their dugouts to occupy the mish-mash of trenches and shell holes left after the British bombardment. As the smoke clouds began to disperse in front of them, their targets soon became clear, and they opened an effective fire. But the real damage came from their artillery, which was effectively augmented by the batteries in Adinfer Wood to the north. Now the consequence of the inadequate counter-battery fire was clearly apparent. As a direct result the attack was an almost complete failure. The only significant incursion into the German lines was made by the 1/5th and 1/7th Sherwood Foresters. They were quickly isolated and a debilitating confusion over the organisation of a combined renewed attack and reinforcement ate away at time deep into the afternoon until eventually the whole idea was abandoned. The surviving Sherwood Foresters were hunted down one by one like rats in a trap.

Meanwhile, on the neighbouring 56th Division front, the German artillery reacted equally violently to the first wisps of the smoke screen that curled towards them across No Man's Land.

> Before we started off we sent up dense clouds of white smoke, under cover of which we started attacking. The moment the Germans spotted this they started with their artillery putting up a wicked barrage of fire – heavy shrapnel at regular distances of about 20 yards covering every inch of ground. They put one in No Man's Land, one over the front line, another over our reserves, and others right along the communication trenches.[13]
>
> Rifleman Frank Jacobs, 1/5th Battalion (London Rifle Brigade), London Regiment, 169th Brigade, 56th Division

Mere smoke certainly could not deflect shells from the massed German artillery who did not need to see to be able to kill their enemies – after all, they knew exactly where they were and where they were going. Notwithstanding this, at 0725 the leading assault companies moved out of the front line and formed up on the tapes laid in front of the British front line to be ready for the final whistle that would launch them on their way. At last the whistles blew at 0730 and one by one the assaulting companies disappeared into the smoke that by then wreathed all of No Man's Land.

From the trenches behind them the attack was an inspirational if somewhat daunting sight.

> It was the finest spectacle I have ever seen. The smoke varied in colour and as each cloud intermingled with the other it formed beautiful tints. By this time the artillery had lifted and carried on with the pounding of the Huns' rear positions and batteries. Mr Fritz was by no means taking this lying down and we soon realised that he had almost as many guns as we had, but it was chiefly heavy stuff that he sent over and this led us to suspect that he had shifted his field guns back. The wood and all the enemy's trenches were now obscured from sight and all that could be seen was the front waves of men advancing to their unknown fate. Line after line advanced and disappeared in the clouds of smoke.[14]
>
> Lance Corporal Sidney Appleyard, 1/9th Battalion (Queen Victoria's Rifles), London Regiment, 169th Brigade, 56th Division

The men amidst the smoke clouds could not really see what was happening but the crescendo of noise, the percussive effects of shell explosions and the rattle of the machine guns gave them every clue that they were engaged in a truly desperate business.

> When we advanced beyond the smoke screens we became an easy target for the German machine guns. I saw many of my colleagues drop down, but this somehow or other did not seem to worry me, and I continued to go forward until I suddenly became aware that there were very few of us in this first line of attack capable of going on. I found myself in the company of an officer, Lieutenant Wallace. We dived into a flat shallow hole, made by our guns, apparently both wanting to decide what we should now do. Lieutenant Wallace asked me whether I thought we should attempt to go on or remain there for the time being. Thinking the position over very rapidly, I came to the conclusion and told him that going on would be suicidal and that the best thing we could do would be to stay there and attempt to pick off any Germans who might expose themselves. We were not very clear as to how we were situated. Lieutenant Wallace said, however, that we had been ordered to go on at all costs and that we must comply with this order. At this, he stood up and within a few seconds dropped down riddled with bullets. This left me with the same problem, and having observed his action, I felt I must do the same. I had thought that a man who could stand up and knowingly face practically certain death must be very brave. I found out that bravery hardly came into it. Once the decision was made to stand up I had no further fear. I was not bothered at all even though I believed that I would be dead within seconds and would be rotting on the ground, food for the rats next day. I am now convinced that when it comes to the last crunch nobody has any fear at all; it is not a question of bravery. In some extraordinary manner the chemistry of the body anaesthetises it. I stood up and was immediately hit by two bullets and dropped down. I did not even feel appreciably the bullets going through.[15]
>
> Private Henry Russell, 1/5th Battalion (London Rifle Brigade), 169th Brigade, 56th Division

His wounds were obviously serious and as the German shells continued to crash down between the lines he was hit again and virtually emasculated as he lay there helpless. Only much later at night would he be able to crawl back to the British lines.

As the attacking waves pushed forwards, despite the heavy casualties they were suffering, the survivors pushed closer and closer to the German front line. Yet as the decisive moment approached the German fire seemed only to increase.

> Officers led the way, most of whom dropped immediately. Machine guns seemed to crackle from every direction, I kept my head down as low as possible, helmet tilted to protect my eyes, but I could still see men dropping all around me. One on my left clutched his stomach and just collapsed. Another, a yard to my right, slumped on to his knees. The din was terrific, stifling any screams. Entangled wire had to be negotiated. Just one opening – on which the German fire was rapid and most accurate. Not many of us got through. The journey seemed endless, but at last a number of us fell into a German trench.[16]
>
> Private Arthur Schuman, 1/5th Battalion (London Rifle Brigade), London Regiment, 169th Brigade, 56th Division

Inevitably, many never made it through the maelstrom of fire that ripped through the hapless Londoners.

> Shells were bursting everywhere, and through the drifting smoke in front of us we could see the enemy's first line from which grey figures emerged and hurled hand grenades. We moved forward in long lines, stumbling through the mass of shell holes, wire and wreckage, and behind us more waves appeared. As we neared the enemy line, a low flying shrapnel shell burst right over my head, completely deafening me. I ducked and slipped head first into a shell hole. Simultaneously several more shells burst close around. We must have been in the midst of the Hun barrage. I felt a sharp pain in my back, and my next recollections are of a medley of Huns and Queen Victoria's Rifles at close quarters with bomb and bayonet. The tide of battle rolled on as our fellows forced their way to the Hun trench, and when I recovered my wits, I found myself bleeding profusely from a wound in my left forearm. There was also a patch of blood on my breeches from the wound in my back. I was by this time, completely dazed and half deafened, but had sufficient sense to appreciate in which direction lay our own front line. I next found myself sliding head first into the old line upon a heap of mangled bodies.[17]
>
> Sergeant Frank Hawkings, 1/9th Battalion (Queen Victoria's Rifles), London Regiment, 169th Brigade, 56th Division

In general, although the British artillery had been unable to suppress the German guns, they had at least managed to cut the barbed wire along most of the 56th Division front. The leading troops, reinforced by the following waves managed to reach and overwhelm the resistance offered by the surviving garrison of the German front line. Here they could see for themselves the visible evidence of the power of their own artillery.

> You couldn't possibly imagine what it was like, but I will do my best to describe it. The place was nothing but a mass of shell holes, some small, some huge. Huge 9.2-in shells lay there unexploded, and the whole place had been smashed to atoms. The German first line was but a ditch and, as we had expected, there were very few Germans there. These held up their hands crying, 'Kamarad, Kamarad!' and some were taken prisoners and some were shot. We went on over the second line and on until we came to the third. This was our objective. Immediately we got there we started consolidating the trench – an awful job – for it was smashed out of all recognition.[18]
>
> Rifleman Frank Jacobs, 1/5th Battalion (London Rifle Brigade), London Regiment, 169th Brigade, 56th Division

The German trenches had indeed been badly battered and the Londoners were quickly into the German front-line trench and the second line was also soon overrun. Sergeant Hawker, the acting company sergeant major of C Company, Queen's Westminster Rifles pushed on as instructed and launched his company against the third line. Here resistance stiffened but as the men surged up the communication trenches the Germans were forced back to their next line of defence at Nameless Farm.

> Between the second and the third lines we were delayed for some moments by uncut wire, and from this point considerable numbers of enemy troops could be clearly seen, evacuating their support trenches and retiring hastily to their rear. They presented an irresistible target to our men who got down behind the wire and opened a strong fire. We now came under a heavy shrapnel fire, and the noise was terrific, rendering fire control difficult. Captain Mott, having found and enlarged a gap in the wire, gave the order to cease fire and push on. It was at this juncture, I believe, that he became a casualty. It was for some moments difficult to communicate the order and to control the fire. I collected a party and advanced as far as a slight back of raised road, which afforded some cover from a withering machine-gun fire, which now enfiladed us from Gommecourt Wood. We had many

casualties here; and, while I was walking to a flank to determine our next move, I was put out of action by a shot through the neck and windpipe.[19]

Sergeant Donald Hawker, 1/16th Battalion (Queen's Westminster Rifles), London Regiment, 169th Brigade, 56th Division

Hawker began to make his way back but was hit twice more and eventually fell down unconscious in the old German front line. While the wounded made their painful and perilous way back to safety, the supporting waves continued to push forward in an effort to exploit the successes that had been achieved before the inevitable German counter-attacks.

The enemy was found in his dugouts in Feast. I saw two taken prisoner and others shot or bombed. On reaching the Maze, which was little more than large shell holes, I bore to the left and took up a position in a large shell hole. I was rather uncertain whether my position was correct, but Captain Harvey arrived and confirmed it as being so. There were about ten men at this point, which we held and commenced to consolidate at once. Snipers were very busy and killed one and wounded two during the first two minutes. We were filling sandbags whilst lying down, until there was sufficient cover to work our Lewis gun.[20]

Lance Corporal John Foaden, 1/5th Battalion (London Rifle Brigade), London Regiment, 169th Brigade, 56th Division

Meanwhile, another party from D Company, London Rifle Brigade sought to consolidate their positions in what little the British artillery had left of the Eck Trench.

Our left was in touch with C Company. One of our Lewis guns was in the left part of Eck and fired half-left across the road in front. The second gun never reached the German trenches. From 8 to 11.30 a.m. the consolidation of Eck proceeded without interruption from the enemy, with the exception of a sniper in the wood on the left and one on the right. Our right was in touch with the Queen Victoria's Rifles until this time. Eck was in such a condition that the company were in isolated groups in holes with heaps of earth between them. These heaps were very large, but communication was maintained between them by men crawling over the top.[21]

Corporal Roland Ebbetts, 1/5th Battalion (London Rifle Brigade), London Regiment, 169th Brigade, 56th Division

Nevertheless, some heroic attempts were made to push on to the final objectives. An amorphous group of Queen's Westminsters, led by an officer from the pioneers of the 1/5th Cheshires launched an attack on the Quadrilateral fortress but were soon repulsed. The moment for further advances had gone and consolidation was now the all-important priority if they were to hold what they had captured.

It was at this point that the utter collapse of the attack of the 46th Division on the left side of the Gommecourt Salient began to severely affect the prospects of the Londoners. Their initial failure was so complete that its ramifications blighted all subsequent attempts to try again later in the day. The British trenches were clogged up with corpses and the wounded being carried back by the hard-pressed stretcher bearers. Under such a strain it was unsurprising that the 'up' and 'down' arrangements for the communication trenches soon fell apart, with the result that these were soon totally blocked and fresh troops could not get forward. Worst of all was the deluge of shells from the German batteries in front and to the north that continued to spatter liberally across the British lines. The failure of the 46th Division to launch a renewed attack meant that the Germans could concentrate all their energies on eradicating the incursion of the 56th Division into their trenches. Although the German front lines had been captured and parties were established as far forward as the Maze, they were isolated and boxed in by the sheer awesome power of the German bombardment falling behind them and splaying across the length and breadth of No Man's Land. The men who had breached the German front line were in effect trapped, cut off from their own front line, from reinforcements and desperately needed new supplies of bombs and ammunition.

German counter-attacks poured in from all sides. Short, sharp artillery bombardments were followed up by probing parties of German bombers, covered by snipers, creeping forward inch by inch along the numerous communication trenches ready to unleash a deadly flurry of hand grenades. Soon the situation was exceptionally confused for the surviving isolated parties left scattered about the various German defence lines. It was in such troubled circumstances that the wounded Sergeant Hawker found himself when he regained consciousness at about 1400.

I found that a party of various units, of whom Sergeant Courteney appeared to be senior, were in occupation of the enemy front line where I lay. Sergeant Courteney told me that they had been driven back by successive counter-attacks from the right (where our attack had not established itself). He asked me for instructions, stating that he had about twenty men with him, that they had no small arms ammunition or bombs, and were expecting a further advance of the enemy from the right. I suggested that they should block a traverse on the right, and endeavour to maintain their position until dusk with any further ammunition they could collect from casualties.[22]

Sergeant Donald Hawker, 1/16th Battalion (Queen's Westminster Rifles), London Regiment, 169th Brigade, 56th Division

Very few orders arrived from behind them and those that did were often impossible to execute. The absolute priority was to establish contact with the neighbouring units to create a continuous defensive line that could not be easily penetrated by the Germans.

A runner appeared over the parapet, having succeeded in a most daring venture from our trenches. He brought a message addressed to 'any officer'. As no officer appeared to be in the neighbourhood, I took the responsibility of opening the message. It ran approximately as follows, 'Aero reports German fourth line unoccupied. Organise party to occupy and secure same'. The runner volunteered to attempt to return, so I had a message given to him, acknowledging receipt of the brigade order and urging support at the earliest possible moment. I then instructed Sergeant Courteney to draw his party along to the left and endeavour to get in touch with the London Rifle Brigade, who appeared to be still putting up a fight near the wood, and to give the message to the first British officer he saw.[23]

Sergeant Donald Hawker, 1/16th Battalion (Queen's Westminster Rifles), London Regiment, 169th Brigade, 56th Division

Lieutenant Petley, who had already been slightly wounded in the shoulder, sent back a message from his outpost in Eck Trench to the previous British front line begging for supplies of bombs and reinforcements.

I sent a message back to you about two hours ago to the effect that I am holding on to Eck with about forty men, including a dozen Queen Victoria's Rifles and one Queen's Westminster Rifle, and *that*

> *I wanted more bombs*. Quite out of touch to right and left. Have held off Germans on our right with barricade. It is quite absurd to lay here at night as we are.[24]
>
> Second Lieutenant R. E. Petley, 1/5th Battalion (London Rifle Brigade), London Regiment, 169th Brigade, 56th Division

Petley's desperate message was just one of many sent back. Officers back in the original British front line appreciated the situation but they could do nothing about it.

> If we could only have got bombs over to them, I think they might have managed to hold on until dark, but the artillery barrage and machine-gun fire put up in No Man's Land was so heavy that it was impossible for anyone to get across or live there. I ordered the reserve company, 'D' to try to get parties across. They made three attempts, but each time all who started became casualties.[25]
>
> Lieutenant Colonel Vernon Dickins, 1/9th Battalion (Queen Victoria's Rifles), London Regiment, 169th Brigade, 56th Division

Orders were given but simple courage was not enough to carry men through the curtain of shells falling in front of them. Lance Corporal Appleyard was one of a party led by Second Lieutenant Ord Mackenzie in a vain attempt to get a fresh supply of bombs across No Man's Land. They had hardly started before most of them were bowled over.

> We started off under Mr Mackenzie with twenty-four bombs per man, and as soon as we advanced over No Man's Land the Germans opened a very deadly machine-gun fire, which laid a good number out. On we went and it seemed marvellous how the pieces missed us, for the air appeared to be alive with missiles. At last after advancing about 30 yards, I was struck in the thigh by a bullet, the force of which knocked me over. The only thing to do was to crawl back, and this I did and explained things to Captain Renton. Knowing that a good number had been hit, I decided to crawl out on top again and give any assistance that might be required. My efforts were fruitless for the only man left out had been shot through the head and killed instantly.[26]
>
> Lance Corporal Sidney Appleyard, 1/9th Battalion (Queen Victoria's Rifles), London Regiment, 169th Brigade, 56th Division

Before the assault some thought had been given to maintaining communications and various detachments had been charged with the task of digging communication trenches across No Man's Land. But in the heat of battle this proved all but impossible.

> Our own particular work was to dig a communication trench between our advanced line and a point known as 'Z' Hedge, from where it would have been possible for our men to carry ammunition and stores fairly safely under cover to the German network of trenches which we had captured and hoped to retain. After three splendid efforts in the face of the overwhelming gun-fire we had to desist. I am sorry to state that Captain Noel, then in command of my company, was in a shocking funk, despite the fact he was wearing a steel body shield. He evidently valued his own life before those of his men, seeing that he attempted to get in the rear of his command by walking on the backs of his men. Fortunately the Colonel came along and prevented him acting foolishly. This murderous fire continued.[27]
>
> Private Sydney Newman, 1/3rd Battalion, London Regiment, 167th Brigade, 56th Division

It soon became apparent that the men that had advanced so bravely across No Man's Land would have to fend for themselves. Major Dickens of the Kensingtons sent various desperate messages back that charted the rapidly deteriorating situation.

> 1.10 p.m.: Shelling fearful. Mackenzie killed. Trench practically untenable, full of dead and wounded. Very few men indeed left. Must have instructions and assistance. 1.48 p.m.: Sap absolutely impassable owing to shell fire. Every party that enters it knocked out at once. Captain Ware has been wounded somewhere there. I have just crawled to the end of it with London Scottish machine-gun party. Could not find him. One of the Scottish had his hand blown off. Our front line in an awful state. Two more men killed and one wounded. Estimate casualties to A and C Companies at least 25 killed and 50 wounded. Impossible to man large lengths of our front line. Digging quite out of the question and position of the Scottish serious. 2.40 p.m.: I have as far as I can find only thirteen left besides myself. Trenches unrecognisable. Quite impossible to hold. Bombardment fearful for two hours. I am the only officer left. Please send instructions.[28]
>
> Major Cedric Dickens, 13th Battalion (Kensingtons), London Regiment, 168th Brigade, 56th Division

It was not just communications with the troops across the chasm of No Man's Land that were cut. The German barrage had severed most of the telephone lines that connected the assaulting battalions with their brigade headquarters. This contributed greatly to the overall confusion. Signaller William Smith was detailed to repair the telephone lines that led back to the headquarters of 168th Brigade.

> I had just been temporarily knocked out by a flat piece of shell and had been attended by a stretcher bearer, who had then left me and proceeded on his way back to a dressing station, whilst I went farther on down the trench to get on with my job. I had not gone many yards when I met a very young private of the 12th Londons. One of his arms was hanging limp and was, I should think, broken in two or three places. He was cut and bleeding about the face, and was altogether in a sorry plight. He stopped me and asked me, 'Is there a dressing station down there, mate?' pointing along the way I had come. I replied, 'Yes, keep straight on down the trench. It's a good way down. But there's a stretcher bearer only just gone along. Shall I see if I can get him for you?' His reply I shall never forget, 'Oh, I don't want him for *me*. I want someone to come back with me to get my mate. *He's hurt*!'[29]
>
> Signaller William Smith, Royal Engineers Signals attached to 168th Brigade, 56th Division

The communications with brigade headquarters were desperately important. It was only by keeping headquarters properly informed that the commanding officers would know where to unleash the power of the British artillery, which was the only real chance of rescuing the situation. One staff officer, Major Philip Neame VC, was able to take over an artillery forward observation post and thereby directly intervene to bring down artillery support for at least one of the isolated parties.

> We had a headquarters up near the front-line trenches in a small dugout which we'd specially constructed, with an artillery observation post for our forward observation officer who came up to the front with us the evening before the attack. When the battle started he was up in this ready to direct artillery fire after the barrage had stopped. Unfortunately a German shell blew the top off this observation post and killed him. As a result of this I had to go up into the trench and carry

out his duties for the rest of the day's fighting. I had to call down into the dugout and transmit messages of any alterations in the artillery fire that was required, telephoned through by my staff captain to the artillery headquarters. The Germans began to launch their big counter-attack against our troops in the German front and support trenches which we had captured, they were starting a very heavy bombing attack. I could see them picking out bombs and starting to throw them and I gave directions for several batteries of our artillery to be concentrated on the German communication trench down which swarms of German troops were coming. Our artillery was most skilfully directed and completely destroyed this counter-attack.[30]

Major Philip Neame VC, Headquarters, 168th Brigade, 56th Division

Yet this was just one of many German counter-attacks that were raining down on the British. Most of the Germans were simply invisible from the perspective of the original British front line as they carefully probed their way through the tangled system of trenches without showing themselves above surface.

As no further supplies of bombs could get across No Man's Land, improvisation was required from the trapped assaulting parties. First of all the British bombs were collected up and sent to where it was considered the pressure was greatest. At the same time diligent efforts were made to locate any remaining German front-line bomb supplies in the areas they had over-run. However, the demand for bombs still far outstripped the supply. Finally, in cases of desperation, men took incredible risks that they would never have considered in the cold light of day.

The Germans were in the same trench slinging over stick bombs from both flanks. I must have been really mad, for in the heat of the moment, I quickly picked up a stick bomb, certain that I had sufficient time to throw it back. But the trench being so high, it hit the top and fell back. With two or three others who were near me, we had to nip into the next bay very smartly.[31]

Private Arthur Schuman, 1/5th Battalion (London Rifle Brigade), London Regiment, 169th Brigade, 56th Division

The German threat was clearly greatest to the right, where the London Scottish had attacked. On their immediate right flank were German troops that had been neither attacked nor bombarded and it was an easy matter for them to organise counter-attacks from this relative oasis of calm. Soon the pressure was beyond endurance.

> I am faced with this position. I have collected all bombs and small arms ammunition from casualties. Every one has been used. I am faced with three alternatives: (a) To stay here with such of my men as are alive and be killed. (b) To surrender to the enemy. (c) To withdraw such of my men as I can. Either of these first two alternatives is distasteful to me. I propose to adopt the latter.[32]
>
> Captain H. C. Sparks, 1/14th Battalion (London Scottish), London Regiment, 168th Brigade, 56th Division

As the London Scottish began to fall back across No Man's Land to the original British front line a domino effect was generated: after the Germans reoccupied their front lines on the right they began to bomb their way along the lines until the neighbouring positions were rendered utterly untenable.

> By this time our numbers were very small, for reinforcements, bombs etc. could not be obtained owing to the heavy curtain of fire put up between the old front lines, and after a consultation I had with the Company Sergeant Major we decided it was a case for every man to do his best to get home, for there was not enough men to get to work with the bayonet in the open. Everybody hung on as long as possible, then small parties began to evacuate, but none got far before they were bowled over by machine-gun fire. It was when I tried to get home that I got one from the left through my thigh and, in getting up, one across my back from the right, just taking the skin off my spine and ripping a nice lump out of my left side in the small of the back. I was able to get up and rush into a shell hole where I remained until 11 p.m.[33]
>
> Sergeant Gilbert Telfer, 1/9th Battalion (Queen Victoria's Rifles), London Regiment, 169th Brigade, 56th Division

All along the 56th Division front, isolated NCOs and officers were left with no choice but to pull back towards the original German front line. The further forward they had got the more difficult it was to withdraw. Even to get back to the previous front line was a real challenge. As the German counter-attack gained momentum, Lance Corporal Foaden and his small force were left increasingly isolated in their outpost in the Maze.

At 4 p.m. Sergeant Hember ordered us to withdraw also, but there being no communication trench, I told him we could not do so until dusk, as we had our Lewis gun and heavy packs of small arms ammunition. Enemy bombers appeared in Fibre and threw bombs at us. I opened fire with the Lewis gun, whereupon the enemy threw up his hands, I took this to be a ruse and fired again. This occurred on three occasions. I then retired towards the Maze taking the gun with me. I saw the enemy again there and once more fired. I was now covering a large shell hole in which were Sergeant Hember and fourteen men. Having but two grenades we decided to try and reach the rest of the battalion, so I stripped the gun, rendering it useless to the enemy. The premature explosion of one of our own grenades wounded Sergeant Hember and five others. I then decided to retire with the remainder and get reinforcements. After several fruitless attempts to find Fen we managed to work round the outer edge of the Maze and reached Exe. On reaching Female we encountered more enemy bombers, at whom we fired and threw our last grenade. We eventually crawled down Exe and reached the remainder of the battalion at the junction of Fen and Exe.[34]

Lance Corporal John Foaden, 1/5th Battalion (London Rifle Brigade), London Regiment, 169th Brigade, 56th Division

One desperate rearguard action was fought by Second Lieutenant Petley as he and his men were grudgingly forced back from their hard-won positions in the Eck Trench.

Sergeant Austin, Corporal Thorpe and myself brought up the rear. Our idea was to try and bring one at least of the wounded back; as soon, however, as the party started we were bombed rather heavily from Female, and, of course, I had to order all wounded to be left alone. We managed to account for two or three of the Huns in Female and kept them down until the rear of the party had passed the top of Exe. We worked our way round to about the junction of Maze and Fibre, Austin and I bringing up the rear. We had no less than four different bombing parties to keep off, and the whole of my party got to the German second trench with only two or three casualties. It was in the independent rushes across the open, of course, that the casualties occurred, but even then, most of us, I believe, got to the German front line, where apparently were the remnants of C and D Companies and

> a lot of Queen Victoria's Rifles. Austin and I lay in a shell hole by the second line to cover as much as possible these final rushes. Our intention was to stay there until dark, but on a bomb bursting in our shell hole we cleared off before the smoke lifted. Austin muttered that he was hit, but we did not wait to argue. We ran in different directions and I have not seen him since. Although the bomb burst practically on us, I was unhurt except for a few tiny places in my legs. I worked my way to the German front trench and joined the others, Harvey, de Cologan, Smith, Cox of the Queen Victoria's Rifles, several other officers and about sixty or seventy men.[35]
>
> Second Lieutenant R. E. Petley, 1/5th Battalion (London Rifle Brigade), London Regiment, 169th Brigade, 56th Division

Soon they had fallen right back to the German front line and had nowhere left to go but back across No Man's Land. The London Rifle Brigade were the last to be forced out. As they hung on scattered remnants from the neighbouring battalions were forced back along the lines into their positions by the relentless bombing and sniping of the Germans. The survivors congregated in Ferret Trench just 200 yards from Gommecourt Park, but the situation was then beyond hope.

> By now I was just petrified. I knew that if I stayed in the trench I would have most certainly been killed. I hardly waited for the order, but it came, 'Everyone for himself!' I did not wait to argue – over the top I went like greased lightening – surviving a hail of bullets. I immediately fell flat. Then trying to imagine I was part of the earth, I wriggled along on my belly. Dead, dying and wounded, feigning death – who knows? The ground was covered with them. I sped from shell hole to shell hole. Never had I run faster. It was snipers, machine guns and shrapnel all the way. About halfway across, I rolled into a shell hole and fell on top of a badly wounded German in a pitiable state – probably an abandoned prisoner. All he said was, 'Sclecht! Sclecht!' – which means, 'Bad!' I don't know what made me do it but I gripped his hand and sped on. When I finally scrambled into our front-line trench I was greeted by our Adjutant Captain Wallis and Regimental Sergeant Major MacVeigh who both solemnly shook my hand. I was told that only twenty had returned so far.[36]
>
> Private Arthur Schuman, 1/5th Battalion (London Rifle Brigade), London Regiment, 169th Brigade, 56th Division

There were other survivors of course, but most were still marooned out in the hostile wastes of No Man's Land. Like a deadly game they had to choose their moment to try and sprint back. Get the timing wrong and the consequences were painful or fatal.

> It was either a bolt back with a sporting chance of getting through, or else surrender. We turned tail and made a blind bolt back about 7.30 p.m. The moment we did so they turned a veritable hail of fire upon us from machine guns and rifles. I got caught in the wire and sprawled headlong, tore myself free and then caught again. Once more I disentangled myself and then plunged into a shell hole and stopped there. How I got as far as there I knew not, for men were falling like flies. None who kept on in this rush for our line got through. There were five of us in this shell hole – three wounded. I sat in a pool of blood and water until it started getting dark, and then we crept out and back to safety. We spent over two hours in that shell hole, but so exhausted were we that even during that time we dozed.[77]
>
> Rifleman Frank Jacobs, 1/5th Battalion (London Rifle Brigade), London Regiment, 169th Brigade, 56th Division

At around 2130 the final party of 'last ditchers' were forced out of the German front line to take refuge in shell holes in No Man's Land as an interim measure before making the last desperate dash across to the British front line.

There was no doubt that the VII Corps attack had been a failure for the Gommecourt Salient still remained intact, thrusting provocatively into the British lines. In retrospect it is clear that the number of British guns assigned to a counter-battery role proved totally inadequate to meet the massed artillery fire of the German divisions, not only to their immediate front, but also from around Adinfer Wood and to the south from around Puiseux on either side of Gommecourt. The result was that the 46th and 56th Divisions faced the heaviest concentration of artillery fire of any sector assaulted on 1 July. In addition the narrow width of the front assaulted meant that the Germans could also utilise their machine guns to deadly effect from both the flanks and from the uncaptured switch lines and Quadrilateral strong point ahead of them. However, one question remained. The Third Army diversion may have totally failed to achieve its local objectives, but had it achieved its wider tactical justification of diverting attention and resources from the main assault? Here, too, there was disappointment. Certainly it was true that the very visible offensive preparations over the past month had caused the Germans to strengthen their forces in the area, but the actual attack when it came had been successfully rebuffed by these local forces without in any way disrupting the German defence further south around Serre and Beaumont Hamel. In essence the attack had been useless and the men of the North Midlands and London battalions had suffered terrible casualties in vain. The 46th Division lost 2,455 casualties, while the 56th Division bore the brunt with 4,314. It was difficult for the men to accept such severe losses in making a peripheral attack that did not and probably could not have affected the overall outcome of the day's fighting.

> The casualties have been very heavy indeed. The trying thing is that many of them are left, wounded or killed, in the German trenches, and whether they are alive or dead we do not know. We are filled with pride for all that has been done, bitterness for the little there is to show for it, and sorrow for those we shall never see again. We are told we have, in fact, helped in the general scheme, and done our job, but the battalion is sadly mauled about. I feel that our job is done as regards actual fighting for many months and for, perhaps, the rest of the war.[38]
>
> Major Samuel Sampson, 1/9th Battalion (Queen Victoria's Rifles), London Regiment, 169th Brigade, 56th Division

But his men would be back on the Somme long before the battle was done.

VIII Corps: *Serre to Beaumont Hamel – disaster on the left of the attack*

THE NORTHERN FLANK of the main assault was the responsibility of the VIII Corps of the Fourth Army. The VIII Corps was commanded by Lieutenant General Aylmer Hunter-Weston who had acquired a very mixed reputation. Born in 1864, he joined the Royal Engineers in 1884 and had seen service in the North West Frontier, Egypt and South Africa before he was appointed as Assistant Director of Military Training in 1911. On the outbreak of war he commanded a brigade in action in 1914 but on promotion was whisked away with the Mediterranean Expeditionary Force to take part in the campaign with which his name will forever be linked – Gallipoli. As the fighting degenerated into a welter of bloody

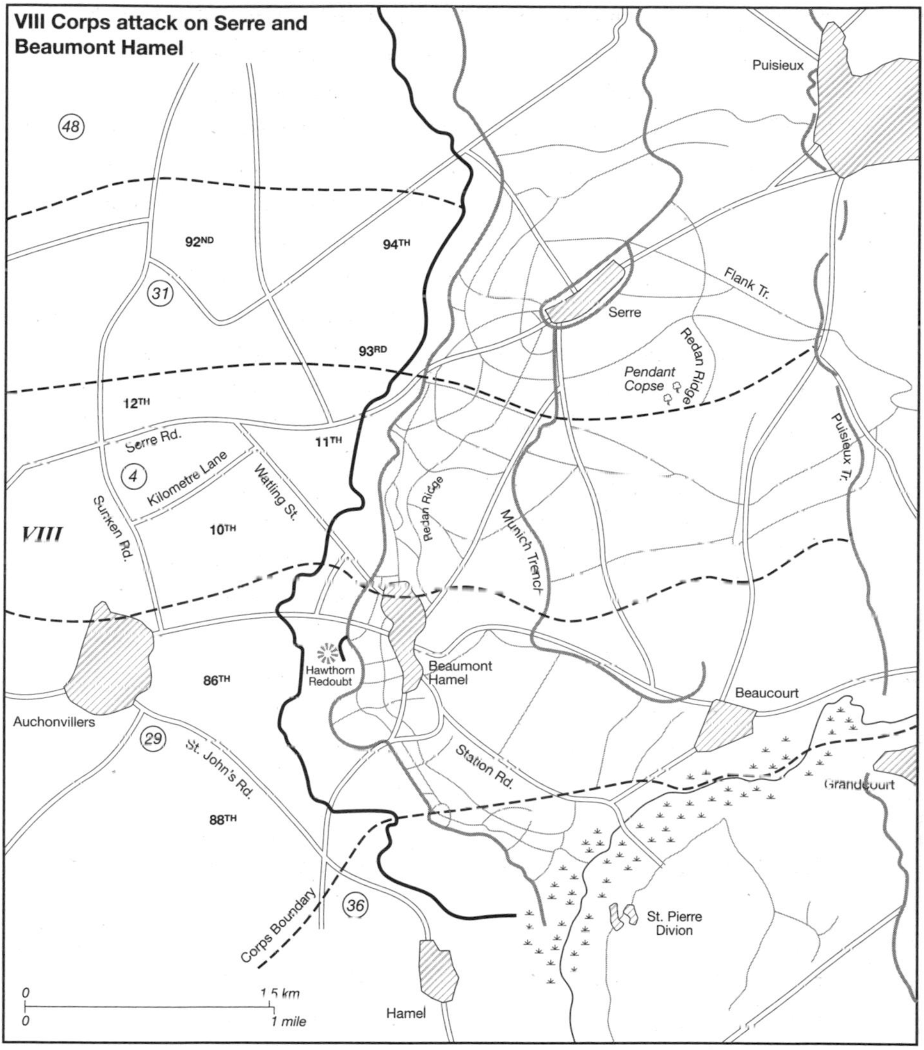
VIII Corps attack on Serre and Beaumont Hamel
Puisieux
48
92ND
94TH
31
Flank Tr.
Serre
93RD
Redan Ridge
Pendant Copse
12TH
Serre Rd.
11TH
Puisieux Tr.
4
Kilometre Lane
Watling St.
Redan Ridge
Munich Trench
Sunken Rd.
VIII
10TH
Hawthorn Redoubt
Beaumont Hamel
86TH
Beaucourt
Auchonvillers
29
St. John's Rd.
Station Rd.
Grandcourt
88TH
Corps Boundary
36
St. Pierre Divion
0
1.5 km
0
1 mile
Hamel

frontal assaults on the Turkish trenches Hunter-Weston soon got a reputation as an unimaginative general who was not overly concerned by casualties. In July 1915 he was evacuated due to the after-effects of severe sunstroke with some evidence of considerable nervous debilitation in the face of the unremitting mental and physical pressures that faced anyone serving on the Peninsula. On his recovery he returned to command the VIII Corps. The Somme would be his first command in a major Western Front battle.

Three of Hunter-Weston's divisions were assigned to the attack; from north to south they were the 31st, 4th and 29th Divisions. His men faced a mighty task ahead of them for they were staring directly across to the fortress villages of Serre and Beaumont Hamel lying on a series of ridges and valleys that formed an almost ideal landscape for defence. The preliminary artillery bombardment had been partially successful: the barbed wire had been cut or at least disrupted in most sectors of the VIII Corps, while the German front lines had been severely battered. Yet the deep dugouts survived almost unscathed. Perhaps even more ominous was the fact that the latent threat of the German artillery had not been dealt with. Here again the counter-battery arrangements had flattered only to deceive the men that relied on them for their lives. Several German batteries had not been put out of action and the location of many others was still unknown.

The plan for the VIII Corps infantry was fairly simple. The 31st Division would advance towards Serre, pivoting on John Copse and occupying the conveniently named German Flank Trench positions to form a strong defensive line facing north. A shallow tunnel had been dug across No Man's Land and would be blown open to leave a trench, thus providing a continuous flank line between the British front line and the expected gain of Flank Trench. The right of the division would ensure that they remained in contact with the neighbouring 4th Division.

The task of the two regular divisions, the 4th and 29th Divisions was daunting in the extreme. They were to advance straight into a natural amphitheatre across the valley in which Beaumont Hamel lay and then climb up onto the Beaucourt Spur to tackle the German second line. A key component of the plans was the mine prepared by the 252nd Tunnelling Company, Royal Engineers underneath the German strong point known as Hawthorn Redoubt, in front of Beaumont Hamel on the 29th Division front. The mine was primed and ready to 'blow' with some 40,000 lbs of ammonal high explosive, yet there was considerable controversy over the best timing of the explosion. Hunter-Weston wanted to set off the mine at 0330, with the intention thereby of seizing and consolidating the Hawthorn Redoubt well before the main assault. This was an optimistic plan and presumed that the British would be successful in getting to the crater first. The Inspector of Mines was very sceptical, and advised the General Headquarters, BEF that previous experience of crater warfare on the Western Front had revealed a definite German superiority in the tactical acumen and speed required to seize control of a crater. He therefore recommended that the mine be detonated only at 0730 as the troops went over the top. After much consultation with the headquarters of the Fourth Army it was finally decided to fire the mine at 0720 – a compromise solution in circumstances where compromise was neither rational nor possible.

The artillery arrangements of the VIII Corps were brought in line with this new deadline. The plan included a simple creeping barrage, but the orders requiring lifts of 50 yards a minute were ignored by the three divisional commanders who preferred to have lifts of 100 yards per minute, and starting from the German front line rather than in No Man's Land. As the mine exploded most of the heavy guns would lift their fire from the German front line to concentrate on their second and third lines. In effect the Germans would be first warned by the explosion of the mine and then left in relative peace to emerge from their dugouts in the ten minutes before the British troops began their advance. Coupled with the fact that a threatening proportion of the German artillery had not been knocked out, it was a recipe for disaster.

The story of the vain assault by 31st Division on the fortress village and ridge of Serre has often been told and has become an essential part of the tragic mythology of the Battle of the Somme. For the most part the division was composed of 'Pals' battalions recruited across the length and breadth of northern England. These were brave men, confident in their own abilities, but they were under-trained and lacked the experience of war to have any realistic chance against a defensive system that could have thrown back even the most battle-hardened troops. As the British climbed out of their trenches the defenders of Serre were ready and waiting for them. Brigadier Rees watched his men of the 94th Brigade going over the top with mingled hope and trepidation. He did not have long to wait before his hopes were dashed.

> Ten minutes before Zero our guns opened an intense fire. I stood on top to watch. It was magnificent. The trenches in front of Serre changed shape and dissolved minute by minute under the terrific hail of steel. Watching, I began to believe in the possibility of a great success, but I reckoned without the Hun artillery. As our infantry advanced, down came a perfect wall of explosive along the front trenches of my brigade and the 93rd. It was the most frightful artillery display that I had seen up to that time, and in some ways, I think it was the heaviest barrage I have seen put down by the defence on any occasion.[39]
>
> Brigadier General Hubert Rees, Headquarters, 94th Brigade, 31st Division

The German garrison and their machine guns had rushed out of their deep dugouts and were in position, ready and waiting. The scything blast of their machine-gun fire hit the Pals with dreadful effect.

> Every man climbed out of the trenches at the whistle of the officers and not a man hesitated. But I was lucky. I was in a part of the trench where the parapet had been battered down as Jerry sought for a trench mortar. When I ran up the rise out of the trench I was under the hail of bullets which were whizzing over my head. Most of our fellows were killed kneeling on the parapet. There was nobody coming forward, only one man, the reserves had been shelled in our lines and blown to smithereens. The Sergeant decided that as the attack was finished we'd go back and try and get into our own line. We wriggled out of this shell hole and then made a dash. Well my rifle got caught on the wire, it stopped there! I hadn't time to take it off and we got back in the line. I noticed higher up the trench one of our chaps laid there with a baulk of timber across his leg, one leg had been cut off – severed. This baulk of timber had cut across his leg and acted as a tourniquet and stopped the bleeding. Well, I ran down the trench looking for stretcher bearers and I bumped into a Bradford officer with about half a dozen men and he stopped me and wanted to know where I was going. I said, 'I'm going for help, there's Jim there with his leg off!' 'Oh!' he says, 'Never

mind him, fall in with my men! So I picked a rifle up, wiped it and fell in with his men. But when I got the first chance I lost him! Well Jim was found, was carried out and sent to 'Blighty' and he's alive to this day![40]

Private Arthur Pearson, 15th Battalion, West Yorkshire Regiment, 93rd Brigade, 31st Division

The German barbed wire had been partially cut by the British bombardment but in some sectors it remained a severe problem, especially protected as it was by concentrated machine-gun fire and the blast of the German artillery fire sweeping across No Man's Land.

Oh, my God, the ground in front it was just like heavy rain; that was machine-gun bullets. Up above there were these great big 5.9-in shrapnel shells going off. Broomhead and I went over the top together. We walked along a bit. A terrific bang and a great black cloud of smoke above us. I felt a knock on my hip which I didn't take much notice of. I turned round and Broomhead had gone. I walked on and I could not see a soul of any description – either in front of or behind me. I presume they got themselves tucked into shell holes. I thought, 'Well, I'm not going on there by myself!' I turned round and came back.[41]

Private Frank Raine, 18th Battalion, Durham Light Infantry, 93rd Brigade, 31st Division

As the Germans manned their front line they were left free of the threat of shell fire as the British bombardment had already lifted to new targets well behind the front line. This was unfortunate in the extreme.

The first line all lay down and I thought they'd had different orders because we'd all been told to walk. It appears they lay down because they'd been shot and either killed or wounded. They were just mown down like corn. Our line simply went forward and the same thing happened. You were just trying to find your way in amongst the shell holes. You can imagine walking through shell-pitted ground with holes all over the place, trying to walk like that. You couldn't even see where you were walking! When you got to the line you saw that a lot of the first line were stuck on the wire, trying to get through. We didn't get to the German wire, I didn't get as far as our wire. Nobody did, except just a few odd ones who got through and got as far as the German

> wire. The machine-gun fire was all trained on our wire. Only a few crept along. I lay down. We weren't getting any orders at all; there was nobody to give any orders, because the officers were shot down.[42]
>
> Private Reginald Glenn, 12th Battalion, York and Lancaster Regiment, 94th Brigade, 31st Division

One of the few that had managed to get further forward was Private Cattell. As the long lines of the infantry melted away behind him he found himself very much alone, marooned in No Man's Land.

> I never saw another man because I went straight on to their wire and I lay there all day. It was very, very hot, a baking hot day, quite different from the previous day, it had been pouring with rain, that was the day we ought to have gone over. Well, I crept back on my belly into the trenches, about nine o'clock, well it was getting dusk. And that was that. I went to a dugout in a trench a lot further back, there were some officers there, they were surprised to see me – they didn't think there was anybody left. I went down into a bunk and I think I slept for eighteen hours. The Germans could have walked through if they wanted, there was nobody there.[43]
>
> Private Douglas Cattell, 12th Battalion, York and Lancaster Regiment, 94th Brigade, 31st Division

For the most part the wounded had to make their own way back to the British front line. Under the German barrage this was by no means a place of safety.

> I saw a few yards away the entrance to a dugout. I thought, 'Well let's see if I can get myself in there.' So I dragged myself along to the steps of the dugout and I managed somehow to get my legs so that I was in a half-sitting, half-lying position on the steps leading down to the dugout. Suddenly the mouth of the dugout fell in and put me into a doubled up position. Some kind of a high explosive shell must have burst very, very near and upset the mouth of the dugout. I wasn't any further hurt, I thought I'd better get myself out of this lot; a dugout's not very safe because by then the rest of the entrance down into the dugout was blocked. So again I dragged myself out and rested a while in the open. Still nothing else hit me. This went on until the evening. I gradually dragged myself in the right direction, I'm glad to say. I passed quite a number of battalions who were going up to take our

places in the firing lines. Eventually, I crawled myself to safety. Who should I see on arriving but an old college friend of mine who was nicknamed Whiskers. I shouted to him, 'Whiskers!' He came over and said, 'Hello, what are you doing here?' I told him the story. He was in the RAMC, he took charge of me, had me put on to a stretcher and conveyed to the medical centre. It took me over a week before I reached England into hospital. I was in the original state that I was in – all covered with mud and lousy.[44]

Corporal Arthur Durrant, 18th Battalion, Durham Light Infantry, 93rd Brigade, 31st Division

Just a few of these gallant men managed to reach the German front line where they were swiftly outnumbered and dealt with by the front-line garrison. Some of the 18th Durham Light Infantry reached Pendant Copse while one brave company of the 11th East Lancashires and a group of the 12th York and Lancasters, despite all the odds stacked against them, may have managed by some feat of determination to break right through and penetrate the village of Serre itself.

Messages now began to pour in. An aeroplane reported that my men were in Serre. The corps and the division urged me to support the attack with all the force at my disposal. I was quite sure that we had not got anyone in Serre except a few prisoners, but the 93rd Brigade on my right, reported that their left had got on, whilst the 4th Division beyond them again claimed the first four lines of German trenches and were said to be bombing down our way. It was obviously necessary to attempt to get a footing in the German first trenches to assist these two attacks. The hostile barrage had eased off by now and was no longer formidable, so I ordered two companies of the 13th York and Lancs to make the attempt. I did not know that the German barrage was an observed barrage, but as soon as this fresh attack was launched down came the barrage again. One company was badly mauled, whilst the other wisely halted short of it.[45]

Brigadier General Hubert Rees, Headquarters, 94th Brigade, 31st Division

The Germans closed in around the isolated parties of men behind the German front line, cutting off all escape and they were gradually hunted down. There are no survivors' accounts. None of these gains were held and everywhere the line stayed exactly as it was. The story of the 31st

Division attempt on Serre was one of truly tragic failure that has become the symbol of everything that went wrong that day. The Pals division had suffered some 3,600 casualties.

MEANWHILE, immediately to their right the 4th Division was attacking in the gap that lay between Serre and Beaumont Hamel. This was not an attractive prospect, but the 4th Division was a regular division with a proud record. Although it had eventually been cut to ribbons as part of the original BEF in 1914, it had been patiently rebuilt with recruits from the original regimental depots and the battalions had largely succeeded in preserving their regular character.

Although the wire had been cut and the German front line trenches severely battered by the bombardment, again their deep dugouts had survived almost unscathed. The initial thrust was made by 11th Brigade with two additional battalions supplied from 48th Division, which was acting as the VIII Corps reserve. They were intended to capture the first two German lines before the 10th and 12th Brigades leapfrogged them to continue the assault on the third line. The lack of surprise after the nearby detonation of the Hawthorn Redoubt mine coupled with the early lift of the artillery on to the German rear areas, meant that as they emerged into No Man's Land they faced an immediate torrent of well-directed machine-gun fire from the front, augmented by sweeping enfilade fire from the Redan Ridge. At the same time the German artillery opened up, drenching No Man's Land and the British front line with masses of exploding shells. Two communication tunnels, named Cat and Rat, had been opened up just short of the German front line and these were occupied by Lewis gun sections. Unfortunately, the Germans soon knocked out the Lewis guns and following up hard and fast with bombing parties; they overran the tunnel ends and proceeded to block the tunnels. This left no safe method of crossing No Man's Land, which was under heavy continuous fire.

In front of the 1/8th Warwickshires was the Heidenkopf Redoubt, part of an earlier scheme of defensive works, which protruded out from the new German front line. The position was indefensible in the event of a concerted British attack and the Germans manned it with only a token garrison and had prepared a substantial mine with the intention of blowing the attacking British troops to smithereens once they occupied the position. Unfortunately for the Germans the mine was detonated far too soon and the 1/8th Warwickshires were able to swarm over what remained, using the chaotic shock of the explosion to advance into the neighbouring support trenches. However, the total failure of the 31st Division on their left flank doomed any hopes of exploiting this relative success. The usual German counter-attacks soon began to push in from Serre pressing hard on the mixed battalions occupying the Heidenkopf Redoubt.

At 0930, in circumstances of considerable confusion and amidst attempts to cancel the attack, half of 10th Brigade began their planned advance from the British front line ready to push on the assault by 11th Brigade. On the left flank of their advance was Lieutenant Colyer and the rest of the men of the 2nd Royal Dublin Fusiliers. They faced a desperate situation.

> Here goes. I clamber out of the front of the deep trench by the scaling ladder, and face my platoon. I am smoking a cigarette and superficially am serene and cheerful – at least, I hope I appear so. As I give the order to advance a sudden thought occurs to me: will they all obey? This is instantly answered in the affirmative, for they all climb out of the trench, and the advance begins. We are advancing in diamond formation, Moffat's platoon is in front, mine on the left corner of the diamond, Stobart's on the right, while the rear platoon is led by a sergeant. So far all has gone as per programme, and there is no reason why it should not have done, for we have simply been traversing more-or-less dead ground. Now as we approach the crest of the rise, we can distinguish hostile rifle fire and shell fire much more clearly in the great pandemonium. Ah! Then the Boche haven't all run away yet! Bullets are flying about and things aren't so comfortable. A communication trench which we have to cross affords us temporary relief from the ordeal. We can see over the ridge now. There are the skeleton trees of Beaumont Hamel. Between is a waste of trench land which is being torn up by shell fire – we are going to have trouble I can see .... We are on top of the ridge and under direct fire. I am trying not to mind it, but it is impossible. I am wondering unpleasantly whether I shall be killed outright or whether I shall be wounded; and if the latter, which part of me will be hit. A traversing machine gun rips up the ground just in front of us. That's enough for me; we can't

> remain in this formation, 'Extend by sections!' I shout. The men carry out the movement well. We have certainly practiced it enough, though we did not expect to have to use it until well past Beaumont Hamel. The Boche artillery and machine guns are terrific. The anticipation of being hit has become so agonising that I can scarcely bear it; I almost wish to God I could be hit and have done with it. I have lost some of my men. I feel an overwhelming desire to swear, to blaspheme, to shout out the wickedest oaths I can think of, but I am much too inarticulate to do anything of the kind. A shell bursts near and I feel the hot blast. It seems to me this is a ghastly failure already. A trench runs diagonally across our path. Half of my remaining men are already in it. My whole being cries out in protest against this ordeal. I am streaming with perspiration. I think I shall go mad. I am in the trench, trying to collect the rest of the men together. Where the devil have they all got to?[46]
>
> Lieutenant William Colyer, 2nd Battalion, Royal Dublin Fusiliers, 10th Brigade, 4th Division

The 2nd Royal Dublin Fusiliers came under heavy fire from both the Ridge Redoubt on Redan Ridge and Beaumont Hamel to their right. The rehearsals in training had seemed a cakewalk and bore no resemblance to the terrifying chaos that faced them. After an abortive attempt to locate his neighbouring platoons, Lieutenant Colyer tried to decide what on earth he was to meant to do next.

> I must go on. That's right; I have that firmly fixed in my mind. I can do no good by stopping here, and the idea of going back could not be entertained for a single moment. But it's rather vague: where am I to go, and what am I going to do when I get there? I certainly never anticipated the extraordinary situation I find myself in now. I have lost touch with half my men in this cursed network of trenches, and in trying to get hold of them again, I have lost the other half. The whole attack as far as we are concerned seems to be completely messed up. Well, if I can't find my own men, I must jolly well collect some others and go forward with them. Let's have a look over the top and try and see what's happening. I climb on to the firestep and look over the parapet. The same scene is there – a desolate waste being churned up by machine guns and shell fire. Shells bursting unpleasantly close too.[47]
>
> Lieutenant William Colyer, 2nd Battalion, Royal Dublin Fusiliers, 10th Brigade, 4th Division

A moment later the necessity of taking such a life or death decision was irrelevant as he was knocked over and concussed by a shell. The sheer force of the blast stripped him of his senses and left him suffering from the classic symptoms of temporary shell shock.

> I was stunned for a moment and thought I was hit. I wasn't hit; how I escaped I can't imagine. Then my whole nervous system seemed to be jangled up and I ran like a hare down the trench. I don't know where I thought I was going. I was much too agitated. I went tumbling along that until I saw what I took to be a dugout opening, which I made for at once. There were a couple of men and an officer sitting just inside the opening. They looked at me as if I had taken leave of my senses – which for the time being, really, I suppose I had. The officer asked me what the matter was and I mumbled something about a shell bursting close to me. He seemed to understand for he was sympathetic and told me to come inside and rest awhile.[48]
>
> Lieutenant William Colyer, 2nd Battalion, Royal Dublin Fusiliers, 10th Brigade, 4th Division

So, feeling muddle-headed and totally confused he took shelter and actually fell asleep in a dugout back in the original British front line.

Meanwhile, elements of the 10th Brigade had struggled on as far as the Munich Trench with a few brave men even being reported to have reached Pendant Copse. But whatever success the 4th Division had achieved was soon negated by the failure of their neighbouring divisions – the 31st Division to the north and the 29th Division to the south – to make any advance. Like the brave Londoners at Gommecourt a few miles to the north they found themselves totally isolated. As desperate attempts to reinforce them failed, the incessant hammering of German counter-attacks forced them back step by step until all that they retained of their gains was the Heidenkopf Redoubt. The German tide surged round them but they held out until early next morning when even that was reluctantly abandoned. The 4th Division was left to lick its wounds back in the trenches from which it had started.

In the dark of the night Lieutenant Colyer slowly began to recover from his temporary shell shock. As he regained some idea of his surroundings he found a renewed commitment to find his unit and do his duty once more. But when he rejoined his battalion he found them back in the support line, behind the original British front line, which by then had been smashed to smithereens by the German counter-bombardment. Once again he tried to settle to sleep, but was haunted by the sheer horror of his experiences.

> I am lying in the corner of a darkened dugout. The night is already far advanced, but I cannot sleep. The sound of heavy breathing within the dugout mingles strangely with the occasional whine of a shell without. Every now and again the doorway is filled with an eerie shivering light, caused by a flare set off from the front line a few hundred yards away. The odour of spent explosives still hangs heavy in the air. What a disastrous day it has been! What a wanton shedding of human blood. And yet, I suppose, only to be expected in war, and all in the day's work of a soldier – I'm no soldier, that's about the truth of it. I cannot sleep, for thinking of my fellow officers; I can scarcely grasp the fact that I shall never see some of them again. It is such a short while ago that I left them in the height of good spirits, and now in the freshness of youth they have suddenly gone off to another world. It is uncanny to think of it. More than that it is sickening–wicked–cruel–impossible. It is only now that I realise how much their friendship meant to me.[49]
>
> Lieutenant William Colyer, 2nd Battalion, Royal Dublin Fusiliers, 10th Brigade, 4th Division

The 4th Division had suffered severely in their brave advance, for overall they suffered 5,752 casualties.

NEXT TO THE 4TH Division was the 29th Division – another regular division. Scraped up from garrisons around the empire, their experiences serving at Gallipoli had succeeded in strimming down the number of original pre-war regulars until survivors were the exception rather than the rule. Nevertheless, since the evacuation in January 1916, the division had been rebuilt and had retained a considerable self-confidence claiming for itself as it did the sobriquet 'Immortal'. Now on the Somme they faced the Hawthorn Ridge and the fortress village of Beaumont Hamel. The ground was devoid of worthwhile cover with the exception of a sunken road near to the left of their sector. In addition the engineers had dug three tunnels reaching forward beneath No Man's Land to near the

German line. Two of these were to be used to establish Stokes mortar sections in posts at the end and the other was for use as a communication trench to the sunken road in front of the 1st Lancashire Fusiliers. As the mine was detonated the Stokes mortar teams, who had squirreled their way to the tunnel exits and taken up positions in the sunken road, would commence a furious bombardment of the front line.

The detonation of the Hawthorn Redoubt mine at 0720 was caught on film by the official British film cameraman Geoffrey Malins. It seems strange to be able to watch such a key moment of the attack, for the film and photographic record is thin for obvious reasons. In a storm of bullets and shell burst any cameraman who exposed himself in the open was no safer than any ordinary infantryman. Despite the natural fears of the men that they would be vulnerable to falling debris the two platoons of the 2nd Royal Fusiliers with machine guns and extra Stokes mortars were to race across and seize the crater. Unfortunately, the Germans were not completely shaken by the enormous explosion. In the immediate area of the crater the effect was truly devastating. But elsewhere the garrison were safe underground in their dugouts. Now they knew the British were going to attack.

> There was a terrific explosion which for the moment completely drowned the thunder of the artillery. A great cloud of smoke rose from the trenches of No. 9 Company, followed by a tremendous shower of stones, which seemed to fall from the sky all over our position. More than three sections of No. 9 Company were blown into the air, and the neighbouring dugouts were broken in and blocked. The ground all round was white with the debris of chalk as if it had been snowing, and a gigantic crater over 50 yards in diameter and some 60 feet deep gaped like an open wound in the side of the hill. This explosion was a signal for the infantry attack, and everyone got ready and stood on the lower steps of the dugouts, rifles in hand, waiting for the bombardment to lift. In a few minutes the shelling ceased, and we rushed up the steps and out into the crater positions. Ahead of us wave after wave of British troops were crawling out of their trenches and coming forward towards us at a walk, their bayonets glistening in the sun.[50]
>
> Anon Officer, 119th Reserve Regiment, 26th Reserve Division, German Army

Stuck in their dugouts for seven days and nights the German soldiers knew that the assault was coming. The only question was when. Before the debris from the explosion had landed they knew the moment was nigh. As they rushed out of their dugouts they found that the British heavy artillery had lifted from what remained of their front line. When Zero Hour arrived at 0730, the artillery barrage moved off the front line in accordance with the plans for a creeping barrage. The German garrison could take up their defensive positions in the remnants of the front line and nearby shell holes without the inconvenience of shells plastering around them. In the race to occupy the lips of the smoking crater, the Germans of course had the enormous advantage of being so much closer to the objective. The entirely predictable end result was that although the 2nd Royal Fusiliers managed to get to the near lip they then found themselves under heavy flanking fire from the German front line, and point-blank fire from a strong party of Germans already in position on the far lip of the crater, a mere 50 yards away.

The main attack at 0730 of the assaulting troops of 86th and 87th Brigades was an utter disaster. They were under heavy scything fire from the moment they left their trenches. In addition in this sector of the front the gunners had failed in one of their basic duties, as the infantry found a sizeable proportion of the German barbed wire remained uncut. From his forward artillery observation post Signaller Dudley Menaud-Lissenburg watched the men of the 29th Division advance in serried ranks to oblivion.

> I watched with mixed feeling the lads mount the firestep and, when at 0730 the barrage lifted, spring up the ladders on to the parapet – many sliding back immediately they had reached the top, killed or wounded. Coolly, it seemed, the survivors worked their way through our barbed wire in the face of fierce shell and machine-gun fire, leaving many of their pals on the wire, dead. On they went up the long incline in perfect order, dropping to the ground every now and then, as though on an exercise on Salisbury Plain. The line thinned as men fell, but never faltered.[51]
>
> Signaller Dudley Menaud-Lissenburg, 97th Battery, 147th Brigade, Royal Field Artillery, 29th Division

The men of the 1st Lancashire Fusiliers, so proud of the six VCs won before breakfast during the assault on W Beach at Gallipoli on 25 April 1915, discovered the reality of war on the Western Front. Once again they were in an open amphitheatre overlooked by an enemy under cover. Once again they drove themselves forward with admirable courage and discipline. But this time instead of having to contend with a mere company of Turks with at most one machine gun, they found themselves facing the mighty defensive strength of a German division as they walked into a scything hell of interlocked machine-gun fire and the withering blast of concentrated shell-fire. This was modern war at its most fiendish.

> It's time to go over the top. It was partly blown down and I'm just stepping on top, there was a corporal lying there, gone – all blown away, I think he'd been hit by a whizz-bang. He looks up at me as I passed him, 'Go on Corporal, get the bastards!' There were bullets everywhere. Run – that was the only thing in my mind. Run and dodge. Expecting at any second to get hit, to feel a bullet hit me. I was zig-zagging, holding my head down so a bullet would hit my tin hat, I seemed to be dodging in between them – I must have been to get there! There was gun smoke. You could hear when a bullet hit somebody, you could hear it hit him! Hear him groan and go down. It was mainly machine guns that cut us up. I was thinking, I've got to get forward that's all. I dove into the Sunken Road.[52]
>
> Corporal George Ashurst, 1st Battalion, Lancashire Fusiliers, 86th Brigade, 29th Division

From the Sunken Road between the lines they couldn't even see the German trenches, which were still a long way ahead of them. After a brief period of reorganisation the men were ready to try again. But the fire pouring into them was still intense and it was impossible.

> Colonel Magniac said, 'Every fit man, come with me – over the top again!' He went over, I ran up the slope, right enough, whether a lot more did I don't know. I ran on and there was nobody with me, I was by myself, so I got a bit frightened then. When I came across this shell hole I dropped in it. I could lie down in it and look back over our lines. I could see our wounded, they would get up and try to go on and then they'd drop, they'd been shot again. I'm lying there; I had a drink out of my water bottle. Looking back I noticed the Royal Fusiliers on the

> left were running back to their trenches. I didn't know what they were doing, but I thought, 'Jerry's counter-attacking, what about me, if he comes over the top here, I'm for it all right, there's nothing for me!' So I made my mind up that I'd got to move and move very quick. I got up and dashed down this slope again and dived into the Sunken Road once more. Safe again – they'd missed again![53]
>
> Corporal George Ashurst, 1st Battalion, Lancashire Fusiliers, 86th Brigade, 29th Division

All along the divisional front the story was one of failure. The attack never reached the German front line but irretrievably collapsed in No Man's Land. The creeping barrage crept forward across the German lines but it was no longer followed by any troops, all of whom had fallen at the first fence. While the British artillery bombarded irrelevant targets the Germans pounded the British trenches and No Man's Land. They knew which way the British reinforcements would be coming and they were determined to break them up before they had a chance to renew the assault. Once again there was a problem with unconfirmed reports, which seemed to indicate that some of the men had got through and were assaulting the German support lines. Although these had no basis in fact the divisional reserve was ordered forward by divisional headquarters to bolster the attack. Ordinary excusable mistakes made in the fog of war can cost hundreds of lives and never was this more apparent than in the futile advance of the 1st Newfoundland Regiment and the 1st Essex Regiment who went over the top at 0905. The Newfoundlanders suffered some 710 casualties. Such losses from a single battalion are beyond the necessity for comment.

Amongst the mass slaughter there were hundreds of individual stories of stoicism and courage in the face of hopeless odds. The last tortured struggle of an anonymous man was watched with physical detachment but a very real emotional involvement by Signaller Dudley Menaud-Lissenburg from the relative security of his observation post.

> I watched a lone figure, a runner no doubt, coming back towards our lines, dropping every now and then into shell holes for cover. On reaching our barbed wire he was about to jump into the trench when a shell burst at his feet and blew him sky high. What a tragedy.[54]
>
> Signaller Dudley Menaud-Lissenburg, 97th Battery, 147th Brigade, Royal Field Artillery, 29th Division

The only toehold made in the Hawthorn Redoubt crater was untenable and the isolated and partially encircled defenders were soon forced back by determined German counter-attacks which would not cede an inch. The Lancashire Fusiliers clung on to the Sunken Road for a while but their position was hopeless. That night they left just a token force to hold it as an outpost.

> Later on in the day a message came across, 'One officer, one NCO and twenty-five men only to man the Sunken Road.' That meant we'd got to stop there all night and all day next day. There was only this officer knocking about. He said, 'That means me and that means you, Corporal!' We got twenty-five men and we put about eight men at the bottom end of the road and about eight at the top of the road and about eight or nine in the middle of the road under the oldest soldier because there were no more NCOs. The thing quietened down, the quiet after the storm, we were practically sleeping all night, just lying there. The stretcher bearers were very busy taking a lot out of it – they were cleared by morning. As dawn came I was against this bit of a barrier we'd built up at the bottom end and I hear some voices the other side of the barrier. I stand up and have a look and there's three Jerries! About 100 yards away stood in a ditch. I said to the lads, 'Jerries!' I took my rifle and I fired at the middle one – he went, but whether I hit him or not I don't know. No sooner had he ducked and the other two followed him out of sight. The officer came down to see what the trouble was. I told him. 'Ooooh, we're all right lads, we can dig in now, Jerry will let us bloody well have it!' He was right you know – he did. He started with *minenwerfers*, you can see them coming. Dropping them here and there, he dropped one right on the body of men in the middle of the road, killed half of them and wounded the other half. One I thought was certainly ours and it was a dud! It dropped about 6 yards past us towards the far end of the Sunken Road. As soon as it was dark word came, a messenger, 'Evacuate the Sunken Road!' So we packed in and ran back as fast as we could.[55]
>
> Corporal George Ashurst, 1st Battalion, Lancashire Fusiliers, 86th Brigade, 29th Division

Soon they were back in the front line. The 'Immortal' 29th Division had lost 5,240 casualties on their introduction to the Western Front.

Overall, there could be no doubt that the attack of the VIII Corps had utterly failed to disturb the integrity of the German defences. Further attempts during the day to resuscitate the attack with reduced objectives centred on Beaumont Hamel all failed in the face of the continued absolute dominance of No Man's Land by the German artillery and machine guns. After their initial failure, the battered remnants of the 31st, 4th and 29th Divisions had no chance of making a successful assault against defences that had already thrown them back when they were at full strength. Mere flesh and blood, whether they be Pals or regulars, could not triumph against such odds.

X Corps: *Thiepval Ridge – a missed opportunity*

NEXT IN LINE TO the south was X Corps who took on the daunting task of attacking astride the Ancre valley. They had been charged with the task of capturing the whole of the Thiepval Spur and Plateau which projected out from the main mass of Pozières Ridge towards the Ancre. At the tip of the Thiepval Spur lay the great Leipzig Redoubt stuffed with machine guns and completely dominating No Man's land in deadly conjunction with two flanking redoubts: Beaucourt Spur across the Ancre, and the Nord Werk on the Ovillers Spur. At the root of Thiepval Spur where it joined the main plateau lay Thiepval village which was less obviously threatening as it had been razed to the ground by the preliminary bombardment. Yet, if anything, the thick layer of rubble that remained only increased the formidable defensive capacity of the reinforced cellars beneath, many of which were expanded and linked to form an underground fortress. In addition the Germans had constructed the Wundtwerk Redoubt on the sheltered reverse slope of the Thiepval Spur, the Schwaben Höhe Redoubt which sat above the spur on the main ridge, and finally the fortress village of St Pierre Divion, which stood sentinel high above the Ancre flank. As if this was not enough, the German Second Line system and intermediate positions ran in interconnected and supporting layers across the breadth of Pozières Ridge bearing names that would come to haunt the British over the next few months: the Hansa Line; Mouquet Switch Line and Mouquet Farm; Stuff and Goat Redoubts. These impressive fortifications reflected the importance of the high ground

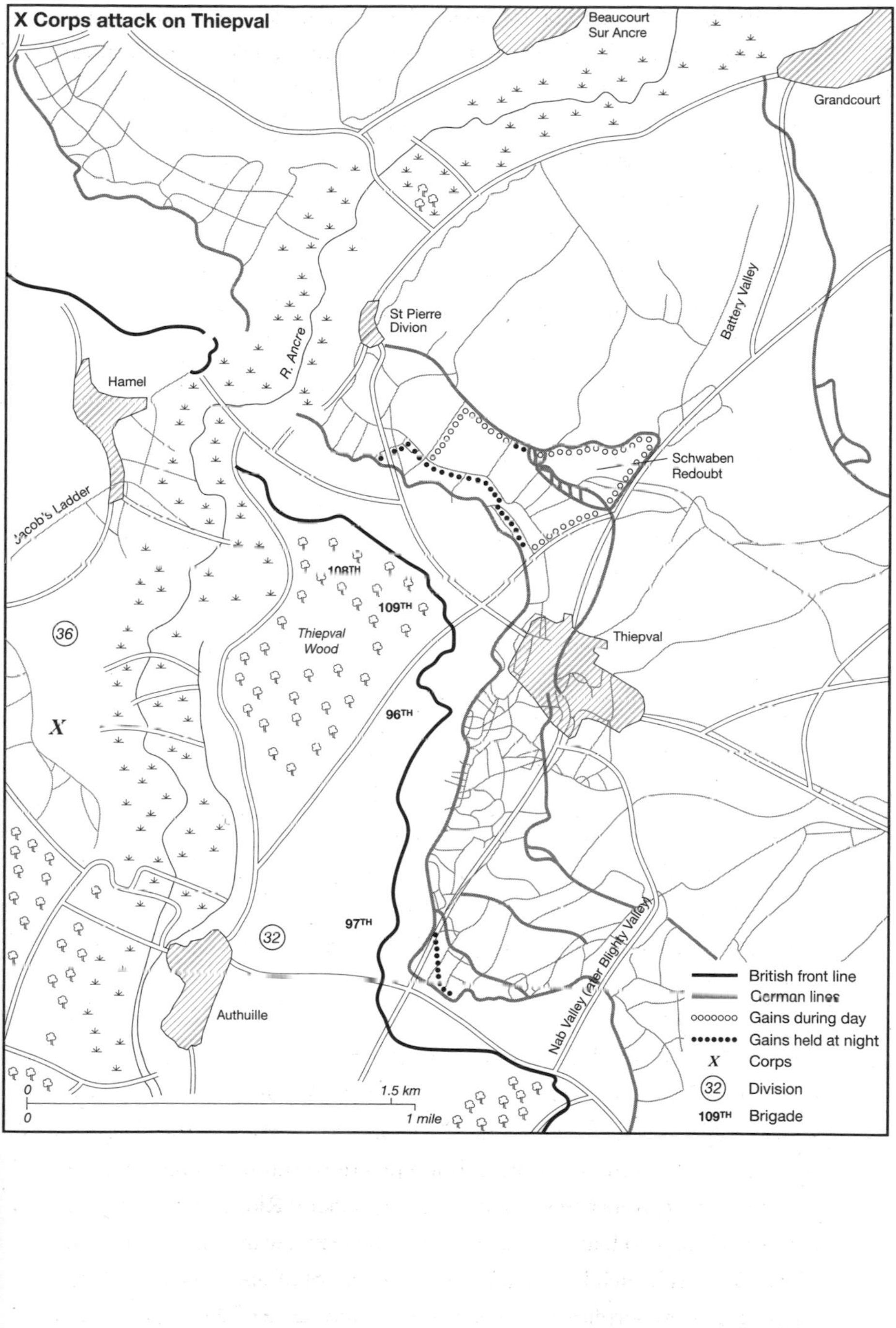
X Corps attack on Thiepval
Beaucourt Sur Ancre
Grandcourt
St Pierre Divion
Battery Valley
R. Ancre
Hamel
Schwaben Redoubt
Jacob's Ladder
108TH
109TH
Thiepval Wood
Thiepval
36
X
96TH
97TH
32
Authuille
Nab Valley (later Blighty Valley)
British front line
German lines
Gains during day
Gains held at night
Corps
Division
109TH Brigade
0
1.5 km
0
1 mile

of Pozières Ridge and Thiepval Spur. If the British could break through here then much of the rest of the German line to the north and south would be overlooked. Taken together, as a multi-layered fortress, it was an almost unparalleled obstacle that faced the attack of the two divisions assigned to the task.

It can be safely said that the plan did not lack boldness. The 36th and 32nd Divisions were to leap with a single bound across the Thiepval Spur and Plateau to take and consolidate the Hansa Line and Mouquet Switch Line. The reserve brigades would move forward to take the German Second Line. The situation was simple: only a faultless display of coordination between the British artillery and infantry would have even a remote chance of cracking open this particular nut. In particular it was obvious that if the 32nd Division failed in front of Thiepval then the 36th (Ulster) Division would be severely exposed from the right flank.

> Before dawn our artillery stepped up their bombardment to the maximum. It was rapid fire by every gun and the noise was like hell let loose. As the shells passed over our heads the air hummed like a swarm of a hundred million hornets. Then at zero hour the shelling stopped abruptly, our troops emerged from the front-line trenches where they had been waiting ready for the signal to advance. Looking up to the front line from our camp I could see men appearing against the skyline, dark against the dawn light and then disappearing as they advanced over the top of the hill.[56]
>
> Second Lieutenant J. L. Stewart-Moore, 107th Trench Mortar Battery, 36th (Ulster) Division

The barrage was intended to lift in stages, jerking back to each German line in succession according to a previously agreed timetable. There was some innovation in that with each lift some of the field artillery guns would move back slowly, tracking along the course of the German communication trenches. The assault battalions of the 108th and 109th Brigades of 36th Division attacked across No Man's Land in successive waves.

> I stood on the parapet between the two centre exits to wish them luck. They got through without delay; no fuss, no shouting, no running, everything solid and thorough – just like the men themselves. Here and there a boy would wave his hand to me as I shouted a good luck to them through my megaphone. And all had a cheery face. Most

> were carrying loads. Fancy advancing against heavy fire with a big roll of barbed wire on your shoulder![57]
>
> Lieutenant Colonel Ambrose Ricardo, 9th Battalion, Royal Inniskilling Fusiliers, 109th Brigade, 36th (Ulster) Division

At least the German barbed wire had been cleared by the bombardment, and to some extent the advancing waves were concealed by the effect of the thunderous bombardment and the additional smoke barrages laid down by Stokes mortars. The Irish battalions smashed into the German trench system and in an amazing feat of arms burst right through to overrun the Schwaben Höhe Redoubt up on the main Pozières Ridge. The German artillery had reacted far too late in this sector but as German shells belatedly dropped down on to No Man's Land they posed a serious threat to the designated support and exploitation troops of the 107th Brigade as they began to move forward. Amongst them was Private Davie Starrett, batman to Colonel Crozier commanding the 9th Royal Irish Rifles.

> We fell in and moved off, woodbines in mouth, across the Ancre swamp. A couple of shells fell. Jerry has woken up! At Speyside we massed on the slopes, our guns thundering over us. Then the enemy artillery broke loose. On past Gordon Castle – into an inferno of screaming shells and machine-gun bullets. Crouching, we slowly moved across No Man's Land. The Colonel stood giving last orders to his company commanders, and I beside him. Bullets cutting up the ground at his feet he watched the advance through his glasses.[58]
>
> Private Davie Starrett, 9th Battalion, Royal Irish Rifles, 107th Brigade, 36th (Ulster) Division

As they reached the forward edge of Thiepval Wood, Crozier could see that Thiepval had not fallen and that the deadly machine guns of the German garrison were still chattering away. The situation looked hopeless when he suddenly espied a brief window of opportunity in the chaos that surrounded them.

> I survey the situation; still more machine-gun fire: they have lowered their sights: *pit pit*, the bullets hit the dry earth all round. The shelling on to the wood edge has ceased. The men emerge. A miracle has happened. 'Now's the chance!' I think to myself, 'They must quicken pace and get diagonally across to the Sunken Road, disengaging from each other quickly, company by company.' I stand still and erect in the

> open, while each company passes. To each commander I give the amended orders. Men are falling here and there, but the guns previously firing on the edge of the wood are quite silent. First passes 'A' with Montey at its head. His is the longest double to the flank. George Gaffikin comes next waving an orange handkerchief. 'Goodbye, Sir! Good luck!' He shouts to me *en passant*, 'Tell them I died a teetotaller, put it on the stone if you find me!' The 'baby' captain of 'C' comes next, 'D' brings up the rear with Berry at the head. Imagine a timed exposure with your camera. The button is pressed, the shutter opens, another press and it again shuts. That is what happened to us. The German shelling ceased for five minutes, we hurried through the gap of mercy.[59]
>
> Lieutenant Colonel Frank Crozier, 9th Battalion, Royal Irish Rifles, 107th Brigade, 36th (Ulster) Division

Together they raced across No Man's Land as fast as their relative burdens allowed them; the heavily laden batman desperately trying to keep pace with his portly little officer. When they got to the Sunken Road they assessed the situation quickly to find that Colonel Bernard of the 10th Royal Irish Rifles had already been killed and Crozier perforce took control of the situation – he was determined to continue the advance up on to Pozières Ridge as planned come what may.

> Between the bursts Crozier doubled to the Sunken Road, his batman making a bad second in the race. 'The Tenth Rifles are wiped out!' he shouted. We reached our own men. They had taken what cover the place afforded. Bernard has been killed. Crozier rallied what was left of the Tenth. 'Sound the advance!' he yelled, 'Sound, damn you, sound the advance!' The bugler's lips were dry. He had been wounded. His lungs were gone. A second later he fell dead at the Colonel's feet. Hine cut the cord and gave the bugle to someone who could play. Crozier was signalling the men on. He walked into bursts, he fell into holes, his clothing was torn by bullets, but he himself was all right. Moving about as if on the parade ground he again and again rallied his men. Without him not a man would have passed the Schwaben Redoubt, let alone reached the final objective.[60]
>
> Private Davie Starrett, 9th Battalion, Royal Irish Rifles, 107th Brigade, 36th (Ulster) Division

With such a man driving them on elements of the 107th Brigade managed to reach and take up positions in Stuff Redoubt. Private Starrett was employed as a runner, moving backwards and forwards between the surviving officers and Crozier's headquarters in a dugout on the edge of Thiepval Wood.

> Trenches and tops were blocked with the dead, but on days like that there's no sympathy in your heart. Over them you go. I found the signals and the office staff, McKinney and Bowers were always exactly in the right place. The dugout was being used as a clearing station. It was hard passing without a word men in terrible pain – men you knew. Kelly, a big lump of a fighting Irishman, in charge of rations, was there too. The fierce shelling continued and the place seemed taped to an inch. Stretcher bearers fell every minute. Most that reached Doncaster Dump were wounded carrying wounded. The barrage, for such it seemed, lifted and caught our rear. Probably Jerry was trying to stop reinforcements. A badly wounded runner brought a message, the Colonel was found, he read and answered it, and went back to our men holding the newly won trenches. The heat and the stench made the day more unpleasant. Prisoners began to arrive, seeming well-pleased to be out of the fight. They were hit badly, too, those who could drag along carrying those who could not. One young German died as he was put down. Half of his face was blown away.[61]
>
> Private Davie Starrett, 9th Battalion, Royal Irish Rifles, 107th Brigade, 36th (Ulster) Division

The wounded were flooding back from the front, where their awful appearance cast a melancholy cloud over their comrades in the divisional rear areas.

> It was a terrible sight to see the wounded coming down in hundreds, the most serious in any conveyance that was handy – in GS wagons, motor lorries, ambulances, or anything they could get. Those that could possibly crawl at all, had to get from the trenches to the dressing station, which was about 3 miles, as best they could. Each time we were coming back from the guns with empty ammunition wagons, we packed as many wounded on as we could, as we passed the dressing station on our way back, but a lot of them were too badly wounded to stand the jolting of the wagon, and preferred to go on their own.[62]
>
> Gunner William Grant, D Battery, 154th Brigade, 36th (Ulster) Division

On the right flank of 36th Division, the 96th and 97th Brigades of 32nd Division launched themselves directly against the Thiepval Spur. The 96th Brigade encountered concentrated machine-gun fire from the German machine guns concealed in the ruins of Thiepval village. Progress was simply impossible and the battalions melted away as they tried to move forward. Next to them the 97th Brigade had slightly more success as it attacked the western face of Leipzig Redoubt. This was possibly due to the innovative tactics of Brigadier J. B. Jardine who ordered his men to creep out into No Man's Land slightly before zero hour and approach as close as possible to the barrage falling on the German front line. When the barrage lifted the 16th and 17th Highland Light Infantry undoubtedly caught the German defenders by surprise.

> At 7.23 we climbed out of the trenches and started to move across No Man's Land. We were loaded down with full kit, and in addition, a spade, shovel or pick. We soon reached the enemy front line and the work of the 'moppers-up' began, shouting down dugouts to the Hun to come up. The battalion had started kicking footballs in front of them. Leipzig Trench was taken and we began to advance towards the Hindenburg Trench. Alas, almost every company officer had been killed. D Company had been almost annihilated.[63]
>
> Private James Jack, 17th Battalion, Highland Light Infantry, 97th Brigade, 32nd Division

The wire in front of that part of the 17th Highland Light Infantry in particular had been well cut and the sheer speed of its attack caught the Germans in the deep dugout somewhat by surprise. Before they could emerge the Scots were in amongst them and the first obstacle had been overcome. But the Hindenburg Trench still lay a good 150 yards ahead of them and as they lurched forward again they soon came under heavy machine-gun fire from the Wundtwerk Redoubt.

> The machine gun swept us down outside the Leipzig Redoubt. It became evident that we, who were working up between two communications trenches, after two or three rushes, that further advancing was impossible without support. We waited for our own reserve waves and the Lonsdales who should have come on behind. But no reserves reached us and we saw our only hope lay in the fact that they had rushed one of the communication trenches and might manage to

bomb out the machine gun. But the bombers were checked out of the range of the gun. We began to work towards the communications trench, but owing to the lie of the ground we were badly exposed.[64]

Private Bentley Meadows, 17th Battalion, Highland Light Infantry, 97th Brigade, 32nd Division

As the men pressed on they encountered more and more intact belts of barbed wire. With the advantage of any surprise lost they found the going was increasingly difficult and the number of casualties swiftly escalated. Amongst them was Private Jack.

Advancing towards the Hun second trench, I felt as if a mule had kicked me above the right eye. Lying prone, I endeavoured to think what had happened. It turned out that I had been sniped, the bullet piercing the steel helmet in the front and circling inside three times had cut a furrow above my right eye. The other eye had swollen up and having crawled into the trench, almost blinded, I was ordered by Captain Laird, my platoon commander to proceed to the rear. Looking back I saw him hit by a shell adding another officer casualty to the growing number. Proceeding round a traverse to the Hun communication trench, I spied a large Hun officer at the top of a dugout. I immediately gave him three of the best as I peered at him. He did not move and getting closer I found that he had been the victim of one of his own shells, part of the casing having fixed his head to the entrance of his dugout. He had not been missed by the 'moppers up' as I first thought.[65]

Private James Jack, 17th Battalion, Highland Light Infantry, 97th Brigade, 32nd Division

Those who remained found themselves increasingly isolated. No reinforcements could get forward to join them and their numbers were rapidly eroding away. Soon there would be no one left.

I at length found myself the only living occupant of that corner. About twelve o'clock I managed to leap the parapet without being hit. I found my platoon officer, Lieutenant MacBrayne, lying shot through the head. Of the others of my platoon I could get no news, except those I saw lying dead or wounded.[66]

Private Bentley Meadows, 17th Battalion, Highland Light Infantry, 97th Brigade, 32nd Division

The remnants banded together for mutual support and resolved on one last attempt to get forward. It was a forlorn hope more born of desperation than any realistic expectation of success.

> An officer suddenly jumped the parapet and shouted, 'Come on the Seventeenth!' I followed him with about twenty others. But we found the barbed wire impossible to cut through and he gave us the order, 'Every man for himself!' Making my way back to the trench I rested in a shell hole occupied by a sergeant wounded in the leg. Whilst talking to him we both fell asleep and slept until about 5 p.m., when the Germans counter-attacked. Their artillery became violent and they attempted to come over the open. We ran for the communication trench and found it disorganised, orders got mixed and some seemed anxious to retire. Fortunately the 17th HLI bombers, who were in the advanced position, held their ground, driving the enemy back with their own bombs, and the attack over the open was checked by our brigade machine guns which had been massed in the German front line.[67]
>
> Private Bentley Meadows, 17th Battalion, Highland Light Infantry, 97th Brigade, 32nd Division

The perspective had changed from the prospect of making a renewed advance to that of a desperate struggle to hold what little ground they had gained.

> Our flanks were exposed and blockades had to be formed at the front line and all lines forward to our advanced posts, which developed into a series of bombing posts. The nature of the Leipzig defences, a maze of trenches and underground saps, made advancing into the salient extremely hard. One was continually attacked in the rear. What seemed dugouts were bombed, and when passed numbers of the enemy rush from them, they being really underground communications with their rear defences. The whole fighting was of a cold, deliberate, merciless nature. No quarter was given or taken.[68]
>
> Private Bentley Meadows, 17th Battalion, Highland Light Infantry, 97th Brigade, 32nd Division

It was at some point in this vicious fighting that one amongst many German soldiers, poor Private Eversmann who was quoted extensively in the last chapter, met his end. How did he die? Whether he was hit by shrapnel, buried alive, shot or bayoneted it surely made little difference to him. His poignant little diary from which the extracts were originally taken was picked up later in the day by one of the Scotsmen. The desperate nature of the fighting in which he died is clearly evident from the account of one of the young German officers of the 99th Infantry Reserve Regiment, which was responsible for holding the German lines in this sector.

> The shout of our sentry, 'They are coming!' tore me out of the apathy. Helmet, belt, rifle and up the steps. On one of the steps something white and bloody, in the trench a headless body. The sentry had lost his life from a last shell, before the fire was directed to the rear – he had paid for his vigilance with his life. It had torn open his head and his brain was lying on the steps. We rushed to the ramparts; there they come, the khaki-yellows, they are not more than 20 metres in front of our trench. They slowly advance, full equipped, to march across our bodies into the open country. But no boys, we are still alive – the moles come out of their holes. Machine-gun fire tears holes in their rows. They discover our presence – throw themselves on the ground, in front of our trenches. Once these were the trenches, now a mass of craters. They are welcomed by hand grenades and gunfire, and now have to sell their lives themselves. With my rifle firing, I felt my right hand hit by a heavy stroke, a bullet from a distance of 20 metres. The gun fell out of my hand, blood is running. I can still see how a rifleman tries to throw himself out of reach of a hand grenade thrown by Kühnel. In vain. It explodes and will probably have finished him. I have my wound dressed by an orderly and take over leading the platoon again. Another half-hour and it becomes clear that the attack has been repelled, at least in our section. I make a reconnaissance of the company positions and cannot recognise it any more. Last night it had been completely smashed. The dugout of the commanding officer is squashed, Hartbrich is alive but stunned by gas poisoning. I find Captain Meschenbier of the 3rd Company suffering from a heart attack. His company has been occupying the notorious corner of the mine explosion and had been surprised and overthrown. Only a few men, who were in the second trench, are left. Volunteers, amongst them Kühnel, begin to drive the intruders out, proceeding from the left

> from breastwork to breastwork, throwing hand grenades and slowly they succeed. Badly wounded 'Tommies' fall into our hands and their rations provide something to satisfy our hunger and thirst. But then we come to a part of the position where the enemy is able stop our advance by flanking machine-gun fire. I return to my company and give orders to restore communications between the various positions and to rearrange the groups to take account of the casualties. Hartbrich has now recovered from his stupefaction, but I feel a weakness overcoming me. At midday, I am aware that I cannot carry on, so I tell Hartbrich that I must retire.[69]
>
> Lieutenant F. L. Cassel, 99th Infantry Reserve Regiment, 26th Reserve Division, German Army

As the young German officer slowly made his way back he found awful evidence of the sheer weight of the British bombardment all around him. The shells seemed to be everywhere.

> On my way back, what a sight! The further you got to the rear, the more the shells whistled, buzzed, hissed and boomed around your ears. Since the attack had started in the morning, the barrage fire had been laid to the rear again. At the commanding officer's dugout, I reported that officers were required at the front. The large dugout looked terrible, full of casualties. The seriously wounded were lying there in rows to be transported further back during the night. Doctors and orderlies worked like butchers in an atmosphere that made me feel like vomiting. I was glad when I was in the open air again, in spite of all those hissing shells.[70]
>
> Lieutenant F. L. Cassel, 99th Infantry Reserve Regiment, 26th Reserve Division, German Army

While the men of 99th Infantry Reserve Regiment fought to hold back the onrush of the 36th Division and 32nd Division of the X Corps, they were greatly assisted by the usual British confusion as to the degree of progress they had made. Erroneous air reports of glinting British helmets seen moving about in Thiepval village encouraged a totally false perception that it was safely in British hands. As a result the artillery did not return to bombard the village and all later attempts to use the reserves to bolster the attack on Thiepval Spur were foredoomed to failure in the face of the untouched German machine-gun nests and massed artillery.

Unfortunately, this total failure knocked on to undermine the heroic success of the Ulstermen to their left. Although the amazing advance of the 36th Division to capture Schwaben Redoubt had threatened to unhinge a vital part of the German line, the Irishmen were at the same time soon totally isolated. The German response was inevitable.

> The Englishman still sits in Schwaben Redoubt. He must be driven out of it, out of our position. The attack is to be pushed with all energy. It is a point of honour for the division to recapture this important point today. The artillery is to cooperate with all possible strength.[71]
>
> Major General von Soden, Headquarters, 26th Reserve Division, German Army

The German counter-attacks pounded away at the hastily established outpost line of the Irish, slowly but surely overrunning their hard won gains. As the bombs and bayonets drew nearer and nearer, some of the Irishmen not unnaturally panicked; all their courage perhaps exhausted by the repeated shocks and terrors of this the longest day of their lives. They found little sympathy as they fell back in desperation.

> A strong rabble of tired, hungry and thirsty stragglers approach me from the east. I go out to meet them. 'Where are you going?' I ask. One says one thing, one another. They are marched to the water reserve, given a drink and hunted back to the fight. Another more formidable party cuts across to the south. They mean business. They are damned if they are going to stay, it's all up. A young sprinting subaltern heads them off. They push by him. He draws his revolver and threatens them. They take no notice. He fires. Down drops a British soldier at his feet. The effect is instantaneous. They turn back to the assistance of their comrades in distress.[72]
>
> Lieutenant Colonel Frank Crozier, 9th Battalion, Royal Irish Rifles, 107th Brigade, 36th (Ulster) Division

Another man dead, and in this case a man who perhaps had done his utmost until he was made an example *pour encourager les autres*. Yet the reality was that if Thiepval was not captured by the 32nd Division then the Schwaben Redoubt could never be held. Therefore, at some point, the 36th Division would have to retire from their exposed and shrinking salient. Slowly, painfully, reluctantly they did indeed begin to fall back. By this time most of their officers and NCOs were killed or wounded. Eventually they managed to stabilise the line in the original German front line. The Stuff and Schwaben Redoubts would not be captured again for three long months.

The attack of X Corps had offered only a brief flicker of hope through the astounding brief success of the 36th (Ulster) Division. Yet the plain reality was that their breakthrough had been the anomaly rather than the rule, the result of raw courage and briefly favourable, localised tactical circumstances. Once the Germans had realised what was happening they were able to swiftly cauterise and seal off the wound and leave only the smallest of scars in their defences. The end result, despite all the excitement of the temporary breakthrough, was a near complete failure at a cost of around 5,104 casualties to the 36th Division and 3,949 casualties to the 32nd Division.

III Corps *La Boisselle – failure in the centre*

NEXT IN LINE TO the south was the III Corps. They too faced a formidable defensive fortress encompassing four distinct spurs with the intervening valleys running down from the Pozières Ridge. From north to south they were named: Thiepval Spur (actually in the X Corps area but the origin of such lethal flanking fire that it cannot be discounted in considering the fate of the III Corps), Nab Valley, Ovillers Spur, Mash Valley, La Boisselle Spur, Sausage Valley and Fricourt Spur. Once again the Germans had used the natural lie of the land to extract the maximum defensive effect, bending their lines into the valleys along the salient and re-entrant contour lines. Anyone venturing into one of the valleys was entering a trap with concentrated interlocking fire from three sides. The front-line fortified villages of Ovillers and La Boisselle were further bolstered by the Schwaben Höhe and Sausage Redoubts. Behind them lay a series of intermediate fortified lines and redoubts before the German second line proper, stretching in this sector from Mouquet Farm to the village of Bazentin-le-Petit.

As with their northern neighbours, the III Corps had been asked to carry out one of the most difficult offensive actions of this or any other war. The 8th Division was centred on the Ovillers Spur while the 34th Division faced the La Boisselle Spur and the valleys on either side. The

III Corps attack on la Boisselle & Ovillers

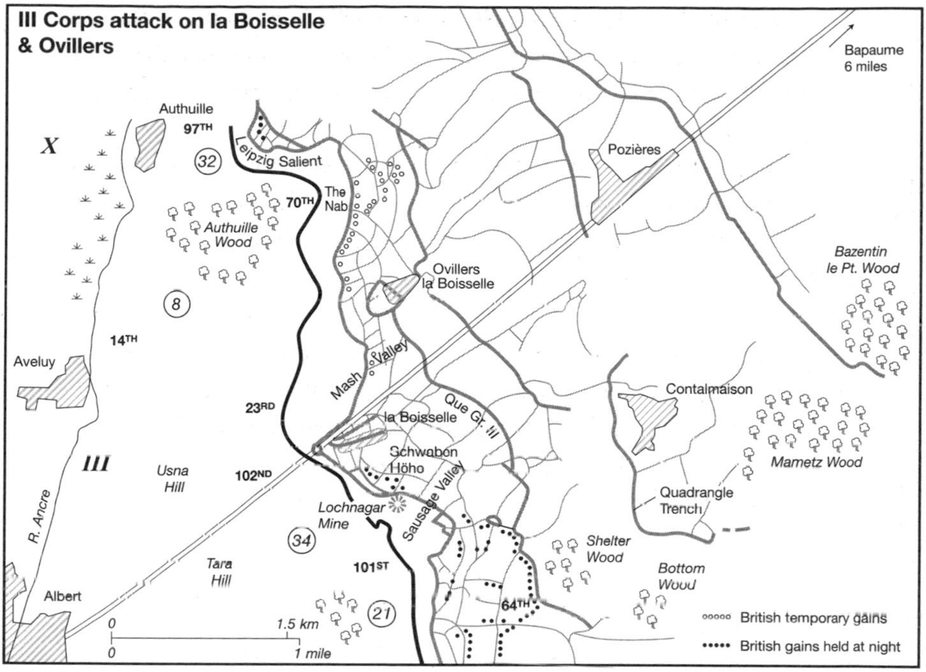

artillery conformed to the generally prevailing arrangements, although some effort was made to allow the field artillery to rake back gradually in short lifts designed to cope with the numerous interlinked defence works between the main lines. It was not a proper creeping barrage as the lifts were 'jerky', in jumps of between 50 and 100 yards. Together the 8th and 34th Divisions were intended to advance to occupy positions just in front of the German second line between Contalmaison and Mouquet Farm.

On the left of the III Corps front, due to the configuration of the ground, the three assaulting brigades of 8th Division commanded by Major General H. Hudson were almost entirely dependent on a successful attack by the divisions on either side of them. Baldly stated, if the 32nd Division of the X Corps did not take the Leipzig Redoubt to the north then a blistering enfilading fire would rake their left flank as they advanced in the exposed Nab Valley. Similarly, if the 34th Division to their right failed in attacking the La Boisselle Salient then their right flank would be savaged from the south as it pushed into the Mash Valley. In view of this total dependence on the success of others, Major General Hudson tried to slightly postpone the 8th Division zero hour to try and reduce their exposure, but had been brusquely overruled by Rawlinson, who realised that a failure to attack at the same time would have allowed the Germans to concentrate their defensive fire on the flanks of the 32nd and 34th Divisions. It was indeed a difficult conundrum.

In the event it happened as Hudson had feared, for the men of his 70th Brigade on the left found the open ground of Nab Valley an utter death-trap. The first wave made some progress breaching the German lines, but as the German defences reorganised and the machine guns began to intervene from the flanks, the supporting battalions found it almost impossible to get across No Man's Land. Amongst them was Corporal Tansley of the 9th Yorks and Lancs.

> Zero Hour, the whistles were blown, ladders were put to mount out of the trench and lanes had been cut through the 30-foot British wire. We had been told, 'There's no need for this short rushes and getting down on your stomach, go straight over as if you were on parade. That's the orders, there's no fear of enemy attack, that's been silenced by the British guns'. Up we went through the lanes cut in the wire, spread out and tried to follow this instruction. Myself, I was a bit sceptical about

> it. Anyway we tried to adhere to it as far as possible. We spread out, I and my section made for this slight ridge marked by an old farm implement. Looked around for where the line was, they seemed to disappear. Lying about on the ground. There was a severe machine-gun fire coming from the region of Pozières, half-left.[73]
>
> Corporal James Tansley, 9th Battalion, York and Lancaster Regiment, 70th Brigade, 8th Division

At this point Corporal Tansley was wounded and soon found himself facing an awful predicament, badly wounded and trapped between the front lines.

> Down we went and my mate who was with me, he went down shot through the legs. I attended to my mate and he had some qualms of conscience in him, because he wasn't facing the enemy when he went down. I didn't realise anything like that myself, but he was an old regular soldier and it troubled him so much. Side by side we were there and he was hit again, hit through the mouth. It killed him. I didn't know when my moment might come – I expected it at any moment. The best thing I could do was to lie low, keep quiet. Another wave came over. As that was passing the enemy fire hotted up of course. They went farther on to meet the same fate. When it died down somewhat, I looked around for a shell hole and found one. It was chock-a-block full – dead, wounded, unwounded – I couldn't get in it! So I had to remain on the surface. I was there until 3 p.m. Just before 3 p.m. I managed to crawl into the trench. I'd stayed the flow of the blood with my own digital pressure in the groin because I'd had some instruction in ambulance work I knew that by applying pressure on the pressure points it would stay the blood, which it did. There was casualties everywhere, more than the RAMC could cope with. I must have lost consciousness some part of the time. I revived a bit and asked them when they would get me away, 'Oh yes, we'll come to you...' It was really a godsend they did pick me up and bring me out because there was so many there who never got picked up at all.[74]
>
> Corporal James Tansley, 9th Battalion, York and Lancaster Regiment, 70th Brigade, 8th Division

As the support battalions tried through sheer guts to get across No Man's Land the German counter-attacks steadily eradicated the survivors of the first wave who had made the initial lodgement in the German lines. This same sad story of failure was repeated immediately to the south where the 25th and 23rd Brigades had their attacking battalions shot to bits by a combination of powerful direct fire from Ovillers and the eviscerating flank fire from La Boisselle. One young staff officer acting as divisional forward observation officer reported back on the results of the attack.

> I was given a place with my signallers about 400 yards behind our front line on a bank where you could see very clearly on a fine day. The troops advanced out of the trenches, but by this time although the sky was clear the shells had thrown up so much smoke, rubble and a reddish dust was over everything. There was a mist to and hardly anything was visible. One saw these figures disappear into the mist and as they did so, so did the first shots ring out from the other side. I thought our men had got into the German trench – and so did the men that were with me. I reported as such to the division. I said, 'I'm going forward, I can't really see what's happened!' I got a message to stay where I was, so I stayed where I was! Presently as the barrage went forward so did the air clear and I could see what was happening. In the distance I saw the barrage bounding on towards Pozières, the Third German Line. In No Man's Land were heaps of dead, with Germans almost standing up in their trenches, well over the top firing and sniping at those who had taken refuge in the shell holes. On the right there was signs of fighting, I saw Very and signal lights go up in the trenches. Then I waited and another brigade was ordered to resume the attack. Providentially for that brigade the order was cancelled with greater realisation came in as to what had really happened. It was the most enormous disaster that had befallen the 8th Division, the whole division was ruined.[75]
>
> Captain Alan Hanbury-Sparrow, 2nd Battalion, Royal Berkshire Regiment, 25th Brigade, 8th Division

The German artillery added to their misery as a severe barrage poured down on the British front line and No Man's Land. In these circumstances it was a tragedy that such secrecy had attended the construction of two substantial communication tunnels some 13 feet below No Man's Land, for it meant that they were not brought into use until it was effectively too late in the day to change the outcome.

MEANWHILE, on their right the 34th Division had the awesome task of capturing the La Boisselle Salient. They were to attack in four 'columns' each marching three battalions deep on a front of about 400 yards. As the assault battalions left the assembly trenches the following battalions would simultaneously set off from the support lines on the low Usna and Tara hills lying behind the British front line. Because of the enormous strength of the La Boisselle village salient it had been decided not to attack this frontally but use pincer attacks to 'pinch' it out. The men were assured that the village had been utterly destroyed but once again the deep dugouts and cellars contained the seeds of disaster for the advancing British troops. In the flanking attacks they had the assistance of two huge mines. On the northern flank was Y Sap, a 1,030-feet-long tunnel which contained 40,600 lbs of ammonal, while on the southern flank the Lochnagar mine had put the phenomenal amount of 60,000 lbs of ammonal under the Germans manning the Schwaben Höhe Redoubt. These were intended to not only cause devastation in themselves, but also throw up high crater 'lips' of fallen debris, which it was hoped would provide substantial cover from enfilade fire as the infantry advanced across the open expanses of No Man's Land. The mines were to be exploded just two minutes before Zero Hour at 0730.

The Y Sap mine was intended to assist the advance of the 102nd (Tyneside Scottish) Brigade as they assaulted the German line immediately to the north of La Boisselle, into the maw of the Mash Valley. The mine caused tremendous damage, but the Tynesiders still had to cross some 800 yards of open ground before they got to the German trenches under concentrated criss-cross machine-gun fire originating from in front and the fortified villages of Ovillers and La Boisselle on either flank. The casualties were horrific. Very few reached the German front line and those that did were soon hunted down.

Just to the right of La Boisselle, the rest of the 102nd and the 101st Brigades were attacking on either side of the Lochnagar mine due to detonate under the powerful Schwaben Höhe Redoubt.

> The mine went up and the trenches simply rocked like a boat, we seemed to be very close to it and looked in awe as great pieces of earth as big as coal wagons were blasted skywards to hurtle and roll and then start to scream back all around us. A great geyser of mud, chalk and flame had

risen and subsided before our gaze and man had created it. I vividly recall as the barrage lifted temporarily and there was just the slightest pause in this torment, several skylarks were singing – incredible![76]

Private Harry Baumber, 10th Battalion, Lincolnshire Regiment, 101st Brigade, 34th Division

Experiments had shown that any debris that might cause physical harm to the advancing soldiers would have crashed back to earth within 60 seconds of the explosion, although naturally the dust and smaller fragments would take longer to settle. But, not unnaturally, many of the men found this difficult to believe and perhaps waited a little longer than was strictly necessary before setting off across No Man's Land.

It went up, the ground suddenly jolting and then rocking below our feet. Muck was thrown some two or three hundred feet into the air to land later like a load of coal dropping for what seemed an age. The instant it stopped we went over the top with 'the lads' to claim the new crater. Amid heavy supporting fire, I and a handful of men brought up the field telephones and the cables essential for the communications between the front-line troops and our artillery.[77]

Corporal John Maw, Royal Artillery, 34th Division

The mine had wreaked terrible devastation blasting out a volcano-like crater, which measured an incredible 270 feet across and 70 feet deep. One of the contact patrol pilots of 3 Squadron, Royal Flying Corps had an amazing view of the explosion as he flew over the battlefield.

Then came the blast when we were looking at the La Boisselle Salient – suddenly the whole earth heaved and up from the ground came great cone shaped lifts of earth up to 3,000, 4,000, 5,000 feet. A moment later we struck the repercussion wave of the blast which flung us over right away backwards over on one side away from the blast.[78]

Second Lieutenant Cecil Lewis, 3 Squadron, Royal Flying Corps

The sheer power of the explosion collapsed many of the German deep dugouts to smother their cowering garrisons, but even so, for all the drama and spectacle, the Lochnagar mine only eradicated the German defences in the immediate area of the crater. The rest were relatively untouched and still functioning. The machine guns from what little remained of the

Schwaben Höhe Redoubt were joined by others flanking the assault from the village of La Boisselle and the Sausage Redoubt.

> By now it was over the top and away up a gentle slope to the German trenches. Line behind line of steadfast men walking grimly forward and wondering what was in store. We soon found out. I noticed men falling thick and fast about me and all the time the tremulous chatter of machine guns. It was akin to striding into a hailstorm and the further you went the less and less became your comrades. Jerry had not been obliterated, his wire had not been destroyed and we had been called upon to walk 800 yards across No Man's Land into Hell. A far cry from the walkover we had been promised.[79]
>
> Private Harry Baumber, 10th Battalion, Lincolnshire Regiment, 101st Brigade, 34th Division

Their officers were equally horrified by the strength of the machine-gun fire. It seemed impossible that they were not hit as the bullets sprayed all around them, flicking spitefully at their uniforms and equipment.

> When we got the orders to advance, we climbed over the top of the parapet. And the enfilade machine-gun fire – the air was full of bullets and the men began to fall all round us. It was tragic. When these men were hit with bullets, they just fell flat on their face and the air was full of bullets. I got one between my fingers, just clipped a bit out of each. When we came to want something to eat, when you got your haversack off your back you found that the bullets had gone through your Machonachie ration or tin of bully beef. Some very near misses.[80]
>
> Lieutenant A. Dickinson, 10th Battalion, Lincolnshire Regiment, 101st Brigade, 34th Division

At last the men reached the smouldering depths of the Lochnagar crater, which was rimmed with lips of fallen debris that stretched up to 15 feet high. In the hurly-burly of crater fighting speed was of the essence and it was vital to consolidate the crater before the dazed Germans could regain their equilibrium.

> When we arrived at the crater, our orders were to man the top, round the lip of the crater. Of course the Germans they soon played their machine guns on that lip and first one would get one through the head and roll down, then one after another would roll down into

> that bottom which tapered down to a point. It was still hot as an oven after just being blown up.[81]
>
> Lieutenant A. Dickinson, 10th Battalion, Lincolnshire Regiment, 101st Brigade, 34th Division

To the left of the crater the 22nd Northumberland Fusiliers broke into the German lines under Major Acklom and managed to carve out a precarious foothold that stretched forward as far as the German support lines. All in all elements of three battalions gathered around the great crater, no doubt drawn by the cover it offered. Yet the flanking fire poured in from all around and crossing No Man's Land was a deadly game. Major Vignoles attempted to get forward with the reserve D Company, which had been assigned to the mundane but essential role of carrying forward ammunition and trench stores that would be needed to consolidate their objectives. It was soon apparent that the task was anything but mundane for even before they left the British front line they came under heavy fire.

> My company got out of the trench to carry forward our stuff and a Boche machine gun kept sweeping over us. I got the men down and while getting them all together I tried to stop a bullet with my left hand! I felt a crack and felt as if a red hot bar had been pushed through my hand. On looking down, I saw that I had been shot through four fingers and felt sure that all were broken. I hated leaving the Commanding Officer in such a hot corner, but I could see by the jet of blood that an artery had also been cut, which necessitated putting on a tourniquet, so I could not proceed. Anderson and Turnbull (the only two officers with me) were OK when I left, but I do not know how they got on afterwards.[82]
>
> Major Walter Vignoles, 10th Battalion, Lincolnshire Regiment, 101st Brigade, 34th Division

Second Lieutenant Turnbull carried on making his way forward, but he was left completely confused by the turmoil of the battle and the sheer complexity of the situation unfolding around him. Pushing across No Man's Land accompanied by his platoon, he found himself just to the left of the Lochnagar crater shortly after 0900.

> Very puzzled with the rotten crater, which was in the wrong place. Used it to screen us from La Boisselle, got as far as the ridge, and goodness knows how many machine guns opened up on us. We all

dropped, and I started to crawl to the crater to see who was there, when I got hit in the back. Corporal Turton helped me in. Unfortunately I couldn't move about much, and felt very dazed. Corporals Barnett and Pearson came into the crater presently unhurt. Tried to sap out to one section not far off, but it wasn't practicable. A Tyneside Irish officer gave me a drop of whisky which cheered me up. There were three unhurt officers there. Got a note from Second Lieutenant Hartshorn, 10th Lincolns and twenty men to say they were in a sunken road in the valley near the Boche lines, and asking for help. Tried to get runner back to headquarters, sent about four, but don't know what happened to them. Later the Tyneside Irish officer went back and got through, but was wounded. I tried to get the other officers to reconnoitre and make an attempt to get forward, but they said it was quite impossible. There were 50–100 unwounded men. We consolidated round the lip of the crater; our parapet was of uncertain thickness and very crumbly. There was a certain amount of cover for all but very shallow. Colonel Howard was there badly wounded.[83]

Second Lieutenant John Turnbull, 10th Battalion, Lincolnshire Regiment, 101st Brigade, 34th Division

All hope of breaching the German lines in front of them had vanished; indeed it was apparent that they had very little chance of surviving the concentrated machine-gun fire.

With enfilading machine-gun fire from the flanks it was simply a massacre and although a few struggled into the German defences, we who were left were simply pinned down where we lay. There was no going forward and at this point no way of going back to our lines – an absolute bloody desolate shambles. If you moved an inch it brought a sweeping crackle of fire and we survivors began to realise our only hope was to wait until dark, but that was a long way off.[84]

Private Harry Baumber, 10th Battalion, Lincolnshire Regiment, 101st Brigade, 34th Division

To the right of them the situation was a little better where the 15th Royal Scots had managed to make considerable progress.

Prior to the attack, the No. 1s of each Lewis gun tossed up for the 'honour' of one gun to go with the bombers detailed to rush the crater

> after the mine had been blown. I tossed for B Company, No. 1 gun and won, amidst muttered remarks from the gun crew that I would ruddy well win a toss like that, and, expecting dirty work we took the reserve gun crew with us, twelve men, and myself in charge, making the thirteenth, as some bright gem quickly pointed out. We went out with the bombers five minutes before zero hour to positions as near as we thought was safe, so that we could work round the crater, after the mines were detonated. This was accomplished with slight loss, and as we lay down, the whole earth seemed to sway sideways. The debris went up hundreds of feet in the air, and above the bombardment we could hear the debris falling, unfortunately burying several of the party. I remember covering my head with my arms and waiting for the first clout. I was lucky and advanced with the rest of the survivors, round the right-hand side of the crater. I was firing at the retreating Germans in front of their third line, when the last remaining Lewis gunner was killed as he handed me another magazine. So I had to carry on with the Lewis gun, spare parts, haversack, and eight full magazines, not forgetting my rifle. When I dropped into their fourth line it was full of Jerries, and, much to the benefit of my trousers, they promptly put up their hands. I made such a noise that they thought my whole battalion had arrived.[85]
>
> Corporal Harry Beaumont, 15th Battalion, Royal Scots, 101st Brigade, 34th Division

Realising they could get no further without considerable reinforcements they dug in where they were in Round Wood, where they managed to link up with the forward parties from the neighbouring 21st Division.

Still flying high above them was Second Lieutenant Cecil Lewis who was desperately trying to work out what was going on down below. He soon realised that there was an unbridgeable gulf between the theory and practice of contacting men in action on the battlefield.

> We had all our contact patrol technique perfected and we went right down to 3,000 feet to see what was happening. We had a klaxon horn on the undercarriage of the Morane – a great big 12 volt klaxon – and I had a button which I used to press out a letter to tell the infantry that we wanted to know where they were. When they heard us hawking at them from above, they had little red Bengal flares, they

carried them in their pockets, they would put a match to their flares. All along the line, wherever there was a chap, there would be a flare and Bob's your uncle! It was one thing to practice this but quite another for them to really do it when they were under fire and particularly when things began to go a bit badly. Then they jolly wouldn't light anything and small blame to them because it drew the fire of the enemy on to them at once. So we went down looking for flares and we only got two flares on the whole front. We were bitterly disappointed because this we hoped was our part to help the infantry and we weren't able to do it.[86]

Second Lieutenant Cecil Lewis, 3 Squadron, Royal Flying Corps

Yet some of the contact patrols were occasionally able to help the beleaguered infantry. Their value was illustrated when at one point later in that awful day the British artillery began to land shells dropping short on to the crater.

For some unknown reason, our artillery started shelling us with whizz-bangs. Our planes were sailing close overhead and though I shone a mirror up they took no notice. In the end I sent an orderly to Colonel Howard to ask for permit to use a red flare, which he gave. As soon as we lit it, our planes went straight off home and our batteries shut up, but of course the Boche redoubled his efforts, though we escaped without further casualties.[87]

Second Lieutenant John Turnbull, 10th Battalion, Lincolnshire Regiment, 101st Brigade, 34th Division

Cut off as they were it was difficult for the officers to make sure that the men kept their sense of purpose and indeed that they did not begin to panic. Although he had been wounded before he reached the crater, Turnbull insisted on staying put with his men. He knew he was needed to help bolster up the men's morale.

I kind of dozed most of the time, but woke up and thought of things now and again, i.e. got Corporal Turton to see rifles were all cleaned etc. He was a brick that day. I found my flow of language, which I am afraid I am rather free with ordinarily, good and bad, very useful several times. Especially when some of the fit men wanted to bolt for it, and leave a good one hundred wounded who couldn't walk. I asked them what the ****** they thought they were doing and ordered them back, and they all meekly went back, much to my surprise.[88]

Second Lieutenant John Turnbull, 10th Battalion, Lincolnshire Regiment, 101st Brigade, 34th Division

Despite all the German pressure the scattered parties around the Lochnagar crater and in Schwaben Höhe managed to maintain their position until nightfall. That night a Russian sap was opened up to provide communications and slowly the positions were connected and consolidated.

Back at the headquarters of the 8th and 34th Divisions the staff officers were left face to face with a failure that was far beyond their comprehension. Many had been worried by their onerous responsibilities, had feared that there might be hard fighting, had dreaded heavy casualties. But they had never imagined anything like this.

I soon realised the ghastly nature of our failure. And, from my advance observation post, I reported, very bluntly I'm afraid, to General Williams that no objectives had been gained and the left wing (102nd Brigade) had suffered heavily in the attack. Soon after sending that message, General Cameron (103rd Brigade commander) was carried into my trench – he had been wounded in the stomach. He smiled, in that nice way of his, told me to carry on, he'd be all right, and was taken down to the dressing station. From then on it was terrible – to see my division wiped out, on the left, in the centre and on the right. In desperation I grabbed a rifle and tried to silence one machine-gun section out in the open near the La Boisselle craters, mowing down our slow-moving infantry coming down on the left of Chapes Spur. After the attack was held, I went down to 102nd Infantry Brigade headquarters, to send messages to divisional headquarters, and I had a few words with General Ternan. He had read some of my earlier messages and was inclined to think I was in error (about the failure of the assault on the left, his brigade) in my estimation of the way the battle was going, but I gave him the details which did nothing to relieve his anxiety.[89]

Captain D. H. James, Trench Mortar Officer, Headquarters, 34th Division

On the whole of the III Corps front the overall picture was one of unremitting failure, which could not really be redeemed by trivial gains and lodgements that would never have been countenanced as success before the attack began. Yet the strength of the German positions was such that, with hindsight, it can be said that the outcome was almost inevitable. The alternate spurs and re-entrant valleys almost guaranteed exposure to deadly criss-crossing machine-gun fire, the British bombardment had been insufficient to destroy the defence works and the inadequate counter-battery fire had left the German guns free to roar their destructive defiance. No troops in the world could have achieved such overly ambitious objectives in front of Ovillers and La Boisselle on 1 July 1916. In trying to achieve what was impossible the 8th Division suffered an appalling 6,380 men killed, wounded and missing with a further 5,121 casualties in the 34th Division.

***XV Corps**: Fricourt and Mametz – hard fighting*

THE XV CORPS was under the command of Lieutenant General Henry Horne. They faced two more of the many little spurs running down from the Pozières Ridge: namely the Fricourt and Mametz Spurs, which were separated by the valley of the Willow stream. Here again the ground was almost ideal for defence and the Germans had taken full advantage. The two villages had been converted into fortresses with a supporting trench system and deep dugouts of labyrinthine complexity. They lay behind a front line that carefully followed the winding contours of the downland to create miniature salients, which time and time again enfiladed much of No Man's Land. Two intermediate lines further bolstered the defence before any interloper could get anywhere near the Second Line system.

The XV Corps plans called for the assaulting 21st and 7th Divisions to overrun both spurs and to make a substantial further advance right up to the second German intermediate line (White Trench to Quadrangle Trench) where they were to consolidate. The village of Fricourt was not itself to be directly assaulted, but pinched out by attacks driving in from either side to isolate the defenders. Later the corps reserve, 17th Division, was to continue the advance through Mametz Wood to a line through Bazentin-le-Grand and Ginchy. Although they were attacking a position that combined natural and man-made defensive strength, one thing in their favour was that in this sector of the front the German artillery had been thoroughly targeted and to some extent silenced. This success rendered the German defences substantially more vulnerable than would otherwise have been the case. The gap between the front lines was also considerably less than in many sectors assaulted – narrowing in places to just 100 yards. A further advantage to the assaulting troops was the use of a definite form of creeping barrage. Although the heavy artillery would lift directly to the next designated barrage line the divisional artillery was to move forward at a rate of just 50 yards per minute.

> The barrages will not exactly lift from one point and be put on to another; they will gradually drift forward, leaving certain lines at certain hours (which may be changed). The line of the barrage must be constantly watched by the infantry, whose front lines must keep close up to it.[90]
>
> Lieutenant Colonel Alfred Fitzgerald, 15th Battalion, Durham Light Infantry, 64th Brigade, 21st Division

On the left, the 21st Division faced the fortress village of Fricourt. They were to be helped by the detonation of three mines of 25,000 lbs, 15,000 lbs and 9,000 lbs under the German lines opposite the small British salient, known as the Tambour, which gave them their collective name. In this case the mines were a pure diversion as the craters were not to be rushed, and it was hoped that the lips thrown up around them would provide an interruption to the deadly flanking fire of the German machine guns. On the left the 64th Brigade, and to a lesser extent the 63rd Brigade, made some considerable progress despite the dangerous irritation of flanking fire from Fricourt itself and La Boisselle on the left. As the leading battalions pushed forward, the support battalions followed hard on their heels. The combination of rattling machine-gun fire, whistling rifle bullets and occasional shells was enough to daunt even the bravest.

> Left trench 7.30 a.m. Couldn't have faced it unless afraid of funking before the men. Scrambled from shell hole to shell hole, through the wire and craters and awful havoc, terrible sights. Terrible slaughter by the Hun artillery and machine guns, the latter with snipers hurling bullets from every direction. Even behind us men were mown down right and left. Hun trenches simply myriads of shell holes. Not so many casualties as expected, as they crowded into deep dugouts and surrendered to attackers. Stopped a bullet on my head about 8 a.m. – dazed for about an hour or so. My steel helmet saved my life without a doubt, it cannot stop a direct bullet hit, but this one was glancing – a

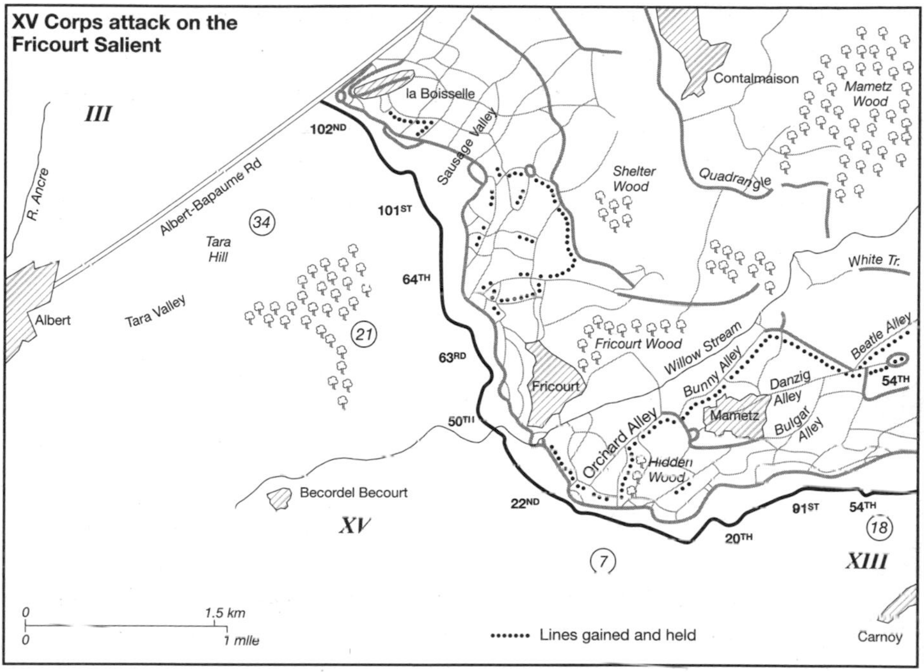
XV Corps attack on the Fricourt Salient
III
R. Ancre
Albert
Albert-Bapaume Rd
Tara Hill
Tara Valley
34
21
la Boisselle
102ND
101ST
64TH
63RD
50TH
22ND
20TH
91ST
54TH
18
7
XV
XIII
Sausage Valley
Contalmaison
Mametz Wood
Shelter Wood
Quadrangle
White Tr.
Fricourt Wood
Fricourt
Willow Stream
Bunny Alley
Beatle Alley
Danzig Alley
Bulgar Alley
Mametz
Orchard Alley
Hidden Wood
Becordel Becourt
Carnoy
0
1.5 km
0
1 mile
Lines gained and held

huge dent. Can remember shooting Hun officer who was shooting into backs of our men in front. Had dozens of close shaves and admit to being in frightened stew throughout the whole advance. One Hun machine gunner held up his hands but this line could not stop to secure him prisoner, leaving this for the second line. As soon as first line passed over he turned his gun and mowed them down from behind. Can vouch for this. Such cases makes you want to skin every Hun you see alive. Never stopped to explore Hun dugouts or prisoners. 9.15 a.m. saw four Hun lines (1,200 yards) cleared. Still murderous machine-gun fire. Dug in.[91]

Captain Rex Gee, 15th Battalion, Durham Light Infantry, 64th Brigade, 21st Division

Later that afternoon, the mixed remnants of the assaulting and support battalions tried to push forward from their positions in Crucifix Trench on to Shelter Wood. The result was disastrous. As they went further forward, away from their reserves and the cover of their field artillery, the Germans just grew stronger and ever more threatening.

Attempted two charges from our hasty trenches, but no use. Was only survivor from second charge. Critical situation, strong enemy position in front, attackers on left withdrawing, leaving our left flank exposed. Held on firmly all day and repulsed two enemy attacks to bomb us out. Very trying. Relieved shortly after midnight. Am only officer left in the company. Cannot understand how anyone escaped alive, never mind capture and hold Hun trenches. Haven't got much left in the way of nerves. Had no sleep for fifty hours and no proper meals or rest. Am dog-tired and not worth much. Everything was horrible, ghastly and awful. May I never experience the same again. Saw scores horribly wounded, horribly killed. Am being converted to conscientious objector. Words cannot express the horrors of it all.[92]

Captain Rex Gee, 15th Battalion, Durham Light Infantry, 64th Brigade, 21st Division

ON THE RIGHT the 20th, 22nd and 91st Brigades of the 7th Division were faced with capturing the village of Mametz. Here six much smaller mines were to be used to assist the attacking troops and to provide a local diversion. The largest of 2,000 lbs was drilled out under Bulgar Point;

most of the others of only 500 lbs each were located opposite Hidden Wood, which was not to be directly attacked. The 20th Brigade had a somewhat complicated set of objectives as it was to move forward and then swing round to form a firm defensive flank facing Fricourt. Once this had been achieved the 22nd Brigade, which initially would remain in the trenches, would advance directly on Fricourt. When the assault went in at 0730, there was little German artillery fire in response although the ubiquitous machine-gun fire caused considerable casualties. Nevertheless, some progress was made, for the German front line was overrun and fierce fighting commenced amongst the maze of trenches, dugouts and machine-gun posts that lay behind.

Amongst the battalions were the 9th Devons charged with advancing through Mansell Copse. Here the poetically minded bombing officer, Lieutenant Noel Hodgson, faced his personal Calvary. No one can ever know what was in his mind as he led his men over the top from the assembly trenches. As the men moved forward they were crucified by lethally criss-crossing machine-gun fire every step of the 400 yards that lay between them and the German front line. One man went forward with them into mortal danger, but did so in an entirely voluntary capacity – their Chaplain Ernest Crosse.

> It was a great thing to think that the church was ready to go where the men had to. Quite apart from anything specific they might do, it is important to realise the significance of their presence on the battlefield. From a military point of view it was far from negligible, because they alone were not under orders to be there – and as such they could hardly fail to encourage the men, who had no option in the matter. From a religious point of view it showed to the men far better than any preaching could do, God's care for them. If a padre's presence was appreciated in the trenches at normal times, it was doubly so in those awful periods in the small hours of the morning waiting for the moment of attack. A young sergeant once remarked to me, 'Damn me, if this isn't the best battalion I ever was in. The CO goes round the tape just before you are going to kick off; the second-in-command comes almost up to the line just to see you get a hot drink at the last possible moment; and the padre follows you over the top!' [93]
>
> Chaplain Ernest Crosse, 8th and 9th Battalions, Devonshire Regiment, 20th Brigade, 7th Division

During a battle the divisional complement of chaplains were carefully allotted to their battle posts. Each field ambulance was given a chaplain and an extra one was assigned to the main dressing station. Only then was permission granted for the remaining chaplains to volunteer to accompany their men into action if they so desired. In this capacity Chaplain Ernest Crosse saw it as his role to work closely with the battalion medical officer and to assist him as and when he could.

> Wounded soon began to come back but our stretcher bearers seemed to move very slowly. Nearly all the first lot of wounded were Borderers. Then the welcomed sight of Boche prisoners passing by looking mad with terror. Doc and I went out to reconnoitre but the CO recommended staying where we were at the junction of 69 and Reserve. I met Trigillis on the top, just going up to support the 9th. Wished A Company of the 8th the best of luck. A journey round our front line revealed four badly wounded in a dugout. I helped Hicton to drag them out and then went for the stretcher bearers. About 3.30 p.m., Doc, Gertie and myself walked down the road to Mansell Copse. The road was strewn with dead. Almost the first I looked at being Martin. In every shell hole all across the valley and up to the German saps were badly wounded who feebly raised a hand or cried out lest they should not be seen. I bandaged up a few as best I could and then went with Gertie to collect all the stretcher bearers. Down Suffolk Avenue I found about eight loafing about with stretchers all over the place. With them and all available stretchers we returned. We now had ten stretchers and about thirty bearers. I gave orders to take the wounded only as far as 67 Support, so as to get as many as possible into our lines before dark, in case the Boche counter-attacked. The RAMC took the wounded back on *our* stretchers leaving us none. I told the stretcher bearers to use trench ladders instead and in this way we got in practically everybody up to the German line before dark. Met Gertie in the road and cursed about the stretchers. A shell pitched 20 yards from us. Went with Doc to examine Boche dugouts for use as an aid post. We could have taken anything we liked but had no time for it. We decided to move up in the morning. Being deadbeat I returned to Wellington Redoubt and lay down till dawn.[94]
>
> Chaplain Ernest Crosse, 8th and 9th Battalions, Devonshire Regiment, 20th Brigade, 7th Division

Meanwhile, on their right, the 91st Brigade attacked across a patch of No Man's Land that narrowed to just 100 yards. They, too, were troubled by machine-gun fire but found sufficient momentum to drive themselves right up to the outskirts of Mametz.

The first rush may have over-run the German trenches but the mopping up had not been sufficiently thorough to eradicate the copious numbers of Germans that subsequently emerged from their deep dugouts. One artillery forward observation officer witnessed the rough justice meted out when German snipers were hunted down.

> The 2nd Gordons were deepening the communication trench to Bulgar support but we had to stop here some time as the sniping was continuing. One captain was sitting in the front line eating his lunch with one hand and shooting the snipers with the other as they came out to surrender. I thought that rather rough as some had their hands up, but he said that he had had several wounded Jocks shot on their stretchers. There were a great many dead lying about, both Gordons and Boche.[95]
>
> Second Lieutenant Y. R. N. Probert, 37th Brigade, Royal Field Artillery, 7th Division

In the early afternoon elements of the hitherto uncommitted 22nd Brigade were ordered forward to carry out the next stage of the plan by making an assault on Fricourt itself. Private Arthur Burke was a reserve Lewis-gun team member when his battalion went over the top.

> All those weary hours the lads remained calm, but very eager to get it over. They did not go over after a strong ration of rum as some people imagine these affairs are carried out, no, they went over feeling themselves. The Colonel watched them mount the steps and his last remarks were, 'Isn't it wonderful?' The way they extended to six paces and walked over at the slope, one would have thought they were at Belton Park.[96]
>
> Private Arthur Burke, 20th Battalion, Manchester Regiment, 22nd Brigade, 7th Division

Their front waves got across No Man's Land almost intact, but heavy machine-gun fire took an increasingly severe toll thereafter. When they arrived in the German lines there was an understandable moment of tension as the excited troops sought to determine what was happening. There were many close shaves.

> I was very nearly bayoneted by a Warwick who was shot about five yards from us by snipers who opened up a fusillade. This was a very noisy, alarming and bloody affair. The cries of the wounded for stretcher bearers, who could not be attended to because of the snipers, were distressing. Although the Boche trenches were flattened by our bombardment the deep dugouts were hardly affected and spewed out snipers who effectively prevented movement until this second attack was made.[97]
>
> Second Lieutenant Y. R. N. Probert, 37th Brigade, Royal Field Artillery, 7th Division

Private Burke was one of those sent to help in mopping up the German front line and dugouts. They were then to bomb their way down the German support lines across the Willow stream valley to penetrate Fricourt itself. It was clearly a vicious affair.

> Then the hand-to-hand fighting started. It was Hell. Bombing was the star turn; many of the Devils were taken unawares and were asleep in their dugouts. We threw bombs of every description down, smoke bombs especially and as the hounds came up, crawling half dead, we stuck the blighters and put them out of time. In one dugout there were about twenty-five in there and we set the place on fire and we spared them no mercy, they don't deserve it. They continued sniping as we were advancing until we reached them and then they throw up their hands, '*Merci, Kamerad!*' We gave them mercy, I don't think! We took far too many prisoners, they numbered about 1,000 and they didn't deserve being spared. What tales they told us, and they would give us anything for souvenirs to spare their lives.[98]
>
> Private Arthur Burke, 20th Battalion, Manchester Regiment, 22nd Brigade, 7th Division

Progress was hard and achingly slow. The further they went forward the more the German resistance stiffened and the inevitable losses weakened the attackers. The arrival of reinforcements could make all the difference in these hard-fought skirmishes.

> We took the first two lines after a hard struggle, but taking the third was Hell. We were all surrounded and had it not been for a very strong

bombing party coming to our assistance, we should have been all 'dicky up'. We captured many guns and all kinds of souvenirs, but the souvenir I treasure most is my life.[99]

Private Arthur Burke, 20th Battalion, Manchester Regiment, 22nd Brigade, 7th Division

Eventually their progress was halted and although small parties of the 22nd Brigade made brief incursions into Fricourt they could not possibly cling on in the face of German counter-attacks and were soon forced to retire. However, further along the line the 91st Brigade was by this time making real progress into Mametz. By 1605 the village had been fully secured and the men had pushed on to consolidate a defensible line based on Bunny Trench.

By around 2000 all the objectives had been secured although the situation was naturally still very confused and the 8th and 9th Devons found themselves badly mixed up in trenches just to the west of Mametz. As evening began to fall some of the men who had been kept out of battle were sent forward. Among them was Private Conn who was sent forward to bring a Lewis-gun team up to strength and to assist at the same time in carrying forward some rations. In an entirely typical manner he was keen to secure the best possible souvenir of the fighting that had raged in his absence.

I lost no time in getting myself dug in. The dead had fallen in many strange, grotesque postures, some on their hands and knees as if they were praying. I did have a bit of a scrounge round though. I thought I might get one of those belts with '*Gott mit uns*' on it or perhaps one of those Prussian helmets. I did come across one bloke, but when I lifted his helmet half the top of his nut was in it – it was full of brains like mincemeat. I'm not very squeamish, but I didn't fancy scraping that out.[100]

Private Albert Conn, 8th Battalion, Devonshire Regiment, 20th Brigade, 7th Division

The attack of the XV Corps had been far more successful than that of its neighbours to the north. The reason was the far more effective counter-battery work that had preceded the assault. The German artillery was almost quiescent and as the narrower space between the opposing front lines allowed the British troops to get across No Man's Land correspondingly quicker, they were able to catch the German front-line troops, in some cases before they had emerged from their dugouts. Ironically, the much vaunted artillery experiments with a creeping barrage, which would later provide a partial template for most infantry attacks on the Western Front, was not particularly relevant to their success. The line of bursting shells was too 'thin' in that there were insufficient shells bursting and there was a lack of the masses of high explosive shells needed to give it a real 'bite'. The over-ambitious speed of advance also meant that in reality the line of shells quickly outpaced the struggling infantry, who were left far behind to fend for themselves. But the successes such as they were had come at a cost. The 21st Division suffered 4,256 casualties while the 7th Division lost some 3,380 men.

XIII Corps*: Montauban – success on the right of the line*

THE SOUTHERNMOST sector of the British assault was to be carried out by the XIII Corps under the command of Lieutenant General William Congreve VC. In this sector the German front line ran out from the main Pozières Ridge across the Montauban to Mametz Spur. Behind it lay the deep Caterpillar Valley, through which the Willow stream ran on its way to pass between Fricourt and Mametz. Montauban had been fortified and there were several self-contained strong points within the trench system, such as the Glatz and Pommiers Redoubts, which had been carefully constructed to break up the smooth flow of any attack that penetrated the front line. Two intermediate defence lines were then backed up by the Second Line system some 3,000 yards back along the Bazentin Ridge. One advantage held by the British was that the Maricourt Ridge behind the British lines provided not only excellent observation of the German forward lines but shelter for the massed batteries of guns on the reverse slopes. Here there was no doubt that a clear British artillery superiority had been established, valuably augmented by the French artillery of the XX Corps, which was next in the Allied line to the south. Here the concentrated counter-battery fire had eroded the numbers of German guns facing the Allies until they were all but silenced on the day that mattered.

The plan produced by Congreve called for the 18th and 30th Divisions to seize all of the Montauban Spur on the first day, reaching forward to Montauban Alley, which ran on the near face of Caterpillar Valley. In reserve would be the 9th (Scottish) Division. The artillery were to use a

XIII Corps attack on Montauban

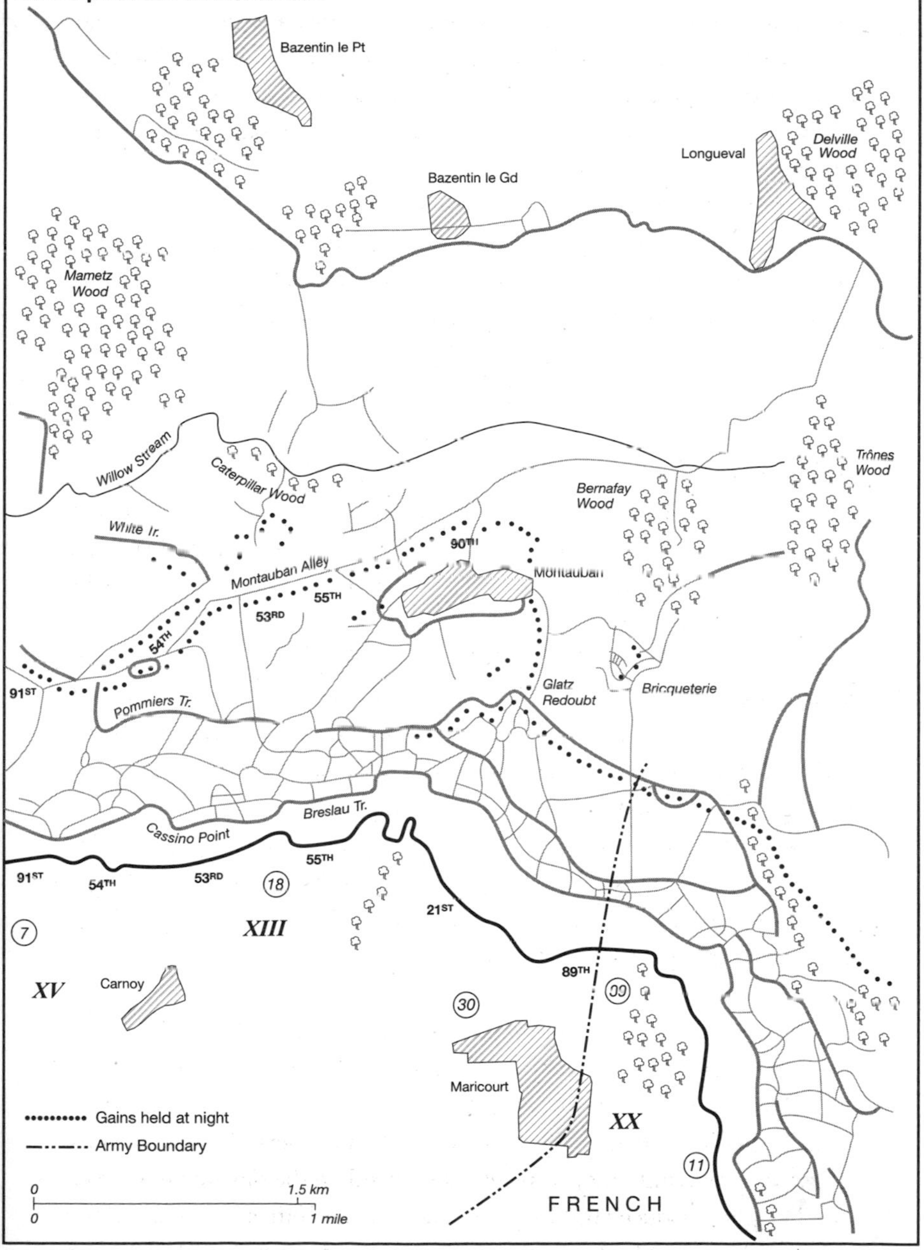
Bazentin le Pt
Delville Wood
Longueval
Bazentin le Gd
Mametz Wood
Willow Stream
Caterpillar Wood
Trônes Wood
Bernafay Wood
White Tr.
90TH
Montauban Alley
Montauban
55TH
53RD
54TH
91ST
Pommiers Tr.
Glatz Redoubt
Bricqueterie
Breslau Tr.
Cassino Point
91ST
54TH
53RD
55TH
18
21ST
7
XIII
XV
Carnoy
89TH
30
30
Maricourt
XX
11
FRENCH
Gains held at night
Army Boundary
0
1.5 km
0
1 mile

simple form of the creeping barrage whereby all the heavy artillery moved in sudden lifts from one objective line to the next, but the field artillery was to creep back in short lifts picking up every previously identified trench between the lines. The VIII Corps orders were reputedly the first to actually use the word 'creep' although the concept was still imperfectly realised.

The 18th Division attacked from in front of the village of Carnoy, directly across the intermediate trenches of Pommiers Alley and Train Alley to seize and consolidate Montauban Alley. Their commanding officer was Major General Sir Ivor Maxse, who had a reputation for attention to detail and meticulous training. He placed all three of his brigades in line for the assault: 54th, 53rd and 55th Brigades. They were assisted by the detonation of two mines, one of 500 lbs on the western edge of the sector intended to remove the threat from a nest of flanking machine guns, and another of 5,000 lbs under the German strong point at the salient of Casino Point. The German line had been much disturbed by previous mine warfare in front of Carnoy earlier in 1916 and as a result the Germans had abandoned their old linear front concentrating instead on a mixture of barbed-wire obstacles and machine-gun strong points in the old craters.

The two mines went up at 0727 and the three brigades surged forward into the attack. Private Henwood was in a support company as the 6th Royal Berkshires went over the top opposite the Casino Point mine.

> We was standing on the firestep just as the attack had started and we had orders that we were going to send a mine up before our men took the front line German trench. But our men were so mad to get there they rushed forward under cover of smoke bombs, a slight wind carrying the smoke towards the German line. One of our companies, being well in front, got to the German parapet and was just landing in the trench when the mine went up and blew most of that company up with it. Just as that happened we had orders to go over the top and extend out.[101]
>
> Private Fred Henwood, 6th Battalion, Royal Berkshire Regiment, 53rd Brigade, 18th Division

Further along the front, Private Cude was with a party designated to remain in the trench as the assaulting troops moved forwards.

> This must be the beginning of the end. 7.22 a.m. Every gun for eight minutes gave of their best and the din was terrific. Punctual to time, 7.28 a.m., two minutes before the line advances, Captain Nevill, 8th East Surreys, kicks off the football that is to take the boys across to Jerry. Now although the line right and left have moved, I am too busy to take in the surroundings other than our immediate front. East Surreys and Queens go over singing and shouting and the ball is punted from one to another.[102]
>
> Private Robert Cude, 7th Battalion, East Kent Regiment, 55th Brigade, 18th Division

One of the footballs had on it 'The Great European Cup-Tie Final. East Surreys v. Bavarians, Kick off at Zero!' while the other had emblazoned on it, 'No referee' to indicate that 'rough stuff' was entirely appropriate to the occasion. Second Lieutenant Alcock wrote to explain to Nevill's family what happened in the following minutes.

> Five minutes before zero time he strolled up in his usual calm way, and we shared a last joke before going over. The company went over the top very well, with Soames and your brother kicking off with the company footballs. We had to face a very heavy rifle and machine-gun fire, and nearing the front German trench, the lines slackened pace slightly. Seeing this Wilfred dashed in front with a bomb in his hand, and was immediately shot through the head, almost side by side with Soames and Sergeant Major Wells.[103]
>
> Second Lieutenant Charles Alcock, 8th Battalion, East Surrey Regiment, 55th Brigade, 18th Division

Such tragedies notwithstanding, the initial attack was reasonably successful. Assisted by the mines the assault battalions burst through the German front line to tackle the first real line of defence along Pommiers Trench and Train Alley. The garrison was thoroughly alert to the danger that faced them and they opened up a heavy fire. Now was the moment that Colonel Irwin considered his men needed the extra push his leadership could hopefully provide.

> When the impetus died down I thought that this was the moment that I might be of some use. I went in and picked up all the chaps I could and went over the parapet by myself, stood well out in the open and

said, 'Come on, come on, come on .... !' They all came on quite smoothly. They didn't know what to do after they'd taken their first objective but I think I acted properly, but I really don't know. It's a very difficult job to know what a commanding officer should or shouldn't do.[104]

Lieutenant Colonel Alfred Irwin, 8th Battalion, East Surrey Regiment, 55th Brigade, 18th Division

As the British barrage line swiftly moved on without reference to the real situation on the ground the prognosis would have been grim but for the minimal nature of the German artillery response. There was no wall of German shells smashing down on No Man's Land to isolate the forward troops and in these circumstances the sheer weight of the superiority of numbers gave the British a greatly enhanced chance of success. Slowly they moved forward, plagued by German strong points, every one of which had to be overrun or outflanked. Nevertheless, the men continued to make progress, greatly assisted by the vaulting advance of the neighbouring 30th Division facing Montauban. There was, however, a very real price to pay – individual machine guns could cause painful casualties in a matter of mere seconds.

All our best men and NCOs are gone and when one sees the remains of a fine battalion one realises the disgusting sordidness of modern war, when any yokel can fire a gun that may or may not – chance entirely – kill a man worth fifty of the firer. But we must bear these losses silently, for it is the way that lies before us and the only way to victory.[105]

Second Lieutenant Alan Jacobs, 8th Battalion, East Surrey Regiment, 55th Brigade, 18th Division

Each man had his own way of dealing with the pain of the losses suffered. For some religion was at the centre of their lives and war was viewed through a prism of pure sanctimony.

Men who had not prayed for years confessed that they did pray that morning, whilst beside the dead body of several were found New Testaments sealed with the blood of men who had remembered that the Eternal God is the only Refuge of us all. A few hundred yards away from where we were fast becoming busy, my good and brave friend, Captain Nevill, led his men into the fight with footballs. And thus he

> died. With the Englishman's way of fighting, he went on his way. The War was a game which was to be played to the end in a clean and straight manner.[106]
>
> Chaplain Leonard Jeeves, 55th Brigade, 18th Division

Although the fighting was savage and in places little quarter was given or asked, prisoners were nevertheless taken and sent back to the rear areas. For men like Jeeves everything and anything was a reinforcement of his warped core beliefs.

> All eyes were turned to the bend in the road, around which came the first batch of prisoners. A more pitiable spectacle of human misery I have seldom seen outside of a madhouse. Worn white and thin with the appalling bombardment, and with hands uplifted, they glanced like hunted animals from side to side as they crept through the lines of wounded men and went back to the place provided for them. And again, and yet again, they came along, many of them never meant for a soldier's life, but driven to it by a State in which a few ambitious leaders made the whole land rise and use all the means that science could teach them in warfare.[107]
>
> Chaplain Leonard Jeeves, 55th Brigade, 18th Division

The prisoners may have looked pitiful, but in the heightened emotions of the day there were some awful incidents as German prisoners were killed out of hand. It is strange that some of the most bloodthirsty reactions came from those who had not actually gone into action themselves.

> I am aghast at the accuracy of the fire. He has plenty of machine guns and is making a frightful carnage. I long to be with the battalion so that I can do my best to bereave a German family. I hate these swines. One feels that one must kill, as often as one can. My hand strays to my pocket. I have two 'Mills' in each, and there are some Jerries against me. They are prisoners and had it not been for the fact that they are being closely watched, I would have put one at least of my bombs amongst them.[108]
>
> Private Robert Cude, 7th Battalion, East Kent Regiment, 55th Brigade, 18th Division

By the end of the day the 18th Division had achieved all of its major objectives and managed to consolidate a new front line that stretched along Montauban Alley and Beetle Alley to make a firm link with the neighbouring 7th Division on their left. As the reserve battalions moved forward they were shaken by the sheer horror of the sights that surrounded them.

> A battlefield in the old days, even though casualties were often far greater, must have been a clean, sweet business compared to one these days. The area over which it is fought is merely the face of God's lovely earth wrecked beyond recognition, except as a plague of volcanoes. Everything about the thing is unlovely and rather dreadful; and to those who are at all weak in the stomach, very dreadful and altogether unbearable. And there are a great many to whom, at any rate in cold blood, it is intolerable. I have two officers both shaken and now useless from mere sights and I suppose there are plenty of men the same.[109]
>
> Lieutenant Colonel Frank Maxwell VC, 12th Battalion, Middlesex Regiment, 54th Brigade, 18th Division

Chaplain Jeeves was watching as some of the thousands of wounded made their uncertain way back to the safety of the rear areas.

> Hour after hour those heroes came, some limping, some helping others who were worse than themselves, some lying still and white upon the stretchers, some asking for the drink which we were only too glad to be able to give to them. So brave, so patient; I felt amidst it all the uplift of a spirit which was not born on earth. I have never seen anything so sublime. Surely in a hall of the brave and good beyond this world we shall meet again, if we walk worthy of all that this sacrifice has won for us?[110]
>
> Chaplain Leonard Jeeves, 55th Brigade, 18th Division

THE HONOUR OF taking the far right flank in the British assault went to the 30th Division commanded by Major General John Shea. The 21st and 89th Brigades attacked directly towards the village of Montauban with the intermediate German line of Dublin Trench and the Glatz Redoubt as their main objectives. Once these had been captured the 90th Brigade was to move forward to capture Montauban itself.

In this sector the British artillery had carried out their task almost to perfection with some considerable assistance from the neighbouring French artillery. As a result of their combined efforts the German artillery was silenced, the barbed wire was largely cut, Montauban had been reduced to rubble and the German trench positions had been thoroughly pounded. At 0722 the artillery was augmented by a furious bombardment from six Stokes mortar batteries, which had been secretly installed at the end of Russian saps dug across No Man's Land. Finally at 0730 the Manchesters went over the top.

> Off we started, about 50 yards between each wave. I was carrying my rifle by the sling on my shoulder with the bayonet parallel to my ear and had not gone many yards, when *whizz* – I felt as if someone had pulled at the top. However, I took no notice as we were at a quick march and it was taking us all our time to keep going. Like nearly every other fellow, I was smoking. No Man's Land was one mass of shell holes, the soil was loose and we had 400 yards of this to go to the first German trench.[111]
>
> Private Albert Andrews, 19th Battalion, Manchester Regiment, 21st Brigade, 30th Division

They came under fire of course, but it bore no resemblance to the deluge of high explosives and massed machine-gun bullets that had haunted the men to the north.

> Over the top! Up lads, good luck and we were away. We went about 25 yards, got through our wire all right, what was left of it. We were going very well; we were in the front wave. All of a sudden I realised what a hell of a weight we were carrying. The No. 1 he carried the gun, put it under his arm, finger on the trigger, and always about 2 yards in front of any infantrymen that were following. The barbed wire was shattered in strands all over the place, twisted round. When we got just off the front line, up pops a machine gun. Chained to this gun was a German. The first thing I did was to put my gun on to my shoulder and sprayed right along the top to keep their heads down. The German gunner went down; whether he was hit or not I didn't know and I didn't care, he was down. They were all down. That gave us a chance of getting in the trench. When we got in the gun team were practically down – not with the exertion of walking up and down shell holes and through wire, but with the damn load they were carrying. It was absolutely inhuman. My immediate concern was to get my Lewis gun on to the back of their trench, Dublin Trench. Our Brigadier General – Stanley – he was up

within our front line within an hour and a half of our taking it. Not standing in the trench but standing in the open with a pair of field glasses looking at the German positions – I can see him now! We stayed about an hour till all the objectives were gained. Once you're in the front line you don't stay there. Then you've got to get forward again to dig in about another 100 yards ahead of our objective – Dublin Trench – and we start digging in. Then the fun did start. We were getting enfilade from right and left. We were the first target. You're not going to worry about a chappie with a rifle, he can only kill one but a Lewis gunner could probably wipe the whole lot out.[112]

Sergeant Ernest Bryan, 17th Battalion, King's Liverpool Regiment, 89th Brigade, 30th Division

Many of the Germans were still caught in what remained of their deep dugouts and only emerged at the very last moment when it was too late to make any real difference. As a result the losses in this sector were held reasonably in check.

As we got nearer, dozens of Germans were running through us towards our lines with their hands up. Others stopped there throwing bombs, firing machine guns and rifles, but those who stayed until we got there will fire no more.[113]

Private Albert Andrews, 19th Battalion, Manchester Regiment, 21st Brigade, 30th Division

Carried away by the adrenaline rush of battle, there were times when war was quite literally murder.

I jumped into the German trench, what was left of it, just near a dugout door. In the doorway there was a big barrel. As soon as I jumped in, a German leapt from behind the barrel, but I was already on guard and I had my bayonet on his chest. He was trembling and looked half mad with his hands above his head, saying something to me which I did not understand. All I could make out was that he did not want me to kill him! It was here I noticed my bayonet was broken and I couldn't have stuck him with it. Of course, I had 'one up the chimney' as we called it, that is a bullet in the breech, so that you only have to press your trigger. I pointed to his belt and bayonet. He took these off, and his hat and water bottle as well, emptied his pockets and offered the lot to me. Just then one of my mates was coming up the

> trench. 'Get out of the way, Andy, leave him to me, I'll give him one to himself!' He meant he would throw a bomb at him, which would have blown him to pieces. 'Come here', I said. The German was on his knees in front of me now, fairly pleading. I said, 'He's an old man!' He looked 60. At the finish I pointed my thumb towards our lines, never taking my bayonet off his chest. He jumped up and, with his hands above his head, ran out of the trench towards our lines calling out all the time. He was trembling from head to foot and frightened to death. I honestly believe he could have 'done me' as I jumped into the trench if he had not been so afraid. This was the only German I ever let off and I never regretted it. Well, with him away, we both bombed the dugout and turned round to go along the trench, when three fine Germans came running towards us with their hands up. They would be about 20 yards away. We both fired and two fell, my mate saying as we let go, 'That's for my brother in the Dardanelles!', and as he fired again and the third German fell, 'That's for my winter in the trenches!' We walked up to them and one moved. My mate kicked him and pushed his bayonet into him. That finished him. This kind of thing was going on all along the line, no Germans being spared. Wounded were killed by us all. We hadn't exactly been told, 'No prisoners!' but we were given to understand that that was what was wanted.[114]
>
> Private Albert Andrews, 19th Battalion, Manchester Regiment, 21st Brigade, 30th Division

On they went, so far ahead of schedule that they had to wait for the artillery to finish knocking hell out of the German trenches that made up the Glatz Redoubt.

> We waited outside Glatz Redoubt, all our guns being turned on this ring of trenches which was right on top of the ridge. We got the order, 'Charge!' and away we went at the double, killing all that stayed there. A good many retreated towards Montauban and we opened rapid fire at them.[115]
>
> Private Albert Andrews, 19th Battalion, Manchester Regiment, 21st Brigade, 30th Division

All in all the Germans that survived could testify that the British gunners had done a superb job in the southern sector of the offensive.

> The troops who had so far held the lines south of Mametz and south of Montauban had sustained severe losses from intense enemy bombardment, which had been maintained for many days without a pause, and for the most part were already shot to pieces.[116]
>
> Lieutenant Colonel Bedall, 16th Bavarian Regiment, 10th Bavarian Division, German Army

Now that the 21st and 89th Brigades had reached their objectives, the 90th Brigade moved up to leapfrog them as planned. As they approached they could see that the French were also making good solid progress.

> As we were going over I could see the French troops advancing on our right. It was a splendid sight to see them, in their coloured uniforms and long bayonets. They advanced in short sharp rushes and they seemed to make very, very good progress. There artillery was giving them plenty of support and as they vanished in the distance, I turned round to some of my comrades and said, 'They're doing very well, very well indeed!' And they did you know![117]
>
> Private Pat Kennedy, 18th Battalion, Manchester Regiment, 90th Brigade, 30th Division

Meanwhile, the artillery was following its prepared programme to the letter. From its perspective everything seemed to be going like clockwork.

> Received news at last from observation post, 'Attack going OK. 1st, 2nd and 3rd lines taken with few casualties.' At 9.56 a.m., lifted from Montauban and put up a barrage on the south-east side of the village to check any reinforcements coming up. Batteries in the rear of us who have to advance first, are now limbering up and trotting forward past our guns! Everything is going top hole – awfully bucked! At 10.10 a.m. received word from OP, 'Infantry have taken Glatz Alley and are now entering Montauban.'[118]
>
> Lieutenant William Bloor, C Battery, 149th Brigade, Royal Field Artillery, 30th Division

The village proved empty when the troops moved into the ruined streets at 1005. By 1100 they had run on to capture their allotted section of Montauban Alley in Caterpillar Valley behind Montauban. The trauma inflicted on the Germans was such that in Caterpillar Valley a number of German guns were captured.

The main role of the artillery in this phase of the battle was to disrupt any attempted German counter-attack. When the army cooperation aircraft of the RFC spotted threatening numbers of German troops moving forward in between Bernafay and Trônes Wood the artillery knew exactly what it had to do.

> At 3.20 p.m. received word that two battalions of Germans had been seen on the road from Longueval, evidently coming up to support. Were warned to be ready to receive them! We *are* ready, and ten times ready, and the more that come, the bigger the target! Am at this moment waiting for further news of them – they are reported by the Flying Corps, and are a mile or two off yet and out of sight![119]
>
> Lieutenant William Bloor, C Battery, 149th Brigade, Royal Field Artillery, 30th Division

As night fell the positions were securely held, but it was obvious that a serious counter-attack would be launched as soon as the Germans could organise themselves. For many men, the collection of souvenirs and a little light looting of German dugouts was a pleasant distraction that might well prove fatal if older, cooler heads had not called them to their duty in consolidating the captured trenches.

> Two or three of us went down in a fine German dugout. There were cigars, tinned food and German helmets. We all took a helmet, cigars and tobacco coming out with these German helmets on we ran straight into our Captain. 'Yes,' he said, 'you all look very nice, but get some fucking digging done!'[120]
>
> Private Albert Andrews, 19th Battalion, Manchester Regiment, 21st Brigade, 30th Division

Of course, the first real line of defence of the captured ground was their artillery. It had the massed slaughtering power to destroy any German counterattack that came within range.

> At 10 p.m. the enemy started a heavy bombardment of the captured village of Montauban and also put up a barrage on his old trenches to prevent us from reinforcing. We started shooting then to cut up his counter-attack which was a failure. From this time until 2 a.m., the fire slackened somewhat, but at that time we commenced another intense bombardment. We received an SOS from Gowland, and fired for an

hour. The attack was foiled. At 4.30 a.m. received by flag from Gowland, that the Boche was advancing in mass. This attack was again repulsed. We fired 834 rounds today.[121]

Lieutenant William Bloor, C Battery, 149th Brigade, Royal Field Artillery, 30th Division

The infantry constructed an improvised line from a mixture of smashed German trenches and hastily linked shell holes. It was a difficult situation and it was soon obvious that many of the young lads in the line were terribly inexperienced.

During one counter-attack I couldn't get my ammunition clips out of my pouches quick enough, so this old soldier with a South African War ribbon said to me, 'Hey lad, get your clips on the top of the parapet, it's more easy for you to do it!' It was a good tip because I could load very, very quick and fire. The counter-attack was beaten off.[122]

Private Pat Kennedy, 18th Battalion, Manchester Regiment, 90th Brigade, 30th Division

Many were haunted by the imagined and all too real terrors of bayonet fighting. They had been trained in England with a straw-filled sack as an enemy; even then many had been shocked by the imprecations of their instructing sergeants who ordered them to scream and yell as if to make their lungs burst. In their makeshift front-line trenches their knees trembled at the thought of cold steel.

When you saw the Germans coming to you with fixed bayonets. The old Sergeant who had been out since Mons, he said, 'By God, Pat, if they get any nearer, we'll have to go and meet them with the bayonet!' I thought, 'Right! I've got a round in my breech, in case I miss him with the bayonet, I can shoot him! Just pull the trigger catch him that way. But they got very near on top of us – a few feet away from us and they were coming full pelt, yelling at the top of their voices. It's a nasty feeling to think of these big Germans, all picked men, they were regular troops, done years and years conscript service. But really, they were on a level with us because it was their first field action they were in, I think.[123]

Private Pat Kennedy, 18th Battalion, Manchester Regiment, 90th Brigade, 30th Division

The attacks were beaten off by a combination of effective British covering artillery fire, well-sited machine guns and the courage of troops determined to cling on to their hard won gains. Their morale was high – after all as far as they knew the British had won a great victory that day.

> We didn't know that the 1st of July was a disaster. The only success was where our division and the 18th Division gained all their objectives. We thought the war would soon be over as our men were flush with success.[124]
>
> Private Pat Kennedy, 18th Battalion, Manchester Regiment, 90th Brigade, 30th Division

Collectively the XIII Corps had achieved all its objectives and thereby smashed through the German front-line trench system. The lack of any real German shell fire in comparison to the more northerly sectors had made a much more feasible operation of war and the two divisions of Kitchener's Army had indeed done very well. Yet it should be emphasised that the British had not by any means broken through. The German Second Line system still lay before them on the ridge extending from Bazentin-le-Grand to Longueval. Behind that a Third Line system was being sketched out on the ground. Nevertheless, on a day of utter disaster, this success offered hope for the future; offered a point of focus for future attacks should Haig and Rawlinson decide to capitalise on the successes achieved. Yet the fighting had still been rough and the cost was inevitably high with the 18th Division totalling some 3,115 losses while the 30th Division incurred 3,011 casualties. Warfare was a painful business even in victory.

French Success on the Somme

THE FRENCH ATTACK alongside the XIII Corps was carried out by the Sixth Army under the command of General Fayolle. The XX Corps attacked north of the river Somme at 0730 and under the cover of a light river mist the French surged forward alongside the British 30th Division and despite stiff fighting in some sectors had overrun the entire German First Line defences. At first it seemed possible that Hardecourt could be attacked later in the day, but the difficulties in coordinating with the British meant that it was decided to hold what they had rather than risk a further advance.

That this was perhaps a wise decision may be seen in the several German counter-attacks emanating from Hardecourt later in the day. South of the river Somme the French I Colonial Corps and the XXXV Corps had managed to attain complete artillery supremacy. The German batteries were almost wiped out and were unable in consequence to put up any real counter-barrage. The attack was delayed until 0930 and this perversely seems to have caught the Germans by surprise. When the French had not emerged alongside the British after two hours the Germans may have thought they were not coming at all. They were wrong and the French stormed through in fine style carrying all before them despite the dangerous flanking fire from the unengaged German positions even further to the south. The French were not a 'New Army' and generally had the benefit of more training and more battle experience than their British comrades – it was no disgrace that sometimes it showed. South of the Somme they pushed straight through the entire German First Line trench system and managed to establish themselves within relatively easy assaulting distance of the Second Line.

Somme Success in the Air

THE MORNING OF 1 July was not the first day of the offensive for the Royal Flying Corps. They had been engaged in a vicious battle for control of the air above the battlefield for the previous six months. Photographic reconnaissance and artillery observation were absolutely essential if the infantry were to have any chance of success on the day when it mattered. At the start of the battle the RFC had been labouring under a considerable disadvantage. The British army cooperation aircraft, the BE2c, was a stable and solid aircraft but it was, however, totally unsuited to the hurly-burly of aerial conflict. Flying against them was the formidable Fokker Monoplane EIII armed with a Spandau machine gun that fired directly through the span of the propellor using a revolutionary interrupter gear. Aware of the importance of their work, the RFC commander, Brigadier General Sir Hugh Trenchard, resolved that his men had to continue to carry out their functions and accept any consequent casualties for the 'greater good' of the army. It was thus fortunate that the technological tide at last began to turn back towards the British in the spring of 1916. The first sign of this was the arrival of the FE2b multi-purpose two-seater

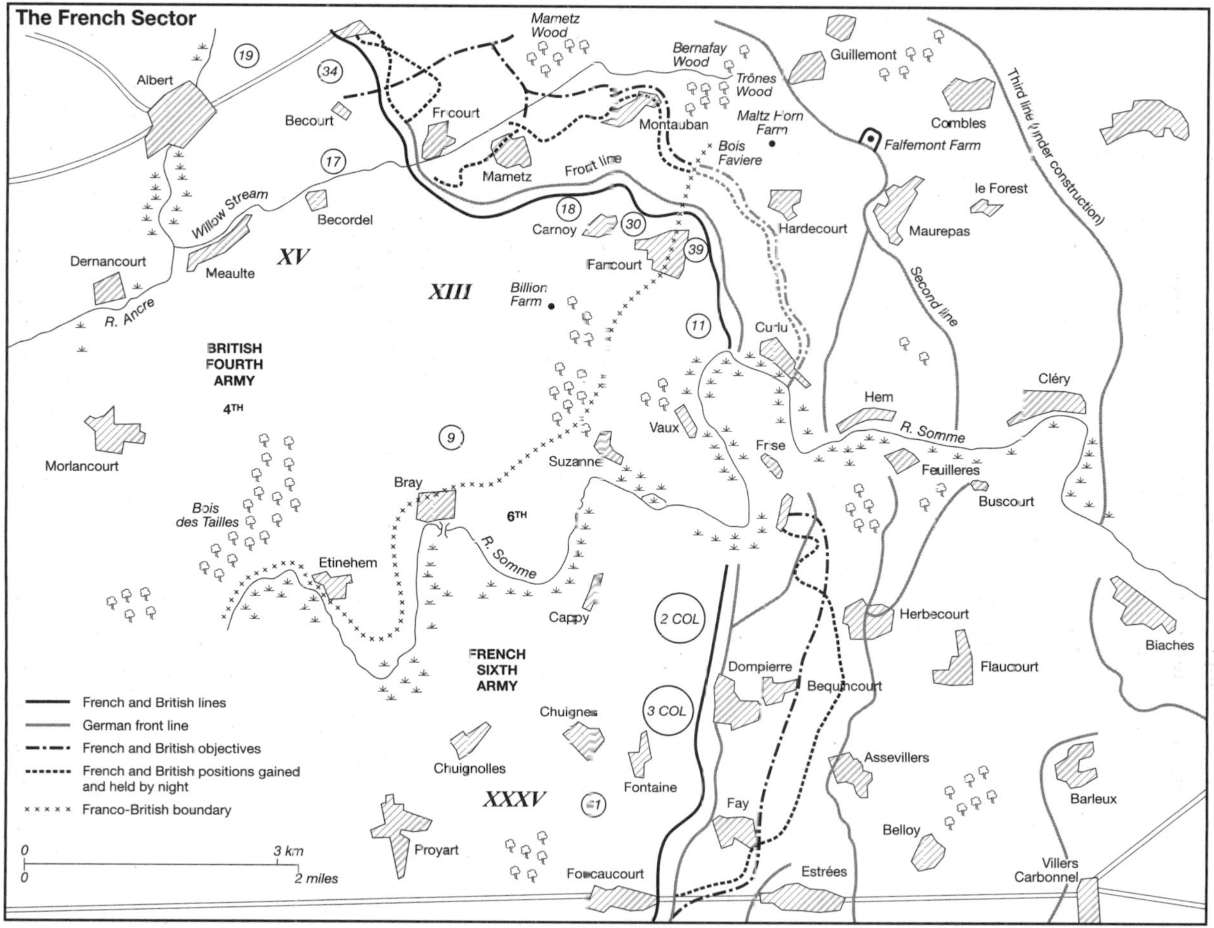
The French Sector
Albert
Becourt
Dernancourt
R. Ancre
Meaulte
Willow Stream
Becordel
Fricourt
Mametz
Mametz Wood
Bernafay Wood
Trônes Wood
Montauban
Maltz Horn Farm
Bois Faviere
Front line
Carnoy
Maricourt
Billion Farm
Guillemont
Combles
Falfemont Farm
le Forest
Maurepas
Hardecourt
Second line
Third line (under construction)
Curlu
Hem
Cléry
R. Somme
Frise
Vaux
Suzanne
Feuilleres
Buscourt
Herbecourt
Flaucourt
Biaches
Bray
Etinehem
Bois des Tailles
Morlancourt
BRITISH FOURTH ARMY
4TH
XV
XIII
XXXV
6TH
FRENCH SIXTH ARMY
Cappy
2 COL
3 COL
Dompierre
Bequincourt
Chuignes
Chuignolles
Fontaine
Assevillers
Fay
Belloy
Barleux
Proyart
Foucaucourt
Estrées
Villers Carbonnel
19
34
17
18
30
39
11
9
French and British lines
German front line
French and British objectives
French and British positions gained and held by night
Franco-British boundary
0
3 km
0
2 miles

machines. This was a 'pusher' aircraft, with the engine behind the pilot and his observer perched in the forward cockpit with a clear field of fire for his Lewis gun. At first the fighting was still hard as the German scouts would often swoop down in ambush when the British patrols were a long way over the lines and far from the safety of home.

> The Fokkers evidently worked on some pre-arranged plan as they were firing small white lights before swooping down. After the first attack which was made between us and the sun, the enemy showed much more caution in approaching near. It was in this first attack I think that Cairn Duff was shot down. Allen had his observer (Powell) shot dead as he was firing back and I rather think he got his man too as three of us saw one Fokker going down anyhow, side-slipping and nose diving. Anyway Powell had his gun right 'on' as the bullet grazed his trigger finger and struck him in the eye. He fell back into the nacelle breaking one of his legs in the fall. Allen was now defenceless and in spite of the fact that the machine was shot to 'bits' just managed to scrape back over the lines, when his engine stopped. He got back into the aerodrome.[125]
>
> Captain Harold Wyllie, 23 Squadron, Royal Flying Corps

The Fokker pilots soon found that the ungainly looking FE2b two-seaters could be dangerous opponents. Yet far more overtly threatening were the new DH2 single-seater scouts. These were also pusher aircraft but they could match the Fokker for speed and manoeuvrability.

> If a Hun sees a De Hav he runs for his life; they won't come near them. It was only yesterday that one of the fellows came across a Fokker. The Fokker dived followed by the De Hav but the wretched Fokker dived so hard that when he tried to pull his machine out his elevator broke and he dived into our lines; not a shot was fired.[126]
>
> Second Lieutenant Gwilym Lewis, 32 Squadron, Royal Flying Corps

Major Lanoe Hawker who commanded the DH2 pilots of 24 Squadron, RFC issued orders to his men that managed to summarise the ethos of the RFC: '*Attack Everything.*'[127] Such an aggressive attitude allowed the RFC scouts to establish such a domination that the hapless BE2cs could carry out their work relatively unmolested.

Now at last though was the day when it really mattered. The RFC had to keep complete control of the skies above the battlefield. The British scouts flew missions roaming far behind the lines and attacking every German aircraft they sighted. Lieutenant Tudor-Hart and Captain Webb flying in an FE2b were about five miles behind the lines when they sighted a formation of German aircraft. The RFC had a strong ethos that no odds were to be considered too great.

> We saw eight German machines approaching from the south-west – they were higher than us, and we flew towards them to attack. Two passed over our heads together about 300 yards or so apart, and I opened fire on one. They both replied together. I gave the signal to Webb to turn so that I could fire at the other machine behind us, but he put the machine's head down. I turned to see what was the matter, and he pointed to his abdomen and collapsed over the joy stick. He died in a few seconds I think, but his last thought was to save his machine. The machine at once began turning towards the German side, and I had to get back to my machine gun to fire at a machine diving at us. This happened again and again, but my fire would always prevent them finishing the dive. Other machines fired from above all the time. I had only time to get the machine pointing towards our lines when I had to get back to the gun. I never got a chance to pull Webb out of the pilot's seat, so I had to steer with my hand over the wind-screen. I didn't expect to get off alive, but tried to put up as good a fight as possible, and tried all the time to keep her towards our lines, but having to man the gun so often made it impossible to make progress, but the erratic course the machine flew probably saved it. At last, still being fired at, I got right down near the ground and proceeded to make a landing, as it was all I could do. I saw a lot of men with rifles, and realised that I might get shot before I could set fire to the machine, so I, at the last minute, put her nose down in order to crash. One wing tip hit first, the whole machine was destroyed. I was hurled out and escaped with a bruised and paralysed side and broken ankle and rib.[128]
>
> Lieutenant W. O. Tudor-Hart, 22 Squadron, RFC

Such casualties were accepted in order to keep back the German aircraft and to give a clear run to the men on the ground. Yet the artillery observation aircraft that were intended to correct the massed batteries fall of shot found themselves struggling with the sheer number of German batteries that opened fire. With every available British gun blazing away it was difficult to work out who was firing at which target and accurate ranging was consequently difficult. Despite this the RFC had at least managed to deprive the German batteries of any chance of their own aerial observation – which in the circumstances was perhaps just as well. The British contact and reconnaissance patrols skimmed unmolested above a battlefield where it was death to show oneself on the ground. One report from Major Lanoe Hawker neatly summarised what was going on below him after a flight along the lines at 1230.

> No Hostile Aircraft seen. About twelve, six-horsed vehicles moving south along Artillery Lane, and two or three moving east from Beaucourt-sur-Ancre. Two or three vehicles moving both ways along St. Pierre Divion–Grandcourt Road. Big high explosive shells bursting on our trenches opposite Thiepval. Hostile trenches from Ancre to Thiepval crowded with dark infantry – presumably Germans. Very few men seen in trenches from Thiepval to Albert–Bapaume Road. Crater north of road empty. Crater south of road and communication trench to north east held by us. Many dead lying on eastern slopes outside this crater. One-horsed vehicles moving in Contalmaison. Our men in communication trenches north of Fricourt facing south. Shrapnel bursting on a line Mametz Wood–Montauban. No indication that Ovillers, Contalmaison or La Boisselle had been captured, but enemy apparently contained in Fricourt. Pilot's impression: enemy holding on to the line Thiepval–Ancre while he evacuates his artillery.[129]
>
> Major Lanoe Hawker VC, 24 Squadron, RFC

The RFC also launched bombing raids designed to slow down and harass the movement of German reserves towards the battlefield by striking at the railway junctions, stations and railheads that were the veins of the German Army. The aircraft used were generally BE2cs, which although sturdy were unable to carry a worthwhile payload without leaving the observer behind. This demanded great courage as they had no means of defence if they were intercepted. The bombing was hardly devastating by any modern standards but the rewards could still be worthwhile, as the interrogation of a captured German soldier late in the war revealed.

> About 3.30 p.m. the first battalion of the 71st Reserve Regiment and the 11th Reserve Jaeger Battalion were at St Quentin Station ready to entrain, arms were piled and the regimental transport was being loaded onto the train. At this moment English aeroplanes appeared overhead and dropped bombs. One bomb fell on a shed which was filled with ammunition and caused a big explosion. There were 200 wagons of ammunition in the station at the time; sixty of them caught fire and exploded, the remainder were saved with difficulty. The train allotted to the transport of troops and all the equipment which they had placed on the platform were destroyed by fire. The men were panic-stricken and fled in every direction. One hundred and eighty men were either killed or wounded. It was not till several hours later that it was possible to collect the men of 71st Regiment. It was then sent back to billets.[180]
>
> Anon German Prisoner

One lucky bomb had devastated and at least temporarily removed from the fray a whole German battalion. On a day of disaster the Royal Flying Corps had finally come of age and achieved almost everything that could have realistically been expected of it.

IT MAY HAVE been a bright sunny day but the fog of war enveloped much of the Somme battlefield throughout 1 July. There was an enormous confusion in trying to interpret accurate situation reports – intelligence that was perfectly accurate in itself when sent, only to be subsequently overtaken by events. Although General Sir Henry Rawlinson was in contact with the lieutenant generals commanding his five corps, they themselves had great difficulty in finding out what happened in front of them. The German shells that flayed the British front lines had cut many of the telephone lines and generally ruined the communication between the Corps and their subordinate formations.

In several sectors where No Man's Land had become a wall of German shells the front-line units themselves had little or no idea where their forward elements had got to. The contact reports from the pilots of the Royal Flying Corps could have helped, but in many cases their reports also further muddied any accurate perception of the overall position: in general, aerial reconnaissance proved unable to distinguish between a properly consolidated British position and a few stragglers cut off and doomed to be slowly pinched out by the inexorable German counter-attacks. Thus false reports of the presence of British troops in Serre, Ovillers and Thiepval created the impression that more had been achieved than was in fact the case. When General Sir Douglas Haig arrived at Rawlinson's headquarters in the afternoon the confusion was unresolved.

> Hard fighting continued all day on front of Fourth Army. On a 16 mile front of attack varying fortune must be expected! It is difficult to summarize all that was reported. After lunch I motored to Querrieu and saw Sir H. Rawlinson. We hold the Montauban–Mametz Spur and villages of those names. The enemy are still in Fricourt, but we are round his flank on the north and close to Contalmaison. Ovillers and Thiepval villages have held our troops up, but our men are in the Schwaben Redoubt which crowns the ridge north of the last named village. The enemy counter-attacked here but were driven back. He however got a position with a few men in the river valley. North of the Ancre, the VIII Corps (Hunter-Weston) said they began well, but as the day progressed their troops were forced back into the German front line, except two battalions which occupied Serre village and were, it is said, cut off. I am inclined to believe from further reports that few of the VIII Corps left their trenches! The attack on Gommecourt Salient started well, especially the 56th Division under General Hull. The 46th Division (Stuart Wortley) attacked from the north side but was soon held up. This attack was of the very greatest assistance in helping the VIII Corps, because many of the enemy's guns and troops were directed on it, and so left the VIII Corps considerably free. In spite of this the VIII Corps achieved very little.[131]
>
> General Sir Douglas Haig, General Headquarters, British Expeditionary Force

Even ignoring the calumny so casually directed against the men of VIII Corps, the diary entry is a typical mixture of truths, half-truths and downright misapprehensions that would take days to settle down into a more accurate assessment of events on that awful day. Yet, on the late afternoon of 1 July, armed with such lamentably incomplete and flimsy evidence Haig and Rawlinson were required to take far-reaching decisions that would shape the future course of the Somme offensive. In particular, it seemed to be clear that the attack of the XIII Corps and the French Army alongside them had been markedly more successful than the central and northern sectors. The question of launching a further attack to exploit the inevitable confusion in the German line was pressing and could not be long postponed. Since the attacks in the northern and central sectors had failed it was decided that a breakthrough was unlikely. Meanwhile, General Sir Hubert Gough was kicking his heels at the Fourth Army headquarters, waiting to take command of the amassed reserves and three cavalry divisions allotted to exploit any significant penetration of the German lines. Haig decided that he would be better used in taking command and, if possible, revitalising the failed assaults of the northern wing of the Fourth Army, thus creating a new Reserve Army out of the VIII and X Corps. In the meantime Rawlinson could concentrate on the central and southern wings of what was left of the Fourth Army – the III, XV and XIII Corps.

While the generals pondered their next move, the British divisions already massed close behind the line, found themselves with nowhere to go as the attack stalled along most of the line. For the men of these divisions the day was just one long utterly dispiriting exercise in disappointment.

> We were in a wood, 2 miles behind the front. Reveille was at half past four, breakfast was at five and we were ordered to be ready to move off at six o'clock. By this time the bombardment had started and the ground shook even where we were and from the edge of the wood we could see the hundreds and hundreds of gun flashes and smoke. I think that every gun that was made was used on that 1st of July. Then we were told of our objective, which was a slag heap near Bapaume which was 5 miles behind the German lines. We were going to have a forced march through the British lines, the German lines and we were going to take this slag heap and we would hold it at all costs. We waited and waited for this signal to move off. We were all ready, everybody was anxious to go, and we waited and waited. At ten o'clock in the morning streams of wounded came back past us, ambulances, walking wounded. The hours went by and then at twelve

o'clock they sent the mess orderlies back to the back of this wood, where the cook carts were and we knew that we weren't going to move. We knew then that the front line had not been cracked. You know, it was a very, very despondent battalion that sat down to their meal of stew.[132]

Sergeant Charles Quinnell, 9th Battalion, Royal Fusiliers, 36th Brigade, 12th Division

Towards the end of the day the rôle of the 12th Division as a whole changed from that of renewing the thrust forward to just reinforcing and relieving the 8th Division, which had been reduced to a husk in the failed assault on Ovillers. The staff officers now had an enormous task ahead of them, and all their organisational skill was required to prevent utter chaos on the roads and communication trenches clogged with the wounded.

During the afternoon, our three brigades were moved up closer in support and at 9 p.m. we got the order to move divisional headquarters up to the front division and double up with them. This was done about 11 p.m., but of course made everything rather a tangle, especially in the dark. Our infantry was ordered to relieve the 8th Division which had not been able to get on. Fortunately it was the same front which we had reconnoitred and over which I had taken the parties of transport officers and staff captains. I had also issued all the bomb store arrangements, water supply, ration supply and maps – so we were all prepared. We had even marked out our transport camps so they all knew where to go. I had also had two lorries fitted up with tanks and pumps, one for drinking and one for animals. Water is a real difficulty about here, unless one is on or near the rivers or streams. We slept where we could.[133]

Quartermaster General Lieutenant Colonel E. H. E. Collen, Headquarters, 12th Division

The 6th West Kents moved up in the early evening to take up their positions in the British front line. They were led by guides from the Rifle Brigade whom they were replacing. It can be safely assumed that the remnants from the morning attack were feeling bitter.

Well our guide took B Company up to the front line with Captain Harris as officer commanding. 'Here you are, Sir!' he said, 'Here is your position.' 'But where is the company?' said Captain Harris. It was now very late at night and dark. 'You will see them in the morning when you look over into No Man's Land!' And surely we did see them: men of that regiment and other regiments lying in lines as hay or corn would lie in a field, all mown down by those German machine guns.[134]

Signaller Sidney Kemp, 6th Battalion, Royal West Kent Regiment, 37th Brigade, 12th Division

In some parts of the line there was evidence of considerable panic as the new battalions took up their positions. The men moving into the line were nervy and unsure of what they were to face, while the men they were relieving had been through hell and were jumpy in the extreme.

At 7 p.m. we moved forward to relieve the 5th West Yorks at Johnson's Post. As we moved forward along a communication trench into this inferno, the men began to turn back – word was passed down we were to retire. I stood in the corner of the trench and pulled out my revolver. 'If any man comes back here I shoot!' I said and after getting order I got out of the trench and ran along the top to rally the men and see what was going on at the front. There was no danger in this as we were not in sight of the German front line. Bland, the Ripon Headmaster's son, however, with the remnant of the 5th West Yorks in Johnson's Post which was below us, caught sight of me running with my helmet off. Thinking I was a German, he ordered his men to fire. I jumped back into the trench as the bullets cracked past me. Luckily the 5th were badly shaken and aimed badly. We eventually relieved the 5th in Johnson's Post and I had a word with Master Bland![135]

Lieutenant Thomas Pratt, 1/4th Duke of Wellington's Regiment, 147th Brigade, 49th Division

Gradually over the next day the battered battalions were relieved and moved back to count their dead and begin the long task of rebuilding.

It was truly the longest day for those men who had been left out of battle by the assault battalions to provide a nucleus for just such a rebuilding process. All day they waited with bated breath to hear how their friends had fared in the attack. This was life or death for the men with whom they had lived and worked for nigh on two years.

It was a glorious day, the sun was merciless and the ground had recovered enough to make it fairly hard for the advancing troops. I went to a report centre with a telephone where spots of news came filtering through from time to time. 'Attack totally unexpected.' 'Doing well in the south of the attack.' 'Five hundred prisoners taken south of Albert.' 'We have advanced 3 miles here.' 'Trench making headway.' But of the bid for Thiepval by our division there was no news.[136]

Lieutenant Edgar Lord, 15th Battalion, Lancashire Fusiliers, 96th Brigade, 32nd Division

News began to trickle back from Thiepval where Lieutenant Lord's battalion was going over the top in the ill-fated attack as part of 32nd Division. The first indications were not promising and the news went downhill from then on.

Two wounded men of our battalion came down the road on a wagon. They told us of several casualties due to an intense bombardment of our trenches before the attack started and hazarded the belief that half of our battalion was *hors de combat* before they went over the top. We did not believe this report to be very reliable, but every few minutes more of our wounded men passed and all told the same story, adding that the Huns seemed to have a machine gun in every trench, that the wire was uncut and he seemed to have the sector extremely heavily manned. It was like following a cricket match on a tape machine, except that the news was desultory and not consecutive, sometimes even contradictory, but one thing was certain – that the fellows one knew so intimately had probably been entirely wiped out.[137]

Lieutenant Edgar Lord, 15th Battalion, Lancashire Fusiliers, 96th Brigade, 32nd Division

Lieutenant Lord was particularly keen to get news of his friend Lieutenant Ivan Doncaster and the bad news merely stoked the fires of his concern. By the end of the day there was incontrovertible proof of the sheer scale of the losses suffered by his battalion.

The scene on the road called Northumberland Avenue leading to Bouzincourt defies my powers of description to do it justice. A broiling hot day, without a breath of wind, and down the dusty road came hundreds of men with wounds of every description. A few of the worst cases came on the ambulances, which were in small supply, but carts, wagons, lorries, limbers, water tanks and any vehicles which could give a lift were crammed to the utmost. The walking cases were choked

Situation at night, 1st July

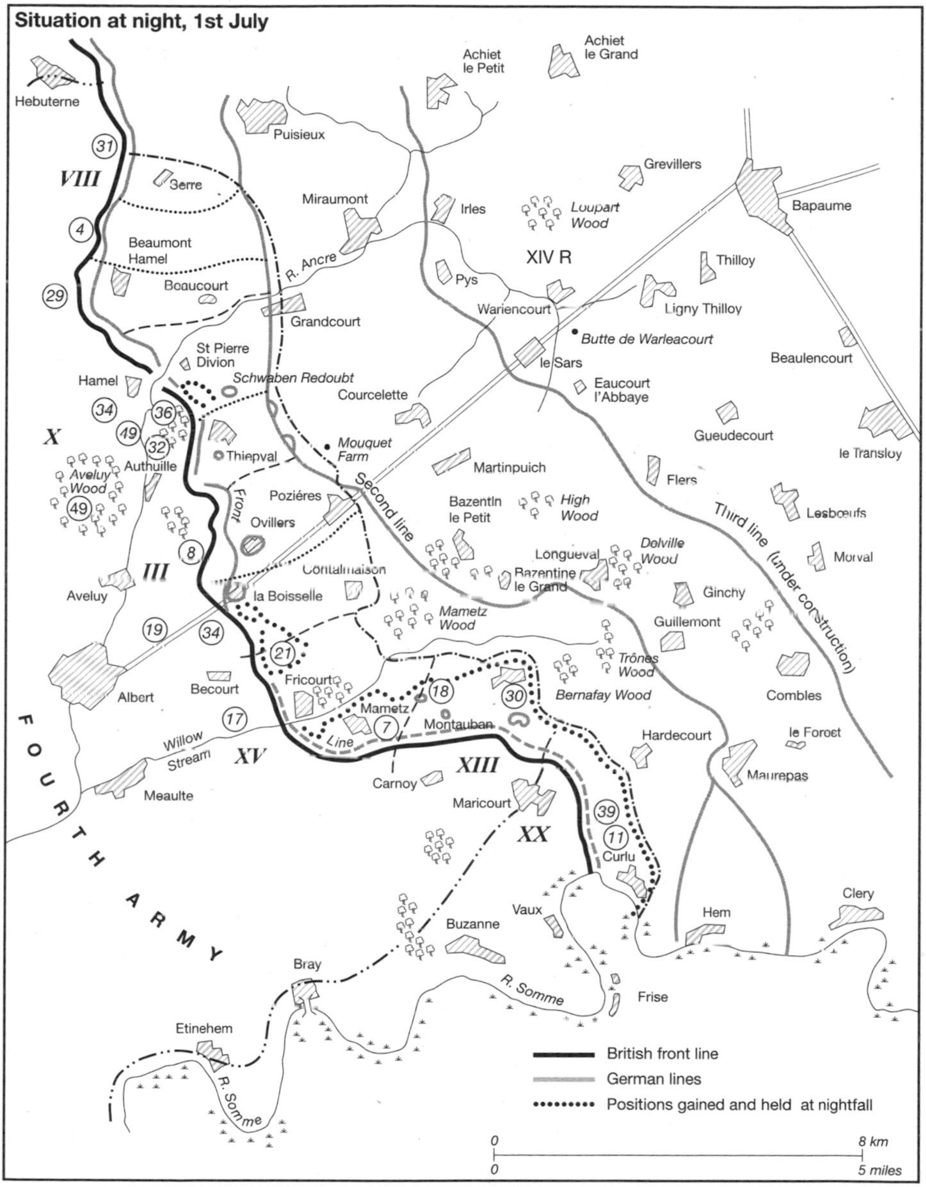

> with dust, staggering along between the limbers, sometimes helping each other forming human crutches, most of them wearing blood stained bandages and many in improvised splints. The agony on their faces told a weary tale of experiences well-nigh beyond recounting, as all had only just escaped the longest journey of all. I helped as I could by buying chocolates, biscuits and giving draughts of water from my bottle, but all along the road men laid down for the last time, being wounded worse than they knew.[138]
>
> Lieutenant Edgar Lord, 15th Battalion, Lancashire Fusiliers, 96th Brigade, 32nd Division

Of his friend Ivan Doncaster there was still no sign. For men like Lieutenant Lord it all seemed frankly incredible. How could this have happened? What had gone wrong?

CHAPTER FIVE

The Morning After

The cost had been horrendous. In one short day the British Army suffered a massive 57,470 casualties of which a staggering 19,240 were dead. This was the worst disaster ever to have befallen the British Army in its entire history. The county regimental system of the British further exaggerated the impact of the casualties. Battalions drawn from a single city area, or a provincial town were slaughtered and whole communities were thrown into mourning.

> There were sheets and sheets in the paper of dead and wounded with photographs where they could get them of the men. Of course everybody rushed to the paper every day to see if there was anyone they knew. When we got to know of anybody at the school, the headmaster announced them if they had been old boys. I was brought out of class to be told that my cousin had been killed. There were numerous services in churches. It was a very, very sad time – practically everybody was in mourning. People were in deep black, the men if they couldn't wear black wore black armbands as a mark of respect. The city was really shrouded in gloom. They were very, very sad and nothing seemed to matter any more.[1]
>
> Miss Llewellyn, Sheffield Schoolchild

Friends who had worked together, enlisted together and trained together had on far too many occasions also died together. This was of no comfort to their grieving families as they faced a future without their children. Then there were the teeming wounded. Some would be restored to full health, but many more would face the consequences of their injuries carrying their scars and gross disfigurements for the rest of their days.

And what kind of a destiny could lie ahead for those who had so far survived unscathed and were still serving at the front in a war that could wreak havoc like this?

The British had failed because they still did not grasp the sheer effort that it took to capture modern fortifications defended by well trained and courageous troops. The much vaunted British bombardment had simply not lived up to its star billing. Although, from the limited perspective of the British front line and observation posts, the bombardment had looked awe-inspiring, what was being seen was merely a one-dimensional viewpoint. Millions of shells had been fired but the total length of the front stretched for nearly 20 miles, while the depth that had to be covered reached back up to 3 miles. The end result was a brutally simple and deadly reality – the number of shells falling along each yard of the successive lines of German trenches was far less than Rawlinson had managed to achieve with his concentrated bombardment of the mere 2,000 yards of front assaulted at Neuve Chapelle. Yet this was not a skimpy, single front line that the British were assaulting, as had been the case in far off March 1915. This was a carefully planned series of deeply dug and revetted trench lines, with interlocking fields of fire, seamed together by communication trenches and switch lines all served by numerous reinforced deep dugouts. When the troops eventually penetrated the original German front line in the days that followed, many of them were stunned by the stark contrast with the basic British trenches they had long grown accustomed to.

> This trench was dug about 15 feet deep and duckboarded. We must have gone through a mile of this, which was just wonderful; each fire bay had a ladder to it, also a deep dugout quite near; and after all our bombardment the trench was little damaged. If it had not been for a big mine we put up, we should surely never have been able to penetrate this system. We then selected a dugout for company headquarters; the best thing in dugouts I have ever seen. It had two entrances being about 40 feet deep, extending underground about 30 yards. The inside room was fitted up with glass doored cupboards, these contained detonators and mining implements. A large stove was fitted, also a periscope looking over the old British line. In an anteroom at one end was an engine for working the electric light of the

trench system. At the opposite end was a tunnel large enough to place about 100 men.[2]

Lieutenant Lionel Ferguson, 13th Battalion, Cheshire Regiment, 74th Brigade, 25th Division

As they explored such dugouts it rendered the events of 1 July rather more explicable. And there were more strings to the German bow: the numerous fortress redoubts and villages had brought the art of defensive military engineering to a new peak. The British shells, whose sound and fury had so much impressed before the attack, were simply not falling in sufficient concentrations to smash this kind of reinforced and layered defence works. Two other factors further weakened the effect of the British bombardment. The British gunners were new to their trade and inevitably the accuracy of their fire was not what it might have been with more training and battle experience. In addition the quality of the British shells had been severely compromised by the intensive efforts of the munitions industry to rapidly speed up their production. Many simply did not explode. All this further diluted the anticipated effects of the bombardment.

If the German dugouts survived unscathed or only lightly damaged then so inevitably did the German garrisons. At the crucial moment the soldiers would file out: shaken, nervous, shell-shocked perhaps; haunted by the privations and crunching detonations they had endured for the previous week – but in the end they still proved capable of firing their machine guns and rifles when it came to the moment of truth. This was made substantially easier for them by the absence of any credible creeping barrage. The British generals cannot be blamed for this – the concept was new and only just being developed. Nevertheless, it was sadly ironic that just as the British troops went over the top into No Man's Land, the British barrage moved smartly off the German front line and began to feel its way back towards the German support lines. As for the German artillery batteries, not all had been properly located and the counter-battery efforts had been too weak to have any credible effect along much of the northern and central sectors assaulted. Of course some German guns were put out of action, but not enough, and time after time the surviving gun teams took their revenge by liberally plastering the British front trenches and No Man's Land with shells.

In the face of this the British infantry tactics were far too simplistic to offer any hope of progress in the face of the withering German artillery and machine-gun fire. Their commanders had generally restricted them to a plodding, slow march in long lines to attack in successive waves with each adding to the weight of the push until an objective was finally secured. But what if the waves were slaughtered before they could exert any meaningful pressure on the German line? Then each successive wave was simply marching forward to their deaths. Perhaps more effort could have been made to 'rush' across No Man's Land, using small squads of lightly equipped troops to try and seize the entrance of the German dugouts before the Germans themselves could emerge from their warrens. But such tactical sophistications had been explicitly ruled out as it was feared the raw, young troops simply did not have the training to cope with such complexities. In the final analysis the real problem was the British disease – hubristic optimism based on over-confidence. They assumed that everything would be all right; that the German defences would be comprehensively flattened; that the German troops would not have the guts to stand up to such an ordeal; that the German artillery would be dealt with. British pluck would, after all, overcome any obstacle – wouldn't it?

Where the success came in the southern sector around Mametz and Montauban, it came because the British and French artillery had managed to break down the resistance of the German artillery and comprehensively demolish the German front line. It also obviously helped if the British front line was close to the German front line – in other words that the gap to be crossed before the Germans emerged from whatever remained of their dugouts was reduced to the point that the British could win the race. It was once again confirmed that artillery was the key to success on the Western Front. Yet to attack on a wide front made the sheer quantities of guns, howitzers and shells needed almost incalculable. Along most of the 20-mile front the British had got nowhere near the phenomenal concentration and domination required to give themselves a chance – so they failed. In the southern sector they had achieved artillery domination – so they succeeded. Such a mechanistic interpretation does much to undermine the old lie of the superiority of pluck or élan or the offensive spirit – however one chooses to put it this belief was exposed as nothing more than an invitation to an early grave.

In the aftermath of such a disaster the sheer weight of human death and suffering was overwhelming. As men moved forward across the battlefields they were appalled at the signs of slaughter that surrounded them.

We literally couldn't walk along the trenches without unfortunately treading on dead bodies: German and British. The stench and the flies on those hot summer days were simply appalling. That was one of my most miserable memories of the Somme. It was pathetic really. I remember particularly a sergeant. He was lying on the ground, dead, and he had his hand on his open bible. I knew it was a Douai bible and from that I knew he was a Catholic. I took his address from that bible, the shrapnel pouring over our heads, it didn't matter. I closed his eyes and closed the bible, put that in my pocket and then we crawled back. I sent that bible to his widow. But we had not to mind – eventually one just got over it, thought nothing of it. Dead bodies all over the place, we couldn't help it – we were alive and that's what mattered. And being alive we jolly well had to get on with it and that's exactly what we did.[3]

Second Lieutenant Montague Cleeve, 36th Siege Artillery Battery, Royal Garrison Artillery

Over the next few days one of the absolute priorities was to try to help those who still clung to life but were too far gone to make their own way back. They lay where they had fallen, unable to move and suffering untold agonies of thirst and hunger with only the pain of their wounds to distract them. Where the attack had made some progress this was relatively easy; but where the failure had been all-embracing it meant trying to get the wounded back from No Man's Land. In front of Gommecourt, once the dust of the fighting had settled, the Germans made an unusually generous gesture to their defeated opponents. In a sense its very magnanimity underlined the completeness of the defeat suffered the previous day by the British.

A figure was observed standing up in the German trenches making friendly signals, which turned out to be an appeal for a truce. Eventually this was agreed to and both sides went out to collect their wounded. The Germans were very particular who went out, and fired at and wounded some men who started out still carrying rifles. Both sides then proceeded to collect their wounded. There were many Germans who had been taken prisoners and sent back, but got wounded or killed crossing No Man's Land. The Higher Command had been rung up and asked to suspend all artillery fire, but unfortunately after a short cessation, whether through necessity or ignorance of the situation, the guns started firing again. The Germans thereupon intimated that they would give our men ten minutes to get back, when the truce would come to an end. Owing to this it was feared that many who might have been saved were missed.[4]

Captain Reginald Lindsey-Renton, 1/9th Battalion (Queen Victoria's Rifles), London Regiment, 169th Brigade, 56th Division

Men were scattered all about the battlefield, many had hidden themselves fearing the Germans, and as their strength ebbed away it was a matter of luck whether they would be found in time by British soldiers.

Breakfast time came and as chaps of 8 Platoon were eating they heard a movement in a small dugout nearby. When they looked they found a young Irish soldier terribly injured, for his stomach had been ripped right down the middle and all his intestines were lying on top of his body. Our doctor was fetched and he couldn't do much, this was a case for the surgeons. The doctor said that if he could soon be got to hospital for treatment he stood a good chance of recovering from the terrible injuries. Volunteers were soon available for the chaps had forgotten about breakfast now. When a stretcher was brought he was laid tenderly on it and carried so carefully by fellows who tried their best to get him to the rear and hospital.[5]

Signaller Sidney Kemp, 6th Battalion, Royal West Kent Regiment, 37th Brigade, 12th Division

Even the unwounded presented a harrowing sight by the time they finally emerged from their ordeal in the line. The first surprise to men left out of the line was how few there were left. Sergeant Stewart Jordan was sent up to a crossroads to guide back the London Scottish as they came out of the line from Gommecourt.

I heard marching feet and after a bit in the dark I could see that they were wearing kilts and guessed that that was our regiment. When I could distinguish them I noticed about 120 men I suppose and the adjutant was leading them. So I said to him, 'Which company is this please?' 'Company!' he said, 'This is the regiment!' About 800 men went over and about 100 came back.[6]

Sergeant Stewart Jordan, 1/14th Battalion (London Scottish), London Regiment, 168th Brigade, 56th Division

Exposure to the realities of war in the twentieth century could wreak havoc with the appearance of men who they had seen march forward with such high hopes of military glory just a couple of days before.

> What a sight this small band presented when we met them: weary, haggard and drawn faces, bodies exhausted and legs that almost could not carry their burden, but their thoughts were too tragic for words. All had lost many friends on that awful day and as I marched along with them, trying to cheer them on, I felt like a warder escorting a condemned prisoner. The band joined us, and as it played 'Keep the home fires burning till the boys come home', I nearly wept with impotence and sadness. For the first time I fully appreciated the horrors of war, the futility and madness of it all.[7]
>
> Lieutenant Edgar Lord, 15th Battalion, Lancashire Fusiliers, 96th Brigade, 32nd Division

Lieutenant Lord was increasingly concerned to trace the whereabouts of his friend, Lieutenant Ivan Doncaster, who was nowhere to be seen. After making enquiries the truth became apparent beyond reasonable doubt. Some of his men thought they had seen him hit in the wrist just 12 yards short of the German wire. He had then been reported hit a second time, this time in the head, while sitting in a shell hole trying to bind up his original wound. It seemed clear that he was dead. Lieutenant Lord was stunned but duty still called. And what a duty it was, as he and the other men left out of battle were repeatedly sent forward to scour the battlefield.

> A skeleton company was sent into the reserve trenches at Ovillers. Our work was to salvage as much equipment as we could: packs, rifles, bayonets, groundsheets, Lewis guns, ammunition, Very pistols, revolvers and suchlike were transported to a central dump to be sorted. Corpses lay everywhere and the stench from the decaying bodies was very unpleasant. A blackened hand protruding from the ground was gruesome to say the least. One night I was detailed with a dozen men to bury some of the dead near our new front line. As some of them had been doing this the day before, they were feeling sick and groggy, so I ordered them to dig holes in the ground and make wooden crosses, whilst I went with a Lewis gunner to handle the corpses. It was a ghastly job in the dark, feeling for their identity

> discs and effects, as most of them were bloated, having been killed some days earlier. We rolled them into adjacent shell holes covering them with earth and placing a cross at the head bearing their names. One man whom we handled had lost both feet and the hand wearing his identity disc had been so badly smashed that the disc was mixed with the putrefying flesh. After a vain attempt to recover it, we interred him as 'unknown'.[8]
>
> Lieutenant Edgar Lord, 15th Battalion, Lancashire Fusiliers, 96th Brigade, 32nd Division

The men that took the responsibility for the mass interments were the army chaplains and padres, who were attached to battalions with the aim of providing the men with spiritual comfort. Now they found themselves ministering to the dead. It was a grim task: identifying where possible the corpse and securing any personal effects to pass on to the family.

> The padre was confronted with the terrific task of burying the dead. It was the only certain way of compiling a correct casualty list. It was no one's job other than the padre to concern himself with burying the dead, unless specifically detailed for the job. Experience showed that in any battle large numbers were merely reported in the first place as 'missing', when in fact their dead bodies were later found on the battlefield. The discovery and identification of the body settled a man's fate beyond all question, and the sooner this was done after the action took place, the more accurate and complete the casualty list would be. It was worth almost any amount of labour to avoid reporting a man as 'missing' unnecessarily. A chaplain who was right on the spot could often seize the opportunity to bury his dead, or at least identify them, taking the red identity disc alone and leaving the green one for the burial party when it should arrive. It was unfortunate that well-meaning, but misinformed persons often removed both identity discs at the same time, without burial, a fact which explains how it was so many unidentified dead had afterwards to be buried.[9]
>
> Chaplain Ernest Crosse, 8th and 9th Battalions, Devonshire Regiment, 20th Brigade, 7th Division

Often they were dealing with men that they knew; men who had perhaps taken communion with them just days before. Chaplain Crosse went forward in the footsteps of the Devons on 1 July. The ground was still littered with corpses. Once they were identified he had to supervise their interment in a rough mass grave and then recite the hackneyed but still moving words of the burial service above the newly disturbed earth.

> All together we collected 163 Devons and covered them up in Mansell Copse. A colossal thunderstorm about 2 p.m. delayed us sorely. At 6 p.m., in the presence of the General, Foss, Milne and about sixty men, I read the funeral service and the 'Thanksgiving for Victory'. The working party was deadbeat and the task of filling in the trench was awfully slow. I got the Pioneer Sergeant to paint a board with red lead borrowed from the Royal Engineers to mark the cemetery. I put up the board
>
> | Cemetery of 163 Devons Killed July 1st 1916 |
> |---|
>
> I placed twelve crosses in two rows and after wiring in the area I rode back.[10]
>
> Chaplain Ernest Crosse, 8th and 9th Battalions, Devonshire Regiment, 20th Brigade, 7th Division

Amongst the bodies buried by Ernest Crosse were the mortal remains of Lieutenant Noel Hodgson who was buried close to where he had fallen in action. The earnest padre's God had indeed met Hodgson's resigned poetic wish: 'Help me to die, O Lord'. But the chaplain's job did not end with the interment of the corpses.

> Once the burial of the dead men was as far as possible completed, the chaplain could tackle the colossal task of writing to the homes of the men who had been killed. But this was such a huge business, that if he was to attempt it at all, some sort of circular letter was the only possible solutions. Even that was abundantly worthwhile, particularly if he was able to add that he had actually buried the man's body.[11]
>
> Chaplain Ernest Crosse, 8th and 9th Battalions, Devonshire Regiment, 20th Brigade, 7th Division

This was also a task undertaken by the regimental officers. Many of them were barely out of their teens and found it excruciatingly difficult to act as the harbingers of misery to the families of the missing and the dead.

> The next heart-breaking task was to write to the next-of-kin of those for whom we could not account. Those who know the difficulty of

sometimes writing an ordinary letter will get only a small idea of the reluctance to start such a job. One would wish to defer it forever, if it were not for the anxiety of their loved ones.[12]

Lieutenant Edgar Lord, 15th Battalion, Lancashire Fusiliers, 96th Brigade, 32nd Division

The letters had much in common. The stumbling phrases, the universal, unconvincing assurances of instantaneous death, which belied the more frequent reality of lonely, agonising deaths marooned between the lines, or life slowly draining away several days later in some anonymous field hospital. Two officers wrote to the grieving family of Captain Wilfred Nevill.

I hardly know how to begin to write this letter at all. It seems almost an impertinence to try to sympathise with you in such a dreadful loss, but I feel it my duty to tell you how your son met his death. He was in command of one of our leading companies in the attack on Montauban on the 1st of this month, and led his company most gallantly and with utmost coolness up to the German front line trench, where he was shot. Death must have been absolutely instantaneous.[13]

Lieutenant Colonel Alfred Irwin, 8th Battalion, East Surrey Regiment, 55th Brigade, 18th Division

Some found fluency and sought to reassure the deceased family of the popularity of the victim, how he would be missed but hastened to reassure them that his sacrifice, although cruel, was worthwhile in the greater scheme of things. Their son had died for his country and all that entailed.

With his brilliance as a soldier he was always my ideal hero as an officer and a gentleman, while as a personal friend it is now that I fully realise that I loved him as boys rarely love one another. It is only by the willing and noble sacrifice of our very best that our country can gradually restore peace and justice to the world. I only wish for your sake and for his country that I could have taken his place.[14]

Second Lieutenant Alan Jacobs, 8th Battalion, East Surrey Regiment, 55th Brigade, 18th Division

It is all too predictable that young Lieutenant Alan Jacobs would indeed die for his country just a month later in August 1916. Yet there is no reason to doubt the sincerity of such emotions. Many men retained a strong belief that there was a very real purpose to what they were doing and the sacrifices that were being made by so many of their friends and ultimately themselves. Not everyone despaired of the future; if they had, the offensive could hardly have continued. Discipline still held firm; men buried their friends, but fought on. A clear majority still believed that there was a real purpose to it all and still trusted their leaders to take them through the hard battles that lay ahead.

> It has been a very wonderful show, one I wouldn't have missed for anything, but it has also been rather terrible. It is still going on of course, in fact it has only just begun! But the centre of gravity has shifted away from us, temporarily at any rate, so you needn't be the least bit anxious about me. The French have had a great show – the Boche thought they were done in and concentrated all his reserves opposite us, so that when the attack took place, the French met with practically no opposition. They have got on splendidly since, and the very latest is that they have broken the Hun line, are through at Péronne and have let loose cavalry to prey on the Boche ammunition columns and supply trains – my word I wish we were down there, it must be a very great show. Everything now depends on the next few days – can we enlarge or keep open the gap, or will the Huns close it again! I want to fight out in the open. I hate this mole life underground, being ceaselessly hammered by heavy guns and never seeing your horses.[15]
>
> Captain Cuthbert Lawson, 369th Battery, 15th Brigade, Royal Horse Artillery, 29th Division

Yet such a response, mixing reason and still vaunting optimism was simply beyond the comprehension of those who had found their preconceptions ripped to shreds by the sheer scale of the catastrophe of 1 July. For them nothing could justify the suffering and death that surrounded them at every side.

> I shall soon be a pacifist and a conscientious objector – to modern warfare anyhow. It becomes more impossible every month, and the ghastly mangling of human beings *en masse* seems disproportionate to any conceivable object. 'A bloody mugs game', said a stretcher bearer.[16]
>
> Chaplain Francis Drinkwater, 139th Brigade, 46th Division

Unfortunately for them all, the Battle of the Somme had only just begun.

CHAPTER SIX

Creeping Forward

For all the pain, mental anguish and crippling losses there was never any going back: a renewed attack was utterly inevitable. The Battle of the Somme was the major Allied offensive of 1916; it was too important to be set aside or evaded because of dreadful casualties. Even if Haig had fully realised the depth and breadth of the losses suffered by his assaulting divisions on 1 July he could not have aborted the offensive without seriously jeopardising the *Entente Cordiale* with France and Russia. The armies of his Continental Allies had been slaughtered time and time again in the first two years of the war while Britain's new armies were given the time to slowly build in relative safety. They were unlikely to look on with any great sympathy if Britain tried to evade her share of the 'butcher's bill'. After all, the unrelenting German pressure on France at the slaughterhouse of Verdun had not miraculously diminished overnight; Germany was still strong. The Somme offensive had only just begun.

A major offensive cannot be held up at will for a detailed situational analysis. Speed is all important in warfare. Time not used by the attacker would inevitably be used profitably by the defender to stifle any forward momentum that might have been generated. The problem for Generals Sir Douglas Haig and Sir Henry Rawlinson was not as straightforward as might be imagined. At the end of the first day they had clearly gained ground in the south, but the tactically significant features still remained a considerable distance ahead of them, securely guarded by the German Second Line system. Furthermore, in the north the assault on the key Thiepval Spur and Pozières Ridge had utterly failed. Success here would have provided vital observation over large sectors of the German defensive system and thus destabilised the whole German line in the Somme sector.

Succinctly put, the British had failed where it mattered and succeeded where it was all but tactically irrelevant. This left a quandary to which there was no simple answer. If the attack was renewed in the south with the intention of capitalising on success, then they would be evading the essence of the tactical conundrum – Thiepval and Pozières would have to be captured before there could be a rapid advance. Yet the sheer scale of the losses already suffered in the attacks there called to mind the wisdom of hitting your head against a brick wall as a means of progress.

At first, Rawlinson was inclined to grasp the bull by the metaphorical horns and batter down the continued resistance to the north before turning to exploit the success gained in the south.

> A large part of the German reserve have now been drawn in and it is essential to keep up the pressure and wear out the defence. It is also necessary to secure, as early as possible, all important tactical points still in the possession of the Germans in their front line system and intermediate line, with a view to an ultimate attack on the German Second Line.[1]
>
> Lieutenant General Sir Henry Rawlinson, Headquarters, Fourth Army

In other words he felt the VIII, X and III Corps would have to 'catch up' by taking their original objectives along the Thiepval Spur and Pozières Ridge *before* the next real assault designed to penetrate the German Second Line all along the original front. This approach can easily be caricatured – 'if at first you don't succeed' – but Rawlinson was responding to the flawed reports of the situation on the ground. After all, he still had large numbers of reserves that had not been committed to the battle.

Haig took an alternative tactical approach. He wanted to push ahead in the south alongside the French, to build on success already achieved. However, this infuriated the French when Haig expressed his intentions at a meeting with General Joffre on 3 July. The natural French propensity for continuously monitoring the performance of 'perfidious Albion' for signs of backsliding and lack of resolve can clearly discerned in his testy reaction.

> Joffre began by pointing out the importance of our getting Thiepval hill. To this I said that in view of the progress made on my right, near Montauban, and the demoralised nature of the enemy's troops in that

> area, I was considering the desirability of pressing my attack on Longueval. I was therefore anxious to know whether in that event the French would attack Guillemont. At this, General Joffre exploded in a fit of rage. He could not approve of it. He ordered me to attack Thiepval and Pozières. If I attacked Longueval, I would be beaten, etc., etc. I waited calmly till he had finished. His breast heaved and his face flushed! The truth is the poor man cannot argue, nor can he easily read a map. When Joffre got out of breath, I quietly explained what my position is as regards him as the 'generalissimo'. I am *solely* responsible (to the British Government) for the action of the British Army; and I had approved the plan, and must modify it to suit the changing situation as the fight progresses. I was most polite. Joffre saw he had made a mistake, and next tried to cajole me. He said that this was the English Battle, and France expected great things from me. I thanked him but said I had only one object *viz* to beat Germany. France and England marched together, and it would give me equal pleasure to see the French troops exploiting victory as my own![2]
>
> General Sir Douglas Haig, General Headquarters, British Expeditionary Force

Joffre considered that the tactical imperative of capturing the Thiepval Spur and Pozières Ridge entirely outweighed the likely price in heavy British casualties. He was very wary of the true British motives in switching the balance of the attack to the south. He feared the French Army might once again end up bearing the brunt of the fighting, thus at a stroke negating any alleviation that the Somme might hope to give them from the crippling pressure they were enduring at Verdun. The end result of the deliberations of the British High Command was fairly predictable in that Haig simply overruled Rawlinson and braved Joffre's wrath. He would accept strategic control from Joffre in the joint Allied cause but certainly would not accept tactical interference on the ground.

They would attack in the south with the intention of securing a position from which the next main thrust would crash through the German Second Line which stretched along the Longueval to Bazentin le Petit Ridge. In addition, there would be a diversionary attack at Thiepval on 3 July as part of an overall aggressive posture north of the Albert–Bapaume road – this would hopefully deflect German attention away from the real targets to be assaulted when Rawlinson was ready. It would take a considerable time to get ready for the next stage of the attack complicated as it was by the need to secure the cooperation of the French: Rawlinson was unwilling to push any further on his southern XIII Corps front towards Longueval and Trônes Wood without a simultaneous French advance as that would form a dangerously exposed salient.

While the great men pondered their next move, down on the ground, 2 July was largely a day of consolidation as the British sought both to complete the capture of the few objectives almost within their grasp, and to secure their meagre gains from the threat of German counter-attacks. Clearly the best chance to move forward without undue trouble was at Fricourt where the German garrison had been placed in an almost insupportable position by the advances pressing in on them from both north and south. Indeed, in the event, the Germans had more sense than to stay put and evacuated during the night. Yet despite reports from patrols that they had found the village clear of Germans, there was still considerable confusion before the village was actually occupied. The Royal Engineers claimed that it was one of their more adventurous officers who finally resolved the situation as the artillery began a somewhat futile barrage of the empty village.

> After all the 'pushes' he was the first to race up to the line to see what was happening, and used to walk up and down the parados, encouraging the men, when it seemed absolute death. The Major had the luck of kings not to have been wounded hundreds of times. After repeated attacks had failed to capture Fricourt and whilst a bombardment of the village previous to another attack was taking place, the Major got out of our front-line trench and waved his hat. Finding no one shot at him, he walked across, in the open, to a point 200 yards in front of Fricourt Farm, an enemy strong point. Finding no one shot here again on waving his hat, he returned to our line and sent this message to Divisional Headquarters, 'Our artillery barrage is only stopping our infantry entering Fricourt!' This report was considered and patrols pushed out, who took the village.[3]
>
> Captain A. C. Sparkes, 97th Field Company, Royal Engineers, 21st Division

Alongside them, the 91st Brigade were charged with advancing to the White Trench and thereby completing the capture of their intended objectives from the previous day. This was easier said than done and Lieutenant

Colonel Frank Maxwell VC, commanding the 12th Middlesex, watched such tentative proceedings with some bemusement. As an experienced veteran he was disturbed at the amateurism of much of what he saw and resolved to assist as best he could.

> I am vain enough to think I helped 'em to succeed at long last by carrying a wire and observing the battle, sending back information to our generals who passed it along to the general concerned. It was a most curious position to be in, actually watching an action from a flank, I was more or less behind the Germans and could see almost from behind. Of course if we could have got artillery up – and I think we could have – we should have boiled the Germans and helped our people out in no time. But we didn't and all I could do was to help with four Vickers guns and my telephone. It was rather a pitiful sight to see our people getting knocked over, hung up, retiring and going forward again. All seemed so unnecessary and badly worked. They only had very inexperienced forward observation officers who knew about as much about fighting as a violet. So I took them in charge and ordered them to send back targets to their people. At length we got things right and the artillery on to a place full of machine guns. It was plastered by the guns for twenty minutes – it did the trick and the whole crowd surrendered – something like 700–800 or so.[4]
>
> Lieutenant Colonel Frank Maxwell VC, 12th Battalion, Middlesex Regiment, 54th Brigade, 18th Division

The end result of these actions was that White Trench was successfully overrun, a link was firmly established beyond Fricourt with the neighbouring 21st Division and the whole line safely consolidated before nightfall.

Further north at La Boisselle the 19th Division had moved forward to augment the generally shattered 34th Division. After considerable delays caused by the general chaos, an attack was ordered to push forward from the captured Schwaben Höhe into La Boisselle itself. After an imaginative artillery ruse had deflected most of the German batteries' attention on to a possible assault on Ovillers, they did better than many must have expected, moving forward under the cover of a solid artillery barrage and managed to fight their way into La Boisselle. The staff officer Captain D. H. James was acting as a liaison officer between the 34th and 19th Divisions.

I went with a colonel of the Cheshire Regiment to explore La Boisselle. On the way, we discovered that the tunnel (Kerriemuir) was choked with dead and wounded. We straightened that out and went across No Man's Land. When we got to the village, about 12.30 p.m., we found an officer and a few men in possession of the left flank – skirting Mash Valley. I took over, and the Colonel went back to bring up reinforcements. The Hun started a bombing attack so I counter-attacked shortly after 1p.m., drove him back until my party was blotted out by shrapnel and I was sent to earth myself. Later on I crawled back out of their bombing range, found I could still walk – I had bullets in my back and right lung, but did not know that – so I decided to hobble back to Divisional Headquarters and report to General Williams. I staggered into my tent, near the mill, and my orderly helped me to change my shirt and tunic, then I saw the General. He gave me some tea, sent for General Kirby, and we had a talk about La Boisselle. By then I was very tired, and all-in. Colonel Parkin helped me across to the field hospital in the mill, where they dressed my wounds.[5]

Captain D. H. James, Headquarters, 34th Division

The position was eventually consolidated after a thorough search to eradicate the Germans still lurking in the linked cellars and strong points hidden below the scattered rubble. A line was eventually established just short of the church in the middle of the village. Bloody, murderously inconsequential, fighting would continue there for several more days.

Meanwhile in the south the process of consolidation and simultaneous preparation for the next phase in the offensive was being carried out all around Montauban. The Scottish territorials of the 9th Division had taken over Montauban from the triumphant Mancunians of 30th Division who had captured it on 1 July. To their immense gratification, in addition to the newly consolidated trenches, they received some intelligence of great practical value.

The Manchesters, before leaving, told us the brick kilns were a vast storehouse of special supplies. Suspected of being booby trapped, they had been ordered not to explore the area until the Royal Engineers had given it a clean bill of health. But a few bold spirits had inspected the labyrinth of storerooms, bringing back canned whole hams of

> delectable mouth watering tenderness, also brandy, chocolate, cigars etc., the Germans obviously building up for their usual generous Christmas handout to troops. Appreciating it was only a matter of time before the 'Boffins' heard about this Aladdin's cave, when the Manchesters reached their rest billets, we hastily dug shallow holes, filling them with the choicest items, then we shaped the mounds like rough graves, complete with wooden crosses inscribed, 'Here lies a German Soldier'. Lies being the cogent word I suppose. As the days passed in preparation for our attack on the fortress village of Longueval across the valley on the hilltop, we revelled in a kind of gastronomic euphoria and it was now evident that the Manchesters had kept the secret and no one was coming to investigate.[6]
>
> Private Barney Downes, 9th Battalion (Scottish Rifles), Cameronians, 27th Brigade, 9th Division

One great boon was that on 3 July patrols discovered that Bernafay Wood had been abandoned by the Germans and that night it was occupied by the 9th Division. In a similar fashion the 18th Division painlessly occupied Caterpillar Wood on 4 July. Yet although the Germans were obviously staggering in this sector, their Second Line system still remained intact. The British field artillery would have to be moved well forward if they were to be able to have the range to deluge these new targets with shells. This was a time consuming and difficult process as all the guns would have to be re-registered on their likely targets from the new observation posts.

The artillery officers were keen to see for themselves at close quarters the effect of their shell fire on the targets in the German lines. By this time Montauban was no longer recognisable as the pleasant village it had once been before total war came to the Somme. Concentrated artillery fire had smashed everything down, rending brick from brick, splintering, powdering and cratering. And, of course, it was not just the British shells that had caused the damage. Since 1 July the village had been targeted relentlessly by the German guns.

> I was appalled by the sight of what artillery fire can do to a place. Nothing of what I had ever seen or even imagined comes near to the destruction which has been wrought here. Many thousands of big shells have been fired into this place by us, and since we took it the

> Boche has never ceased to pound it with 5.9s. It now represents a mass of huge shell craters and some heaps of bricks, among which, every now and then, more unpleasant sights come in view. Along the north edge of the ruins, the Royal Scots had now scratched a sort of trench in which at the time I was there, they all slept – all deadbeat. Picking my way along this trench, I could not tell which were men sleeping and which dead men, both were lying side by side. I found a spot out of which one could get a good view of Longueval and Bazentin, and then went back and got a wire laid out to this spot.[7]
>
> Lieutenant William Bloor, C Battery, 149th Brigade, Royal Field Artillery, 30th Division

The work of the guns remained of paramount importance, the next set of targets had to be identified, registered and destroyed. There was no room for sentiment.

3 July 1916

WHILE THE ARTILLERY prepared for the next great leap forward in the south, it was considered crucial to try and pin the Germans in the more northerly sectors – to keep the German attention firmly fixed on the Pozières Ridge and away from where the next assault would actually be made. To this end early on the morning of 3 July, it was planned to make twin diversionary thrusts on Ovillers and Thiepval. These were to be carried out by the 12th and 32nd Divisions who had fallen under the command of General Gough and his newly constituted Reserve Army. Unfortunately, like many diversionary actions, these were to prove excessively grim and sanguinary affairs. As the men of the 12th Division awaited the attack, they had few illusions as to what lay before them. Amongst them were two brothers.

> Fred and I talked together for a few minutes. We then shook hands and wished each other good luck tomorrow. Much has been written about men saying goodbye to each other before going into battle, but we were brothers and the only sons of our parents and looking at what had happened to the 8th Division our chances of survival looked slender. He told me that the parents of Captain Matthews had sent him out a bulletproof waistcoat, but he didn't intend wearing it when

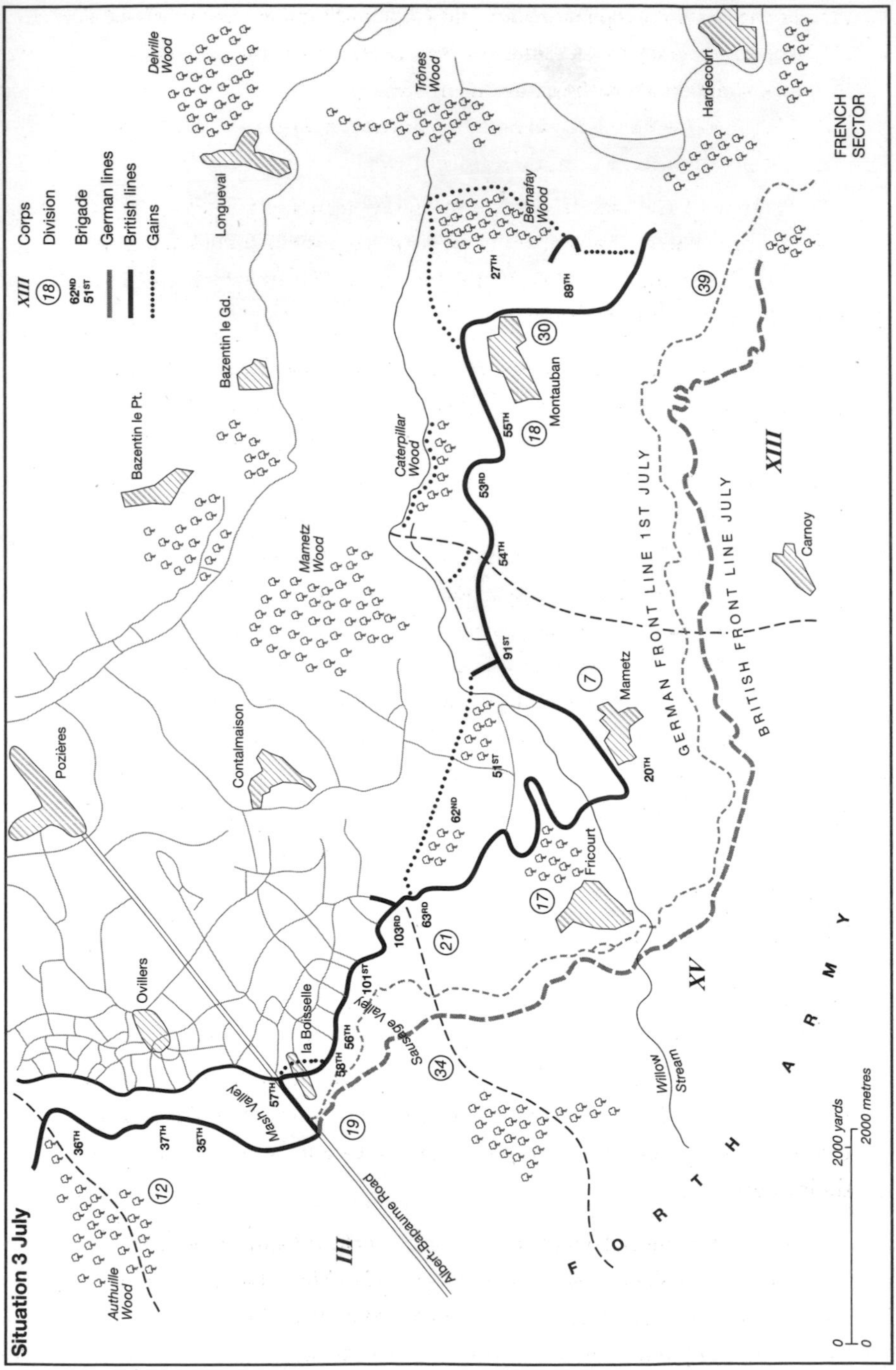

Situation 3 July
XIII Corps
18 Division
62ND 51ST Brigade
German lines
British lines
Gains
Delville Wood
Longueval
Trônes Wood
Hardecourt
FRENCH SECTOR
Bernafay Wood
Bazentin le Gd.
Bazentin le Pt.
Montauban
Caterpillar Wood
Mametz Wood
GERMAN FRONT LINE 1ST JULY
BRITISH FRONT LINE JULY
Carnoy
Pozières
Contalmaison
Mametz
Fricourt
Ovillers
la Boisselle
Mash Valley
Sausage Valley
Albert-Bapaume Road
Authuille Wood
Willow Stream
FOURTH ARMY
III
XV
XIII
36TH
37TH
35TH
57TH
58TH
56TH
101ST
103RD
63RD
62ND
51ST
20TH
91ST
54TH
53RD
55TH
27TH
89TH
12
19
34
21
17
7
18
30
39
0
2000 yards
2000 metres

we went over the top in the morning. Captain Matthews had told Fred that he was going to die tomorrow, waistcoat or no waistcoat, so why wear chain mail, which was an encumbrance.[8]

Signaller Sidney Kemp, 6th Battalion, Royal West Kent Regiment, 37th Brigade, 12th Division

The attitude of the men in the 'jumping off' trenches was understandably sombre. The veterans of previous battles who had already had some experience of going over the top affected a pragmatic calm that amazed newcomers from recent drafts.

Jack Webb, and I, and a new chap whose name I didn't know, who had only recently joined us from a big draft of chaps, were to be B Company's signallers, with me in charge. Being old soldiers, now, Jack Webb and I found a dugout, we lit candles, got out our next day's rations, ate the lot and washed it down with water, feeling that at least if we were to die the rats wouldn't get our grub. Our poor mate was petrified with fear and there was nothing we could do to help him. Well we had a smoke or two, talked about anything except what was happening later on today and the time went. Afterwards we met another new chap who told us that while Jack Webb and I were eating and talking, he was lying petrified on his stomach on the bottom of the trench outside, too frightened to move, yet able to listen to our conversation and he thought us marvellous. We told him we had just got used to that sort of thing and that was the truth. You can get used to almost anything if you try.[9]

Signaller Sidney Kemp, 6th Battalion, Royal West Kent Regiment, 37th Brigade, 12th Division

Their fatalism would be tested to the limits of human tolerance. The artillery bombardment began at 0215 and after an hour they attacked Ovillers at 0315. The German front line was initially only lightly held, but when the West Kents moved forward the machine-gun fire gradually increased in density as the German garrison emerged from their dugouts.

We signallers moved out of the dugout just before 3 a.m. We found that part of B Company was already out in No Man's Land. We got up over the parapet and went towards the German lines. I went over to the German trench and there wasn't anyone else about and it wasn't yet quite light. I went back a bit looking for Webb and the other signaller, when suddenly the German machine guns went into action. I was suddenly standing alone out in No Man's Land, with everyone else either killed, wounded or the few that were left, down on the ground, I could feel the bullets going past me and yet I didn't get hit by any. I then got down on the ground still having my telephone and my rifle. I saw Captain Harris get up as he was going to advance again and he toppled over dead. I crawled to where Webb was and together we crawled nearer to the German trench and there we stayed with a few of D Company who hadn't gone over into the second line of German trenches with Captain Matthews. He was killed, as well as Captain Barnett of A Company and the captains of both the other companies. When daylight really broke, there we were, Webb and I and those few chaps from D Company, tucked up right under the German trench, against the wire. I was lying on the outside, trying with Webb's help to grub a bit of soil from under me, when suddenly a German sniper saw me moving and aimed two shots: one behind and the other at my head. They hit my tin hat a bit too high up and glanced off into the air. I lay still and let him think he had killed me. On my left lay a chap badly wounded, who begged me to help him. I told him I couldn't save myself and said be quiet! But being in pain, he continued to move about and was soon killed by a sniper's bullet. We stayed under that German trench all that day and wasn't it a long hot day too? The sun blazed down and yet we couldn't move off.[10]

Signaller Sidney Kemp, 6th Battalion, Royal West Kent Regiment, 37th Brigade, 12th Division

The horror and desperation of their situation needs no false emphasis. Marooned under the very noses of the Germans they had no alternative but to endure or die. Kemp lay out there all that long summer's day until at last the light began to fade.

We whispered that as soon as it got dark enough, we would make a dash for our lines. Suddenly from about 15 yards from where we were a chap who was lying facing the German lines got up in a kneeling position and put his rifle up to his shoulder and fired over me. I looked round and just behind me was a German soldier coming through their wire, but our chap had toppled him. We then got up and bolted, as we

> thought, towards our lines. Instead we ran parallel with the German line. When we came to a deep shell hole we got into it. There was a sergeant from D Company with us and he said it was our wire. I told him, 'It's German wire and if you wait as soon as some more Very lights of ours go up, I will take you to our lines!' I did this but not before the chap who shot the German was himself shot when he got tangled on our barbed wire.[11]
>
> Signaller Sidney Kemp, 6th Battalion, Royal West Kent Regiment, 37th Brigade, 12th Division

Very few men of the five battalions that had attacked Ovillers that morning managed to return to the British lines unscathed. Kemp was fortunate, but his brother was wounded and had to be evacuated to hospital. Many of the others had been shot to bits. The cost of failure came to nearly 2,400 officers and men.

If anything the attack made three hours later on Thiepval was an even worse disaster. The scale of this attack had been reduced due to the intervention of Haig and instead of the best part of three divisions just two brigades were to be sent into the fray. On the left was the 14th Brigade of the 32nd Division while on the right was the 75th Brigade, which had been attached specially for the attack from the 25th Division. It is fair to say that many of the officers of 75th Brigade were unhappy with the prospect of what lay before them.

> Colonel Cotton had done all he could to dissuade a damn fool brigadier not to attempt it; a damn fool to whom the vital decision had been left by the divisional commander. A brigadier who had never reconnoitred the ground nor read a map intelligently. A brigadier who had collapsed when almost the first shell fired in retaliation for our barrage landed outside his headquarters killing his staff captain and three of the four adjutants in his unfortunate brigade.[12]
>
> Second Lieutenant Sydney Stevenson-Jones, 2nd Battalion, South Lancashire Regiment, 75th Brigade, 25th Division

The frontage of attacks had been varied late in the day and on their way up into the line that night the 75th Brigade had been severely delayed, which caused a postponement for three hours. Unfortunately, most of the supporting artillery were not informed and hence fired off their barrage at 0315 as originally intended, leaving little ammunition for when it was needed. All the battle arrangements were utterly rushed and an atmosphere of utter chaos prevailed. Second Lieutenant Sydney Stevenson-Jones was with the reserve company of the 2nd South Lancashires when the attack went in at 0615 on the morning of 3 July.

> Word came down to 'stand to' for the attack. I grabbed my equipment and had hardly got it on when the order came along to: 'File out for the charge!' and our guns ceased firing. We, that is, B Company, rushed up the communication trench only to find it hopelessly blocked by a company of another battalion coming down. By then there wasn't more than a handful of D Company left, who had gone over first on our right. I just saw Captain Bill Gates lead the head of A Company out under a withering machine-gun and rifle fire and the fag end of C going out on our left dropping like rabbits. We shunted again to let another company pass and I came up again to see Gates rally the last of A for another rush. Captain Charles Rathbone told me to keep in touch and come back and report to him. I saw nothing but bravery on all sides that day. I saw Captain Alexander Blair lead out his company with a cane in his hand as on parade, still lead on when almost alone. I saw big Lieutenant Eric Fletcher, his senior subaltern walk on alone right up to the German wire (which was totally uncut, in spite of what we had been told) empty his long-nosed Colt into the Germans standing on their parapet firing at him, but they could not bring him down, until one got him and he fell across the wire and hung there all day, the Colt swinging from the lanyard buttoned under his shoulder strap. I saw big Company Sergeant Major Collins, all 6 feet 3 inches of him walk out under fire and pick up the slightly wounded Second Lieutenant Poundall and carry him in. Idiotic – but very brave. Poundall was far better on the ground than being carried shoulder high. I had been watching from a sap that ran forward out into No Man's Land so I kept pace with Gates down it on the left flank of his company. I must have nearly reached the end of it when I decided to go back and report, there were so few up. I turned and out of the tail of my eye saw a heavy HE explode which blotted out everything where Bill was and I was sent flying. Dazed for a moment, I opened my eyes to stare into the eyes of a face on the same level as my own. I tried to move my legs and arms, they all

> worked well enough but the left arm was stiff and hurt. The face asked me if I was all right and an arm tried to drag me down into the Vickers gun emplacement below ground which I hadn't noticed as I passed going out. I told the face I mustn't, I must go back and report. My friend the machine gunner gave me a drink of water. I thanked him, scrambled up and pushed off to report to Charles Rathbone. My cross belt fell off, a piece of case from the shell that killed Bill had sliced through to the bone of my left shoulder blade, a neat cut two inches long and that was the first time I knew I was hit.[13]
>
> Second Lieutenant Sydney Stevenson-Jones, 2nd Battalion, South Lancashire Regiment, 75th Brigade, 25th Division

The attacking companies had been slaughtered by a lethal combination of enfilading machine guns and heavy shell fire. When Stevenson-Jones reported back to Captain Charles Rathbone he was immediately sent off to contact the neighbouring Border Regiment.

> Followed only by my orderly, Golding, I set off down a long straight trench entirely empty till I came to a place where a young officer had mounted his Vickers gun on the top of the high parapet and was blazing away at something, his gun boiling with a tell-tale cloud of steam. On and on till I came to the end of the trench and there was still no Border Regiment. Just shell holes and fragments of trench now, but on we went, running and dodging from shell hole to shell hole, we seem to be fired at from all around, could we be in No Man's Land now – or what? I stopped, looked around, but I was alone. I waited but Golding never came on, had he been hit? I must get back if I can, retrace my steps, find him, report to Charles Rathbone, there is no one here, and we couldn't bring the company here if there was. A maze of shell holes, I tried to keep the general direction as best I could, but I never saw Golding again. A lad I was fond of – he would never have gone back without telling me, I heard afterwards he was killed. I came to the place where the young machine-gun officer had mounted his gun on the top of the too high parapet. The gun was askew, pointing skywards, still steaming, the young subaltern spread-eagled head downwards, shot through the centre of the forehead, his eyelids just fluttering. When I got to Charles a shell had just landed almost plumb on top of him. He was on the floor, very badly

> wounded, with his company sergeant major alongside him, and various others dead and wounded all around. So far as I knew, I was then the only officer left. I couldn't go back to get my wound dressed.[14]
>
> Second Lieutenant Sydney Stevenson-Jones, 2nd Battalion, South Lancashire Regiment, 75th Brigade, 25th Division

Afterwards Stevenson-Jones was required to report on why the attack had failed and why he had not renewed the attack in the absence of Colonel Cotton, who had by that time been called to assist in sorting out the chaos by then existing at the 75th Brigade Headquarters. His report was short and to the point.

> Your report is called for by the divisional general and will go direct to him. Two questions. Two answers. In pencil, on one page of the Field Message Book. 'The attack failed because too few men can get across No Man's Land, which is under direct observation from high ground behind Serre and Beaumont Hamel and swept by shrapnel and machine-gun fire from behind the enemy front. Thiepval will never be taken by frontal attack. *A glance at the map will suffice.*'[15]
>
> Second Lieutenant Sydney Stevenson-Jones, 2nd Battalion, South Lancashire Regiment, 75th Brigade, 25th Division

At the end of the day, the 2nd South Lancashires had suffered the loss of some 14 officers and over 300 men in the abortive attack. Second Lieutenant Sydney Stevenson-Jones always believed that he was the direct cause of the dismissal of the brigadier the following day. Whatever the truth of the matter, Brigadier General N. F. Jenkins certainly was dismissed, although in fairness he had a variety of excuses for what appeared to his junior subordinates as gross incompetence. The delays at the start had been beyond his control and he had been forced to ask for the fatal postponement. Not all the charges laid by the querulous Stevenson-Jones can be easily dismissed, but the origins of the failure certainly lay with officers far more senior than the hapless brigadier. The actions at Ovillers and Thiepval had been small scale, on narrow fronts, launched in isolation at differing times and with inadequate preparation. The resulting failure was inevitable and it is difficult to believe that the attacks were in any way seriously effective as a diversion. Such piecemeal assaults could be swatted away without any necessity for the German command to divert extra defensive resources to the area.

Piecemeal Attacks: *7–13 July 1916*

THE NEXT PHASE of the offensive was a series of attacks launched on 7 July by the X, III and XV Corps on Ovillers, Contalmaison and Mametz Wood. These were essentially local affairs designed to maintain the pressure on the Germans and to improve the local tactical position prior to the next concerted big effort to break through the German Second Line in the sector between Bazentin le Petit and Longueval. Yet although the attacks were localised in their nature Haig was much concerned to impress on Rawlinson and his corps commanders the vital importance of securing these objectives.

Unfortunately, it is apparent that whatever the intentions of Haig and Rawlinson they soon lost control of events. Once the responsibility had been devolved down to the corps and divisional commanders each went their own way in planning the actions in the area for which they were responsible. The plans prepared show clearly that each was planned in isolation with all that entailed. The outlook was made worse by an untimely break in the summer weather. Thunderous rain showers did not improve the ground conditions and naturally made movement more difficult for the teeming thousands of Haig's army.

In the more northern sector occupied by the X Corps, the 12th Division were charged with making yet another attempt on capturing Ovillers. This time the 74th Brigade of the 25th Division was temporarily attached to them for the attack. They were ordered to go over the top at 0800, with the thankless task of pushing up from the south, across the head of Mash Valley, while the 36th Brigade would attempt to drive straight across to Ovillers half an hour later at 0830.

> Our barrage, which had been heavy all night, became intense at 7 a.m., lasting till zero hour. The enemy reply was also very heavy and although this caused a few casualties in No. 1 Company we were not touched; most of the shells falling in the ground between the two companies, and in the very spot we had been asked to assemble in. All sorts of dirt was flying about now and we had to lie very low to avoid being hit. The rim of my hat was punctured, also a brick fell on it, which thoroughly put the wind up me, my heart was once again in my mouth, but this time I knew I had complete self control.[16]
>
> Lieutenant Lionel Ferguson, 13th Battalion, Cheshire Regiment, 74th Brigade, 25th Division

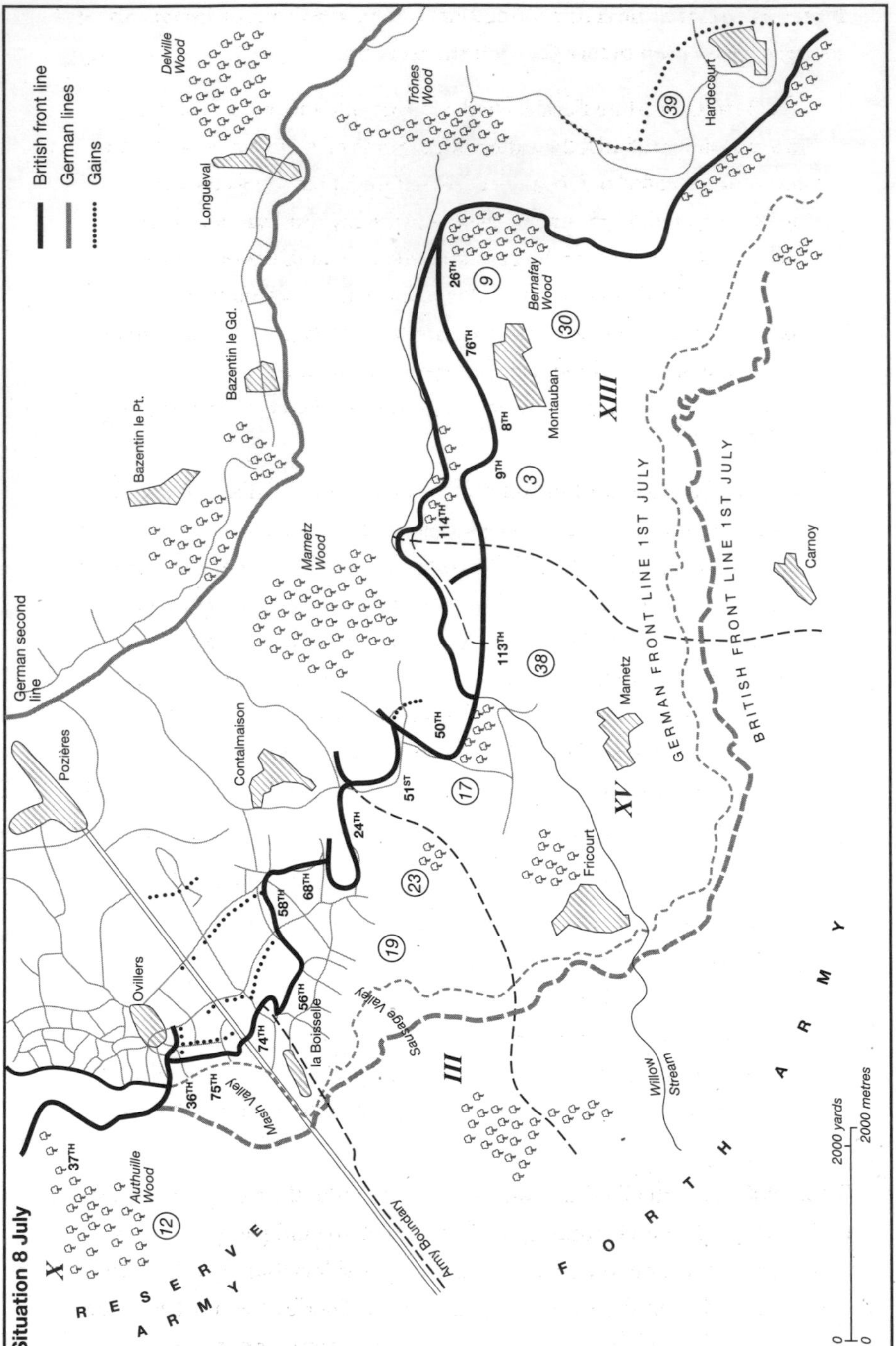
Situation 8 July
British front line
German lines
Gains
German second line
Pozières
Contalmaison
Ovillers
la Boisselle
Mash Valley
Sausage Valley
Authuille Wood
Bazentin le Pt.
Bazentin le Gd.
Longueval
Delville Wood
Trônes Wood
Mametz Wood
Bernafay Wood
Montauban
Hardecourt
Mametz
Fricourt
Carnoy
Willow Stream
Army Boundary
GERMAN FRONT LINE 1ST JULY
BRITISH FRONT LINE 1ST JULY
RESERVE ARMY
FOURTH ARMY
X
III
XV
XIII
37TH
36TH
75TH
74TH
56TH
58TH
68TH
24TH
51ST
50TH
113TH
114TH
9TH
8TH
76TH
26TH
12
19
23
17
38
3
30
9
39
2000 yards
2000 metres
0
0

It was as well that he had retained his self possession, for he was to be severely tested even before they left the trenches.

> The 11th Lancashire Fusiliers had come up into the position also, in order to support and follow afterwards. Some of them got 'windy' and one of them called out to get back. What might have looked nasty nearly occurred. I held one of them up with my revolver, refusing to let any past till I found out who gave the order, but at that moment the order came for them to return, when at once they took up their positions again. I was very pleased with No. 3 Company, for not a man moved out of his position lying up against the parapet.[17]
>
> Lieutenant Lionel Ferguson, 13th Battalion, Cheshire Regiment, 74th Brigade, 25th Division

Lieutenant Ferguson and his men were in a tactically difficult position. They were occupying a communication trench that ran between the former German first and second lines. They were to attack German positions in another communication trench some 250 yards away and then swing to the left to capture the Ovillers Post. As the Germans were defiantly still occupying sections of their front and second line the Cheshires would have to advance under fire from three sides. The Cheshires' officers felt sure that it would have been far better to bomb their way along the German trenches rather than launch themselves across this deadly expanse of open ground. Orders, however, were orders.

> I had a few old hands round me, as I was taking a platoon over and they kept me cheery. One man in particular was fine, keeping us all laughing by his wit. We gave out a good rum ration at 7.30 a.m. and it did us a power of good. The waiting to go over is most unnerving work. I kept calling out the time, 'Five, four, three, two, one more minute to go. Over the top and the best of luck!' [18]
>
> Lieutenant Lionel Ferguson, 13th Battalion, Cheshire Regiment, 74th Brigade, 25th Division

So at 0800 the 13th Cheshires went over the top into their very own 'Valley of Death' with the German guns blazing all around them. They were supposed to have been covered by a heavy artillery barrage, including smoke shells but in the event the barrage was feeble; the smoke screen nonexistent. Both merely drew attention to the imminent attack.

The barrage lifted and we were up to our front line before we knew it, but here we got it hot. Stewart in charge of No. 1 Platoon was killed outright, the best officer in the battalion, I saw him a few moments later, quite dead, his lighted pipe still between his teeth. The Hun now could be seen all round. He had machine guns mounted on three sides of us, it seemed as if our barrage had been ineffective. From this point we were just mown down. My blood was up now, my fear had gone and I wanted to kill. I rushed on. Colonel Finch I saw in the middle of No Man's Land, trying to direct No. 1 Company who now seemed to have lost direction. It appeared that all their officers were hit. He called to me to get on and lead them to the enemy machine guns now doing so much havoc. I did my best and with Brown my batman, ran up forward. I felt a pain in my shoulder and found my arm was useless. I did not realise I was hit, but fell headlong into a shell hole, Brown following beginning to tie me up with a bandage. I remember telling him off and began to fire at the machine-gun crew, now not 30 yards away. Of course I never hit them, but I kept seeing them fall, and quite had the idea it was my work. I must say I admired them, for no sooner than the man who was working the gun was hit, than another took his place on that seat of death – in fact they seemed endless. At this point Brown was hit by a shrapnel ball in the cheek. It settled under his skin, giving him the appearance of having toothache. I had to tie him up and he informed me he was going back. Myself, I did not want to go, but he said I was badly hit and was losing a lot of blood – this I could not see as it was running down my back. I was beginning to feel weak also, so decided to try and get back. We started by running, but after two falls, I rested in a shell hole. Brown ran on, getting safely into our old front line, from which he beckoned for me to follow. I had 50 yards to go and the ground all round was being torn by bullets, so I had grave doubts about doing it. But beginning to feel faint, and not wishing to be left lying out, I started to roll from hole to hole, in time reaching the trench.[19]

Lieutenant Lionel Ferguson, 13th Battalion, Cheshire Regiment, 74th Brigade, 25th Division

Unsurprisingly, Ferguson now began to lose all semblance of control under the extraordinary stress of his situation.

> I was now rather excited and seeing a number of prisoners, all of which had put Red Cross armlets on, I started calling them nasty names, not realising that I was still carrying my revolver in my hand – but they did realise – they were putting their hands up and falling on their knees. The stretcher bearer who was putting on my bandage, unloaded my revolver, which gave them a bit more pluck.[20]
>
> Lieutenant Lionel Ferguson, 13th Battalion, Cheshire Regiment, 74th Brigade, 25th Division

As walking wounded, Ferguson and his batman, Private Brown, were expected to make their own way all the way back to the town of Albert. Brown had his work cut out as Ferguson was losing strength and with it his mind began to wander. He wandered across to the French 75-mm gun batteries determined to remonstrate over the number of shells falling short into the British front lines. He also tried to pass on his experiences to troops moving up into the lines; the stumbling incoherent officer must have bemused them. At last, the long-suffering Brown got him back to the dressing station.

> We entered a large hall filled with wounded. I saw Captain Dean getting a dressing put on and other friends lying dead or dying. The sight was so cruel that my nerve went and I fell down on the floor and started sobbing. I had had no sleep and little food for sixty hours, also was weak from loss of blood – so I had some excuse.[21]
>
> Lieutenant Lionel Ferguson, 13th Battalion, Cheshire Regiment, 74th Brigade, 25th Division

Eight of the Cheshires' officers had been killed and 243 NCOs and men were killed or wounded. Lieutenant Ferguson had escaped relatively lightly as the bullet through his left shoulder had not broken the bone.

The omens did not look good for the neighbouring attack on Ovillers, due to be launched by the men of the 36th Brigade just half an hour later at 0830. Three battalions were to go over the top: the 9th Royal Fusiliers, the 7th Royal Sussex and the 8th Royal Fusiliers.

> I was scared, I'd seen these bodies. Now's the time to show 'em what we're made of! But we were all very quiet, never spoke or said anything – just grin at one another. You knew you had a job to do and you were going to do it but you weren't so lively![22]
>
> Private Tom Bracey, 9th Battalion, Royal Fusiliers, 36th Brigade, 12th Division

They were to launch the attack from assembly trenches already dug in the middle of No Man's Land.

> The objective was 250 yards away. Every man had a sandbag with twenty Mills bombs in it, and each Mills bomb weighs 2 lbs, so that was 40 lbs of weight. We had two extra bandoliers of 50 rounds in addition to our 150 rounds in our pouches. Every alternate man had a shovel or pick. The bombardment started at 4.15 and at 8.15 we were to go over – a four hours' bombardment. As soon as the bombardment started the Germans' retaliation came and for four hours we had to sit there and take everything he slung at us. We lost 25 per cent of our men before we went over.[23]
>
> Sergeant Charles Quinnell, 9th Battalion, Royal Fusiliers, 36th Brigade, 12th Division

The guns splattered the British jumping-off trenches with a mixture of shrapnel and high explosive shells. Even before they went over the top battalions were decimated again and again in circumstances where they could do nothing meaningful to protect themselves or harm their enemies.

> We were badly shelled for about two hours before Zero by the guns that practically enfiladed the trench from the north, our left. We actually lost more men then, I think, than in getting across No Man's Land. Captain May, my company commander, got a shrapnel wound through his tin hat about fifteen minutes before we went over; although this was, I think, the wound which killed him, he kept on his feet and walked up and down the trench talking to the men till we attacked. He must have held out till Zero and then dropped.[24]
>
> Captain Henry Sadler, 7th Battalion, Royal Sussex Regiment, 36th Brigade, 12th Division

When they went over the top some of the Royal Sussex officers had impressed on their men that speed was of the absolute essence. Even though they were heavily laden they must get across No Man's Land as fast as possible – the only safety on offer lay within the German trenches.

> I myself went across like a scalded cat, and when I got to the German front line I had to wait for a moment for our guns to lift. As I was travelling light and the men were loaded with all sorts of junk, I got to the enemy line all alone. It was blown all to hell, but the dugouts were

obvious. There was not a soul in the trench and I realised I had got there before the Germans had come out of their burrows. I sat down facing the dugout doors and got all the Germans as they came up. They had no idea I was there even, the ground was so blown up and I was in a hole; they never knew what hit them.[25]

Captain Henry Sadler, 7th Battalion, Royal Sussex Regiment, 36th Brigade, 12th Division

Captain Sadler was lucky. Many of the waves of troops were caught in the open as the enfilading machine guns began their deadly chatter.

The first wave went over and as soon as they had gone I gave the orders to: 'Advance!' Up the ladders, over the top. When I got through our wire, the first wave were down, two machine guns played on them and they were absolutely wiped out. Everybody was either killed or wounded. We went through. We got halfway across and then the two machine guns found us. They traversed, they played on us like spraying with a hose. At the finish I was the only man standing, but I'm not one of those heroes who want to take the German Army on my own and so I went to earth, got down behind the lip of a big shell hole. I kept looking to see where these two machine guns were. I couldn't see them, but there was a German in the trench about 100 yards away, standing up on the parapet and flinging bombs, so I shot him. The machine-gun crew spotted me and they opened up. I ducked my head down and the dirt was just spraying down the back of my neck. 'You bastard!' I said. He thought he'd got me and he played his machine gun somewhere else. I put my head up again and back came the machine gun, down I had to go. I stopped down for about quarter of an hour. By this time the machine gun had stopped and I took a convulsive leap over into the shell hole and there were seven wounded men in there. Well, we bound one another up and there we stopped all day.[26]

Sergeant Charles Quinnell, 9th Battalion, Royal Fusiliers, 36th Brigade, 12th Division

Quinnell's men had paid a terrible penalty, but the company on their right were more fortunate and got through to their objective. In some ways it was a terrible lottery. Corporal Razzell of the 8th Royal Fusiliers had a chilling view of the deadly lash of the machine gun.

> I noticed that the first two lines were practically all down because there was terrific machine-gun fire coming from the Jerries. I came to a road which ran at a slight angle to our line of advance. I noticed that every man that attempted to cross the road went down. It was obvious to me that there was a fixed machine gun or guns firing down the road. I noticed how deadly it was, it was there in front of my eyes. A man would drop, hit in the lower limbs and in a few seconds he was cut to pieces. The machine gun is a cutting machine.[27]
>
> Corporal Arthur Razzell, 8th Battalion, Royal Fusiliers, 36th Brigade, 12th Division

Razzell moved along the slight drainage ditch that ran alongside the road. It did not provide much shelter, but it was far better than risking his life in a mad dash across the road.

> I scuttled along until I came to the German wire, which was intact, breast high and about 20 feet in depth. I dropped into a shell hole under the wire and I was immediately joined by another man. I hadn't chosen a very deep shell hole but he was of the opinion, same as mine, that this attack had failed. There we were under the wire, you couldn't possibly get back again in daylight and in July it was a long time till darkness. The Germans knew we were there because they began throwing their potato-masher bombs, but we were just out of range. We could feel the concussion when they exploded, but provided we kept below they did us no harm. All we could think of doing was to stay put for the moment.[28]
>
> Corporal Arthur Razzell, 8th Battalion, Royal Fusiliers, 36th Brigade, 12th Division

To Corporal Razzell the situation seemed utterly hopeless; but further along the line the troops had managed to break through. They immediately began the deadly task of exploitation by bombing their way sideways along the German trenches – every traverse was a new block to their progress and it was essential to maintain momentum and not to give the Germans a chance to collect their wits and reorganise.

> I saw Mills bombs going through the air and the German bombs going back. It was obvious that our men had got in somewhere on the left and were bombing the Germans out. When they got opposite

to us the Germans left the trench and ran back, they were gone in seconds before we could drive at them.[29]

Corporal Arthur Razzell, 8th Battalion, Royal Fusiliers, 36th Brigade, 12th Division

Colonel Osborn of the 7th Royal Sussex had moved forward with his Headquarters Company and temporarily took shelter in two huge shell holes in No Man's Land. He was determined not to give up and rallied his men for another attack.

We reorganised for a further rush into the German front line. Before we got off Lieutenant Gordon, the bombing officer, was killed, and Lieutenant Wilton, the signals officer, wounded; also three of the men were killed. In the German lines things were a little chaotic. Some shots were being exchanged and bombs thrown on the flank and into dugouts. A few German snipers had stuck to their posts. I shot one and frightened off another with a rifle I picked up from a casualty. Our own liaison aeroplane then came over to look us up and flew most gallantly right into a barrage of shrapnel. We tried to signal him, but I don't think he saw us. Our flares were ready, but we had not time to light them before he was gone. When there is hand-to-hand fighting it is impossible to light flares at a fixed hour.[30]

Lieutenant Colonel W. L. Osborn, 7th Battalion, Royal Sussex Regiment, 36th Brigade, 12th Division

Trying to communicate their progress was difficult especially as most of the regimental signalling team had been badly wounded earlier in the attack and had to be left lying in No Man's Land. Despite his wounds the signal officer, Captain Wilton, desperately tried to signal their progress to the contact patrols of the RFC skimming above the battlefield.

Corporal Chevis was badly wounded as he was getting into the shell hole. At the time he was carrying one of the two large signalling shutters on a pole. This was smashed by the piece of shell which went through his thigh, while shortly afterwards he was wounded again in the same leg, and died the following morning. No words could express his bravery during the pain he suffered. I took one of the signalling shutters on my knees, and as our contact aeroplane came over I kept sending our battalion call-sign – which I think was seen, because the plane came down quite low, and the observer waved what looked like a muffler before flying away.[31]

Captain John Wilton, 7th Battalion, Royal Sussex Regiment, 36th Brigade, 12th Division

The men of the 7th Royal Sussex who had breached the German front line were equally aware of the importance of consolidating their tenuous grip on success. Time was a precious commodity, never regained once squandered. Almost invariably the Germans would be on them before they were ready.

> While going round the lines organising the defences I went into a German dugout occupied by some nine or ten Guard Fusiliers who had surrendered to our men and the 9th Royal Fusiliers. I was questioning them about water-supply and bombs, when the Germans rushed the trench above from a flank.[32]
>
> Lieutenant Colonel W. L. Osborn, 7th Battalion, Royal Sussex Regiment, 36th Brigade, 12th Division

Colonel Osborn found himself trapped in the dugout with the Germans swarming all over the trench above him and directly controlling the only exit.

> I started five men making a block on our left and told them to hold on there. While I was busy on our right the enemy attacked on our left, captured our block, killing the men I had left, and occupying the trench where the battalion headquarters dugout, with Colonel Osborn inside it, was situated. German stick bombs were going off all over the place and things were a bit windy for a moment, but directly the men knew the colonel was 'in the ditch' they wanted no leading. We just went for the Germans and they could not withstand the combination of Mills bombs and the 7th Battalion bereft of their commanding officer. When we had cleared them well back and made good the line again, I hared to the top of the steps of the dugout where the colonel was; there was someone lying dead at the bottom, and I thought for a moment it was the colonel and shouted, 'They have got the CO!' He heard me and, sticking his head round the corner, said, 'Oh no they haven't!' I then went into the dugout myself and the CO tied up my head. I did not take any further part in the show, as I found I was full of little bits of bomb.[33]
>
> Captain Henry Sadler, 7th Battalion, Royal Sussex Regiment, 36th Brigade, 12th Division

Colonel Osborn had spent the intervening minutes somewhat anxiously watching the different coloured legs rushing past the dugout entrance.

In the end the operation could be considered a success. Eventually the first two German lines were overrun and during the night a link was established with the far less successful 74th Brigade. The question of the brutal trade-off between gains made and casualties suffered soon began to surface both at the front and behind at divisional headquarters.

> We have held on to what we have gained this morning but it has been slow and not without loss. The people on our right did not get on far enough to join up so we have got to do it ourselves. This and machine guns have delayed things a bit. Very little news of any sort today. The rain has been vile, converting everything again into quagmires and emergency roads into bogs. It really has been a cruel fate. Men are all wet through and no shelter. The conditions the last three days could hardly have been worse – it seems always to be like that when we attack. But still we have done a good bit and the brigade attacked most gallantly and the men are pleased with themselves.[34]
>
> Quartermaster General Lieutenant Colonel F. H. F. Collen, Headquarters, 12th Division

The men of the 7th Royal Sussex may have been pleased with themselves but the majority of the 74th Brigade had suffered nothing but pain and death. They had a very different perspective of the days fighting.

> When we got back to the transport I saw our regimental sergeant major standing on the road. As soon as he saw me, 'Fall out the 8th Battalion!' I went to him and I said, 'I'm the only one left!' 'You can't be, you can't be!' he said. They came down in ones and twos. When there were no more coming down we moved back to Albert. Next day we moved back to some woods in huts and we had a roll call. Apparently the colonel was killed, the adjutant was killed, all four company captains were killed, no officers came back, they were either killed or wounded; there was one NCO, that was myself; a corporal, one lance corporal and sixty-three privates.[35]
>
> Corporal Arthur Razzell, 8th Battalion, Royal Fusiliers, 36th Brigade, 12th Division

As his skeleton battalion moved back out of the line it was just a husk of the unit that had marched forward only a few days before. But Corporal Arthur Razzell had not yet seen the last of his former companions – or of Ovillers.

> A couple of days after we came out, I was sent back with five or six men to collect the pay books of our men. The Germans had been pushed over the ridge so that we could go up in daylight. They were all our own men, some were from the attack that had happened on the 1st July. We had to turn them over to get to their breast pockets where they always kept their pay book, collected them in sandbags. Of course we were face to face with the absolute horror of war, men decapitated, empty brain cavities, entrails where they'd been disembowelled – horrible really. There was a corpse every odd yard, halfway up the 700 yards, very few got past that because they were being mowed down by machine-gun fire. In fact that day at Ovillers is absolutely engraved on my brain. I've thought about it all my life.[36]
>
> Corporal Arthur Razzell, 8th Battalion, Royal Fusilers, 36th Brigade, 12th Division

AS PART OF THE same uncoordinated series of attacks launched on 7 July, the 17th and 23rd Divisions launched an entirely unsequenced series of clumsy thrusts directed against Contalmaison and the neighbouring German strong points. A day of desperate attacks and counter-attacks followed as both sides fought over the ruins. In the afternoon the reserves began to move forward to push on the attack and consolidate the gains made.

> We saw a fine sight on our right; the second and successful attack on Contalmaison. It was thrilling to see the lines of infantry advancing in extended order despite the shrapnel bursting all around them. They disappeared into the trees and presently we heard the attack had been very successful.[37]
>
> Sergeant Roland Mountfield, 10th Battalion, Royal Fusiliers, 111th Brigade, 37th Division

At 2100 that night they were pushed forward in support of the attack made by the 13th Rifle Brigade toward Pozières. The situation was confused and so were the men.

> The Rifle Brigade were holding our front line and we were under the impression we were to relieve them. The way up was over ground for a little way, then along some trenches and then up a light railway line for

> nearly half a mile, from which the trenches turned off to the left and right. We moved off in the evening without knowing definitely what we were going to do and with many maddening halts and crawls got up near the tram line. Suddenly we saw that in front they were starting to run. Our captain stood at the corner where we came out on to the line yelling, 'Buck up, they've gone over!' and off we went at the double. What was meant to happen I don't know now. What did happen is that the Rifle Brigade went over the top to the German trenches opposite them; then we came running up the line past the trenches the Rifle Brigade had vacated and on towards the German line. The attack ought never to have been made and an order was sent up cancelling it. But the Rifle Brigade were already in the German trenches and we were nearly there. We came on, not knowing where we were, where we were going, or what we were going to do when we got there. The Germans, of course, had got the tram line taped. Shrapnel was flying all over the place and a machine gun on the left caught us. We seemed to go on for a year. Men were going down every minute, and since there had previously been bodies lying all the way, the place began to look a bit rotten. Here and there the lines had been torn up by shells and the holes had filled up with water, so that often we were nearly knee deep and one or two I saw struggling up to their waists. Then just as I became sure that there was nobody leading us and we should just go on running till there was no one left, there was a check in front and the order came down to retire. The advance had been steady enough, but I am afraid that the retirement was a bit of a scramble.[38]
>
> Sergeant Roland Mountfield, 10th Battalion, Royal Fusiliers, 111th Brigade, 37th Division

They fell back to the original front-line positions to the left and right of the tram line.

> Our orders were to spread out and man the parapet, which we did. The trenches were being heavily shelled, we didn't know what was happening and consequently when we saw men advancing towards us fire was opened for a few moments until we saw that some were English. They proved to be the Rifle Brigade bringing back wounded and prisoners. Of the latter over 200 came or were brought in and some of them are supposed to have said that if we hadn't fired there

> was a whole battalion ready to come over and surrender. We were shelled all night, but the rottenest part was the unsettled state of things. The Rifle Brigade had now received the order to retire and they came back from the German trenches. We heard the Germans return to it presently, chucking plenty of bombs about by way of precaution.[39]
>
> Sergeant Roland Mountfield, 10th Battalion, Royal Fusiliers, 111th Brigade, 37th Division

Sergeant Mountfield was then ordered to carry rations forward along a communication trench that linked the front line with a party clinging on to an isolated outpost. It was a journey he could only try to forget; but the horror of it was surely imprinted on his mind for the rest of his life.

> I wonder what the people at home who say, 'We will fight to our last drop of blood!' would think if they were taken up that trench. For 500 yards it is paved with English dead. I don't know what happened, but they were evidently caught there by awful shell fire – some say our own. In places you must walk on them, for they lie in heaps. I went up with rations and again to help carry down a casualty on a stretcher. I won't describe that trench until I have forgotten it a little. We slept in our little excavations at the side of the trench. The man in the one next to mine tried to deepen his a little and struck sacking. Suspecting nothing he went on and got as far as a blood stained cap and then he went to dig a new hole. I had already found sacking in mine but providentially had stopped there, so didn't trouble to move. What the eye doesn't see.....[40]
>
> Sergeant Roland Mountfield, 10th Battalion, Royal Fusiliers, 111th Brigade, 37th Division

There seemed to be little point to their horrific experiences and the terrible blood sacrifice they had made. Even the normally neutral regimental history commented that: 'The men preferred attack when losses sustained went to pay the price of some tangible success, or at least to further an obvious purpose.'[41]

MEANWHILE, on this day of futile sacrifice, another tragedy loomed just to the right of the struggling 37th Division, where the 38th (Welsh) Division had been ordered to attack the brooding menace that was Mametz

Wood. It was to be the first of a series that would indelibly mark out a link between the pride of Wales and this hitherto obscure little French wood. The 16th Welch and the 11th South Wales Borderers of the 115th Brigade were to be the first over the top at 0830 that morning.

> Rations for the day were issued. For fifty-two of us I was allocated one and a half loaves of bread, a piece of boiled bacon weighing about 16 ounces after the Somme mud had been removed, a small quantity of biscuits, some currants and sultanas and a petrol tin of tea. As I displayed the rations which would not be the 'last supper' but the 'last breakfast' for some of us, I reminded my lads of the parable of the 'loaves and fishes', adding that as I had not the miraculous powers of Our Lord Jesus Christ, section commanders should toss up – the winner taking the lot. At this, one of the lads said, 'Say Sarge, the buggers do not intend us to die on a full stomach, do they?'[42]
>
> Sergeant Albert Perriman, 11th South Wales Borderers, 115th Brigade, 38th Division

Primed with such examples of gallows humour the men awaited the signal to attack.

> We were crouched down, I had all these magazines round me, Jack had the machine gun and we crouched down behind a ridge overlooking the wood. We had our eyes on the officer, Lieutenant Eddie Williams. He had a whistle in his mouth and he was looking at his wristwatch. Then a blast on the whistle and a wave of his hand and we were up and over. It was just like a referee starting a football match.[43]
>
> Private Victor Lansdown, 16th Battalion, Welch Regiment, 115th Brigade, 38th Division

The attack was launched from Happy Valley towards the fringe of Mametz Wood. This was a considerable expanse of ground that they would have to cross. They could only hope that the guns had forced the Germans back. At first the prognosis seemed good.

> Our artillery barrage was raised to form a cover for our forward push, it also anticipated that the time had arrived for us to go 'over the top'. The battalion leading advanced slowly in waves of platoons, No. 1 Platoon of A Company leading. There was something of a distance of 10 yards between each platoon. The advance was made in stages,

moves made alternatively to a point where a mass attack on enemy positions could be launched. The ground we were covering was undulating and afforded plenty of cover, but when the apex was reached some 150 yards from the fringe of the wood, the ground fell away, leaving us completely exposed to German fire. The lack of enemy fire made the situation somewhat unrealistic, and gave the impression they had retired further than we expected. The battalion was now ready to make its final attack, with A Company some 50 yards from the wood. The trouble started when the next move was made. Without warning, not that we expected any, the whole front we were holding was subjected to murderous machine-gun fire. What had happened was the Germans had provided a rear-guard protection with three machine guns dug deeply into the ground. Our advance was watched by means of periscopes and fire was held until we provided an ideal target. Casualties were thick and heavy and our advance halted. There was nothing for it but to lie prone and hoping for the best as thousands of bullets whizzed over our heads. Slight rain did not add to our comfort.[44]

Sergeant Albert Perriman, 11th South Wales Borderers, 115th Brigade, 38th Division

The other assaulting troops of the 16th Welch Regiment had also been cut to ribbons by heavy machine-gun fire. The attack broke down before the men had the chance to reach the fringes of the wood.

The bullets were whistling past our ears, this man was holding up his hand. He had his rifle in it but only the finger and thumb was holding it because three fingers had been shot off. He said, 'Look what the bastards have done!' I said, 'Lie down, make yourself as small as possible!' We kept going, Jack and I, till the officer gave the signal to get down. We spotted a shell hole which we dived into head first. The tops of our bodies in the shell hole and our legs stuck up in the air. Jack fixed up the gun, fired a blast into the wood and that brought the revenge. A hail of bullets and I passed out – I was unconscious. It wasn't till later that we came to the conclusion that a bullet had hit my steel helmet and stunned me! At the same time a bullet had gone through my leg, so Jerry had given me an anaesthetic and I never felt any of it! But poor old Jack had a bullet through both legs and he felt

> both of them. When I came to my senses, Jack asked if I could get at my water bottle, so I turned over on my back, we were face down before. I handed him my water bottle. And then I could see my leg. The bullet had ripped my puttee and the two ends were hanging down soaked in blood. There was nothing much I could do about it. I'd lost so much blood I was too weak to do anything.[45]
>
> Private Victor Lansdown, 16th Battalion, Welch Regiment, 115th Brigade, 38th Division

He would only crawl back into the British lines when night fell.

Meanwhile, Sergeant Perriman had no officer with him and he was ordered back to the jumping-off point in Happy Valley. Here his company commander told him the glad tidings that he had been selected with his platoon to accompany him in an effort to capture the three machine guns before the main attack was relaunched at 1630.

> Our expedition was a hazardous one, to put it mildly. The German shelling on our position had intensified so as to become a living hell. What our individual feelings were as we moved off remained inexpressible. Led by our officer we moved off in single file up through Caterpillar Wood to a pathway which would take us to a farmyard and our first objective.[46]
>
> Sergeant Albert Perriman, 11th South Wales Borderers, 115th Brigade, 38th Division

They did not get far before they were forced once more to ground. To continue was simply suicide; a useless sacrifice, entirely without military meaning.

> Shrapnel and heavy machine-gun fire all around us spelled instant death. My officer was the first to go. I was a yard or so behind him when he fell. He fell without uttering a sound. I examined him and found he was dead. I took over, but for short duration – I became the second casualty. I received multiple wounds – in leg, stomach and hands by shrapnel. Unable to continue, I handed over to the senior NCO and I managed to crawl back to Happy Valley the best way I could. Progress was slow and painful.[47]
>
> Sergeant Albert Perriman, 11th South Wales Borderers, 115th Brigade, 38th Division

The situation was obviously hopeless and the planned resumption of the attack at 1630 was abruptly cancelled. The 38th Division had undoubtedly failed, but the reports that fed back along the line of command severely under-represented the difficulties the troops had faced. When the reports reached Haig he reacted harshly.

> Although the wood had been most adequately bombarded the division never entered the wood, and in the whole division the total casualties for the 24 hours are under 150! A few bold men entered the wood and found little opposition. Deserters also stated enemy was greatly demoralised and had very few troops on the ground.[48]
>
> General Sir Douglas Haig, General Headquarters, British Expeditionary Force

From the perspective of Private Lansdown, Sergeant Perriman and all the others who had tried their best this was manifestly unfair, but Haig could only respond to the reports he had received. From his perspective the attack had been a failure and he sought reasons or culprits. And, after all, it had not been a divisional attack – just two battalions had gone forward. Might more have been achieved with a more concentrated effort? Who *was* to blame? Rightly or wrongly, Haig blamed Major General Phillips and he was summarily removed from his command.

The 38th (Welsh) Division had certainly not finished with Mametz Wood. After a period of licking their wounds, three days later at 0415 on 10 July the men were ordered forward again. This time it was the turn of the 113th and 114th Brigades. The wood was bombarded for forty-five minutes before they went over the top, partially covered by a smoke screen. On the left of the wood ready to lead the attack in eight waves were the 16th Royal Welch Fusiliers, who had the dubious pleasure of an inspirational address from their colonel.

> Make your peace with God. You are going to take that position, and some of us won't come back – but we are going to take it. This will show you where I am.[49]
>
> Lieutenant Colonel Ronald Carden, 16th Battalion, Royal Welch Fusiliers, 113th Brigade, 38th Division

So saying Carden tied a coloured handkerchief to his walking stick and led them over the top. He could hardly have been a more obvious target for the Germans if he tried. He was undoubtedly brave, but to what end? He was soon hit, but managed to struggle forward until he was hit again and killed as he got to the wood. Behind the 16th Battalion came the four waves of the 14th Royal Welch Fusiliers.

> Presently the silent waves of men started moving forward, and I, with my third wave, joined in. Machine guns and rifles began to rattle, and there was a general state of pandemonium, little of which I can remember except that I myself was moving down the slope at a rapid rate, with bullet holes in my pocket and yelling a certain amount. I noticed also that there was no appearance whatsoever of waves about the movement at this time, and that the men in advance of us were thoroughly demoralised.[50]
>
> Captain Glynn Jones, 14th Battalion, Royal Welch Fusiliers, 113th Brigade, 38th Division

As the two battalions wavered and bunched up together short of the wood the situation looked hopeless. Then, a seeming miracle.

> From the wood in front a number of Germans – about forty – came out, with hands up. Suspecting a trick, I ordered my men to cover them, but allowed them to approach us. When they got about halfway, I went out to meet them, accompanied by a sergeant, and sent them back to our headquarters. As this appeared to point to the wood being unoccupied, I sent a small patrol to examine it; and then we all moved forward. Crossing the trench on the fringe of it, we entered the wood at the entrance of the main ride.[51]
>
> Captain Glynn Jones, 14th Battalion, Royal Welch Fusiliers, 113th Brigade, 38th Division

To the right of the Royal Welch Fusiliers were the 13th and 14th Welch Regiment. As soon as they came clearly into the view of the German machine gunners the ominous clattering began.

> We moved forward, quite open country; we had nearly 500 yards to go across towards the wood. It was breaking day and as we went up a little bit of a rise, as soon as we got where the Germans could see us they started machine gunning us right away. It was just tree stumps and all the broken branches were all down. They were wiping us down with enfilade fire. I don't know how we got to the wood but we did get to it and we engaged them in hand-to-hand fighting. It was hectic. We were so

reduced in numbers that we couldn't hold them and they drove us back out into the field. We were there for a while and our reserves came up to give us a hand and we made a second attack then. I was about 20 yards from the edge of the wood when I was wounded, I had a bullet through my left leg and then I was laying on the field there and a shell burst above me and the shrapnel came down and hit me in the hip. Nearly took half my hip away. As far as I was concerned that was the end of the war, but I dare not move because I was afraid that the snipers would catch me. I saw the Germans that had come out of the wood bayoneting our wounded – I saw the downward motion of their rifle which indicated to me that that was what they were doing – bayoneting our wounded boys. I think some of the men in our reserve battalion, the 10th and the 15th must have seen that, because they passed me in a screaming temper. I think that was the turning point of that battle. By pulling myself on the grass I had crawled into a shell hole and I lay there. I fell with my hip on the mud and that may have stopped the bleeding.[52]

Sergeant Tom Price, 13th Battalion, Welch Regiment, 114th Brigade, 38th Division

Sergeant Price lay there alone and untended until late in the afternoon of 11 July. In Mametz Wood itself the fighting continued unabated. It was a desperate scramble in conditions for which no training could have prepared the soldiers adequately.

Everybody for themselves. The brambles; trees falling. Almost like barbed wire in a sense except it was trees interwoven with one another, one across another. You had a battle to get over the trees and get out of their way in case they fell on you. You've got to experience it yourself to actually know. Our main concern was keeping alive. They wouldn't come too close to me with the Lewis gun. I was going along firing from the hip. We managed to drive them out. They shelled us and it was making craters. We believed in the old axiom, that lightning never struck twice in the same place. If a shell had made a crater, we jumped into that for our protection.[53]

Private George Richards, 13th Battalion, Welch Regiment, 114th Brigade, 38th Division

The attack managed to push the Germans back to within 40 yards of the northern edge of the Mametz Wood. That night there was near total confusion. Amorphous parties of men frequently fired on each other as they had no idea what was happening amidst the pitch darkness and deafening clamour. All night British and German shells crashed aimlessly down into the wood to kill and maim according to chance. Not unsurprisingly some men began to panic.

> Our own guns were firing short, and in spite of our attempts to communicate with the rear this continued. The numerous casualties we sustained because of this had the effect of making the men very panicky. Further, the difficulty in seeing more than a few yards in front caused ignorance amongst the men as to where the front lay and whether any of our fellows were there; any noise in the bush in front meant a hail of bullets. I, myself, saw an officer of the 15th Royal Welch Fusiliers killed in this way.[54]
>
> Captain Glynn Jones, 14th Battalion, Royal Welch Fusiliers, 113th Brigade, 38th Division

The vicious fighting would continue until the wood was finally secured on 12 July. In all the 38th Division suffered casualties amounting to 190 officers and 3,803 other ranks. Mametz Wood would cast a long shadow over Wales for many years.

All told the attacks launched on 7 July were an uncoordinated disaster that achieved next to nothing. The men were condemned to advance with their flanks gaping open allowing the Germans the freedom to concentrate their artillery and machine guns to deadly effect. The all-important artillery support was also lacking in concentrated power and failed to destroy the German barbed wire, trench positions, deep dugouts and artillery gun positions. Worst of all the guns of neighbouring formations not involved in the offensive failed to chime in to add the weight of their shells to the overall bombardment of the targeted German defences and covering artillery. This *was* futile; men were dying in their thousands for no reason.

> Death is a very dreadful thing to those who are not flung into slaughter. It will take months for me to gain a truer perspective. When the dead lie all around you, and the man next to you, or oneself, may puff out, death becomes a very unimportant incident. It is not callousness, but just too much knowledge. Like other things, man has ignored death and treated it as something to talk of with pale cheek and bated

> breath. When one gets death on every side, the reaction is sudden. Two chaps go out for water and one returns. Says a pal to him, 'Well, where's Bill?' 'A bloody "whizz-bang" took his bloody head off' may not appear sympathetic, but it is the only way of looking at the thing and remaining sane. You may be certain however, that the same man would carry Bill 10 miles if there was any chance of fixing his head on again.[55]
>
> Medical Officer Captain Charles McKerrow, 10th Battalion, Northumberland Fusiliers, 68th Brigade, 23rd Division

AT LAST, on 8 July, the fighting belatedly expanded to cover the XIII Corps front to the south of XV Corps. By this time over a week had elapsed since the successes of 1 July when, for a couple of days, the woods and villages that would a few days later become symbols of senseless slaughter lay tantalisingly open before the British. The days spent by Rawlinson and the Fourth Army in reorganising on this southern right flank can easily be characterised as a lost opportunity. Yet the much maligned British staff officers had a complex task in arranging for the relief of exhausted battalions whilst simultaneously moving in the fresh divisions to hold the line and make the next leap forward. It was difficult in the extreme to ensure a relatively clear passage through the crowded roads and tracks without running the risk of a horrendous traffic jam well within range of the German heavy artillery. Troop movements were just the beginning of an administrative nightmare in preparing for a renewed offensive. Stores and munitions were being consumed in prodigious quantities and everything had to be got forward to the right place at the right time. In addition all their efforts to plan the next offensive were complicated by the requirement to secure agreement in advance with the neighbouring French.

The French were still doing reasonably well south of the Somme but there was little sign of urgency and the German resistance had begun to stiffen. To the French the crux of the matter lay north of the Somme and the responsibility was firmly with the British. There was a definite 'chicken and egg' situation here. Both sides were waiting for the other. If they did not move forward in harmony then Rawlinson's XIII Corps would be advancing into a pronounced salient and the Germans would inevitably not hesitate to exploit any open flanks that would inevitably be left exposed. On the other hand, it is equally valid to point out that they managed to get new divisions forward for the futile attacks on 3 and 7 July further to the north where the opportunities for progress were by no means so obvious. Risks were taken with exposed flanks there – why not take them with an overt thrust towards Longueval or Trônes Wood?

While the British prepared and got everything 'just so' for the attack, the Germans were naturally not idle. Where once Trônes Wood had stood open, penetrated with impunity by British patrols, now the Germans had managed by dint of sheer hard work to incorporate the wood once more into a coherent defensive line. This did not bear any comparison with the veritable fortresses that had faced the British on 1 July, but it did not have to reach such heights of military engineering as it would not have to face such a prolonged bombardment. What was important was that more German gun batteries had been moved up into their positions behind the lines, troops were safely ensconced in trenches, barbed wire had been hastily erected and machine guns were ready and waiting.

To make matters worse the XIII Corps also made no effort to launch any kind of a concerted mass attack on 8 July. Tragically the initial attempts by the 30th Division to take Trônes Wood were made by isolated companies, or at best single battalions, with derisory preliminary bombardments. Under these circumstances it is no surprise the troops made little headway. Even if they did make some small inconsequential gains the German artillery would open up, shells would isolate the incursion and then search backwards and forwards across the area before the inevitable counter-attacks threw any bedraggled survivors back to their start lines. It is incomprehensible that having waited so long the British should fail to attack in force covered by the full power of their guns. Over the next few days Trônes Wood became a place of horror. When Lieutenant William Bloor was sent up as a forward observation officer he was appalled by what he found there.

> The place beggars description quite – there has been the fiercest fighting here for four days, and both sides have taken and lost the wood several times. Wounded have not been cleared away, and there are some who have been all that time without food or any attention. The horror and misery and countless tragedies of this war – even the little

of it I have seen – are much too awful to let the mind dwell on it and I am surprised that more men do not go mad with the horror of it. Many of the infantry that I saw and spoke to were in a state of 'daze', their senses were all blurred and dull, and they neither cared if they lived or died, nor if they went forward or backward. I suppose it is as well that they can get that way.[56]

Lieutenant William Bloor, C Battery, 149th Brigade, Royal Field Artillery, 30th Division

Much of the British and German artillery within range concentrated their guns on this one small patch of woodland. Shells tore up and down between the trees like a huge rake, searching out their weedy human prey with a grim inevitability. Attack after attack was ordered. On 13 July it was the turn of the 55th Brigade, 18th Division to try their luck. The troops went forward bravely, many even managed to enter the bounds of the wood, but once inside they were lost, isolated in a tangled jungle of smashed trees, heavy undergrowth and the unmentionable mangled debris of men and equipment.

At 6.30 p.m. we started the preliminary bombardment, and at 7.30 p.m. lifted into Guillemont. At 10 p.m. I was ordered to go forward to the infantry to report progress and send down any information obtainable. At battalion headquarters found everything in confusion. It appeared that 55th Brigade had attacked from their different points and were to have joined up after getting through the wood. They had no real news as every messenger had been laid out in getting through the heavy barrage which the Boche put up. The only information to be got was from their wounded who had contrived to get as far as us – the spot was 300 yards south-west of the wood. They said the attack was a complete failure and that they had been cut to pieces.[57]

Lieutenant William Bloor, C Battery, 149th Brigade, Royal Field Artillery, 30th Division

14 July 1916 *The Battle of Bazentin Ridge*

ALL TOLD, the flurry of attacks on Contalmaison, Mametz Wood and Trônes Wood that characterised this period were launched with the express aim of securing a better jumping-off position and securing the flanks for the main attack, which it had by this time been decided would commence on

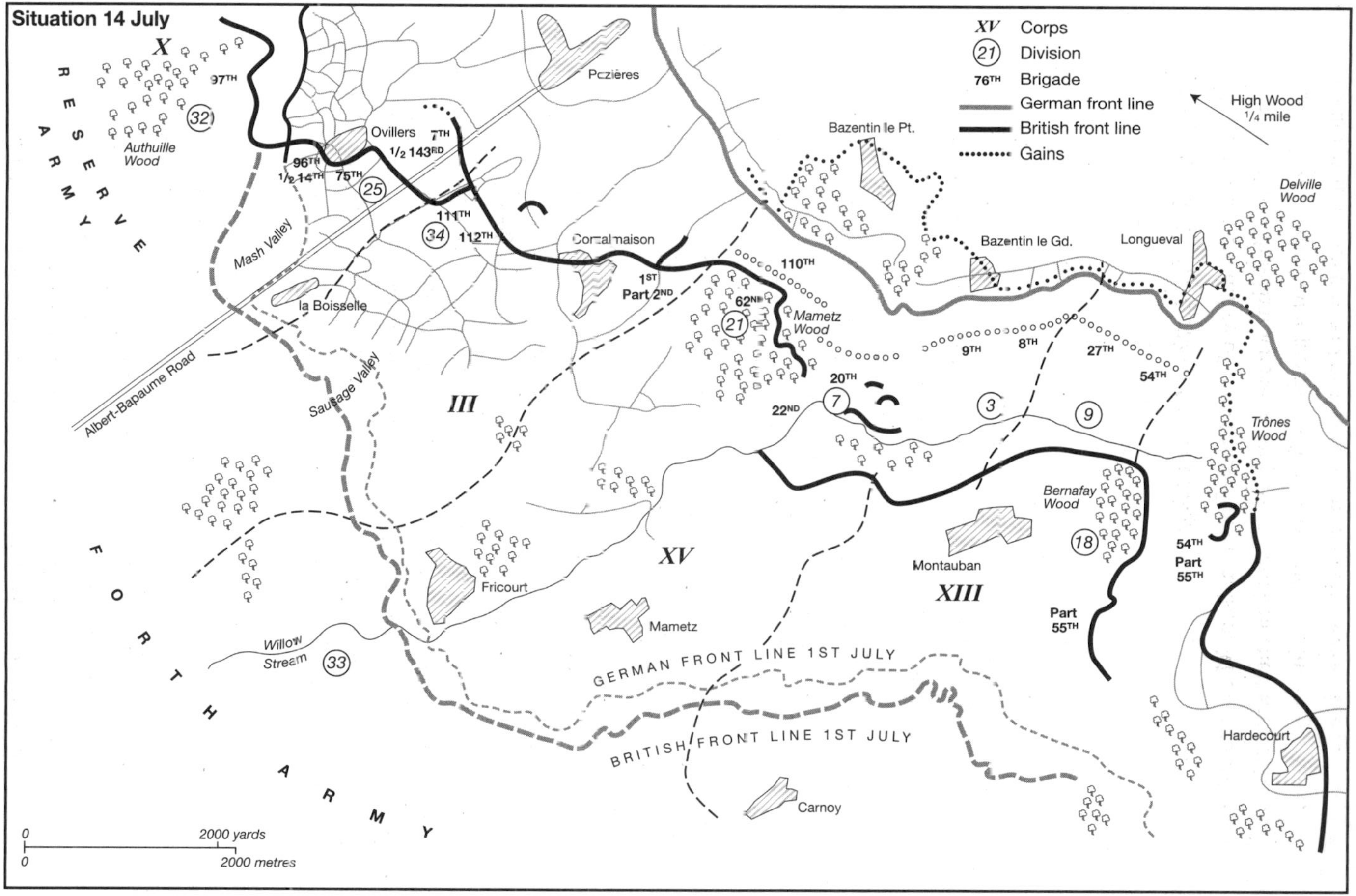

Situation 14 July
XV Corps
21 Division
76TH Brigade
German front line
British front line
Gains
High Wood
1/4 mile
X
RESERVE ARMY
FOURTH ARMY
Authuille Wood
32
97TH
Ovillers
7TH
1/2 143RD
96TH
1/2 14TH
75TH
25
Pozières
Mash Valley
la Boisselle
111TH
34
112TH
Contalmaison
1ST
Part 2ND
Albert-Bapaume Road
Sausage Valley
III
Bazentin le Pt.
Bazentin le Gd.
Longueval
Delville Wood
110TH
62ND
21
Mametz Wood
20TH
7
22ND
9TH
8TH
27TH
54TH
3
9
Trônes Wood
Bernafay Wood
18
54TH
Part 55TH
Montauban
XIII
Part 55TH
XV
Fricourt
Mametz
Willow Stream
33
GERMAN FRONT LINE 1ST JULY
BRITISH FRONT LINE 1ST JULY
Carnoy
Hardecourt
0
2000 yards
0
2000 metres

14 July. As each attack failed, so another was ordered. The commanders seemed to have become objective fixated, possessing a tunnel vision that prevented them from looking around them, or to pause for even a moment's reflection as to *what* they were doing or *how*. Generalship had been reduced to noting the failure of the latest attack and ordering a repeat. Small-scale attacks that might have succeeded on 3 July were doomed in the face of reconstituted German defences. The absence of any meaningful coordination exerted at divisional, corps or army level meant that these attacks signally failed to exploit the British overall superiority in raw numbers or the sheer bludgeoning power of their massed artillery. Unfocused attacks, launched against powerful trench works with varying start times, squandered all such advantages and inevitably left individual British battalions exposed in No Man's Land to superior concentrations of German firepower from flanking machine guns and the artillery batteries of neighbouring sectors left free from attack. The end result was mounting losses – not this time the stunning single blow as suffered on 1 July – but a trickling incremental drain that over days added up to serious losses that approached some 25,000 casualties in just under fifty separate attacks. Even then, Trônes Wood still remained partially in German hands while the distance between the hard-won British front line and the original German Second Line system still stretched to nearly a mile.

The collective failure of generalship within the Fourth Army can never be adequately explained or excused. Rawlinson should have knocked his corps commanders heads together, should have insisted on a properly coordinated attack or attacks. But Rawlinson was a believer in the convention that the general in command merely 'pointed the gun' by setting the overall objectives and then left the 'details' to the subordinate commanders. It was clear that this 'laissez-faire' view of generalship was endemic and stretched down to encompass Rawlinson's corps commanders and many of his divisional commanders. Such a view was, in fact, an abrogation of clear responsibility to personally oversee the performance of command tasks. Not everything can be delegated if hundreds of thousands of men in disparate units are to successfully operate together with a coherent common purpose. The bulk of the Fourth Army were left as hapless bystanders as their comrades fought and died under their very noses. If lieutenant generals and major generals evade their responsibilities then their brigadiers and colonels can only order attacks by battalions or even mere companies – and so it came to pass. Men serving in the proud battalions that were smashed in these attacks would nurse a grievance against 'High Command' that would endure throughout what remained of their lives. Such men could only judge with the evidence of experiences seared into their very beings. They had seen little evidence of any 'learning curve'. If anything these attacks were a dreadful step or two backwards to the dark ages of military tactics so tragically symbolised by the battles of Aubers Ridge and Festubert in 1915.

Fortunately for the overall reputation of Sir Henry Rawlinson he was at the same time making plans for a new attack that was as well conceived as the so-called preparatory attacks that led up to it were monstrously foolish. The first emphasis was in securing an adequate artillery bombardment tailored to destroy the known menace of the German barbed wire, trenches, strong points and artillery batteries. This time there was no evading the necessity for concentration. In all 1,000 guns were amassed, of which some 311 were the all-important heavy artillery. Although numerically less than that used in the bombardment prior to 1 July, this was actually a far more potent assemblage. For instead of being required to fire on a front line of 22,000 yards and attempting to saturate the multiple defence lines that lay behind it, the artillery was to attack on a front of just 6,000 yards, behind which the Germans had not yet had time to build a multi-layered new trench system to match the original Byzantine complex of strong points and switch lines. In essence it has been calculated that 66 per cent of the original guns available would be firing on just below 5 per cent of the original total of targets.[58] This meant that the bombardment would have the real power that it was mistakenly believed to have had prior to 1 July. This time it would not just look impressive, but would guarantee to land large numbers of shells on and in close proximity to all of the German defence works and to allow far more British batteries to be devoted to suppressing any identified German artillery batteries. This unprecedented concentration of artillery was to fire half a million shells over the three-day preliminary bombardment.

Yet not all the artillery lessons of 1 July had been properly digested. Counter-barrage fire was still low on the list of the priorities of the artillery batteries, despite the clearest possible demonstrations on 1 July of the killing power of unfettered German guns. Furthermore, it was obvious that the concept of the creeping barrage was still regarded as merely theoretical, and was not yet built into the overall framework of recommended attack tactics for the assault divisions.

One serious problem, certainly, was boldly addressed by Rawlinson and his planning staff. It was clear that the attacking troops would, even at best, be facing a No Man's Land that would stretch uphill over 1,500 yards in front of them. Rawlinson proposed that a night attack would allow the attacking battalions to edge forward under the cover of darkness to take up position on carefully laid white marker tapes, ready to launch an attack at dawn from right under the Germans' noses. This was an audacious plan that required careful planning, an exact reconnaissance of the ground and a skilful execution by the attacking troops. There was clearly little or no room for error. Disaster would be likely if the alarm was raised amongst the Germans. Given the risks it is easy to see why these plans worried Haig and on 11 July he took the unusual step of intervening to forbid the employment of such tactics on a grand scale.

> Our troops are not highly trained and disciplined, nor are many of the staff experienced in such work, and to move two divisions in the dark over such a distance, form them up, and deliver an attack in good order and in the right direction at dawn, as proposed, would hardly be considered possible even in a peace manoeuvre.[59]
>
> General Sir Douglas Haig, General Headquarters, British Expeditionary Force

Put in such a forceful manner, Haig's views certainly had some resonance. His alternative proposals were, however, nonsensical. He envisaged a breakthrough from a narrow-front attack to be launched by the XV Corps from Mametz Wood towards Bazentin-le-Grand Wood, followed by a vigorous exploitation to roll up the German line. If all went well, there would be an all-out direct assault next day by the XIII Corps on Longueval. This over-ambitious plan was ill-conceived and laid so many hostages to fortune that it was never properly spelt out – at a conference called later that day even Rawlinson's corps commanders summoned the nerve to express their doubts about attacking Bazentin-le-Grand and Longueval separately. Backed up by his subordinates, Rawlinson decided that he must protest and with considerable courage engaged in a direct dispute with Haig in an effort to retain his original concept of a night attack. To Haig's credit he treated this opposition to his wishes seriously and reconsidered the proposals root and branch.

> I thought carefully over Rawlinson's amended plan and discussed it in detail with Kiggell, Butler and Davidson. General Birch also gave me his opinion of the artillery situation, which was satisfactory viz. that advancing certain guns he felt fairly sure that we could dominate the enemy's artillery. I put four questions to the General Staff:
>
> Can we take the position in the manner proposed?
> Can we hold it after capture?
> What will be the results in case of a failure?
>
> What are the advantages, or otherwise, of proceeding methodically, viz. extending our front and sapping forward to take the position by assault? They all agreed that Rawlinson's new plan materially altered the chances of success, and there seemed a fair chance now of succeeding. They thought we could both take the position and hold it. In the case of failure, the supporting points must be held, and we can then proceed by deliberate methods – extending our front and sapping up. The disadvantage of the deliberate method at once is that we must hold the German troops in our front. If the attack was allowed to die down, they might continue the attacks at Verdun or elsewhere. The news this morning shows the Germans again attacking at Verdun. Also to encourage the French, we must keep on being active.[60]
>
> General Sir Douglas Haig, General Headquarters, British Expeditionary Force

Finally, Haig was convinced that the British artillery would be strong enough to guarantee the kind of domination of the German artillery on the battle front that made his earlier concerns almost irrelevant. Rawlinson was given the go-ahead on condition that he addressed more attention to the vital importance of suppressing the German artillery by organising a far more comprehensive programme of counter-battery fire. So it was agreed that there would indeed be a combined attack by the XV Corps (21st and 7th Divisions) and the XIII Corps (3rd, 9th and 18th Divisions). In all, four divisions would be launched forward in the main dawn attack with the 1st (III Corps) and 18th Divisions engaging in flanking attacks. The 2nd Indian Cavalry Division was earmarked to exploit any breakthrough by swooping forward on High Wood and then on to the village of Flers. In view of all the time that had been spent waiting to secure French cooperation in a joint attack it was particularly ironic that the

French looked on the whole Rawlinson plan with utter horror and refused to have anything to do with it – they would remain on the defensive until the British had captured the German Second Line along the Bazentin Ridge. Nothing would budge them and all the waiting had been in vain.

Even before the plans had been finalised, the massed British artillery had begun their three-day bombardment. The field batteries were tasked to cut the German barbed wire well before the attack and to that end sent observers into No Man's Land, where they edged as close as was physically possible to ensure that there was no mistake. Meanwhile the heavier guns and howitzers pounded all identified German strong points. At night the guns kept up a harassing bombardment meant to hamper the damage repairs and targeted their communications behind the lines.

To preserve the maximum possible surprise as the infantry formed up in No Man's Land it was planned to unleash the final hurricane bombardment just five brief minutes before the moment of assault. The infantry lined up on their tapes deep in No Man's Land with nothing to protect them but darkness and their own disciplined silence. Even such an imperturbable character as Sir Douglas Haig seemed to have some difficulty in sleeping that night. His, after all, was the ultimate responsibility.

> Very heavy artillery bombardment about 2.30 and then at 3.30 a.m. I looked out at 2.30, it was quite light but cloudy. Just the weather we want. The noise of the artillery was very loud and the light from the explosion of the shells was reflected from the heavens on to the ceiling of my room...[61]
>
> General Sir Douglas Haig, General Headquarters, British Expeditionary Force

The men crawling forward were aware of the risks they were being ordered to take. The 8th Devons had already felt the vicious impact of a German barrage line and the lash of concentrated machine-gun fire two weeks earlier on 1 July. They knew what would happen if anything went wrong.

> From 2.30 a.m. to 3.20 a.m. was a period of horrid suspense. Everything depended on whether or not the Boche got wind of what was happening. The 8th were engaged during this time in crawling up the 1,000 yards that separated Caterpillar Wood from the Snout. If the Boche had spotted them a few shells and machine guns might have spoiled everything. I listened and listened. The night seemed quieter

> than usual and only an occasional shell fell on either side. Still the suspense continued till 3.20 when I knew the hurricane bombardment of five minutes was due to start. 3.00 all quiet; 3.05 all quiet; 3.10 a few of our own machine guns just behind me pipping away; 3.15 all quiet again; 3.18; 3.19; 3.20. Then every gun for miles around gave tongue and as the shells hurtled overhead I almost felt sorry for the Boche. One thing was already certain. The surprise had succeeded.[62]
>
> Chaplain Ernest Crosse, 8th and 9th Battalions, Devonshire Regiment, 20th Brigade, 7th Division

It may have been only five minutes; but what a five minutes .... This was everything that the original Somme bombardment was supposed to have been, but in the end had failed to deliver. This truly was the essence of destruction.

> The whole world broke into gunfire. It was a stupendous spectacle – the darkness lit up by thousands of gun flashes – the flicker of countless bursting shells along the northern skyline, followed a few minutes later by a succession of frantic SOS rockets and the glare of burning Hun ammunition dumps.[63]
>
> Major Neil Fraser-Tytler, D Battery, 149th Brigade, Royal Field Artillery, 30th Division

Under the cover of the bursting shells the infantry moved still closer to the German line, intent on giving the survivors no chance of recovery when the barrage lifted. Although the artillery arrangements had once again been left in part to the discretion of the attacking divisions, there was overall a much greater emphasis on creating a genuine creeping barrage, moving in lethal synchronicity just in front of the attacking infantry, lifting some 50 yards in range every one and a half minutes to keep pace with their advance. So that the troops could get as close as possible to the barrage, it was even arranged to fire only HE shells with delayed action fuses to avoid them being detonated early from contact with any remaining trees and thus exploding prematurely, directly above the troops. The end result was a stunning success. At 0325 the assaulting infantry pressed forward on the very heels of the line of bursting shells and they crashed into the remnants of the German front line, where they found little but the dead and dying. In many sectors there was almost no serious opposition: there was no one left to oppose; there were no trenches left worthy of the name. The Germans had been simply swept away in the tide of bursting shells.

In the 9th Division sector the Scots burst through the front line and vaulted across two more trench lines in their initial impetus preceded as they were by the barrage of bursting shells. Naturally, in places, there remained pockets of resistance that had to be broken down. The 9th Scottish Rifles were involved in some bitter hand-to-hand fighting as they attacked the Longueval Redoubt.

> A German fired point-blank at me and I thought he had blown part of my face off, the pain was so intense, but instinctively lowering my rifle like a pistol, I blew the top of his head off as he came up at me; my reaction to this being, 'Gosh, just like lifting the lid off a boiling pot!' In the light of the flares going up all over the front, I saw that the bullet fired point-blank at me had hit the German stick bomb I was carrying in my left hand, taking a crescent shaped piece out of the rim, to make a scar which is still with me today. The remainder of the garrison seemed to be centred on the middle of the redoubt and I found myself in a trench with several other ranks from various units. A private of my own company and my shadow since the action began, Bill Crowe, was a slightly built lad from Lancashire and it was remarkable how this sprat had been caught up in the mesh of war, for he was obviously still under age, his driving force the ambition to win a medal for his mother. We all tried to shield his tender years and frail physique, but Billy regarded danger as a part of the apprenticeship he had to serve. His moment of glory was near. The other three in the trench with me comprised of a lieutenant and sergeant of the Royal Scots and a sergeant of the Royal Scots Fusiliers. We decided to winkle Jerry out from our end by lobbing bombs over the traverses and under cover of the explosion, dash round the traverse to put him to the bayonet. Rushing round into one of the bays there was a rather undersized black-visaged private of the Bavarian Regiment crouched on the firestep, and as I lifted the stick bomb to club him, the arm he lifted up in defence of the blow was just a gory mess. While I attended to his wound, the lieutenant was speaking urgently to him in German, ordering him to take a message to his commandant that the fort was now surrounded, but that if he surrendered with his men, they would

> guarantee safe conduct to the rear and then to England. Our commiseration for his young soldier must have impressed the garrison commander favourably, for suddenly about 200 soldiers erupted from the trenches to crowd into the sunken road leading back to Montauban, milling round crying, 'Kamerad! Kamerad!' until the tall figure of a German captain appeared to line them up in the roadway and they were marched off, dazed and shaken from their ordeal.[64]
>
> Private Barney Downes, 9th Battalion, Cameronians (Scottish Rifles), 27th Brigade, 9th Division

They were escorted off by young Private Bill Crowe. Downes himself did not have long to savour their triumph. As he gazed at the relatively unspoilt countryside that lay behind the village of Longueval he was caught all unawares, in a near-fatal moment of inattention.

> The increasing daylight showed corn growing in the fields with trees no longer defoliated with the recurrent blasts of war. While enjoying this rustic scene in the morning sunlight, I was caught off guard when a sniper who had crept back to our new positions shot me point-blank through the chest. The impact was frightful, and the pain terrific as the thrust of the bullet leaving me pitched me forward. The bullet went through my right lung, just missing my spine. I started losing consciousness as the severe haemorrhage drained the lifeblood from a chilled body, warming only when the flow of blood streamed down my back. As the stretcher bearer carried me away, I was told that the sniper had been winkled out and, 'Left as full of holes as a pepper pot!' But I was singularly free of animosity for this brave man. Now barely conscious of events, I was handed over to a stretcher bearer of the new Red Cross unit, the 'Non-Combatant Corps' mainly recruited from the white-livered element of our society – the so-called conscientious objectors. On the way to the field hospital they dumped me in a shell hole, one saying to the other, 'Come on, leave the big Jock here, he's not going to live anyway!' And off they went.[65]
>
> Private Barney Downes, 9th Battalion (Scottish Rifles), Cameronians, 27th Brigade, 9th Division

During the highly pressurised fighting the inexperienced troops of the South African Brigade moved into the attack. As they pushed forward it was apparent that the German resistance was stiffening.

We all knew that we were going against a pretty tough enemy – but we didn't expect anything like what actually happened. While going up to Longueval my friend next to me said, 'Man, but there're a damn lot of bees around here!' I said, 'Bees be blowed! Those are bullets flying around.' Unfortunately about four minutes afterwards a bullet caught him and killed him right out. Then I began to see that things were getting bad. Then another went over. Then another. Then I thought, 'It's my turn next.' There were machine-gun posts at the flour mill at Longueval and we got it very heavy from there. I got hit at the beginning of the wood. The lower part of my jaw was shot away, they reckon by a ricochet. It felt like a mule-kick.[66]

Private Sidney Carey, 1st South African Infantry Regiment, South African Brigade, 9th Division

The pace of the 9th Division advance slowed to a crawl as the troops fought their way slowly through Longueval, and finally washed up against the fringes of Delville Wood and the German strong point at the Waterlot Farm sugar refinery. Here, as German opposition stiffened and casualties inexorably mounted, the advance was finally halted.

To their left, the 3rd Division had substantially more problems with uncut wire but still managed to get forward towards the main Bazentin Ridge. The original German Second Line system was breached and overrun as the men swarmed forwards. In the excitement and trauma of mopping up the nobler virtues of war were not always observed.

Dead and wounded were lying all around. One of our infantrymen was kicking a wounded German, crying out, 'You may be the bastard that killed my brother.'[67]

Sapper John Cordy, 56th Field Company, Royal Engineers, 3rd Division

The troops pushed forward and began struggling their way through the village of Bazentin-le-Grand. Sappers were a useful adjunct to the infantry in such close-quarter street fighting.

We got into the buildings which were on one side of the street in the village. It was an old brewery, half of it below street level. The Germans had made a first aid dressing station here, and German wounded lay in bunk beds both sides of the room. We moved them from the street-side bunks and put them all together on the other side,

> so we were able to stand on the beds and open up the air vents in the walls for our snipers to get rifles through. In my working party I had five pioneer infantrymen and I sent them to dig a trench past an opening between the houses. I left them, and went into the cellar to see how the fellow was getting on cutting the holes. I thought I would have a shot and went to step up on a bed, but spotted a sniper lying dead on the other side, a bullet through his head. As soon as I got outside again I saw an observation balloon go up over the houses and after a few moments over came the shells, one burst right near and a piece of shrapnel took the top off a fellow's shoulder. The first aid chap with the bandages and dressings was very frightened, 'What shall I do?' he cried, 'Get the fellow in the cellar and dress his shoulder!' was the quick reply. Another shell exploded and the shrapnel knocked me down with pieces hitting my leg and shoulder, and another piece piercing the middle of my knee.[68]
>
> Sapper John Cordy, 56th Field Company, Royal Engineers, 3rd Division

It was, of course, crucial to get artillery support in attacking the deeper objectives where the preliminary bombardment was obviously neither so heavy nor accurate. The gun batteries sent forward observation parties who followed hard on the heels of the first wave. It was naturally an extremely confusing environment.

> We were walking over this open ground and this thick mist was rolling about. There's bullets flying about and Locking said, 'Well for stray bullets, it's bloody good shooting!' Just then we heard a voice yelling, 'Get down you silly so-and-sos!' We dropped flat and crawled up. There was a bank about two feet high and there was some infantry; it was the 8th East Yorks. There was about 200 of them left of 800 and it was only twenty minutes from the start. They were pinned down. One chap was making a run from behind, we were in a shell hole then, and this chap was hit right in the ear and he pitched amongst us. Just for a few moments blood was spurting out of his ear, I suppose his heart was still beating. Then it gradually died away. Then Jerry put a 'box barrage' down, to cut them off, so I thought, 'That means he's going to attack and he's cutting off reinforcements'. I said to the officer, 'We'd better get out of this, there'll be a counter-attack in a minute!' He wouldn't move, so I said, 'You bloody well stay there but I'm going!'

> We started crawling out. We had some rations with us. I had a sandbag with some tins of bully and I put that across the back of my neck. We were crawling flat on our faces to get through this barrage. Fortunately, most of it was going into the ground and not doing much damage, it wasn't bad. I'm crawling through this and suddenly there's a terrific clout on the back of my head, knocked me out for a moment. Then I felt something move and what had happened was a big clod of earth had dropped on the back of my head and bashed me. My nose was bleeding, my chin was cut.[69]
>
> Signaller Leonard Ounsworth, 124th Heavy Battery, Royal Garrison Artillery

When forward observation posts were eventually established with a reasonable view over the German lines, the observers began the difficult task of communicating with their batteries to ensure that shells were falling accurately. In many cases the telephone wires had not yet been laid, but even where they were they did not stay intact for long under the German barrage. Observation post work was an extremely dangerous task for if sighted by the Germans the signallers became a prime target.

> During the afternoon our artillery concentrated their fire upon Bazentin-le-Petit and Shelter Wood. This wood is, or rather *was* situated upon a slope, and at the top in a small clearing there stood a crucifix made of wood. As our position was close by, we used this place to signal from – with flags. It was also not very far from the first-line trenches and could be plainly seen from the German lines. We were busy signalling from this spot when Fritz caught sight of us and, of course, put one of his guns on us. The first shell dropped just in the rear and then he got the range all right, for he absolutely levelled the ground, or rather made holes in it, smashing the crucifix to smithereens and turning the trees round about into sawdust. As for ourselves, we dived at once for the nearest shelter we could find. Some of us were lucky enough to get there, but two of the chaps were not. One of them was blown to smithereens and the other's head was completely cut off. That finished our signalling there for that day. The body of the one chap and the few pieces we could find of the other were buried where they fell.[70]
>
> Signaller F. J. G. Gambling, B Battery, 97th Brigade, Royal Field Artillery, 21st Division

Later in the day when the telephone line had been laid and duly broken by shelling, Signaller Gambling was sent back to locate and repair the break.

> As we were passing through Mametz Wood, I pulled out a couple of fags from my pocket, gave my chum one and then found I had not got a match. My chum felt in his pockets and found that he had none either. We had been walking on for some distance when I saw a chap crouched against a tree. At first I thought he was getting a light. Then I saw he was not moving so I turned to my chum and said, 'What's he doing down there?' My chum stopped and said, 'God knows!' So I went up to the chap and dropping my hand on his shoulder. I said, 'Got a match, old chap?' But I got no answer from him so I shook his shoulder gently, and was about to ask him again, when he fell over and I could see then he was stone dead. It seemed as though he had taken to that tree for cover when advancing and just as he got there, he must have been shot, and that is how he fell. He had a full pack on and his rifle was gripped tightly in has hands.[71]
>
> Signaller F. J. G. Gambling, B Battery, 97th Brigade, Royal Field Artillery, 21st Division

In one sense the British had been unfortunate in their timing of the attack for 14 July. Local German counter-attacks had been anticipated, but the attack had coincided with the arrival in the battle area of the forward elements of the relief 7th Division. These fresh troops, unaffected by the prior bombardments, began to launch a series of counter-attacks that hammered time and time again against the villages of Bazentin-le-Petit and Bazentin-le-Grand. This effectively prevented any further forward movement, as the troops on Bazentin Ridge were fully occupied in holding what they had. Even if this had not been the case, Rawlinson had ordered the XV Corps to hold back from an assault on High Wood until the XIII Corps on their right had managed to capture Longueval.

As the infantry began to run out of steam this, if any, was the moment at which the much-vaunted mobile power of the cavalry should have been swiftly deployed to push through the infantry and so exploit the German confusion. In one sense it was strange that Rawlinson had allotted such a considerable role to his cavalry. Before the original assault on 1 July he had not at any time actually envisaged a breakthrough and, despite Haig's prodding, had not assigned the cavalry a significant role. Yet, on 14 July, conscious of the relative weakness of the German defences existing behind the front line, he had assigned a very definite task to his cavalry. Once Delville Wood and Bazentin-le-Petit were captured it was to deploy forward to seize the brooding High Wood before advancing to capture Flers and Eaucourt L'Abbaye. This was ambitious in the extreme.

> Our fire continued at a rapid rate until 10.30 a.m., when we got news of the capture of the objective, and soon after, on the skyline west of Montauban, we could see the silhouettes of cavalry and horse artillery moving forward, a thrilling sight after the weary round of trench warfare.[72]
>
> Major Neil Fraser-Tytler, D Battery, 149th Brigade, Royal Field Artillery, 30th Division

The Germans were in some disarray, but the difficulties in moving large bodies of mounted troops across a cratered battlefield, constantly snagged by barbed wire, had not simply disappeared. The cavalry consequently found it almost impossible to get across the broken ground and most were stymied well behind the new front line. Indeed, by the early evening only the 7th Dragoon Guards and 20th Deccan Horse of the 2nd Indian Cavalry Division finally managed to make their way forward on to the high ground that stretched between Delville Wood and High Wood.

They deployed ready for action, but horsemen were still a tempting and large target, unable as they were to take cover without dismounting. A few connected patches of barbed wire, a machine gun or a surviving battery of artillery would spell disaster. As they moved forward the bruised, but otherwise unharmed, Signaller Leonard Ounsworth saw a most unusual sight from his observation post.

> A Morane-Saulnier, a French aeroplane that we had at the time, kept diving down on to the corner of the field on our left front. I saw this Indian cavalry, the Deccan Horse they called them, and this plane was diving down and up again. Suddenly the officer in charge of the cavalry cottoned on. He stood up in his stirrups, waved his sword above his head and just charged across that field – like a shot out of a gun, like bats out of hell. The two outer lots split, so they made a pincer and encircled them – it was all over in a matter of seconds. The next thing we saw was thirty-four Jerry prisoners, some with heavy machine guns. They were waiting while the Cavalry got a bit nearer –

my God, they'd have slaughtered them. The plane was trying to draw their attention, just diving down on top, I suppose distracting these machine gunners, because a plane coming down close above your head is enough to draw your attention.[73]

Signaller Leonard Ounsworth, 124th Heavy Battery, Royal Garrison Artillery

Despite such minor successes, the Deccan Horse soon found that they had bitten off more than they could chew. As they moved forward the machine gunners forced them to ground and they took up a dismounted line stretching from Longueval to the southern corner of High Wood. By the early evening sufficient infantry reserves had arrived to allow a partial resumption of their advance and elements of the 7th and 33rd Divisions managed to gain a fairly solid foothold in High Wood. It has been suggested that if Rawlinson had not waited for the cavalry then the infantry could have advanced much earlier and taken High Wood almost without opposition. The Royal Flying Corps had reported on several occasions that the wood was free of Germans during the afternoon. Yet this vista of lost opportunities totally ignores the difficulty experienced along most of the new line as the infantry struggled to hold back the German counter-attacks. And whatever the RFC observers may have thought they had seen, their gaze could not penetrate the leafy bowers and inner fastness of the woods – the Germans *were* there in some strength. There were indeed opportunities for further advance, but it would be ludicrously over-optimistic to discount the prospect of further stiff German opposition. It probably would have been hard going; on the other hand, suffering endured then may have been an easier option than the subsequent torments the Fourth Army underwent over the next two months in High Wood.

One man truly grateful for the arrival of the cavalry was the seriously wounded Private Downes of the 9th Cameronians. He had been left abandoned in a shell hole by a pair of stretcher bearers who had clearly believed he was beyond mortal help.

A young trooper of the Dragoon Guards, whose horse had been shot from under him, jumped into the shell hole for protection. Finding me alive, he called to his comrades, also horseless and on foot, who despite my stretcher being full of blood, hoisted it onto their shoulders and raced over the ground to hand me over to an Indian cavalry unit waiting in reserve, who completed my journey to the field ambulance unit – a journey with the smoothness of a magic carpet ride compared to the one with the troopers. As always it was the combat men who showed their humanity towards comrades in distress.[74]

Private Barney Downes, 9th Battalion, Cameronians (Scottish Rifles), 27th Brigade, 9th Division

WHILE THE MAIN advance was progressing a separate but related tussle was taking place on the right flank of the main thrust on 14 July. It had been considered axiomatic that Trônes Wood would have to be captured before the launch of the next phase of the attack. It stuck out right into the side of the intended attack on Bazentin Ridge and promised a scything flanking fire that could have cost thousands of lives. Yet, as night fell on 13 July, the bulk of the wood still remained in German hands; time had all but run out when Rawlinson ordered a last desperate attempt by the 54th Brigade of the 18th Division. They were to advance in the dark, seize and consolidate their hold on the wood and form a defensive flank along the eastern face, thus covering the advance of the neighbouring 9th Division. In view of the prevailing communication difficulties Colonel Frank Maxwell of the 12th Middlesex was placed in charge of the attack.

From 11 p.m. onwards kept busy for an attack on the Trônes Wood which had been taken (more or less), lost and retaken about three or four times. Finally it had to be taken and kept at all costs. The Northants and my regiment, under myself, were ordered to do it. Not a pleasant or easy job to take on and be warned off for at 2 a.m., to get across the open before daylight to the edge of the wood or be Maxim-gunned out of existence.[75]

Lieutenant Colonel Frank Maxwell VC, 12th Battalion, Middlesex Regiment, 54th Brigade, 18th Division

It looked hopeless at such short notice for there were severe organisational difficulties to be overcome. His unit was not expecting to be ordered forward and had been scattered about by the various conflicting orders received that day. Maxwell only had two Middlesex companies ready in the right place at the right time and he was forced to send the 6th Northants in first. In the event they were delayed to such an extent that they were attacking broadly at the same time as the main assault that morning.

Yet at first things seemed to go well as the Northants disappeared into the maw of the wood.

> We crossed just as dawn was breaking the half-mile of open ground to the wood, passing through a very thick enemy barrage of shell. The edge of the wood we were aiming for was held by a battalion that had managed to stay in at the last attack. We got over wonderfully well and only one or two parties were blown away which was wonderful. Men were very good and steady. On arrival at wood my orders were for the battalion to halt at the edge and reform. But the CO got muddled and didn't do this, and consequently hadn't a dog's chance of doing anything except be killed just in the same way that other regiments had been for the same fault. Fortunately, I stopped mine inside and kept them in hand. Then waited for reports to come back from the Northants. None came, nor could come as they were soon lost and broken up into small bodies playing just the same game the Germans like for it let them fire at them from sideways and behind.[76]
>
> Lieutenant Colonel Frank Maxwell VC, 12th Battalion, Middlesex Regiment, 54th Brigade, 18th Division

Realising things were going wrong Maxwell went forward himself to see what he could do. As he looked into Trônes Wood, Maxwell realised the sheer magnitude of the task that lay before his men. The English language no longer seemed to have appropriate words to encompass what lay before him.

> To talk of a 'wood' is to talk rot. It was the most dreadful tangle of dense trees and undergrowth imaginable, with deep yawning broken trenches criss-crossing about it. Every tree broken off at top or bottom and branches cut away, so that the floor of the wood was almost an impenetrable tangle of timber, branches, undergrowth etc. blown to pieces by British and German heavy guns for a week. Never was anything so perfectly dreadful to look at – at least I couldn't dream of anything worse – particularly with its dreadful addiction of corpses and wounded men, many lying there for days and days. So dense is the tangle that even if one finds a man, gets someone to bandage him and then leave him, you have lost him probably, simply because you can't find your way back to him.[77]
>
> Lieutenant Colonel Frank Maxwell VC, 12th Battalion, Middlesex Regiment, 54th Brigade, 18th Division

Realising that the Northants had been smashed, Maxwell then devised his own method of dealing with the ferocious problems of fighting in woodland. Modern commentators may jeer at the 'hunting, shooting and fishing' mentality of the old-style regular officers that filled the pre-war Regular Army, but in these circumstances that kind of experience certainly seemed relevant as Maxwell considered the problem. He would form a single line and 'beat' the woods from end to end as if he were flushing out pheasants for a shooting party.

> Well I formed a line with fragments of the Northants and two companies of my own with a job lot of about five very young officers – all the rest being *hors de combat.* After infinite difficulty, I got it shaped in the right direction, and then began the advance very, very slowly. Men nearly all very much shaken by the clamour and din of shell fire and nervy and jumpy about advancing in such a tangle of debris and branches. I had meant only to organise and start the line, and then get back to my loathsome ditch, back near the edge of the wood where we had entered, so as to be in communication by runners with the brigade and the world outside. It is a fundamental principle that commanders of any force should not play about but keep in touch with the higher authorities behind. But though an old enough soldier to realise this, and the wrath of my seniors for disregarding it, I immediately found that without me being there, the thing would collapse in a few minutes. Sounds vain, perhaps, but there is nothing of vanity about it really. So off I went with the line, leading it, *pulling* it on, keeping its direction, keeping it from its hopeless (and humanly natural) desire to get into single file behind me, instead of a long line either side. Soon I made them advance with fixed bayonets – and ordered them to fire ahead of them into the tangle all the way. This was a good move and gave them confidence and so we went on with constant halts to adjust the line. After slow progress in this way, my left came on a hornets' nest and I halted the line and went for it with the left portion. A curtain may be drawn over this, and all that need be said was that many Germans ceased to live, and we took a machine gun. Then on again, and then began what I hoped for: the Germans couldn't face a long line offering no scattered groups to be killed. They began to bolt, first back, then, as the wood became narrow they bolted out to the sides, and with rifle

> and automatic guns we slew them. Right up to the very top this went on, and I could have had a much bigger bag, except that I did not want to show my people out of the wood too much, for fear of letting the German artillery know how we had progressed and so enable them to plaster the wood *pari passu* with our advance. So far they had only laid it on thick, strong and deadly in the belt we had left behind. And, finally, the job was done, and I was thankful, for I thought we should never get through with it.[78]
>
> Lieutenant Colonel Frank Maxwell VC, 12th Battalion, Middlesex Regiment, 54th Brigade, 18th Division

Maxwell and his men had not only achieved their physical objective of capturing Trônes Wood but also been successful in preventing the German garrison from firing into the exposed open flank of the 9th Division during their advance. But capturing the wood was less than half the job. After all, it had been captured before; the problem was keeping the wood in the face of concentrated German artillery fire and hard-pressed counter-attacks.

> Having cleared the wood of live Germans I had then to think of keeping what we had got with the utterly tired men. Poor things, they thought, as one always does, that having done one job, somebody else would pop up and do the next. But there was nobody else. every man in the wood was now needed to cram on the edge facing the Germans, to hold it against them – in fact, far more than were available.[79]
>
> Lieutenant Colonel Frank Maxwell VC, 12th Battalion, Middlesex Regiment, 54th Brigade, 18th Division

As soon as he had set his men in place Maxwell attempted to make his way back to the place where he had first entered Trônes Wood. This he found more difficult than he had expected, both geographically and emotionally.

> I completely lost my way, adjutant and orderly with me. It was a black, clouded day and smoke of shells hung over the shattered tree tops – those that had tops! We simply seemed to walk in circles round and round the incredibly horrible debris, amongst which were more sights to make one weep. Men wounded and lying there, some for days, unbandaged and with every sort of shattered limb. One could only do what one could do for the moment, bandage till they ran out, water till

that ran out, and tell them we should send for them, but all the time knowing that if we were losing our way in hell we should never be able to lead or direct anybody else to bring them in, even if there were any available to send.[80]

Lieutenant Colonel Frank Maxwell VC, 12th Battalion, Middlesex Regiment, 54th Brigade, 18th Division

Maxwell's inability to proffer any kind of immediate succour to the wounded caused him considerable distress and he attempted to get stretcher bearers and medical officers to move further forward to give some real practical assistance.

Not a doctor came to the wood – thought it wasn't their job, not properly realising the ordinary battle conditions (an aid post in some sort of security a little distance behind the battle line) of fighting did not exist in wood fighting. Repeatedly I sent back messengers for doctors and stretcher bearers, but the Germans 'barraged' the open ground all over the route from our own rear and it is an axiom I believe that the RAMC must not run undue risks in getting to wounded. Regimental stretcher bearers – only eight per battalion – carry the cases out of the really dangerous zone to RAMC people who then dress and send them back with their stretcher bearers. In the evening as I went out of the wood, on a summons to brigade headquarters I met the Northants doctor coming in, but he was killed a few yards after passing. But I found our own right away back at brigade headquarters and told him I thought his post should be in the wood and not outside – custom or no custom. Good little man that he is (a Canadian) he immediately went off and has been in it since, searching for wounded with his three men, which is like searching for a needle in a haystack with three fingers. However, it was good his getting there, though the only other man who followed him was also killed.[81]

Lieutenant Colonel Frank Maxwell VC, 12th Battalion, Middlesex Regiment, 54th Brigade, 18th Division

Maxwell's character bemused most of the men that encountered him on what seemed to be his natural battlefield habitat. He seemed immune to fear or any of the traumas that afflicted so many other men in the slaughterhouse of Trônes Wood. As he remarked in an earlier letter to his wife:

> A man may be squandered over me without any more feeling about it, than being sorry for his poor mother or wife. I mean of course, that it does not incapacitate my system in the least.[82]
>
> Lieutenant Colonel Frank Maxwell VC, 12th Battalion, Middlesex Regiment, 54th Brigade, 18th Division

This was not an entirely normal reaction and there is little wonder that many of his men had difficulty in living up to his standards of conduct during battle situations. Maxwell was a hero; he had already won a Victoria Cross and he was not as other men. He set a standard they could perhaps aspire to but with little hope of success.

The aftermath of the fighting that day was truly ghastly to behold. Signaller Leonard Ounsworth could barely believe his eyes when a day later he was sent across into what remained of the 'wood'.

> Well good God, there was no trees intact at all, just stumps, tree tops and barbed wire all mixed up together. Bodies all over the place, Jerries and ours. Robbins, he pulled some undergrowth up and there was a dead Jerry shot away right up his hip, all his guts were out and flies on it. He just had to step back and this leg up the tree became dislodged and fell across him on his head. Good Lord, he vomited on the spot, terrible....[83]
>
> Signaller Leonard Ounsworth, 124th Heavy Battery, Royal Garrison Artillery

Most men reacted to death and destruction with deep gloom and a gradually encroaching fatalism. Soon it would be them, there was nothing they could do, no way out of the trap.

> Seeing Buffs colours on the sleeve of a wounded man's tunic I cross over to see him. It happened to be my old Signal Sergeant Lustead. As fine a man as ever breathed. He was finished, although not quite dead, shot through the throat. It makes one feel gloomy. How long will I be able to dodge the end, still I must not be too morbid. If it comes, well it comes and I daresay that I can be replaced.[84]
>
> Private Robert Cude, 7th Battalion, East Kent Regiment, 55th Brigade, 18th Division

THE ATTACK ON 14 July, known subsequently as the Battle of Bazentin Ridge, had undoubtedly been a triumph in its declared intention of capturing the German former Second Line. Yet for all this tactical success, it remained true that the Fourth Army had emphatically not succeeded in achieving the true breakthrough that might have beckoned towards a strategic success. Even when pushing in the area of his greatest triumphs Rawlinson was still playing catch-up for the original objectives meant to have been taken on 1 July. This perhaps is not so much a criticism of the objectives and achievements of 14 July but more a condemnation of the disaster that had preceded it. Nevertheless, some real hope existed of an accelerated British advance in the weeks that would follow in late July and early August. The German defences were steadily weakening as they struggled to recreate in just a few days from scratches in the ground, the fortress lines that had served them so well on 1 July. And now that the British stood on Bazentin Ridge the French Army would at last rejoin the attack north of the river Somme. If the British kept their nerve and pushed forward then surely victory would be theirs.

CHAPTER SEVEN

Stumbling to Disaster

The atmosphere of optimism engendered by the dramatic successes of 14 July was to prove the cruellest false dawn of the whole Somme campaign. During the next few weeks it seemed as if every lesson that might have been learnt from that success – the devastating use of massed artillery in support of an attack on a reasonably wide front using imaginative infantry tactics – had been deliberately and perversely cast to the winds and replaced with the tactics of a lunatic asylum. If this was a learning curve then it was a sad travesty of geometry. For the infantry the 'High Summer' on the Somme was a dispiriting litany of suffering, failure and 'successes' that were so expensive in lost lives that only the criminally short-sighted would regard them as worthwhile. Once again obscure villages, woods and trenches would attain a notoriety that would still strike a real resonance of despair some decades later.

General Sir Henry Rawlinson certainly appreciated that the situation had changed as the German reserves arrived in some considerable force. He consequently intended a moratorium on piecemeal attacks before a properly coordinated attack on a broad front could be organised – which eventually occurred on 23 July. The sense of drift in the Fourth Army was heightened by the realisation that whatever its army commander may have intended, his subordinates were still intent on launching isolated attacks to attain local objectives. Time after time his divisional commanders launched attacks that had little or no chance of success. All the old faults so evident in the period that had preceded 14 July were once more fully in evidence.

Inevitably, the overall character of the battle changed as the Germans moved up more of their artillery. Although the Royal Artillery still had superiority in the number of guns deployed, they had a far more onerous role in that it was required to destroy the whole fabric of the German lines, whereas the German guns merely had to break up British attacks and support infantry counter-attacks. Whenever either side launched an attack the guns would redouble or triple their efforts, flaying the front-line sectors and reaching back to seal off the area from reserves.

Delville Wood

PERHAPS THE MOST futile series of attacks were launched against a small wood with a burgeoning reputation as a hell-hole and the name to match – Delville Wood. Indeed part of the official nomenclature for the Somme refers glumly to the period 15 July to 3 September as the 'Battle of Delville Wood', as the British struggled to capture and then hold the blighted wood and the ruins of the adjoining village, Longueval. In peacetime the 156-acre wood had a typically sylvan aspect, with mingled oak and birch trees interspersed with thickets of hazel and undergrowth, the whole divided into sections by a series of 'rides' or breaks in the trees. But by mid-July the trees were smashed down, ripped into tangled heaps by the shells and the 'Devil's Wood', as the troops unsurprisingly called it, presented a fearsome prospect.

On 15 July the 9th Division, who had captured the bulk of Longueval on 14 July, were given the task of completing the capture of the wood. Few could have imagined what a protracted saga they were embarking on. The South African Brigade was ordered to capture the wood at 'all costs' on 15 July. The three attacking battalions were placed under the command of Lieutenant Colonel William Tanner the commanding officer of the 4th South African Regiment, and the attack duly went in at 0615.

> We arrived at the edge of the wood at about dawn, everybody on tenterhooks and just as the last man got in old Fritz opened fire with big and little guns, rifle and machine-gun fire. What a time we had! Our men were being rolled over like ninepins, but on went the boys and by 8.30 we had accomplished our task. We gave old Fritz the time of his life. I took a slow and steady aim and made every shot tell. My only regret was that I did not get my bayonet into him. Later there was a lull and it was during this lull that I was hit. I was on guard at the time

Longueval and Delville Wood

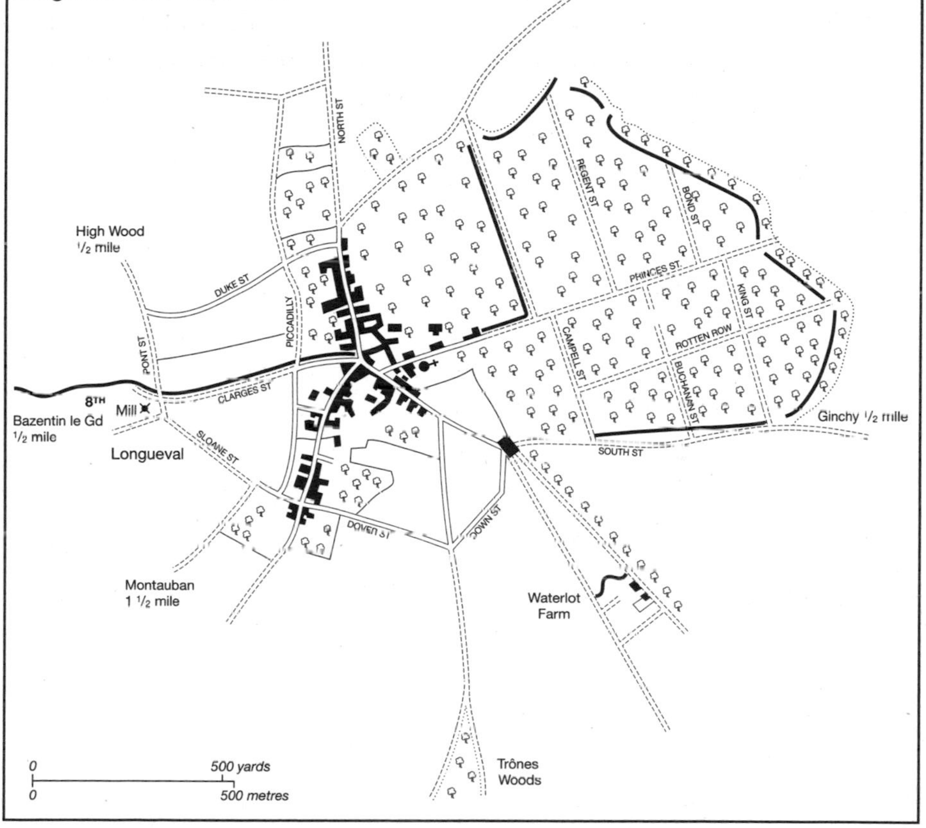

NORTH ST
High Wood
1/2 mile
DUKE ST
PICCADILLY
PONT ST
REGENT ST
BOND ST
PRINCES ST.
KING ST
CAMPELL ST
ROTTEN ROW
BUCHANAN ST
8TH
Mill
CLARGES ST
Bazentin le Gd
1/2 mile
Longueval
SLOANE ST
SOUTH ST
Ginchy 1/2 mille
DOVER ST
DOWN ST
Montauban
1 1/2 mile
Waterlot
Farm
Trônes
Woods
0
500 yards
0
500 metres

> and it was my duty to keep a sharp lookout over the parapet. I had only been on a few minutes when old Fritz sent a huge shell right in front of our trench. It blew away a portion of the trench and knocked a tree over on top of us. One of the splinters of the shell landed me one on the right cheek, which of course put me out for a few moments. It made a nasty hole. I did not wish to leave, but I was told to take another wounded man into safety. We were shelled all the way to the dressing station, but I got him away without any further mishap. On my way through the wood I saw many of our brave lads dead.[1]
>
> Private Hugh Mallett, 2nd Battalion, South African Regiment,
> South African Brigade, 9th Division

There was considerable confusion over the tactical position in and around the wood as no one could say for sure where exactly the amorphous front line was.

> We are engaging troops advancing on wood from south and east. There is some uncertainty as to who they are. Can you say whether French or Huns? Am much perturbed as to uncertainty who we are fighting.[2]
>
> Captain E.V. Vivian, 3rd Battalion, South African Regiment,
> South African Brigade, 9th Division

They managed to capture all but the north-western portion of Delville Wood but, as the severity of the German counter-attacks increased from all around the salient, almost every available man was needed to repel them.

> In view of the fact that there is no wire in front of my firing line – neither is there any in front of the Huns and No Man's Land is only about 300 yards – I think an ample supply of ammunition for Lewis Guns chiefly should be on hand with me. It was most difficult work getting the men to husband their ammunition – especially as we had to allow several hundred Huns to go in peace at a range of 800 yards. But it paid as we caught them at 500 yards. My supply of ammunition is very short.[3]
>
> Captain Medlicort, 3rd Battalion, South African Regiment,
> South African Brigade, 9th Division

The South Africans held on till nightfall and set to entrenching the wood perimeter – no small task in ground filled with twisted roots and mangled trees. This, however, was only the beginning: there would be no relief for days and the South Africans were ordered to hold their ground – again 'at all costs'. Inspirational orders are undoubtedly easier to give out than to follow. Since Captain Vivian had been wounded, another young officer had taken over command of the company and was desperately struggling to cope.

> The enemy continued shelling the wood very heavily all last night, inflicting many casualties. The Vickers machine gun has been put out of action and the gun withdrawn. Nothing has been heard or seen of the 3rd Division. I was given to understand that they were attacking at dawn. My company has been so depleted, and the remaining few are now so exhausted that I do not consider we could put up an effective resistance if the enemy were to attack.[4]
>
> Lieutenant Owen Hubert de Burgh Thomas, 3rd Battalion, South African Regiment, South African Brigade, 9th Division

The German shells were raking across the wood, the ceaseless roar gradually increasing in volume as more and more guns were brought up to the line. To allow the Germans free rein across the wood the German garrison of the north-west section were pulled back. On 18 July it has been calculated that around 20,000 shells fell on the single square mile of Devil's Wood reaching a crescendo at the phenomenal rate of seven crashing down per second.

> Absolute hell turned inside out. I never expected to get out whole. Shells dropping everywhere. We get orders to return in the afternoon late. I think, in fact I am almost sure, that our lives were saved when a very brave officer, Captain Hoptroff, made his way to our position. He wasted no time, 'Get out!' he said, and was almost immediately hit by a bullet and killed outright. It is strange how, in the most urgent and tragic circumstances, one notices things of minor importance. For as Captain Hoptroff dropped, my eye caught sight of his very beautiful gold wristlet watch; and I have never ceased to regret that I did not take it off, and send it to his family. I am sure that they would have appreciated it.[5]
>
> Private Frank Marillier, 2nd Battalion, South African Regiment, South African Brigade, 9th Division

All around the wood perimeter young South African officers were recognising the prosaic truth that human courage alone cannot withstand huge quantities of high explosive and shrapnel.

> I am now the only officer left in A Coy. One Lewis Gun crew have been blown up. Can you send another crew? I have wounded men lying all along my front & have no stretchers left, and they are dying for want of treatment, my field dressings being all used up. Can you obtain stretcher bearers? Urgent. I consider the position is now untenable, and have had my breastworks all blown in. It is impossible to spare men to take wounded away, and my front is now very lightly held with many gaps. To save the balance of men it will be necessary to withdraw. Most of the men here are suffering from shell shock and I do not consider we are fit to hold the position in the event of an enemy attack.[6]
>
> Lieutenant Owen Hubert de Burgh Thomas, 3rd Battalion, South African Regiment, South African Brigade, 9th Division

The South Africans had given all they could give. Despite their orders to stick it at all costs several reluctantly began to fall back on Prince's Street, as the Scots had quaintly named the main ride that cut across the wood from Longueval to its eastern border. Colonel Tanner had been evacuated wounded and Colonel Thackeray of the 3rd South Africans had therefore taken effective command of the brigade. Their new positions were amongst what remained of the wood, and a new and deadly threat soon made itself apparent.

> We made our way back, joining Colonel Thackeray and about seventy survivors in a reserve trench. Here we set up our Lewis gun with tragic results. In succession ten of my mates were killed and it looked as if my own turn was next. Whilst at the gun, one bullet grazed the side of my face, near the eye. Another hit the stock. But the bullets were not coming from the direction our gun was facing. After our tenth comrade had been killed, one of our chaps thought he saw a slight movement in a tree, some distance to our rear. We gave the tree a burst, and out dropped a German sniper. A brave man, he must have crept into the wood in the darkness of the previous night, and set himself up, well hidden, in the branches.

> I am sure he would have known that his chances of survival were very slight. I was indeed lucky not to be his next victim.[7]
>
> Private Frank Marillier, 2nd Battalion, South African Regiment, South African Brigade, 9th Division

Although by this time exhausted, running out of food and water, the increasingly shell-shocked South Africans clung on to their makeshift shallow trenches. As each hour passed there were fewer men left standing to face the next German counter-attack.

> D Coy retired without passing up any word, so did those on their left. *My orders were to hold on.* I was on point of salient and furthest force pushed out. A and C Companies on my right not being dug in were scattered – one platoon D Company did well on my left. I used 4th Regt in reserve trench as reinforcements. Ammunition scarce. Mud caused ammunition to be useless – also wounded men's rifles jammed with mud. No cleaning material – all consumed. Two guns, one Lewis and one Maxim knocked out. Our own field guns killed and wounded many of us. Difficulty owing to this to extend to my left. D Coy retired when the attack came at probably 5 p.m. or later; however beat Germans off. Many killed 7 yards from my trenches. Remnants of A and C Companies overpowered. I learnt this after heat of attack abated, with machine guns enfilading us from my right. By passing up five rounds at a time from each man I kept machine guns and one Lewis gun going sparingly. Killed many Germans. I divided my front i.e. alternate men facing alternate fronts. Sent bombing party and patrol under officer to try and clear my right and get away to retire to Waterlot Farm or our old Regimental Headquarters. German held trenches at latter place and machine guns up trenches on my right. Determined to hold on.[8]
>
> Captain Medlicort, 3rd Battalion, South African Regiment, South African Brigade, 9th Division

Despite all their valiant efforts, Captain Medlicort and his men were finally overrun by the Germans at dawn on 19 July.

> Exhausted machine gun ammunition. Drove off attack from wood but had to chuck it soon after 8 a.m. Handed back, sorry to say, all German prisoners captured during the day. I got not a wink of sleep for four nights. Could not sleep in the night of the 18th. Got

> Lieutenants Guard and Thomas in a safe place (both wounded) with German prisoners. I was satisfied at our marksmanship, so many dead Germans round us in the wood. I was too busy waiting for the moment of attack which was maturing during the day. The enemy shell fire was chiefly 5.9-in. Too intense to think of retiring. The Germans were rattled with our gunfire. Our men, who at that time owing to want of water and sleep were cold and stiff, were calm and had a 'don't care a damn' appearance.[9]
>
> Captain Medlicort, 3rd Battalion, South African Regiment,
> South African Brigade, 9th Division

Amongst the thoroughly exhausted prisoners was Private Victor Wepener.

> We were shelled from all sides. At times men were killed next to me while I was talking to them. Though I always had ammunition, the rain and mud got into our rifle bolts and caused them to jam. When the Germans eventually overran us, I was impressed by a very aristocratic officer who wore a cap instead of a steel helmet. He kept his hand over his pistol holster whilst we 'remnants' were being collected in an open glade. A German soldier with a bandaged head and his rifle and bayonet slung over his shoulder called me, '*Kamerad*'. I didn't quite know what to say as I didn't fancy being his comrade. The German soldiers on average were jolly good chaps. I then helped carry Lieutenant Guard who had been shot in the leg. Some of the wounded had to be left behind. I was one of the few to escape unscathed. We were then marched through their lines and we saw many Germans lying there waiting to attack. A couple of our chaps carried a German with a stomach wound on a groundsheet. Our artillery opened up and we were amused to see our guards ducking away and running for cover. After what we had been through we didn't worry about shell bursts anymore.[10]
>
> Private Victor Wepener, 3rd Battalion, South African Regiment,
> South African Brigade, 9th Division

Colonel Thackeray and the scattered remnants of the 3rd South Africans were left clinging on to the last line of defence running along Prince's Street and then bending back along Buchanan Street. Grimly hanging on by their fingertips to just a small corner of the wood they waited for the long promised relief. Time and time again they were promised assistance but nothing concrete resulted. To add injury to insult the South Africans were constantly plagued by British shells dropping by accident or design right into the wood.

> Urgent. My men are on their last legs. I cannot keep some of them awake. They drop with their rifles in hand asleep in spite of heavy shelling. We are expecting an attack. Even that cannot keep some of them from dropping down. Food and water has not reached us for two days – though we have managed on rations of those killed, but must have water. I am alone with Phillips who is wounded and only a couple of sergeants. Please relieve these men today without fail as I fear they have come to the end of their endurance.[11]
>
> Lieutenant Colonel E. F. Thackeray, 3rd Battalion, South African Regiment, South African Brigade, 9th Division

At last the news came the men had been praying for. The 53rd Brigade of the 18th Division was temporarily attached to the 9th Division and duly sent forward to relieve the beleaguered South Africans. When the South African Brigade finally emerged from what remained of the wood there were only 780 of the 3,153 men present to answer the roll call. The South Africans would never forget Delville Wood.

So it was that on 19 July it fell to the 53rd Brigade to move forward without prior reconnaissance to make an attempt to recapture the southern half of Delville Wood. It is the sheer ubiquity of such attacks that gave them an aura of futility and horror that resounds to this day. This time it was the turn of Private Thomas Jennings of the 6th Royal Berkshires to go forward with his friends into the maw of battle in Delville Wood. Just reaching the wood was a trial of biblical proportions.

> Shovels were in the proportion of five to one of picks. A pile of these were passed along the line, and all of us replacements found ourselves with a pick stuck down our back under our haversack. This wasn't by chance for the older members of the Berkshires had a spade, a much lighter and easier tool – we live and learn. There was only one entrance to the wood on the south side and the way from Longueval to this entrance was under direct machine-gun fire. The 8th Norfolks went in first, then the 10th Essex and the 6th Berks in the centre. At the sound of a whistle we moved forward. It is amazing, indeed astounding, that in spite of the enemy's barrage of HE, we went on in columns of four. It

> seemed ages before the order to thin out in extended order was given. We now passed the field gunners who were stripped to the waist, and gained the cover of the sunken road. We stopped there for a while, then went on a yard or so, then stopped again, and so on. It seemed such slow progress, it must be that A Company was finding it difficult to push forward, they were in front. As we crouched against the bank there came from out of the blue a terrific explosion, the air was thick with black smoke and a thousand bells rang in my head. When everything cleared I saw in front of me a soldier lying on his back in a pool of blood from a gaping wound. He called out, 'Mother, take 'em away, take 'em away!' He died a few minutes later. I then realised that another chap in front of me didn't move. I almost touched him and I could see that his water bottle was dripping water tinged with blood. A further look at him told me he was dead, indeed I heard his last gasp. My feelings were awful; this was just plain murder. To make things even worse a dozen or so soldiers were crying and staggering about with shell shock.[12]
>
> Private Thomas Jennings, 6th Battalion, Royal Berkshire Regiment, 53rd Brigade, 18th Division

As Jennings neared the front, the shelling steadily increased and the awful sights and sounds pressed deeply on his bewildered senses.

> We moved on again and reached a communication trench running alongside a road and a wood the other side. A couple of Jerry soldiers passed us on the way back; these were prisoners, and scared to hell, making signs that they were not officers. It still seemed slow progress as we made our way along that trench. Shrapnel pegged us down somewhat and the evidence of this was the 'ping' on the tin hat. As Captain Hudson was talking to the regimental sergeant major, a German sniper saw them, killed the RSM and put a bullet through the captain's tin hat. Looking above the trench at times I could see stretcher bearers with their burdens lying dead. The red cross on their sleeves didn't protect them from being killed. Slow progress was made again along the trench with the dead and dying all around us. We halted many times for several minutes. On one occasion I found myself squatting on a corpse that was covered with earth, except for his head, which was minus his scalp and hair worn away by the traffic of heavy boots.[13]
>
> Private Thomas Jennings, 6th Battalion, Royal Berkshire Regiment, 53rd Brigade, 18th Division

At last they reached the end of the trench where it met a road. Ahead of them lay the terrible tangle of Delville Wood.

> Our captain was there to give us the signal when to go. I shall always remember his words, 'Follow your sergeant – go!' The sergeant was a tall heavily built chap, who shot across the road as if from a gun. Each man ran singly under withering machine-gun fire and shelling, which increased in severity once the attack had been launched. I followed suit, but lost my sergeant and myself in the wood. I wandered around for a moment or so and then dived into a shell hole. That action didn't give me much consolation. The thoughts that ran through my head were, 'If the Germans saw me there, would they take me prisoner or lob a couple of hand grenades at me?' I was duly relieved of these thoughts by seeing a couple of our lads approaching and they asked me what I was doing. I had no answer, but was glad to get out of that hole and set forward in the direction we thought we should go. With a bit of luck we found a platoon of khaki uniformed soldiers in a waist-high trench. On speaking to them we learned that they were South Africans. One of them told us that he had been a Boer soldier and fought against us in that war in 1901. He proved to be quite a decent chap. All the time the din, the racket and the fearful noise continued, machine gun and gunfire, trees crashing down from HE. We were then prompted by our South African friends to go in the direction they thought we might find our company of the 6th Berks. We did eventually find them on the extreme edge of the wood with a mound of earth in front of their heads and equipment piled in front of that. This was the only quick way to protect their heads against rifle fire; it was all bewildering to me.[14]
>
> Private Thomas Jennings, 6th Battalion, Royal Berkshire Regiment, 53rd Brigade, 18th Division

Having reached the wood they were confronted by the usual problems of fighting in a woodland, smashed by shell fire and haunted by ambushing snipers. The Berkshires had no Colonel Frank Maxwell VC to seize the situation by the scruff of the neck. Thwarted by the Germans in front and on either side, they were cut off by the barrage line of German shells falling behind them from any chance of reinforcements or supplies.

> There was great difficulty with regard to water, the only well in the wood was close to where the enemy was strongest, and we received no

> food supplies the whole of the time we were in the wood. In parts of the wood, patrols, and even single men of the opposing forces were hunted and stalked, one after the other. The air was thick with a horrible stench from dead bodies and the pungent odour of gas. The 'Devil's Wood' was indeed a terrible place. Nightfall came and with it a silence of a kind. No gunfire, just the occasional crack of a rifle. We moved around like ghosts in the darkness, which gave the fellows an opportunity to search the dead for their water bottles. Sergeant Bygraves, one of our senior NCOs, crept over to a severely wounded German prisoner to give him a drink of water. That poor Jerry had been propped up against a tree for at least thirty hours or more. Whenever one of us got near him he feebly put his hands up as a token of surrender. I remember the aide-de-camp to the commander of 53rd Brigade coming up to the front line to see how things were progressing. When this one-armed Guards officer had seen Lieutenant Colonel B. G. Clay, he came across the wounded German. Turning to me he said, 'Shoot the bastard!' I thought to myself, 'He has a revolver, why doesn't he do it?' This staff officer then went on his way without waiting for me to carry out his order. As no one else pursued the matter, I decided not to do his dirty work and walked away apprehensively.[15]
>
> Private Thomas Jennings, 6th Battalion, Royal Berkshire Regiment, 53rd Brigade, 18th Division

They could get no further and their position remained extremely tenuous. Finally, having achieved nothing, they were eventually relieved on the night of 21 July. Their brigadier summed up the operation in a lacerating report that did not mince its words as it lashed home the sheer futility of the 'gesture' his 53rd Brigade and the men of the 6th Royal Berkshires had made. The tactical problem of taking Delville Wood was almost insuperable without a large-scale general advance that encompassed the wood. Without that the only effective way of clearing the wood was by utilising the power of the artillery, but once occupied the victors were equally vulnerable to the same treatment.

The Germans, too, were suffering as they launched costly counter-attacks that had little real purpose, but their tactical naivety faded into insignificance beside the confused, headstrong, wilful stupidity of some of the British attacks, which cost the Germans only ammunition to repel. Not only did the continuation of such futile British piecemeal attacks leach away the fighting strength of the Fourth Army to no purpose, but the feeling of events spiralling out of control was exacerbated by an unfortunate break in the weather that brought rain and dull overcast skies. This hampered the work of the Royal Flying Corps, led to further delays and gave more invaluable time to the Germans. Minor attacks could be defeated with the defences and resources in place, but the Germans were in a race against time to knit together the integrated defence they would need to hold back another pile-driven assault. Every day counted.

23–29 July 1916:

THE PLANS FOR the next major attack envisioned a thrust forward of both the Fourth and Reserve Armies in conjunction with the French in the early morning of 23 July. Of all the valuable lessons that could be gleaned from the successes achieved on 14 July it seems perverse that General Sir Douglas Haig and Rawlinson should, at least on the surface, have drawn little more than a near-superstitious belief that a night attack could deflect the power of massed German machine guns and artillery. The skilful tactical use of the cloak of darkness to amass and deploy troops to secure a stunning surprise had indeed been a vital component in the success achieved at the Battle of Bazentin Ridge. Yet the crushing preliminary bombardment was far more crucial in its ability to smash the German front lines, destroying the machine guns and the battery-gun positions. If they were not dealt with then the Germans retained the potential, whatever the degree of visibility, to open a deadly fire on previously determined fixed lines and pre-registered targets. Furthermore, it was unfortunate for the British artillery that the next lines of German trenches were tucked away on the reverse slopes of the low ridges, and hence far better concealed from direct observation than had been the case before 14 July. The British gunners were heavily dependent on artillery registration from the BE2cs of the RFC for their accuracy and the weather had severely hampered flying. When the sun finally re-emerged on 20 July it left far too little time for the hundreds of guns to be registered before the preliminary bombardment began in earnest on 22 July.

The Allied High Command was under pressure while preparing for the next stage in the offensive, for speed was necessary if the Germans were not further to consolidate their positions. In bowing to this imperative plans were conceived, considered, approved and disseminated in excessive haste. In these circumstances it is not surprising that when the reconnaissance flights of the RFC brought back photographs that clearly delineated a newly dug German trench stretching forward of the switch line in front of Bazentin-le-Petit the High Command failed to act in a considered or logical fashion. The new line, unimaginatively christened the 'Intermediate Trench' had not been catered for in the original plans but at that late stage all that could be thought of on the spur of the moment was to bring forward the time of attack in the affected sector to 0030 on 23 July. The Intermediate Trench would be rushed at that time, after which the presumed 'victors' would join in the main assault at 0130 on the switch line that still lay ahead of them. A similar approach was adopted to deal with Wood Trench, which interfered with the main plans for the attack in the sector between High Wood and Delville Wood, although this time the attack would start even earlier at 2200 on 22 July.

A further complication was provided by the necessity of the XIII Corps to hammer out a compatible assault plan with the neighbouring French, which had resulted in a negotiated start time of 0340 on 23 July. Yet worse was to follow. Perhaps sensibly, the French were anxious not to be 'rushed' and at the last moment they announced that they would not in fact be ready to attack until the next day – 24 July. Rawlinson was thrown into an invidious position, but reluctantly decided that the British had gone too far down the line to postpone the attack. He therefore reluctantly accepted that the right of his line would be attacking towards Guillemont with their right flanks exposed and, as it was by then too late to change the orders, they would still go over at the anomalous start time of 0340. Last minute changes generated their own confusions and in the event not all the assault divisions along the line received their final start times correctly before it was simply too late.

An additional complication was the decision to increase the contribution made by General Sir Hubert Gough and his Reserve Army to the overall offensive effort. Although it had by no means been inactive, Reserve Army operations since 1 July had largely been conducted on a small scale. Costly localised attacks had been made to 'improve' the tactical position and indeed the village of Ovillers had finally fallen on 16 July.

> Ovillers has been of special interest to us the last six days. My battalion has seen some sticky fighting. By continually harassing

> the Boche and working our way round him, we eventually got him out of the village. In his last trench on the outskirts of the village he left a number of wounded, all of whom were agreed that they had had a damnable time. Here I collected all the Germans who could in any way hobble along and sent them back to our brigade dressing station. Would you believe it our damned brigade staff cursed the man in charge of the escort for not sending them down on stretchers. I only wish I had been there. I would have let the blasted maniacs have a bit of mind. As if we were not already busy enough dealing with our own wounded and carrying them back, and using every available man we had got to man the trenches as we collared them. It is this sort of damned impudence from people sitting on their haunches miles in the rear, who not only have no idea of the conditions and strain under which people are working up in front, but also are too idle to come up and find out – which makes the regimental officer despise the staff.[16]
>
> Lieutenant H. G. Wood, 1/7th Battalion Worcestershire Regiment, 144th Brigade, 48th Division

As ever, an objective captured merely moved the focus on to the next perceived target. In this case it was the village of Pozières, which now lay before the British on the Albert–Bapaume road. The village was strongly defended as part of the original German Second Line defence system on the Pozières Ridge. It was a tactically important location as its capture would not only to some extent destabilise the rest of the German Second Line in that sector, but it would also begin to unravel the German stranglehold on the fortress of the Thiepval Spur, which still barred the way to any advance in the northern sector of the Somme battle front. Several small-scale attempts on the village had done little more than inflate the number of casualties suffered. It was at this point that Haig ordered Gough to capture Pozières as soon as possible, in conjunction with the general night attack being launched by the Fourth Army on 23 July. Gough decided to throw the newly arrived 1st Australian Division into the fray. They would attack at 0030 on 23 July, striking across from the south-east at the junction of the Reserve Army and the Fourth Army rather than straight up the Albert–Pozières road. To their left would be the 48th Division who, in attacking towards the head of Mash Valley, would depend for their lives on an Australian success.

The planned assault on 23 July would, therefore, be no single smashing blow, but in essence nothing more than a succession of isolated attacks, each of which would succeed or fail essentially on the basis of its own merits. With each complication and last-minute adjustment to the plans, the overall concept of a single coordinated blow was fatally diluted. The end result was a crazy mélange of start times amongst the X, ANZAC, III, XV and XIII Corps that spread out across a period of some five and a half hours between 2200 and 0340. It was a recipe for disaster.

The preliminary bombardment for the attacks commenced at 1900 on 22 July. The first assault was made three hours later by the men of the 5th Division, who attacked Wood Trench, which ran between Delville Wood and High Wood. The troops went over the top at 2220 that night – for the survivors it would prove an unforgettable experience.

> It was a night of such kaleidoscopic effects that I can still see them vividly. It must have been terrifying in its utter inhumanity to the men of the new drafts from England. Every variety of sound, colour and odour assailed and overwhelmed our senses, so that we felt immune to the perpetual threat of death or mutilation – until it came. Loaded with rifle, bayonet, extra ammunition and an unwieldy field telephone in the hope of keeping contact with the rear, I went sprawling in the fitful darkness into a shell hole just short of a new explosion. When I recovered, I moved on, but not before glancing around the whole scene into which I was trudging at a half-trot. The wood was alive with points of light from machine guns, vivid with shell flashes and coloured by the urgent signal flares of Bengal lights; patches of black smoke and flickering red came from the burning debris. From Longueval, almost behind me came the reflected flashes of an exploding dump.[17]
>
> Private Francis Fields, 15th Battalion, Warwickshire Regiment, 13th Brigade, 5th Division

Before they were spotted the 15th Warwicks made some considerable progress until they crossed the ridge and found themselves in view of the Germans. Lost in a nightmare the survivors were forced to take shelter in a scratch trench that offered only an illusion of protection.

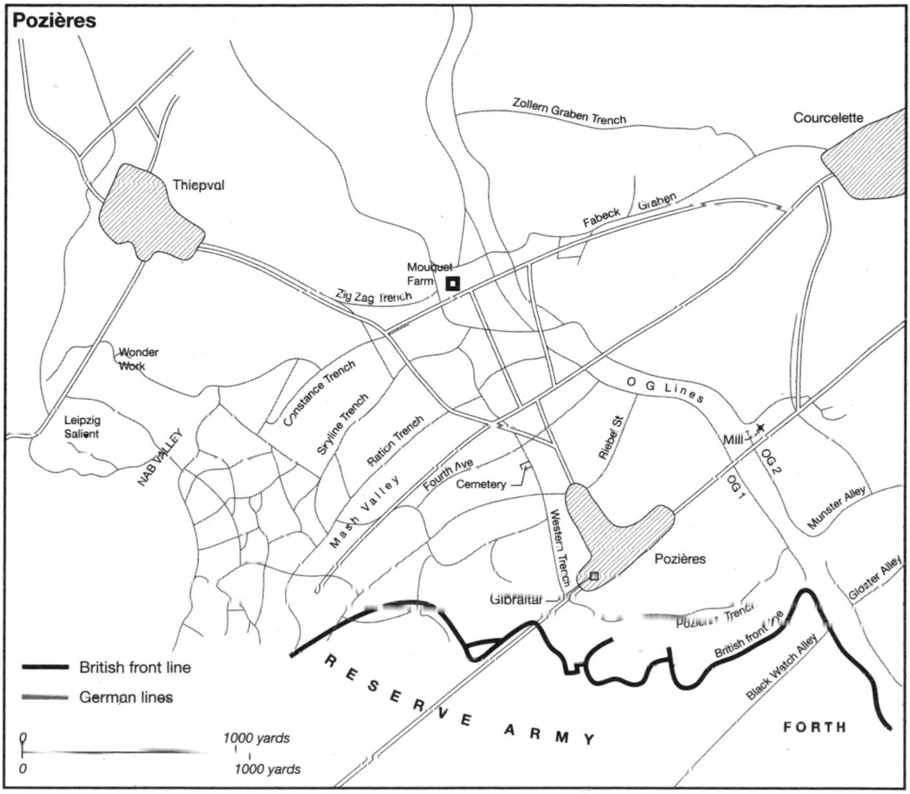

Pozières
Thiepval
Zollern Graben Trench
Courcelette
Fabeck Graben
Mouquet Farm
Zig Zag Trench
Wonder Work
Leipzig Salient
NAB VALLEY
Constance Trench
Skyline Trench
Ration Trench
Mash Valley
Fourth Ave
Cemetery
O G Lines
Riebe St
Mill
OG 1
OG 2
Munster Alley
Western Trench
Pozières
Gibraltar
Gloster Alley
British front line
Black Watch Alley
RESERVE ARMY
FORTH
British front line
German lines
0
1000 yards
0
1000 yards

> Some of us, survivors of two platoons of A Company manned a trench about an eighth of a mile in advance of the British front line, and beyond the limit reached by the British and Indian cavalry after their charge through waving corn up the slope topped by the ill-famed woods. Behind, bodies of horses and men lying under the hot sun did not let us forget the incident. The trench itself was a mere ditch and poor protection from the exploring German gunners, especially shrapnel as I knew to my cost when a red hot particle lodged near my left eye. We turned corpses out to improve the parapet. Here, a plane would come over at dawn, just visible through the mist, to assure headquarters we still held the position. We were surprisingly immune from attack and could watch that sector, all around us, without inhibitions. Once, there was a short liquid fire attack on the edge of High Wood; again, on the far corner of Delville Wood there were yells and a few running figures. The ground was littered with the blackened remains of Highlanders and Fusiliers. As a signaller I was either alone or working with a companion, Harry Ellis usually. Exploring this area for wire and souvenirs, I came face to face with a figure round a small shrub – a Highlander on all fours – staring, rigid, forever immovable. I guided a complete stranger who was utterly helpless, abandoned with 'shell shock'. He moved leaning forward, his head projected, arms limp, all control of his face had gone. He could not hear me; he did not respond in any way, just slouched steadily forwards.[18]
>
> Private Francis Fields, 15th Battalion, Warwickshire Regiment, 13th Brigade, 5th Division

Fields was sent to establish whether there was any contact between the right of his company and the neighbouring village of Longueval. Amongst the ruins was a strange reminder of more innocent times.

> I was tracing a wire up an old German trench towards the village defences. Advancing boldly towards me came a tiny friendly little ball of fur, something utterly incongruous in that setting; a kitten, mewing and tail erect. Evidently the village pet, still surviving the devastation.[19]
>
> Private Francis Fields, 15th Battalion, Warwickshire Regiment, 13th Brigade, 5th Division

On the right of the line the 30th Division had the task of attacking Guillemont without any support from the neighbouring French. The 19th

Manchesters moved out from the edge of Trônes Wood, heading directly across the open ground to the battered village at 0340 on the morning of 23 July.

> We attacked just before dawn, I being told off to carry a coil of barbed wire on a stake. We had 1,000 yards to go over the open. I soon dropped the barbed wire and lost the spade off my back – the Germans were waiting for us![20]
>
> Private Albert Andrews, 19th Battalion, Manchester Regiment, 21st Brigade, 30th Division

This was unsurprising as the British had by then been sending in isolated attacks for four hours. Yet despite all the problems and the added stress of uncut barbed wire, the Manchesters managed against all the odds to burst through to capture Guillemont. This, however, was just the opening gambit in a battle that would rage all day long. The inevitable German counter-attacks hit home hard, isolating and destroying the first two waves of Manchesters, and taking a heavy toll of the rest. Private Albert Andrews was one of the casualties, receiving a wound in the right shoulder. With considerable difficulty, battling with increasing faintness and thirst, he made his way back as one of the walking wounded.

> I was just about done and was staggering along, I think I would have given up some time since, but my nose was towards home. A parson saw me nearly fall, picked me up and carried me into the dressing station at Billon Farm, where he gave me a drink of tea. While I was drinking this a general came, looked at my shoulder and said, 'Manchesters', asking where I was wounded. I told him, 'Guillemont!' He seemed as if he could hardly believe it, until a Yorks said to him, 'Yes, Sir, the Manchesters are in Guillemont.' He turned to me and said, 'Are they in it now?' I said, 'They were when I left, but were being hard pressed in a counter-attack by the Germans!' He waited no more and off he went with some other officers. I asked who he was, with him being so anxious, and was told it was General Rawlinson.[21]
>
> Private Albert Andrews, 19th Battalion, Manchester Regiment, 21st Brigade, 30th Division

Of course their heroism proved all in vain. Cut off by the German artillery and hounded by ceaseless counter-attacks the Manchesters could not hold on to their cherished gains and ultimately fell back to their start lines by the early afternoon. They had fought hard but the odds were always against them. The situation was replicated more or less all along the front of the Fourth Army during their attacks on 23 July. Rawlinson had presided over an unfocused attack and his men had paid a grim price. No ground was gained and the casualties were made all the more painful by the sacrifices being all in vain.

MEANWHILE, on the Reserve Army front, the 1st Australian Division, fresh from all their wasted endeavours at Gallipoli, were experiencing for the first time the reality of warfare on the Western Front. The supporting British artillery flayed the ruins of Pozières from 19 July with an ever-increasing intensity in preparation for their attack, which was scheduled for 0030 on 23 July. At about midnight the Australians moved out to their jumping-off tapes and many crept out into No Man's Land to get as close as possible to the barrage line when it fell, thereby accepting the risk of casualties from shells that dropped even a few yards short. At 1228 the massed guns roared out together and the Australians saw for the first time the stupefying lethal power of an artillery bombardment.

> Down came our barrage on to the enemy lines and Pozières village, the Germans replying with artillery and machine-gun fire. As we lay out among the poppies in No Man's Land we could see the bullets cutting off the poppies almost against our heads. The flashes of the guns, the bursting of the shells and the Very lights, made the night like day, and, as I lay as flat to the ground as possible I was expecting to stop one any time. Jamming my tin helmet down on my head I brought the body of my rifle across my face to stop anything that might happen to drop low. In the tumult it was impossible to hear orders. My ears were ringing with the cracking of bullets. A man alongside me was crying like a baby, and although I tried to reassure him he kept on saying that we would never get out of it. Suddenly I saw men scrambling to their feet. Taking this to be the signal for the charge I jumped up and dashed across.[22]
>
> Sergeant H. Preston, 9th Australian (Queensland) Battalion, 3rd Brigade, 1st Division, Australian Imperial Force

The surviving German machine guns gave the Australians the unwanted chance to judge the killing potential of these guns in the relatively open fields of the Somme battlefields compared to the enclosed gullies of ANZAC. When Zero hour came the officers' whistles went for the most part unheard, but their men followed them forward as fast as they could. The bombardment had done its grim work and they soon forced their way into Pozières Trench, which barred the way to the village.

> At the point where I entered there was a German doctor, who afterwards did good work among the wounded. Private Jack Rogers, who reached the trench with me, bayoneted two Germans, and after a sharp fight the trench was cleared, and we immediately set to work to improve our position. Captain S. N. Lawrance was in charge of this work. The trench was in good order, with dugouts let into the sides. The dead bodies, which had to be thrown out, were used in building up the parapet.[23]
>
> Sergeant H. Preston, 9th Australian (Queensland) Battalion, 3rd Brigade, 1st Division, Australian Imperial Force

The 9th Battalion were on the right flank of the Australian attack and thus had to contend with the threatening presence of the German OG1 and OG2 lines. A German strong point immediately to their right was still holding out. Private John Leak was awarded a VC as he rushed a machine gun and bayoneted the whole crew. The fighting that ensued had a particularly vicious intensity.

> I was with a party that was ordered to the right in an endeavour to force a way into the stronghold. This, however, proved difficult as it was strongly held by the enemy whose egg bombs could be thrown farther than our Mills. After a sharp fight our bomb supply ran out, and we were forced to barricade the trench and rely on rifle and bayonet until more grenades arrived. Men were spread out along the trench and the bombs were passed from man to man. The Germans at first tricked us by putting helmets and caps on their rifles and walking along with them held above the parapet. When our men put their heads up and attempted to shoot them, they were shot by other Germans farther along the trench. But it did not take us very long to wake up to this ruse, and very soon we were playing the same game. While all this was going on we were tunnelling under a road into the strong post, and by this

> means we succeeded in getting into the enemy trench. This movement startled the Germans, who dashed out and across the ridge towards Pozières village, making an excellent target for our rifles and machine guns. In the meantime, other Australians had entered Pozières and driven out its garrison who were making their way to the stronghold. So out over the top we went and chased the confused and panic-stricken enemy over the ridge in the direction of the old windmill. A good many were overtaken and shot or bayoneted.[24]
>
> Sergeant H. Preston, 9th Australian (Queensland) Battalion, 3rd Brigade, 1st Division, Australian Imperial Force

The capture of most of the village meant that consolidation was the priority as the troops awaited the inevitable violent German reaction. Once it realised the situation the German artillery was not idle, it took a steady toll of the Australians; it isolated them, in an attempt to cut them off from reinforcements and basic supplies. This tactic was obvious and expected, but almost impossible to counter without a concerted prior attempt to knock out the German batteries.

> Most of the fire was in enfilade, and as the line ran parallel and close to the main road, our position was accurately marked down. As fast as one portion of the trench was cleared another was blown in. There were no dugouts in which men on post could take shelter, and the only thing to do was to grin and bear it. The shells, which were dropping almost perpendicularly, could be clearly seen in the last 40 feet of their descent, and the whole trench was methodically dealt with.[25]
>
> Captain J. R. O. Harris, 3rd Australian (New South Wales) Battalion 1st Brigade, 1st Division, Australian Imperial Force

This bombardment was not falling on virgin ground; by this time it had been thoroughly pounded, thrown up time and time again until it was merely a treacherous amalgam of loose earth, bricks and helpless soldiers.

> The men who were not wounded were kept busy digging out men who were buried alive by the explosions caving in the trench sides. I had occasion to bless my 'tin hat' for in our portion of the trench the parapet was composed of the debris of a ruined house – and a shell pushed over a barrow load of bricks on to my head with no other ill effect but some bruises on the shoulders.[26]
>
> Captain J. R. O. Harris, 3rd Australian (New South Wales) Battalion, 1st Brigade, 1st Division, Australian Imperial Force

There was nothing for the survivors to do but endure as best they could.

> Without doubt Pozières was the heaviest, bloodiest, rottenest stunt that ever the Australians were caught up in. The carnage is just indescribable. As we were making our attack after the 3rd Brigade had gone through we were literally walking over the dead bodies of our cobbers that had been slain by this barrage. I can't imagine anything more concentrated than the artillery barrage of the Germans at that particular stunt. He was even shelling our front line with great 'coal boxes'. His artillery was registered right smack on it. The bay on our left went in, two or three chaps were killed; the bay on our right went in. I said to this chap, 'Its our turn next!' I hadn't said it before we were buried. I was quite unconscious, buried in what had been the German front-line trench. I was picked up and sent back to the battalion first aid post. I was given a bottle of *sal volatile* or something – I wish it had been rum! I was sat in a corner of this aid post for a little while, but then the wounded just streamed in and the chap in charge of the post said, 'Oh well, you've had enough rest, you'd better get back again!' And I went back. During the whole of that period I can't remember anything more nerve-wracking than the continuous shelling day and night.[27]
>
> Private Frank Brent, 2nd Australian (New South Wales) Battalion, 1st Brigade, 1st Division, Australian Imperial Force

Whatever the men did, whether they moved to left or right they could not second guess the random machinations of high technology and blind fate that guided the shells to their final resting place.

> The heavy shells were falling, so it was estimated, at the rate of three a minute. It was not long before the area became unrecognisable, and as time went on even the unwounded felt sick. Food and water were not too plentiful, and we did not know when any more would be available. After our iron rations had gone we were compelled to fall back upon any that could be found on the dead.[28]
>
> Private P. Kinchington, 3rd Australian (New South Wales) Battalion, 1st Brigade, 1st Division, Australian Imperial Force

In such circumstances, it was imperative that risks were taken if the Australians were to maintain a foothold in Pozières. Ration parties were sent back towards Contalmaison to try and get some desperately needed water. Sergeant Preston volunteered to lead a party in this prosaic but excessively dangerous mission.

> Big shells were falling thickly. We could see them like black streaks coming down from the sky just before they hit the ground. Often times we were thrown to the ground with concussion, great clods of earth showering us and making our steel helmets ring. One member of the party, Private Fitzgerald, was partly buried, but was quickly dug out and left in the nearest trench to await the stretcher bearers. Eventually we reached Contalmaison, got some water in benzene tins, and made our way back to the front. On the way we passed Fitzgerald, badly wounded, but still alive. The water, as can be imagined, had a strong benzene flavour.[29]
>
> Sergeant H. Preston, 9th Australian (Queensland) Battalion, 3rd Brigade, 1st Division, Australian Imperial Force

At 0830 on 25 July the long-expected, major counter-attack at last materialised from the direction of the windmill further along Pozières Ridge.

> As I happened to be on the right flank, I found myself right in the thick of it. The enemy came over the ridge like swarms of ants, rushing from shell hole to shell hole. Our men, full of fight and confidence, lined the parapet and emptied magazine after magazine into them. Some of the boys, anxious to get a shot at the Germans, pulled one another down from the firestep in the midst of the fight. Under this fire and that of our machine guns and the artillery, which tore great gaps in the advancing lines, the enemy attack withered. The survivors were later seen retiring beyond the ridge, which was barraged by our artillery.[30]
>
> Sergeant H. Preston, 9th Australian (Queensland) Battalion, 3rd Brigade, 1st Division, Australian Imperial Force

The Australian lines held, but by the time they were finally relieved by their comrades of the 2nd Australian Division they had lost over 5,000 casualties.

Gough was a vigorous commander and he remained determined to launch a resumption of the drive through Pozières as soon as possible. Partly in consequence the 2nd Australian Division was inveigled into launching an attack without adequate preparation. The fresh troops had no chance to settle in to their new surroundings and reconnoitre the ground ahead of them. At 0015 on 29 July, the 7th Australian Brigade attacked the OG1 and OG2 lines and then the Pozières Windmill that lay beyond them. A stretcher bearer watched the doomed advance of the proud ANZACs of the 28th Battalion.

> They marched across No Man's Land as if they were on the parade ground with their own shells screaming in droves over their heads and the German shells blowing them to bits. The men dropped like flies, the German wire remained intact and they could go neither forward nor back. They tore at the barbed wire with their hands, searching for openings under one of the most intense machine-gun barrages Australians ever faced.[31]
>
> Private Tom Young, 27th Australian (South Australia) Battalion, 7th Brigade, 2nd Division, Australian Imperial Force

Trapped in front of the thick barbed wire the survivors had little or no chance and most took shelter in shell holes. On their flanks the other battalions of the 7th Brigade faired better and overran part of the OG1 line, but floundered against the wire of the OG2 line. This was of small consolation to the men of the 28th Battalion.

> We left a long line of the best and bravest boys that Australia ever produced lying along that wire; some fell across it with the wires in their hands. Others died with the wire cutters still on the wire, but they were glorious lads every one of them. I got into a shell hole right under his wire and could go no further forward, so I sent my supply of bombs in the direction of his machine gun right in front of me. I cannot vouch for the result. By this time everything was in a state of chaos and I took the risk of going from shell hole to shell hole trying to get the boys together for another try. The word came up for us to withdraw to our original front line. They all did this, but I stayed and did my best for several wounded fellows.[32]
>
> Corporal Percy Blythe, 28th Australian (West Australia) Battalion, 7th Brigade, 2nd Division, Australian Imperial Force

Amongst the men he was able to assist was Private Norgard, who had been badly hit in the first rush.

> I 'stopped it' and promptly dropped into a shell hole. I took what was left of my boot off and bandaged the wound as quickly as possible. Our poor chaps were falling like ninepins everywhere. I assumed a very painful crawl and got back to our starting point with a couple more minor hits on the ribs. Percy Blythe got me safely back to the aid post.[33]
>
> Private E. R. Norgard, 28th Australian (West Australia) Battalion, 7th Brigade, 2nd Division, Australian Imperial Force

For his earlier determination and courage in assisting the wounded Blythe was awarded the Military Medal. A few trivial gains were made but on most of the 7th Brigade front the men ended up back in their jumping-off trenches. Their casualties had been sobering – the 28th Battalion lost some 467 men.

As the news trickled back Haig blamed the over-confident attitude of the ANZACs for the failure. It is easy to see why the brash confidence of the Australians might grate on his more restrained susceptibilities, but it was still unfair.

> The attack by the 2nd Australian Division upon the enemy's position between Pozières and the windmill, was not successful last night. From several reports I think the cause was due to want of thorough preparation. After lunch I visited headquarters Reserve Army and impressed upon Gough and Neill Malcolm that they must supervise more closely the plans of the ANZAC Corps. Some of their divisional generals are so ignorant and (like so many Colonials) so conceited, that they cannot be trusted to work out unaided the plans of attack.[34]
>
> General Sir Douglas Haig, General Headquarters, British Expeditionary Force

Sometimes it seemed that the proverb, 'more haste less speed' could have been coined with the Somme in mind. Yet it was unwarranted to blame the Australian commanders, as they had been pushed into the attack with no chance for proper groundwork. To add further insult Haig took the opportunity to personally berate Lieutenant General Sir William Birdwood, during a visit to ANZAC Corps Headquarters by sharply lecturing him that they were not fighting the Turks now!

Early August 1916 *Pozières Ridge*

BEFORE THE AUSTRALIANS had any chance to redeem themselves with another attempt on the redoubtable OG1 and OG2 lines, the 8th Royal Fusiliers and the 6th Buffs of the 12th Division, who stretched alongside them to the left of Pozières, launched a night attack at 2315 on 3 August. Their objective was Fourth Avenue.

> There were 300 or 400 yards to go to their trench and because of the attacks that had gone before, there was no wire – we knew there was no wire between us and the Germans. We lay out under cover of darkness about 100 yards in front of our front line. There was a short five minutes or so of mortar barrage, no artillery barrage. When the mortar barrage ended we were to advance. We did and jumped into the trench which was full of Germans. They were sheltering from the bombardment of our mortars. We were all armed and they immediately surrendered. There was as many Germans in the trench as their were British soldiers, it was a bit embarrassing for a bit but they were gradually ushered away and forced to go back over No Man's Land. We had wounded Germans in the trench and unfortunately they had to stay there because our stretcher bearers were so busy that they took our own men first, naturally. Our men were kind to them, they gave them water, cigarettes, it depends how badly they were wounded. We tried to tie them up or put a tourniquet on.[35]
>
> Corporal Arthur Razzell, 8th Battalion, Royal Fusiliers, 36th Brigade, 12th Division

They took ninety-two prisoners in all. Some British bombers managed to work their way up the communications trenches to gain a tenuous foothold in Ration Trench, which marked the next major obstacle to progress. The next day the 2nd Australian Division attacked towards Courcelette, finally overrunning the tough German resistance centred on the strong OG1 and OG2 lines. At the same time, 2115, the neighbouring 12th Division made another gallant attempt to take Ration Trench.

> The order came, 'Platoon sergeants to come to headquarters!' Well, we went along and there was Captain Cazalet, and this is the sort of orders we got: 'We are going in behind curtain fire, we don't know exactly how far this trench is, but it's between 200 and 300 yards. Sergeant Turnbull will take the first wave, I will go over with the first;

Mr Firefoot will go over with the second; Sergeant Quinnell, with your platoon, you'll be in the second wave. Now go along and tell your men to be ready and as soon as the curtain fire starts, we move!' Back along the trench we went and told our men what to do. Well my men in the second wave, the tip I gave them was to: 'Run like hell and catch up with the first wave!' That wasn't an order it was just a tip, because my experience told me that when you're out in No Man's Land you're standing there naked, but if you catch the first wave, the sooner you get over and get your job done, the fewer casualties you'll have.[36]

Sergeant Charles Quinnell, 9th Battalion, Royal Fusiliers, 36th Brigade, 12th Division

The British knew there was no barbed wire in front of them, which of course simplified matters enormously. The Germans had not had any chance to attend to this defensive necessity in the maelstrom that was Pozières Ridge.

My men got over, we caught up with the first wave behind this curtain fire and we were into the Germans with the first wave – we ran like hell. When we got to the German trench, there was this German kneeling on the floor of the trench and the poor bugger was dead scared. At any rate, while I'm wondering whether to stick him or shoot him, a German jumped out of the trench away to my left, another one on the right, so I jumped down on this German, pinned him down, knelt on his shoulders, shot the German on my left, worked my bolt, put another one up the spout and shot the German who was running away on the right. By this time all our men had reached the trench and I went along to report to the captain. He said, 'Good, now let's have a quick roll call!' I counted my men and I'd only lost three coming over, which was a marvellous performance. It was a surprise attack you see, and the Germans didn't have time to drop their barrage down. Once we were over there and in the German trench, the barrage came down behind us and my tip paid off, otherwise we would have caught the barrage.[37]

Sergeant Charles Quinnell, 9th Battalion, Royal Fusiliers, 36th Brigade, 12th Division

As this incident illustrates, the learning curve did not only apply to the generals. The ordinary soldiers that had the good fortune to survive their first experience of battle swiftly learnt how to maximise their chances of staying alive in the most deadly of environments.

The German bombardment, when it came, was a dreadful experience for the 8th Royal Fusiliers in Ration Trench as it eroded their strength one by one.

> Of course they knew the range to the yard and they began a terrific bombardment which went on hour after hour. About two in the morning, when the bombardment had been on for a couple of hours or more, a sergeant asked me to see how many men we had left in our platoon, because we were getting casualties all the time. The trench was no longer a trench it was just a series of shell holes. I went along where the trench had been and I found an odd man here and an odd man there. I went back to him and I wrote a little chit saying we had six men in our platoon. He was sitting at a 'T' junction with a communication trench and at that point the trench was in rather good condition. So I sat next to him on the floor, gave him the chit and was talking to him when there was an explosion quite near and I felt my helmet go and I realised that I was wounded.[38]
>
> Corporal Arthur Razzell, 8th Battalion, Royal Fusiliers, 36th Brigade, 12th Division

As Corporal Razzell set off back to the rear for medical assistance, for those left behind in Ration Trench there was little or nothing to alleviate the overall gloom. In the absence of a general advance in that sector they were left merely occupying a tenuous lodgement in the German front line. Barricades were established to both left and right flank and in all communications trenches leading forwards and then the men sat down to await their fate. Sergeant Quinnell and his men were fortunate in that they entirely escaped the German shelling that had devastated their neighbours. It was their considered opinion that in the mad tangle of trenches the German artillery simply did not know where they were. But there were other weapons available to the Germans and their response was to use one of the most loathed advances in the noble art of warfare – the *flammenwerfer*.

> Over this barricade on our right flank came a German with a canister of liquid fire on his back; squirting liquid fire out of a hose he burnt twenty-three of our chaps to death. I plonked one into his chest, but he

must have had an armoured plated waistcoat on, it didn't stop him. Someone threw a Mills bomb at him and it burst behind – he wasn't armoured plated behind, he went down. But at any rate he'd done a lot of damage. The bombers bombed the Germans back from the barricade. Plenty of chaps were wounded with this liquid fire as well as those that were killed; it practically wiped out Tubby Turnbull's platoon. Then we got an order from the Captain. I hope I never hear it repeated again. We must shorten our front – so he gave us an order to make a barricade of the dead, the German dead and our dead. We made a barricade of them and retreated about 40 yards back towards my platoon. Now I'd got a barricade on my left to look after, there was the front, plenty of Germans out there and sniping from behind. I'd got these chaps – green as grass! When we went over we only had two bombs apiece which we had in our tunic pockets. Everybody handed their bombs into the right-hand flank, because that was the danger point, all our bombs were taken to the barricade there. That afternoon these Germans behind us were winkled out of their trench and that night our pioneer battalion dug a 7-foot communication trench from our own British front line to where we were. They must have worked like Trojans – they were a battalion of Northamptons.

As soon as the trench was dug, up came a Stokes trench mortar, also boxes and boxes of rifle grenades, like a pineapple on a stick. I'd been trained for firing rifle grenades – they had to be fired by a very powerful blank cartridge, it was a specialist job. By this time Tubby Turnbull was wounded, Mr Firefoot was wounded and that left Captain Cazalet and I. We had a consultation as to where to site this Stokes trench mortar, we put it about 50 yards back from the barricade. I trained three of these rookies how to load and prepare the rifle grenades. The next time an attack came over this barricade – the same performance: a man coming over with a liquid fire canister – he got a very, very hot reception. The Stokes trench mortar opened up and dropped the mortars just the other side of the barricade. I'd three men loading up these rifle grenades and I peppered the whole line – I couldn't miss, I was in the same trench you see – peppered it from 75 yards to 200 yards and judging by the shouts and screams I was taking a very good toll. The Stokes was the barrage that prevented them coming over and I was doing the peppering with the rifle grenades. All told we had five attacks over this barricade. The first was the disastrous one, for which we paid very heavily, but in the other four we took a very, very heavy toll and we didn't lose a man.[39]

Sergeant Charles Quinnell, 9th Battalion, Royal Fusiliers, 36th Brigade, 12th Division

Alongside the 12th Division, the battered 2nd Australian Division was finally relieved on 6 August by which time it had suffered some 6,800 casualties in two attacks. It had eventually attained the crest of the Pozières Ridge and thereby secured a tactically valuable vista extending over Courcelette, and Martinpuich towards Bapaume. As the tattered remnants moved back out of the line they were replaced by the 4th Australian Division. As the men of the 14th Australian Battalion moved up through Sausage Valley they had to cross the devastated hinterland, which all too clearly bore the scars and detritus of the awful events of the last few weeks.

We gained the entrance to the communication trench and passed along it in single file. The trench was a particularly long one and uncomfortably narrow. Loaded up as we were, it was difficult to worm our way along it, and the knuckles of the hands became skinned in consequence. Ghastly sights were witnessed on that journey through the sap. Scores of bodies had been partially buried in the soft earth, and bloody hands and feet protruded at frequent intervals. Boxes of rations and ammunition were scattered about, telling plainer than words that the fatigue parties had come under violent artillery fire and had been annihilated.[40]

Corporal Charles Smith, 14th Australian (Victoria) Battalion, 4th Brigade, 4th Division, Australian Imperial Force

Corporal Smith who served with 5th Platoon was fortunate indeed in his officer, for it was none but the renowned Lieutenant Albert Jacka, who had already won a Victoria Cross as an acting lance corporal, when he had led a desperate counter-attack to throw the Turks out of their trench at Courtney's Post, during the Turkish offensive on the small ANZAC beachhead at Gallipoli on 19 May 1915. But as all the Aussies of the 4th Division had discovered, the conditions on the Turkish peninsula were nothing compared to those on the Somme.

Dead were scattered everywhere. Broken trenches, twisted barbed

> wire, mutilated rations and military equipment, stretchers with their once human contents, and bearers now cold and stiff – all gave mute evidence of the recent carnage. Lieutenant Jacka was in charge of the platoon and such a cool level-headed officer seemed strangely suited to such grim surroundings, for he inspired confidence in all with whom he came into contact. Here indeed was a test of courage even before the firing line was reached. Leaving the company in the sap, Lieutenant Jacka and the officer commanding (Major Fuhrmann) hopped over the sandbags and went to investigate. After a time he returned and told us to leave the trench in parties of two and three and double across the open in a direction half-left, they leading the way. We did so, bullets whizzing uncomfortably the while. A number of partly connected shell holes formed the firing line, and into these we jumped.[41]
>
> Corporal Charles Smith, 14th Australian (Victoria) Battalion, 4th Brigade, 4th Division, Australian Imperial Force

The Victorians thought they had taken up positions in the support line following the advance made by the 2nd Australian Division the previous day. However, in the chaos they were actually in the front line and hence liable to be counter-attacked by the Germans at any moment.

> The most remarkable thing about the trench was the number of dead that blocked access to it. Many of the previous occupants had been killed by concussion alone, for they were sitting as if asleep in little 'funk-holes' dug in the earth. Before commencing deepening operations in the sap, we first had to eject these corpses – a very unpleasant job. That done we removed our equipment and worked furiously with picks and shovels.[42]
>
> Corporal Charles Smith, 14th Australian (Victoria) Battalion, 4th Brigade, 4th Division, Australian Imperial Force

It was as well that they did. They had been lucky to travel up the communication trench without coming under German shelling. Now they were to receive the full force of the German artillery in all its destructive majesty.

> A fearful bombardment from the enemy commenced. He seems to have registered our range perfectly. Several men near me were killed by falling earth, and others killed outright. Some who had recently

> joined up as reinforcements were killed in their first night or two under fire. Many were literally blown to fragments. Our little stretch of trench was fast losing all semblance to one, and it seemed we were completely at the mercy of the German artillery. For myself, I was temporarily stunned, on one or two occasions, by the concussion, and the wonder of it is that anyone survived to tell the tale. Few did, in fact. My party of three were still unwounded, but their nerves, of course, like my own, were not unshaken. Communication had long since been severed with the remainder of the platoon on the right, and on the left it was as bad – a dead end. Neither was there communication with the rear. We tried to continue our task of digging during that infernal uproar, but all to no effect. The trench was blown in faster than we could empty it.[13]
>
> Corporal Charles Smith, 14th Australian (Victoria) Battalion, 4th Brigade, 4th Division, Australian Imperial Force

Smith had been sent with a small party of men to cover the left flank of the platoon, where the 'line' they were occupying inconsequentially petered out into nothingness, with a yawning 60-yard gap before the next elements of the battalion. As the shells crashed down and the casualties mounted he decided to pull back.

> Common sense told me to lead the way to the survivors of the platoon, whatever the risks. Better to be killed thus than as rats in a trap. Finally, acting partly from the entreaties of my comrades, and partly from what I judged best, I decided on the move. How it was accomplished I do not know, for it was indeed hard to find the course of the one-time trench in the darkness. At times we had to dash across the open, then jump over corpses in shallow shell holes, always amid the infernal bursting of the high explosives. Not a living soul did we see. Suddenly, in the lightning-like flashes of the shells, the dugout entrance sprang invitingly into view, and into this we disappeared without ceremony. Friendly voices hailed us and we soon discovered that the remainder of the platoon had taken refuge there.[44]
>
> Corporal Charles Smith, 14th Australian (Victoria) Battalion, 4th Brigade, 4th Division, Australian Imperial Force

Despite, and because of, the searing traumas of the day, nature had its way and the exhausted men fell asleep in the stygian darkness of the dugout. Perhaps the best security blanket was the reassuring knowledge that the redoubtable Lieutenant Jacka had survived and stood alongside them, ready for anything.

> About 3 or 4 a.m., someone asked Lieutenant Jacka the time, I forget what he answered, but he announced his intention of leaving the dugout to have a look around on top to make sure everything was OK. This he did, and returned shortly afterwards with the information that things were just the same.[45]
>
> Corporal Charles Smith, 14th Australian (Victoria) Battalion, 4th Brigade, 4th Division, Australian Imperial Force

The absolute confusion of the Pozières Ridge battlefield was such that the men had not yet realised that they were in the front line and still firmly believed that they were holding the support lines – in other words that there was an additional line of soldiers protecting them as they tried to recover and make sense of the day's events in that dark dugout. They were soon to be rudely disabused of this comforting notion.

> Just before daylight, a terrific explosion occurred at the bottom of the dugout steps, and two revolver shots rang out almost simultaneously. What had happened was this: the bombardment was but a preliminary to a counter-attack by the enemy. This barrage at 4.45 a.m. had gradually lifted off our front line, the enemy following in its wake. Passing our dugout, a German had thrown a bomb into it, and Jacka had immediately replied with a couple of revolver shots. Naturally, the explosions awakened all of us, and, grasping the situation immediately, a wild scramble towards the steps resulted. It was still pitch dark down there, and I don't think any of us ever expected to reach the top alive. Certainly, I did not. Two of our chaps had been badly hit by the bomb and lay groaning at the foot of the stairs. Cruel though it seemed, we had to climb quickly over their bodies to meet the enemy. Reaching the top we looked around and saw Germans everywhere. We were surrounded![46]
>
> Corporal Charles Smith, 14th Australian (Victoria) Battalion, 4th Brigade, 4th Division, Australian Imperial Force

Unsurprisingly, it was Lieutenant Jacka who had reacted first. He raced up the dugout steps and pitched straight into the Germans who were threatening to overrun their trench. This was no time for thought; instinct, luck and the primal urges were all that could help him

> There were four Huns in a shell hole. All I could see were their heads, shoulders and rifles. As I went towards them, they began to fire point-blank at me. They hit me three times and each time the terrific impact of the bullets fired at such close range swung me off my feet. But each time I sprang up like a prize fighter, and kept getting closer. When I got up to them, they flung down their rifles and put up their hands. I shot three through the head and put a bayonet through the fourth. I had to do it – they would have killed me the moment I turned my back. I think another fellow must have fired at me and missed. I looked round and saw a Hun who must have weighed 17 or 18 stone. I aimed at his belly and he almost fell on me.[47]
>
> Lieutenant Albert Jacka VC, 14th Australian (Victoria) Battalion, 4th Brigade, 4th Division, Australian Imperial Force

His men were still stumbling round far behind him with no idea what was happening or where their officer had gone.

> Jacka had disappeared somewhere, as had all our NCOs. The Germans appeared to be bombing parties, for they did not seem to possess rifles; instead they were throwing stick bombs – some with effect. As most of our chaps, including myself, had left their rifles and equipment in the shell holes when deepening the line, we were unarmed. Action was needed if we were to escape with our lives. I picked up an old rifle, choked with dirt, nearby, and, grabbing a bandolier of ammunition that someone handed up from the dugout steps, let fire for all I was worth.[48]
>
> Corporal Charles Smith, 14th Australian (Victoria) Battalion, 4th Brigade, 4th Division, Australian Imperial Force

In the absolute chaos the two sides were thrown together in a haphazard confusion where the surreal mixed with the grim certainties of close-quarter fighting, when men gave quarter only at vastly increased risk to their own safety.

> A specially venturesome German was walking toward the dugout entrance, evidently with the intention of again bombing it. No one seemed anxious to stop him, and the peculiar part was that he could

> not be taken prisoner, as his mates were all around us. He could not very well be shot, at a range of a few yards, so the only alternative was to bayonet him. I looked around for a bayonet, but could see none. The rifle I had picked up out of the mud had a pair of wire-cutters attached to the muzzle, and, as these were sharp at the points, I decided to use them instead. I therefore gave the German a sharp prod with them in the back, and he gave a howl. I was afterwards told that Jacka had shot him. I had lost sight of the gallant Jacka.[49]
>
> Corporal Charles Smith, 14th Australian (Victoria) Battalion, 4th Brigade, 4th Division, Australian Imperial Force

In the cold light of dawn, the fight had a strange aspect for the men watching it from the trenches scattered across the ridge around them. It was impossible to intervene from a distance without killing their own men as the Australian and German soldiers appeared randomly intermingled in close combat.

> Through my glasses I could see some of our boys standing up and firing point-blank at other men. Some figures I could see on their knees in front of others praying for their lives, and several were bayoneting Huns. It was one of the queerest sights I've ever seen – Huns and Aussies were scattered in ones and twos all along the side of the ridge. It was such a mix-up that it was hard to tell who were Huns and who were Aussies. Each Aussie seemed to be having a war all on his own.[50]
>
> Sergeant Edgar Rule, 14th Australian (Victoria) Battalion, 4th Brigade, 4th Division, Australian Imperial Force

Lieutenant Jacka was undoubtedly by this time in a very bad state. He had been wounded several times but once again he drew on his phenomenal inner strength in his determination to survive.

> A stretcher bearer came, took off my tunic and fixed me up. I asked him to go and bring a stretcher. He went away and I never saw him again. I lay there for a long time, and then began to think of the wounded that were never found. I made up my mind to try and get back by myself, I don't know how I managed it, but I got back quite a way and some men found me.[51]
>
> Lieutenant Albert Jacka, 14th Australian (Victoria) Battalion, 4th Brigade, 4th Division, Australian Imperial Force

When his broken body was eventually put on a stretcher and carried back towards ultimate safety the departure of such a legendary figure caused much comment amongst those who witnessed it.

> Stretcher after stretcher went by interspersed with the walking wounded. I called out to one set of bearers, 'Who've you got there?' 'I don't know who I've got, but the bravest man in the Aussie Army is on that stretcher just ahead. It's Bert Jacka, and I wouldn't give a Gyppo *piastre* for him; he is knocked about dreadfully!'[52]
>
> Sergeant Edgar Rule, 14th Australian (Victoria) Battalion, 4th Brigade, 4th Division, Australian Imperial Force

The situation was still terribly confused. To his regret Sergeant Rule was the man chosen to go forward and sort it out.

> Even after all the Huns had been taken to the rear, our officers were in doubt as to who held the ridge, and a few minutes afterwards word came for Lieutenant Dean to advance and clear up the situation. As he was not present, I had to act. I got my boys together and we went along the communication trench leading to the front line, until we came to Major Fuhrmann's headquarters. He was in charge of B Company. I did not like the job at all, because I knew nothing about the locality, and, what was more, no one else seemed to know. The Major told me to wait a little while before going over, and after a good wait he said he did not need me and my men, as a scout had been across our ridge and reported it free of Huns.[53]
>
> Sergeant Edgar Rule, 14th Australian (Victoria) Battalion, 4th Brigade, 4th Division, Australian Imperial Force

The Australian front line had once again been secured and all the Germans had either been butchered or surrendered.

Pozières had been secured but the next vital objective lay before them – Mouquet Farm, which still barred the way to Thiepval. The Australians were by no means finished with the Somme. Attack after attack was launched but, as so often before, piecemeal assaults led to little more than an accelerated rate of slaughter. An enduring horror had enfolded the Australians struggling on the Pozières Ridge. Insignificant humps and farms had become both the prime focus and unnatural bane of their lives. Advances and retreats were measured in yards and all semblance of objectivity was lost as the Australians and German troops fought to the death over near-worthless ground soaked with the blood of the men that had gone before them.

Just one of these numerous affrays took place at 2230 on 14 August when an Australian attack was directed at the Fabeck Graben Line which lay between the OG1 and OG2 lines in the maze of trenches that criss-crossed the ground to the right of Mouquet Farm. The 13th Australian Battalion went over the top at 1030 p.m. and were fortunate enough to capture their objectives. Unfortunately, in an oft-told tale, it soon became obvious that they were isolated as the flanking units failed to get forward. Once again brave men found themselves facing death in an atmosphere of blended chaos and terror.

> Soon it became evident that the enemy was trying to cut us off; and, at the same time, were delivering strong frontal bombing attacks along his communication trench. Immediate retreat was essential, and to effect this under such hostile pressure it was necessary to hold the enemy in check, while retreating along the captured trench, falling back successively on to a number of hastily thrown up strong points. Unfortunately, we had run very short of hand grenades, and the cool, heady, courageous men who pressed us, were well aware of our disabilities and pushed their advantage relentlessly. Cleverly they mixed their attacks, twice trying an 'over the top' enveloping movement, but each time a fierce and deadly response from our riflemen and Lewis gunners taught them the futile and dangerous nature of such tactics. From thence onwards they relied on bombing entirely.[54]
>
> Captain H. W. Murray, 13th Australian (New South Wales) Battalion, 4th Brigade, 4th Division, Australian Imperial Force

Captain Murray had no choice but to fall back down an old communication trench that providentially led back towards the Australian front line. With the Germans hard on their heels it was an extremely difficult situation demanding both tactical skill and an iron nerve. Maintaining control of his men was all-important as they fell back in stages from one barricade to the next. It was a desperate business, but his men held their nerve even in retreat – potentially the most demoralising of circumstances.

> We kept the enemy well in check all the time, and got all our wounded away. Our men were cool, confident and grimly determined, despite

ABOVE LEFT General Sir Douglas Haig (Q 23659)

ABOVE Lieutenant-General Sir Hubert Gough (Q 35835D)

LEFT Lieutenant-General Sir Henry Rawlinson standing on the steps of his head-quarters at Querricu Château (Q 4032)

KING'S ST
FIRING LINE

ABOVE 8-inch howitzers of the 39th Siege Battery, Royal Garrison Artillery in Fricourt-Mametz Valley (Q 5817)

OPPOSITE PAGE

TOP General Joffre, General Sir Douglas Haig and General Foch walking in the gardens at Beauquesne (Q 992)

BELOW The 1st Lancashire Fusiliers fixing bayonets prior to the assault on Beaumont Hamel, 1 July 1916 (Q 744)

TOP Lochnagar mine crater at La Boisselle (Q 4000)

ABOVE British 18-pounder in action in the Carnoy Valley (Q 4066)

OPPOSITE PAGE

TOP A 15-inch howitzer in action at Englebelmer Wood, 7 August 1916 (Q 4196)

BELOW Troops of the 34th Division advancing on La Boisselle, 1 July 1916 (Q 54)

TOP British troops in the entrance to a German dugout in the Dantzig Alley trench in Fricourt (Q 814)

ABOVE Two German dead in a front line trench (Q 126)

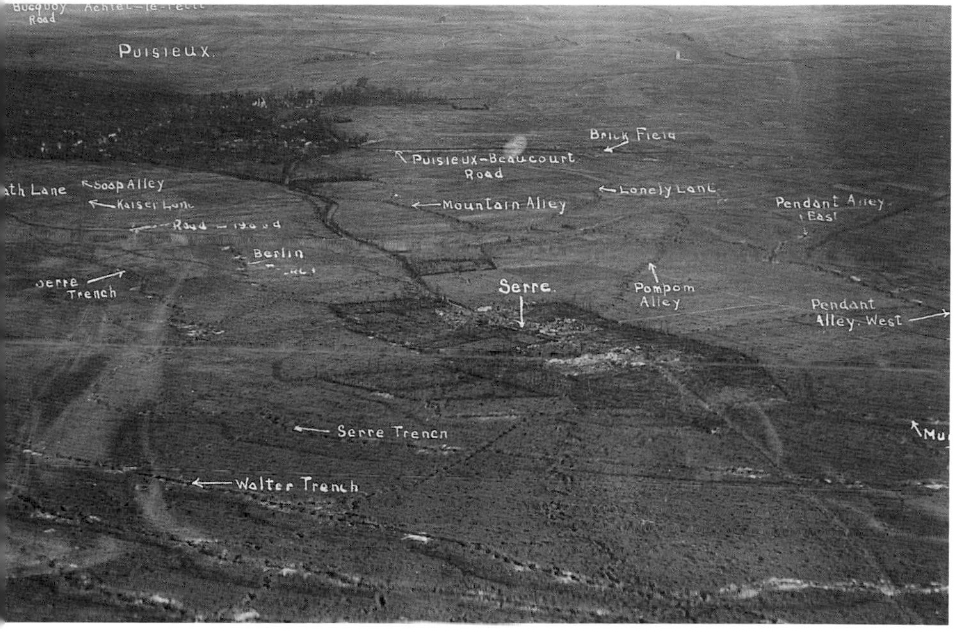

TOP Aerial photograph showing the sector between Puisieux-au-Monts and Serre (Neg No 21 Box 7003 1916)

ABOVE German observation post in Trônes Wood, 10 August 1916 (Q 862)

ABOVE New Zealand troops on the Amiens–Albert Road, September 1916 (Q 1244)

OPPOSITE PAGE

TOP Men of the 4th South African Regiment cleaning their Lewis Guns in Carnoy Valley, July 1916 (Q 4018)

BELOW Australians resting by the side of the road (E (AUS) 19)

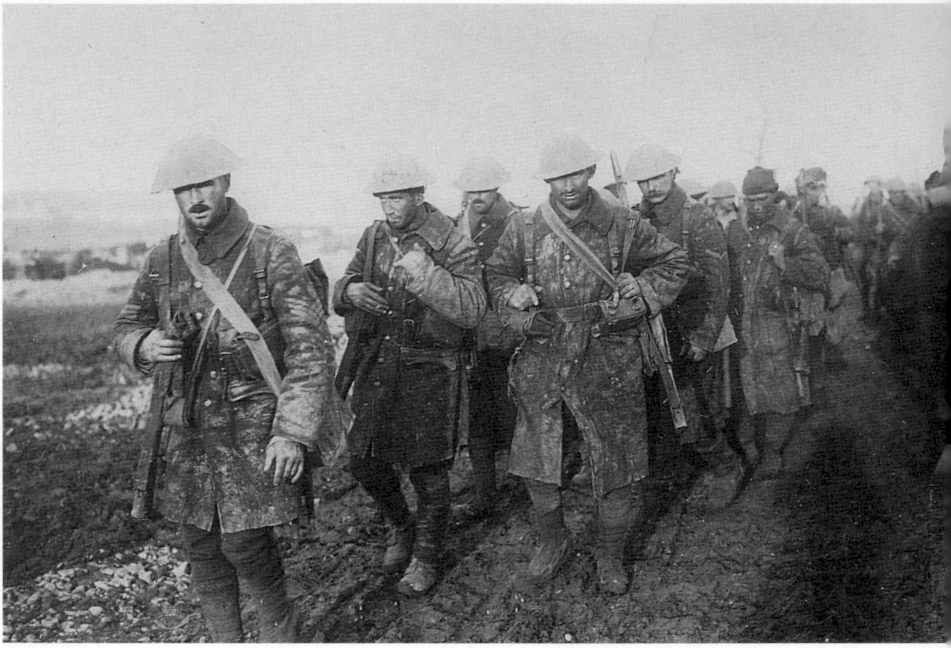

TOP Mud-bespattered Canadians returning from the trenches (CO 997)

ABOVE Thiepval, September 1916: the heap of bricks in the centre is the remains of the Château (Q 1439)

OPPOSITE PAGE

TOP A group of Royal Fusiliers after the capture of Thiepval on 26 September 1916 (Q 1398)

BELOW A dead British soldier in a trench near Guillemont, September 1916 (Q 3964)

180

TOP & ABOVE Aerial photographs showing the effects of artillery fire on Mouquet Farm (Q 56399 and Q 56397)

TOP A Mark I tank (C19 Clan Leslie) of 'C' Company in Chimpanzee Valley prior to the attack, 15 September 1916 (Q 5574)

ABOVE German prisoners captured at Thiepval, 26 September 1916 (Q 1336)

TOP A 6-inch howitzer being hauled by manpower through the mud near Pozières (Q 1490)

ABOVE German gun captured by the Royal Naval Division at Beaucourt, November 1916 (Q 4570)

TOP German dead covered in flies at Guillemont, September 1916 (Q 4253)

ABOVE Digging a communication trench through Delville Wood (Q 4417)

TOP The skeleton of a dead German at Beaumont Hamel (Q 2041)

ABOVE A group of French and British troops, December 1916 (HU 92014)

> the continuous pressure. After each successive minor retirement, Freddy Doust would send a message to me that he was OK, and that was the signal to send most of the front post back, giving them a couple of minutes start, while we made all the show we could. Then we sent the last few remaining riflemen back, following a minute later with the two last 'diggers' and the officer.[55]
>
> Captain H. W. Murray, 13th Australian (New South Wales) Battalion, 4th Brigade, 4th Division, Australian Imperial Force

Captain Murray was responsible for timing the breaks between barricades and, of course, as the officer, it was his duty to bring up the rear. As the supply of bombs began to run out they found it difficult to keep the encroaching Germans at bay as they pressed ever closer during the final desperate scramble up the narrow confines of the communication trench.

> Just before reaching the fifth post, and it looked as if we were clear, a bomb dropped one of the two men in front of me. The survivor, half-dazed by the explosion, wounded superficially by metal fragments, and not really comprehending what had happened, continued his flight. I jumped over the body of the prostrate man, who appeared to be dead, but just as I did so his eyes opened, and it was plain he was alive, but how badly wounded it was impossible to say. His leg was doubled and twisted, and although he did not speak his eyes were eloquent.[56]
>
> Captain H. W. Murray, 13th Australian (New South Wales) Battalion, 4th Brigade, 4th Division, Australian Imperial Force

Behind him were the Germans and the thought of their naked, cold steel bayonets sent tremors through the length of Murray's spine. It was a defining moment in his life. He had a simple choice to make: to escape alone in ignominy, or to risk everything for the sake of a wounded man who might well die anyway.

> It was then I fought the hardest battle of my life, between an almost insane desire to continue running and save my life, or to comply with the sacred traditions of the Australian Imperial Force and stop to help a wounded comrade. Surely I must be bayoneted if I stopped for an instant. The enemy were coming up at the double. I often dread to think of what I might have done. I was safe enough at the time, and all I had to do was to keep on going; there was only a straight run of 50 yards to my mates. Despite that poor, twisted leg, those mute lips and

pathetic eyes, it was really only the mechanical habit engendered by strict discipline, that forced me to do what I did. I dropped on to my shaking knees, caught him in my arms, and pulled him on to my back. He helped like a hero with his one sound leg, and off we staggered, with Fritz just coming into our bay. We outpaced him, however, largely because the impetuosity of his advance had more than once been checked. Already he had been pulled up with a jerk four times, and such things test the mettle of the bravest and most seasoned troops. At last I had reached a haven of temporary safety, and now had others to support us. I was once more among my mates.[57]

Captain H.W. Murray, 13th Australian (New South Wales) Battalion, 4th Brigade, 4th Division, Australian Imperial Force

Slowly the Reserve Army inched its way forward on the Pozières Ridge edging towards Mouquet Farm. The old adage of two steps forward, one step back may well have exaggerated the speed of the advance, the ground was so hotly contested.

IT WAS EVIDENT that the fighting had descended into an attritional battle of the worst kind. The constant barrages of the British guns were gradually grinding away at the bedrock of the German Army. The rain of shells probed everywhere behind the German lines, causing a ceaseless trickle of casualties which rose to a crescendo in the larger barrages. Yet the incompetent and often uncoordinated tactics of the British meant that when they went into the attack they were losing men wholesale to achieve very little. Both sides were suffering dreadfully and there was no end in sight.

CHAPTER EIGHT

From Bad to Worse

While the Australians were being so brutally introduced to the horrors of the Western Front in July and August, the Fourth Army had once again embarked on a difficult period of trying to seize a string of local objectives, which would serve to ease and prepare the ground ready for the next big assault on the integrity of the entire German line. On the left of the Fourth Army links had to be maintained with the Reserve Army. In the centre High Wood dominated the thinking, then came Longueval and Delville Wood, while on the far right Guillemont was to be captured in conjunction with the neighbouring French.

On 27 July, Rawlinson had demonstrated that there was a way of making local attacks a success when he completed the capture of Longueval and finally managed to seize most of Delville Wood. The method was simple: the combined firepower of all the available guns of the two adjoining XV and XIII Corps were concentrated to create a stunning bombardment that hosed down thousands of shells across the village and the splintered remnants of the wood. All descriptions of previous artillery bombardments were rendered linguistically superfluous as some 125,000 shells fell on this narrow sector in a bombardment that commenced at 0610. Only the luckiest could hope to survive such a deadly, all-embracing combination of bursting high explosive and the deadly splatter of shrapnel shells. After an hour, at the designated zero hour of 0710, no less than four infantry battalions charged into the wood where they found that the few German soldiers who had managed to survive were in no fit state to resist. Once again the overwhelming supremacy of massed artillery had been demonstrated. When the leading troops pushed through to the Prince's Street trench – scene of the last stand of the gallant South Africans – they found the smashed German machine guns, their dead and wounded, but no one capable of resisting.

> A German prisoner said that our artillery fire on the Delville Wood was worse than Verdun. I had tried to deny food and rest to the enemy in the wood and it seemed I had more or less succeeded.[1]
>
> Brigadier General Hugh Tudor, Commander Royal Artillery, 9th Division

Then, inevitably, the awful mindless game of tit-for-tat began. It was simply the turn of the Germans to train their massed artillery on what remained of the wood. The fighting would go on in Delville Wood until it was finally overrun and retained in early September.

But even while the Fourth Army was demonstrating the effect of concentrating resources on a single focused objective, it was also guilty of repeating most of the mistakes made on 23 July. After an Anglo-French conference on 26 July it was decided on a joint attack to take Guillemont and the village of Maurepas on 30 July. This might have been acceptable, except at the same time 'diversionary' operations were planned further along the line. These achieved nothing but to distract the British themselves. Once again the attacks had different start times, the artillery was not concentrated and the result was not only predictable but predicted. The 89th Brigade commanded by Brigadier F. C. Stanley was on the right of the British line and had the complicated task of taking the German line between Falfemont Farm and Guillemont.

> About our new venture, which was to take place on the 30th, I must confess that we were not happy, and we expressed ourselves on these lines to the division, and I believe they, in their turn, had expressed the same views to the corps. It was not for us to criticise the plans of those above us, but we one and all recognised the enormous difficulty of the task which had been allotted to us. Our own particular job depended too much upon what happened to our flanks. If one or both of them did not succeed – and they each of them had an exceedingly difficult task to perform – then the success of our operation was out of the question.[2]
>
> Brigadier General F. C. Stanley, Headquarters, 89th Brigade, 30th Division

His fears were realised and this local failure was entirely symptomatic of the wider disaster experienced that day. The British artillery failed to subdue the German batteries and they consequently ran riot. The territorial gains made were infinitesimal at a cost of over 5,000 British casualties. The French had not done any better as initial gains in their attack towards Maurepas were swiftly eroded to nothing by German counter-attacks.

BY THE END of July the politicians in London were becoming edgy as to the lack of visible progress on the ground on the Somme. From their perspective the enormous sacrifices that were being made needed to have some clearly visible results other than just the intangible claim that the operations had relieved the pressure on the French at Verdun. One of the most trenchant critics was Winston Churchill, who had returned to his parliamentary duties after his brief period of service on the Western Front – penance for the Gallipoli debacle he had initiated. Churchill argued his case in a confidential memorandum, which was circulated to the War Cabinet. Having stressed the serious nature of the British casualties and the failure to gain ground, he bluntly questioned the purpose of continuing the offensive.

> The month that has passed has enabled the enemy to make whatever preparations behind his original lines he may think necessary. He is already defending a 500 mile front in France alone, and the construction of extra lines about 10 miles long to loop in the small sector now under attack is no appreciable strain on his labour or trench stores. He could quite easily by now have converted the whole countryside in front of our attack into successive lines of defence and fortified posts. What should we have done in the same time in similar circumstances? Anything he has left undone in this respect is due only to his confidence. A very powerful hostile artillery has now been assembled against us, and this will greatly aggravate the difficulties of further advance. Nor are we making for any point of strategic or political consequence. Verdun at least would be a trophy – to which sentiment on both sides has become mistakenly attached. But what are Péronne and Bapaume, even if we were likely to take them?[3]
>
> Winston Churchill MP

In response to this kind of criticism, Haig vehemently defended the achievements of the Somme offensive so far in a note to the Chief of

Imperial General Staff, Sir William Robertson. This, in turn, was later printed as a Cabinet paper to refute Churchill's arguments.

> (a) Pressure on Verdun relieved. Not less than six enemy Divisions besides heavy guns have been withdrawn.
> (b) Successes achieved by Russia last month would certainly have been stopped had enemy been free to transfer troops from here to the Eastern Theatre.
> (c) Proof given to world that Allies are capable of making and maintaining a vigorous offensive and of driving enemy's best troops from the strongest positions has shaken faith of Germans, of their friends, of doubting neutrals in the invincibility of Germany. Also impressed on the world, England's strength and determination, and the fighting power of the British race.
> (d) We have inflicted very heavy losses on the enemy. In one month, 30 of his Divisions have been used up, as against 35 at Verdun in 5 months! In another 6 weeks, the enemy should be hard put to it to find men!
> (e) The maintenance of a steady offensive pressure will result eventually in his complete overthrow.
>
> Principle on which we should act. Maintain our offensive. Our losses in July's fighting totalled about 120,000 more than they would have been, had we not attacked. They cannot be regarded as sufficient to justify any anxiety as to our ability to continue the offensive. It is my intention:
> (a) To maintain a steady pressure etc.
> (b) To push my attack strongly whenever and wherever the state of my preparations and the general situation make success sufficiently probable to justify me in doing so, but not otherwise.
> (c) To secure against counter-attack each advantage gained and prepare thoroughly for each fresh advance.
> Proceeding thus, I expect to be able to maintain the offensive well into the autumn.
> It would not be justifiable to calculate on the enemy's resistance being completely broken without another campaign next year.[4]

General Sir Douglas Haig, General Headquarters, British Expeditionary Force

Haig followed this reasoned defence with a delightfully waspish attack on Churchill himself during a conversation with King George V, who visited Haig's headquarters on 8 August 1916.

> We must not allow them to divert our thoughts from our main objective namely 'beating the Germans'! I also expect that Winston's head is gone from taking drugs.[5]
>
> General Sir Douglas Haig, General Headquarters, British Expeditionary Force

Yet, at the same time as he robustly fended off the politicians, Haig was becoming frankly exasperated himself with the lack of progress being made by Rawlinson and his Fourth Army. He perceived a lack of control over the course of operations and it is difficult not to agree with him. Numerous small-scale tactical operations were being launched in the most haphazard, disorganised fashion and even when larger assaults were begun the planning had been botched, resulting in what were effectively a series of small-scale attacks united only in the date of their launch. Overall there was no sense of cohesion or a guiding hand at the tiller in the Fourth Army attacks.

By then it was becoming apparent that careful preparation was a two-edged sword. Time to prepare for an assault gave time for the Germans to repair and prepare their defences, and bring up fresh divisions and more gun batteries to duel with the British artillery for control of the battlefield. Yet to attack without proper preparation would simply guarantee defeat as had happened so many times before. This tactical conundrum was fundamentally unsolvable without introducing the concept of the 'wearing out battle'. This was a fairly classical, military tactical philosophy, which considered that most battles resolved themselves into a fight to wear down the front-line troops and reserves of the enemy, whilst reserving a strike force to be launched into decisive action at the critical moment of the battle. This process had once taken hours, but given the strength of the armies involved on the Somme and the sheer scale of the fighting, it now seemed that this phase would last for weeks. It was an awful prospect, but Haig had the dour determination to see the job through. In consequence, he was determined that Rawlinson would not fritter away precious reserves in meaningless attacks that did not materially harm the Germans and did not, therefore, contribute to 'wearing' them out.

> To enable us to bring the present operations (the existing phase of which may be regarded as a 'wearing out' battle) to a successful termination, we must practice such economy of men and material as will ensure our having the 'last reserves' at our disposal when the crisis of the fight is reached, which may – and probably will – not be sooner than the last half of September.[6]
>
> General Sir Douglas Haig, General Headquarters, British Expeditionary Force

Haig was convinced that the Fourth Army should be concentrating on their right flank in an effort to overrun the German positions that threatened the French left flank in any projected joint advance. His instructions clearly reveal the inherent dichotomy between the necessity for speed to prevent the Germans tightening their grip, and the equal priority to make sure the next assault did not go off half cocked.

> The first necessity at the moment is to help the French forward on our right flank. For this we must capture Guillemont, Falfemont Farm and Ginchy as soon as possible. These places cannot be taken, however – with due regard to economy of means available – without careful and methodical preparation. The necessary preparations must be pushed on without delay, and the attack will be launched when the responsible commanders on the spot are satisfied that everything possible has been done to ensure success.[7]
>
> General Sir Douglas Haig, General Headquarters, British Expeditionary Force

Haig hammered home the point and insisted that the Fourth Army should concentrate its collective minds and resources on this sector to the exception of all other distractions.

> No serious attack is to be made on the front now held by the XV and III Corps (extending from Delville Wood to Munster Alley). Preparations for a subsequent attack on this front must, however, be carried on with energy and method by pushing forward sap heads and connecting them up, capturing important posts held by the enemy within easy reach, and, generally, by such procedure as will enable us, with due regard to the local conditions and to a wise economy of men and munitions, to secure the ground we have gained against counter-attack and to place ourselves in a good position for the resumption of the

offensive there when the time for it arrives. The decision as to when a serious offensive is to be undertaken on this front is reserved by the Commander-in-Chief.[8]

General Sir Douglas Haig, General Headquarters, British Expeditionary Force

In addition, the Fifth Army operations were to be severely limited to carefully planned operations to gain possession of the German Second Line trenches on the Pozières Ridge with particular reference to Mouquet Farm.

The operations outlined above are to be carried out with as little expenditure of fresh troops and of munitions as circumstances will admit of, but in each attack undertaken a sufficient force must be employed to make success as certain as possible, and to secure the objectives won against counter-attack. Economy of men and munitions is to be sought for not by employing insufficient force for the objective in view but by a careful selection of objectives.[9]

General Sir Douglas Haig, General Headquarters, British Expeditionary Force

Haig was certainly guilty here of trying to have his cake and eat it. His generals were being ordered to be perfect; to employ just the right amount of men to ensure that they secured and retained carefully chosen objectives. But this was easier said than done.

It is remarkable that August would demonstrate that Haig was as impotent in controlling the actions of his subordinates as Rawlinson had been. Had his instructions been merely verbal then it is possible that Haig's legendary inarticulacy might have led Rawlinson astray, but these instructions were repeated in a written memorandum. There could have been no mistake or illusion as to what Haig intended. Yet confusion did result. It soon became apparent that Rawlinson and his subordinates considered that operations to capture objectives previously considered essential prior to the next major assault were not to be included in the ban but to fall under the ambit of 'preparations' and were not in themselves 'serious'.

Initially, Rawlinson paid lip service to Haig's requirements at the conference held amongst the senior commanders of the Fourth Army on the morning of 31 July. Guillemont was to be the first target with careful arrangements being made to try to ensure the kind of overwhelming artillery support required. Yet when the attack was launched on 8 August the resources allocated were still not adequate to overcome the deadly combination of enhanced German defences, the open and enfiladed nature of the ground to be crossed by the assaulting troops and the increasing necessity of bombarding the whole of an area – every shell hole had the potential to conceal their enemies. The attack was a dreadful failure. In addition, Rawlinson had also ignored Haig's overall strictures by continuing to launch numerous small-scale, localised attacks aimed at High Wood, the Wood Lane Trench and, of course, Delville Wood. These were all costly failures with little or no serious chance of success. Rawlinson was wasting men and munitions.

Haig responded with yet more pointed prompting, for he sent his Chief of General Staff Lieutenant General Launcelot Kiggell to urge Rawlinson to take personal control – and hence the undiluted responsibility for the success or failure of the next attack. This would clearly leave Rawlinson dangerously exposed to direct criticism if the attack failed, indeed it is evident that Haig was making it utterly clear that he was not happy with the way that the Fourth Army was approaching the task at hand. Haig was not the only member of the Allied High Command who was becoming frustrated by the progress of the Somme offensive. General Joseph Joffre was also fretting at the interminable sequence of minor uncoordinated attacks, which seemed to achieve nothing concrete. He therefore proposed that the French should join in a combined assault across the board from High Wood to the Somme.

Yet again 'the most thorough preparations' were made for the joint attack, which took place on 18 August. There is no doubt that some of the lessons of earlier fighting had been taken on board, for this was a broad-front attack delivered on a standard zero hour of 1445 but, on the other hand, the artillery bombardment was still not adequate. The importance of countering the new German tactics of placing their machine guns in shell holes meant that a whole sector needed to be drenched with shells rather than a concentration as before on only the obvious trench lines. The counter-battery work had also failed to dominate the German batteries. Once again the Germans had raised the stakes required for success. Unless the British could counter the new tactics then their attacks were doomed to failure.

Amongst the troops going over the top at 1430 on 18 August was Private Arthur Russell and his Vickers machine-gun team who were

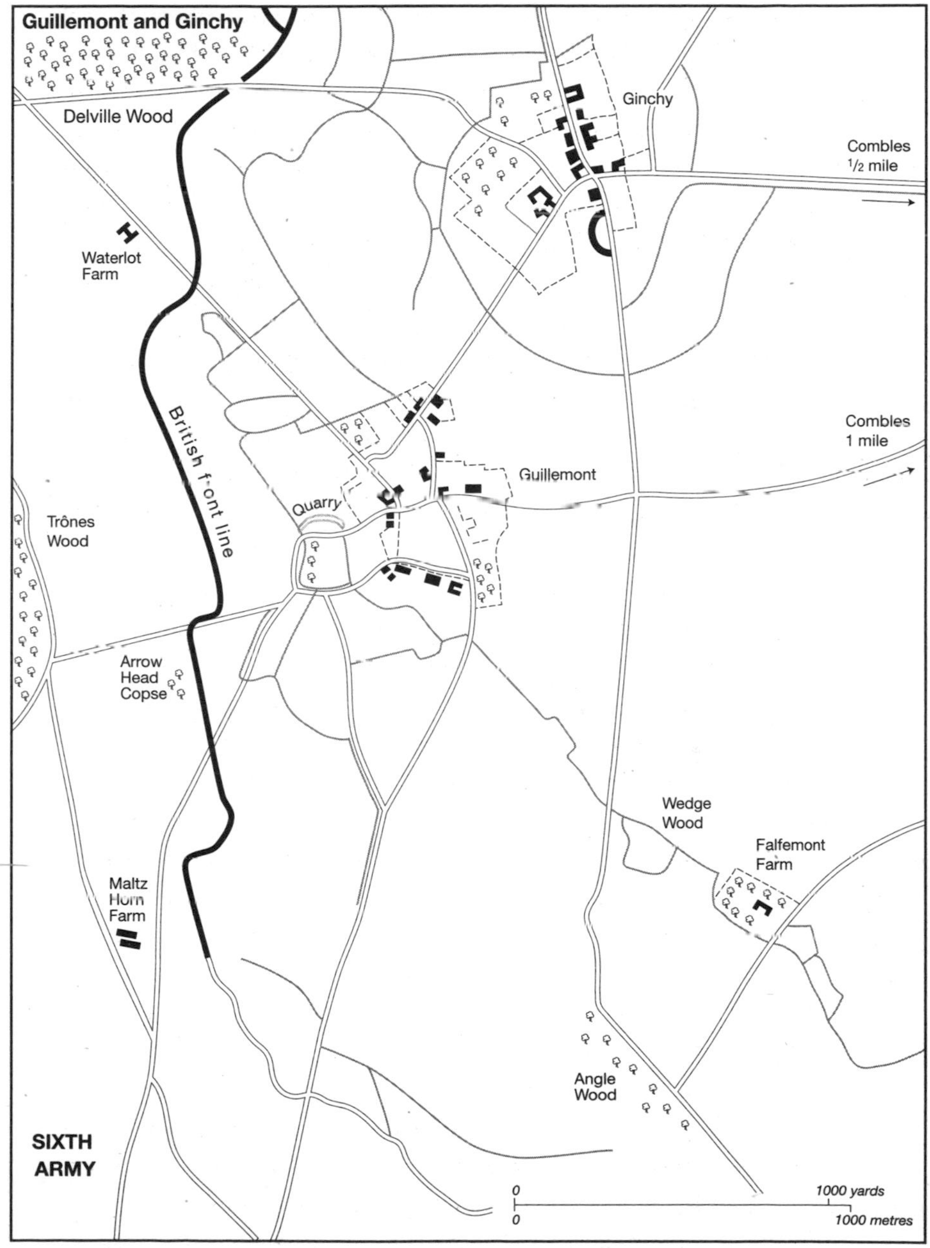

Guillemont and Ginchy
Delville Wood
Ginchy
Combles
1/2 mile
Waterlot Farm
British front line
Combles
1 mile
Guillemont
Quarry
Trônes Wood
Arrow Head Copse
Wedge Wood
Falfemont Farm
Maltz Horn Farm
Angle Wood
SIXTH ARMY
0
1000 yards
0
1000 metres

assigned to accompany the 4th King's Liverpools as they attacked the Wood Lane Trench, which ran toward Delville Wood from High Wood. They were to move out to occupy specially dug machine gun posts in No Man's Land so that they could provide strong covering fire as the Liverpools went over the top. Unfortunately, they had got held up in the crowded trenches whilst moving up.

> Shrill blast from the whistles blown by the company and platoon commanders warned us that it was three o'clock and time to attack. The infantry commenced to scramble over the parapets and our crews of Vickers machine gunners to move up the saps in No Man's Land. Almost at the same moment the German front which for several hours had been uncannily quiet, broke into violent action with a great crash of artillery, trench mortars, field guns, howitzers and siege guns – everything they had. At the same time their trench garrisons let off into the ranks of the attacking British troops a blaze of rifle and machine gun fire, and a shower of stick bombs.[10]
>
> Private Arthur Russell, 13th Company, Machine Gun Corps, 13th Brigade, 5th Division

Private Russell with the Vickers gun and the supporting team of four other gunners and one ammunition carrier did not get far towards the head of the sap before disaster struck.

> A terrific explosion blew me off my feet; earth and sandbags cascaded down and the sides of the trench caved in on top of me. Stunned and dazed I dragged myself out of the tumbled debris and retrieved the Vickers gun which had fallen off my shoulders into the trench bottom. Two yards in front of me the gunner who had been carrying the tripod lay face down in the bottom of the trench with a large gory gash across the small of his back where a large piece of shell had ploughed its way through his equipment and clothing cutting deeply into his flesh in its path – he was groaning and just conscious. Where were the rest of my mates? Turning round I saw another gunner on his knees, a great wound at the back of his neck from which blood was spurting freely, his head had gone forward and his steel helmet held suspended by its strap was hanging down below his face; it was full of blood and overflowing – he was dead. Then I saw the attached infantryman extricate himself from the tumbled heap of earth and sandbags, apparently

> unhurt. There were still two of the team to be accounted for. Pulling at the sandbags and earth piled in the trench their limp and lifeless bodies were soon revealed.[11]
>
> Private Arthur Russell, 13th Company, Machine Gun Corps, 13th Brigade, 5th Division

The 4th King's Liverpools were on their own in a maelstrom of fire as it was impossible for Russell and the one ammunition carrier infantryman to get the gun forward and into action. The result was a slaughter and there were very few survivors left to return to the British lines when the attack fell apart. It is almost unnecessary to say that High Wood was not captured.

The experience of Russell and the 4th King's Liverpools was typical of a very bad day for the Fourth Army. A few trenches were gained but the cost was utterly exorbitant. Although this time the attacking divisions went across at the same time, they did so in isolated pockets of a battalion here and there, interspersed along the line. To make matters even worse some of the attacking battalions only sent a couple of companies forward. The attacking troops were consequently still rendered vulnerable to deadly local flanking fire from the German positions on either side of them, which were not under direct attack. Furthermore a succession of minor attacks along the rest of the Fourth Army front north of High Wood had once again dissipated the artillery effort to no practical diversionary purpose. In no way was this a coherent mass assault to punch its way through to the objective – the artillery barrage was not yet concentrated enough to clear the way and there were simply too few troops committed to swamp resistance and consolidate any gains. The painful failure meant that Rawlinson was in trouble up to his neck. Haig's mind was already turning to the next great attack all along the German Third Line of the original Somme defences that would mirror the efforts on the First Line system on 1 July and the Second Line system on 14 July. Yet, as ever, before they could attack the Third Line they needed to secure a good start line not too far away and with no flanking menaces like the German fortresses at High Wood, Ginchy, Guillemont and Falfemont Farm. Rawlinson had been floundering since mid-July and was getting nowhere in attaining these vital objectives. He simply had to get a grip on affairs and Haig hammered home the point in no uncertain terms.

> The only conclusion that can be drawn from the repeated failure of

> attacks on Guillemont is that something is wanting in the methods employed. The next attack must be thoroughly prepared for in accordance with the principles which have been successful in previous attacks and which are, or should be, well known to commanders of all ranks. The attack must be a general one, engaging the enemy simultaneously along the whole front to be captured, and a sufficient force must be employed, in proper proportion to the extent of front, to beat down all opposition. The necessary time for preparation must be allowed, but not a moment must be lost on carrying it out.[12]
>
> General Sir Douglas Haig, General Headquarters, British Expeditionary Force

There was no mistaking the threatening tone. He even lectured Rawlinson on his personal responsibilities as an army commander.

> In actual *execution* of plans, when control by higher commanders is impossible, subordinates on the spot must act on their own initiative, and they must be trained to do so. But in *preparation* close supervision by higher commanders is not only possible but is their duty, to such extent as they find necessary to ensure that everything is done that can be done to ensure success. This close supervision is especially necessary in the case of a comparatively new army. It is not *interference* but a legitimate and necessary exercise of the functions of a commander on whom the ultimate responsibility for success or failure lies.[13]
>
> General Sir Douglas Haig, General Headquarters, British Expeditionary Force

It was some time before Haig's strictures could be put into action. The onset of rain severely delayed preparations and the date for a new attack was finally set for 3 September. This time it was intended that all the 'start-line objectives' prior to the next big offensive would be finally overrun: High Wood, Ginchy, Guillemont and Falfemont Farm. Rawlinson was determined to make no further mistakes and had tried to ensure that he had amassed sufficient resources to guarantee success, despite the difficult tactical situation that faced his troops. In addition, an attempt was made to improve the tactical positions by digging trenches in No Man's Land to the north-west of Guillemont, which would allow the attacking troops the chance to take the Germans holding the village from the flank. Yet the artillery support was still not adequate to support such an extended front. It was becoming apparent that this was another intractable problem: if they attacked on a narrow front then a crushing bombardment could be achieved, but the German artillery and machine guns could pour in fire from the flanks; yet if they attacked on a wide front then the concentration of shells was inevitably reduced, which left German defensive positions intact and able to resist the troops directly attacking them. It was extraordinarily difficult to square the circle.

When the attack went in the results were patchy in the extreme, except in Guillemont where the German resistance finally crumbled to the concentrated attack of the 20th Division. Alongside it, aligned next to the French, the 5th Division was facing the dreaded Falfemont Farm. For the attacking infantry it was certainly difficult to discern the trappings of victory amidst the usual misery.

> I lay crouched in a shell hole in No Man's Land. My leg, arm and side were numb and bleeding fast and I was half blinded by blood from a slight shrapnel wound above one eye. With my teeth and right hand, I struggled to tear the first aid dressing and iodine phial from my tunic lapel. I began to realise I was not alone in that shell crater. Two still figures hung over the lip. Spouting earth and soft 'phuts' made me thank my lucky stars they were protecting me from the traversing machine guns. A voice was sobbing nearby, 'Water!' or 'Mother!' I could not tell which. An Edinburgh lad from the earlier King's Own Scottish Borderers attack was lying beside me, his thigh and knee shattered. Already his eyes were beginning to glaze. I pressed my water bottle to his lips, and took the last sip myself, as the burning thirst from loss of blood was becoming intolerable. Then I realised that the clean face turned towards me from one of the protecting corpses was Larry. Larry, from one of the May drafts, was precise in manner and dress and would go to any lengths to perform a clean shave. Early that same morning we had scrounged some extra tea dregs for him to shave. Only one arm hung over the crater lip from the other inert figure. I looked casually at the hand, then again, a long glance, for a few black hairs curled over the lower arm and wrist. I tugged at the arm with all the final strength of despair, pulling the body down the incline. Yes – it was George .... His face was completely relaxed, at peace. The sweeping bullets had twice cut across Larry and George breast high; the same sweeps had only caught my arm and side. I slipped down beside them, utterly exhausted.[14]
>
> Private Francis Fields, 15th Battalion, Warwickshire Regiment, 13th Brigade, 5th Division

In between periods of merciful oblivion, he was prepared to fight to the last should it be the German who found him in his shell hole in No Man's Land.

> With my right hand and using my head as a butt, I forced the rifle out of Larry's grasp, checked the magazine, and then wedged it between his limbs so that it was sighted on the irregular rim of the nearby German trench line. As all four of us carried an extra belt of ammunition, I could hold out for quite a time, I thought. I then remembered that, as a signaller in the first attacking wave, I carried a Mills bomb in each pocket. These I laid out in a row. It would be easy to remove the pins with my teeth before lobbing them into the enemy line after drawing their fire with my rifle. Then came a blank. My next recollection is of a complete metamorphosis, for I was lying on my back. Darkness was above me, save for the stars and occasional flashes like distant summer lightning. There was a heavenly silence, but for the jingle of harness, creaking wheels and groans beside me when the wagon lurched. Spasms of cramp and still the burning thirst. For us at least the Battle of the Somme was over.[15]
>
> Private Francis Fields, 15th Battalion, Warwickshire Regiment, 13th Brigade, 5th Division

The gains made, however, had to be defended. Everyone was aware that the Germans were unlikely to react with passive acquiescence. The counter-attacks would be deadly. Lieutenant Paviere was ordered forward with a machine gun section from the 61st Machine Gun Company to reinforce the front line.

> The ground was strewn with mud and multiple shell holes full of water. Shelling was intense and accurate. I therefore ordered the section to crawl forward, each gun crew keeping a good distance from one another as there were no communication trenches. By the time I reached the company and reported to the commander, I was covered in foul mud. Pieces of dank, decaying, stinking flesh clung to my fingers which had pierced the bodies of corpses as I moved forwards. There, after consultation with the commander, I placed the four machine guns with their crews in positions with good fields of fire. The parapet of the so-called trench consisted mainly of stacks of German and British dead. As the afternoon wore on and night fell, shelling

> became more and more intense resulting in the death of the captain and his two subalterns who were killed in front of my eyes. There were numerous other casualties. Two of my guns with the majority of their crews were blown to pieces and the others rendered useless. Mustering the troops in my own vicinity, I counted twenty–thirty all told, including the survivors of my own crews out of a total of more than one hundred the afternoon before. Communication with the rear was lost entirely through the destruction of the field telephone system. Soon afterwards, our own artillery began to shell us also, assuming that we had lost the trench, having received no message for support. The troops around me were dazed, one young boy begging me to take him home to his mother. Convinced that my own end was near, I prayed that death might be other than by being bayoneted. I dreaded the thought of my body being pierced by a bayonet in the event of a German charge. Gradually, a strange peace of mind followed, and all fear of death disappeared. I felt that passing on was to be so simple and easy.[16]
>
> Lieutenant Horace Paviere, 61st Company, Machine Gun Corps, 20th Division

All this was in the sector of the front where the attack had been relatively successful. Elsewhere the situation was simply disastrous. Any progress made in front of Ginchy, Wood Lane and High Wood was soon reversed by strong German counter-attacks that simply swept the British back to their start lines. Here there was no 'victory' to console the wounded and mentally shattered men. Rawlinson reacted by simply ordering a series of renewed attacks over the next week, which centred on Ginchy. This phase of the fighting seems almost Kafkaesque to the modern mind as the valiant troops of the 7th Division lurched forward time and time again in utterly futile isolated attacks, till there were simply too few left to hold their place in the line. The artillery did its best, but it was all so totally confusing.

> It was difficult to keep direction. Ran into the tail end of our own 18-pounder shrapnel barrage – very unpleasant! Mist cleared about 9 p.m. Ginchy very much knocked about. Coldstream Guards hold the north-west edge of the village. Crept up to a point from which I could see the strong point on the north east corner of Delville Wood which

> had caused us so much trouble. As usual we found the line cut and had to send a signaller back to try and mend it. This was very exasperating because from where we were lying in a shell hole I could see a row of Huns in enfilade in Pint Trench which looked very battered. They were about 150 yards off. There was an officer standing next to a machine gun looking through his field glasses. I saw him tap his gunner on the shoulder to swing the machine gun on us and fire a burst. The noise of the battle was terrific. Our shell hole was rather shallow and the guardsman next to me got a bullet which entered his shoulder and ran for about 10 inches along his back just under the skin. There was another guardsman and a sergeant in our shell hole. We patched up the wounded one and as I could not do any good there with no line, I returned down the line to see what had happened to my linesman. Communication during a battle was a desperate business, one was lucky to get through to the battery for more than a few minutes at a time. If I had a line to the battery I could have blown the Hun out of Pint Trench in a few minutes.[17]
>
> Lieutenant Y. R. N. Probert, 35th Brigade, Royal Field Artillery 7th Division

In front of High Wood the 1st Division had taken over the line and they were flinging themselves forward in penny-packets in the same old style. On 9 September they were responsible for a diversionary attack on High Wood, while Rawlinson ordered a concentrated full-scale effort by the 16th Division on Ginchy. The diversionary attack was a depressingly inevitable failure. The 1st Northamptonshires attacked High Wood itself. The story remained the same.

> At 3.50 p.m. we mounted the firesteps and at 4 p.m. the signal – by Stokes mortar – was given and 15 and 16 Platoons, about sixty men including myself, went over. I was carrying rifle, bayonet, haversack with rations, entrenching tool, 260 rounds of ammo, two gas helmets, one gas goggles, two Mills bombs in each pocket, six more bombs in a bag slung around my neck, two empty sandbags and a first aid packet. One or two men had to carry a shovel extra. Our barrage stopped the instant we went over and consequently we were at the same time met with intense machine gun fire and shrapnel. Of the four on my firestep, one got a bullet in the shoulder and fell back in the trench, my mucking-in mate, Lance Corporal Wymet was killed

> and Private Huggins badly wounded a few yards on. I got about 16 yards across No Man's Land and seeing the officer in charge, Captain Martin, taking cover in a shallow shell hole, I dropped in beside him, as also did Private Blount and a second lieutenant. Huggins crawled in with us, with the help of a puttee we slung him and we applied a dressing, but he was in a bad way and attempted to crawl back. He was immediately hit, we pulled him back and he died in the shell hole with us. A message to Captain Martin was later thrown out attached to a stone, to say that the attack was abandoned and to crawl back after dark, the situation being hopeless. After it got dark, the German lit the place up with parachute flares and kept up the fire in bursts. However we four all managed to crawl back one at a time.[18]
>
> Private Bernard Whayman, 1st Battalion, Northamptonshire Regiment, 2nd Brigade, 1st Division

Of the sixty men who attacked, the roll call would reveal only twenty left to answer their names. Forty were killed, wounded or missing. Alongside them the 2nd Royal Sussex had the dubious pleasure of attacking Wood Lane Trench. Private Walter Grover was a member of a new draft joining the battalion. It was to be a rough baptism of fire.

> You had to clamber out of the trench on a scaling ladder and then double across No Man's Land. Not knowing what we were going into, we'd never heard a bullet whizzing past. There were the dead lying all over, the Cameron Highlanders and the Black Watch – all their kilts. We had to stumble over those; you couldn't go in a straight line because it was all pitted with shell holes. Bullets were coming from High Wood they could enfilade us; bullets were coming from in front of us from Wood Lane Trench. So we were getting it all ways. Shrapnel was coming down overhead, all the German artillery banging away at us. We had our own artillery firing over that way. You can hardly credit what it was like; it's only those who have been through it who know what it was like. We got to the wire and then we got held up. The wire cutters came along, cut the wire and we got through. Then we were held up again in front of Wood Lane Trench and we laid there until it got dark. Then a sergeant came along, got us in line and we got into the German trench. That had to be seen to be believed. The Germans were buried in the sides of the trench

still holding their rifles, in grotesque postures; the trench was full of the dead, ours as well as Germans.[19]

Private Walter Grover, 2nd Battalion, Sussex Regiment, 2nd Brigade, 1st Division

The main attack on 9 September was to be made by the 16th (Irish) Division on the benighted village of Ginchy. Amongst the men going over the top that morning was Lieutenant Tom Kettle who was a prominent Irish Nationalist MP. He was born in Dublin in 1880. A leading intellectual he was elected the first president of the Young Ireland Branch of the United Irish League and became editor of *The Nationalist* newspaper. In 1906, his burgeoning political career culminated in his victory in the East Tyrone seat for the House of Commons. His life changed when he was in Belgium on a mission to purchase rifles for the Republican volunteers in 1914. Kettle was caught up in the outbreak of war and soon repulsed by witnessing the brutality of the German Army. He firmly identified with invaded Belgium whose position he compared to Ireland and in the end, despite his republicanism he had enlisted into the British Army. His experiences up to that point of war utterly appalled him.

If God spares me I shall accept it as a special mission to preach love and peace for the rest of my life. If He does not, I know now in my heart that for anyone who is dead but who has loved enough, there is provided some way of piercing the veils of death and abiding close to those whom he has loved till that end which is the beginning. I want to live, too, to use all my powers of thinking, writing and working to drive out of civilisation this foul thing called war and to put in its place understanding and comradeship.[20]

Lieutenant Tom Kettle, 9th Battalion, Royal Dublin Fusiliers, 48th Brigade, 16th (Irish) Division

Yet from the misery of war at least he had been vouchsafed a kind of hope for the future of Ireland, born from the shared experiences of Protestants and Catholics within the 16th (Irish) and 36th (Ulster) Divisions.

Had I lived, I had meant to call my next book on the relations of Ireland and England: *The Two Fools: A Tragedy of Errors*. It has needed all the folly of England and all the folly of Ireland to produce the situation in which our unhappy country is now involved. I have mixed much with Englishmen and with Protestant Ulstermen and I know

> that there is no real or abiding reason for the gulfs, saltier than the sea, that now dismember the natural alliance of both of them with us Irish Nationalists. It needs only a *Fiat lux*, of a kind very easily compassed, to replace the unnatural with the natural. In the name, and by the seal of the blood given in the last two years, I ask for Colonial Home Rule for Ireland – a thing essential in itself and essential as a prologue to the reconstruction of the Empire. Ulster will agree. And I ask for the immediate withdrawal of martial law in Ireland and an amnesty for all Sinn Fein prisoners. If this war has taught us anything it is that great things can be done only in a great way.[21]
>
> Lieutenant Tom Kettle, 9th Battalion, Royal Dublin Fusiliers, 48th Brigade, 16th (Irish) Division

The intellectual man of letters also conceived a real respect and love for the endurance and good spirits of his men, serving alongside him.

> We are moving up tonight into the Battle of the Somme. The bombardment, destruction and bloodshed are beyond all imagination, nor did I ever think the valour of simple men could be quite as beautiful as that of my Dublin Fusiliers. I have had two chances of leaving them – one on sick leave and one to take a staff job. I have chosen to stay with my comrades. I am calm and happy, but desperately anxious to live.[22]
>
> Lieutenant Tom Kettle, 9th Battalion, Royal Dublin Fusiliers, 48th Brigade, 16th (Irish) Division

One of those reasons for living had been born just a few days before – his daughter Betty, whom he had never seen. He tried to encapsulate his feeling in a poem written on 6 September.

> *The Gift of Love*
>
> In wiser days, my darling rosebud, blown
> To beauty proud as was your mother's prime –
> In that desired, delayed, incredible time
> You'll ask why I abandoned you, my own,
> And the dear breast that was your baby's throne
> To dice with death, and, oh! They'll give you rhyme
> And reason; one will call the thing sublime,
> And one decry it in a knowing tone.
> So here, while the mad guns curse overhead,
> And tired men sigh, with mud for couch and floor,

> Know that we fools, now with the foolish dead,
> Died not for Flag, nor King, nor Emperor,
> But for a dream, born in a herdsman's shed
> And for the secret Scripture of the poor.[23]
>
> Lieutenant Tom Kettle, 9th Battalion, Royal Dublin Fusiliers, 48th Brigade, 16th (Irish) Division

He had survived the earlier attack made on Ginchy and on the 8 September was put in charge of the remnants of B Company. One of his subalterns was Second Lieutenant Emmett Dalton.

> I was with Tom when we advanced to the position that night and the stench of the dead that covered our road was so awful that we both used some foot powder on our faces. When we reached our objective, we dug ourselves in and then at 5 p.m. on the 9th we attacked Ginchy. I was just behind Tom when we went over the top. He was in a bent position and a bullet got over a steel waistcoat that he wore and entered his heart. Well, he only lasted about one minute and he had my crucifix in his hands. He also said, 'This is the seventh anniversary of my wedding' I forget whether seventh or eighth.[24]
>
> Second Lieutenant Emmett Dalton, 9th Battalion, Royal Dublin Fusiliers, 48th Brigade, 16th (Irish) Division

The bullet that struck down Tom Kettle also killed part of the hope for a peaceful solution to the long standing 'Irish problem'. His body was never found after the fighting had ceased and he eventually took his place amongst the legions of the lost commemorated on the Thiepval Memorial. His little daughter, Betty, would live her life without ever knowing her father except perhaps through the medium of the sad poem he wrote her. She would die some eighty years later in a Dublin nursing home on 20 December 1996.

Kettle had been hit early on in the attack, but the men of 48th Brigade moved gradually forward across No Man's Land. They were joined by the 7th Royal Irish Fusiliers from the divisional reserve of 49th Brigade.

> Our shells bursting in the village of Ginchy made it belch forth smoke like a volcano. We couldn't run. We advanced at a steady walking pace, stumbling here and there, but going ever onward and upward. [A shell] landed in the midst of a bunch of men about 70 yards away on my right. I have a most vivid recollection of seeing a tremendous burst

> of clay and earth go shooting up into the air – yes, and even parts of human bodies – and that when the smoke cleared away there was nothing left.[25]
>
> Second Lieutenant Young, 7th Battalion, Royal Irish Fusiliers, 49th Brigade, 16th (Irish) Division

Still the men went on against what was officially described as 'slight opposition'. They overran the German front line and burst through to the powdered remnants of Ginchy, which they eventually managed to consolidate. Alongside the 48th Brigade, the 1/6th Connaught Rangers, commanded by Colonel Rowland Feilding, found themselves in even more trouble. Colonel Feilding had only just taken over command of the battalion, which had already suffered severe casualties early in the month.

> The commanding officer had been killed, the second in command had been killed. Various other people had been killed and we were sort of re-forming under a new CO – a Guards officer. We got this Colonel Feilding, an elderly gent in the Coldstream Guards who was not a regular soldier, but a nice man. But he was a Roman Catholic they thought 'Ah, Send him to the Connaught Rangers!' So Feilding turned up, a very large rubicund man.[26]
>
> Second Lieutenant Francis Jourdain, 6th Battalion, Connaught Rangers, 47th Brigade, 16th (Irish) Division

Colonel Feilding brought his new battalion no luck at all. The increasingly flexible new German defensive arrangements had fooled the British artillery and the Connaught Rangers were facing an untouched strong point.

> The trench in front of us, hidden and believed innocuous, which had in consequence been more or less ignored in the preliminary artillery programme, had – perhaps for this very reason – developed as the enemy's main resistance. This, in fact, being believed to be the easiest section of the attack, had been allotted to the tired and battered 47th Brigade. Such are the surprises of war! Supplemented by machine-gun nests in shell holes, the trench was found by the few who reached close enough to see into it to be a veritable hornets' nest. Moreover, it had escaped our bombardment altogether, or nearly so.[27]
>
> Lieutenant Colonel Rowland Feilding, 6th Battalion, Connaught Rangers, 47th Brigade, 16th (Irish) Division

It was the 18-year-old Second Lieutenant Jourdain's first experience of battle. He found it an experience that tested him to his limits.

> When the battle started it was all very horrifying, shells shooting over the trench and knocking the sand off the parapet. The troops went forward and they very soon came back, they were really knocked to bits by the Germans. I did not take part in the actual movement because it wasn't my business to do so. I was the signal officer and I was in the front-line trench looking after whatever signal communications there were, D3 telephone and lines which kept on being broken. The only useful communication was back to brigade. I had one or two NCOs and soldiers with me trying to keep a line going down the communications trench. One single wire on which everything depended. That kept on being bombarded and the thing got cut and several brave men kept on mending it. The whole thing developed into some glorious muddle and there wasn't anything very coherent sent back. In the middle of the battle the adjutant decided to go sick with trench fever! He retired from the war in fact and was never seen again. Which was not a very good thing for an adjutant to do in the middle of a battle! Feilding, who took a certain liking to me, thought I was reasonably intelligent and made me the adjutant on the spot. I was militarily speaking of no height and only 18! The point was I was there! The thing finished as a shambles.[28]
>
> Second Lieutenant Francis Jourdain, 6th Battalion, Connaught Rangers, 47th Brigade, 16th (Irish) Division

Jourdain's efforts were appreciated by his colonel. In his published memoirs, Feilding mentions Jourdain as having, 'wisdom far beyond his years'[29] and found he performed well under pressure: 'The boy Jourdain is still acting adjutant and is doing it marvellously well, in spite of his extreme youth.'[30]

In some ways the study of August and early September is the least rewarding and most utterly depressing chapter in the whole tragic epic of the Somme offensive. The British had the troops, the guns, the ammunition and even the weather – the perpetual enemy of British generals – was reasonably favourable. Yet the period went by unredeemed by anything that could be considered a success. At the end of 9 September the Fourth Army had still not been able to capture High Wood, Wood Trench or Falfemont Farm. All in all, nothing had changed, nothing had been achieved. As the fresh troops moved up they were soon made aware of what lay before them.

> We had to go up to the top of a little rise. Strewn up the hill, in rows like corn that had been mown, lay hundreds of our chaps that looked as though they had run into a machine-gun nest. It was a warm muggy day and the poor chaps' faces and exposed flesh were smothered in flies. The smell was awful. They lay so thick we simply could not avoid running over some of them. The horses of course stepped over, as a horse, unless absolutely forced to, will not tread on a prone body. But we could not help the wheels going over a few.[31]
>
> Driver James Reynolds, 55th Field Company, Royal Engineers, 3rd Guards Brigade, Guards Division

And all this sacrifice for what? A few German trenches and strong points had been captured, but new ones had blossomed behind the German front. There seemed to be no end in sight.

> I am afraid we are settling down to siege warfare in earnest and of a most sanguinary kind, very far from our hopes in July. But it's always the same: Festubert, Loos, and now this. Both sides are too strong for a finish yet. God knows how long it will be at this rate. None of us will ever see its end and children still at school will have to take over.[32]
>
> Captain Philip Pilditch, C Battery, 235th Brigade, Royal Field Artillery, 47th Division

After 9 September it was obvious that nothing more could be done before the next great leap into the unknown that was being planned by Haig and Rawlinson for 15 September. The stage was set for the decisive phase of the Battle of the Somme. This was to be the great offensive that would make all the losses and suffering worthwhile by finally breaking the power of the German Army – or condemn the BEF to at least another year in the trenches.

CHAPTER NINE

You are not Alone

There is an understandable tendency in considering the massacres of the Somme to concentrate on the legions of the dead. Yet, throughout the Battle of the Somme, as in most battles, three or four were wounded for every man that was killed. The term 'wounded' covered a multitude of varying conditions, and there was no denying that a relatively minor 'Blighty' wound could come as a blessed relief to some:

> Fred and I smoked, shielding with our cupped hands the glowing tip of our fags. We had to keep pressing back against the side of the trench to allow small parties of walking wounded to pass. I had my leg braced against the trench when I was jolted out of my sleep by a sharp blow on the inside of my left leg, just below the kneecap. It was just as though somebody had kicked me. I felt it with my hand in the darkness and my hand came away sticky and wet. I knew that the flesh was torn. A piece of shrapnel had gone deep in my leg. I had received what every soldier prayed for – a perfect 'Blighty'! I told Fred, he, too, felt the edges of a jagged wound, tied a field bandage on it and called me a lucky bastard.[1]
>
> Private Albert Conn, 8th Battalion, Devonshire Regiment, 20th Brigade, 7th Division

The problem was that no one knew where the bullet or shrapnel might hit. It was a complete lottery. Corporal Arthur Razzell was another of the lucky ones. When he was hit it was almost an anti-climax as a shell exploded right next to him. For a moment he went into a surrealistic, muffled dream world.

> I had no sense of pain, I was sort of deafened and the noise in my head from the blowing in of my ears. When I realised I could walk I

> did the same as everybody else – you got back. I scrambled over a heap of soil that was in front of me, blown up by the shell and as I scrambled across it I felt it moving. There were evidently people buried underneath who were struggling to get out. A few more yards along the communicating trench I realised where I was, I suppose I'd recovered from the blow. I realised if I kept to the communicating trench I'd have about a mile to go, whereas there was a road nearby that went direct towards Albert.[2]
>
> Corporal Arthur Razzell, 8th Battalion, Royal Fusiliers, 36th Brigade, 12th Division

Razzell found he had been wounded in the face and as one of the walking wounded he was therefore in the vast majority. There was no chance of them all being stretchered back – there were simply not enough stretchers. And the longer they waited in the front-line area the more likely they were to be hit again. Slowly the wounded staggered back, stumbling and struggling as best they could.

> So I climbed up on to the road and walked as fast as I could until I came to the glow of a cigarette burning on the side of the road. I said to the fellow who was smoking, 'Can you tell me where there is a dressing station?' And he pulled back a blanket that had been screening a little dugout in the bank of the road. He was an RAMC man. Inside there were a couple of stretchers with some wounded men on them. He sat me on a box and fumbled with my breast tunic buttons. I said, 'Oh, it's not there, it's my face - my jaw!' He said, 'Yes, OK!' and still went on. What he was doing was giving me an anti-tetanus injection in the chest. They'd found out in France that so many wounds were getting tetanus, the soil was infected quite heavily with tetanus germs. I said to him, 'Is this a Blighty one?' He said, 'My lad, this time next week, you'll be sitting in a deckchair drinking iced drinks through a straw!' He was right![3]
>
> Corporal Arthur Razzell, 8th Battalion, Royal Fusiliers, 36th Brigade, 12th Division

Many men who walked were actually quite severely wounded and the journey back taxed them to the utmost. Often they helped each other along as best they could. Guardsman Norman Cliff was wounded in the right thigh and could hardly walk when his officer sent him back.

> On the way I caught up with another man staggering along and we clung to one another, each holding the other up. I was shocked to see that the top of his head was a mass of blood and the crown seemed to be missing. I marvelled that he was still conscious and still able to use his limbs. Encouraging one another to keep going, we finally stumbled into an advance first aid post and dropped exhausted.[4]
>
> Private Norman Cliff, 1st Battalion, Grenadier Guards, 3rd Brigade, Guards Division

For the seriously wounded there was no chance of walking. Most had no option but to lie where they fell. In a pregnant second they had been dashed from the peak of manhood to utter ruin. Sergeant Kerr was one of those who went over the top in a state of exaltation.

> Fear? I had no fear at all. All the pent up dread and tension had completely left me. Like a shot I was up and over the top of the trench. In no time bullets were flying, and a wicked machine gun had opened up against us on my right. One or two of my section who had had most difficulty climbing out of the trench had barely got up into line and I gave them an encouraging wave of my arm. Barely had I straightened myself forward again, when something with the force of a cannon ball hit me full in the chest. I believed I had been killed, and in the two seconds it took me to crumple up, my lips had only time to murmur, 'Oh mother!' Then nothingness.[5]
>
> Sergeant William Kerr, 5th (Western Cavalry) Battalion, 2nd Canadian Brigade, 1st Canadian Division

For so many men, such thoughts *were* the end. But although he had indeed been terribly wounded Sergeant Kerr had also, in a warped sense, been fantastically lucky. When he was later examined, he was told that from the location of the entry and exit wounds his heart must have been in the act of contracting at the instant the bullet smashed through his chest. The battlefield was the most hostile environment in the world and hardly any one had the time to dawdle and help such severely wounded men. If they were to have any chance of survival, the first thing a wounded man had to do was to care for himself as best he could. Every soldier carried a field dressing in the inside pocket of his tunic and this was to prove a life-saver for Sergeant Kerr.

> I opened my eyes and had a minute or two to realise I was still alive. After a while I began to feel about my chest, for I didn't know how bad

> I had been wounded, or what had got me. I felt my left breast pocket sticky with blood, managed to undo the button, and pull out what was in it. It was my pay book, stained with blood and a bullet hole through it. I knew then it was 'only a bullet' that had got me, not a cannon ball as it had felt like. Elation at finding myself still alive helped greatly to ease the pain and sense of helplessness I felt, but fear of loss of blood began to take hold of me. It was then I remembered the first aid dressing carried in the little pocket at the bottom of my tunic, and I reached down to feel if it was still there – it was. I got it out. It comprised two small pads with bandaging. Gingerly I opened up my tunic and shirt, located the wound with my finger and placed one of my pads over – and buttoned up again. Already aware of more blood under me, I hoped I could get the other pad on to the wound that must also be there – the hole where the bullet had gone out. It had clearly gone right through my chest. I finally managed by bending my left hand to slide the other pad far enough under to what I hoped was the right spot. Then I just lay still. How long I lay like that, I had little idea. The sun was going down when I became aware of footsteps.[6]
>
> Sergeant William Kerr, 5th (Western Cavalry) Battalion, 2nd Canadian Brigade, 1st Canadian Division

It was essential to stop any bleeding because the wounded would almost certainly be left out until darkness fell. There were very few battalion stretcher bearers to pick the wounded up from the battlefield and as they followed behind an attack they were soon swamped.

> Up they went and then we stretcher bearers went over with them. We were quickly very busy: picking up the wounded, taking them to regimental aid posts. As the day went on there were other regiments going through and other wounded. As you were going along with the stretcher you'd hear faint calls, 'Stretcher bearer, stretcher bearer!' from the wounded men. You'd go over, look on his shoulder; you were concerned with your own regiment, 'Sorry chum, we're Yorks!' If you collected all and sundry back to your aid post, your medical officer had his hands full already with his own wounded. If you're going to take every wounded man back – they were strewn all over the shop like. Going backwards and forwards, picking up. A hell of a noise.[7]
>
> Private Basil Farrer, 2nd Battalion, Green Howards, 21st Brigade, 30th Division

Despite his apparent indifference, Basil Farrer was merely trying to do his best in impossible circumstances. He had to have some criteria to sort out the collection of so many wounded. He was a brave man; nearly all the stretcher bearers were. Alongside them, the more conscientious chaplains and padres would often scour the battlefield trying to bring what comfort they could to the desperately wounded in the long hours before they could be picked up.

> I have a confession to make that may sound ghoulish and brutal. If I had to be on a battlefield, the more dead and wounded there were, the happier I was. This was not due to lack of sympathy or imagination, but, I think, to a simple psychological fact. As a non-combatant, a chaplain was under no definite orders, and with nothing to do, he had nothing to think of but his own skin. But with work, and the highest work, abounding, he might to some extent forget his own fears in ministering to the needs of others. In going from one wounded man to another, he would have endless opportunities of ministration. He could often relieve the torment of thirst, perhaps by a drink from the man's own water bottle which he was unable to reach (never, of course, giving spirits to a man with an open wound lying out in the open). He could take down a message from dying lips. I recall one lad in the Shropshires, lying in a shell hole, whose one thought was, 'I don't know what my mother will do'. I could at least write to that mother and tell her how her boy had forgotten his pain in his thought for her. And one could speak, often in dying ears, the Saviour's precious Name, and of the Blood that cleanses from all sin.[8]
>
> Chaplain Roger Bulstrode, Senior Chaplain, 20th Division

When at last the injured were picked up by the stretcher bearers they would often be taken to the regimental aid post where the medical officer attached to each battalion would roughly bandage and administer palliative morphia. In Sergeant Kerr's case he was carried by stretcher to a deep German dugout, which was being used as an advanced dressing station. Here he was laid on a rough wire-mesh bed, surrounded by other seriously wounded men.

> The dead and the walking wounded would be somewhere else. That was to be a terribly long night, pitch dark as it was down in the depths of the place. Two of the most seriously wounded screamed with their

> pains for most of the night, until one of them passed away. He was at the far end of the dugout, but I could hear the murmur, 'He's dead. He's gone.' His passing brought a hush in the darkness, a kind of two minutes silence, in which even the remaining demented one seemed to join. In no time, though, he was at it again, but only for a few minutes longer. 'For Christ's sake can't you stop that bawling, you are not the only one who is suffering!' Strange to say this reprimand from a hitherto quiet one was to do the trick. From then all that could be heard was the utter silence of the underground darkness. For myself, with a dull pain all over my chest, I just lay without moving all through the night.[9]
>
> Sergeant William Kerr, 5th (Western Cavalry) Battalion,
> 2nd Canadian Brigade, 1st Canadian Division

Such advanced dressing stations were operated by the men of the Royal Army Medical Corps. While the men on both sides sought to destroy the lives of their enemies, it was their task to try and patch up the results of the general mayhem. The crunching, flensing power of the shell splinters, the scything of machine guns, the sudden shattering impact of the sniper's bullet – all caused bodily wounds that needed urgent medical treatment. It is not surprising that the RAMC was one of the most hard-pressed units in the whole of the British Army on the Somme. Its work never ceased for a moment. Someone, somewhere always needed to be swiftly diagnosed, tended, bandaged, splinted, vaccinated, stitched, operated upon, or simply drugged with morphine till all pain and life ebbed away. The medics' efforts went largely unsung, but they are worthy of earnest admiration.

One field ambulance unit – the 45th Field Ambulance, RAMC – can stand as an example of all these brave men trying their best to stem the tidal wave of death on the Somme. The field ambulance was the basic unit. It was the staging post between the regimental aid posts and the casualty clearing stations further back. Early in August a group of its officers moved forward to examine the sector on which they had been assigned to operate in the service of their parent body the 15th (Scottish) Division. At their head was one Captain Hamilton.

> Fricourt is to be our headquarters. There is an excellent big deep dugout made by the Hun as a headquarters. There is a long passage and from it open off numerous rooms. There is room for about fifty

officers and men. The mess is nearer the surface in a cellar, not very big, but light and airy compared to other rooms. From the passage run several shafts which serve as bolt holes and also air shafts. For patients there is very poor accommodation as one couldn't get a stretcher down into the big dugout. There is a more or less sheltered spot where one could put half a dozen stretchers or perhaps twenty sitters who would be safe, except for a direct hit which would clean them out. Of course there is no idea of keeping patients here. It is only a place for our headquarters and a reserve of men.[10]

Medical Officer Captain Eben Hamilton, 45th Field Ambulance, Royal Army Medical Corps, 15th Division

The headquarters was in fact just a staging post; a link between the advanced dressing station post and the main dressing station situated still further back in Albert. The organisation for relays of ambulances was crucial if they were not to maroon the wounded at the front or leave them lying in the open at Fricourt.

Two cars are kept here and one at the advanced dressing station at Contalmaison. As the car from Contalmaison comes down, it is loaded by a medical officer who sees that all patients are properly bandaged etc. and does anything necessary for them. This car goes on at once back to Albert, and one of the other cars goes up to Contalmaison. As the first car passes the wagon lines which are back a couple of miles on the road to Albert, another car there moves up to Fricourt. When the first one discharges its patients at a main dressing station, it returns to the wagon lines.[11]

Medical Officer Captain Eben Hamilton, 45th Field Ambulance, Royal Army Medical Corps, 15th Division

The advanced post was to be stationed at the Contalmaison Chateau. Captain Hamilton went forward to check whether it was suitable for their specific needs as medics. He found that little remained of the chateau.

Contalmaison: a ruin with a dead and very stinking horse at the cross-roads. The advanced dressing station is in the cellar of the chateau, there is still a bit of wall standing. There are four small rooms in the cellar: the patient goes down the stairs through 'A' and 'B' where he waits his turn, to the dressing room 'C' where there are trestles on which to set the stretchers and chairs for the sitters. Then when

> dressed and labelled, he is sent through to 'D' there to be fed and await evacuation. 'D' might hold nine stretchers and about a dozen sitters on a bench down the side. The whole place is lumbered up with beds and quite unnecessary stuff, which I shall clear out. The officers' room is small but beautifully finished, all boarded over with a fixed table and a bed. Two stretchers can just fit in, so it holds three people with a squeeze. There is a blow hole for air and a certain amount of light. But artificial light is necessary all the time.[12]
>
> Medical Officer Captain Eben Hamilton, 45th Field Ambulance, Royal Army Medical Corps, 15th Division

The 'facilities' seemed adequate for their requirements, although the absence of a functioning water supply meant that all they needed would have to be laboriously sent forward in petrol tins. The advanced dressing station also needed to be kitted out with all the medical supplies they would need once the casualties started to flood in. Large numbers of stretchers were necessary and plenty of blankets, for even in summer wounded men suffering from shock could feel cold. Huge numbers of bandages and splints of all different shapes, types and sizes were obviously essential as were oceans of simple medical stores such as disinfectant. All this had to be brought forward across some of the most dangerous ground on earth.

After Hamilton had scouted out the position, the rest of the 45th Field Ambulance moved up a few days later. As they approached their destination, Lieutenant Lawrence Gameson found that the directions given to him by Hamilton, although eccentric, were peculiarly effective at guiding them through the last stages of their journey.

> Contalmaison is quite completely ruined. We were told to turn left at the second *bad* smell. The directions proved to be as accurate as a precise map reference. We live in the remains of a chateau. A few chunks of wall and part of one room is all that is left above ground. The cellars are sound. There are German dugouts many feet below the original cellars. Our mess is at this depth. It is a small, square, box-like room having connection with the relatively fresh air outside by means of a long wood-lined shaft; which, being of German make, naturally faces the enemy. A good shot would lob down the shaft and burst in our box. Already a shell has exploded almost on the edge of the opening - it sent down a great 'whoof' of smoke, stink and dust

which put out our lamp. Seems an odd place for a living quarters; but I always anticipate the worst. I am not always wrong. Here at Contalmaison I feel most curiously and disturbingly isolated, as if one was going to be stuck here forever.[13]

Medical Officer Lieutenant Lawrence Gameson, 45th Field Ambulance, Royal Army Medical Corps, 15th Division

These miserable, claustrophobic surroundings were to be their home for the next month. Whatever the gloomy prospects down below, the world outside was rather more dangerous as the shells rained down, making no discrimination between fighting men and those wearing the Red Cross brassard.

Soon the wounded began to arrive: some walking, some carried, some just helped along; the usual bloody, patient battered crowd, without a grouse and with scarcely a groan.[14]

Medical Officer Lieutenant Lawrence Gameson, 45th Field Ambulance, Royal Army Medical Corps, 15th Division

The arrival of the wounded converted the cellars into a macabre combination of waiting room, surgery, abattoir and crypt. For the wounded men and the desperate doctors who tended them it was a subterranean hell.

The flow of work in our cellar was uncertain. Times of slackness alternating with times of great stress, when the place was filled with scores upon scores of reeking, bleeding men. These times of great stress were not isolated incidents, to be dealt with, cleaned up, then forgotten, like a railway accident. They recurred regularly. They went on and on and on. Stretchers blocked the cellar floors, the passages, the battered shelter that remained above ground and the approaches outside. Often we worked for hours on end without respite; at the crude dressing tables, at men grounded on stretchers, at men squatting or sticking. It was emphatically not sheer muddle, but the congestion beggars description. Our working space was limited. We got in each other's way. There was a constant movement of bearers shuffling and staggering with stretchers, negotiating the cellar stairs, seeking a way in or out and a bare space whereon to deposit their burdens. Walking wounded sat on benches or squatted between the stretchers on each available foot of floor, patiently waiting their turn to be dressed or get their shot of anti-tetanus serum. Sometimes a man on a stretcher would vomit explosively, spewing over himself and his neighbours. I have seen mounted troops brought in with liquid faeces oozing from the unlaced legs of their breeches. Occasionally a man would gasp and die as he lay on his stretcher. All this was routine and the waiting crowd looked on unconcerned. No one spoke much during these seemingly endless periods of congestion. For the most part, the wounded showed little tendency to talk and to exchange the customary quips. They waited patiently, while we got on with our work with no needless words. This was done in the poor light of candles and reeking lamps. There was little water and of course no running water. Dressings and filth accumulated, to be burnt outside with the minimum of smoke. The air became rank; worse when gas was about for airways had to be partially blocked. Blood was the general background: dried, drying or wet. With the means then available we did our best for the wounded's immediate needs and for their rapid evacuation by ambulance to Fricourt.[15]

Medical Officer Lieutenant Lawrence Gameson, 45th Field Ambulance, Royal Army Medical Corps, 15th Division

Even simple tasks became complicated beyond belief by the extreme nature of the situation. Tetanus was a constant threat on the ravaged battlefield and injections were given to almost every casualty. This in itself posed a problem.

One of our troubles was the shortage of serum needles. It was impossible to keep sharp what we had. To shove a large, blunt needle into a man already tried almost beyond endurance was no nice task, but it had to be done. It was then that orders came from a distance, forbidding all but medical officers to inject serum. The orders would have been more convincing had the supply of new needles been increased. It was not.[16]

Medical Officer Lieutenant Lawrence Gameson, 45th Field Ambulance, Royal Army Medical Corps, 15th Division

The endless hours at work up to their arms in other men's innards left them looking like apprentice butchers.

There is a continuous stream of wounded through at all hours. The pips on my tunic cuffs are shiny with polished blood, blood of someone else, of infantry mostly. Although but a middleman, one gets sick of blood's smell and of the endless procession of red raw human meat passing through our hands.[17]

Medical Officer Lieutenant Lawrence Gameson, 45th Field Ambulance, Royal Army Medical Corps, 15th Division

The blood, the 'meat', the vomit, the ripped, torn and loosened bowels brought into sharp focus a further pest – swarms of bloated flies. In a world filled with 5.9-in shells it might be considered that little harm could result from the buzzing of a few flies. But the flies, with their natural predilection for faeces, accelerated the spread of disease and somehow amplified the overall horror simply by dint of their ceaseless buzzing and thoroughly nauseating lifestyle.

This evening I killed fourteen flies with one swipe with a rolled up copy of an ancient *Times*. They are infinitely numerous, leisurely and deliberate in movement, and have large sticky feet. The neighbourhood is an incubator for them. Eggs are laid in corpses of Germans and horses, hatching in the rotting semi-liquid flesh. The rest of their lives, for the most part, is an ephemeral gluttonish revel amongst all that is most revolting in this revolting region of putrefaction and decay. They swarm upon food, they buzz. Night and day this room resounds with their buzzing. The drone becomes a background, it even steals into one's sleep.[18]

Medical Officer Lieutenant Lawrence Gameson, 45th Field Ambulance, Royal Army Medical Corps, 15th Division

Behind the all-pervasive background buzzing lay the horror of fly eggs hatching out in the bodies of the wounded and the dead. It was almost too horrible to bear for boys brought up with heroic, fictional images of superficial arm wounds. The reality of war could turn, or indeed colonise, the stomach.

I saw more torn human tissues than one would have thought possible in so short a time. There was hardly any part of the body I did not see cut or exposed. Maggot invasion was common. One unconscious man arrived with part of a frontal lobe protruding from a hole in his skull. The protruding portion of his brain was moving with maggots. There was a man with a loop of gut sticking out of a gash in his uniform. It was a bayonet wound. The loop of gut had been lightly dressed with gauze, beneath which there was a wriggling mass of maggots. The man had been lying out wounded and the flies never missed a chance.

> His condition was deplorable. When men had been left out wounded for some time, often their shoulders, buttocks or whole back were invaded by the creatures in the areas of skin compressed by the weight of their immobilised bodies. One man I saw had been lying out because both legs were wounded. Prolonged pressure had caused necrosis of the skin over his buttocks and of the superficial portions of muscle beneath it. Maggots had invaded the deeper tissues, I had to pick them out with a long forceps. The man was unaware of his condition. Maggot invasion was always accompanied by a foul smell, since it flourished only in tissues undergoing some degree of decomposition. As a rule, the patient did not notice the stink, or did not know that it came from his own body, if sensitive enough to notice it.[19]
>
> Medical Officer Lieutenant Lawrence Gameson, 45th Field Ambulance, Royal Army Medical Corps, 15th Division

Of course, there were many men who could not be saved; their broken bodies afterwards awaited removal, acting as a haunting reminder of the medics' impotence, when it came down to it, to save their mangled patients.

> Two bodies in room, covered with blankets – head one end, feet the other. It's the repetition which gets on one's nerves. Stiff and still. They obtrude. Seem to fill the place. Can't look away from them. Turned back the blankets and looked at their faces. Covered them up and went to doorway. But, God! The world seems stiff and still today and death is everywhere.[20]
>
> Medical Officer Lieutenant Lawrence Gameson, 45th Field Ambulance, Royal Army Medical Corps, 15th Division

Helping them, on occasion, were the padres sent to comfort and pacify the dying with promises of eternal life. Sometimes the medics found the presence of these padres deeply depressing.

> A certain unhumorous Presbyterian priest haunted our cellars in those days. Padres were always welcome, but this man was rather exceptional. In addition to the usual armaments of cigarettes and field service postcards, he carried a concertina. An eeriness clung to him. His favourite pitch was at the distant end of the cellar floor, beneath the vaulted roof. Here he squatted. A figure not easily forgotten: long lugubrious face peering above the wheezing bellows, swaying from side to side in the flickering candlelight, playing dour tunes to those on the stretchers around

him. He was quite beyond my ken. He suggested impending doom. He gave me the creeps. Most of our patients were Scotsmen; beyond question they valued highly the ministrations of this terrifying priest.[21]

Medical Officer Lieutenant Lawrence Gameson, 45th Field Ambulance, Royal Army Medical Corps, 15th Division

Stressed by constant danger and the sheer ubiquity of the sordid physical and mental horrors that surrounded them, it is not surprising that the atmosphere was tense as the over-worked medical officers found themselves *in extremis* and locked underground with only each others' company for weeks at a time.

My vividest memory is that of enforced and confined companionship with those who constantly jar and irritate; a torture less easily endured than some which touch the flesh only, as everyone knows who has had to put up with it. It was quite unimportant, but added to one's unease. That unease, which just then was almost overwhelming, derived in part from the sense of separation from a normally ordered world. Being cut off from the land of dreams where I used to live in that other life on the other side of the war.[22]

Medical Officer Lieutenant Lawrence Gameson, 45th Field Ambulance, Royal Army Medical Corps, 15th Division

When the doctors had bandaged them up as best they could the seriously wounded would be sent back on the ambulances. These relatively unsprung ambulances jolted unmercifully down what remained of the endlessly shelled roads. This was an experience that many men never forgot as their broken bones grated against each other. After being severely wounded in his hip and left leg at Mametz Wood, Sergeant Tom Price faced such an ordeal.

We were put on a Ford ambulance van with rubber tyres, hard wheels. There were six of us, three on each side and I don't know which of the six of us screamed the most on that journey down over the rutted, shell-holed roads.[23]

Sergeant Tom Price, 13th Battalion, Welch Regiment, 114th Brigade, 38th Division

When the wounded finally reached safety, well behind the lines, there was a new awakening. Many had almost given up hope of ever returning to a normal life and the presence of the women nurses seemed to epitomise the promise of a whole new life away from the horrors of the front line.

> I looked up in a sort of half coma to see a Red Cross nurse looking down at me. I was never to forget this, because I have always thought of it as the most beautiful sight I have ever seen in my life. I never saw this girl again, and I only know her name to be Miss Jones. I have been asked what is the most beautiful thing I have ever seen and I have always given the same answer – a woman. I have seen the sunrise on the Jungfrau, sunset at Corbiere, the midnight sun in Northern Norway, evening light on the Taj Mahal, the Mediterranean blue, England and Paris in the Spring, the glory that was Greece. I can therefore claim to have seen a lot of wonderful sights, but I still give the same answer.[24]
>
> Private Henry Russell, 1/5th Battalion (London Rifle Brigade), 169th Brigade, 56th Division

There were plenty of men, however, who came round only to find that new horrors surrounded them. When Private Norman Cliff awoke in a tented hospital his senses were almost overwhelmed.

> I looked around and my nostrils were assailed by the sickening odour of suppurating wounds and soiled bandages. There were badly disfigured men, pale-faced lads from whom life was ebbing, heavily bandaged stumps indicating this or that limb missing. Saddest of all was a youngster who had been reduced to a trunk, minus arms and legs. How could it be possible that he was not only alive but that his spirit seemed undaunted? Glancing at the bandages swathing his stumps, he challenged his nurse in a strong Scottish accent, 'How about three rounds with me tonight, Sister?' Humour even *in extremis*. Mercifully, before day dawned the spark of life went out of him …[25]
>
> Private Norman Cliff, 1st Battalion, Grenadier Guards, 3rd Brigade, Guards Division

Even when wounds responded to medical treatment the process of healing was often agonising. There was no penicillin and many of the methods of packing and draining pus from wounds seem almost primitive in their nature.

> My wound is dressed twice a day and is more awful every time – a sign as I am assured, that it is healing up nicely. It has to be 'packed' at the lower entrance, which means that a few yards of bandage are poked up with a knitting needle, to keep it open and allow it to discharge. It consists of a little blue mark on the top of my shoulders where the

> bullet went in and a long deep slit a few inches down my back, where it came out.[26]
>
> Sergeant Roland Mountfield, 10th Battalion, Royal Fusiliers, 111th Brigade, 37th Division

The lightly wounded would be patched up ready to fight again, but the prospects for the seriously wounded were extremely bleak. There was no underpinning concept of the welfare state. People earned a living or existed in dire poverty. The war crippled, with their prosthetic legs, wheel chairs, missing arms, emasculated bodies and mutilated faces, were a nuisance to a society that believed in standing on your own two feet – if you had them.

One man's story may stand for those ruined lives and the cruel impact of war that could reach down through the generations to torment its victims. Private George Dray was wounded with the 6th Northamptonshires during the battle to take Trônes Wood on 14 July 1916. After the war the multiple wounds suffered in his various battles took a terrible toll, as his son, John Dray, relates.

> He was the deputy pier-master on Woolwich ferry. I was born in 1926 and in December 1928, two years old I was, he came home from work, just before Christmas and he said, 'I've got a headache I think I'm going to bed' It was December 23rd. My sister went up with a cup of tea for him and she came running down, 'There's something funny with daddy's eye!' The eye was bulging on one side. They ran him into hospital and this blood clot was pushing the eye from behind. They took the eye away and they thought that was the end – that he'd be 'One-Eyed George' for the rest of his life. But the blood clot had turned and was going back. The next day, 24 December, was my mother's birthday. About eight at night she went up to the hospital. He was dozy, half unconscious. All of a sudden he came very clear, and he said, 'Elsie, have you hung the children's stockings up?' She said, 'Not yet!' He said, 'I would go home if I was you and do the stockings! I'll see you tomorrow!' Well she did, and before she got home he was dead – this blood clot had touched his brain and killed him. Christmas Eve, my mother's birthday and she was six months pregnant with my last sister.[27]
>
> John Dray

CHAPTER TEN

When Push Comes to Shove

The origin of the Battle of Flers–Courcelette, which commenced on 15 September, lay back in the middle of August when Haig sent a memo ordering Rawlinson to prepare plans for an all-out offensive with the aim of capturing the original German Third Line defensive system. Haig considered that the second half of September 1916 would mark the decisive phase of the 'wearing out battle' that the Fourth and Fifth Armies had been waging on the Somme. This was the time to amass all the British reserves and strike the tottering Germans.

> The general plan of the attack projected for the middle of September will be to establish a defensive flank on the high ground south of the Ancre, north of the Albert–Bapaume road, and to press the main attack south of the Albert–Bapaume road with the objective of securing the enemy's last line of prepared defences between Morval and Le Sars, with a view to opening the way for the cavalry.[1]
>
> General Sir Douglas Haig, General Headquarters, British Expeditionary Force

The trials and tribulations of much of the fighting in August and early September had originated in the pressing need to attain a good start line – one that was not fatally undermined by the presence of German strong points, which could catch the advancing British troops in enfilade in the next attacks. All that agonising, long drawn out struggle had still left some key strong points in the German's grasp – most evidently in the splintered remnants of High Wood. By the time the British were ready for the next stage the Germans had, of course, significantly strengthened their defensive positions. That the 'last shall be first' was now literally true, as the German Third Line, such as it was on 1 July, was now the German First Line.

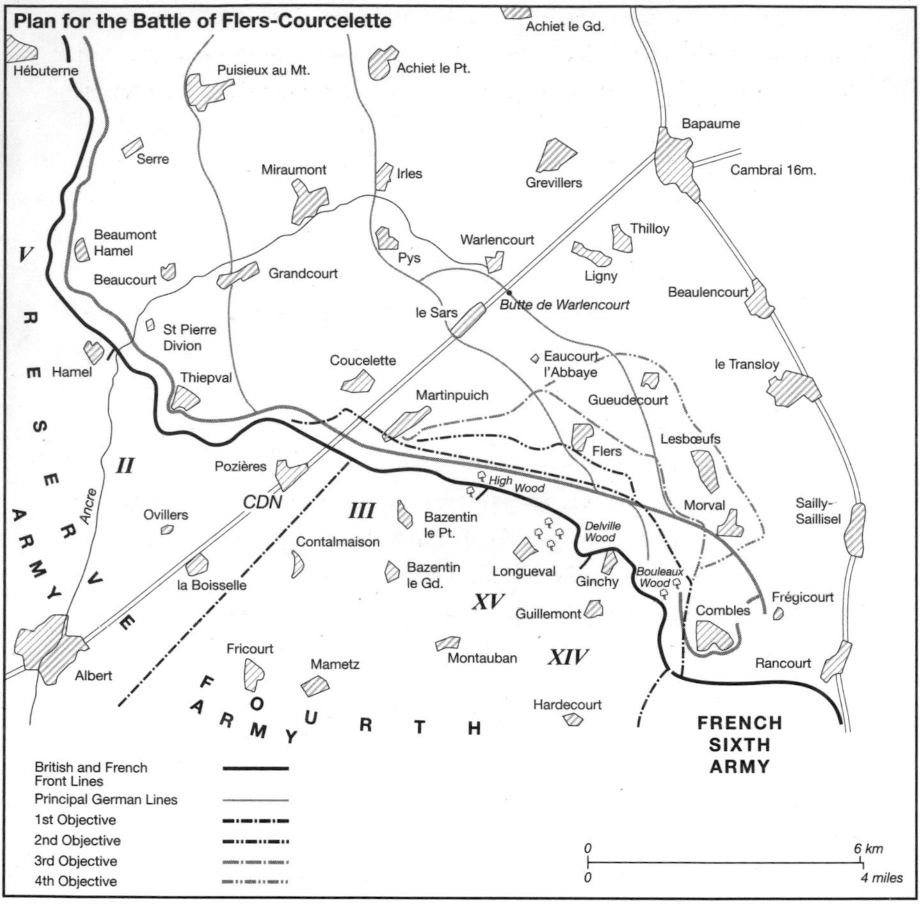

Plan for the Battle of Flers-Courcelette
Achiet le Gd.
Hébuterne
Puisieux au Mt.
Achiet le Pt.
Bapaume
Serre
Miraumont
Irles
Grevillers
Cambrai 16m.
Beaumont Hamel
Thilloy
Warlencourt
V
Pys
Ligny
Beaucourt
Grandcourt
Beaulencourt
Butte de Warlencourt
le Sars
St Pierre Divion
Coucelette
Eaucourt l'Abbaye
le Transloy
Hamel
Thiepval
Martinpuich
Gueudecourt
RESERVE ARMY
Lesbœufs
Flers
II
Pozières
High Wood
CDN
III
Morval
Sailly-Saillisel
Ancre
Ovillers
Bazentin le Pt.
Delville Wood
Contalmaison
Bazentin le Gd.
Longueval
Bouleaux Wood
la Boisselle
Ginchy
XV
Frégicourt
Guillemont
Combles
Fricourt
Montauban
XIV
Albert
Mametz
Rancourt
FOURTH ARMY
Hardecourt
FRENCH SIXTH ARMY
British and French Front Lines
Principal German Lines
1st Objective
2nd Objective
3rd Objective
4th Objective
0
6 km
0
4 miles

Although the new obstacles did not have the deep sunk dugouts of the original defences, they were still a formidable obstacle to further progress. In addition, the development of German tactics to encompass placing machine gunners in neighbouring shell holes was particularly effective, and it should be remembered that in many sectors the forward German defences had been reduced to little more than a line of connected shell holes after the recent attentions of the British artillery. Unfortunately the ferocious fighting in August had demonstrated that every string of shell holes left by the crashing shells of the British high explosive barrage was a potential additional line of defence for the Germans. Artillery bombardments had to cover not just the main lines but also all the cratered area that surrounded them – this meant that ever more guns and shells were necessary to attain the same results.

Yet just as the British were encountering the renewed logistical problems that such a huge artillery effort thrust upon them, so there appeared a new weapon of war that offered a slim hope of shattering the deadlock on the Somme. The origins of the tank lie in a number of simultaneous brainwaves by an army desperate for some kind of armoured vehicle that could both burst through barbed wire to clear a way for the infantry and carry guns or machine guns across No Man's Land.

After a fairly prolonged gestation the results were two variants of a tracked vehicle: the lozenge-shaped Mark I 'tank', as the new weapon of war was known – probably in recognition of its outward resemblance to a water tank. The 'Male' tank was armed with two 6-pounder guns held in protruding sponsons clamped on to either side, with an additional four machine guns for good measure; the 'Female' tank had six machine guns. These machine guns could enfilade German trenches to great effect, while the 'Male' tank's guns could blast away fortified posts. Tracks on the tank enabled it to surmount difficult ground conditions, crush its way through barbed wire, cross trenches and generally surmount obstacles at an overall top speed of just under 4 miles per hour. Yet its abilities should not be over-exaggerated. The tank was armoured, but this was no defence at all against any shell fire, and small arms weapons could cause 'splashes' of white hot metal to whirr round inside the tank to painful effect. Wide trenches, deep craters and mud, and tree stumps all brought the tanks sooner or later to a halt. The crew of eight were also severely limited in what they could achieve by the dreadful working environment inside the tank. Visibility was extremely restricted through the narrow slits, which made it difficult to avoid dangerous obstacles or to seek out enemies. Although the tanks looked big the engine filled most of the available space and it made its presence felt in no uncertain terms: the noise was deafening, the heat utterly enervating and its noxious fumes quickly poisoned the atmosphere. After a few hours the crews were good for nothing. Unfortunately, the sheer mechanical unreliability of the tanks meant that this was usually of little importance as the tanks often broke down well before the crew's health became a problem.

Haig was probably the most effective champion of the tank in the early days in that he not only quickly appreciated its potential but also, unlike so many of the vainglorious buffoons who subsequently made the Tank Corps their career, he had the power to get things done.

> I saw Colonel Swinton with Generals Butler and Whigham (the Deputy CIGS) regarding the 'Tanks'. I was told that 150 would be provided by 31 July. I said that was too late. Fifty were urgently required for 1 June. Swinton is to see what can be done, and will also practise and train 'tanks' and crews over obstacles and wire similar to the ground over which the attack will be made. I gave him a trench map as a guide and impressed on him the necessity for thinking over the system of leadership and control of a group of 'tanks' with a view to manoeuvring.[2]
>
> General Sir Douglas Haig, General Headquarters, British Expeditionary Force

Already Haig was thinking about how the tanks should be used in action and pondering on some of the command and control problems that would bedevil the tanks in action. It was also apparent that the question of integrating these tanks into the complex mix of artillery and infantry tactics would not be a simple matter. The Heavy Section, Machine Gun Corps were themselves short of training and most of the infantry had had little or no opportunity to train alongside them.

> I was present at a demonstration in the use of 'Tanks'. A battalion of infantry and five Tanks operated together. Three lines of trenches were assaulted. The Tanks crossed the several lines with the greatest ease, and one entered a wood, which represented a 'strong point'

> and easily walked over fair sized trees of six inches through! Altogether the demonstration was quite encouraging, but we require to clear our ideas as to the tactical handling of these machines.[3]
>
> General Sir Douglas Haig, General Headquarters, British Expeditionary Force

Some people have claimed that Haig should have withheld the use of this 'super-weapon' until there were sufficient numbers to end the war in a single mighty stroke. Such fantasies ignore the natural weft and weave of weapon development. The 1916 Mark I tank was by no means the fully fledged article of war: there were simply too few available, they were mechanically unreliable in the extreme, too slow and cumbersome and with limited powers of both offence and defence. Until weapons have been used in active service conditions it is almost impossible to judge their efficacy in action, to carry out the development work to eradicate technical problems, or to train the crews under the pressures of battle and generally to develop the tanks as effective weapons of war within the total effort. After all, the Battle of the Somme was no skirmish – it was the major Allied effort of 1916, and Britain was very much the junior partner in the coalition with France. As such it was a 'kitchen sink' battle – everything was thrown in that might add weight to the battering ram of British arms and thereby finally overthrow the brick wall of German resistance in September 1916.

> There was much discussion as to their use – whether we should wait until we had built up a bigger form of them, and had the personnel more highly trained. The main argument in favour of their use was that the Germans did definitely know we had some new instrument, but had not yet found out what it was. If we waited, they would find out and might – we do not know – have found a suitable reply. Also we learn more by one day's active work with them than from a year's theorising. When we use them next time we shall have improved by this experience; it is still not too late to make an alteration in design if necessary. Above all, this is a vital battle and we should be in error to throw away anything that might increase our chance of success.[4]
>
> Brigadier General John Charteris, General Headquarters, British Expeditionary Force

THERE WERE MANY sources of raw data as to the state of German morale both at the front and back at home. One key indicator that all was not well was the recent change in the German High Command. Commanders are not usually replaced while their strategies are bearing fruit and the replacement on 29 August 1916 of the Chief of General Staff General Erich von Falkenhayn by General Paul von Hindenburg and his First Quartermaster General Erich Ludendorff was a sign that the German plans for 1916 were in ruins. The Verdun offensive had rebounded against them, the Somme was one long nightmare for the German Army, the Russians were once again stirring on the Eastern Front and Romania had joined the Allies on 27 August. Translations of German newspapers exposed a great deal about the country's internal tensions, while reports from neutral countries, captured orders and briefings revealed the German tactical plans and fears. Letters and diaries provided snapshots of morale and often details of scandals and food riots occurring in Germany that the newspapers did not always report. Even the German corpses revealed their units and helped the Allies draw up an accurate list of which divisions were in the line at any one time. Obviously prisoners were a fertile source of information: by their very age it was plain to see where the Germans had reached in their conscription of young men. Subsequent interrogations showed much about their personal morale and often revealed recent unit movements. There was thus much evidence to delineate the declining state of German morale, but at the same time there is no doubt that Brigadier Charteris had an optimistic approach to the interpretation of intelligence on the state of the German Army. He took all the reports of chaos in Germany, all the depressed letters and despondent prisoners and extrapolated from that the conviction that the Germans must be on the very point of collapse. This therefore was the advice he gave Haig.

On the ground the outlook was a good deal less optimistic. Faced once again with three German lines to overcome before any breakthrough could possibly be achieved, Rawlinson reverted to his usual caution and the proposals that he initially submitted to Haig were once again for a carefully staged approach. He was minded to attack at night, pause for a day or so, move up his artillery, and only then attack again. He considered that the gap between the new First, Second and Third German lines was cumulatively too wide to allow his field artillery to bombard the rear lines without moving forward. In this he was undoubtedly correct as the 18-pounders and 4.5-in howitzers, which made up the bulk of his artillery, only had an effective range of about 6,500 yards and they could not reach such distant targets. In addition, even the medium and heavy batteries that were capable of firing at long range were hampered by the carefully sited rear-slope positions of the German Second and Third Lines. Even with the best observational assistance of the Royal Flying Corps this was a crippling handicap to an accurate barrage.

When it came to the use of tanks, Rawlinson was equally cautious. When he had seen the tanks training in late August he was impressed by their obvious potential but was equally aware of their unresolved problems. He was left with a neatly balanced quandary that he found somewhat difficult to resolve.

> The presence of the fifty 'tanks' however raises entirely new, but at the same time somewhat problematical, possibilities. Should they prove successful we might lose valuable time and miss an opportunity by confining our operations only to the capture of system (a) [the Combles–Martinpuich line] On the other hand we may, by expecting too much of the 'tanks', be tempted to undertake an operation which is beyond our power, and which might cause very heavy losses to the 'tanks' themselves and to the infantry engaged in their support. Moreover, if the attack failed, the secret of the 'tanks' would be given away once and for all. Setting aside the enormous value of first surprise the chief asset of the 'tanks' will be lost when they cease to be an unknown quantity. Till the enemy know exactly what they have to deal with they cannot arrange or prepare an antidote. We must therefore endeavour to keep them a mystery as long as possible.[5]
>
> Lieutenant General Sir Henry Rawlinson, Headquarters, Fourth Army

It is unsurprising that he built this desire to keep the nature of tanks a secret for as long as possible into his overall plan for a night attack aimed only at overwhelming the German front line. He reasoned that having seized their objectives before dawn the tanks could be withdrawn before daylight and hence leave the Germans none the wiser as to their true nature. Sadly, although he had grasped the tanks' vulnerability to artillery fire he had failed to realise that in the dark, with their already severely restricted visibility, the tanks could not be driven over a rough, obstacle strewn terrain without very quickly coming to grief.

There is no doubt that Haig was considerably under-whelmed by the cautious nature of Rawlinson's plans. Once again he felt Rawlinson was not aware of the necessity of maximising the potential gains of the attack. Already disgruntled by the overall failure of the August operations Haig was not willing to compromise.

> I studied Rawlinson's proposals for the September attack and for the use of the 'Tanks'. In my opinion he is not making enough of the situation and the deterioration of the enemy's troops. I think we should make our attack as strong and as violent as possible, and go as far as possible.[6]
>
> General Sir Douglas Haig, General Headquarters, British Expeditionary Force

Haig still hoped for a breakthrough battle. He was increasingly aware of the agitation from dissatisfied politicians and the 'stellenbosched' generals who had their own reasons for criticising the conduct of operations on the Western Front. And, of course, he was egged on by the encouraging intelligence reports originating from Charteris. Haig was keen to capitalise on the 'known' weakness of the German Army by making a vigorous effort to cut the Gordian knot of trench warfare once and for all.

> During the two months that the Battle of the Somme has lasted the enemy has suffered repeated defeats and heavy losses, and has undergone many hardships. All this has undoubtedly told on his discipline and morale, and signs of deterioration in his troops are not wanting. The general offensive on all his fronts, which will be continued, has placed a great and prolonged strain on his power of resistance which strain will now be increased by the entry of Romania into the war. The reserves at the enemy's disposal to meet a renewed attack are very limited and consist mainly of tired troops which have already suffered severely. Moreover, it is not unlikely that he will be compelled to transfer some of his reserves to his Eastern Front. The combined attacks to be launched by the French and British troops during the first week of September, and the counter-attacks by the enemy that are likely to result, will weaken him further and wear down the divisions now opposed to us. On our side several fresh divisions are still available to be thrown into the scale after these combined attacks have been carried out. We shall also have a new weapon of offence (some fifty tanks) which, coming as a surprise to the enemy, are likely to be of considerable moral and material assistance to us. In short, we are

> approaching a stage in the battle when bold and energetic action may give great – perhaps decisive – results, provided the requisite preparations are made in time and all ranks put forth their utmost efforts.[7]
>
> General Sir Douglas Haig, General Headquarters, British Expeditionary Force

At this stage in the Somme campaign Rawlinson was not in any position to attempt to contradict or thwart his increasingly impatient commander-in-chief. Any credit he had earned for his bold plan for 14 July had long since evaporated in the arid six weeks that had followed, devoid of any significant success. Yet Haig's proposals were themselves flawed.

> The general officer commanding Fourth Army, while pressing the attack on his whole front, will direct his main efforts to the capture, as quickly as possible, of Morval, Lesboeufs, Flers and Gueudecourt. Then, as soon as the necessary gap in the enemy's defences in that area has been made, as strong as possible a force of cavalry, supported by other arms, will be passed through to establish a flank guard of all arms on the general line Morval–Le Transloy–Bapaume, and assist rolling up the enemy's lines of defence to the north-westwards by operating against their flank and rear in cooperation with the attack which will continue to be pressed against their front. All arrangements are to be made with a view to overwhelming the enemy at the outset by a powerful assault, and following up every advantage gained with rapidity and vigour.[8]
>
> General Sir Douglas Haig, General Headquarters, British Expeditionary Force

These proposals were radical indeed and repeated some of the mistakes made on 1 July. In trying to take all three lines and break through the German defences, Haig was running the risk of diluting the artillery preparation and thereby falling at the first hurdle. He was also intent on committing almost all the available reserves to the initial attack, which left little capacity to respond to unexpected developments, be they good or bad. The plan was also noticeably optimistic as to the chance of getting cavalry forward across the broken ground that would inevitably result from such a battle. Yet Rawlinson had no choice but to back down and he duly conformed to Haig's intentions. They would indeed attack on a wide front, with each attacking corps using all three divisions on narrow fronts to maximise the impact of the attack. The main thrust, however, would be concentrated on the narrower front centred on Flers.

Once again, the artillery bombardment would be at the very centre of the British plans. Over the previous months the Royal Artillery had gained much experience in both theoretical and practical gunnery. The debate as to the best type of artillery barrages in support of major attacks had been heated. Should they be long and pounding or short hurricane waves of destruction? Should the infantry be covered by creeping barrages of high explosive or shrapnel shell? How close could the infantry get to the back of the barrage before the 'friendly-fire' casualties outweighed the advantages? How many guns should be brought up ready to go forward just behind the infantry to extend the support given by the artillery in the event of success?

For the Battle of Flers–Courcelette to be launched on 15 September 1916, there would be approximately one field gun per 10 yards of front, with a medium or heavy gun every 29 yards of front. This was approximately twice the concentration achieved on 1 July. The day of the really heavy bombardment was dawning. In the three day preliminary bombardment some 828,000 shells were fired. The concept of a creeping barrage was now firmly accepted by all, although the attacking corps still made its own arrangements in dividing up its artillery between a creeping barrage moving at 50 yards per minute some 100 yards ahead of the advancing infantry and a stationary barrage continually pounding the objectives. The vital question of counter-battery fire was still not sufficiently well appreciated, but, on the other hand, improvements had been made, with some fifty-six guns and howitzers being specifically assigned to the task with observation supplied by the Royal Flying Corps. Meanwhile, arrangements were made to move as many of the guns as close to the front as possible. This would allow the heavier guns to continue to support the advance for as long as possible, while batteries of field artillery were readied to move forward with special bridges to allow them to cross the trenches as soon as it was feasible after the infantry had taken their objectives. The power of the guns was growing exponentially.

After closely debated discussion it was decided that the tanks would be employed in small groups scattered along the front line with the aim of moving ahead of the attacking troops to suppress identified German strong points. More imaginatively some eighteen tanks were to spearhead the XV Corps assault on the village of Flers, which Rawlinson considered to be the key to the integrity of the new German Second Line defences.

Despite this important role assigned to the tanks, there could be no doubt that Rawlinson was not to any great extent pinning his hopes on the success of the tanks. To him they were a potentially useful auxiliary weapon and nothing more.

> I do not think the tanks will actually capture anything for you. They are only accessories for the infantry and the latter must work in conformity with them … I think we had better issue some definite instructions in regard to the employment of tanks with the artillery. Personally, I am strongly in favour of not making any changes in our ordinary method than is absolutely necessary, in order to allow the tanks to work, ... we will place ... chief reliance on the methods which we are practising, looking on the tanks as an auxiliary to help us by every possible means.[9]
>
> Lieutenant General Sir Henry Rawlinson, Headquarters, Fourth Army

Whatever the differences in opinion over tactics there is no doubt that both Haig and Rawlinson were still absolutely wedded to the concept of the primacy of artillery. The tanks were seen as a promising addition to the book of war, not yet deserving any greater status than an addendum. It is therefore particularly ironic that, in their efforts to accommodate the tanks into their plans, they fatally diluted the power of the guns and thereby rendered the infantry appallingly vulnerable if the tanks failed.

> Tanks will start movement at a time so calculated that they will reach their objectives five minutes before the infantry. The infantry will advance as usual behind a creeping barrage in which gaps, about 100 yards wide, will be left for the route of the tanks, some minutes before their arrival at these objectives.[10]
>
> Instructions for the Employment of Tanks, Headquarters Staff, Fourth Army

In these seemingly sensible arrangements the seeds of disaster were planted. In the attack on the most dangerous German strong points, there would be no creeping barrage and if the tanks failed the infantry would be left to their own devices. This was made worse by the natural caution of artillery batteries, who inevitably left the gap wider to avoid possible mistakes and thus exacerbated the already dangerous situation. In assaulting the second objectives it was decided that the infantry and tanks would, wherever possible, advance together under a renewed uniform creeping barrage.

The third objectives were far beyond the range of the field artillery, so it was intended that the tanks would be employed to flatten the wire for the infantry and then use their weapons to try to suppress the inevitable German defensive fire. Overall, it was clearly emphasised that if the tanks were held up for any reason, the infantry were not to wait but were to push on regardless; yet if the tanks succeeded and the infantry were checked the tanks must turn back and endeavour to assist them. The infantry were still the primary force on the battlefield.

MEANWHILE, the old story was being relived as the assault battalions began to move up into the line. The 47th (London) Division was one of the divisions earmarked for the attack and was assigned the particularly dangerous task of taking the dreaded High Wood. The Londoners seemed perfectly sanguine and indeed, like some chivalrous knights from a semi-mythical past, many were delighted that such a post of honour had been granted them in the coming battle.

> The postmen from quiet little hamlets, or clerks who had spent their lives hitherto in snug offices, talked about these future regimental mortuaries with the homely names, with astonishing calmness. Rumour set an early date for the grand attack. The Guards and the ANZACs were concentrated in the region, and the Londoners thought it quite natural that they should march with them, so high had risen the *esprit de corps* of the London Division. But bad weather set in and no orders came. Day followed day and on the fringe of the vortex that would engulf them in turn, the battalion continued serenely to train. Not a detail was overlooked and by long hours of work in common, the officers got to know intimately their men, and the men the officers who were to lead them. Particular attention was given to night work. More than once in pitch darkness and blinding rain, companies were deployed in the broad stubble fields south of Framvilliers to practise keeping in touch and finally dig in as noiselessly as possible. Farewell joy rides were taken to Amiens, a dusty journey by lorry, but where to share even briefly the animation and intense throb of life was like imbibing a tonic.[11]
>
> Lieutenant Etienne de Caux, 1/8th Battalion (Post Office Rifles), London Regiment, 140th Brigade, 47th Division

For many of the men a good 'blow out' in the local *estaminet* represented a last chance to enjoy themselves come what may before they went into battle. These were simple pleasures for men with simple tastes.

> Most of us turned over the very few francs and centimes we happened to have and spent it. 'Oeufs' and 'pommes de terre' were on sale. Plus plenty of 'Plink Plonk' a cheap red or white wine. The shadows were darkening, particularly when at short notice one late afternoon we were all hustled on parade. The 'high ups' were going to give us a dose of moral courage. In one of the largest, recently harvested cornfields, that I remember, we were marched to join up with other regiments in the area. It was called a drum head service and in the far distance from where our company stood at ease, one could see two figures in white. We presumed they were padres and doing their duty.[12]
>
> Private Albert Whitehurst, 1/8th Battalion (Post Office Rifles), London Regiment, 140th Brigade, 47th Division

Unsurprisingly, on the eve of battle, the padres found themselves in unprecedented demand from men determined to improve their chances in this world and the next.

> We had some wonderful services on Sunday. To see fifty or sixty men in a dark building, lighted by only a few candles and one acetylene lamp is wonderful! Your cross is on the wall, two candles on the altar, the Union Jack underneath 'a fair linen cloth', and the singing very enthusiastic. The men are in great form. A good few are inwardly anxious, but they put a cheery face on it all. Sometimes this is from a highly religious motive, at other times a kind of fatalism, or, resigned dependence on God. 'What has to be, will be' they often say.[13]
>
> Chaplain David Railton, 1/19th Battalion (St Pancras), London Regiment, 141st Brigade, 47th Division

Finally, during the afternoon of 12 September, the Post Office Rifles left their billets at Framvilliers and marched down the long Albert road. They were largely silent.

> The great highway was dry and dusty, the morning air fresh. Steadily the long column marched towards the quavering lights ahead. Colonel Whitehead rode at the head of the battalion with the adjutant and myself. At hourly halts he dismounted and spoke to Captain Mitchell,

or walked a little distance down the column. The men were silent, but for an occasional snatch of song. The usual unconscious irony, 'There's a sneaking feeling round my heart that I'd like to settle down ....' The merry words of the popular 'Follies' ditty floating out into the fields bordering the tree-lined highway, were laden with unconscious pathos. Dawn had come as the battalion breasted the last long hill, where the ragged screens of the old French camouflage still lined the road. Down in the hollow the red brick houses of the once prosperous little town, clustered round the remains of the red brick basilica with its shattered tower. Near the railway station a tall, slim factory chimney still defied the Hun. Beyond the valley, towards the rising light, stretched the grey slopes scarred by the white chalk of the old front lines.[14]

Lieutenant Etienne de Caux, 1/8th Battalion (Post Office Rifles), London Regiment, 140th Brigade, 47th Division

Here there were no comfortable billets. After all, this had been part of the battlefield and hard fought over just scant weeks before.

That night we slept rough in some village that was uninhabited – in amidst the ruins – and thought of the comfortable heap of straw in the open cowshed of the farmstead at Framvilliers. The windy or nervous ones said, 'See all them Red Cross vans going back – that's where I'd sooner be!' They expressed what others stifled; for the odds of survival on the Somme inferno were, to say the least, very poor. The utter darkness and devastation of the night's shake down did not inspire one to think otherwise. Yet, were we not seasoned trench troops?[15]

Private Albert Whitehurst, 1/8th Battalion (Post Office Rifles), London Regiment, 140th Brigade, 47th Division

Thousands upon thousands of troops were moving forward in readiness for the attack during the night of 14 September. Laden like mules they moved forward across the wastelands of the Somme. The march was both exhausting and nerve-racking as every step took them closer to the German guns.

We were laden with all the extras needed for such an attack: pick or a spade, extra ammo, two Mills bombs, one man in every section had a petrol tin of water and the signallers had D3 telephones, wire, liaison shutter for aeroplane contact or signal flags. On the move again, but a shade more slowly at a pace like a pack animal's. At last we entered a

> communication trench which brought us to Delville Wood and through it. The trench had been hastily dug and hanging from its sides were telephone wires and above broken branches of trees. For a long time there could be heard, 'Wire overhead!' 'Mind the wire!' 'Mind your head!' and occasional curses as some poor Tommy caught his equipment on a wire and had a struggle to extricate his impedimenta from it. Frequent pauses whilst those leading the column waited for the unfortunate last men to catch up. They never got a breather – only the leading men as they patiently awaited the stragglers. Along with two PH helmets each man carried lachrymatory goggles. These were hastily donned two or three times as Jerry pumped gas shells all around. Some men wept copiously, some sneezed a lot and some coughed. Apparently Jerry heard nothing of these sounds and fired not a shot.[16]
>
> Lance Corporal Gerald Dennis, 21st Battalion, King's Royal Rifle Corps, 124th Brigade, 41st Division

As the troops moved forward they became aware of an overall sense of secrecy and mystery that surrounded the new weapon that had been added to the armoury of the British Army for this offensive.

> On our way up to the trenches we passed groups of large objects concealed under camouflage netting, but in the dark could not see what they were. Also we noticed that at intervals white tapes had been laid on the ground leading in the direction of the trenches. When we got into position we had the job of filling in the trench at each place where the tapes met it to provide a crossing place for the 'tanks'. After we got into position, we were told that 'tanks', a kind of armoured vehicle, were coming up to lead the attack.[17]
>
> Sergeant Harold Horne, 1/6th Battalion, Northumberland Fusiliers, 149th Brigade, 50th Division

Wild rumours had abounded as to what the mysterious shapes cloaked beneath the tarpaulins were. That night, the tanks moved forward the last couple of miles, with the constant drone of low flying aircraft intended to cancel out the tell-tale roar of their infernal engines. The tank crews were tired for they had had little opportunity for rest in the previous 48 hours and the task of moving the tanks forward was somewhat fraught. Although the route had been reconnoitred and a white tape put down to show the intended route, the tanks were cumbersome beasts and moving them over such rough ground was a slow, time-consuming business. The crews had little knowledge of the terrain and often needed guides. One such was Private Gray of the Queen Victoria's Rifles who was ordered to help the three tanks (C-13, C-14 and C-16) allotted to the attack in the 56th Division sector. Unaccompanied, the journey would normally have taken him about twenty minutes.

> Leaving brigade headquarters at eight o'clock we followed a track marked with tape for some little distance, the tanks following one behind the other. The ground over which they had to go was very soft and nothing but a mass of shell holes, some of them very large indeed, and as it was dark the drivers could not see where they were going. Before long they were in difficulties, as one caterpillar might go well down in a shell hole and the other remain on the level, but owing to its capabilities it would not capsize although it required extra power to get it into position, when after a struggle it would be ready to move off again. There being but one guide, if one tank got into difficulties the remainder had to wait until it was able to move on again. This sort of thing kept on occurring till at last the officer in charge, who was in the leading tank, got out and said, 'I think we should get on much better if you had my torch and walked 5 or 6 yards in front of the leading tank, picking out the most suitable ground for the tanks to take, throwing the light on the track so that the driver may follow'. One of the tanks had broken down and had to be left behind on account of one of its caterpillars having gone wrong. With the aid of the torch we were able to get along much better though the pace was still very slow.[18]
>
> Rifleman W. J. Gray, 1/9th Battalion (Queen Victoria's Rifles), London Regiment, 169th Brigade, 56th Division

As the tanks approached closer to the front line, Private Gray not unnaturally became increasingly apprehensive as he realised the enormous risks they were running.

> We were now not far from battalion headquarters and naturally I did not like the idea of continuously showing a light to guide the tanks, so only gave them a flash now and again, whereupon the officer alighted and wanted to know what was the matter. I explained that we were getting close to the line and the light would no doubt attract attention

> and bring over some 'whizz-bangs', which were pretty common in this part of the world, but he replied that we were very late and as they must get the tanks up at any cost they must take the risk. Shortly after we arrived at battalion HQ and considering all things and especially the flashing of the torch I think we were lucky to have done so without mishap.[19]
>
> Rifleman W. J. Gray, 1/9th Battalion (Queen Victoria's Rifles), London Regiment, 169th Brigade, 56th Division

Gray was ordered to push on with one of the tanks to guide it into its actual jumping-off position ready for the assault.

> I left headquarters with plenty of wind up as the tank I had now to lead had to be taken practically up to the front line with myself leading and flashing the light, which I was anxious to get rid of, you bet! The tank once more got into difficulties halfway to its position, and the torch had to be brought into use more than ever. A strafe took place while we were trying to get a move on. It may have been only the usual strafe or it may have been brought about by the use of the torch, but whatever was the cause it was none too healthy and I didn't enjoy it a bit. After a kick and a splutter the tank was ready to move and we were off again. The ground was still very bad and sloshy and the tank pursued its noisy way. The strafe was over and things were now pretty quiet for that part of the line, but Jerry may possibly have heard the noise of the engine, which would travel far. Anyhow, he showed all sorts of lights, and a searchlight was also put up seeking aeroplanes, though none were up. Shortly after the tank found its position and my job was over, for which I was profoundly thankful.[20]
>
> Rifleman W. J. Gray, 1/9th Battalion (Queen Victoria's Rifles), London Regiment, 169th Brigade, 56th Division

All in all along the front out of the forty-nine tanks meant to go into action only thirty-six arrived at their jumping-off stations.

Everything was ready for the big attack. This was no local affair. It was a major Allied thrust. Not only were the three corps of the Fourth Army (III, XV and XIV) involved, but also the Reserve Army, the Canadian Corps and the French Army would be attacking. Ten British divisions would attack with the odds roughly at two to one in their favour. It was the last chance of winning the war in 1916.

FRIDAY 15 SEPTEMBER was a typical, sunny early autumn day. The guns roared and the infantry waited in their assembly trenches for the whistles to blow.

> Mostly in shell holes we awaited zero hour. Very little was said – all just busy with their own thoughts. Seconds seemed minutes and minutes seemed hours during this wait. The grey light of dawn was appearing over the German lines and then we had a sight of the first enemy trench to be taken – Tea Support Trench – and could vaguely make out the nature of the broken ground in front of us. The ground sloped away and then rose abruptly and on the top of this ridge was that enemy trench. All around were shell holes reeking of tear gas and fumes. One sudden burst from a German machine gun was a little disturbing. Had we been seen?[21]
>
> Lance Corporal Gerald Dennis, 21st Battalion, King's Royal Rifle Corps, 124th Brigade, 41st Division

The minutes ticked by with unbearable slowness. But, at the same time, every minute that passed was irrecoverable for the men sweating in the trenches.

> The hour before zero, while crouching in the trench and looking at one's watch, was an almost unbearable strain. Eventually we heard the hum of machinery coming up behind us, and saw through the mist great toad-like things with caterpillar tracks, a gun projecting forward and at the back a tail with two small wheels, come lumbering over the shell-holed ground at walking pace. One tank followed the tape to the filled in place in the trench where I was and went on towards the German line. A few moments later it was our zero time and we got out of the trench and followed. Once in the open and going forward the tension and fear lessened to some extent and a feeling of excitement took over, helped in this case, I suppose, by curiosity about the tanks.[22]
>
> Sergeant Harold Horne, 1/6th Battalion, Northumberland Fusiliers, 149th Brigade, 50th Division

One man described his feelings in homely terms, which somehow caught the very essence of his apprehension.

> Up to this time my nerves had not been troubling me, but now I began to experience a feeling of – not weirdness, but the kind of

> feeling just before a tooth extraction – a sort of, 'I'm not afraid, but I hope it won't hurt!' sensation.[23]
>
> Lance Corporal Charles Morden, 1/7th Battalion, London Regiment, 140th Brigade, 47th Division

On the left of the assaulting British formations was the Canadian Corps, which formed part of General Gough's Reserve Army. The Reserve Army only had a subsidiary, supportive role to the Fourth Army attack, but Gough had been forewarned by Haig that if Rawlinson's efforts were once more thwarted, then the whole emphasis of the offensive might switch over to the Reserve Army front, with the overall intention of capturing the Pozières Ridge as a winter stronghold and a base for renewed attacks in 1917. The Canadians had a difficult 'nut' to crack if they were to build on their burgeoning reputation. They were to push out from Pozières towards the village of Courcelette. It is unfortunate to record that there was a vicious practicality about the orders given to the Canadians that provided an easy excuse for men inflamed beyond reason by the terrors and fierce joys of battle.

> We were given strict instructions to take *no* prisoners until our objective had been gained. The reason for this was that so often in British advances, when the Germans had thrown down their arms in surrender and our men had moved through them, at the same time indicating to them to go to our rear where they would be collected as prisoners, the Germans had picked up their rifles again and shot our men in the back, thereby bringing the advance to a halt. No such risks could or would be taken in this important advance.[24]
>
> Private Lance Cattermole, 21st Battalion (Eastern Ontario), 4th Brigade, 2nd Division, Canadian Expeditionary Force

Immediately in front of the 21st Canadian Battalion was the sugar refinery, just to the north of the main road passing through from Pozières via Courcelette to Bapaume. The Germans had converted the factory into a veritable fortress with several well-concealed machine guns.

> My platoon was in the third and last wave in the advance – the waves were 20 yards apart. We crawled over the top of the parapet and lined up on a broad white tape, jut discernable in the growing light, immediately in front of the trench and behind the first two waves which were already in position. It was almost zero hour. I looked at my wristwatch

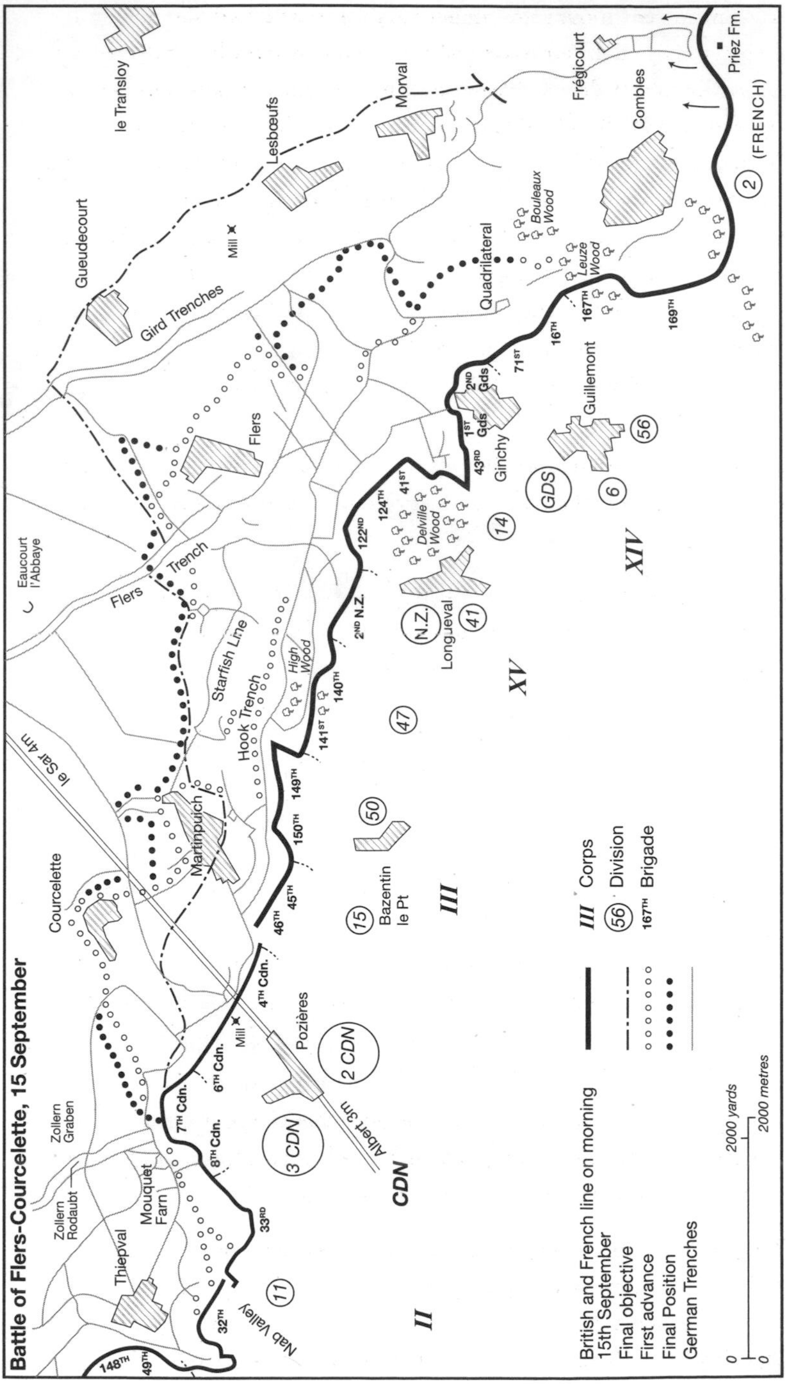
Battle of Flers-Courcelette, 15 September
148TH
49TH
Thiepval
Zollern Rodaubt
Zollern Graben
Mouquet Farm
Nab Valley
32TH
33RD
8TH Cdn.
7TH Cdn.
6TH Cdn.
4TH Cdn.
Mill
Pozières
3 CDN
2 CDN
CDN
Albert 3m
le Sar 4m
Courcelette
Martinpuich
46TH
45TH
150TH
149TH
141ST
140TH
2ND N.Z.
122ND
124TH
41ST
43RD
1ST Gds
2ND Gds
71ST
16TH
167TH
169TH
15
Bazentin le Pt
50
47
III
XV
XIV
N.Z.
41
Longueval
14
Delville Wood
GDS
6
56
Ginchy
Guillemont
Hook Trench
Starfish Line
High Wood
Flers Trench
Eaucourt l'Abbaye
Flers
Gird Trenches
Gueudecourt
Mill
Lesbœufs
le Transloy
Morval
Quadrilateral
Bouleaux Wood
Leuze Wood
Combles
Frégicourt
Priez Fm.
2
(FRENCH)
11
II
British and French line on morning 15th September
Final objective
First advance
Final Position
German Trenches
III Corps
56 Division
167TH Brigade
0
2000 yards
0
2000 metres

> and saw we had about three minutes to go. I never heard our officers' whistles to signal the advance, and I don't suppose they heard them either because of the terrible crash with which the creeping barrage opened up, exactly at 6.20 a.m. The air over our heads was suddenly filled with the soughing and sighing, whining and screaming of thousands of shells of all calibres, making it impossible to hear anything. We stood up and I looked around behind me; as far as the eye could see, from left to right, there was a sheet of flame from the hundreds of guns lined up, almost wheel to wheel, belching fire and smoke. It was an awe-inspiring sight.[25]
>
> Private Lance Cattermole, 21st Battalion (Eastern Ontario), 4th Brigade, 2nd Division, Canadian Expeditionary Force

When they went over the top, they entered a veritable inferno of German shell fire raking across the battlefield. Private Cattermole was a lucky man that morning.

> I had only taken three paces when an enemy shell fell exactly in front of me. All I saw was a great fountain of loose earth, of which I received a mouthful, and I was flung on my back. I believe it was only a second or two before I struggled to my feet, thinking I was blown to bits! I felt myself all over, and to my amazement I had no injuries whatsoever; I was simply winded. The shell must have been a dud. At this I started to laugh, which I presume was a sign of nervous relief that I was not hit, and I continued my walk forward. An added noise made me look upwards and, through a break in the swirling morning mist, I saw one of our spotter planes, the wings golden in the rays of the rising sun against a blue sky, showing the red, white and blue roundels of the Royal Flying Corps. This gave me a cheerful feeling.[26]
>
> Private Lance Cattermole, 21st Battalion (Eastern Ontario), 4th Brigade, 2nd Division, Canadian Expeditionary Force

As they approached the refinery the attack stalled under the weight of German fire and the infantry went to ground. It was at this point that one of the attached tanks made a dramatic appearance.

> The attack had been held up at this point, and a party of us had to rush up with more ammunition, bullets and grenades, to the 21st Battalion, lying in shell holes in front of the refinery. As we reached them, we saw a 'landship', named the *Crème de Menthe*, pass ahead, and

go right up to the walls of the refinery, its guns blazing. It seemed to lean against one of the walls which collapsed, and the monster roared into the fort, while we could see the Germans streaming out of it, offering an excellent target to the riflemen in the shell holes.[27]

Private Magnus McIntyre Hood, 24th Battalion (Queen Victoria's Rifles), 5th Brigade, 2nd Canadian Division

The *Crème de Menthe*, a 'male' tank commanded by Captain Arthur Inglis, was more formally known as C-5 of C Company, Heavy Section, Machine Gun Company. The dramatic appearance of the tanks certainly had a traumatic effect on the already shell-shocked Germans.

A man came running in from the left, shouting, 'There is a crocodile crawling into our lines!' The poor wretch was off his head. He had seen a tank for the first time and had imagined this giant of a machine, rearing up and dipping down as it came, to be a monster. It presented a fantastic picture, this Colossus in the dawn light. One moment its front section would disappear into a crater, with the rear section still protruding, the next its yawning mouth would rear up out of the crater, to roll slowly forward with terrifying assurance.[28]

Feldwebel Weinert, 211th Infantry Regiment, German Army

With the fearsome arrival of the tank the sugar refinery was captured and the Canadian infantry swept into the network of trenches that lay behind and to the east.

We came upon an enemy trench to our left. In keeping with our 'no prisoners' order, this trench was being mopped up and the occupants eliminated. The trench was already half full of dead enemy and here and there little columns of steam rose above the cool, morning air, either from hot blood or from the urine I understand is released on the death of any human body. Two Canadians stood over the trench, one in the parapet and the other on the parados, and they exterminated the Germans as they came out of their dugouts. One young German, scruffy, bareheaded, cropped hair and wearing steel rimmed spectacles, ran, screaming with fear, dodging in and out amongst us to avoid being shot, crying out, '*Nein! Nein!*' He pulled out from his breast pocket a handful of photographs and tried to show them to us – I suppose they were of his wife and children – in an effort to gain our sympathy. It was all of no avail. As the bullets smacked into him he

> fell to the ground motionless, the pathetic little photographs fluttering to the earth around him.[29]
>
> Private Lance Cattermole, 21st Battalion (Eastern Ontario), 4th Brigade, 2nd Division, Canadian Expeditionary Force

There were reasons – but no excuses – for this appalling conduct: there was simply no necessity for the murder of this poor soldier. The terrifying pressures of war and the fig leaf of 'official' sanction for these barbarous acts had turned ordinary, decent men into beasts.

The 4th and 6th Canadian Brigades held on to their positions perched along the southern border of Courcelette, despite the strenuous German counter-attacks that streamed out of the shattered ruins. At around 1815, the reserve 5th Canadian Brigade arrived and with the help of a renewed artillery barrage it swept forward through the village. Alongside it, elements of the 3rd Canadian Division managed to gain a substantial foothold in the Fabeck Graben Trench. All told the Canadians of Gough's Reserve Army had done well in extremely difficult circumstances on the flank of the main assault.

MEANWHILE, the Fourth Army had a day of mixed fortunes. The III Corps (15th, 50th and 47th Divisions) under the command of Lieutenant General Sir William Pulteney were charged with the dual role of protecting the flanks of both the main thrust towards Flers and the Canadian assault on Courcelette. Their own objectives were the German lines running along the reverse slopes of the ridge running between the villages of Martinpuich and Flers.

On the left the 15th (Scottish) Division surged forward and succeeded in capturing Martinpuich, which allowed it to keep pace with its neighbours in the 2nd Canadian Division. Alongside, the 50th (Northumbrian) Division was faced with severe enfilade fire from the fringes of High Wood. This was, of course, the very reason that so many lives had been expended in vain attempts in previous weeks to capture the wood.

> It was as quiet as the grave, there wasn't a shot fired. And then, just in the twinkling of an eye, it was hell let loose. Every gun fired at the precise second, hundreds of guns. Just about 50 or 60 yards to the right of where we were we saw this tank come forward. Our infantry the 5th Yorks were alongside and behind him. Billy Fielding, he said, 'A sight

for the Gods! A sight for the Gods!' Which it was! Mr Wilson said, 'Come on, never mind about the sight for the Gods!' So we got out, following out, running this wire out. I think the Germans were startled. They opened out with everything they had, but you couldn't hear a shell, what I mean was it was noise. You didn't know if it was our shells or their shells, our guns or their guns. There wasn't a great deal of small arms fire, mainly shell fire you see. We went forward, running the wire out and we were relaying information back to our guns. One time the wire broke and we went back to repair it. I was on my knees, fastening the wire together, tying a reef knot in it, pull it tight, clip the ends short and wrap it in insulation tape. Billy says, 'Look at them buggers there!' I just turned to look and here was a fellow with a cinematograph taking photographs of me mending the wire. I turned and looked; I waved my hand at him.[30]

Signaller George Cole, C Bty, 253rd Brigade, Royal Field Artillery, 50th Division

The Northumbrians struggled manfully despite the scything nature of the flanking fire and partially switched the direction of their attack to send parties of bombers into High Wood to help out the struggling 47th Division. They successfully gained their first objective – Hook Trench – but efforts to capture and consolidate the second objective of Starfish Trench were severely compromised. The German bombardment crashed vindictively all around them and eventually the surviving parties were pulled back to try to make good the grip on Hook Trench. The tanks had cooperated and performed valuable services in despatching various German strong points, although their intervention was inevitably somewhat random and unpredictable.

The key to success in the III Corps area was High Wood. Here the 47th (London) Division had been given a daunting task of overrunning that benighted wood, and its task had been made complicated by a blistering clash of opinions over the best means of employing the attached tanks. This controversy enveloped the 50th Division, whose senior staff officers were certainly much exercised at the nature of the plans for their neighbours upon whom they realised their own survival would depend.

On September 15th the attack of the division I was with depended for its success on the subjugation of fire from High Wood. My divisional commander therefore begged that the tanks available should move in

> single file on our right just outside the wood. He pointed out that the tanks were bound to be stopped by the tree stumps if they attempted to go through the wood. He was overruled with the result that both 47th Division and the 50th Division lost terribly from fire from High Wood, the tanks failing to get into the wood and being quite useless.[31]
>
> Lieutenant Colonel Henry Karslake, Headquarters, 50th Division

Lieutenant General Sir William Pulteney, the III Corps commander responsible, was guilty of an egregious blunder for which the men of the 47th and 50th Divisions would suffer the consequences. Pulteney had feared that the British and German lines were too close together at High Wood and he thought that any massed creeping barrage would cause the British unacceptable casualties. Therefore, he decided to use his tanks to capture the German front line and to rely on the artillery barrages only for the subsequent objectives. Major General Sir Charles Barter commanding the 47th Division made his views on these proposals more than plain but he was brusquely overruled.

So it was that the 141st Brigade and half of the 140th Brigade of the 47th Division were launched into the unwelcoming maw of High Wood. It was a scene daunting to anyone no matter how brave.

> The guns thundered continuously with deafening crescendo. Shrapnel burst over the whole area. Black, acrid smoke from German 'coal box' heavy shells did their best to obliterate the early dawn and rising sun. Above all, I think it was the deafening noise of our own forward 18-pounder field guns that thundered with shrieking velocity into the German front and rear lines.[32]
>
> Private Albert Whitehurst, 1/8th Battalion (Post Office Rifles), London Regiment, 140th Brigade, 47th Division

As the 15th Londons moved forward they found themselves half in and half out of High Wood. Wherever they were, they were as close as makes no difference to a living hell.

> That day I saw sights which were passing strange to a man of peace. I saw men in their madness bayonet each other without mercy, without thought. I saw the hot life's blood of German and Englishmen flow out together, and drench the fair soil of France. I saw men torn to fragments by the near explosion of bombs, and – worse than any sight – I heard the agonised cries and shrieks of men in mortal pain who

were giving up their souls to their Maker. The mental picture painted through the medium of the eye may fade, but the cries of those poor, tortured and torn men I can never forget. They are with me always. I would I had been deaf at the time.[33]

Corporal M. J. Guiton, 15th Battalion (Civil Service Rifles), London Regiment, 141st Brigade, 47th Division

Poor Guiton lost his leg in the mad press of the fighting. In the absence of any creeping barrage sweeping all before them, and in the absence of the promised tanks the infantry found themselves criminally exposed. Crouching down in their jumping-off trenches, the second wave awaited the inevitable orders to attack. They pressed their bodies up against the front of the trench in an effort to avoid the German shells tumbling amongst them, and the liberal spray of machine-gun bullets that sped overhead served only to remind them of what they were about to receive.

The deafening inferno continued: time had ceased. In moving along the tortuous quaking trench to a supposedly better vantage point of protection, I stumbled in rounding a corner, upon Rifleman Rankin. He was slumped against the parados, tin hat all askew, mortal terror shone in his glassy eyes, his left breast was gaping open; deep red blood in profusion soaked his khaki tunic. Shrapnel had killed him. A very short distance away and the six foot corpse of our captain – Captain Mitchell, No. 1 Company – lay full length in the trench with an ominous bloody wound in the forehead. They were not the first soldiers I had seen killed, nor were they to be the last.[34]

Private Albert Whitehurst, 1/8th Battalion (Post Office Rifles), London Regiment, 140th Brigade, 47th Division

For a moment some of the troops had hope of some kind of a reprieve as at last they sighted the tanks manoeuvring behind them.

Someone who had been looking out of the back of the trench cried out, 'Look boys, what the hell's this?!!' I saw for the first time the 'Tanks' or as we called them the 'Caterpillars'. Somehow the feeling of what these would do among the Jerrys lightened the tight and desperate feeling I had at heart. It was with a yell that my crowd went over the top. The yells were soon death screams.[35]

Rifleman Donald Cree, 1/8th Battalion (Post Office Rifles), London Regiment, 140th Brigade, 47th Division

The tanks in which the Londoners had invested so much hope, and for which they had been deprived of a creeping barrage, achieved absolutely nothing amongst the tree stumps. One ditched in a shell hole, another in No Man's Land, while only one succeeded in moving forward inside the wood and got as far as the German front. The final tank lost its way around the southern border of the wood and in turning east in a desperate effort to find clear ground only ditched itself in the British front line. In the depths of nerve-racked confusion the crew made a dreadful error and opened fire on their own comrades.

As they left the useless tanks behind them the infantry moved deep into the wood.

> I was 'over the top' amidst the tangled undergrowth, plus many hefty branches strewn in all directions by shell fire which had peppered the wood. I stumbled upon two dead bodies of our 'kilted soldiers' slain no doubt in a previous attempt to drive Jerry from High Wood, their bodies so hidden that stretcher bearers had not found them. The deafening roar of the guns had lessened, so that one only heard the more distant thunder rumble of our heavy guns giving Jerry's supply lines a continuous hammering.[36]
>
> Private Albert Whitehurst, 1/8th Battalion (Post Office Rifles), London Regiment, 140th Brigade, 47th Division

The clatter of the German machine guns went almost unheard amidst the dreadful din, but it was impossible to be unaware of their menacing presence.

> Man after man went down to that awful machine-gun fire of the enemy. Within 50 yards of the trench we left, there was but a bare handful left of half a company. I looked behind to see the second half of the company come on, led by the company officer, who as he neared us shouted, 'Get on damn you!' Just then he fell dead. Our platoon officer led us on. He had a walking stick in his hand, a revolver in the other and his face was set in a set smile. A big fine looking man he was. Men were falling on all sides, some in their death agonies. The officer's runner stopped with a terrible scream, crumpled and fell behind a tree stump. The platoon sergeant next collapsed and began crawling back to our lines. In between the groans and cries of the men

and the eternal awful fumes of cordite, that 100 yards to Fritz's line is the most fearful memory I have.[37]

Rifleman Donald Cree, 1/8th Battalion (Post Office Rifles), London Regiment, 140th Brigade, 47th Division

While the fighting was chaotic, one man's courage and initiative seemed on many occasions to make a difference. For example, Lance Corporal McIntyre's quick thinking certainly saved the lives of many of his section.

On we pushed and suddenly we came to a small clearing in the wood, with a near straight trench full of men, and a machine gun blazing down it. The officer was on top exhorting his men to climb out. I dropped on one knee and fired my rifle grenade at the machine gun. My aim proved good, the grenade burst at the point from which the machine gun was spluttering and the firing ceased. Immediately, I fired another grenade for good measure.[38]

Lance Corporal John McIntyre, 1/8th Battalion (Post Office Rifles), London Regiment, 140th Brigade, 47th Division

It may perhaps have been an illusion, but the effect on morale was considerable and seemed to give the men a renewed sense of purpose. At last they were there on top of the Germans: still not safe but at last there was the promise of shelter in what remained of the German trench and the chance to wreak their vengeance for all the casualties they had suffered.

As we reached the trench a lance corporal laughed and coolly walked back with blood spurting from his trouser leg. Germans were lying all over and at the back of the trench. A group of six of seven had been hit together by a shell and were the bloodiest and most battered humans I had seen. Some of the less severely wounded put their hands up, while their comrades in the trenches behind kept up a machine-gun fire and rifle fire among friend and foe alike.[39]

Rifleman Donald Cree, 1/8th Battalion (Post Office Rifles), London Regiment, 140th Brigade, 47th Division

The fight for High Wood was clearly hanging in the balance. High above pilot Lieutenant Eric Routh was flying on a contact patrol and he could see all was not well.

At High Wood things were not going so well. Just behind the wood a battalion had put out 'XX' denoting 'Held up by machine-gun fire'.

> This was immediately taken back and dropped at Railway Copse, the Corps artillery station. Returning we found same place had put out 'OO' which means barrage wanted but before we could send it, it was taken in. It therefore remained unsent. The first signal would probably get what was required. The tanks in High Wood were not successful. One had gone over both trenches, rather beyond the Boche line and there had stuck. It was very heavily shelled for about ten minutes, probably by a trench mortar, so much so that after smouldering for some time it burst into flames. The other two turned over on their side in our own trenches.[40]
>
> Lieutenant Eric Routh, 34 Squadron, Royal Flying Corps

On the ground the situation was clearly desperate. Unless something was done soon the whole attack would collapse and once again the Germans would hold on to High Wood to act as a thorn in the British flesh.

> When I got clear of the trench, I could only see the officer and about a half-dozen men who were somewhere on my left. The officer waved me over but before I could move a shell landed beside him and he was practically covered with earth and mud – dead. All I could see was his helmet which had been covered with a piece of sacking to keep it from glinting in the sunlight. I had won clear of the wood and was lying on an open piece of ground on a downward slope. On my left the rest of the battalion were having a terrific fight. Shells were crashing into our men from the German batteries, the incessant machine-gun fire made my mouth so dry I could hardly draw breath.[41]
>
> Rifleman Donald Cree, 1/8th Battalion (Post Office Rifles), London Regiment, 140th Brigade, 47th Division

Respite came from an unexpected quarter. Lacking either the assistance of tanks, or of a creeping barrage, it was the shattering detonations of the Stokes mortar shells fired at a phenomenal pace by the 140th Trench Mortar Battery that finally cracked the German resistance. In just a quarter of an hour, 750 shells were fired.

> A few men with a comparatively new weapon, a Stokes Trench Mortar machine operated one of these at a pocket of resistance to our left. I could see about eight to ten of these cylinder shells going through the air like a long row of single sausages. Soon afterwards twenty or so Germans came over the open battlefield holding up their hands above

their heads. With other men of our company I happened to, as it were, 'receive' these prisoners and much regret that from one of them I accepted a proffered gift, thrust into my hand. It was a small box, a snuff box.[42]

Private Albert Whitehurst, 1/8th Battalion (Post Office Rifles), London Regiment, 140th Brigade, 47th Division

By this time Rifleman Cree was totally isolated in a former German trench behind High Wood. The crowded battlefield had to all intents and purpose emptied before his very eyes.

There was not a soul beside me and it was with heartfelt gladness that I saw a group of khaki clad figures through the haze ahead on my right. I went over there, dodging from shell hole to shell hole. In one of them I found a man with a terrible hole in his body. His eyes looked at me so pitifully, but I could do little to help. Our instructions were, 'Any man stopping to help a fallen comrade is liable to be shot.' The inhumanity of it all. That lad, who although I could do little for him, made me marvel at his courage. I am sure that by the time I reached the others he would be past all pain and horror.[43]

Rifleman Donald Cree, 1/8th Battalion (Post Office Rifles), London Regiment, 140th Brigade, 47th Division

He made his way to the right towards the blurred figures, hopping from shell hole to shell hole and soon found himself amongst a mixed bag of troops from various other London battalions of the 47th Division.

I found an officer, a sergeant and a dozen men of different companies. How they got there I don't know. We advanced about 60 yards, when we were enfiladed by snipers and machine guns. The officer gave the order to run back 50 yards and dig for our lives. We started to run the gauntlet two at a time. The officer and myself were last. Just as we made our dash one of the two in front was hit and dropped. We got to him and pulled him into a shell hole. He was hit through the shoulder and was moaning, 'Don't leave me'. That officer was a brick. He got hold of the wounded chap and ran with him to where the others were digging in. I was left to make the last dash. I got there but it was awful expecting to get one in the back all the time. As I dropped beside the others, thinking that I was lucky not to have been killed with my back to the enemy. Now, that seems weird, because if I had been killed it

> would have made little difference how I was facing. We dug ourselves in with anything we could lay our hands on. I had a shovel but it was God knows where by this time.[44]
>
> Rifleman Donald Cree, 1/8th Battalion (Post Office Rifles), London Regiment, 140th Brigade, 47th Division

From their hastily dug 'trench', Cree saw the 1/6th Londons begin to move forward to continue the attack through the Starfish Line and on towards the Flers Trench. Cree watched in disbelief at their method of approach.

> All of a sudden, the German batteries opened up and the ground all over the slope we were on was churned up with hissing metal. We were amazed to see coming over the ridge a battalion in platoon formation. They nearly all had their rifles slung over their right shoulders. Shells dropped amongst them and they must have lost hundreds by the time they reached our position. As they passed, one said, 'Cheer up, boys, we'll see you all right!' Another beside him had a pipe in his mouth and a bag of bombs or rations on their backs. Mostly the faces were set and white, but not a falter as they went on to hell in front. Later that night they came back and went right back, as our officer would not take responsibility for them. A mere handful, some whimpering and crying like babies. Poor devils they had it rough. They belonged to our own brigade.[45]
>
> Rifleman Donald Cree, 1/8th Battalion (Post Office Rifles), London Regiment, 140th Brigade, 47th Division

The 47th Division had finally captured High Wood and gained a foothold in the Starfish Trench. When the men were eventually withdrawn from the front line a few days later they were all but a shadow of what they had once been. The division had suffered some 4,544 casualties over the period.

> On our way back, Major General Barter met the battalion and as our company passed him, he said, 'Well done, 20th, you have done splendid work, I am proud of you'. He might with reason be proud of us, for the battalion of which I am more than proud to be a member, had done that day what many other battalions on previous occasions had failed to do – namely, had driven the Germans out of the wood and kept them out. We have had to pay the price however.[46]
>
> Lance Sergeant Reginald Davy, 20th Battalion (Blackheath and Woolwich), London Regiment, 141st Brigade, 47th Division

They may have been proud men, but they had little to celebrate. There were scenes of indescribable pathos as the battalions took stock of those who were unscathed, at least in body, after the horrific battle.

> From tea time to well after dark, Major Vince and the adjutant, seated at a deal table out in the open, made a detailed roll call of the battalion. The men, clean-shaven, though haggard still, stood round in their mud-soiled, creased slacks. 'Rifleman "X"?', the Major's voice would call. No reply. 'Anyone know anything about him?' 'Yes, Sir', answered a voice from the crowd, 'He went over besides me, I last saw him as we got up to the German trench.' Then silence. No one else knew anything more. 'Rifleman "Y"?' No reply and no one knew anything about him. By the light of guttering candles, question and answer went from the flame-lit table to the dark circle and back. Nor did anyone move until the work was completed. The result gave 63 killed, 50 missing and 185 wounded.[47]
>
> Lieutenant Etienne de Caux, 1/8th Battalion (Post Office Rifles), London Regiment, 140th Brigade, 47th Division

Lieutenant de Caux was the French interpreter attached to the 1/8th Londons and as he watched the roll call he mused that the relationship established between the two traditional enemies had been truly consummated in the fires of war.

> A hollow square of jaded muddy figures standing in an orchard open at one side to the after-glint of the sun that set red. Mist begins to float up the valley, but the glint of light on some clouds high up has still the hardness of silver. A strong voice calls one name after another from a roll lit by a fluttering candle shaded by the hand of the one remaining sergeant major. A dark mass of tall trees in the background. There should never, never be anything but brotherly feeling amongst Frenchmen for their English comrades after this war.[48]
>
> Lieutenant Etienne de Caux, 1/8th Battalion (Post Office Rifles), London Regiment, 140th Brigade, 47th Division

THE XV CORPS (New Zealand, 41st and 14th Divisions) under the command of Lieutenant General Henry Horne was at the centre of the attack and was to be responsible for the capture of Flers. To assist it in this somewhat daunting task were eighteen tanks of D Company, Heavy

Section Machine Gun Corps although only fourteen of these managed to drag themselves even as far as their starting points. The New Zealand Division were on the left of the XV Corps. It was to seize the German lines stretching to the north-west of Flers. As the men advanced they, too, initially suffered from flanking machine-gun fire from High Wood. The tanks were also late coming up into the line and contributed little of value in the initial stages as the New Zealanders closely pursued the creeping barrage and managed to overrun the Switch Line before, after a pause, sweeping on to the outlying trenches of Flers. As they began to encounter stubborn resistance from the Flers Trench, the tanks caught up to lend assistance and a further advance was made to the Flers Support Trench. Here the German resistance stiffened and the attack finally spluttered out of steam.

Adjoining the New Zealanders was the 41st Division. It was to seize Flers itself and then advance on the neighbouring village of Gueudecourt. It was allotted ten tanks to assist it, of which no more than seven actually got forward. In many accounts the advance is seen as a walkover – but there is no doubt that to the troops involved it was a tremendous battle. Many of the men of the leading battalions started out in No Man's Land, sheltering in shell holes. They would advance, clinging as close as possible to the creeping barrage, willing to risk casualties from the occasional shells falling short.

> The flames, the shrapnel, the acrid fumes, the clouds of smoke and the uplifting of tons of earth. All these conjured up a vision of awfulness and yet of tragic grandeur. Then a lot of the noise seemed to fade away as we jumped or rather struggled to our feet to get on with the job of going forward. No sooner had we started than the enemy had begun a very useful reply to our guns by dropping a barrage around the Tea Support Trench. The tank wallowed along, not fast enough for the keen troops, so it was left behind us with its gallant section to guard it. We lost some men. The stretcher bearers were doing their best for our first casualties – some were beyond their help. German machine gunners were already successful and our numbers were being gradually thinned. The creeping barrage moved on; and the first objective was captured.[49]
>
> Lance Corporal Gerald Dennis, 21st Battalion, King's Royal Rifle Corps, 124th Brigade, 41st Division

There was a pause to consolidate and to allow the 'moppers up' to complete their grim task. Then they lurched forward again.

> On again, as the rain of iron from our guns moved slowly forward. Heavy shells continued to sing overhead, more earth was being churned up and smoke slowly drifted in the wind. Although our main aim was to press on, we did look to the right and left now and again to see our troops moving on. An occasional glance revealed one man stumbling head foremost, another blown in the air, another collapsed in a heap, nearby one with blood streaming from his face. Our lines were getting thinner and thinner.[50]
>
> Lance Corporal Gerald Dennis, 21st Battalion, King's Royal Rifle Corps, 124th Brigade, 41st Division

Alongside the 124th Brigade to their left, the men of the 122nd Brigade were directly facing Flers and were assisted greatly in this attack by the presence of the tanks. Amongst them was D-17 commanded by Second Lieutenant Stuart Hastie, and which he had named *Dinnaken*. His second gearsman in the tank was Gunner Reiffer.

> We were a male tank and carried two 6-pounder guns with several hundred rounds of ammunition and some Hotchkiss light machine guns with .303 ammunition. Our tank was filled up with stores of all kinds: drums of engine oil, gear oil, iron rations, gas masks, equipment, overalls, revolvers, anti-'bump your head against the roof of the tank' leather helmets, carrier pigeons in a basket, semaphore signals. We even went into action with ten 2-gallon tins of petrol (flaming red in colour) on the outside of the tank on either side of the exhaust pipes.[51]
>
> Gunner A. H. R. Reiffer, Tank D-17, D Company, Heavy Section, Machine Gun Corps

As the infantry and tanks went over the top, Lieutenant Cecil Lewis was up on contact patrol at the vital moment. From high up in the skies he truly had a grandstand view and could even see the red petrol cans carried on the tanks.

> There was this solid grey wool carpet of shell bursts, but it was just as if somebody had taken his finger in the snow and pulled it through the snow and left a sort of ribbon. There were four or five of these ribbons running back toward High Wood. Through these lanes at zero hour

> we saw the tanks beginning to lumber. They'd been cleared for the tanks to come in file. They came up three or four in file, one behind the other. Of course they were utterly unexpected, the first lot went sailing over the trenches and we thought, 'Well this is fine!' Because the whole thing was the year was getting a bit late, 'If we don't get through now, we never shall!' This was the great opportunity and hope was high. We thought, 'If they can get through the third line defences, we can put the cavalry through and the whole war will become mobile again!' And so we watched pretty carefully to see how things went. Amongst the grey wool of shell burst these lumbering chaps. One or two of them with red petrol tanks on their back; one even with a little mascot, a little fox terrier running behind the tank. Then one would stop and we had no idea why. Obviously it had been hit, or somebody had thrown a grenade at it, or it had a breakdown. At the end of two hours they had moved about a mile and we thought everything was going well and we came back because our petrol was finished.[52]
>
> Lieutenant Cecil Lewis, 3 Squadron, Royal Flying Corps

Unfortunately, a somewhat farcical incident soon removed two of the tanks trundling towards Flers. Tank D-9, commanded by Second Lieutenant Victor Huffam, was following Tank D-14, commanded by Second Lieutenant Gordon Court, when they came to grief in embarrassing fashion.

> Before he had gone 200–300 yards he attempted to cross a disused support trench. As he crossed it – the tank weighed 28 tons – the parapet crumbled beneath him. His tail end, the backside of the tank, disappeared into the trench. He scrambled out of his tank – quite a job – and he came back to me. Now we had been equipped with very large iron hooks on the stern of our tanks and we had wire hawsers coiled on the roof. Court was a particular friend of mine, so I manoeuvred up behind him and attempted to come alongside of him, to cross in front of him and to try and tow him out. But in manoeuvring alongside of him, my sponson got tangled with his and the two tanks were locked together.[53]
>
> Second Lieutenant Victor Huffam, Tank D-9, D Company, Heavy Section, Machine Gun Corps

There was nothing more they could do but climb on to the roof and watch the rest of the battle. What the infantry thought of this wretched display of bad luck and ineptitude can easily be imagined. Passing close to them D-17 continued up the main road, heading directly into Flers.

> There was a terrific amount of noise in the tank made up by the engine, the tracks, and the tumbling about of the drums of oil and various paraphernalia that we had to carry. Our own barrage was going on outside and the German barrage, but really we couldn't hear a lot of this because of our own noise.[54]
>
> Gunner A. H. R. Reiffer, Tank D-17, D Company, Heavy Section, Machine Gun Corps

His officer, Lieutenant Hastie decided to push on alone in support of the infantry. Ahead of him was the battered village of Flers.

> It was up to me to carry on alone. Having crossed the front German line I could see the old road down into Flers which was in a shocking condition having been shelled by both sides. At the other end of this road, about a mile away, which was about the limit of my vision from the tank, I could see the village of Flers, more or less clouded with smoke from the barrage which had come down on top of it and the houses, some of them painted white, some seemed to be all kinds of colours. Across the front of the village, we could see the wire of a trench named Flers Trench and this formed a barricade in front of the village on the British side. We made our way down the remnants of this road with great difficulty. Just as we started off our steering gear was hit and we resorted to steering by putting on the brake on each track alternatively and trying to keep the tank following the line of the Flers–Delville Wood road. When we got down to Flers Trench and passing into the village, there was a great deal of activity from the eaves, under the roofs of the cottages and also from a trench which appeared to be further through the village but which we couldn't just locate at that point.[55]
>
> Second Lieutenant Stuart Hastie, Tank D-17, D Company, Heavy Section, Machine Gun Corps

The tank was targeted by German machine gunners and the sides were liberally splattered with bullets. The multiple impacts caused slivers of hot steel to whip round the confined interior of the tank.

> We were fired on by German machine guns. First of all they were firing on the starboard side and the impact of their bullets was making the inside of the armour plate white hot. And the white hot flakes were

> coming off and if you happened to be near enough you could have been blinded by them. Fortunately, none of us on the starboard side caught it. But there was a gunner, Gunner Sugden, on the port side who was wounded that way. We went on and Percy Boult was rather upset about this machine gunner and he said, 'I can spot him, I think, he is up in the rafters!' He was a pretty good shot and he scored a bull's eye on the target and brought him down.[56]
>
> Gunner A. H. R. Reiffer, Tank D-17, D Company, Heavy Section, Machine Gun Corps

Above them a contact patrol of the RFC sighted D-17 moving through Flers and the observer's sober message, 'Tank seen in main street Flers going on with large number of troops following it' was transmuted and thereafter immortalised by the press as, 'A tank is walking up the High Street of Flers with the British Army cheering behind'. Whatever the impression may have been from the air, D-17 was soon deep in trouble. Second Lieutenant Hastie could achieve little by crashing around the ruins of Flers without solid infantry support. Although elements of the 122nd Brigade had managed to enter the village, they had naturally gone to ground in the heavy shelling and were invisible from D-17.

> Having steered the engine by using the brakes up to this point, the engine was beginning to knock very badly and it looked as if we wouldn't be fit to carry on very much further. We made our way up the main street, during which time my gunners had several shots at various people who were underneath the eaves or even in the windows of some of the cottages. We went on down through the High Street as far as the first right-angle bend. We turned there and the main road goes for a matter of 200–300 yards and then turns another right angle to the left and proceeds out through towards Gueudecourt. But we did not go past that point. At this point we had to make our minds up what to do. The engine was really in such a shocking condition that it was liable to let us down at any moment. So I had a look round, so far as it was possible to do that in the middle of a village being shelled at that time by both sides. I could see no signs of the British Army coming up behind me. So I slewed the tank round with great difficulty on the brakes and came back to Flers Trench and turned the tank again to face the Germans.[57]
>
> Second Lieutenant Stuart Hastie, Tank D-17, D Company, Heavy Section, Machine Gun Corps

Having rejoined the main body of the infantry, Second Lieutenant Hastie tried to find out what was going on and what he should do. It was fairly obvious that D-17 was all but finished.

> I got out of the tank and contacted an infantry officer who asked me if I could take the guns out of the tank if the tank was unable to go any further forward and help them meet the counter-attack which they were certain was going to come. I had to explain to him that it was impossible because the guns are fixtures in the tanks and the machine guns are fitted in ball mountings which when you took the machine gun out it could not be mounted on anything else – it had no mounting of its own. By this time the infantry did not show any particular anxiety to go on, they were more concerned with consolidating in Flers Trench. We made up our minds that nothing could be done with the tank except get it back. We eventually turned the tank off the road to the left, pushed it up against a small hillock which gave us a certain amount of cover – and at that moment the engine packed up and did not start again.[58]
>
> Second Lieutenant Stuart Hastie, Tank D-17, D Company, Heavy Section, Machine Gun Corps

Shortly afterwards one of their tracks was hit and the tank was finally immobilised and abandoned. Later that day two other tanks (Second Lieutenant Arthur Arnold in D-16 and Second Lieutenant L. C. Bond in D-18) helped break down the German defences around Flers by making a determined approach towards the west face of the village.

> A tank appeared on the left front of my company position which I immediately attacked with machine-gun and rifle fire and also, as it came closer, with hand grenades. These unfortunately caused no real damage because the tank only turned slightly to the left but otherwise just carried on. He crossed the trenches in the area of the company on my left, caused us heavy losses with his flanking machine gun fire on trenches which had to a large extent been flattened, without my men being able to do anything against it.[59]
>
> Leutnant Braunhofer, 5th Bavarian Infantry Division, German Army

The tanks then took up a position from which they were able to provide useful machine-gun support fire for the advance of the New Zealanders towards the northern section of Flers. They were also ideally placed to deal with German counter-attacks.

> We were rewarded with the sight of long lines of Germans advancing in open formation, and opened fire with our port-side Vickers guns at 900 yards range. It was impossible to tell just what effect our fire took, but it certainly checked the advance. *Dracula* cruised about for a while in front of the village and then came under what seemed to be direct fire from a field gun. A difficult matter to judge, but someone was making useful practice against us. One shell in particular seemed to miss us by inches. I had, in the meantime, collected a bullet through my knee, while outside. It was now late afternoon, and as our infantry had been reinforced, I judged it was time to get back.[60]
>
> Second Lieutenant Arthur Arnold, Tank D-16, D Company, Heavy Section, Machine Gun Corps

The situation remained chaotic for some time until finally a staff officer, Major Gwyn Gwyn-Jones, came forward to investigate and, after taking personal control, led the various disparate groups forward to finally secure Flers.

Meanwhile, a tragic breakdown in communications led to disaster for the survivors of the 21st King's Royal Rifle Corps, who were in the fields to the right of the village looking towards Gird Trench. Although it had been intended they should remain there and consolidate their positions, a fatal confusion in the definition of the objectives in their latest orders meant that a further attack was ordered. Their colonel, the Earl of Faversham, led them forward to destruction.

> The scanty remains of the two battalions drew intense machine-gun and cannon fire and many fell amidst the growing corn. The Colonel knelt down and as he peered through his binoculars he fell back, killed. Signallers Baker and Gunson were wounded at the same time: the former a nasty wound in the neck. He was made comfortable in a shell hole, which was deepened a little to protect him. A liaison aeroplane appeared above and the Queen's colonel suggested that a message be attempted. The battalion sign was laid out and the shutter used. The message was acknowledged by the airman on his klaxon horn, though all did not hear the acknowledgement owing to the din. A shell dropped where the regimental sergeant major, police sergeant, pioneer

> sergeant and corporal lay. Two were wounded and two were killed. Immediately afterwards the signal officer, 'Tockie' Turner, was hit in the stomach and was writhing in agony. The intelligence officer was then killed, and the adjutant, Captain Honey, was hit in the eye. Jerry had held his intense fire whilst the men ascended a slight slope and then had mown them down. It was impossible to hold any positions thereabouts and the depleted ranks fell back down to the bottom of the slope amid a knee high hail of machine-gun bullets.[61]
>
> Lance Corporal Gerald Dennis, 21st Battalion, King's Royal Rifle Corps, 124th Brigade, 41st Division

The attack on Flers may have been a success but the men of the 41st Division had suffered severe losses in the course of the long day. Alongside them, the 14th Division faced what looked like a dangerous extra complication of straightening out the German 'pocket' pressing into the British lines just to the east of Delville Wood. A preliminary operation was ordered to commence at 0515, but in the event the Germans abandoned it without much of a fight. When the main advance came the division would have much more hard fighting before it was able to successfully conform to the general advance made by the XV Corps.

THE XIV CORPS (Guards, 6th and 56th Divisions) on the right of the Fourth Army was attacking the German front stretching from Ginchy to Combles. The Guards and the 6th Division were to move forward, while the 56th Division moved out to form a defensive right flank to the whole advance. They were allotted fifteen tanks, nine for the Guards Division and three each for the 6th and 56th Divisions.

It was here on the XIV Corps front that the assault tactics broke down in total disarray. After the Royal Artillery had carefully left the 100-yard gaps required for the tanks in its artillery barrage, the infantry found to their horror that the tanks either failed to get forward or lost their way as they set off into No Man's Land. The results were predictably disastrous. Without a creeping barrage to flay across the German trenches and the shell holes where German machine-gun teams were, the infantry were exposed to deadly fire from all sides. Although the Guards made fair progress, they suffered badly from flanking fire originating in the centre of the line. Here, the unfortunate 6th Division was faced with the German

Sydow Höhe Redoubt known to the British, who seemed to have lacked much imagination in these matters, as the Quadrilateral. The preliminary bombardment also seems to have been badly directed and lamentably failed to destroy the trenches. When they were also left without a proper creeping bombardment the British infantry stood naked before their enemies.

The tanks achieved nothing in the chaos and confusion that seems to have enwrapped them. Everything started to go wrong the night before as they moved up. Of the three original tanks one, C-20, commanded by Second Lieutenant George Macpherson broke down while moving forward and had to be left behind. Shortly after, C-19, commanded by Captain Archie Holford-Walker suffered a broken axle on the tail unit. As Holford-Walker was unfortunately not aware that the tank could still be steered without the tail unit (which, indeed, was later discarded from use) he felt obliged to stop for repairs, which effectively excluded him from any part in the battle. This left only one tank to carry forward the hopes of the 6th Division next morning: C-22, commanded by Second Lieutenant Basil Henriques.

The progress of this tank has frequently been analysed without much firm agreement emerging as to what actually happened. It has been claimed that Henriques inadvertently opened fire on soldiers of the 9th Norfolks while behind the British lines and then compounded this by moving forward too early, thus arousing German suspicions with the result that they dropped a brief but damaging artillery barrage on the British troops waiting for zero hour. Whatever occurred,[62] it was still not Zero Hour when C-22 began moving across No Man's Land heading towards the Quadrilateral. The Germans seem to have been effectively stupefied by its strange appearance and somehow failed to open fire as C-22 slowly rumbled across to their lines. As Henriques and his crew crossed the German trench his gunners opened up a vicious fire on both sides. Coming to their senses the Germans opened a heavy small arms fire, which included armour piercing rifle ammunition normally used to penetrate the metal shields used by British snipers.

> All the time I had the front flaps open, for visibility was far too restricted if they were shut; but after a hail of machine-gun fire, I closed them tightly for the first time. Then the periscope got hit away; then the small prisms got broken one after another; then armour piercing bullets began

> to penetrate, in spite of the fact that tanks were said to be completely proof against them. Then my driver got hit; then one of my gunners; then I got splinters in the face and legs. Meanwhile the gunners claim to have killed or hit twenty or thirty of the enemy. I could see absolutely nothing. The only thing to do was to open the front flap slightly and peep through. Eventually this got hit so that it was hanging only by a thread, and the enemy could fire in at us at close range.[63]
>
> Second Lieutenant Basil Henriques, Tank C-22, C Company, Heavy Section, Machine Gun Corps

Just as Second Lieutenant Henriques and his battered crew were discovering that German infantry were not entirely helpless against tanks, the British barrage burst out at 0630. Fortunately, for C-22 at least, the barrage was not directed at the Quadrilateral as it was located within one of the tank 'lanes' left in the barrage. But the tank had not the firepower to deal with the Quadrilateral, indeed the garrison seemed to be on the point of overwhelming it and adding its machine guns to the existing bristling defences. As the men of the 6th Division moved forward across No Man's Land they were met with a hail of fire.

> As the infantry were now approaching and as it was impossible to guide the car, and as I now discovered the sides weren't bulletproof, I decided that to save the tank from being captured I had better withdraw. How we got back, I shall never understand. We dodged shells from the artillery and it was just a preserving hand which saved us. It was like hell in a rough sea made of shell holes. The way we got over the ground was marvellous; every moment we were going to stick, but we didn't. The sight of thousands of men dying and wounded was ghastly. I hate to think of it all.[64]
>
> Second Lieutenant Basil Henriques, Tank C-22, C Company, Heavy Section, Machine Gun Corps

The slight inconsistencies in his story are not necessarily serious, but it does seem remarkable that he should retire, seemingly able to see well enough to steer from the field of battle just as the infantry most needed him. The infantry attack, it hardly need be said, was a dreadful failure. The reason for the disaster was not the failure of the tanks – they were, after all, only an adjunct to the artillery and infantry that together still ruled the battlefield. The problem lay in the deliberate weakening of the artillery to allow for the tanks and then the inability to respond swiftly by filling the gaps when it became apparent that the tanks were letting them down.

When the infantry tried again a little later, three more tanks had been optimistically ordered forwards. One, C-12 from the XIV Corps reserve, commanded by Lieutenant Vincent, came up only to ditch at the rendezvous by Guillemont crossroads. A second tank, C-9, commanded by Second Lieutenant Murphy, had originally been assigned to the Guards Division, while the third was C-20, repaired after its breakdown the night before. Second Lieutenant George Macpherson was about to take this tank forward to its destiny when he encountered his friend, the somewhat battered and bedraggled Second Lieutenant Basil Henriques.

> Just as I was reporting to the brigadier commanding the infantry, I met George, who had got his tank to go. He looked aghast at my blood-stained face, and then with a smile got into his tank and went off to follow up the slowly advancing infantry. It was the last I saw of him. I never heard how his tank fared. I only know he was a great hero off the field of battle and I am sure he must have been one on it.[65]
>
> Second Lieutenant Basil Henriques, Tank C-22, C Company, Heavy Section, Machine Gun Corps

The situation was chaotic as the never robust battlefield communications surrendered to the disruptive attentions of German shell fire. In the event the second attack planned for 1330 was cancelled, but the tanks seem to have gone forward anyway.

> Our tank commander was Second Lieutenant Macpherson, a fine and likeable young fellow, but he, like all of us, had never been in an actual battlefield or in action before. The briefing and instructions regarding objectives were quite inadequate and there was little or no cooperation between the infantry and the tanks. We reached a point which we believed was our objective and after a while as petrol was getting low, we had to return some distance, where we were joined by the other tank in our section. Both it and ourselves came up against machine-gun fire with armour piercing bullets and while we had quite a few holes I counted upwards of forty in the other tank. I regret to say however that Lieutenant Macpherson, when going back to headquarters to report, was killed by enemy shell fire.[66]
>
> Gunner William Dawson, Tank C-20, C Company, Heavy Section, Machine Gun Corps

His crew never really knew what happened to their officer; for tragically all was not as it seemed. Brigadier Osborne, who commanded the badly mauled 16th Brigade, later explained what had happened to George MacPherson.

> I was ordered to space them out evenly over the area attacked and their lines of advance were marked with tapes as far as possible by the divisional Royal Engineers. I was then told to issue the orders for attack. In answer to my protests that I could not make a plan of any worth I was told to get on with it as GHQ had issued orders for the tanks to move in this way. The result as you know was heavy and useless casualties to 1st Buffs and 8th Bedfords. It may interest you to know the true history of the three tanks with 16th Infantry Brigade on 15th September. One went north of the Quadrilateral and wasn't much use to me. Then the tank which reported a broken tail came back, and while the subaltern in charge was waiting for a minute while I heard another officer's report, he shot himself and left a paper on which he wrote, 'My God, I have been a coward'. I concealed the manner of his death to save his parents unnecessary grief. The third tank was absent, lost its way.[67]
>
> Brigadier Osborne, Headquarters, 16th Brigade, 6th Division

Perhaps Osborne was overly harsh in his judgement of a young officer driven over the brink of despair by the horrors of battle and a sense of responsibility for the failure that manifestly surrounded them. George Macpherson did not die instantly, but was taken back to a casualty clearing station for treatment where he succumbed to his injuries. Certainly Second Lieutenant Basil Henriques could testify to the strain imposed on young and inexperienced officers charged with the responsibility for the success of unreliable tanks.

> The nervous strain in this first battle of the tanks for officers and crew alike was ghastly. Of my company, one officer went mad and shot his engine to make it go faster, another shot himself because he thought he had failed to do as well as he ought, two others, including myself, had what I suppose can be called a nervous breakdown.[68]
>
> Second Lieutenant Basil Henriques, Tank C-22, C Company, Heavy Section, Machine Gun Corps

Lieutenant Henriques's splinter wounds looked far worse than they actually were, but in the confusion generally prevailing he was evacuated right back and eventually ended up in an ophthalmic hospital in London. He was haunted by feelings that he had not done his duty and had in a sense fled the battlefield.

> If only we had been able to reconnoitre, if only we had some kind of training with the infantry, if only there had been some semblance of cooperation with the artillery, if only there had been proper practice over ground that was like the Somme, and if only we had a little more sleep and a little less showing off, what a marvellous story might this Somme battle have been.[69]
>
> Second Lieutenant Basil Henriques, Tank C-22, C Company, Heavy Section, Machine Gun Corps

Eventually he retrained as a tank reconnaissance officer, in which role he returned to the Western Front in 1917. He never commanded a tank in action again.

Their neighbours to their right in the 56th Division were forthright in their condemnation of the contribution of the tanks to their flanking operation. Hopes had been so high before the battle that the tanks' failure caused a bitter reaction.

> We were allotted one of the first tanks to land in France to do some training with our brigade. Everybody was staggered to see this extraordinary monster crawling over the ground. We did what training we could with this one tank, learning to follow it at suitable intervals. We knew it had to make gaps in the enemy barbed wire and a little column of infantry had to follow through the gap. Everybody thought it was a terrific thing until the first battle and then we rather lost our faith. Of the three tanks allotted to my brigade: one broke down before it reached the front line, one broke down in the front line, only one got across the front line and it broke down before it reached the German front line, so that they were a complete failure.[70]
>
> Major Philip Neame VC, Headquarters, 168th Brigade, 56th Division

This was quite unfair; once again tanks were getting the blame for the tactical decision that had been taken in the Fourth Army to leave 100-yard gaps in the creeping barrage, which the troops depended on for any realistic chance of success. The whole of the 56th Division only had three tanks and as we have seen one failed altogether as Private Gray was leading them up to their jumping-off places the night before. Another one also ditched in the early stages of the attack in Bouleaux Wood but the other, C-16 under the command of Second Lieutenant Eric Purdy, got well forward before it was hit by a shell while firing into the Loop Trench. Although the detail of Neame's statement is therefore incorrect, the overall gist reflects his experience as a brigade staff officer. Offered a new solution he found that normal methods of working were undermined by measures taken to facilitate a new weapon that proved unreliable and of minimal impact.

In analysing the overall performance of the tanks it is difficult to avoid the use of the word 'failure'. Although Haig had ordered a large number of tanks as soon as he was aware of their potential, there had been a manifest disappointment in the inability of the hard-pressed British munitions industry to deliver them on time. The officers and crews had not had time to be properly trained; the infantry units that surrounded them in action had usually no chance to train with the tanks. The tanks that went into action were plagued with mechanical failure and their speed was too slow to keep up with the infantry when things were going well; too slow to rush to the point of need when things were going badly. The visibility from within the tanks and the environment of a mechanical hell meant that the efficiency of tank crews in fighting was severely compromised. Where things went well the tanks were a useful adjunct to the overall all-arms battle, but where the tanks failed the artillery could not respond to sudden changes in plan and the infantry were left on their own.

Sensible officers avoided hyperbole and saw the tanks for what they really were. At this stage in the development of the tank, common sense counted for far more than specialist military knowledge in analysing their worth.

> Reading about the tanks is amusing. I have been in them and examined them and know exactly what they have done in our area. Of course their virtues are exaggerated, but they are only in their infancy and did well – really well in some places. I would like to see them with double the horsepower; less impotent when they get sideways, and with some contrivance to reduce the noise.[71]
>
> Chaplain T. Guy Rogers, 2nd Guards Brigade, Guards Division

As one new weapon came into blurred focus the cavalry once again found itself marooned on the sidelines of the war. They never quite seemed to be in the right place, in the right numbers, at the right time. When any fleeting opportunities did appear the cavalry always seemed to be easily thwarted.

> We have made good progress, but I don't think there is much chance of the cavalry being used today. Of course, everyone in high places was very optimistic and they thought that the chance would come. It may still come tomorrow, but today it is getting a bit late for a large forward movement. It would appear that if the cavalry does not get a chance this time it will be the end of them. I suppose that people at home are howling about the expense and so on. Today we used tanks for the first time. They seem to have been very successful in some places, especially towards Flers. We now hold most of the ridge – I shall be very sorry if we don't get a chance this time, but it may come later when we least expect it.[72]
>
> Brigadier Archibald Home, Headquarters, Cavalry Corps

The cavalry officers must have had an inkling of the future as they gazed at the slow, rumbling, stinking tanks that seemed to have stolen their thunder.

> The tanks as a whole have been a success, the idea will probably be developed and we shall come back to the steel armour on land once more. This time it will be petrol driven, as opposed to the horses of the old days.[73]
>
> Brigadier Archibald Home, Headquarters, Cavalry Corps

The Battle of Flers–Courcelette marked the writing on the wall for the old *arme blanche* as the world slowly awoke to a new era of mechanised warfare. A thousand years or more of cavalry achievements and tradition were being consigned to the dustbin of history.

CHAPTER ELEVEN

Hammering On

Compared with the nadir of the August and early September operations the Battle of Flers–Courcelette had been a startling success. A considerable stretch of the German front line had been captured and their Second Line system had been significantly breached in the Flers sector. Even the long overdue capture of High Wood and the final portions of Bazentin Ridge can be seen as a success of sorts. High Wood opened up a far better tactical situation for the British with the much enhanced observation it offered over the German lines. A couple of days later the Germans bowed to the inevitable and made a limited, local tactical retreat back onto the low Le Transloy Ridge.

> Went for a walk to reconnoitre the ground towards Flers and walked to the Switch trench between Delville and High Wood. It is from here that one can see the value of the ridge we have gained and the reason why the Boche hung on to it. The ground on the other side lies in front of one like an amphitheatre. Le Sars, la Barque, Ligny Thilloy, Beaulencourt could all be easily seen and identified. The ground is open and even in its present state of shell holes could be quickly crossed by cavalry.[1]
>
> Brigadier Archibald Home, Headquarters, Cavalry Corps

However, the British casualties all along the line had been atrocious and were comparable in percentage terms with the debacle of July. It has been estimated that the Fourth Army suffered over 29,000 casualties. In simple terms the army had captured about twice the number of square miles of territory, but twice not very much is still not much. Once again,

Haig's insistence that the Fourth Army should attempt to break through, and thus, by definition, smash its way through all three of the German trench-line systems meant that the available artillery resources were fatally diluted in the front lines that mattered. In any case, the German first line that had been taken was only the original German Third Line. Since early July new lines, redoubts and switches had been dug to replace those the Allies had so painstakingly captured. In the final analysis although the German line had been put under severe strain by the offensive on 15 September it still held. German morale was failing, but it had not failed completely; the artillery was struggling, but had not been overwhelmed by the British counter-battery fire; supplies and reserves were running short, but had not run out. There was no imminent prospect of a breakthrough and the German defensive system retained its amazing resilience. Contrary to the more optimistic intelligence forecasts the great German nation state was not yet ripe for defeat.

The successes won in the centre by the New Zealand, 41st and 14th Divisions have been over-exaggerated in many ways. True, they had got forward and captured tactically significant German positions, but in doing so the three divisions had suffered severe casualties and there were no fresh reserve divisions lying behind the lines ready to surge forward and leapfrog to victory. The tanks had also clearly shot their bolt, brought down by a combination of persistent mechanical problems, heavy casualties and a general exhaustion amongst the shattered crews. Most significantly of all the German artillery were still not prevented from opening fire when the crucial moments of decision occurred. Though the Germans suffered from the attentions of the fifty-six British guns specially assigned to counter-battery work, the Royal Artillery undoubtedly needed to assign many more guns to the task if it was ever to have a chance of silencing the massed roaring batteries of German guns in the never-ending gunnery duel of the Somme.

Rawlinson immediately ordered a further push all along the line of the Fourth Army, with the pious hope that the cavalry might be unleashed if the German line crumbled under the hammer blows. Yet his divisions were fully committed already and there were no immediate reserves to lend fresh push to the attack. The result was that little was achieved. One exception was the success of the men of the 6th Division who atoned in some senses for their perceived failure on 15 September when on 18 September they captured the Quadrilateral, backed by a strong preliminary bombardment and an effective creeping barrage. This, however, was not a breakthrough by any definition, merely another tactical objective achieved at high cost. By this time the rain had also started, which threatened to turn the battleground into a swamp.

There was another problem facing the British High Command. The Battle of the Somme was envisaged from the start as a joint operation with the French Army. Despite the leaching away of French reserves necessitated by the never-ending horror of Verdun, the French were still needed to make a contribution on the Somme. They, too, had attacked on 15 September but had been repulsed with painful losses. In the days that followed it became apparent that the French had lost much of their enthusiasm for further attacks on the Somme.

> I cannot help thinking that we want more fresh troops here before we can break the line, also we must make an attack at the same time as the French so as to drive the Boche back on a broad front, I am afraid that the French are very difficult to deal with. I certainly think they are very jealous especially in the higher command. In a way it is natural as to commence with we had such a small army that they commanded us and now things are quite different. If only we can bring off a combined effort it might succeed. There is no doubt in my mind that the Boche is deteriorating. His counter-attacks lack sting and I also think he is tired. Prisoners are not as confident of winning the war now as they were. His whole attitude is chastened. This rain is real bad, it will make attacks impossible for some days to come. It will be better for us as we shall have more men. The French also may be ready.[2]
>
> Brigadier Archibald Home, Headquarters, Cavalry Corps

The Battle of Morval

AFTER TAKING HEED of the state of their Allies, it was decided that new troops would have to be moved forward before any joint attack could be attempted. The next stage of the offensive was eventually scheduled for 25 September and would become known as the Battle of Morval. In

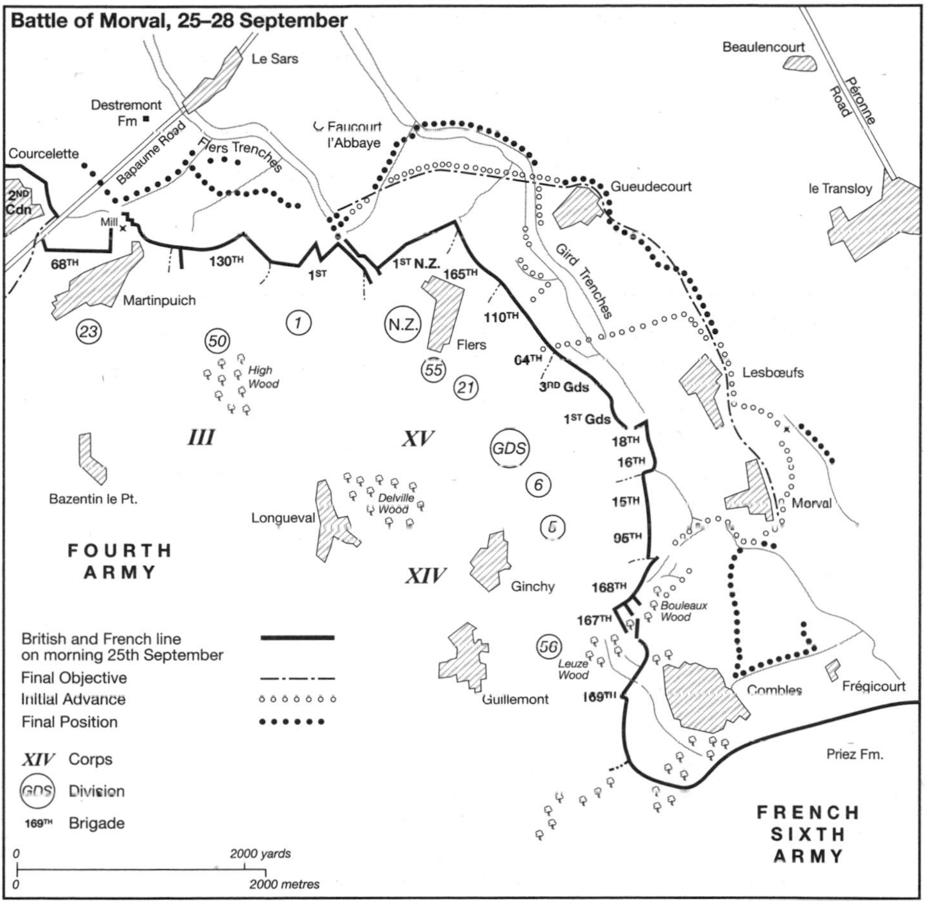
Battle of Morval, 25–28 September
Le Sars
Destremont Fm
Bapaume Road
Flers Trenches
Faucourt l'Abbaye
Courcelette
2ND Cdn
Mill
68TH
130TH
1ST
1ST N.Z.
165TH
Martinpuich
23
50
1
N.Z.
Flers
110TH
64TH
3RD Gds
1ST Gds
55
21
High Wood
Gueudecourt
Gird Trenches
Beaulencourt
Péronne Road
le Transloy
Lesbœufs
Morval
18TH
16TH
15TH
95TH
168TH
167TH
169TH
III
XV
GDS
6
5
Bazentin le Pt.
Delville Wood
Longueval
FOURTH ARMY
XIV
Ginchy
Bouleaux Wood
56
Leuze Wood
Guillemont
Combles
Frégicourt
Priez Fm.
British and French line on morning 25th September
Final Objective
Initial Advance
Final Position
XIV Corps
GDS Division
169TH Brigade
0
2000 yards
0
2000 metres
FRENCH SIXTH ARMY

many ways this battle was a signpost to the future. It was a real 'bite and hold' affair, with objectives limited to the new German front-line system and a total advance of just 1,200–1,500 yards. The objectives were designed to achieve what had not been managed on 15 September. This simple change of plan allowed the British artillery to concentrate all its venom and bile on the targets that affected the initial progress of the troops. It also meant that the infantry would not advance beyond the range of their field artillery – which made up the bulk of their artillery support. As a result the guns could cover the infantry throughout the course of the battle and stand ready to defend the troops against German counter-attacks without having to move forward and re-register targets. The artillery bombardment opened on 24 September and the thousands upon thousands of shells poured down on the German trenches to devastating effect. The Germans simply did not have the time to deepen their trenches or to prepare that deadly combination of deep dugouts, concreted machine-gun posts and massed belts of barbed wire.

The tanks were now to be more sensibly integrated into the attack plan. Instead of sending them forward in advance or level with the assaulting infantry, they would follow behind and be directed to the capture of German strong points that were proving difficult. In particular, it had been recognised that tanks would be invaluable in the capture of the fortified villages. At a stroke the tanks had been placed in their proper context; they were not the war-winning machines of myth but merely a *potentially* useful adjunct to the deadly combination of infantry and artillery. This time there would be an all-embracing creeping barrage sweeping forward in front of the infantry with no gaps as hostage to fortune. There was also a significant further advance in the counter-battery fire arrangements for the day of the assault. By dint of the various methods of observation some 124 German batteries were identified and forty-seven were engaged with the result that twenty-one appeared to have been silenced. Whilst still only a partial success, nevertheless, the loss of such a significant element of their artillery power was a handicap to the overall German defensive effort.

The infantry went over the top just after noon at 1235, a time chosen mainly to coincide with the simultaneous assault to be carried out by the French, who once again had been inveigled to join the assault. The troops went over clinging as closely as possible to the skirt tails of the creeping barrage. In many places they found that the German front line had been utterly devastated by the concentrated power of the British guns. There were few deep dugouts available for the German garrison to ride out the storm of shells and for most there was nowhere to hide. The XV Corps (New Zealand, 55th and 21st Divisions) made some progress towards Gueudecourt, but the village was still holding out when night fell. The real success was on the right on the front of the XIV Corps (Guards, 6th, 5th and 56th Divisions) which was faced with the daunting task of capturing the fortress villages of Lesboeufs, Morval and Combles. The four divisions were again packed into a narrow frontage with the idea of maximising their penetrative power. Without the confusion inherent in using the tanks the infantry swept forwards to a dramatic success, seizing the whole of the German front-line system and securing possession of Lesbouefs and Morval.

> We were all ready at ten o'clock, waiting to go over. They promised a good artillery bombardment and everybody was ready. We were sat talking and smoking, making sure all your equipment was ready to be used, that everybody was in line and you knew who your corporal, sergeant or officer was that you had to follow. Prompt at the time, the whistle went and over we went. Out of the trench and there was no barbed wire in front. We met the usual machine-gun fire, the mistake to me was blowing a whistle before the attack; another way could have been found which was silent. As soon as the whistle went the Germans must have known the attack was on its way and they were ready.[3]
>
> Guardsman Horace Calvert, 4th Battalion, Grenadier Guards, 3rd Guards Brigade, Guards Division

That afternoon, Private Arthur Russell had a good view of the attack across No Man's Land from his position lying behind rocks at the top of a nearby quarry.

> We could look across No Man's Land and follow the movements of both British and French infantry as they streamed across towards the German trenches and the village of Morval. The shells of our dense creeping barrage being placed upon the German positions rushed over our heads with a frightening intensity, but above all that we could hear the humming rushing sound of the thousands of bullets from the eight machine guns of the 13th Machine Gun Company to make

that almost impassable barrier between the enemy reserves and their hard-pressed front-line troops.[4]

Private Arthur Russell, 13th Company, Machine Gun Corps, 13th Brigade, 5th Division

Generally things were going well, although Guardsman Horace Calvert ran into some localised heavy resistance.

It was a green field, you could see the village of Flers just on the top and on the right was a German redoubt; we were getting fire across from that. Machine-gun fire and some artillery shells. We had to bomb the Germans out of one position. I was just a few yards away from where the bombers were throwing the bombs and when I passed it the corpses were piled up – our bombs had done a lot of work there. We were losing a few and the section corporal wasn't far away from me when he was hit in the right arm. He said to me, 'Keep going, I've got a Blighty, I'm no good, I'll have to go back!' He set off walking. Usual thing – there were snipers waiting and they got him on his way back. He was killed. We got near to the front-line trench when I got mixed up with some German bombers. These bombs came fast and furious amongst us. And I and one or two more caught the nasty side effects, shrapnel in the right shoulder. I couldn't use the rifle – I knew I was no good, so I did what was usual. I dropped my equipment and rifle to be used in case it was necessary as a reserve and I set off back – I got back all right.[5]

Guardsman Horace Calvert, 4th Battalion, Grenadier Guards, 3rd Guards Brigade, Guards Division

Although Calvert had come to grief, this was the nature of such attacks: even successes concealed minor disasters and personal tragedies. In many places along the line the troops of the XIV Corps met little opposition from the front-line Germans and simply smashed their way through. No tanks were involved in these successful operations as they could not keep up with the marauding infantry. This achievement left Combles so isolated that the Germans were forced to abandon it without any further fighting next day.

The results of this first day's fighting of the new battle were promising, but once again the cavalrymen were thwarted. Their chance to play a significant role before winter rains made the going impossible for horses was slowly slipping away.

> Another most disappointing day for the cavalry. We had the 1st Indian Cavalry Division up ready with Neil Haig commanding the leading brigade. The attacks went splendidly except at the point at which we hoped to push through. The Guards took Lesboeufs and the 15th Division Morval. We got two battalions into Gueudecourt, but they were beaten back again. The French took Rancourt and advanced towards Fregicourt. It can be looked at as a successful day as a whole except for the cavalry. My heart bleeds for them, All they want is a chance and yet as today the chance was very near, but just out of reach. It has been a lovely day and we are all very disappointed. Kavanagh is a brick, he is very disappointed but does not show it at all. I suppose we shall now move backwards until the next big attack. I am certain that Douglas Haig means to go on pushing and if so our chance will come yet.[6]
>
> Brigadier Archibald Home, Headquarters, Cavalry Corps

In truth there was never any hope of such a cavalry breakthrough. This was the inevitable quid pro quo of 'bite and hold'. By only attempting to capture one trench system at a time there would always be at least two systems left still intact and barring any cavalry exploitation. The underlying problem with 'bite and hold' was that it was a slow and measured process that could not be rushed depending, as it did, on tremendous logistical and artillery preparations. As such, it also gave the Germans time to build new lines of defence. Thus, as the British edged forward the Germans dropped back, occupying the new lines as they went. The Royal Flying Corps uncovered the disturbing, but unsurprising, fact that the Germans had already constructed a more than adequate replacement trench-line system stretching from Thilloy to Le Transloy, while preliminary work could be discerned from the aerial photographs for a further two defensive lines.

Following the successful action of 25 September it was obvious that Gueudecourt was vulnerable to a further attack and the next day 21st Division was once more ordered forward. This time a single 'female' tank showed the potential value of tanks in dealing with 'hold ups'. The capture of the Gird Trench was the objective and the D-14, commanded by Second Lieutenant C. E. Storey, moved along the trench parapet pouring machine-gun fire into the trench and backing up the action of a party of bombers from the 7th Leicesters. In an early example of all-arms cooperation, a contact patrol aircraft above them not only brought down artillery support fire as required, but actually intervened itself with machine-gun fire. The Germans suffered heavy casualties having some 370 taken prisoner, while the British startlingly only lost five wounded. Gird Trench was captured with the help of the 15th Durhams and Gueudecourt was finally overrun later that afternoon.

Thiepval Ridge

TUESDAY 26 SEPTEMBER also marked the beginning of one of the most amazing battles in British military history. The fight for Pozières had been as an aperitif for the titanic struggle that would engulf the Reserve Army at the end of September 1916. Haig was utterly convinced that the moment had come when the German reserves and resolve were finally failing and he ordered Gough to strike hard to attain some of the original objectives of 1 July. Once the *bête noire* of Thiepval Spur was captured, Haig planned an advance towards Serre, pushing out from Beaumont Hamel. Gough, too, was optimistic that the moment had come to strike hard.

> The Reserve Army had not so far been in a position to attack on so broad a front or to deploy so many divisions. The front of attack was well supported by artillery, and from many positions south-west and west of Thiepval we swept the defenders in enfilade and exposed them to a heavy cross fire.[7]
>
> Sir Hubert Gough, Headquarters, Reserve Army

The attack was to be carried out on a total front of some 6,000 yards by the II Corps (18th and 11th Divisions) alongside the Canadian Corps (1st and 2nd Canadian Divisions). The artillery support would of course be crucial and some 230 heavy guns and 570 field guns were soon blazing away supplemented by the artillery further north, which could strike deep into the rear of the German positions. The Vickers machine guns were also used to supplement the artillery barrage, with a constant hosing stream of bullets directed into the air, carefully calculated to fall back to earth spattering across the German positions.

The attack was once again timed for 1235. On the right of the front, the Canadians pushed forward from Courcelette, striking out towards the

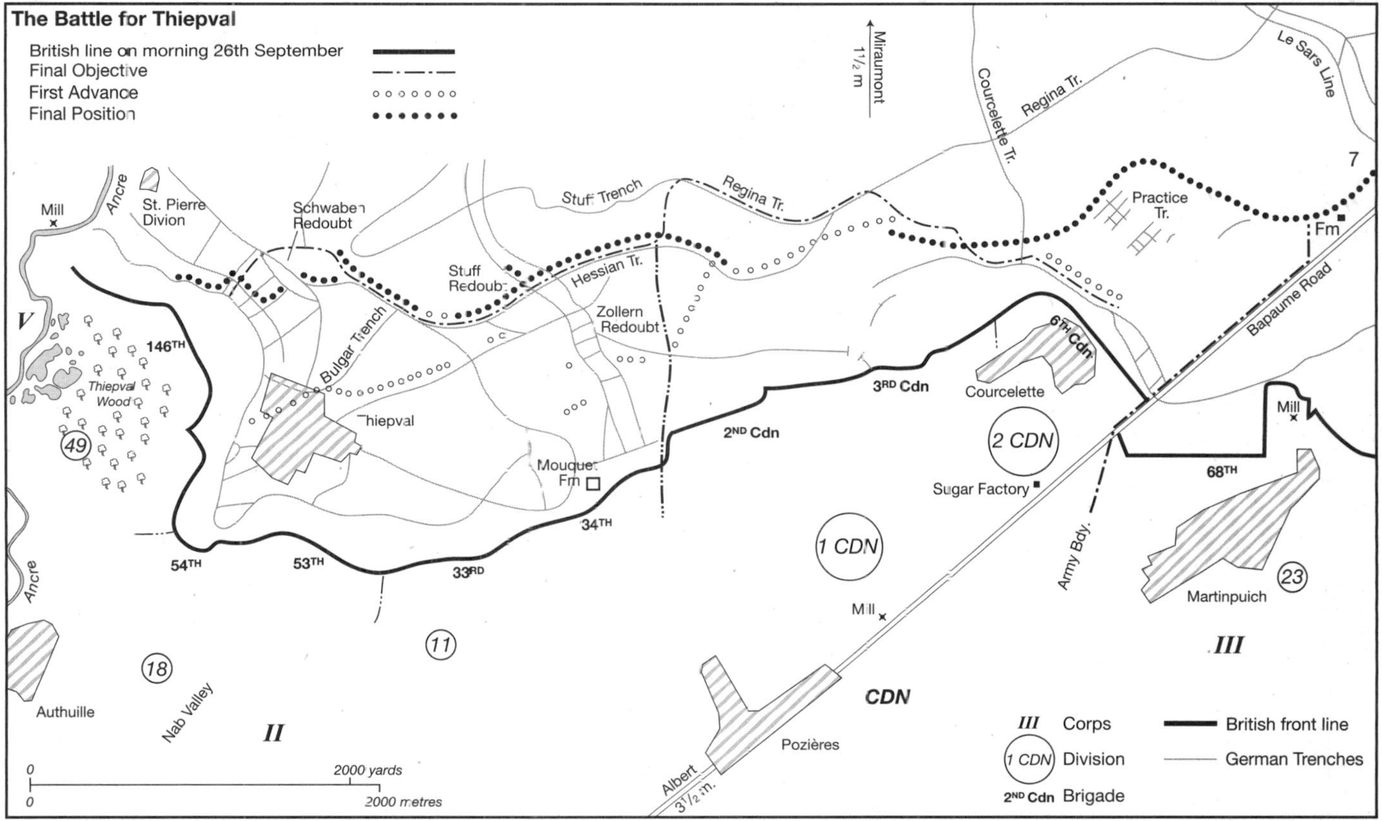
The Battle for Thiepval
British line on morning 26th September
Final Objective
First Advance
Final Position
Miraumont
1½ m
Le Sars Line
Regina Tr.
Courcelette Tr.
7
Practice Tr.
Fm
Bapaume Road
Mill
Ancre
St. Pierre Divion
Schwaben Redoubt
Stuff Trench
Regina Tr.
Stuff Redoubt
Hessian Tr.
Zollern Redoubt
Bulgar Trench
V
146TH
Thiepval Wood
Thiepval
49
Mouquet Fm
3RD Cdn
6TH Cdn
Courcelette
2ND Cdn
2 CDN
Sugar Factory
68TH
34TH
1 CDN
Army Bdy.
Martinpuich
23
54TH
53TH
33RD
Ancre
Mill
11
III
18
Authuille
Nab Valley
II
CDN
Pozières
Albert
3½ m.
0
2000 yards
0
2000 metres
III Corps
1 CDN Division
2ND Cdn Brigade
British front line
German Trenches

Zollern Trench and Zollern Redoubt. Next to the Canadians the 11th Division was faced with the task of capturing the ruins of Mouquet Farm; a task that had defeated the best efforts of all-comers in the previous month. The 8th Northumberland Fusiliers went forward alongside the 9th Lancashire Fusiliers, with the assistance of two tanks.

> I was housed in a small dugout about a quarter of a mile behind the jumping-off trench. I had a periscope from inside the dugout to above ground level and it was thought I would be able to obtain a good view of our whole front and report progress to brigade headquarters. It was known that the Germans had machine guns and mortars in the dugouts beneath the farm and two tanks were allotted to us for the purpose of mopping up, while the infantry went straight on up the hill. The tanks had to remain under cover about a mile behind the farm until zero hour. It was a bright sunny day when, promptly at 1235, our barrage opened up and our men swarmed out of their trenches and began walking up the hill. The German response was very quick and I found that with all the dust flying about, I could see nothing through my periscope. I had a signaller with me, so I informed brigade headquarters that I was going to leave the dugout and would lie outside. Communication was more difficult there, but at least I could see something. Unfortunately, my first view was not very encouraging. The two tanks were coming down the hillside behind towards Mouquet Farm. The first went into a large shell hole on our side of the farm and remained stuck there. Very soon the second did likewise. Neither was able to neutralise the Germans in the farm who continued to shoot into the backs of our troops advancing up the hill. The farm was not subdued until the evening when our pioneer battalion, 6th East Yorks, dealt with it.[8]
>
> Second Lieutenant Alan Angus, Headquarters, 34th Brigade, 11th Division

The failure of the tanks left the infantry exposed to a lashing crossfire from the German machine guns concealed in Mouquet Farm. The Germans were clearly still determined to fight every inch of the way across Thiepval Spur and Pozières Ridge.

To their left the 18th Division was faced with Thiepval village and chateau, and behind them the grim fastness of Schwaben Redoubt. The 18th Division had earned itself a great reputation for their performance in the opening attack on 1 July and in the capture of Trônes Wood. This time the 54th Brigade was charged with taking Thiepval itself: the 12th Middlesex and 11th Royal Fusiliers would lead the way with the 6th Northamptons coming up in reserve as required. When the orders were given to Lieutenant Colonel Frank Maxwell VC of the 12th Middlesex, he knew that all his accumulated military skills and a large slice of sheer good fortune would be required if he and his men were to have any chance of surviving their daunting task.

> July 1st was a playground compared to it and the resistance small. I confess I hated the job from the first. So many attempts had been made, and so many failures, that one knew it could only be a tough thing to take on and I hadn't personally any particular hopes of accomplishing it. More especially as the distance to be covered, nearly one mile, was enormous for these attacks under any circumstances, and under the special one of country absolutely torn with shell for three months it was, I considered, an impossibility.[9]
>
> Lieutenant Colonel Frank Maxwell, 12th Battalion, Middlesex Regiment, 54th Brigade, 18th Division

The artillery opened up and provided a concentrated barrage, which crashed shells liberally across the German defences.

> Shells crashed over and around our trenches, machine guns chattered as their fire swept to and fro across our path as we stumbled forward though No Man's Land doubled up in the faint hope of dodging bullets. We had been told not to bunch up together as that would be an easy target, so from the first each man was on his own. Here and there were men tangled up in barbed wire, many dead. The ground was up hill and we did not have far to go to reach the German front line smashed by our artillery, where we found a few Germans.[10]
>
> Private Reginald Emmett, 11th Battalion, Royal Fusiliers, 54th Brigade, 18th Division

Here the surviving Fusiliers took their awful vengeance, hunting down their quarry in a manner that combined bloodlust with a murderous efficiency.

> We met Boches running about, scared out of their wits, like a crowd of rabbits diving for their holes. Men were rushing about unarmed, men were holding up their hands and yelling for mercy, men were scuttling

> about everywhere, trying to get away from that born fighter, the Cockney, but they had very little chance. I had the pleasure of shooting four of them before I was wounded in the wrist. After this everything seems blurred.[11]
>
> Second Lieutenant George Cornaby, 11th Battalion, Royal Fusiliers, 54th Brigade, 18th Division

With the German First Line successfully overrun, the men of the 11th Royal Fusiliers pushed further forward as fast as they could in the appalling conditions. Private Emmett was heading for what little remained of Thiepval Chateau.

> We shot anything that moved and dragged ourselves out and on to the next trench. We had been told to make for the ruins of a castle and, dazed and exhausted as I was, I dragged myself to a little hill where there was a pile of stones – all that was left of the castle I supposed. Here the German machine gun fire became fiercer than ever, just sweeping above the ground. I threw myself into a shell hole and seizing my chance as the bullets whistled over my head, I slid from shell hole to shell hole into a third German trench where some of our boys were held up.[12]
>
> Private Reginald Emmett, 11th Battalion, Royal Fusiliers, 54th Brigade, 18th Division

At this point the men were told by an officer that they had reached their objective. Emmett's company had been assigned the role of mopping up the German dugouts. The wounded Second Lieutenant Cornaby watched them in action.

> I found myself in a shell hole with one of my men who was also wounded. We patched each other up, and then went on. I have visions of excited men tearing after the Boches, visions of men sitting over dugout entrances waiting to shoot the first Boche that appeared.[13]
>
> Second Lieutenant George Cornaby, 11th Battalion, Royal Fusiliers, 54th Brigade, 18th Division

Emmett was one of the men lurking at the top of the dugout steps.

> I started by shouting down telling any Germans left to come up. If there was no response I fired a few shots and then threw a bomb down. We got quite a few – some came up holding their hands up and

shouting, 'Kamerad!'; others held up photographs of their wives and children. We had to be very quick on them, for some still had a bit of fight left in them and pulled out revolvers, but we soon knocked them off. The survivors were sent back down the line in charge of a corporal, but many got shot on the way, for many of our boys were mad with what they had gone through and the strain of it all, and just shot anything in a German uniform.[14]

Private Reginald Emmett, 11th Battalion, Royal Fusiliers, 54th Brigade, 18th Division

Private Fuller of the 8th Suffolks of the neighbouring 53rd Brigade saw an awful sight as they hunted down any resisting Germans.

One was lying buried almost to the neck by a shell which had dropped near, but still alive. I shall never forget the expression on this man's face – ghastly white, his eyes staring with terror, unable to move, while our chaps threw bombs past him down the dugout stairs, and the enemy inside threw their bombs out.[15]

Private Sydney Fuller, 8th Battalion, Suffolk Regiment, 53rd Brigade, 18th Division

The 12th Middlesex also fought its way through to the ruins of the Thiepval Chateau, which Colonel Frank Maxwell immediately made his battle headquarters. His responsibilities were fast expanding as both Colonel Carr of the 11th Royal Fusiliers and Colonel Ripley of the 6th Northamptons were knocked out in the fighting. The simply irrepressible Colonel Maxwell took effective command of all three battalions.

It was an extraordinarily difficult battle to fight, owing to every landmark, such as a map shows, being obliterated – absolutely and totally. The ground was, of course, the limit itself, and progress over it like nothing imaginable. The enemy quite determined to keep us out as they had so many before. And I must say that they fought most stubbornly and bravely. Probably not more than 300–500 put their hands up. They took it out of us badly, but we did ditto, and – I have no shame in saying so – as every German should in my opinion be exterminated – I don't know that we took *one*. I have not seen a man or officer yet who did anyway.[16]

Lieutenant Colonel Frank Maxwell, 12th Battalion, Middlesex Regiment, 54th Brigade, 18th Division

This was the old cruelty of the medieval wars. Fight to the end and no mercy given or to be had at the last. Small isolated parties of soldiers from both battalions fought their way down the trenches that filled the village area. Bombs were the main weapon, followed by the quick deadly rush with the bayonet. It was incredibly difficult to determine what was going on, and even more difficult to keep General Maxse at the 18th Division Headquarters abreast of the situation.

> Perhaps the most trying business is to keep your generals informed of how things are going. It is extraordinarily difficult, for on a field like that at Thiepval, telephone lines don't remain uncut by shells for more than five minutes. And yet they *must* know things of course, and must get their information by lamp or runner. By lamp it is laborious for no answer to say, 'Message', or rather 'Word received' is possible in case the enemy should see the replying lamp and put artillery on to its position. If the message is sent by runner, it means long distances on foot – by day the runner is usually killed or wounded, by night he gets lost![17]
>
> Lieutenant Colonel Frank Maxwell, 12th Battalion, Middlesex Regiment, 54th Brigade, 18th Division

When night fell they held the entire village except for the north-west corner where a strong German machine-gun post still held out. Consolidation was all important for they were sure there would be a German counter-attack sooner rather than later.

> We started to get the trench ready to resist, building up the parapet facing the other way round. This meant heaving the German dead bodies over the top, a gruesome job which covered us with blood. This done we waited through the night. Some explored the dugouts which were well supplied with drink and cigars and came up wearing German helmets. Those who had them divided up their rations and tried to get a little sleep through sheer exhaustion. The counter-attack never came.[18]
>
> Private Reginald Emmett, 11th Battalion, Royal Fusiliers, 54th Brigade, 18th Division

Colonel Maxwell spent that night at the Thiepval Chateau.

> I had a safe place in a pile of ruins which managed to ward off shells and all the other unpleasant things of a modern battle. It was a very

busy night for me though, and not unmixed with anxiety – in fact very much to the contrary.[19]

Lieutenant Colonel Frank Maxwell, 12th Battalion, Middlesex Regiment, 54th Brigade, 18th Division

As Maxwell wrote these words in a letter home he was being observed by a slightly awed young officer of the 11th Royal Fusiliers, who was experiencing the full force of Maxwell's slightly irascible personality for the first time.

For some hours during the night Colonel Maxwell was writing diligently page after page – it was supposed popularly to be a letter to his wife. Shells were passing over and dropping all the time, and one runner who had the wind up gave a groan every time one came. Suddenly Maxwell got up from his writing, saying, 'I can't stand this any longer – send that man here!' He then told everyone round to stand in line, said, 'I'll give him the first kick – the rest of you pass him along!' and the runner was passed out into the dark.[20]

Second Lieutenant George Cornaby, 11th Battalion, Royal Fusiliers, 54th Brigade, 18th Division

BY THE TIME night fell on 26 September, the assault battalions of the Reserve Army were simply exhausted and the reserve battalions were moved forwards. In doing so they were threatened by the vicious German counter-bombardment that fell all across the newly captured trenches. Of course, the Germans had the range taped to an inch.

Dusk was creeping up fast and then came the biggest barrage Jerry ever sent over and well we knew it. We rushed about in all directions and dived into the old trenches that were knee deep in oozy, greasy mud, running from bay to bay, to escape the jagged metal showering down from the HE. It fell like white hot cinders around us and sizzled in the wet earth of the trench. This went on throughout the hours of darkness until dawn came, when the enemy gunners ceased firing, as they didn't want to be spotted by our aircraft. What a sight met our gaze in daylight. The trench must have been a terrible hot spot during the past few weeks, for buried in its walls were dozens of bodies, both British and German, rotting in the wet earth. A khaki-clad leg or arm

> protruded from the sides and a couple of Jerries wrapped in blankets, complete with jackboots, were acting as silent sentinels either side of a dugout. During the night my mates and I had been close companions to all these corpses. The 'lull before the storm' as we called the silence that daylight brought, enabled us to leave the 'mortuary' and look further afield. More horrors were brought to our eyes. What a sight! A huge crater about 50 yards away, its occupants were the dead of our soldiers who made the advance on the 1st July – nearly three months before. They lay, sat or reclined in all positions, skeletons covered with the greenish skin and flesh of decomposition. One that I noticed in particular was lying on his back, his belly a moving mass of maggots. I was about to retreat to the trench when our captain came across to reprimand us for being away from our positions. Then he ordered us to search the bodies for their personal belongings and pay books. This helped to clear up the 'missing believed killed' problem. We found out that they were from the West Country – the Dorsets in fact. It wasn't a very pleasant task.[21]
>
> Private Thomas Jennings, 6th Battalion, Royal Berkshire Regiment, 53rd Brigade, 18th Division

In a state of shock, Jennings and his Lewis gun team were allotted a dugout for the night. Here further horrors awaited them.

> With the light of a candle we looked round our new quarters. A German officer, bare from the waist up was lying on a bunk with a mass of bandages around his middle. He had died from a severe wound. Another Jerry was lying dead on the floor. Rather reluctant to haul them up the twenty odd steps, we covered them with blankets and promptly forgot them. It was a case of 'out of sight out of mind'.[22]
>
> Private Thomas Jennings, 6th Battalion, Royal Berkshire Regiment, 53rd Brigade, 18th Division

Next morning there were further reminders of the bitter fighting that had gone on over the last three months on Thiepval Ridge.

> We investigated all the trench, from one end to the other. In the next bay were three Jerries kneeling in a pool of blood. Their tunics were blood-red instead of field grey, their faces from the forehead to the chin were missing, completely blasted away. But why were they kneeling? Had they been at prayer? Going in the other direction we

came across a strange sight. There were perhaps a dozen or more Jerries on steps that appeared to be emerging from a dugout. They were as dead as doormats and I was prompted to give the first one a push and send them all tumbling to the bottom. Well I didn't succumb to the temptation.[23]

Private Thomas Jennings, 6th Battalion, Royal Berkshire Regiment, 53rd Brigade, 18th Division

That same night the 7th Bedfords also infiltrated their way forward to relieve the captors of Thiepval; ready to spring forward to clear the remaining north-west of Thiepval village before dawn on the morning of the 27th. Amongst them was Lieutenant Tom Adlam who was temporarily in command of a company. At the colonel's briefing he was given his deceptively simple instructions: under the cover of darkness they were to break into the German trench and then bomb their way along to establish strong outposts on the trenches leading directly into the heart of the threatening Schwaben Redoubt, slightly to the north of the village.

The guides that were taking us up all got lost except in my company. I thought, 'Yes, it would be us!' Luckily, just before we started the attack my company commander came and took over. It had taken us so long to get into position that it was quite daylight. I knew that we weren't supposed to do this in daylight but he said, 'Well, get along!' And we got over. I was lucky because the part my platoon was opposite was only about 100 yards, then the trench swung back 45 degrees. We got a certain way then the machine guns started and we all went in the shell holes.[24]

Lieutenant Tom Adlam, 7th Battalion, Bedfordshire & Hertfordshire Regiment, 54th Brigade, 18th Division

Lieutenant Tom Adlam was certainly no ordinary young man. He was not prepared to sit around and wait for something to happen. He would make things happen and trust to his own luck come what may.

I thought, 'We've got to get in this trench somehow or other. What are we going to do about it?' So I went crawling along from shell hole to shell hole, till I came to the officer in charge of the next platoon. I said, 'What do you think about it, "Father"?' We always called him 'Father', that was his nickname. He said, 'I'm going to wait here till it gets dark then crawl back, we can't go forward'. I said, 'Well I think we can!

Where I am, I'm not more than 50 yards from the trench and I think I can get in'. He shook hands with me solemnly and said, 'Goodbye, old man!' I said, 'Don't be such a damn fool, I'll get back all right, I'm quite sure I can get back!' It didn't worry me, it seemed – of course, I was abnormal at the time, I didn't feel that there was any danger at all at that moment. I got back to my platoon. I went across to them and said, 'You all got a bomb?' We always take two bombs with us. And I said, 'Well, get one in your hand, pull out the pin. Now hold it tight, as soon as I yell, "Charge!" stand up and run, two or three yards, throw your bomb, and I think we'll get into that trench, there's practically no wire in front of it.' [25]

Lieutenant Tom Adlam, 7th Battalion, Bedfordshire & Hertfordshire Regiment, 54th Brigade, 18th Division

His men could easily have taken a very jaundiced view of Adlam's zeal and determination to get forward at all costs. Their lives were at stake, but they knew that they had no real say in the matter. Yet Adlam's powers of leadership and his blowtorch style of courage seem to have inspired them forward.

They went like a bomb, they really did. They all up and ran and we got into our little bit of trench. There was no trench to the right of us, they'd all been blown away. We were in this narrow bit of trench and by this time we had no bombs. There were bags of German bombs like a condensed milk can on the top of a stick. On them there was written '5 secs'. You had to unscrew the bottom and a little toggle ran out. You pulled that and you threw it. I'd noticed that the Germans were throwing them at us, seen them coming over, wobbling about as they did, pitching a bit short of me, luckily. I could count up to nearly three before the 'Bang!' came. So I experimented on one. I pulled the string and took a chance, counted, 'One, two, three …' My servant beside me was looking over the top of the trench and he said, 'Bloody good shot, Sir, hit him in the chest, hit the bugger!' The Germans found their own bombs coming back at them, I think it rather put the wind up them. There were bags of them in the trench. With my few men behind me, I got them all to pick up bombs.

I dumped all my equipment except my prismatic compass, I thought, 'I bought that myself and I don't want to lose it!' I kept that over my shoulder. The men brought these armfuls of bombs along. I just went gaily along, throwing bombs. I counted every time I threw, 'One, two three …' and the bomb went – it was most effective. Then we got close to where the machine gun was and it was zipping about. We daren't look up above. I got a whole lot of bombs ready and I started throwing them as fast as I could. My servant, who was popping up every now and again, said, 'They're going, Sir! They're going!' I yelled, 'Run in, chaps, come on!' We just charged up the trench like a load of mad things, luckily they were running, we never caught them, but we drove them out. Then we came to another machine-gun post, they were keeping down the other people who had the longer journey to go over. In the end, with these few men I had, we got right to our objective that the battalion was down to do. They came up and cleared up. They took nearly 100 prisoners out of the dugouts, it was lucky they didn't come up behind us, but they were more frightened than we were. I was frightened, I don't mind telling you.

Then the CO saw two trenches leading up towards Schwaben Redoubt, and he said, 'It would be a good idea to get an advance post up there!' They started off and a man got killed straight away. I said, 'Oh, damn it! Let me go, I can do it, I've done the rest of it, I can do this bit!' So I went on. I bombed up the trench, put some men to look after that, bombed along this one there, it wasn't much of a trench at all, nearly blown to pieces, that was an easy job. Then I got to the other corner, bombed them out of there, bombed back down the way. We took more prisoners down there in dugouts. So we had our two advanced posts out towards the enemy.[26]

Lieutenant Tom Adlam, 7th Battalion, Bedfordshire & Hertfordshire Regiment, 54th Brigade, 18th Division

His words long after the event still conjure up some idea of the desperate mad excitement of the trench fighting, the sheer exhilaration that overcame any idea of self-preservation, or basic commonsense, as to what was and was not possible. Although he probably barely noticed it at the time in his frenzied state, Adlam received a leg wound but it was not that serious and sheer pumping adrenalin kept him going. He would be awarded a VC for his desperate courage that morning.

You did a job out there and I never realised that there was anything unusual about it. There was a job to be done and you just got on and did it. I was more frightened going up to the trenches, sitting, waiting to start, I was very frightened then, very frightened indeed. But when we got going … You've got a group of men with you, you're in charge of them. We were taught we had to be an example to our men and that if we went forward, they'd go with you, you see. And you sort of lose your sense of fear, thinking about other people.[27]

Lieutenant Tom Adlam, 7th Battalion, Bedfordshire & Hertfordshire Regiment, 54th Brigade, 18th Division

A day later Adlam was in the thick of the action again when the 18th Division was ordered to take the Schwaben Redoubt itself. The 53rd and 54th Brigades were again earmarked for the assault, supported by the reserve battalions of the 55th Brigade. Amongst the troops lined up for the attack was Lieutenant Tom Adlam of the 7th Bedfords. He had suffered very little reaction to his slight leg wound and had been able to stay with his unit. Once more he suffered the tension of waiting to go into the attack. Perhaps even he was aware that he had used a fair amount of any normal reserves of luck the day before at Thiepval. As the Zero Hour was set for 1300, on 28 September he and his men had plenty of time for waiting and thinking.

They put us in the last line of attack and the other people in front, three companies. We sat waiting until one o'clock, but we got into position at twelve. We sat down waiting. We sort of chattered away to keep the spirits up. Waiting for an hour for an attack is not a very pleasant thing. There was a nasty smell about there and of course we all suggested somebody had had an accident. But it wasn't; it was a dead body I think. We joked in that way, in a very crude manner, just to keep them alive.[28]

Lieutenant Tom Adlam, 7th Battalion, Bedfordshire & Hertfordshire Regiment, 54th Brigade, 18th Division

The artillery barrage, when it opened up, certainly seemed to have done the soldiers justice. The blasted earth of Schwaben Redoubt was thoroughly rearranged.

Then when the shells started, they put everything in. You'd never think anything could have lived at all in the Schwaben Redoubt. And the old earth piled up. We went forward and you'd see one lot go into a trench, then another line going into a trench. Three lines had all met up and mingled altogether, some of them were killed so they weren't as strong as when they went in. We caught up with them, our last lot. By this time we got this close to the Schwaben Redoubt there was a huge shell crater, a mine crater I think, because it was about 50 feet across. It was all lined with Germans popping away at us. So I got hold of the old bombs again and started trying to bomb them out. After a bit we got them out of there and started charging up the trench, all my men coming on behind very gallantly. We got right to within striking distance of Schwaben Redoubt itself. Just at that minute I got a bang in the arm and found I was bleeding. So being a bombing officer who could throw with both arms, I used my left arm for a while and I found I could bomb pretty well with it as I could my right. We went on for some time, holding on to this position and working our way up the trenches as far as we could. The men sort of lose all control. There was a German soldier, he'd been wounded, he was in a bad way. He was just moaning, 'Mercy, kamerad, mercy, kamerad'. And this fellow in front of me, one of the nicest men I had in my platoon, he said, 'Mercy you bloody German, take that!' He pointed point-blank at him, just in front of me, but he jerked and missed him. I gave him a shove from behind and said, 'Go on, he won't do any harm. Let's go and get a good one!' It was so funny, the fellow said to me afterwards, 'Sir, I'm glad I missed him!' It was just the heat of the moment you see. Then my CO came up and said, 'You're hurt, Tom', I said, 'Only a snick in the arm!' He said, 'Let's have a look at it' and he put a field dressing on it. He said, 'You go on back, you've done enough'. So I sat down for a while. The fight went on, but what happened afterwards, whether they actually took Schwaben Redoubt, I don't know. I waited for some time and the CO said, 'Well, you've got to go back, take this batch of prisoners!' I took about a dozen prisoners with me. They filed in front of me and I just had my old gun, I walked back.[29]

Lieutenant Tom Adlam, 7th Battalion, Bedfordshire & Hertfordshire Regiment, 54th Brigade, 18th Division

Behind him the men of the 18th Division swept over the great German fortress. It was a truly ding-dong battle conducted in tight trenches, and battles raged over saps, corners, dugout entrances. Finally, as the 55th Brigade came up to throw themselves into the fray, the German garrison began to give way. But the constant counter-attacks meant that only on 5 October was the whole of the Schwaben Redoubt within the British grip.

The fighting had the grim complexion of a true soldiers' battle as the two sides fought tooth and claw for every single inch of the ground. The story never seemed to change: the place names altered hour by hour, but the essential plot remained the same. So it was that on the morning of 27 September another young officer, like Adlam temporarily commanding his company, was ordered to attend a colonel's briefing. This time it was Second Lieutenant Geoffrey Pratt who found himself in command of B Company of the 9th West Yorkshires when he was briefed by his colonel for an attack planned for the mid-afternoon.

> We both produced our maps which had been issued the previous day and the CO proceeded to give his orders. 'Our barrage,' he said, 'will be on the enemy trench from three o'clock until eight minutes past, and you two, with your companies, are to be there and take Stuff Redoubt and this part of Hessian Trench (indicating it on the map). You must go at once over the top and do your best. The Canadians are somewhere on your right. Take care you do not mistake them for Boche, and the intermediate trench (Zollern Trench) is already held by our own men. Until you get there I think you will be fairly safe'.[30]
>
> Second Lieutenant Geoffrey Pratt, 9th Battalion, West Yorkshire Regiment, 32nd Brigade, 11th Division

In fact, the attack was postponed, but the runner failed to reach the West Yorkshires who consequently launched the attack as planned. In the final minutes leading up to the Zero Hour, Second Lieutenant Pratt found himself almost bereft of hope as he looked at the open ground that lay in front of them, which seemed devoid of all cover.

> There was no possibility of explaining anything to the men and there seemed no chance that we should be there before the German counter-barrage should prevent all possibility of getting there alive. It seemed next to certain that we should give our lives for a failure. 'Well,' the CO said, 'I am very sorry, but it is an order, and I am afraid you will simply have to do your best.' I felt angry and depressed – mostly angry! I could scarcely have borne to tell my company about it even if there had been time. The men had only just come out of a previous attack, and none had been home for ten months. All one's hopes were to come to this, to be shot down in a hopelessly muddled failure.[31]
>
> Second Lieutenant Geoffrey Pratt, 9th Battalion, West Yorkshire Regiment, 32nd Brigade, 11th Division

Left with nothing to say, he wisely said nothing, and he started off down the trench followed by his men.

> Bullets were crackling round us in an alarming way. A lad named Hirst was by me and suddenly he fell down shouting, 'Oh! I am shot!' He looked round and put his hand on his back, evidently thinking the bullet had come from behind, but it was a wound straight through the chest. He then put his head on his hands and lay still, breathing stertorously. I lifted him over and called his name, but he gave no sign of recognition and I perforce left him. As I went on, I saw some signs of what effect machine-gun fire had had. One man was in a sitting posture with his eyeball hanging out, mercifully dead. I glanced at him and recognised Corporal Sadler. My sergeant major had a face wound which was bleeding freely.[32]
>
> Second Lieutenant Geoffrey Pratt, 9th Battalion, West Yorkshire Regiment, 32nd Brigade, 11th Division

At last they reached Zollern Trench. Here they found a party of Manchesters who were to follow them over at 1600. The state of tension and near-panic was such that one of the Manchesters' officers threatened to shoot them if they didn't go on. It was then 1520. They still had 500 yards to go before they reached Stuff Redoubt. Resigned to his duty, Pratt went on. A fair number of his men followed.

> We advanced about half the distance under heavy fire, now at close range. I could see the Boche lines with what looked like wire entanglement in front. The machine-gun fire was at this time very alarming. There were constant stinging spurts of dust in one's face as a bullet buried itself close by, and I remember a sudden hot smarting sensation across my face, although I paid no attention to it at the time. It was still visible a week after, and showed the track of a bullet from ear to ear, just grazing the skin. It really seemed that one could go no further. I looked round, to the right, and the advance seemed to have stopped. Almost at the same time I stumbled into a deep shell hole in which there were six or seven of my men.[33]
>
> Second Lieutenant Geoffrey Pratt, 9th Battalion, West Yorkshire Regiment, 32nd Brigade, 11th Division

Despite it all, they were still a long 200 yards from their objective.

> We had all had enough of it. It seemed a miracle that under the hail of bullets, we had escaped so far. In addition the men were dispirited because, as they said, they 'Hadn't been given a chance.'[34]
>
> Second Lieutenant Geoffrey Pratt, 9th Battalion, West Yorkshire Regiment, 32nd Brigade, 11th Division

Just as any lingering vestiges of hope were evaporating the men trapped in the shell hole saw an evidently successful attack being made by the men of the 18th Division to their left. Taking heart, they seized the moment and thrust forward to break into Hessian Trench and managed to fight their way along it to the southern face of Stuff Redoubt itself.

> Just at the corner was a dugout full of Boche. I fancy we might have passed it but a German was looking out and as soon as he saw us he shouted, 'Kamarad!' They were all standing on the stairs in a perfectly hopeless position. One bomb would have blown them all to bits. But I felt that we could not kill them, yet on the other hand we could not let them out. So we waved pistol and rifle at them till they retreated downstairs and I told a sentry to guard them. Whether the sentry stayed there or not I do not know, but they gave us no more trouble, and on revisiting the place later I found that someone had put a bomb down.[35]
>
> Second Lieutenant Geoffrey Pratt, 9th Battalion, West Yorkshire Regiment, 32nd Brigade, 11th Division

The young officer pushed on, moving down the west face of Stuff Redoubt, which stretched about 150 yards with Germans concealed in about five deep dugouts that were dotted along.

> We shouted to them to come out. If they came out, well and good. If not, we rolled a bomb down. Each dugout had two entrances into the same trench. A bomb went down one and the Boche came up the other like rabbits all scrambling to get out first. Some of them were pitiably wounded by the bombs and I felt very sorry for them. From the bottom of one dugout the Boche fired a rifle at a man looking down. The bullet just crazed his cheek. At the mouth of another, a Boche who seemed terrified, would not go down the trench as he was told. We shouted at him but in the end he scrambled down the parapet and was off. One of the men put up his rifle, 'Shall I shoot, Sir?' I could not think what to say, but Sergeant Cox hastily shouted, 'Yes, of course!' and the man fell.[36]
>
> Second Lieutenant Geoffrey Pratt, 9th Battalion, West Yorkshire Regiment, 32nd Brigade, 11th Division

The prisoners were becoming a problem as they seemed to outnumber the available British troops and many seem to have been shot out of hand. Pratt sent a message back to headquarters, then started to establish a series of bombing posts in the west-face trench of Stuff Redoubt with a mixed group of men from various battalions. He tried to encourage his men to dig a new firestep and make funk holes in the side of the trench.

> I had thrown my pack off on arriving at the trench and during the night I went back to find it. It was there but the water bottle was gone and I had nothing with which to open the tin of bully beef I had brought. Bowman and Hurst I found, eating German bully in which I joined with some success. But thirst was the worst – brought on by over-excitement. We explored the dugout and found a few cigars, some of which I smoked. There were hundreds of soda water bottles but all empty. There were water bottles on the equipment left behind by the Boche and some of these were filled with cold coffee. Thus we were not altogether without drink; but nothing seemed to assuage the tremendous thirst.[37]
>
> Second Lieutenant Geoffrey Pratt, 9th Battalion, West Yorkshire Regiment, 32nd Brigade, 11th Division

Although the men's efforts had been crowned with success they were, nevertheless, still in great danger. The situation was by no means clear to the staff officers behind them and as a result Second Lieutenant Alan Angus was sent forward to try and see exactly what was going on. By this time there were mixed parties of various battalions in the redoubt.

> Zollern Redoubt had been taken and part of Stuff Redoubt. During the afternoon, I spent a very uncomfortable hour or so, trying to find out what was happening in Stuff, when a lively barrage opened up and 'whizz-bangs' were passing over very uncomfortably close to me and my signaller. At the same time, I saw waves of our troops coming up the hill towards Stuff Redoubt and very nearly in my direction. I decided I had better stay put until I could see what was happening, and as there was a convenient shell hole near at hand, we took to it. It was as well that we did. I found later that part of the redoubt which I had been approaching somewhat light-heartedly, was still in German hands, and was very nearly in the line of fire. The situation cleared

fairly rapidly after this and when I reached the redoubt, I found it crowded with our own troops from 34th Brigade. I found they were already in touch with Brigade HQ and that I could serve no useful purpose by remaining there, so I set off on the long trek back.[38]

Second Lieutenant Alan Angus, Headquarters, 34th Brigade, 11th Division

During the night several more officers appeared and Pratt was ordered to lead an attack on the south face of Stuff Redoubt next morning. It was a mixed bag of troops that he would take forward.

There were about twelve under a big strong fellow of a sergeant. I said I was sorry I was not an officer of their own regiment, but that I would try to do what I could. We talked the thing over and I divided them up into a bombing party with the sergeant as the bomb thrower. I warned the sergeant though not to throw any bombs unless I gave him orders. We set off rather gingerly and found the trench, though tolerable at the start, badly blown in so that we were practically walking in the open. There was one dugout, possibly two, and we put bombs down which elicited no response. We were soon at the place where the trench forked which was where I had been ordered to stop. Here the trench was slightly improved and I selected a place where there was a good outlook forward, in which to build a post. We had brought sandbags with us and the men began filling them. All was quiet; not a thing stirring.[39]

Second Lieutenant Geoffrey Pratt, 9th Battalion, West Yorkshire Regiment, 32nd Brigade, 11th Division

Nervous that they were not in the right place, Pratt went back and paced out the eighty long paces to check. Then, still uncertain, he went back to the headquarters to report. But the headquarters no longer existed.

Smoke and fire was coming from the entrance. Every dugout in the redoubt had two ways in, so I went down the other and found that a shell had come straight down the stairs blowing everyone there to pieces. I found two men and we set to work clearing out the debris. Soon we came across mangled portions. I came across a man's shoulder and chest mutilated and raw, and part of a severed head. There was an acrid smell of blood – peculiarly repulsive, and the debris soon resolved itself into merely a mass of loose earth in which

> the dead men were all mushed up together. We poked about a bit with our fingers, then turned our attention to a lad who had been sitting on the bottom step when the shell entered and was now half-buried. As soon as we cleared him up a bit, I could see that his back was broken, as he could not feel his legs and they lay twisted away from his body in an impossible position. He did not seem to feel much pain, but was very much scared when he saw where his legs were. I gave him a dose of morphia, I had a bottle of tablets, and he said it made him feel better.[40]
>
> Second Lieutenant Geoffrey Pratt, 9th Battalion, West Yorkshire Regiment, 32nd Brigade, 11th Division

He returned to the trench where he found himself pestered by a German sniper who, in taking pot shots at them, was occasionally making himself just visible.

> A lad near me was taking aim at him, 'I'll just give t'begger another one!' he said as I passed, and both sniper and he shot simultaneously. He fell down quite unconscious in the trench and in an unearthly voice cried out, 'Mother! Mother!' Then he seemed to come to and tried to pick himself up. The bullet had ploughed through the top of his head, taking part of his brain with it. I picked him up, but he said he could not move his left arm and leg. This seemed to daunt him at first, but he soon picked up spirits and cheerily said he could get away given a little help. A man who seemed to be a pal of his took him off and I never saw him again. He was a lad of about 18. Soon after, I saw a shell drop near the sniper, and I imagined that I saw parts of him go up in the air. Anyway he troubled us no more.[41]
>
> Second Lieutenant Geoffrey Pratt, 9th Battalion, West Yorkshire Regiment, 32nd Brigade, 11th Division

The pressure around the margins of their position in the Stuff Redoubt was slowly building up.

> Those in the post told me that they were worried with bombs from two Boche posts beyond, and whilst I was there the Boche threw two or three egg bombs and a stick bomb which landed near. There was no hope of reaching the Boche with our bombs, as I threw one to find out – the distance must have been about 60 yards. I therefore thought it wise to retire our post out of reach. We did this for about five minutes,

> but, after considering the position, determined to go back, as the new position was very far from being as good as the old. It was foolish to attempt to retire at all, but I was sick of blood and carnage.[42]
>
> Second Lieutenant Geoffrey Pratt, 9th Battalion, West Yorkshire Regiment, 32nd Brigade, 11th Division

Then Pratt noticed he could actually see some of the harassing German bombers and snipers. Despite the risks of being sniped himself, Pratt took them on.

> I climbed on the trench side and tried to pick off a few Boche with a rifle. They replied readily enough and every shot I fired they sent me one back. At one time we aimed simultaneously – the Boche had a round German cap on – and I saw his cap fly up in the air and imagined I saw his face fall back. So I shouted to the men in the trench that I had shot one, and I did not see this particular man fire again. After this a Boche in a steel helmet took me on, and my place in a shell hole on the left side of the trench began to be too hot for me, for whenever I put up my head, they fired both with rifle and machine gun. I therefore shifted over to a shell hole on the right where there were some pieces of old timber sticking up. By moving about between these two shell holes I got in several more pot shots.[43]
>
> Second Lieutenant Geoffrey Pratt, 9th Battalion, West Yorkshire Regiment, 32nd Brigade, 11th Division

He then was called to a conference and told that he and his men must take the rest of Stuff Redoubt at all costs. Pratt was to push round the north side, while two platoons of the West Ridings were to go round the south side. All German prisoners were to be bayoneted and thrown over the parapet.

> If it came to bombing, it would be soon over one way or the other. I had made up my mind from previous experience that it was no use advertising our presence by chucking bombs forward as we went along. My idea was to go round quickly and silently, and only throw a bomb if absolutely necessary.[44]
>
> Second Lieutenant Geoffrey Pratt, 9th Battalion, West Yorkshire Regiment, 32nd Brigade, 11th Division

Pratt had difficulty in amassing a trustworthy bombing party with their nerves intact after their experiences over the last 24 hours.

> One man begged not to be moved, as he had made a nice funk hole and had a wife and children. I told him not to be a fathead and he reluctantly left the place. Sawyer, Crochan and Doyle I selected and they asked a man called Parkinson to come as well. Parkinson had always been a good sturdy fellow, but I found that he was trembling like a leaf. He said he could not understand why. He was so bad that I told him to sit in a dugout till he felt better. I rooted Westcott out of his dugout, told him the scheme and determined he should come on at the back. I asked Sergeant Beaumont to come with me as NCO. He started to make excuses – he knew nothing about bombing and so forth. 'Alright!' I said, turning away, 'You will come Corporal Welsh, won't you?' Welsh said he would and we moved up to our position in the post. I then started explaining the scheme to everyone, saying nothing about the bayoneting business. I gave the job of handing the bombs out and seeing to the ammunition to a lad named Gallagher and I divided the party up, making Crochan and Sawyer the throwers. It was now nearly six o'clock and we waited for the barrage. Ten minutes, a quarter of an hour went and nothing happened.[45]
>
> Second Lieutenant Geoffrey Pratt, 9th Battalion, West Yorkshire Regiment, 32nd Brigade, 11th Division

At 1815 there was still no sign of the anticipated artillery barrage though two men were killed by a single shell that appeared to be dropped short by one of the British heavy guns.

> Just after 7 p.m. the barrage started. We were quite close and could see every shell. They seemed all on the mark right along the trench. I had cleared away the barrier and entanglements and immediately the barrage was over we set off. I got some distance bent double and then looked back. I found that I had got a good deal beyond the others. I went back and we all came on. We went about 30 yards, rather too slowly as the men were laden with bombs etc., and I turned back and whispered to Crochan, 'Have a bomb ready!' as we were nearing the post. At that moment some bombs exploded close to us. It was dark, but I could see little spurts of green flame and loud cracks. At first I thought someone had dropped some of our own bombs. But immediately after it dawned on me that it was the Boche. I chucked two bombs I was carrying as hard as I could in the direction of the

> German post and fired my pistol. Then a whole shower of bombs seemed to fall at once and I felt pieces enter my foot, hand, legs and side. I can remember a sort of wail of alarm that we all set up together and I hobbled back as best as I could. I felt knocked to pieces and sure that I could not live long.[46]
>
> Second Lieutenant Geoffrey Pratt, 9th Battalion, West Yorkshire Regiment, 32nd Brigade, 11th Division

For the moment at least the gallant Pratt was finished and was evacuated back out of the line. It took days of this murderously heavy fighting before the capture of Stuff Redoubt was finally completed. Another German redoubt had fallen. Another step to the British domination of Pozières Ridge and Thiepval Spur.

BOTH SECOND LIEUTENANT Pratt and Lieutenant Tom Adlam were clearly resourceful leaders with the stuff of heroes manifest within them. But not everyone could be a hero. One nervous young officer, Second Lieutenant James Meo, had already been out in France for fifteen months before he finally came up into the line for the first time in late September. His experiences may well strike more of a chord in the psyche of the average person.

> I went over the top to three listening posts to encourage the new draft men. It was a very wonderful experience, very tiring, especially dodging rifle grenades all day, the same incessant bombardment. What hell it all is. Blood-stained articles still lie about as memories of the slaughter the night before last. The men seem very good, and mixed, old and young. In the afternoon I patrolled alone from 2 p.m. to 4 p.m. Came under shell fire at 3.45 p.m. owing to Germans seeing some of our B Company at work in communications trench. It was hell; it proves to me I am not strong enough to stand it all. From 10.45 p.m. to 2.30 a.m. the Germans bombarded with *minenwerfers* – hell again. Thank God no one was hurt.[47]
>
> Second Lieutenant James Meo, 11th Battalion, Royal Sussex Regiment, 116th Brigade, 39th Division

Just two days later the young officer had already realised that he could not cope. Meo was quite simply terrified and not afraid to admit it to anyone who would listen to him. Call it windy, call it nerves, call it neurasthenia – whatever it was poor Lieutenant Meo had it, and he was desperate to get away.

> Was sent to doctor yesterday afternoon. The doctor is going to have a board of inquiry, I shall probably get the sack as my nerves are no good.[48]
>
> Second Lieutenant James Meo, 11th Battalion, Royal Sussex Regiment, 116th Brigade 39th Division

Everything seemed to conspire against his well-being, even his family and friends.

> My thirtieth birthday. An awful day. Still in these trenches. In the afternoon I was called to see the doctor. It seems possible that if I live that I may be invalided away. This night I was sent on an ammunition job conducting a party of fifty bombers to stores in close support lines. It was hell! I was already tired and ill. This night we prepared a scheme to draw enemy fire. Oh it was hell! I came back and found a terrible letter from my dear mother, all scrawly and obviously ill. It was an awful night. Yvonne never writes warmly now. She takes absolutely no notice of my birthday. If it had been Captain Fisher or some 'interesting' person she would have thought about them and written warm letters.[49]
>
> Second Lieutenant James Meo, 11th Battalion, Royal Sussex Regiment, 116th Brigade, 39th Division

On the day that Second Lieutenant Pratt was being wounded deep within the death-trap of Stuff Redoubt and while Lieutenant Adlam was earning imperishable glory in the attack on Schwaben Redoubt, the timid Meo was almost beside himself as he heard the thunderous echoes of that titanic battle.

> 1 p.m. – a terrible bombardment has started, it is simply awful to hear. As I write the guns are crashing, roaring and the din is like a collision of hundreds of bad thunderstorms. God knows what mothers are losing their sons now.[50]
>
> Second Lieutenant James Meo, 11th Battalion, Royal Sussex Regiment, 116th Brigade, 39th Division

The next two days seemed to last for ever. Ironically, both Adlam and Pratt by this time were being evacuated home to Blighty with their heroes' wounds.

At last. Reported to 134 Field Ambulance at 9 a.m. with servant. Sent to casualty clearing station at 3, arrived at 5. Examined, and am now going on, but staying the night. Officer in next bed with awful shell shock, also airman with broken nerves. God what sights.[51]

Second Lieutenant James Meo, 11th Battalion, Royal Sussex Regiment, 116th Brigade, 39th Division

No hero's wound for Meo. But he was just glad to be getting away with his life. Even as he boarded the hospital train he could not conceal his delight.

At 3.30 I was warned I was going on. At 5 p.m. I was put on the hospital train with crowds of wounded officers. The train is packed with wounded soldiers. Most of the officers wear Tommies' uniforms. This is all rather a wonderful experience. The thought of being alive for my dear mother is so great in me. My 'ticket' is marked with medical signs and 'nerves and debility', ear trouble etc.[52]

Second Lieutenant James Meo, 11th Battalion, Royal Sussex Regiment, 116th Brigade, 39th Division

He was finally sent back to England on 8 October. It should not be forgotten that for all his obvious nerves and possible cowardice, Meo had in fact tried his level best to do his bit and in the end had managed eight days under fire in the trenches. He was, after all, a volunteer. It was just unfortunate that he could not endure the manifold horrors of war. Nevertheless, if he had been a private soldier he would have run the risk of being shot.

I hear I am now off to England at 4.30 p.m. Thank God I am about to leave this miserable country. I hope to God I never return. I have been tortured all the morning by dreadful thoughts. How I wish I had a girl to care for me, waiting in England for me.[53]

Second Lieutenant James Meo, 11th Battalion, Royal Sussex Regiment, 116th Brigade, 39th Division

THE PATTERN OF the fighting on the Somme had now been clearly established. It was fundamentally a battle of the artillery. The British could not advance without it; the Germans could not defend without it. The roar of the guns was unceasing. It could grind away and erode the courage of all but the bravest.

> During the night we carried out the (by now) usual programme of continuous shelling. This has been found by statements of prisoners and from captured documents to have a most demoralising effect on the enemy, and to prevent his supplies coming up. Every track and road for miles back is systematically searched, and I have no doubt we pip a good many that way, I didn't sleep a wink. The incessant noise (to which I am not yet used, after a month's quiet) kept me awake. We fired 200 rounds, and as we are one of about fifty batteries in the valley all doing the same, and the heavies lined up behind the next crest did their share (about one third of that), there must have been about 15,000 explosive shells from our guns – not to speak of the Boches who don't take much without giving a receipt for it![54]
>
> Lieutenant William Bloor, C Battery, 149th Brigade, Royal Field Artillery, 30th Division

Nothing could slaughter like the guns. A mistake in full view of their muzzles was an invitation to disaster for the Germans.

> Up at the OP in the morning, and at about 10 a.m. I saw a mass of Boches in open order coming out of Bapaume. My mouth fairly watered for them, but they were right out of my range. They advanced a bit towards Ginchy, and I thought they were going to dig a trench there and I rang up the 'heavies' and told them about it. Then to my joy they started advancing again, and I began to think I should have a shoot yet. I got an angle down to the guns, our utmost range, and waited. Started at 'em in about two minutes and had the time of my life. They – there were about two companies – scattered every way and ran down into a fold of ground, nearer me, but out of sight. Put a few more over there, and then gave up till they came into sight again. Three stretcher parties left the place shortly, so I certainly got a bull's eye. The best shoot I have ever had in my life – the sort of thing that hasn't happened since the open fighting of 1914. Later on saw another large party near Le Transloy, and the 'heavies' made mincemeat of them. This is the life! A gunner comes into his own in this place![55]
>
> Lieutenant William Bloor, C Battery, 149th Brigade, Royal Field Artillery, 30th Division

The Somme was becoming a mincing machine for the German Army. Fresh divisions were sent into action, where the British artillery simply chewed them up over a period of days to spit them out as mere shadows of their former selves. Herbert Sulzbach spent some time in St Quentin while *en route* for leave in Brussels.

> In the two hours we had to wait there, a very large number of troops, some in column of route, moved through the town, coming from the Battle of the Somme, on their way to rest stations. They were ragged and filthy, with blunted nerves and indifferent expressions; while other troops, all fresh, clean and without a notion of what it was like, were pushing the other way towards the Somme, to be sent straight into action.[56]
>
> Sergeant Herbert Sulzbach, 63rd (Frankfurt) Field Artillery Regiment, German Army

The decisive moment of the battle had dawned. The Germans were staggering under the weight of the British attacks, the wearing out battle had reached its peak – the question was, would the Germans crack?

CHAPTER TWELVE

October Attrition

Even though the Somme campaign was now moving deep into autumn and the onset of winter was approaching, there was no still no question of abandoning the offensive. On the contrary, to General Sir Douglas Haig and the General Headquarters it seemed that the hammer blows of the previous months seemed to be bearing fruit at last. There were some indications that the German resistance was weakening and the tantalising possibility that they might at long last be on the very verge of collapse. This was in contrast to his own divisions which Haig felt were being bound by their experiences on the Somme into a real army as opposed to a conglomerate of half-trained divisions that had no experience at the sharp end of war. In a letter written to King George V he summarised his confidence for the immediate future.

> I venture to think that the results are highly satisfactory, and I believe that the army in France feels the same as I do in this matter. The troops see that they are slowly but surely destroying the German Armies in their front, and that their enemy is much less capable of defence than he was even a few weeks ago. Indeed there have been instances in which the enemy on a fairly wide front (1,400 yards) has abandoned his trench the moment our infantry appeared! On the other hand our divisions seem to have become almost twice as efficient as they were before going into the battle, notwithstanding the drafts which they have received. Once a division has been engaged, all ranks quickly get to know what fighting really means, the necessity for keeping close to our barrage to escape loss and ensure success, and many other important details which can only be really appreciated by

> troops under fire! The men too, having beaten the Germans once, gain confidence in themselves and feel no shadow of doubt that they can go on beating him.[1]
>
> General Sir Douglas Haig, General Headquarters, British Expeditionary Force

Haig was more than ever convinced that the Germans stood on the brink of collapse and he was not prepared to give them any chance to recover. Any break would allow them to restore their equilibrium and all the sacrifices of the previous months would be undermined.

> We had already broken through all the enemy's prepared lines and now only extemporised defences stood between us and the Bapaume ridge: moreover the enemy had suffered much in men, in material, and in *morale.* If we rested even for a month, the enemy would be able to strengthen his defences, to recover his equilibrium, to make good deficiencies, and, worse still, would regain the initiative! The longer we rested, the more difficult would our problem again become, so in my opinion we must continue to press the enemy to the utmost of our power.[2]
>
> General Sir Douglas Haig, General Headquarters, British Expeditionary Force

It was an increasingly technical business as his intelligence staff attempted to work out the state of the available German reserves. Bluntly put, this was the cold-blooded business of monitoring the wholesale slaughter of the youth of Germany.

> We have now got a very full and thorough examination of the *Soldbücher*, both of prisoners and of dead, with a view to identifying their classes. In most cases where we have found a man of the 1917 class he has turned out to be a volunteer. Still, if the 1917 class is now beginning to appear, and if the weather holds we shall have worked through them pretty quickly, though I do not think we shall get the 1918 class in the front line before December at the earliest, and probably not before the end of the year.[3]
>
> Brigadier General John Charteris, General Headquarters, British Expeditionary Force

War between industrial nation states was a ruthless business that was emphatically unsuitable for the faint-hearted. And certainly, whatever Haig's faults, he was not faint-hearted. Yet the evidence was seen through the prism of what might be about to go wrong for Germany, rather than how the Germans might yet endure despite all the privations. It was the age old question of whether the German glass was half empty or half full.

> There is no doubt that the German is a changed man now when opposed to British infantry. His tail is down, he surrenders freely, and on several occasions has thrown down his rifle and run away. Altogether there is hope that a really bad rot may set in any day. Do not think that this means I am very sanguine. Nobody can be who sees the ground over which the men are fighting here. Still there is a possibility.[4]
>
> Brigadier General John Charteris, General Headquarters, British Expeditionary Force

There was indeed that possibility. But although the morale of some of the German soldiers undoubtedly *was* at a low ebb, the mood of the majority or the way that they would fight could not be effectively judged by those that were captured. Miserable letters home did not mean that the men would not fight when they had to – otherwise half the British Army would have been good for nothing. Indeed, if Charteris had applied the same criteria to the British he may well have come to the same conclusions: the British soldier was hardly averse to moaning immediately after becoming a prisoner of war. The British Army was getting through its manpower at a fast rate and there were food shortages, strikes and unrest back at home. However, the British proved to have plenty of 'go' left in them. Likewise, the Germans were suffering but they would endure. Perhaps the men who fought to the last in the labyrinthine trenches of the Schwaben Redoubt served as a better indication of how the German soldier would respond when put under pressure.

Yet, if the British did not persevere, they would never know what might have been achieved. This was both the temptation and the trap. If they suspended the battle for winter then the Germans would have in effect five months to bind their wounds, reorganise and dig new defence lines to thwart the British advance. In 1914 Haig had seen the Germans stop attacking just as they were about to break through to victory during the First Battle of Ypres and he had sworn never to make the same mistake. He would keep on going forward and trust that the German collapse was imminent.

By this time 'the plan' was fairly simple – to keep attacking and load all possible pressure on to the 'staggering' Germans – culminating in another concerted attack all along the Somme front on 12 October. The Fourth Army would continue the attack ranging along the Le Transloy Ridge, the Reserve Army would thrust forward again on Pozières Ridge, and the Third Army would re-enter the fray with another push to pinch out the Gommecourt Salient.

In the meantime, the Fourth Army continued to occupy centre stage as it changed the axis of its attack to move on a more northerly or north-easterly orientation. On 1 October it pushed forward again, attacking the villages of Eaucourt l'Abbaye and Le Sars in an attempt to finally eradicate a salient that bulged into the British lines. The contact patrols of the Royal Flying Corps had a perfect view of the attack and were given a textbook example of the key role of the creeping barrage and why the troops must stick as close to it as was humanly possible.

> At 3.15 p.m. the steady bombardment changed into a most magnificent barrage. The timing of this was extremely good. Guns opened simultaneously and the effect was that of many machine guns opening fire on the same order. As seen from the air the barrage appeared to be a most perfect wall of fire in which it was inconceivable that anything could live. The first troops to extend from the forming up places appeared to be the 50th Division who were seen to spread out from the sap heads and forming up trenches and advance close up under the barrage, apparently some 50 yards away from it. They appeared to capture their objective very rapidly and with practically no losses while crossing the open. The 23rd Division I did not see so much of owing to their being at the moment of Zero at the tail end of the machine. The 47th Division took more looking for than the 50th, and it was my impression at the time that they were having some difficulty in getting into formation for attack from their forming up places, with the result that they appeared to be very late and to be some distance behind the barrage when it lifted off the German front line at Eaucourt l'Abbaye, and immediately to the west of it. It was plain that here there was a good chance of failure and this actually came about, for the men had hardly advanced a couple of hundred yards apparently, when they were seen to fall and take cover among shell holes, being presumably held up by machine-gun and rifle fire. It was not possible to verify this

owing to the extraordinary noise of the bursting shells of our barrage. The tanks were obviously too far behind, owing to lack of covered approaches, to be able to take part in the original attack, but they were soon seen advancing on either side of the Eaucourt l'Abbaye–Flers line, continuously in action and doing splendid work. They did not seem to be a target of much enemy shell fire. The enemy barrage appeared to open late, quite five minutes after the commencement of our own barrage, and when it came it bore no resemblance to the wall of fire which we were putting up. I should have described it as a heavy shelling of an area some 300–400 yards in depth from our original jumping off places. Some large shells were falling in Destrémont Farm but these again were too late to catch the first line of attack, although they must have caused some losses to the supports. Thirty minutes after Zero the first English patrols were seen entering Le Sars. They appeared to be meeting with little or no opposition, and at this time no German shells were falling in the village. Our own shells were falling in the northern half.

To sum up: the most startling feature of the operations as viewed from the air was:

1) The extraordinary volume of fire of our barrage and the straight line kept by it.

2) The apparent ease with which the attack succeeded where troops were enabled to go forward close under it.

3) The promiscuous character and comparative lack of volume of enemy's counter-barrage.[5]

Major John Chamier, 34 Squadron, RFC

Over the next couple of days Eaucourt l'Abbaye was captured, but the onset of blanket rain delayed the next step forward and Le Sars did not actually fall until 7 October.

The artillery still took pride of place at the centre of everything the British planned, and not for nothing was its proud motto '*Ubique*'. Yet the gunners were suffering from an accumulation of problems by this stage of the campaign. The men that served the guns were suffering from the relentless nature of the long drawn-out battle. The artillery did not come in and out of the battle like the infantry; gunners tended to stay in position fighting day in and day out. Ground down, the officers and men began to suffer from the effects of physical and mental exhaustion. The sheer physical hard labour of serving the guns cannot be underestimated, but it was compounded by the German counter-battery fire, which placed a terrible mental strain on the men. Thus Lieutenant William Bloor and his long-suffering battery came under fire from some German heavy 8-in guns. It was the seemingly random nature of the shells that unnerved them. Of course, they had been aimed with all the care and skill that the science of gunnery allowed but the results seemed to be totally random.

> As we were not shooting at the time, the Major and I, as well as every man on the position cleared out to a flank and lay there until the 'bumping' ceased at about one o'clock. It was lucky we did as about twenty or more fell right on top of us, scattering things every way. Thanks to our uncanny luck, we escaped with only one casualty; although I thought the Major had gone – one bursting at his very feet and burying him. One 4.5-in howitzer was lifted and thrown 30 yards, falling muzzle downwards on the roof of an officer's dugout. It sank in the floor up to the wheels, and the trail and spade stuck through the roof. The officer who was in the place got a slight bruise only! What might be called a 500 million to one chance![6]
>
> Lieutenant William Bloor, C Battery, 149th Brigade, Royal Field Artillery, 30th Division

Such incidents happened day in and day out for months on end. Gradually, the near escapes scratched away at the brittle veneer of courage with which the men protected their inner feelings. But the guns were needed by the infantry, so the men could not rest.

When the massed batteries of the British field artillery were moved forward into their new gun positions following the advances, they found that the configuration of the ground meant that there was very little space in which to pack all the hundreds of guns.

> There is a very great difficulty here which is causing our staff a good deal of anxiety, and that is that all the batteries have to be crowded into this one little valley as it is absolutely the only spot that is not under direct enemy observation. If we advance over the crest there is a gradual forward slope right up to Bapaume. It is entirely destitute of any form of cover and is in full view from three sides, and any battery

> on it would be blown sky high at once. There is a tiny dip (a sort of sunken road) just south of Gueudecourt, which 148th Brigade are going into; I don't envy them the position a wee bit. The whole brigade is jammed in axle to axle, covering a front of about 110 yards, whereas one battery alone is supposed to have a frontage of 100 yards. In this small spot the New Zealand Division, the 5th, 12th, 21st, 41st, Guards Divisional Artillery and ourselves (30th) are all crammed together. Every bit of ground is taken up, and it is only with the greatest difficulty we could find any spots unoccupied in which to dig holes for ourselves. There are three infantry brigade headquarters, several signal stations and a Royal Flying Corps wireless in a little gully just on our left, and their orderlies etc., have burrowed all over the place like rabbits. Everyone spent the day digging hard, endeavouring to get a little shelter. Currie and I kept ourselves warm by digging a hole six feet long, five feet wide and three feet deep, and roofed with ground sheets, praying devoutly that it would be rainproof. It wasn't, however; but that is a trifle in our present state. The sides of the 'mess' fell in at lunch time, the rain having loosened the clay and half buried me. The Major and I got ourselves warm in the afternoon by digging it out. There are three lines of guns and howitzers here, about 20 yards or so apart, and the risk of prematures is fearful, but no one seems to think anything about it at all. One shaves and washes and stands about generally with two rows of muzzles spitting it out behind you for all they are worth.[7]
>
> Lieutenant William Bloor, C Battery, 149th Brigade, Royal Field Artillery, 30th Division

Another officer of the same brigade found himself forced forward into an extremely exposed and muddy position actually under the nose of the Germans on the forward slope. The position seemed suicidal yet there were benefits.

> Everywhere round the guns and ammunition dumps is knee deep, while the banks of the road are so soft that it is very difficult to make anything except scoops for cover, and they also become rapidly filled with mud. But to this there is one great sell off – that here we appear to be quite immune to shell fire. We are on a forward slope, in full view of Hunland on the ridge round Bapaume, and I am sure that no Hun

has yet suspected that anyone can be mad enough to have put a battery in such a place. Consequently the whole of the heavy shelling goes over our heads into the crowded Delville Valley.[8]

Major Neil Fraser-Tytler, D Battery, 149th Brigade, Royal Field Artillery, 30th Division

Lieutenant Bloor could certainly testify to the amount of German shell fire that they were forced to endure in their supposedly superior gun positions just behind the cover of the low ridge. The Germans also had the remnants of the roads covered.

What was the road from Longueval to Flers runs just on our left, and this the Boche has registered to an inch, and all day and all night he bumps it with HE and shrapnel. It is always packed with traffic, and he can't shoot at it without hitting somebody. It is only 50 yards from us, and we have seen some terrible sights. Today he hit a six-horse team in a GS wagon; two minutes later he dropped a 5.9-in on a water cart, and just after that another fell in the middle of a platoon of ANZACs, coming out of action, killing and wounding about twenty. The road is thick with dead horses and derelict vehicles and is a perfect death-trap. I wouldn't volunteer to go down it unnecessarily for £50![9]

Lieutenant William Bloor, C Battery, 149th Brigade, Royal Field Artillery, 30th Division

And this, as they say, was when £50 *was* £50!

The guns were also wearing out through continuous firing. The barrels needed replacement once a certain number of shells had been fired as the rifling was worn down. Such limits were massively exceeded and as the barrels wore out the shells rattled their way up the barrel to emerge 'wobbling' in their flight rather than spinning, thereby losing all accuracy and often dropping short with painful consequences for their own infantry. The whole of the gun mechanism needed a through overhaul and a period of tender loving care from its artificers. In the absence of such basic maintenance misfires and devastating premature shell bursts became much more common. This did nothing to improve the gunners' morale.

This afternoon, one of Major Kirkland's howitzers, about 50 yards from us, burst on discharge. Horrible groans and screams broke out on all sides, and it fairly chilled the blood to hear them. I have never seen

> anything so horrible done by a hostile shell. We had one man hit in the stomach, but thirty at least were laid out by it. One man near me had his knee blown off, and another I saw lost an arm.[10]
>
> Lieutenant William Bloor, C Battery, 149th Brigade, Royal Field Artillery, 30th Division

A further problem for the Royal Artillery was securing accurate aerial observation. The Royal Flying Corps was increasingly handicapped by the rain and overcast conditions and could do little to correct the accuracy of the guns. Yet the weather was not the only problem facing the RFC; the German Air Force was definitely emerging from its long quiescence. Aircraft had been diverted from Verdun and the new Albatros scouts were making their debut.

> About 4.30 p.m. five Boche planes come sailing over our heads and flying (for them) quite low. This was colossal cheek as our air supremacy here is absolute, and the Hun never seems to challenge the fact, which is rather surprising. Our 'Archies' get on to them, and in less than a minute one of them was hit and a flame burst out of it, and turning round and round it crashed to the ground about 200 yards away from us. The others cleared off with great celerity, and everyone started cheering. This was one of those little passing tragedies, which was gleefully described in a hundred dugouts over tea.[11]
>
> Lieutenant William Bloor, C Battery, 149th Brigade, Royal Field Artillery, 30th Division

Such triumphs could not disguise the increasing confidence of the German pilots. The Albatros DI was a truly awesome weapon of war with the power to cut a swathe through anything the British could put up against it. It was faster, more powerful and far better armed than any British aircraft. Its twin Spandau machine guns firing through the propeller could fire some 1,600 rounds a minute in sharp comparison to the pathetic 47-round drum fired by the Lewis gun with which most of the British scouts were equipped. It was an unequal battle in the skies but at least the RFC still had the advantage in numbers. Like the artillery they guided, the pilots knew their prime duty was to serve the infantry. The BE2c carried on its photographic and artillery reconnaissance duties, accepting casualties, while the increasingly obsolescent DH2 scouts tried their best to keep back the Albatros.

> We shall have to bring out some very fine machines next year if we are to keep up with them. Their scouts are very much better than ours now on average . . . the good old days of July and August, when two or three DH2s used to push half a dozen Huns onto the chimney tops of Bapaume, are no more. In the Roland they possessed the finest two-seater machine in the world, and now they have introduced a few of their single-seater ideas, and very good they are too, one specimen especially deserves mention. They are manned by jolly good pilots, probably the best, and the juggling they can do when they are scrapping is quite remarkable. They can fly round and round a DH2 and made one look quite silly.[12]
>
> Second Lieutenant Gwilym Lewis, 32 Squadron, Royal Flying Corps

Haig may have wanted to keep hammering on to prevent the Germans reorganising their defences but the weather intervened to thwart him. A near-continuous downpour began on 1 October and proceeded to teem down for the next four days. The all-pervading wet and mud disrupted everything and with air observation all but impossible, the operations were perforce postponed until 7 October.

Once again the 47th (London) Division came up into the line ready for the next attack. The sorely tested 1/8th Londons were warned off to be ready to attack the Snag Trench that guarded the approaches to the Butte de Warlencourt. The misery of the cold and wet can hardly be imagined for men who were under no illusions of what lay in store for them after their recent experiences in the hell of High Wood. On 7 October the artillery barrage began at 1300 and an hour later they attacked into heavy machine-gun fire. Strung out in extended order they advanced up the slight slope with the NCOs keeping them in line as best they could.

> At 2 p.m. on a grey mournful afternoon of Saturday 7th October, 1916 I was again over the top. Within a few minutes we had rushed forward with fixed bayonets, a distance of about 60 yards when Jerrys' machine gun caught our sparsely distributed wave of onslaught. I was bowled over, so were men on my left and right. My first recollection, within seconds of falling, is that of still being alive. The next is of pressing my body closer to the rough short winter-weathered grass that clothed this hump of semi-downland to avoid if possible the machine-gun bullets that screamed and whined over and around me.[13]
>
> Rifleman Albert Whitehurst, 1/8th Battalion (Post Office Rifles), London Regiment, 140th Brigade, 47th Division

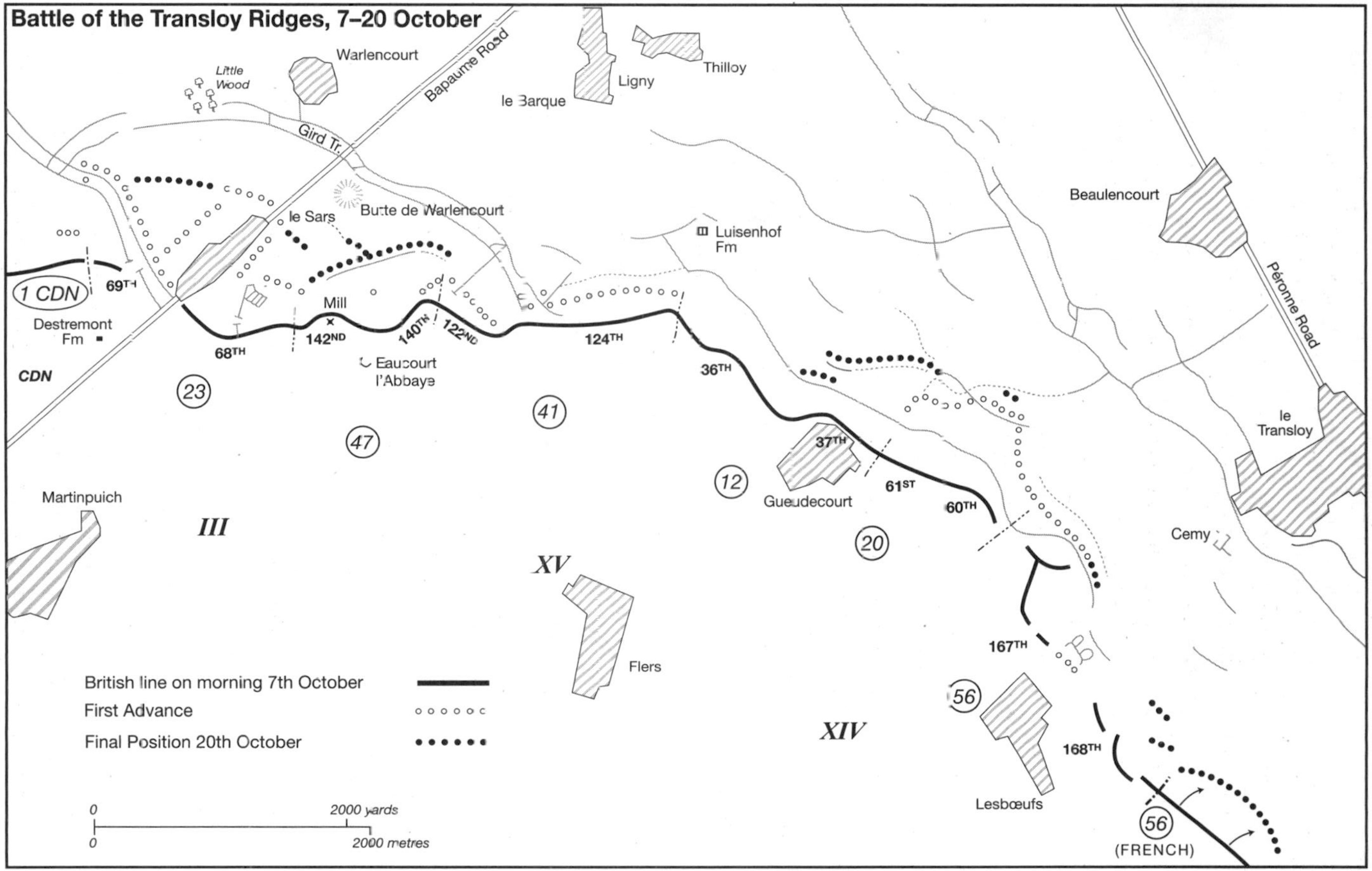

Battle of the Transloy Ridges, 7–20 October
Warlencourt
Little Wood
Bapaume Road
Ligny
Thilloy
le Barque
Gird Tr.
Beaulencourt
le Sars
Butte de Warlencourt
Luisenhof Fm
1 CDN
69TH
Destremont Fm
CDN
Mill
142ND
140TH
122ND
124TH
68TH
Eaucourt l'Abbaye
36TH
23
41
47
37TH
Péronne Road
le Transloy
Martinpuich
III
12
Gueudecourt
61ST
60TH
20
Cemy
XV
Flers
167TH
56
XIV
168TH
Lesbœufs
56
(FRENCH)
British line on morning 7th October
First Advance
Final Position 20th October
0
2000 yards
0
2000 metres

Corporal William Howell was a little more fortunate in the first instance and survived the first passes of the chattering machine guns.

> As we drew closer to the German lines, I could see gaps in our lines. I remember seeing poor old Bill Bolton, father of six children go down. Then we were in the thick of it. Terrific machine-gun and rifle fire. No orders were being given. Could not see anybody on their feet. Knew I had to keep going. Could see Bapaume burning in the distance. Suddenly through the long grass, I saw them. They were in a half-dug trench. Thick as fleas. A lot of them were kneeling. They were jostling each other to get the bolts of their rifles open. The trench was hardly touched. In front of me was a German machine gun. It had stopped firing and the infantry were picking off our chaps. Didn't know what to do. Had just been made full corporal, and was very proud of my stripes. I thought the others were bound to come up shortly, and when they did I would lob a Mills bomb right in the middle of that nest and we would stand a good chance of getting in. I took out the pin in anticipation, kneeling in the grass waiting for the second wave.[14]
>
> Corporal William Howell, 1/8th Battalion (Post Office Rifles), 140th Brigade, 47th Division

Coming forward behind them with the second wave was Private William Harfleet as part of a Lewis gun team. He, too, could not but be aware of the concentrated machine-gun fire.

> We left 50 yards behind the first wave, on slightly rising ground, and as the first wave reached the higher point they just disappeared under the most intense machine-gun fire imaginable. We in turn were suffering heavily; our team now only had one other man and the wounded corporal with the gun. We dropped into a shell hole to take stock, but the least movement was met by bullets, apparently enfilading us.[15]
>
> Private William Harfleet, 1/8th Battalion (Post Office Rifles), 140th Brigade, 47th Division

Ahead of them young Corporal Howell, weighed down with the responsibility of command, was waiting for the second wave. He was still ready to leap forward, but he soon became aware that the whole attack was breaking down in total confusion.

> There was no second wave, or reinforcements. They were all casualties and the attack had been called off. There I was, on my own, waiting, when two bullets hit me in the abdomen. They spun me round and knocked me into a deep shell hole. I thought, 'This is it!' A bullet in the stomach – they wouldn't waste a bandage – and I had got two! I did not seem to worry about dying. The immediate problem was the Mills bomb. I felt myself getting weaker and I knew I should not be able to hold the spring down much longer. The thought occurred to me to try and get the first aid dressing out, having succeeded with some difficulty, using one hand, I forthwith tied the lever to the bomb case, thus making it harmless.[16]
>
> Corporal William Howell, 1/8th Battalion (Post Office Rifles), 140th Brigade, 47th Division

The dangers of trying to get back in daylight with machine-gun bullets and shrapnel liberally spraying across the battlefield were fairly obvious, but many of the wounded were so desperate to get back that they would risk anything.

> During the afternoon we were joined by a runner who somehow dragged in Second Lieutenant Leon, who was wounded high in the thigh. We dressed his wound, but he insisted on trying to get back, and fell within a few paces, shot through the head and neck.[17]
>
> Private William Harfleet, 1/8th Battalion (Post Office Rifles), 140th Brigade, 47th Division

Many of the badly wounded men, like Private Whitehurst and Corporal Howell, had no choice but to lie still where they were – helplessly awaiting the next burst of machine-gun fire or the near-inevitable crunch of the German defensive barrage.

> After a period of utter stillness, I dared to cautiously raise my head, to better view the enemy line, fearful that Jerry might counter-attack our depleted force and I'd be killed or captured. The October mist persisted, a thin drizzle of vapour beneath the low grey clouds. The machine gunning gradually ceased. I became numb with cold, sheer fatigue and my unknown injury. With a fervent utterance to God, I fell asleep.[18]
>
> Rifleman Albert Whitehurst, 1/8th Battalion (Post Office Rifles), London Regiment, 140th Brigade, 47th Division

In such circumstances many essentially irreligious men found that God could manifest himself in many ways as their minds reeled through the combined effects of shock and loss of blood.

> I was never a great churchgoer, but I always had a conviction that there was a supreme being. I was convinced I was dying. Whether it was a fatalistic attitude which comes to a lot of us, after prolonged hardship, I don't know, but I felt quite calm and peaceful – almost happy. In my confused mind, I could imagine there was an orange glow around the lip of the shell hole, and what appeared to be a misty golden ball immediately overhead in the sky. I derived great comfort from these apparitions. I was getting very drowsy, and had a feeling of floating on a cloud. This was where I thought I died. I regained consciousness, to my amazement, and it was pitch-dark. There was a lot of activity going on, I took a peep out of my hole, and could see several parties of Germans foraging. I suddenly realised they were collecting the wounded. I didn't fancy ending up as a prisoner – especially as I was a sniper. The wound did not appear to be so bad after all. The bleeding had stopped, so I decided to have a go to get back. I managed to get out of the shell hole, and crawled through the long grass. Seemed to get a reserve supply of strength. Made good progress, crawling and resting, and was eventually spotted by a patrol of South African Scottish who took me in.[19]
>
> Corporal William Howell, 1/8th Battalion (Post Office Rifles), 140th Brigade, 47th Division

Amongst the South Africans combing No Man's Land looking for casualties was Corporal Walter Reid, who had accompanied the battalion padre on a mission of mercy to rescue the wounded.

> I was one of a party of men who were 'instructed' by Father Hill, one of our padres, to get up and follow him into No Man's Land and collect the wounded. He had on his white surplice and carried a brass cross carried aloft. His instructions were to see who was alive, put them on a stretcher or ground sheet, and carry them back to our trench. My half section and I carried a wounded man, wounded in the stomach. He was in agony and kept pleading with us to give him a drink of water, but we knew that might be fatal. He was in such pain that we had to tie him down to stop him falling off.[20]
>
> Corporal Walter Reid, 4th Regiment, (Scottish) South African Brigade, 9th Division

Their own stretcher bearers were also out between the lines rescuing comrades. The Germans usually left them in peace, but not always – it was still an extremely risky business that was certainly not for the faint-hearted.

> I awoke to the reality of the Butte de Warlencourt. It was almost dark. With an effort I knelt up, thankful that it was possible. Behind me I heard the sound of English voices. One of our company was lying about 5 yards to my left. Having stumbled to my feet, I went to him, he was dead. Our company first aid men reached me, 'You hurt, Bertie?' said Ben Tyler. I fell as he spoke. He helped me up and we returned to our trench.[21]
>
> Rifleman Albert Whitehurst, 1/8th Battalion (Post Office Rifles), London Regiment, 140th Brigade, 47th Division

For Bertie, at last, Blighty beckoned. Behind him the battalion had to come to terms with the total failure of its attack: it was another grim casualty list for the readers of the London evening papers to digest.

About the only achievement of any note during the attacks on 7 October was the completion of the capture of the village of Le Sars. As the generals tried to work out what had gone wrong, one thing was apparent: the German resistance had, once again, stiffened.

> He has had time to recover since previous attack. Our advance has been delayed by wet and so enemy has been given time.The reason for this was quite simple. They were not the same troops.[22]
>
> General Sir Douglas Haig, General Headquarters, British Expeditionary Force

Just as the British were capable of bringing in fresh troops, so too were the Germans. Many more batteries of artillery were moved to the Somme from Verdun where the German line was carefully rationalised. Although the hectic nature of the fighting in late September had made it difficult to carry out an organised relief of their exhausted front-line infantry divisions, the rain had given them the chance and they had taken it. *Gott mit uns* indeed.

ONE OF THE MAIN problems during the attack on 7 October was a small valley opposite Gueudecourt from which deep-lying German machine guns had taken a dreadful toll firing into the flank of the advancing infantry. Major Fraser-Tytler of the 149th Brigade, Royal Field Artillery was asked to try and establish an observation post in the front-line positions in the village of Gueudecourt itself. This was an extremely difficult proposition.

> I felt sure that once there I would get a grand view of the valley we wanted to pound, so accordingly in the afternoon I started off with my signallers and laid a cable as far as two blown-up tanks. Leaving one of the signallers at the tanks, we started off across the open trailing a D3 cable as we ran. We had to get through a nasty lot of Hun shells, but reached the shelter of the village safely, where we found an entire troop of cavalry horses all killed, apparently while waiting during dismounted action in the attack which captured the vehicle about ten days ago. We were just working our way through the ruined village when, without the slightest provocation, the Hun infantry had one of their frequent afternoon panics and sent up SOS rockets; within three minutes down came the 5.9-in and 8-in barrage. These barrages always ran on the same line – usually close behind our front line – with the idea of preventing supports coming up, and we happened to be in the centre of the cyclone. It was some hot corner! Just before our cable was cut in a thousand places, I managed to speak to Wilson, back at our OP on the ridge behind the guns, and told him to give the Huns 200 rounds quickly, as we seemed to be in for it and might as well have a good 'send off'! He could see the turmoil from the OP and certainly never expected us to win through alive; it was quite the hottest shop I had ever been in. However, at last with much ducking and dodging, we worked our way back to the tank, and from there to the battery.[23]
>
> Major Neil Fraser-Tytler, D Battery, 149th Brigade, Royal Field Artillery, 30th Division

Major Fraser-Tytler was not the kind to give up, even after such a reverse, and he now considered it a point of honour to establish an OP in the village outskirts. Once again, in the early hours of 9 October, he and his signallers made their way forward to the wrecked tank. There they established a signal base.

From the tank we started across the open, laying two parallel lines, as it was hardly a place where it was safe to mend the line during the daylight. Guided by the smell of the troop of dead horses we soon found the point of entry into the village, where we rested for a bit. It had been a tough walk, and dodging intermittent night shelling is trying work. The everlasting stumbling and treading on 'things' in the dark is very unpleasant, and whenever one dived in a crater to escape a close shell it generally resulted in the discovery that some noisome horror had already made its home there. By 5 a.m., we had reached the front-line trench near the desired point, but it took us nearly an hour longer to work down the narrow trench, as stretchers with wounded were being carried up it ...

When at last we reached the spot from which I intended to observe we tacked on the telephone and got a reply from the battery immediately. It is an exciting moment when the earth pin, usually an old bayonet, is driven into the ground; the next minute one will know if all is well or whether somewhere behind the line is hopelessly broken! The battery had been 'standing to' and the first salvo went over my head within thirty seconds. In these stunts I register in salvoes at high speed as many targets as possible. If the line is then cut the officer at the guns can still shoot with confidence throughout the day; if, however, the line continues to hold, I recommence and register each gun more accurately. I detected an uneasy stirring of heads in a mass of trenches, or rather connected shell holes. By careful spying I soon found that the bulk of the enemy hid there during the day. Thereupon I warned the 18-pounder batteries to be ready, and shelled the spot hotly with my own guns. In the first five minutes alone 170 rounds were fired, not bad for four howitzers. The Huns stood it for about five minutes, but then lost their heads and started to bolt in every direction. There was no connected trench up which they could escape, so the 18-pounders were then turned on and for nearly forty-five minutes we converted that torn hillside into the best imitation of Hell that one could want to see. The Huns were now throwing away their rifles in every direction, and scattering as fast as they could move, and all the time we were only 400 yards off, while the division on our right was 200 yards nearer to them still. All along the parapet our Lewis gunners were sitting up and doing their share too. The wretched victims had to run for it over 300 yards before reaching any cover, and very few escaped. The men were delighted.[24]

Major Neil Fraser-Tytler, D Battery, 149th Brigade, Royal Field Artillery, 30th Division

The relentless small-scale infantry attacks went on throughout the first two weeks of October. Many were failures, but some managed to drag themselves forward a few yards. It was often difficult to see why some attacks succeeded where others failed. On 9 October, the 10th Cheshires were charged with finally taking Stuff Redoubt. It is fair to say that the situation did not look promising.

At 12.35 p.m., we put an intense barrage on to the German front line, on to their communication trenches leading backwards, and on to neighbouring trenches on our flanks. Stokes mortars conformed to the artillery barrage. Heavy artillery shelled German dugouts behind, and places where the enemy was known to keep his supports. Our machine guns covered our flanks, and swept the German communications trenches with overhead fire. At the same moment, our fellows climbed out of our trenches and formed up in No Man's Land. For a moment I was a bit anxious, as our barrage, instead of being on the German front line was over it, so that there was really no reason why the Germans should not man their parapet. I counted six or more of their sentries standing up and firing at our fellows, but fortunately their firing was wild, and none of our chaps were hit. The men were splendid. There was no faltering. They went straight over without bunching or losing direction, and were in the German trench before they could get their machine guns in action.[25]

Lieutenant Colonel A. C. Johnston, 10th Battalion, Cheshire Regiment, 7th Brigade, 25th Division

Perhaps some accident of battle had befallen the Germans trapped in a deep dugout; perhaps the barrage had broken their morale; perhaps their machine gun jammed at the wrong moment. Sometimes things just went well and, difficult as it is to pinpoint now why that should have been, it was almost impossible in the confusion of battle to explain why a tactic sometimes worked and more often did not. Stuff Trench had fallen at last.

IT WAS EVIDENT that the British were falling seriously behind their schedule, but the deteriorating weather was conspiring against them. What was meant to be another great leap forward was in reality just another series of dogged attempts to attain the same objectives. Fresh troops were moved into the line ready for the next attack scheduled for 12 October. But many of these were making a return visit to the Somme after a thorough blooding in previous chapters of the never-ending story. The battalions were nowhere near at full strength and many of the soldiers were recent drafts sent to replenish the torn ranks. The basic training experienced by the new soldiers was quite inadequate to prepare them for such a vicious baptism of fire. One such battalion was the 2nd Lancashire Fusiliers who were temporarily attached to the 12th Division and found themselves ordered forwards from between Gueudecourt and Lesboeufs to attack the ridge that lay some 1,500 yards in front of Le Transloy. The attack went in at 1404 and the battalion soon ran into dreadful trouble.

> 2.50 p.m. Fifty per cent of company already down. Whole brigade appears to be held up. Lance Corporal Fenton, one of my Lewis gunners, has got his gun going in a shell hole on my left. Awful din, can hardly hear it. Yelled at Sergeant Manin to take the first wave on. He's lying just behind me. Hodgkinson says he is dead. Sergeant Mann on my right, of 7 Platoon, also dead. Most of the men appear to be dead. Shout at the rest and get up to take them on. Find myself sitting on the ground facing our own line with a great hole in my thigh. Hodgkinson also hit in the wrist. Awful din still. Most of the company now out. I put my tie round my leg as a tourniquet. Fortescue about 5 yards on my right still alive. Yell at him to come over to me. Show him my leg and tell him what to carry on. He gets into a shell hole to listen while I tell him what to do. Shot through the heart while I'm talking to him. Addison also wounded and crawling back to our lines. That's all the officers and most of the NCOs. Can't see anything of Sergeant Bolton and 8 Platoon.[26]
>
> Lieutenant Victor Hawkins, 2nd Battalion, Lancashire Fusiliers, 88th Brigade, (attached) 12th Division

Further to their left the 2nd Royal Scots of the 30th Division were cut to ribbons as they breasted the ridge and came under heavy fire.

> We had to attack up a reverse slope, where we were quite protected from the Boche, and then over the top of the hill, the Boche had his lines down there. The Boche had a very powerful machine-gun barrage rigged up and the preliminary bombardment didn't disturb it. The result was we attacked in four lines, one after the other, and as each one went over the top, it got caught in this machine gun barrage and pretty well wiped out. I was in the last line; I found myself the only one on his feet – as far as I could see – so I got down into a hole and stayed there until it was dark. How I wasn't hit in that attack . . . . I had bullets through my hat, I had a belt with a pistol and a bullet had gone inside the belt and out through the buckle, through my trousers – all over the place. I wasn't touched.[27]
>
> Lieutenant Ralph Cooney, 2nd Battalion, Royal Scots Fusiliers, 90th Brigade, 30th Division

The attacks were a failure. Very little progress had been achieved and any minimal successes had been pyrrhic victories. The German defensive tactics were still mutating under the direct pressure of the British artillery barrages. Not only were the Germans utilising the scattered shell holes that surrounded their trenches as part of their defensive structure, but they were also establishing hidden machine-gun posts farther back beyond the main barrage lines of the British field artillery, but still with sufficient range to allow them to cover the open ground near their front line. They had used their breathing space well and once again the German front seemed solid.

FROM MID-OCTOBER the sombre complexion of the Somme nightmare darkened still further to match the lengthening nights. The long cold frontal depressions of late autumn began to sweep across in ever-increasing frequency. Even when it wasn't raining it was still damp and the ground had little or no chance to dry out.

> A wretched place it was, I can assure you, in many senses. The trenches were flooded through the heavy rains, we were exposed to all observers, the trench being only about three feet deep, instead of at least six. The sight of the dead in front and behind us, told us of a recent engagement for the possession of a most important position.

> Not far from our bombing post was a sergeant quite dead and who, apparently, died in the attitude of prayer. His hands were clasped and his head bowed in reverence. I went close to him at dusk and his face had a beautiful expression upon it. Evidently the man had died of shock, but I thought as I went away that that man was one who had known and experienced a Godly life. I thought he was a splendid example for the men who passed that spot continually, all of whom had come there with the same object – to work, to watch, to fight, and to die if need be for the maintenance of nation's honour, liberty and justice.[28]
>
> Private John Lawton, 1/5th Battalion, King's Liverpool Regiment, 165th Brigade, 55th Division

The rain made life a misery for the infantry, but it also led to the onset of swampy ground conditions, which severely hampered the effective deployment of the artillery. It was difficult to move the heavy guns and limbers, and the thousands of shells across the flooded moonscape. The roads leading forward to the front line had been destroyed by the relentless action of countless wheels, tracks, hooves and feet pounding away at them – to say nothing of the thousands of shells crashing down day in and day out for months on end. When new artillery units moved forward into the line they could no longer bring up their long cherished guns. It was simply impossible to get them forward.

> We got our orders to leave horses and guns and to take our gunners and officers up the line to take over the battery we were to relieve *in situ*. We knew it meant handing over our good, well-tended weapons for old, filthy, worn out guns, and we didn't like it. A subaltern from the other battery arrived to guide us up. We didn't quite like the undue haste he showed to get us up there, nor his relief at handing over. In fact he gave the impression that all he wanted was to get away out of it as quickly as possible.[29]
>
> Lieutenant Kenneth Mealing, A Battery, 308th Brigade, Royal Field Artillery, 61st Division

When the gunners got to their gun positions it was worlds apart from anything they could have dreamed of. Nothing could have prepared them for the vista of desolation that lay before them.

> Not a blade of grass nor anything green was in sight. We were in a huge morass extending almost as far as the eye could see – mud and shell holes and wreckage. Dotted around were little mounds with small khaki figures moving about them. Occasionally a stab of bright flame would shoot eastward from one of the mounds and simultaneously the 'Bang-zee-eew!' of the departing shell would reach the ear. At last we reached a small collection of four of these mounds and were met by the captain commanding the battery we were to relieve. He promptly invited us to the mess, and the skipper and I went with him, while Smith went off with their subaltern to 'take over' and install our gunners in their new quarters. The mess was dug out of the ground, 6 feet down with timber rafters laid across at ground level, corrugated iron and two layers of mud-filled sandbags on the top. The stairway was a mud slide, the floor was six inches deep in wet watery mud. The furniture, one rickety kitchen table, two benches cut out of the earth and covered in sandbags. Nothing else, just room for four men to stand upright inside! And still the rain came down – the mud oozed down the 'stairway' and dripped down the walls. The men's quarters were, if possible, worse. In fact they mostly slept round and under the guns.[30]
>
> Lieutenant Kenneth Mealing, A Battery, 308th Brigade, Royal Field Artillery, 61st Division

As a junior officer Lieutenant Mealing was required to go up to the forward observation post. It was located near the once dreaded Zollern Redoubt, which was now in British hands.

> I set off with Captain Smith, to find the observation post. This was close to the Zollern Redoubt, in the remnants of a trench, now reduced to a shallow ditch half full of water and dead bodies, both British and German. It was about 200 yards behind the front line – which was a similar ditch only without the dead bodies. To get to the OP we had to dodge from shell hole to shell hole for the last few hundred yards as we were well in sniping range and on the wrong side of a slope. By the time we arrived there we were, of course, soaked to the skin and covered in mud and thus we sat, peering over the edge through our field glasses, picking out the salient points, stumps of trees, bits of trench, contours to the ground etc. behind the German Line

> and identifying them on our maps. Our telephone line to the battery was useless and a fresh one had to be laid. Apart from keeping our guns ranged the OP work was practically useless, but had to be done, day in and day out by the three of us. And how we hated that hour of hard struggle, mostly under fire, through the clogging mud, those eight or nine hours in the stinking bullet riddled ditch, and the struggle 'home' to the battery, which formed our OP duty every third day.[31]
>
> Lieutenant Kenneth Mealing, A Battery, 308th Brigade, Royal Field Artillery, 61st Division

Every so often the benighted infantry would be sent forward into the cloying mud. Unfortunately, the German batteries were beginning to recover their confidence as the problems multiplied for the Royal Artillery. As the British guns opened up they found that they themselves became a target.

> About a week after we had settled in, orders came round for a special night firing programme to last until 3 a.m., then to be followed by a half-hour's barrage on the German reserve line, an intrusive ten minutes on their front system, and raise on to their reserve line. The infantry were to 'go over' at 3.40 a.m. It was a night of horror. The Germans knew something was in the wind and shortly after midnight they opened up their artillery on the British batteries who were harassing them. Their fire, on counter-battery work, was better organised than ours. They would put four or five batteries – two 5.9-in, two 4.2-in and a 77-mm all on the same target. High explosive, shrapnel and gas, all at once, for ten minutes. Then they would move on to another target. Twice they came on to us that night. A gun was blown up, a small heap of ammunition went up, an NCO killed and several men were wounded. We were lucky to get off so lightly. With our three remaining guns we turned on the intensive stuff at 3.30 a.m. and from then on we lived in one screaming holocaust of light and sound. Sound! Deafening, screaming, shrieking sound, the whole range of the eardrum, like 50,000 express trains tearing through the air – colliding and tearing on again. Orders could only be passed by signal, no one could hear a verbal order however loudly shouted. It was like daylight. The flickers and flashes as the shells left the guns, not only our gun, but every gun for miles, the yellow flash of bursting

> shells, the white glare of Very lights and star shells lit up the landscape as in one continuous lightning storm. Indeed man's efforts outdid the worst electric storm I have ever seen both in light and sound – rendered it a puny imitation – yet it is the only thing I know which gives any idea of the sensations of that night.[32]
>
> Lieutenant Kenneth Mealing, A Battery, 308th Brigade, Royal Field Artillery, 61st Division

After only a few days the men's morale was rotting away in the mud, blood and gathering exhaustion. Everything was so difficult; nothing was easy; there never seemed to be any respite from the tension.

> Nights like the first attack were becoming more frequent. Our smashed gun was replaced from another battery – it took us four hours to manhandle it 200 yards through the mud. Our senses were becoming numbed – we were fatalists, but jumpy ones at that. I had stopped trying to sleep in the mess and had made myself a shelter of earth-filled ammunition boxes with one sheet of corrugated iron above and one below. Rather like a tin coffin on the ground. Bits and pieces rattled on my roof, but none came through and I had no dread of the roof falling in as it had no heavy load of sandbags to bury me. We only left our guns to go forward to our OPs. We were never dry or clean, our food was always cold, gritty, out of tins, bread generally wet, nothing ever appetising, the noise of gunfire was practically continuous, if not in our immediate neighbourhood, then up or down the line to the north or south of us, so that the nerves were constantly stretched, listening and assaying continuously or subconsciously the depth and nearness of shell bursts. The skipper was getting nervy and jumpy. He was a decent chap, but sensitive and somewhat depressing to live with. He had a conviction he would be killed, although I believe I saw him in a London crowd after the war, so his premonition was not justified, but his moral force was not towards that Spartan attitude which a commander needed to inculcate in his command. I had no such premonition, but the Battle of the Somme seemed as if it might go on forever! Shells could not go on missing one for ever – the time must come when one would be standing on an unlucky spot at the wrong time – and then? The ever-present unforgettable knowledge that, if not today, then tomorrow, if not tomorrow, then some day later,

> but in any case *eventually*, your turn would come. That conviction would grow as the stalemate continued, week after week, month after month, world without end, Amen. This was what caused all your pals to get thin in the face, haggard and jumpy. They knew it too; that some day some beer-swilling Kraut would load a shell into a Krupp gun, and an invisible hand would write in invisible ink *your* name on that shell before the trigger was pulled. And what would it do to you? A clean 'blot out' or blinding insanity, incurable crippling – searing white-hot pain?[33]
>
> Lieutenant Kenneth Mealing, A Battery, 308th Brigade, Royal Field Artillery, 61st Division

Some could not stand it and used all their wiles to get away. The men they left behind had little sympathy and saw this as a simple case of desertion.

> We were already short-handed and a casualty set us back to three officers only. A fourth was sent us. A nasty little worm whose name I forget. He was with us three days and then disappeared, an official note coming up from the local casualty clearing station to say that, 'Lieutenant "X" had reported sick and been sent down the line with scabies!' Hard words went after him from us: three days in the line and gets scabies.[34]
>
> Lieutenant Kenneth Mealing, A Battery, 308th Brigade, Royal Field Artillery, 61st Division

After a few days Lieutenant Mealing was appointed as liaison officer to an infantry brigade with its headquarters deep in the bowels of the captured German fortress at Mouquet Farm.

> I reported there to the General and his staff and was allotted a tiny room 30 feet below ground. It was indeed a marvellous place. Fully timbered, it had five entrances, a large mess, private rooms for the General, the members of his staff, for the telephonists, runners, ambulance men and clerks. My duty was to keep in touch with my divisional artillery headquarters by telephone, and with the three brigades of artillery covering the front under this general's command. I was not supposed to leave the place from the time of my arrival until I was relieved. I had little desire to do so as, for whilst one was safe enough in Mouquet Farm, one was by no means safe going to or from

it. Shells fell on, or near it, practically day and night – but it was impregnable with 30 feet of solid earth as its roof![35]

Lieutenant Kenneth Mealing, A Battery, 308th Brigade, Royal Field Artillery, 61st Division

Relative physical safety may have been secured, but Mealing found there were moral dilemmas that could turn a man's knees just as surely to water.

My telephone buzzed and an excited voice came over the wire, 'SOS! Gas! SOS! Gas!' At any time an attack might develop – a cloud of grey-coated Germans rise out of the ground and steadily march over No Man's Land to attack our trenches. In this case the infantry would fire a rocket which would burst into three vertical red lights. These would hang in the sky, the artillery lookouts would call the guns into action, and within thirty seconds a hail of shells would descend on No Man's Land to discourage the German advance. Sometimes the grey cloud would be gas, with gas-masked Germans following it, in this case a rocket with two greens and a red light would go up and the batteries respond, whilst all the men were warned to don their gas masks. When this message came through therefore *if it were authentic* no time was to be lost. But was it authentic? It was at night. I knew our infantry had a number of working parties out putting up barbed wire in No Man's Land. If we 'opened' on our gas lines of fire, these men would be wiped out by our own guns. On the other hand men lived with their fingers on a hair-trigger, and if a gas attack was developing, failure of the artillery to get busy at once might cause a great disaster. For a young man of 21 this was no light responsibility. I dashed into the General's room, 'Have you any confirmation of SOS Gas, Sir?' I asked. He said he had not, but that the brigade major was finding out. 'Do you authorise the artillery to open fire on the gas lines, Sir?' I asked. 'No, I don't,' he said, 'but that doesn't relieve you of responsibility if it *is* confirmed!' he added. 'Then I ask your instructions, Sir, do you want artillery support or not?' Before I got a reply, my signaller rang up to say that division wanted me on the line. The other end was the divisional artillery general. 'What's this about SOS gas?' he said. 'And why haven't we heard from you?' I replied that the infantry general refused to confirm or ask for artillery support and until I could obtain some confirmation I was not ordering fire to be opened. To my great relief he agreed with me - and to my greater relief, the alarm proved to be a false one, so no more was heard of it. There is no doubt I saved many men's lives that night by keeping my head, but was I right? *Supposing it had not been a false alarm* – we should have 'opened' too late![36]

Lieutenant Kenneth Mealing, A Battery, 308th Brigade, Royal Field Artillery, 61st Division

Many of the gunners were becoming dispirited as the power of the guns faded and they found themselves unable to help the infantry, who were desperately struggling for their very existence in front of them.

The difficulty here is that we have to advance up a gentle slope giving absolutely no cover at all, and the Boche puts machine guns by the dozen in shell holes and bits of trenches well back (say 1,500 yards) from his real trenches. This means that there is a tremendous extent of ground for our artillery to try and cover, and although we sweep and search thoroughly, as soon as we lift from one spot, a machine gun jumps up there, and when our fire comes back there it goes to ground, and they come up in other places. It is costing us thousands of men to take two or three hundred yards of trenches, and until we have worked our way right up to the crest (the Bapaume–Péronne road) we shall always have to suffer the same. It is simply heart-breaking for the infantry who call it 'pure murder', but we gunners cannot possibly help more than we are doing, and the infantry don't blame us at all. In fact they say our fire is very good, and that we are killing large numbers of the enemy for them.[37]

Captain William Bloor, C Battery, 149th Brigade, Royal Field Artillery, 30th Division

As the Royal Flying Corps slowly lost their iron grip over the battlefield, so the German army cooperation aircraft began to emerge, flying above or even across the British front line. With them came the onset of much more accurate counter-battery fire.

Enemy aeroplanes were very active and flew over our batteries at a great altitude. Very soon an intense bombardment with 5.9-ins and 8-ins was started on the Delville Valley, no doubt directed by their planes. We escaped loss, but my old battery (C/149th) had a direct hit on 'E' gun, killing the detachment, B/149th lost two guns and several men,

A/149th had a direct 8-in hit on a gun, and D/149th (the howitzer) battery had a gun blown up and several dugouts also. A terrible day for my poor brigade.[38]

Captain William Bloor, B Battery, 150th Brigade, Royal Field Artillery, 30th Division

In this benighted place no one was safe. Many of the generals were exposed to severe danger as they toured their front-line areas.

On the 16th, Colonel Bartholemew, Prideau and I went for a tour at an hour at which we hoped the enemy would not be too frightful. We entered Lesboeufs just as dawn was breaking and I made straight for the large pile of masonry, which had been the church. Lesboeufs, by daylight, was quite impossible at that time owing to the shelling and we had no troops in it. We scrambled to the top of the masonry and had a look over the depression a few hundred yards in front, in which lay the much fought for gunpits. We couldn't even then get a clear view. A lot of mist hung about the ground and the shrapnel, which kept rattling in the masonry, made even Prideau express his joy when we decided to get away. We went out at the north end of Lesboeufs and found a vantage point in the next brigade area, from which we got a splendid view. The enemy's observers saw us however and belted us with 5.9s, several being too close to be at all pleasant. We wound up the morning by being shot at by a sniper, who made extremely good practice at some 1,200 yards as we were going home. It was rather a lively morning and very tiring, 10 or 12 miles over mud shell holes, varied by running short stretches doubled up is no light amusement.[39]

Brigadier General Hubert Rees, Headquarters, 11th Brigade, 4th Division

Even back at headquarters Rees was vulnerable to the attentions of the Germans.

The enemy had marked down my headquarters and had registered it. Shortly after the action began, they started shelling it with disconcerting accuracy with salvos of 5.9-ins which burst close enough to blow all our candles out. A little later, there was a cry of 'Gas!' and we had to don our gas masks. Our value as a directing centre of operations was practically nil. Luckily the gas was only lachrymatory and we all wept copiously. At 10 a.m., I came to the conclusion that it was useless to stay there, so went back to Guillemont about three miles behind.[40]

Brigadier General Hubert Rees, Headquarters, 11th Brigade, 4th Division

The Royal Artillery commander of the 9th Division also found that his guns were all too willing to accidentally pay him their 'respects' by dropping a 'short' close by him while he was in the front line.

> I went down with Thorpe to the front trench to check our barrage which looked very effective. There was a lot of mutual shelling. An 18-pounder HE shell landed short where a communication trench joined the front trench – just where we were standing while I was talking to Moorhead, a company commander of the South African Brigade. The shell hit the corner of the rear parapet and as the earth was very sodden from the recent wet weather, it collapsed on us and buried us both up to our chins. The heavy, wet, sandy soil was deep over us and we could not move a limb. A party began at once to dig us out, and in the process I know I hoped the 18-pounder battery had discovered the mistake – a repeat would have been most unfortunate for the men digging and for Moorhead and me. It was a brave action by the men digging. I got home in the dark unhurt; my nose is scratched, probably by a splinter.[41]
>
> Brigadier General Hugh Tudor, Commander Royal Artillery, 9th Division

This incident had been watched with considerable ironic amusement by one of the infantry officers, who had been trying to persuade the gunners that their shells often fell short of their targets. It is noticeable that the two accounts still do not agree as to which British battery was responsible!

> Our CRA was nearly killed here by one of our shells. We had repeatedly complained of short shooting on the part of the 4.5-in howitzers – nothing very original in that! It was difficult to bring it home to any particular battery, because every group always assured us that they were not firing at the time we complained of. Tudor was up as usual one day when our howitzers were indulging in their nasty little habits. Making us clear the trench he went forward into a sap; the next shells buried him. He was then perfectly satisfied that our howitzers were shooting short![42]
>
> Lieutenant Colonel W. D. Croft, 11th Royal Scots, 27th Brigade, 9th Division

It was all too apparent that generals also risked their lives on a daily basis on the Somme battlefields.

THE BRITISH FOURTH Army generals considered their tactical approach at length at a Fourth Army conference on 13 October. The meeting examined the reasons for recent failures and found a disconcertingly large number of cogent explanations. These included a total lack of surprise, not helped by using the same start times for successive attacks, a tactically difficult start line for the assaulting troops, the short and inadequate preliminary bombardment, and the increasing use of deep-lying German machine guns. The solutions proposed were largely wishful thinking: a heavier and longer bombardment, the usual dreaded preliminary minor actions to improve the tactical position of the start line, a deeper creeping bombardment to take out the machine guns, the greater use of smoke-screen barrages to cover the attack and better communications all round. These things were far easier to conceive than to achieve in the Somme wastelands when faced by a resurgent German Army.

The next important attack was launched at 0340 on 18 October. It, too, was a total disaster. The fate of one battalion can well serve to illustrate the nature of the fighting that day. The 9th Norfolks made some slight progress in taking Mild Trench in front of Le Transloy, but at what cost and to what point was dubious indeed.

> I clambered over the top and walked slowly forward till I fell in a shell hole. I crawled out of the shell hole, then walked blindly forward again until I came to the Boche trench, shattered and with many dead. There was one live German in that trench, a few yards from me, with a bomb in his hand; but when our boys came over the parados and leaped into the trench, up went his hands and he shouted, 'Kamarad! Kamarad!' I felt exceedingly tired and would have liked to have slept, but we'd got that trench and I wasn't keen on losing it. The Boches were coming down the communication trench towards us, but my little party of bombers – only seven strong – bombed them back, three being killed in doing it. That left me with one lance corporal and seven men to hold the trench. Picking up captured German rifles (our own being caked with mud and it raining in torrents) we sniped over the parapet. I called for a volunteer to take a message back to headquarters for reinforcements. Within five minutes one was on his way. I saw an officer and four men crawling towards me under heavy fire; two of the party were killed,

> but the officer, Lieutenant Blackwell, got here with the other man. He took over, and I went to sleep in the mud.[43]
>
> Lieutenant Terence Cubitt, 9th Battalion, Norfolk Regiment, 71st Brigade, 6th Division

Under constant artillery fire and repeated German bombing attacks the small party managed to hold out until they were relieved a day later.

The new tactics had not failed – they had not been tried. The artillery barrage was substantially the same, and as such it was inadequate for the changing nature of the battlefield. There was no smoke barrage; there simply weren't enough smoke shells available to make a decent smoke screen blanketing the area under attack. More seriously there were not enough ordinary shells, as it proved impossible to get sufficient forward in time to feed the ever-voracious mouths of the guns. The Decauville light railways had not been pushed far enough forward and they did not serve the whole front. This was a concrete example of the importance of logistics, for the lack of shells meant that the creeping barrage could not be extended to sweep across the areas well behind the front line to encompass the lurking deep-sited machine guns. The barrage was also substantially inaccurate since the observation problems that had plagued the previous attacks had not been resolved. In particular, the continuing bad weather had given the RFC no chance to carry out any detailed photographic reconnaissance or comprehensive artillery registration of identified targets. Only a prolonged Indian Summer could give the army cooperation aircraft a realistic chance to catch up with all they needed to do. As the rain continued to pour down it did not seem to be a likely prospect.

The last week of October was marked by repeated rainstorms and intermittent offensives. Both were utterly predictable. The rain just got heavier, the water could not drain away and there was no chance of the drying sunshine that might have evaporated away some of the army's problems.

> The whole night was continuous heavy rain and all day today. The weather conditions are so bad that the push is out of the question at present and so we have another day's reprieve, thank goodness. From what we can hear it is going to be a short and sweet affair, but damned hot while it lasts – chiefly on the Schwaben Redoubt, so rumour says! We are jolly glad it is off today, as the prospects of marching 10 miles

in the rain and then pitching tents on sodden ground is not exactly cheerful. It rained today the whole time and everything is filthy – mud on one's food, blankets and kit – in fact mud everywhere and it tastes rotten.[44]

Captain Arthur Hardwick, 59th Field Ambulance, 19th Division

Water and mud surrounded the men when they were awake; it filled their horizons and penetrated the fastness of their dreams at night.

It started to rain and for 36 hours without a break the skies did their worst, so a description of our doings on a really wet day might amuse. Maclean and I sleep in the mess, and we woke up to find a vast pool at the ends of our bed bags; also, as usual, the trench outside had had a landslide, which on this occasion thoroughly blocked the exit from the mess. After breakfast we waded about in mud over our knees, trying to repair things. The back of No. 1 gunpit had fallen in, half burying the gun, and No. 2 pit seemed to have bred a spring during the night and was nearly a foot deep in water. We spent the morning rescuing ammunition from the worst of the water and patching up the dugouts and gunpits. Hickey, my servant, and I baled out the mess with cigarette tins, and dug a sump hole under the table to collect the water.[45]

Major Neil Fraser-Tytler, D Battery, 149th Brigade, Royal Field Artillery, 30th Division

The much maligned staff officers tried their best to plan the next attacks. On 23 October the 11th Brigade of the 4th Division was required to attack from Lesboeufs towards the village of Le Transloy. Brigadier Rees and his headquarters staff tried their best to consider every eventuality and to ensure that it was catered for.

This was one of the occasions where any defects in the capacity of the brigade staff would make the completion of the arrangements nearly impossible. I was never better served from the two staff officers down to the brigade chief clerk, who came away as if he was recovering from a severe illness. It was not necessary to dot the 'i's or cross the 't's for any of them. To suddenly increase an attacking force by five times its original strength, in trench warfare and on a narrow frontage, requires time and multitudinous matters of detail settling. For instance, headquarters for battalion commanders, extra ammunition, bombs, water, rations, telephonic communication, allotment of assembly trenches,

> timetable for moving into trenches, boundaries, spheres of command, liaison with neighbouring troops, prisoners, reserves etc. Add to this the reports of the situation and fighting activity of two battalions holding the front line, who have to be relieved by the assaulting battalions. Intelligence reports and aeroplane photos may cause a change in the plan at any moment. One lives at very high pressure on occasions.[46]
>
> Brigadier General Hubert Rees, Headquarters, 11th Brigade, 4th Division

The attack was to be made by the 1st Hampshires and the 2nd Royal Dublin Fusiliers, who had been attached to Rees from the 10th Brigade. They were the right-hand unit of the British Army and would be accompanied in the assault by elements of the neighbouring French Sixth Army. On the morning of the attack there was an immediate complication.

> The morning of the 23rd was foggy for which I was duly grateful as I was by no means satisfied that the large numbers of men assembled would have enough cover to escape observation until 11.30 a.m., the hour of the attack. I should not have been sorry to attack in the fog, but the authorities thought otherwise apparently, for the time of the attack was altered to 2.30 p.m. We only just had time to get the alterations through to the troops before 11.30.[47]
>
> Brigadier General Hubert Rees, Headquarters, 11th Brigade, 4th Division

His men went forward but they were soon stopped dead in their tracks. Detailed planning at brigade level was all very well, but it could not cope with the ground conditions. One could not plan a way through deep liquid mud covered by machine guns. Brigadier General Rees went forward to see what was happening for himself.

> I started off up the line to see the conditions. I was soon convinced that further operations were hopeless. Where the mud wasn't up to one's knees, it was so slippery one couldn't stand and one slid off the brink of the shell holes into a foot or so of mud and water every few minutes. The only communication trench to battalion headquarters was being shelled and nearly impassable from the festoons of telephone wires hanging across it every few yards. My orderly and I were plastered with mud and drenched to the skin before we returned four hours later. The rain came down in a steady stream and, even for the Somme, it was an awful night.[48]
>
> Brigadier General Hubert Rees, Headquarters, 11th Brigade, 4th Division

There would be two more attacks on 28 and 29 October. Small-scale local attacks, with an inadequate bombardment and exposed to the combined fire of every German gun that could reach them. The attacks were a tragic sight to men watching.

> The attack was on – the noise concussion and smell of powder fumes was fearful, and the whole ground rocked and quivered to the shock of the guns and bursting shells. 'Fritz' was putting a deluge of shells on our infantry who were advancing on the Redoubt. I got up and peeped over the parapet and I was glad I did. One could see men like ants moving steadily forward, many falling never to rise again, until they were lost to sight in the shell fire from 'Fritz' batteries which was raising the earth in clouds in No Man's Land where his defensive barrage was smashing down in a thick wall in front of his trenches.[49]
>
> Signaller Ron Buckell, 1st Artillery Brigade, Canadian Expeditionary Force

The German artillery were beginning to operate in parity with the British gunners. Major Fraser-Tytler found that the sunken road position, which had served him so well, had finally been identified by the Germans. Now he was really for it in his exposed forward positions.

> I saw an ominous sign – four huge craters – and realized that we had been registered by an 8-in howitzer battery. On the previous day hostile aeroplanes at a low altitude had circled round our position, and it looked as if our number was up. A Hun 8-in battery, evidently directed by an observation balloon began shelling our positions, and, after about four rounds short and over, they got the range of the road, and then the trouble began. Trouble only for material however, because we had made every plan for evacuating the position, as we knew that sooner or later we would get knocked out. We had already fitted up an emergency telephone exchange in a dugout, which was 200 yards to the flank of the battery, and where there was also accommodation to shelter all the men. At an order from the officer at the guns every man left the doomed position and assembled at the flank dugouts, the limber gunners carrying their dial sights, and everybody else their most precious belongings. From my OP in the front line, I could see the fall of every shell in the position, and the exploding one by one of our many ammunition dumps. After the usual two hours

> struggle through the mud I got back to the battery to find everybody busily engaged in attempting to clear up the mess. The bombardment lasted just over an hour and a half, in which time the Hun fired 120 8-in shells. His shooting really was wonderful, but luckily he had mistaken for gunpits two large ammunition dumps to the flank of the battery, and therefore his fire only extended over one half of the position, Every ammunition dump except one had been blown up, No. 4 gunpit had been hit three times – the gun literally had disappeared. No.3 gunpit was empty, its inmate had been slightly damaged the previous day and sent back the same night. It got hit twice and all the men's dugouts had been completely destroyed. The officers' mess and telephone dugout were the only ones that escaped. The sunken road itself had been hit about twenty times and it was impossible for any vehicle to pass along it. Our position being now known to the Hun, it was no use attempting to carry out our game from that spot any longer, so we got orders from the brigade to retire.[50]
>
> Major Neil Fraser-Tytler, D Battery, 149th Brigade, Royal Field Artillery, 30th Division

As conditions worsened in the front-line areas, feelings began to run high. Medical Officer Lieutenant Lawrence Gameson, who had been posted by this time from the 45th Field Ambulance to the 73rd Brigade, Royal Field Artillery, was thrown into a state of veritable apoplexy when he received a communication on the subject of trench feet from Colonel Bruce Skinner, the Deputy Director of Medical Services of the II Corps.

> It was feckless effusions of just this kind which earned for some of the distant cushioned-staff the derisory title, 'Plush-arsed buggers', a coarse, happily-chosen phrase which I gladly put on record without apology. The letter opened with the following sentences, 'Now that the wet season is approaching … .' It reached me on October 26th. Since the end of September conditions had been bad almost beyond belief. I will pass over the error of at least four weeks implicit in 'is approaching', for that was not the most damning part of this opening sentence. Lightly to dismiss the season as wet was scarcely short of criminal meiosis. Many of the trenches were waist deep in liquid mud. Batteries were shockingly housed. Communications in the forward areas were heart-breaking of all infantry movements, for carrying parties and

> horses. With this in mind, and I have done little more than hint at the conditions, it is instructing to see what the letter goes on to suggest, 'The loose trouser offers no constriction … the over-lapping of the loose trouser will prevent rain from falling into the top of the boot.' The letter is before me as I make these extracts which are so revealing of its writer's dreadful innocence. The effusion was lengthy, with inanities as the above incorporated among bits of the obvious. The following sentence, in conjunction with much of the letter, thereby was somewhat pointless and made sour reading, 'You must bear in mind that experience has shown that the presence of trench feet in a unit is an index that these hygienic rules have not been carried out'. And the document itself was an index. It indicated one of two alternatives: that the deputy director of medical services was waiving his responsibilities; or, and more probably, that he was culpably, complacently ignorant of the conditions in which the troops were slaving. We felt that his attitude was gracelessly lacking in reality. Actually we put our feelings in slightly different language! The communication ended, 'It is your duty to point out these matters to the commanding officer, and to all ranks in the unit to which you are attached.' I did that, quoting without embellishment. We needed something to laugh at just then.[51]
>
> Medical Officer Lieutenant Lawrence Gameson, 73rd Brigade,
> Royal Field Artillery, 15th Division

Of course, Gameson had already been trying his very best to ensure the health of his men's feet. But in the circumstances it was almost an impossibility.

> The feet of the gunners were sometimes shockingly clad. I happen to know, because it was part of my job to inspect their feet. Some men had only one pair of socks (don't ask me why it was so) and in that pair of socks I have seen both heels worn threadbare. When people at home, as they constantly did, asked me what they could send for the troops, my invariable reply was SOCKS. In a single consignment from home I once received a sack full; compressed to reduce bulk and so increase the number of pairs. At various times I distributed scores of pairs from private sources; and not as a luxury, but as a downright necessity.[52]
>
> Medical Officer Lieutenant Lawrence Gameson, 73rd Brigade,
> Royal Field Artillery, 15th Division

Yet even amidst his concern and fury, he could not but observe the strange survival of humour in even the most difficult of circumstances.

> One of our Scottish infantrymen was perched on a ledge in the wall of a sodden trench. The trench was almost knee-deep in liquid mud. The ground outside and the approaches was a viscid, glutinous morass. Pitiless rain was pouring down. He was pulling a sock through the clenched fingers of his left hand. Mud oozed through his fingers and around the top of his sock as he pulled the sock, which, saturated with mud was as slimy as an eel. I asked him what he was doing. He answered simply, with no dangerous Scottish twinkle in his eyes, 'I'm doing a bit of washing, Sir!'[53]
>
> Medical Officer Lieutenant Lawrence Gameson, 73rd Brigade, Royal Field Artillery, 15th Division

As the misery of the troops increased there was a need to define more closely the medical conditions that could offer an escape from this hell on earth. One sign of this more rigorous approach was the definition and treatment of 'shell shock' cases. Shell shock was a difficult and somewhat controversial matter, complicated by the fact that some of the symptoms were caused by prolonged fear and stress, rather than proximity to an actual shell burst.

> I have today examined a second lieutenant who had been admitted into this hospital, I understand marked 'Shell Shock W (Wounded)'. Considering the present symptoms, and the previous history, I have no doubt that the case ought not to be regarded as a battle casualty. In his own words, 'To tell you honestly it was not *that* (the shell) that made me fall; it was the horrible sight of the arm (blown off by the shell from a neighbouring soldier) flying in front of me'. I recommend that the diagnosis be changed to 'Shell Shock S (Sick)' His condition is mainly due to congenital and acquired nervous instability.[54]
>
> Lieutenant Colonel C. S. Myers, Royal Army Medical Corps

Many front-line medical officers were incensed by this approach. It was not so much the particular example as the overall approach that worried them.

> Rough justice and rough psychiatry, though probably fair and right in this particular case; a case which the Deputy Director of Medical

Services offers so chirpily as 'a useful illustration'. Indeed it is. It usefully illustrates the incompetence of the board and the system which ultimately passed this plucky unfortunate man as fit for combatant service. There is a minor point arising from Colonel Myers' letter. The remark, 'He was neither buried nor lifted by the shell' seems to imply that there were no other means, barring actual wounding, by which shells could damage a man. Concussion, to my certain knowledge, could play a major part in the after-effects of the near explosion of a shell. For instance, I have seen men killed outright by concussion alone without a vestige of evidence of external injury. And there were lesser degrees of concussion. It was probably not an important factor in the cited case, but this factor should always be taken into account, especially as concussion means 'W'. All this 'W' versus 'S' stuff seemed a shade tendentious, and it did not only apply to the admittedly difficult shell shock cases. Once a man had been officially labelled 'W' – and here is the point – he was in a much better bargaining position than one marked 'S'. From the DDMS's letter there emerged, I fancied, a thinly veiled invitation to diagnose 'S' in preference to 'W'. I may have been wrong but I doubt it. We all knew that shell shock was a highly debatable matter. When the diagnosis was questionable, as clearly it could be, how often, I wonder, did the official view err in the patient's favour. I do not wonder, really.[55]

Medical Officer Lieutenant Lawrence Gameson, 73rd Brigade, Royal Field Artillery, 15th Division

As October staggered to a close, the situation on the ground was degenerating into a miserable spiral of despair for the men fighting on the Somme. Things just seemed to get worse and worse, an escalation that never seemed to end. It had never been easy, but the conditions the men at the front now had to endure were the stuff of nightmares.

I will never forget that trench – it was simply packed with German corpses in the stage where face and hands were inky black with a greenish tinge from decomposition and whites of the eyes and teeth gave them a horrible appearance. How so many came to be in one trench I cannot tell, unless one of our 'tanks' caught them there. Fritz had tried to get rid of some, for they were laid in rows on the parapets at the level of one's head, stuck into walls, buried in the floor and felt like an air cushion to walk on, and one was continually rubbing against heads, legs, arms etc., sticking out of the walls at all heights. The floor one walked on was in a fearful state, in some parts covered several deep with bodies or a face with grinning teeth looked up at you from the soft mud, and one often saw an arm or a leg by itself and occasionally a head cut off. Everywhere are Prussian helmets with their eagle badge, belts and equipment, many bodies had wristwatches etc. We did not collect many souvenirs, for our own skin was the best souvenir we could think of that day. Why in war does a trip over decayed bodies in every position and showing fearful expressions of pain on their black faces not affect one? No one liked them of course but all were cheerful, and walked on them as though they were oat sacks, all that one did was to step between them wherever possible. Possibly the danger from bullets and shells was sufficient to take away all fear of the bodies which were of course perfectly harmless.[56]

Signaller Ron Buckell, 1st Artillery Brigade, Canadian Expeditionary Force

Some of those clinging to life were in not much better condition than the corpses that surrounded them. Men were trapped in No Man's Land, in shell holes and in dugouts for days on end, before they summoned the strength to move or were rescued by stretcher bearers.

A young Hun about 21 was brought in this evening who had been lying out for six days in a shell hole with multiple slight bomb wounds. He was in an awful condition and smelt like a badger. Had had to eat a few stray biscuits and to drink his own urine. Wounds not deep but maggoty. He said that they were all sick of the war and that people in Germany had no idea of the real state of affairs out here – but neither have ours![57]

Captain Arthur Hardwick, 59th Field Ambulance, 19th Division

Few men could endure such horrors without a desperate longing for the normalcy of home. In desperation, men reached to religion and thoughts of their loved ones to comfort them through their ordeal.

The Germans were flinging those awful trench mortars over and causing a terrible lot of damage. I laid down in my dugout and thought of you and Nellie. I prayed to God that I might be spared for it was an awful day. One shell burst over my head causing a dreadful crash, a lot of stuff like cinders and earth fell over me, but still I am thankful to say I am still alive and hope to come out all right.[58]

Private Albert Abrey, 1/23rd Battalion, 142nd Brigade, 47th Division

The miserable month of October had in effect decided the outcome of the Battle of the Somme. The high hopes of a German collapse had dissipated in a quagmire of rain and blood. The threat posed by the British onslaught had been held. And yet the battle still dragged on.

CHAPTER THIRTEEN

Last Shake on the Ancre

By the beginning of November, no one any longer seriously believed that the British Army could ever break the resolve of the German Army in 1916. The Germans had ridden out the storm: battered and torn to be sure, but they *had* survived. Despite the twin horrors of the Somme and Verdun they still had the strength as a nation to ensure that they could endure the tremendous strain of a global war for at least another year. The enforced winter lull would give them time to recover and as such it was also apparent that the British would have little to show for all their Herculean efforts during the pitiless summer and autumn of 1916. Yet the fighting continued as new priorities emerged for the British. Gradually the attitude of the British High Command had changed over the course of the seemingly never-ending month of October. As optimism faded with the pouring rain, Haig, Rawlinson and Gough all found their thoughts turning to the necessity of securing the best possible positions for their winter lines.

The problem was simple. The advance towards the Le Transloy Ridge had left the British lines running along the bottom of a shallow valley overlooked by the Germans. It was obviously not an ideal place to spend what looked like being a long hard winter. If they did not want to stay where they were then the choice was plain: they could either advance and wrest the next ridge from the Germans, or they could effectively fall back, metaphorical tails tucked between their legs, back up on to the Bazentin Ridge, leaving only an easily overrun outpost line in the valley. They would thereby surrender all their painfully won gains of the last month, but could winter in relative comfort.

The changing situation brought on by the failure of the October attacks forced a notable revision in Haig's plans for the next big push. The idea of the Third Army rejoining the fray with a repeat of its early attack on Gommecourt was quietly shelved and it was decided that instead Gough's Fifth Army would attack astride the river Ancre with the assistance of the left of the neighbouring units of the Fourth Army. The bad weather inevitably caused repeated postponements from the original date, which had been pencilled in for 23 October.

By this time Haig himself was aware of a resumption of the rumblings emanating from the Home Front. The Battle of the Somme had been fought for several compelling reasons, prime amongst which was the necessity of playing a serious role within the alliance, while her main partner, France, was under severe pressure. It was also attritional in the sense that any battle or campaign had a 'wearing out' phase after the initial clash of conflict before one side or the other could gain the decisive advantage. The Battle of the Somme was evidently just this phase writ large by the sheer scale of the conflict on the Western Front – the greatest extended battle the world had ever known up to that time. Yet at times, Haig had promised more than that. There had been occasional loose talk of breakthroughs, of throwing back the Germans in confusion. Politicians by their nature need and fixate on quick results, thus, when it became apparent that all the British sacrifice had been made as part of a long grind, they began to rebel and seek alternatives. As the fighting continued into November, officers with influential connections at home began to hear echoes of political skulduggery.

> There is a most persistent talk of intrigues at home to oust Douglas Haig and Lloyd George and Lord F and Winston Churchill are all mentioned as being in it. I suppose if there is any truth in it, it must be because D.H. is too strong a man for them. The successors to D.H. suggested are Ian Hamilton and Gough – two men as poles apart. The story of the latter being a favourite is too comic as I don't think they could ever make him do what they wanted. But one hears whispers such as a useless waste of life in this offensive with nothing to show for it!!! Again I must hope that it is pure gossip, such a thing at this period is unthinkable.[1]
>
> Brigadier Archibald Home, Headquarters, Cavalry Corps

The plotters scurried around, but they would soon discover that the upper echelons of the British Army offered no realistic choice to Haig as commander-in-chief. Only by subverting the British Army to direct French command could they hope to discover a genuine alternative – and as Joffre was even more committed to the Western Front and the concept of the 'wearing out' battle they had nowhere left to go.

While the politicians manoeuvred at home the Fourth and Fifth Armies were finding that their attacks were increasingly floundering in the mud. This was not just the physical problem of getting infantry across the flooded wastelands. The British method of attack had been founded on the pre-eminence of her artillery, but the gunners found that they had 'shot their bolt' as they were slowly overwhelmed by the glutinous mire in which they had to work. It was a near-insuperable problem to sort out the logistics of getting the thousands upon thousands of shells that were needed up to the guns across the flooded maze of shell holes that lay behind the gun lines. The ever-increasing mechanical problems reduced the effectiveness of the massed batteries as gun after gun dropped out with worn barrels or faulty recuperator springs. In the deep mud there was no chance to drag a gun out for repairs and it was almost impossible to get a replacement gun forward.

> Very wet weather still continues and trouble with guns on the soft ground. The three guns do the work of the battery and keep up the fire well. No. 4 out of action owing to glands leaking, so right section did all the firing which was still fairly heavy every day. No. 1 gun was out of action for twelve hours after firing 65 rounds in an hour. No. 4 gun was dismantled and owing to heavy rains the pit again flooded axle deep. Dugouts both at battery and billets falling in and all looked somewhat hopeless in the water and mud.[2]
>
> Second Lieutenant Robert Blackadder, 151st Siege Battery, Royal Garrison Artillery

The performance of the gun batteries was falling away. The conditions simply made good gunnery impossible. Gunnery required precision in all things. A small movement caused by a gun firing from an unstable platform would inevitably mean that the shell would land hundreds or even thousands of yards from its intended target and many more shells than usual would come crashing to earth around the long-suffering heads of the British front-line troops. Of course, the German artillery suffered similar problems, but as they were going backwards across hitherto virgin country and their gun positions and communications had consequently not been flayed by millions of shells over the last three months, they were naturally in a better position. The end result was that although the British artillery was still a massively destructive force, there was a decline in its overall efficiency. As battles are surely fought and won at the margins of endeavour then this represented a significant blow to British hopes.

The great offensive that had begun with such a fanfare all along 25 miles of the Somme front had by this time shrunk to much closer, more limiting horizons. Ceaseless pressure had to be exerted on the Germans and as a result, the hopeless small-scale attacks were still being launched for no more logical reason than to straighten the line or improve a local tactical position. The Battle of the Somme encompasses countless dramatic tales that have a tremendous resonance in particular localities across Britain and the empire. The loss of so many men struck home not only to mothers, fathers, wives and sweethearts, but it also cast a longer shadow over the whole community. For the people of County Durham, the fighting that raged over the Butte de Warlencourt in early November 1916 affected the lives of thousands who have never consciously heard of it. The Butte, an ancient burial mound from a prehistoric era, had an appropriately sinister appearance. About 50 feet high it stood out from the man-made swamp that surrounded it as a battered mass of muddy white chalk on a low ridge, and as such in theory it provided useful observation for the Germans towards High Wood and Martinpuich. The Butte was honeycombed with tunnels and dugouts, which provided shelter for the bulk of the German garrison. They had already resisted numerous British attacks over the last month.

Now it was the turn of the 151st (Durham) Brigade who moved into the line as part of the 50th (Northumbrian) Division on 3 November. Even that simple-sounding manoeuvre was no easy task. The communications trenches that meandered across the shell-blasted landscape were full of glutinous, thigh-deep mud that could exhaust a man beyond reason. The tired men of the 1/9th, 1/6th and 1/8th Durhams took over the front-line positions, while the 1/5th Border Regiment came up behind them as the reserve battalion. In view of the atrocious conditions Brigadier General B. G. Price decided to hold his brigade frontage with just one company of

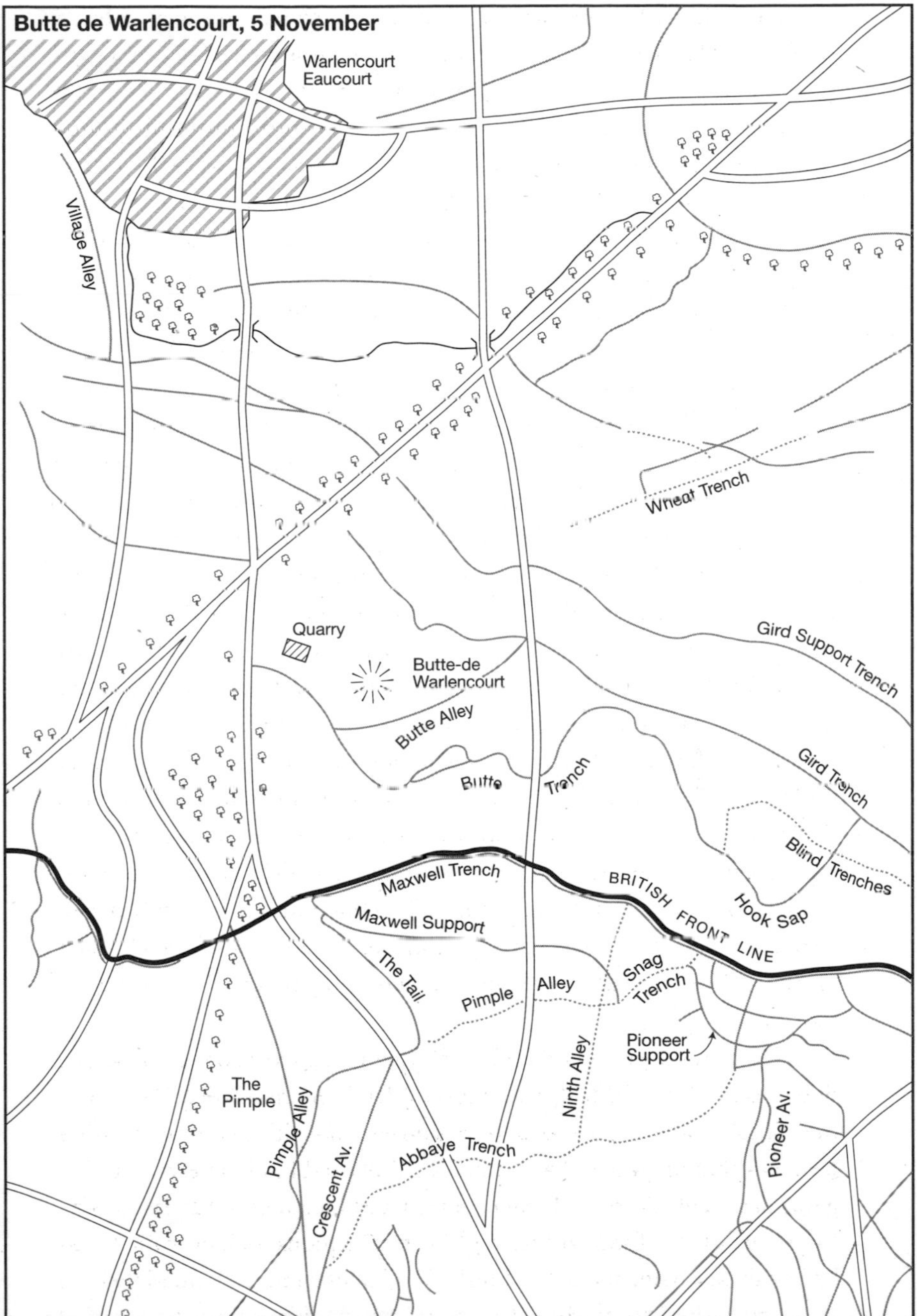

Butte de Warlencourt, 5 November
Warlencourt Eaucourt
Village Alley
Wheat Trench
Quarry
Butte-de Warlencourt
Gird Support Trench
Butte Alley
Gird Trench
Butte Trench
Blind Trenches
Maxwell Trench
BRITISH FRONT LINE
Hook Sap
Maxwell Support
The Tail
Snag Trench
Pimple Alley
Pioneer Support
Ninth Alley
The Pimple
Pimple Alley
Crescent Av.
Abbaye Trench
Pioneer Av.

each of the Durham battalions. On the left were the 1/9th Durham Light Infantry – the 'Gateshead Ghurkhas' as they optimistically hoped they would be known to posterity – who were under the command of a truly remarkable young man, Lieutenant Colonel Roland Bradford. Although just 24 years old, this naturally brilliant soldier had already demonstrated a combination of considerable administrative abilities and tactical skills of the highest order, all underpinned by a raw courage that inspired all who met him. In the centre were the 1/6th Durhams, a battalion recruited mainly in Bishop Auckland and the upper valley of the river Wear, who to the rest of the Durham Light Infantry were cheerily known as the 'black-buttoned bastards'. On the right of the brigade front were the 1/8th Durhams. Together they were to attack the Butte on 5 November 1916.

The German guns never seemed to stop and the weather was truly awful. The all-important artillery support was ready, but there was no real confidence amongst the gunners that they could deliver the barrage needed for such a desperate enterprise.

> The attack is fixed for tomorrow, in spite of the weather. It seems rather hopeless expecting infantry to attack with any success in this mud. The trench mortars have only their muzzles showing above it. Yesterday we had two barrages by brigades. They seemed fairly good; but I should like more guns. To be effective, a barrage should be an 18-pounder to every 7 yards of enemy front, and the guns should be capable of firing 4 rounds a minute, at least to start with, without the recuperator springs giving out.[3]
>
> Brigadier General Hugh Tudor, Commander Royal Artillery, 9th Division

The 1/9th Durhams were charged with capturing the Butte and a quarry beside its west face. Meanwhile, the 1/6th and 1/8th Durhams were to seize the Gird Trench and Gird Support Trenches. The 1/6th and 1/4th Northumberland Fusiliers were in support on the left and right respectively, while the 1/5th Border Regiment stood ready in reserve. Zero Hour was set for 0910 on 5 November.

> Time passed on leaden wings up to the Zero Hour. The Lewis gunners and bombers were heavily laden with their extra ammunition but calmly awaited the time for action. Rain fell during the whole time and early on the morning of Sunday Nov. 5th 1916 the companies in close support moved forward to man the front-line trench. The distance

> between the close support was not great, but owing to the boggy ground progress was dreadfully slow. I was a lance corporal in X Company in command of two Lewis gun sections composed of seven men per section carrying gun, spare parts and old-fashioned panniers holding four magazines each. Lieutenant Ludgate was acting-captain in command of my company. Owing to the slow progress of the troops it was daylight when we reached the front-line trench to be greeted by the gallant W Company. The trench was in such a deplorable state that we marched along the parados in order to reach our places quicker. As we were in full view of the enemy he met us with a terrible hail of shell, machine guns and rifle fire, and we were glad to take advantage of the slimy trench and reach our places as best we could.[4]
>
> Lance Corporal Harry Cruddace, 1/6th Battalion, Durham Light Infantry, 151st Brigade, 50th Division

Corporal Cruddace found himself acting as the link with the neighbouring 1/8th Durhams to his immediate right. That night was hell: heavy rain, a howling gale, there were rumours circulating that men had drowned in the mud and it was bitterly cold. Worst of all they had a good idea of what lay ahead of them in the morning.

> Every man then looking to the loading of his rifle and the fixing of his bayonet as the Zero Hour was almost upon us. Serious men gazed eagerly into one another's faces and some muttered thoughts of God and their loved ones at home. Chums clasped hands and said, Cheerio! not knowing what the day had in store for them. Officers were in eager conversation with the senior NCOs regarding the readiness of the men. The enemy kept up a ceaseless bombardment of our trenches in conjunction with the merciless rain and cold.[5]
>
> Lance Corporal Harry Cruddace, 1/6th Battalion, Durham Light Infantry, 151st Brigade, 50th Division

As Zero Hour struck, all the available guns in the area laid down a barrage some 200 yards in front of the jumping-off line.

> Nothing but HE was used. We began with a stationary barrage of four minutes whilst the infantry were getting out of their trenches and thereafter the creeping barrage was lifted in range 50 yards every minute and firing continued at the rate of 4 rounds per minute.[6]
>
> Brigadier General Hugh Tudor, Commander Royal Artillery, 9th Division

As the moment came, the Durhams went over the top on their modern day 'forlorn hope'. With mud high above their knees, wading, slipping, stumbling and falling forward, laden as they were with the usual infantry equipment necessary in an attack: rifle, packs, grenades, entrenching tool, pick, Lewis gun drums – it was worse than they could have ever imagined.

> At last the Zero Hour arrived and the officers' whistles sounded the advance. Immediately the first wave mounted the trench and made off in the direction of the enemy trenches. They were met by terrific and annihilating fire and crumpled up like snow in summer. The second wave was by this time on its way. I was in that wave and placed my gun sections in single file to make a less target. The enemy barrage was doing enormous damage and our fighting strength was fast diminishing.[7]
>
> Lance Corporal Harry Cruddace, 1/6th Battalion, Durham Light Infantry, 151st Brigade, 50th Division

Whatever the hopes, the Germans were clearly not caught by surprise and on such a narrow-front attack they were able to concentrate a devastating machine-gun fire from all around on to the hapless Durhams and the Australian brigade that was also advancing alongside them, immediately to the south. It was also apparent that the British artillery had by no means succeeded in eliminating the German batteries designated to fire in support of the Warlencourt sector. Inevitably, the German guns opened up with a roar and splattered a barrage of shells all along the threatened sector. The Germans were deliberately isolating the British front line in an attempt to cut off the assaulting troops from any reserves that were intended to continue the assault or consolidate any gains. That impenetrable wall of bursting shells meant that the Durhams would have to fight the battle on their own.

On the right the 1/8th Durhams were badly hit by a combination of both German shell fire and British shells dropping short. Even the long-distance, indirect machine gun barrage that was meant to be supporting them was inaccurately ranged and their parapet was laced with machine-gun bullets from behind. Many of the men could barely get out of the trenches because of the mud and individuals were forced to help each other out – all under heavy fire. Although, with exemplary heroism, the left of their line managed to get within 30 yards of the Butte the fire eventually overwhelmed the Durhams and the few survivors fell back in disarray to their original front line. The wounded were left scattered around No Man's Land, marooned in shell holes and slowly sinking down. Many who were too weak to save themselves must have slowly drowned – an awful death.

Meanwhile, the 'black-buttoned bastards' of the 1/6th Durhams were dying one by one as they found themselves marooned between the lines.

> By this time the whole line was held up and Lieutenant Ludgate ordered me to proceed and engage the enemy machine guns, a task almost impossible. Out of my two sections of fourteen men there were two of us left – a No. 1 on the gun by the name of Private Allen and myself. I pushed on with one gun and a quantity of ammunition to about 30 yards from the German trench and took up a position in a shell hole. We opened fire on the opposing troops who formed an excellent target. In taking up my position, in the excitement I placed myself on the right side of the gun instead of on the left, which was fortunate for me. After firing one or two magazines, the enemy found us with a machine gun and succeeded in wounding my No. 1 in four places down his left side. Thinking him dead, I pushed him aside and carried on until want of ammunition forced me to withdraw to our troops in the rear. I took back my gun and spare parts, and came in contact with an officer of another company, to whom I made my report. A few minutes later I saw my No. 1, who was out in front lifting an arm in an appealing manner, and I knew he whom I had thought dead was still alive. I immediately ran out in a zig-zag method and brought him back to the shelter of the shell hole we were then manning. After tending to his wounds we set about organising and consolidating in preparation for a counter-attack from the enemy.[8]
>
> Lance Corporal Harry Cruddace, 1/6th Battalion, Durham Light Infantry, 151st Brigade, 50th Division

The only success came on the left where the 1/9th Durhams who directly faced the Butte de Warlencourt, advanced with considerable success, under the influence of the dashing young Lieutenant Colonel Roland Bradford. Why they should have succeeded is unclear – perhaps it was just a fluke and the Germans here had simply sunk into a fatal lethargy dragged down by the dreadful conditions. Whatever the reason, the 1/9th

Durhams broke through to sweep up and over the Butte. The watchers crouched in the British line even caught a glimpse of one man caught in dramatic silhouette as he paused for a moment on the very peak of the Butte, some even said he waved, before plunging on down the other side. By 1000 such men had grabbed most of the low mound and the surrounding trenches.

> Four posts were established in the Gird front line, the left one being on the Albert–Bapaume Road. There were four posts between the Butte and the Gird front line. The front edge of the Quarry was strongly held and two company headquarters were situated in the Quarry in telephonic communication with battalion headquarters. Each of the assaulting platoons had a reserve platoon in Butte Alley, the trench running immediately south of the Butte. Two machine guns were sited in Butte Alley and a 2-in Stokes Mortar in the Quarry. Two battalion observers were on the Butte. The reserve company of the battalion was in Maxwell Trench. Eight Bavarian prisoners had been sent back to battalion headquarters. Some other prisoners who were on their way back had together with their escorts been annihilated by the German artillery fire. The Germans were still holding a dugout on the north-east side of the Butte. The parties who should have 'mopped up' the Butte dugouts had either gone forward without completing their work, carried away in the enthusiasm of the assault, or had been shot by German snipers while at their work.[9]
>
> Lieutenant Colonel Roland Bradford, 1/9th Battalion, Durham Light Infantry, 151st Brigade, 50th Division

With the wall of shells falling behind them and an awareness burning within them that the German reserves would be making their way forward they knew they had to consolidate as fast as possible.

> The ground had been so pulverised by our bombardments and was so muddy that it was not possible to do much in the way of consolidation. But the men were ready with their rifles.[10]
>
> Lieutenant Colonel Roland Bradford, 1/9th Battalion, Durham Light Infantry, 151st Brigade, 50th Division

In the event it proved that the failure to complete the 'mopping up' was crucial. It was soon apparent that over a hundred German soldiers were lurking in the dark warren of dugouts and tunnels beneath and around the Butte. A murderous game of chance began to be played out with bomb and bayonet, with little or no quarter on either side.

> The Germans in the dugout on the north-east edge of the Butte had brought a machine gun into position and were worrying us from behind. Many gallant attempts were made throughout the day to capture this dugout but without success. All our parties who tried to rush it were destroyed by the German machine-gun fire from the direction of Hook Sap and by the fire of the large number of snipers in Warlencourt. However, a party did succeed in throwing some Mills grenades into the dugout and this made the Boches more cautious.[11]
>
> Lieutenant Colonel Roland Bradford, 1/9th Battalion, Durham Light Infantry, 151st Brigade, 50th Division

The first German local counter-attack was launched at about 1200 and this began a series of harassing bombing attacks, all of which were only repulsed after hard fighting. Over the afternoon the Germans were heavily reinforced and their counter-attacks began to hammer home with a real menace. The 1/9th Durhams were entirely cut off from any reinforcement by the German artillery and well-directed machine guns and as their numbers dwindled they were forced gradually back. At 1530 they held a line that stretched round the north of the Quarry to Butte Alley, south of the Butte, and then by shell hole positions to where the1/6th Battalion had its block. At 1700, Colonel Bradford sent one of a series of messages back to his brigade headquarters.

> We have been driven out of the Gird front line and I believe my posts there were captured, and have tried to get back but the enemy is in considerable force and is still counter-attacking. It is taking me all my time to hold Butte Alley. Please ask artillery to shell area north of Bapaume road, as Germans are in considerable force there. Enemy is holding Gird front line strongly on my right and in my opinion a strong advance to the right of the Butte would meet with success. I have a small post in a shell hole at the north-western corner of the Butte, but the enemy still has a post on the Butte on the north side. I am just going to make another attempt to capture this post.[12]
>
> Lieutenant Colonel Roland Bradford, 1/9th Battalion, Durham Light Infantry, 151st Brigade, 50th Division

In between the cool situation reports were interspersed periods of desperate hand-to-hand fighting, the impact of which the dry language of his laconic reports cannot possibly convey.

> We are holding Butte Alley. We have a post on the north side of the Butte. The enemy still has a post on the northern slope of Butte, but I am hoping to scupper this. I am now endeavouring to establish posts in the Gird front line. Germans are still attacking and a good deal of hand-to-hand fighting is taking place. We killed large numbers of enemy on the Butte and in the Quarry and, owing to heavy fire could not take so many prisoners as we might otherwise. If another battalion were attached to me I could probably take the Gird front line. The work on the communication trench to Butte is progressing.[13]
>
> Lieutenant Colonel Roland Bradford, 1/9th Battalion, Durham Light Infantry, 151st Brigade, 50th Division

Despite the desperate need for urgent reinforcements the sustained German barrage crashing down behind them on the communications trenches and rear areas would have destroyed any that tried to get forward in a gesture that could only have added to the casualty figures. The 1/9th Durhams would have to fight on alone supported only by a few machine-gun teams from the 151st Machine Gun Company.

> About 6 p.m. the Germans made a determined counter-attack preceded by a terrific bombardment and were able to get to close quarters. A tough struggle ensued. But our men who had now been reinforced by the reserve company and who showed the traditional superiority of the British in hand-to-hand fighting, succeeded in driving out the enemy. The 9th DLI was getting weak, but it was hoped that the Boche had now made his last counter-attack for that day.[14]
>
> Lieutenant Colonel Roland Bradford, 1/9th Battalion, Durham Light Infantry, 151st Brigade, 50th Division

Unfortunately, just as Bradford thought they were weakening, the Germans received yet more reinforcements and their attacks took on a new and deadly lease of life. The showers of bombs and the desperate bayonet charges bit deep. The exhausted Durhams had been fighting all day with no respite. As the Germans pressed forward, retreat had become inevitable. One by one the precious morning gains were surrendered back to the Germans.

> At about 11 p.m. battalions of the Prussians delivered a fresh counter-attack. They came in great force from our front and also worked round from both flanks. Our men were overwhelmed. Many died fighting, others were compelled to surrender. It was only a handful of men who found their way back to Maxwell Trench and they were completely exhausted by their great efforts and the strain of the fighting.[15]
>
> Lieutenant Colonel Roland Bradford, 1/9th Battalion, Durham Light Infantry, 151st Brigade, 50th Division

Eventually the survivors fell right back across No Man's Land and the hard-pressing Germans were soon threatening even the jumping-off positions in the British front line. Back in the front line the Durhams rejoined their comrades of the 1/6th and 1/8th Battalion, who had fallen back hours before.

> The brigade position now ran in an irregular line, but despite extremely heavy casualties we held on. As night drew in we were made stronger by our comrades from W Company in linking up and gathering the Lewis guns from the men who had fallen. The expected happened and the enemy counter-attacked under cover of darkness, but we staved off the assault at a great price. Despite our weakened condition we held on till the night of 6th November.[16]
>
> Lance Corporal Harry Cruddace, 1/6th Battalion, Durham Light Infantry, 151st Brigade, 50th Division

After hard fighting the Germans were held back and so, after a day of drama and death that brought misery to countless Durham homes, the situation was exactly as it had been before they started. On the evening of 6 November, they were relieved by the 1/5th Durhams who formed part of the 150th Brigade.

> It was a very rotten job. Approaches to the line were completely water-logged, and one was continually meeting stretcher parties and walking wounded which made going up a very slow and tedious business. C and D Companies, taking over the front line, experienced a heavy barrage after passing the Pimple. This barrage set on fire an ammunition dump near company headquarters and we thought that another

> Boche attack was coming. However, some of us went ahead and found things all right, and after what seemed an awful long time we were able to send 'relief complete' to battalion headquarters.[17]
>
> Lieutenant Herbert Green, 1/5th Battalion, Durham Light Infantry, 150th Brigade, 50th Division

The signs of battle were all around them. This was the battlefield as a flooded charnel house. Bodies were everywhere. Some were 'fresh meat', many others were definitely not.

> Snag Trench was full of mud and water with bodies sticking out all along. It is in fact no exaggeration when I say that in our part we had to tread from body to body to get past. Dead from all regiments were there, including our division, South Africans, and Jocks of the 9th Division, and hands, arms and legs were sticking out of parados and parapet where the dead had been hastily buried.[18]
>
> Lieutenant Cuthbert Marley, 1/5th Battalion, Durham Light Infantry, 150th Brigade, 50th Division

The front was in a state of complete confusion with stragglers coming in and several wounded soldiers still trapped out in No Man's Land.

> But all that night, whilst trying to reorganise and make a fairly continuous front line, one came across isolated posts of the outgoing battalions who knew nothing of the relief. No Man's Land was an equally weird sight. Patrols came across wounded men and men just sitting there exhausted and unable to move.[19]
>
> Lieutenant Herbert Green, 1/5th Battalion, Durham Light Infantry, 150th Brigade, 50th Division

Surrounded by corpses and shattered bodies, enduring the relentless pouring rain and the cold that froze them to the very marrow – it seemed nothing could make the situation worse. But it could ....

> The last straw was when one of the company commanders gallantly arrived at the posts with the rum jar – imagine everyone's horror when he 'dished' it out and the first man who tasted it said it was whale oil.[20]
>
> Lieutenant Herbert Green, 1/5th Battalion, Durham Light Infantry, 150th Brigade, 50th Division

The casualties of this 'insignificant' action are difficult to determine, but each and every one caused pain somewhere. It has been estimated that the 1/6th Durhams lost 11 officers killed, wounded or missing, with 34 other ranks dead, 114 wounded and 111 missing – which, of course, usually meant dead. The 1/8th Durhams lost 9 officers killed, wounded or missing, 38 other ranks dead, 100 wounded and 83 missing. Worst of all the 1/9th Durhams paid the full penalty for 'success' losing 17 officers killed, wounded or missing, 30 other ranks dead, 250 wounded and 111 missing presumed dead. The 151st Machine Gun Company who accompanied them lost 3 dead, 20 wounded and 8 missing. The dreadful total for the 151st Brigade was nearly 1,000 casualties. So why in the end had the Durhams failed? Lieutenant Colonel Roland Bradford was emphatically not a man to pull his punches. His views were made characteristically plain.

> There were many reasons why the 9th DLI was unable to hold its ground. The failure of the troops on the right to reach their objectives and the fact that the division on our left was not attacking caused both flanks of the battalion to be in the air. The positions to be held were very much exposed and the Germans could see all our trenches and control their fire accordingly. It was a local attack and the enemy was able to concentrate his guns on to a small portion of our line. The ground was a sea of mud and it was almost impossible to consolidate our posts. The terribly intense German barrages and the difficult nature of the ground prevented reinforcements from being sent up to help the 9th DLI. Four hundred yards north of the Butte the enemy had a steep bank behind which they were able to assemble without being molested. The terrain was very favourable to a German counter-attack.[21]
>
> Lieutenant Colonel Roland Bradford, 1/9th Battalion, Durham Light Infantry, 151st Brigade, 50th Division

It was Bradford's contention that it was not so much that they had failed, as that the task had been impossible for an isolated battalion within a narrow-front attack against superior forces. After the battle Bradford looked back to see if he could make sense of it all, of why so many lives had been sacrificed in vain.

> On looking back at the attack of the 5th of November it seems that the results which would have been gained in the event of success were of doubtful value, and would hardly have been worth the loss which we

would suffer. It would have been awkward for us to hold the objectives which would have been badly sited for our defence. The possession of the Butte by the Germans was not an asset to them. From our existing trenches we were able to prevent them from using it as an observation point. The Butte would have been of little use to us for purposes of observation. But the Butte de Warlencourt had become an obsession. Everybody wanted it. It loomed large in the minds of the soldiers in the forward area and they attributed many of their misfortunes to it. The newspaper correspondents talked about 'that Miniature Gibraltar'. So it had to be taken. It seems that the attack was one of those tempting, and unfortunately at one period frequent, local operations which are so costly and which are rarely worthwhile. But perhaps that is only the narrow view of the regimental officer.[22]

Lieutenant Colonel Roland Bradford, 1/9th Battalion, Durham Light Infantry, 151st Brigade, 50th Division

He would receive some personal compensation for his disappointment shortly afterwards when he was awarded a Victoria Cross for his earlier exceptional courage and leadership during an attack in October. Promoted to brigadier, one of the youngest ever in the British Army, he did not live long to enjoy his new rank as he was killed in 1917. He was just 25 when he died.

Actions like the attack of the 151st Brigade on the Butte de Warlencourt on 5 November had no real importance within the context of the huge Somme offensive. However, they surely contained a seed of truth within them – this kind of attack was achieving nothing but swollen casualty lists.

However unpleasant it is to think about, there is one thing that is certain and that is that Napoleon's 'fifth element' viz: 'mud' is now victorious and that we shall have to go into winter quarters. By that I don't mean that we are to sit down and do nothing, but that an offensive on a large scale is out of the question. It is now a great labour to get supplies up to the men in the front trenches, to say nothing of the ammunition for the guns. Guns cannot be moved at all. Men fall into shell holes full of liquid mud and are drowned. Horses stick in the mud and have to be shot. As regards the wounded, it is terrible. They cannot be got back by day in some places and so their sufferings are increased many times. People can have no conception of what

> this warfare means. We shall win through however in time and this is the one consolation.[23]
>
> Brigadier Archibald Home, Headquarters, Cavalry Corps

Any change in tactics would be too late for the gallant Durhams. Their wooden commemorative crosses afterwards marked the top of the Butte de Warlencourt, but the choice of the words used may not readily be seen as appropriate; *'Dulce et decorum est pro patria mori.'* After all the horrors and the countless disillusionments of the Somme, it seems that with unintended irony the dead of the Durham Light Infantry were to be considered as an advertisement for the glories of war.

WHILE MEN DIED in futile local attacks the main offensive remained stalled by the weather. Every time a new date was set the resumption of rain forced a rethink and the date slipped well into November. Haig was worried by the ever-deteriorating ground conditions and he decreed that Gough's main attack should not be launched until the ground was dry enough to let the infantry advance with relative freedom of movement, thereby, of course, enabling them to keep pace with the all-important creeping barrage. Not only that, but the weather forecast must also hold the reasonable prospect of fine weather for the two days following the assault. Finally, after a meeting with Haig's Chief of Staff Lieutenant General Launcelot Kiggell and a conference with his corps commanders on 8 November, Gough took the plunge and provisionally scheduled the attack for 13 November – with the proviso that no more heavy rain fell in the interim. During this period Gough was under considerable pressure of the 'damned if you do and damned if you don't' persuasion. Haig was urging Gough forward by pointing out the huge benefits of ending the Somme operations with a crowning success, but at the same time he warned of the serious consequences of failure.

> I rode to Toutencourt and saw General Gough. He had been round all the divisions and most of the brigades detailed for the attack. Their commanders all now thought that we had a fair chance of success. He himself recommended that the attack should go on. I told him that a success at this time was much wanted – firstly, on account of the situation in Romania, we must prevent the enemy from withdrawing

> any divisions from France to that theatre. Next the feeling in Russia is not favourable either to the French or to ourselves. We are thought to be accomplishing little. The German party in Russia spreads these reports. Lastly on account of the Chantilly Conference which meets on Wednesday. The British position will doubtless be much stronger (as memories are short!) if I could appear there on the top of the capture of Beaumont Hamel for instance, and 3,000 German prisoners. It would show, too, that we had no intention of ceasing to press the enemy on the Somme. But the necessity for a success must not blind our eyes to the difficulties of ground and weather. Nothing is so costly as a failure! But I am ready to run reasonable risks. I then discussed with Gough what these risks were, and why he thought our chances of success were good. Finally, I decided that the Fifth Army should attack tomorrow.[24]
>
> General Sir Douglas Haig, General Headquarters, British Expeditionary Force

So it was that after two relatively dry days, Gough fixed the time of the attack for 0545 on 13 November. The II Corps, under the command of Lieutenant General C. W. Jacob, was to drive forward from the Schwaben Redoubt attacking north towards St Pierre Divion and thereby to clear the south bank of the river Ancre. The V Corps (3rd, 2nd, 51st and 63rd Divisions), commanded by Lieutenant General E. A. Fanshawe, was to attack along the front from Serre to Beaucourt north of the river Ancre where it would establish a common front line with the II Corps. This seemed an awesomely difficult proposition. They were facing the very defences that had withstood all that could be thrown at them on 1 July.

How had the situation changed? What hope could they have of success at this late date in the campaign? There was, in truth, a certain amount of the usual optimism in the preconceptions of Gough and his commanders. It was assumed that the Germans, battered by their collective experiences on the Somme over the last five months, would not be capable of mounting a stern resistance. The artillery barrage would encompass all that had been so painfully learnt with the creeping barrage and counter-battery arrangements at the centre of British plans. In addition, assiduous sapping had drastically narrowed the width of No Man's Land while the Royal Engineers had revisited their old haunts opposite Beaumont Hamel

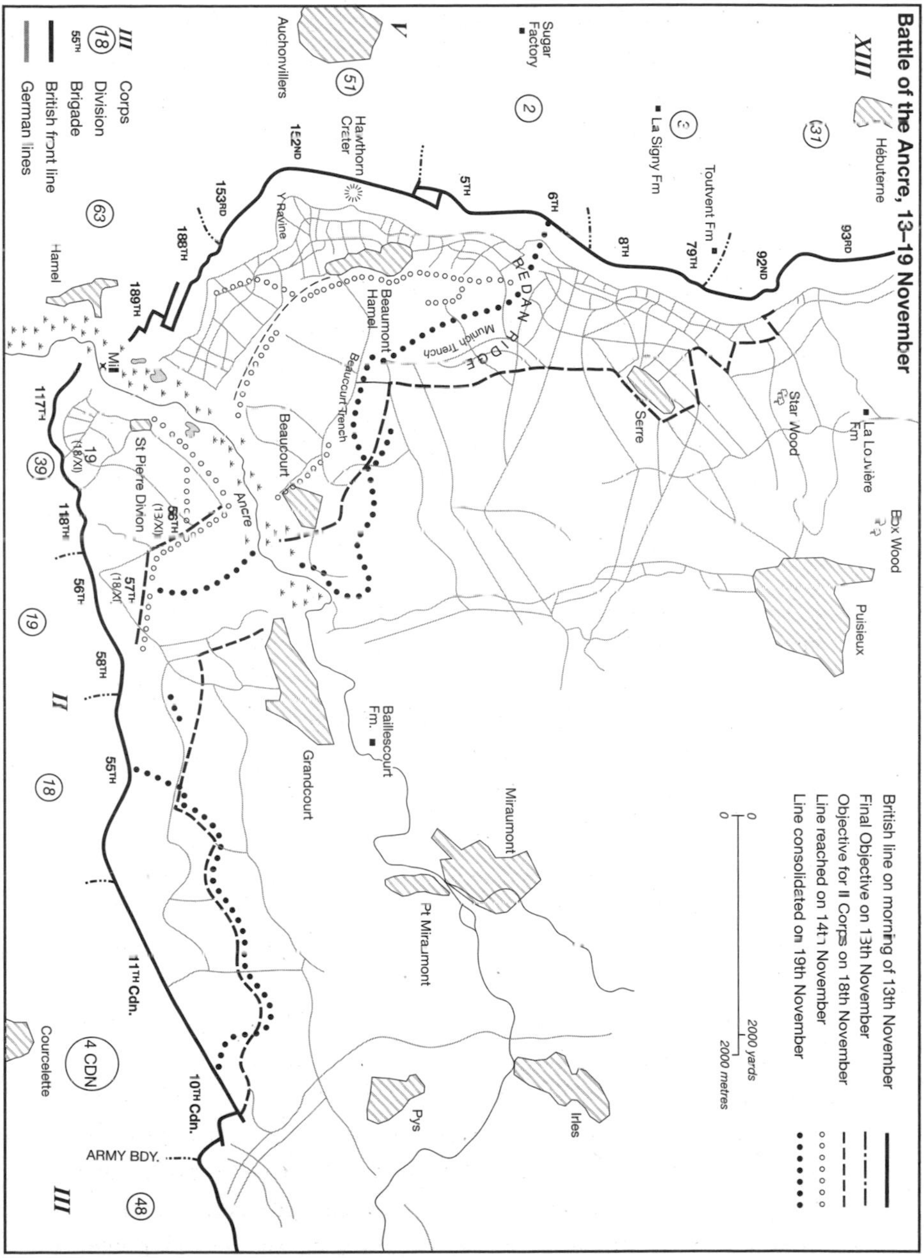

Battle of the Ancre, 13–19 November
British line on morning of 13th November
Final Objective on 13th November
Objective for II Corps on 18th November
Line reached on 14th November
Line consolidated on 19th November
0
2000 yards
0
2000 metres
III
Corps
18
Division
55TH
Brigade
British front line
German lines
XIII
V
II
III
Hébuterne
Toutvent Fm
La Signy Fm
Sugar Factory
Auchonvillers
Hawthorn Crater
Y Ravine
Hamel
Mill
Serre
Star Wood
La Louvière Fm
Box Wood
Puisieux
REDAN RIDGE
Munich Trench
Beaumont Hamel
Beaucourt Trench
Beaucourt
Ancre
St Pierre Divion
Grandcourt
Baillescourt Fm.
Miraumont
Pt Miraumont
Irles
Pys
Courcelette
93RD
92ND
79TH
8TH
6TH
5TH
152ND
153RD
188TH
189TH
117TH
118TH
56TH
58TH
55TH
11TH Cdn.
10TH Cdn.
19 (18/XI)
56TH (13/XI)
57TH (18/XI)
31
3
2
51
63
39
19
18
4 CDN
48
ARMY BDY.

and Serre. New mines were driven out to the old mine crater on Hawthorn Ridge while the Russian saps across No Man's Land were rebored and once again ready for use. This time all would be well ....

The divisions designated for the attack prepared themselves as best they could for the task in hand. When units arrived on the Somme front late on in the campaign, it was as if they were coming to a strange new world. For the 63rd (Royal Naval) Division, which really was fresh from the very different horrors of Gallipoli, this change was even more marked, and there was a prolonged period of acclimatisation before it was considered ready to be properly deployed in action. The veterans of the war against Turkey were stunned at the relative largesse encountered as they entered the war on the decisive front as opposed to their previous sideshow.

> Then came the first revelation of what had been going on while we were starving in Gallipoli. We had come to a land of plenty. From tip to toe we were re-equipped; new transport, new machine guns, new rifles, new uniforms, new generals. At Gallipoli we had made our own bombs out of jam tins; in France we were given whole cases of new and deadly bombs, not more than 10 per cent defective, to play with. France was not the East – we were told proudly, and again and again. Everything had to be done properly or not at all. No hurried rush to the line, but a steady progress of training behind the lines, with courses for officers and instructional visits to the line. Then, in due course, we might be allowed to hold a small piece of the line of our own. But only if we were very, very good.[25]
>
> Captain Douglas Jerrold, Hawke Battalion, 189th Brigade, 63rd (Royal Naval) Division

The madness of the Somme had crept up on the men serving there month in and month out. The incremental developments of total war in its rawest form had slowly changed their views of what was normal or acceptable. The newcomers looked on the battlefield with baffled amazement.

> The Somme area was a God-forsaken battleground created by earnest staff officers now slightly hysterical about their still incomplete labours. An atmosphere of over-elaborated brusque inefficiency pervaded the hinterland of slaughter. Too many men, too many officers, far too many generals, and a thousand times too many jacks-in-office, railway

> transport officers, town majors, assistant provost marshals, traffic control officers, laundry officers, liaison officers, railway experts and endless seas of mud. And no more *estaminets*. This was war.[26]
>
> Captain Douglas Jerrold, Hawke Battalion, 189th Brigade, 63rd (Royal Naval) Division

When its original divisional commander was wounded the 63rd (Royal Naval) Division was given a new man rooted in this strange new world. It is fair to say that Major General Cameron Shute did not make a good impression with his new charges. There was an immediate cultural clash between what he, as a long-standing regular soldier considered acceptable, and the distinctly slapdash naval traditions of the Royal Naval Division. Shute had never been a man to suffer fools gladly and certainly never courted popularity, as his officers in his previous command of the 59th Brigade in the 20th (Light) Division could easily testify.

> Shute was another of those men who had the misfortune to soldier in the wrong sort of army. Had he been a German or Frenchmen he might have become Commander-in-Chief, whereas it was only his indomitable tenacity coupled with unquestionable military ability, which enabled him with difficulty to overcome unpopularity. What a strange man he was; brutal and merciless with fools, he rarely allowed merit to pass without praise or reward. Always sure of himself, knowing exactly what was wanted, he was never at a loss for a decision even in the moments of the greatest stress. One felt that as long as the brigade was in his hands no harm would come to it. It is a pity we do not have more generals like him.[27]
>
> Lieutenant Colonel Ronald Bodley, 10th Battalion, Rifle Brigade, 59th Brigade, 20th Division

The Royal Naval Division had originally been formed from naval reservists by the First Lord of the Admiralty Winston Churchill in 1914. Although most of the original reservist sea-dogs had long since departed, eroded away by the severe casualties in Gallipoli and the inevitable recalls to sea service, they still affected a large number of nautical habits in a manner guaranteed to infuriate any 'landlubber'. It was a situation that might have been designed to irritate the choleric Shute, who considered them not only pretentious but also dangerously inefficient and in this he may well have been right. Although it had lost many of its 'glitterati' in the Dardanelles, the RND still had several louche young officers who regarded themselves as the cultural elite of their generation. Captain Douglas Jerrold, the adjutant of the Hawke Battalion, was one such literary gentleman, with his allegiances tending to the New Georgian School. There was also the wonderful light poet and all-round intellectual Captain A. P. Herbert, and the insouciant figure of Captain George Peckham, who seems to have specialised in 'winding up' those in authority to deadly effect. Peckham was a man who truly deserves to be remembered by posterity.

> I was standing in a communication trench talking to George Peckham about everything in the world except the war, when we were surprised by the general's arrival. Foolishly, we were standing in a blind corner and there was no avenue of escape. A rain of questions descended, which we were fortunately able to answer, and all seemed to be going well. Alas, the general had a habit when standing still of striking the ground rather forcibly with the point of his walking stick. Our trenches were innocent of duckboards and more than ankle-deep in mud. The general's stick went in deeper and deeper, till suddenly it struck something hard. Instantly there was an ominous bristling. After much kicking and scraping a perfectly good box of small-arms ammunition was revealed. 'Ammunition boxes lining the communications trenches,' the general exclaimed, drafting out loud another report to corps headquarters on the iniquities of the Navy. 'Good God, Sir,' cried George Peckham, with a credible imitation of pietistic, but tolerant horror, 'I believe you're right!' He stood looking at the general, who was now quite white with rage, as if he were a lunatic to be humoured and then, on some pretext or other, shown off the premises. 'And you were deliberately standing there trying to conceal it from me. It's a damned disgrace!' 'Good God, Sir,' says George with a broad smile, 'If I'd known you were coming, this is the last place on earth where I should have been standing!'[28]
>
> Captain Douglas Jerrold, Hawke Battalion, 189th Brigade, 63rd (Royal Naval) Division

Major General Shute was not to be deflected by such insults. When it eventually emerged that the entire communication trench was paved with ammunition boxes he was almost incandescent with fury. In Captain

Jerrold's considered view the boxes *must* have been dumped by some Army working party. The row that ensued went on for some time. Shute made an only slightly better impression on the men of the Hood Battalion when he inspected them.

> It was still raining, raining like hell, wet through. The whole battalion were on parade, all there, and Major General Shute inspected us. He starts off, the usual stunt, you know, 'Blah, Blah, Blah!' What wonderful men we had both on Gallipoli and in France, he'd done this and done that, he was reliable. He says that the place we were going to attack now was one of the most formidable parts of the firing line of the whole of the Western Front, the Germans had been there umpteen months, we know it was all honeycombed with dugouts, we know this, we know that, we've had five different attempts – but we must get that ridge at all costs – because if we don't get that the whole of the advance on the Somme further down towards Bapaume and Pozières would be in danger of being encircled like a pincer movement. He said, 'I'm going to tell you this much, you know what you have got to do, the more prisoners you take, the less food you'll get, because we have to feed them out of your rations!' Now that's honest God's truth! That's General Shute's instructions to us.[29]
>
> Ordinary Seaman Joe Murray, Hood Battalion, 189th Brigade, 63rd (Royal Naval) Division

The men of the Hawke Battalion were treated to much the same kind of harangue during their inspection by Shute. Captain Jerrold still remained resolutely unimpressed.

> Shute came to inspect us. He wished us luck and told us no prisoners were required. I am afraid we were not amused. After Shute, Sir Douglas Haig. This, of course was our death warrant; only those about to die salute the commander-in-chief.[30]
>
> Captain Douglas Jerrold, Hawke Battalion, 189th Brigade, 63rd (Royal Naval) Division

The Hawke Battalion had been carefully drawn up in companies for the inspection but the men were surprised by the amount of interest that Haig took in them. They may have been unaware of Haig's strong suspicion over the quality of the divisions that had served at Gallipoli.

> Sir Douglas Haig made no speeches, but talked to all the officers and to most of the NCOs, and forbore from all comment when George Peckham, who had been summoned at the eleventh hour from the *estaminet*, burst through a hedge to find the inspection of his company actually in progress. George proceeded to explain, after being introduced, that he was a Marine, the implication presumably being that he had only just returned from a long sea voyage and that nothing but wind and tide had made him late.[31]
>
> Captain Douglas Jerrold, Hawke Battalion, 189th Brigade, 63rd (Royal Naval) Division

As the relationship between the officers of the RND and their grim general simmered nicely to the boil, Captain A. P. Herbert finally hit back hard with his weapon of choice – the pen – in a devastating broadside of doggerel aimed right over the head of Major General Cameron Shute.

> The General inspecting the trenches
> Exclaimed with a horrified shout
> 'I refuse to command a Division
> Which leaves its excreta about'
>
> But nobody took any notice
> No one was prepared to refute
> That the presence of shit was congenial
> Compared with the presence of Shute
>
> And certain responsible critics
> Made haste to respond to his words
> Observing that his Staff advisors
> Consisted entirely of turds
>
> For shit may be shot at odd corners
> And paper supplied there to suit
> But a shit would be shot without mourners
> If somebody shot that shit Shute.[32]
>
> Captain A. P. Herbert, Hawke Battalion, 189th Brigade, 63rd (Royal Naval) Division

The dislike demonstrated by such RND officers was entirely reciprocated and General Shute repeatedly reported numerous examples of what he considered to be their deplorable efficiency to General Headquarters. But the Fifth Army plans for the Battle of the Ancre demanded that the last reserves be thrown in and thus, despite it all, the RND was at last earmarked for serious action for the first time on the Western Front.

> It was just the last throw of the year's campaigning, and we were the last piece. It was a last desperate gamble against all odds, as it seemed; had not our dyspeptic General Shute reported on us time and again as unfit to go into action, and it was by mere chance, not intent, that our still-despised Naval Division and the 51st (Highland) Division, had landed up side by side in front of Beaucourt and Beaumont Hamel. The positions we were to attack were reputed unassailable and we were reputed utterly unworthy assailants. The weather was doubtful; the ground conditions lousy. As usual there were no reserves.[33]
>
> Captain Douglas Jerrold, Hawke Battalion, 189th Brigade, 63rd (Royal Naval) Division

Many of the men knew what was coming. They remembered reading about Beaumont Hamel in their newspapers way back in July. They may not have grasped all the tactical details, but they knew enough to get the general idea of what they were facing.

> We've got in mind what we got to do. We know we're for the slaughter-house. We know that the 29th Division, the Newfoundlanders, the Essex and everybody else got slaughtered. We know that! We knew that since then there'd been five attempts all beaten back – five![34]
>
> Ordinary Seaman Joe Murray, Hood Battalion, 189th Brigade, 63rd (Royal Naval) Division

Following in the footsteps of its predecessors the attacking battalion moved up into the lines on 12 November. The men certainly did not all go forward in a spirit of uncomplaining self-sacrifice. Some of them were voluble in the extreme as they considered their woes.

> We were issued with two 'P' bombs. Phosphorous bombs, they were new things to us, we'd never seen them before. They were like an elongated jam tin. We had a couple of Mills bombs. Then we got two sacks per section of bombs. Bless my heart and soul if they didn't come along with the rations. We were given a tin of jam each. Now we'd never had a tin of jam each in the whole time we were in the blinking

army. A glass jar of piccalilli, never seen the damned stuff before. Cups hanging here, a mug hanging here, entrenching tool at the back beating a tattoo on the backside, you've got your haversack on this side, you've got a sack of bombs round your neck, like a blinking Christmas tree. Lousy things, coming up the communication trench, you got tied up with this telephone wire, you pull like hell, then you trip over and the sack would fall in the mud. A wet muddy sack is an uncomfortable thing. We were the front-line attacking troops, we were ahead of everybody, every time all the time. It was still daylight, round about five o'clock. We couldn't go forward because of the observation balloons and planes flying across the top. We hid in these trenches just outside Hamel. We opened and ate the tin of jam and we ate the piccalilli! Well whether the piccalilli didn't agree with the jam, or the jam didn't agree with the piccalilli, I don't know, but we knew the results afterwards! Anyhow we got rid of that lot.[35]

Ordinary Seaman Joe Murray, Hood Battalion, 189th Brigade, 63rd (Royal Naval) Division

The fact that they went forward into at least partially sketched out assembly trenches was largely as a result of the much maligned General Shute, who had gained much hard practical experience whilst in command of the 59th Brigade at Guillemont. When it came to the actual fighting, the fussy characteristics that they had so deplored in their leader began to appear in another light. His usual nickname was not only a classic pun 'Tiger', but it also suited his aggressive character. 'Tiger' Shute was a general who led from the front, who demanded the highest levels of performance from his subordinates; in turn, he used all his experience to try and ensure that his men's efforts would be crowned with success in battle – where it counted. Shute was well aware that the trenches they were moving up into for the assault were not suitable as jumping off trenches and he had ordered an entire new system dug. The working parties that had to do the work may well have cursed him, but this was to prove a wise precaution.

We had to line up in four waves, so we had to have four jumping-off trenches near enough. We were the first ones, behind us was the Drake, and behind them was the Honourable Artillery Company. So when we got to our own front line we had to count the trenches. One, two, three, four – that's the HAC; one, two, three, four – that's the

Drake and one, two, three, four – that's the Hood – so we know where we are. They were only about a foot or two feet deep in places. At that particular place the line ran along and then moved back towards the Ancre. We got to our assembly point at seven o'clock, official records say nine – but that was when it was complete, we were the first ones. The attack was due at 5.45 the next morning. We'd got hours to wait. In the open! In the mist it was, and the rain, people will swear falling into water, awful lot of noise although we tried to keep quiet. We didn't know where the Germans were, but we knew they were in front. If they knew that 200 yards from them, there was thousands of troops lying out in the open for hours, goodness knows what would have happened. We knew that, we knew the danger we were in. We knew what we had to attack, we were getting a bit shaky, no doubt about it. We'd done all the donkey work and now we have to do all the fighting, why doesn't somebody else have a go at this lot? We were getting a bit shaky. We ceased to have any conversation, we weren't quite sure what each man was thinking. We were lying there.[36]

Ordinary Seaman Joe Murray, Hood Battalion, 189th Brigade, 63rd (Royal Naval) Division

It was a long time to wait. The November night was cold and wet, they had no shelter, no hot food and only the thought of what lay ahead of them to keep them warm.

We of the Hoods, under Colonel Freyberg, were right on the right flank, almost on the river. In fact the river was our boundary. It was dark, misty, there was a slight drizzle; it may have been the mist. So I was lying in this hole, the next man to me was about 5 or 6 feet away. I've got a sack of blinking bombs for my head; that was my pillow. It must have been about midnight, but I saw someone come along. I thought to myself, 'Ooooh blimey, who's that walking about in front here?' Normally you would fire, anyone in front of me was an enemy unless you were warned. I heard this fellow talking and I find out its Colonel Freyberg. He'd come along to inspect his troops before the attack. The generals do it 10 miles away, quite safely, but Freyberg he was coming along. He went past me eventually and went on to see his old pal Kelly of B Company. There was Asquith, Freyberg and Kelly were the only three officers left out of the whole crowd, that left

> Avonmouth on the *Grantully Castle* in February 1915. Asquith had been pardoned off, they wouldn't let him go, but Kelly was in charge of B Company. Freyberg said to me, 'Oh, you here!' He was quite cheerful, wondering how we were getting on. 'Do try and get some sleep!' I suppose we did sleep; exhausted sleep I suppose.[37]
>
> Ordinary Seaman Joe Murray, Hood Battalion, 189th Brigade, 63rd (Royal Naval) Division

What sleep the men were able to get was fitful, broken by the sounds of battle and a penetrating cold.

> In the early hours of the morning, round about five o'clock, we were all woken, perishing cold. A little bit towards Kelly's place, B Company, there was a little bit of bombing going on. I think our patrol slung a couple of bombs and cleared out, came back again, but that didn't affect us. There was a Very light up there and this shell hole in front of me, the edges were frozen and every time a gun went off you'd see the quivering of the water. The official record says that someone brought round some tea at five o'clock, quarter past five. I never saw any tea. I'm not saying they didn't have it but I didn't have any! About 5.30, most of us started getting warmed up a bit, dancing about, quietly! Then we had to fix bayonets. There's always a noise with fixing bayonets, a clink, a metallic noise, so you put your tunic round it to deaden it. Up to now, for at least a month at 5.45 in the morning the artillery had an intensive bombardment on the Jerries, always at 5.45. Of course the Jerries, first of all, took that as the prelude to an attack. Nothing happened, the next morning, nothing happened again, after five weeks we did attack, they didn't think we would having been mislead for five weeks.
>
> At 5.45 – all the watches were synchronised – *'Bang! Bang! Bang!'* All of sudden, behind us, the whole sky was red, it reminded me of home a couple of miles across the valley from Conset Iron Company, when they used to draw the furnaces there, it was the same thing. Immediately afterwards you could hear the shells going over your head and really and truly you could almost feel the shells. Then you heard the sound, the light was first, the shell was next and then the sound! There was a lot of them falling short. We expected to be shelled by Jerry, we didn't expect to be shelled by our own men, but you knew by the thrust

which way they were coming. You knew they were your own because they were coming forward. But at the same time, you know, were it not for the artillery barrage then we'd all have been slaughtered we wouldn't have advanced at all. So it was the lesser of the two evils. We accepted they were doing a brilliant job. We knew we had seven or eight minutes, then the Germans would retaliate, they would bombard beyond the front line to the reserves coming up – which they knew would be there. So the quicker we got out of our positions towards the barrage, in a way the safer we were. When the attack opened at 5.45, we were up, we'd got our gun at what you call the 'high port'.[38]

Ordinary Seaman Joe Murray, Hood Battalion, 189th Brigade,
63rd (Royal Naval) Division

Alongside the Hood Battalion were the men of the Hawke Battalion. Captain Douglas Jerrold was with the battalion headquarters party as they, too, watched the seconds ticking down to zero hour.

I had my watch by me, and it was the second hand that I was watching. Wilson, graver than I had ever seen him, was doing exactly the same. The horrible thing, for us, was that it was not *our* battle. In a matter of seconds the 400 officers and men would have passed out of our knowledge and control. We were to go forward and establish our headquarters in the German front line as soon as it should be occupied.[39]

Captain Douglas Jerrold, Hawke Battalion, 189th Brigade,
63rd (Royal Naval) Division

When the men went forward, Jerrold's habitual cynicism was, for once, overwhelmed as he watched his men go forward into the unknown.

I shall never see a sight more noble. I was, you see, in the front row of the stalls. Eight lines of men passed me so closely that I could see every expression on their faces as they faded into the mist, and among all those men walking resolutely to wounding or death, I saw not one expression of fear or regret, or even of surprise.[40]

Captain Douglas Jerrold, Hawke Battalion, 189th Brigade,
63rd (Royal Naval) Division

On the right the Hood Battalion went forward in fine style attacking towards Dodders Green Lane line. They achieved this without much difficulty, but on their left the Hawke and the Howe Battalions ran into far more severe resistance from the Whaleback Redoubt located between the German First and Second Lines. Coming up behind the Hoods were the 1st Battalion, Honourable Artillery Company.

> It was very dark and misty and several times got hung up in the Huns' barbed wire. I eventually lost touch with our battalion and arrived in the Huns' front-line trench by myself and found a chap belonging to the RND in there. We at once started bombing and throwing smoke bombs down into the dugouts and it was some time before we got them out. The first one to come out went down on his knees and cried for mercy. I did not have the heart to stick him although I would have liked to. Between us two we took forty or more prisoners.[41]
>
> Private Stanley Hawkins, 1st Battalion, Honourable Artillery Company, 190th Brigade, 63rd (Royal Naval) Division

Thankfully, General Shute's more bloodthirsty command not to take prisoners had been ignored by at least some of his mopping-up teams. Back at the various battalion headquarters there was no clue as to what was happening.

> We stood there for a quarter of an hour, and I remember turning to Leslie Wilson and saying, 'No one has come back.' We wanted, of course, a message to say, quite comfortably, that we had captured the front line. Then we could have sent a message from our own notebooks, and everybody would have been pleased and we should have gone forward to establish our 'report centre'. That would have been charming. But it had just not happened. And there we were lost in the fog of war.[42]
>
> Captain Douglas Jerrold, Hawke Battalion, 189th Brigade, 63rd (Royal Naval) Division

The pain of responsibility was intense. There was no real evidence as to what was the right course of action; a mistake might well, and probably would, be fatal.

> Wilson was looking more and more troubled; then suddenly his face cleared of anxiety. I knew him so well that I was ready for his question, 'Hadn't we better go on and see what's happening?' 'Go back?' would have been a question. 'Go on!' was an order. So we went. I had laboriously acquired a revolver for the battle, but in my right hand I carried

all the documents adjutants are supposed to carry, including even the orders for the battle, in case we ever arrived there. We knew enough by now, however, to realise, that if we got anywhere at all it would be by luck, and if we got anywhere near our destination it would be by using our wits. Then suddenly, as I was trying to think if I had forgotten anything, I felt a blow and realised my arm had been shot off. I looked round and found my arm hanging somewhere at my back, but, alas, no revolver. Oddly enough, I hadn't been knocked out. Indeed I walked on a few yards, looking for my arm, and was really only overcome with the pleasure of finding that it was still there. Then I subsided into a shell hole, and Wilson relieved me of such papers as he wanted, while one of our own orderlies stayed with me and bandaged my arm, with very great skill incidentally. So that was the end of my dream. No heroic exploits, no triumphs, not even a 'triumph of organisation'.[43]

Captain Douglas Jerrold, Hawke Battalion, 189th Brigade, 63rd (Royal Naval) Division

Meanwhile, the Hoods were pondering their next move. Their support in the Drake Battalion had been sucked into the battle raging on the left. It was at this moment that Colonel Bernard Freyberg showed evidence of the decisiveness and the charmed life that would take him to the highest echelons. He personally took control of the situation and led the Hoods off in a pell-mell attack on the shattered ruins of the Beaucourt Railway Station, which was their objective.

I forget how long we had to wait, but the time was getting on. Freyberg decided the Drakes can't go by themselves so we'll have to go. We arrive on the river bed and off we go. The barrage lifted and off we go again. There was firing going on all over the place: our own shells falling short, the Jerries firing from left and right, our left flank was vacant. They say run, but you stumble, there's shell holes, you can't go direct, you go this way and that way, picking your way round the shell holes. Sometimes there are two or three of you together, sometimes there was nobody. They'd got behind or blown up, you don't know. All the time there was this fumes and the shelling going on. We get to this point on the other side of the sunken road and we capture it. I was almost near the station. We had to go down this road and up the side. There was a lot of dugouts there, well we got our 'P' bombs out and chucked them down there. As you went along you could smell these phosphorous bombs – a rotten lousy smell. I saw some crowd over here, I thought they were our men, but they were really prisoners. We started talking to these fellows, they couldn't understand, we couldn't hear there was so much bloody noise, but a soldier knows what the point of a bayonet means, 'Quick, quick, quick! Get back!' Some of them wouldn't behave themselves and we shot them. No doubt about it. You'd tell a bloke, some of them wouldn't behave themselves, wouldn't take any notice, or making threatening gestures – 'BANG' – you had no time to fool around with them.[44]

Ordinary Seaman Joe Murray, Hood Battalion, 189th Brigade, 63rd (Royal Naval) Division

Murray had fought his way all the way through the gullies of Gallipoli without a scratch and had earned himself the sobriquet, 'Lucky Durham'. In the total confusion that prevailed in front of the village of Beaucourt he finally ran out of luck.

We'd got to still go forward. We go on to this Green Line and there seems to be more prisoners giving themselves up than what there was fighting men. We the Hood were at least three or four hours ahead of our time, we shouldn't have been there until the Drakes had captured it and we'd reorganised. In the afternoon our artillery was firing on the Yellow Line. That was wrong to us. We'd been told that at that time it would move forward on to the village of Beaucourt. We move up and then somebody realised, 'Look the barrage hasn't lifted!' It was there or thereabouts that I got blown up. There was a shell burst very near, it hit me crouched down and I got wounded in the abdomen, little bits of shrapnel in here and a bit of a shell took off the skin and pubic hair, nasty. The abrasion was worse than the wound. I can remember thinking what to do and – 'BANG!' – something else, I don't know what. The next I knew I was in Mesnil, lying on a stretcher and somebody washing the mud off my face.[45]

Ordinary Seaman Joe Murray, Hood Battalion, 189th Brigade, 63rd (Royal Naval) Division

Freyberg moved to consolidate the newly captured position.

The colonel sent me out on battle patrol, just twenty or thirty men and you go ahead of your trench. You're really there to hold up a counter-

> attack as long as you can. You were there to do as much damage as you can and to warn the front line so that they can be getting ready. One of our men went out and came back in great glee, he'd been to the back of the village some how or other, he was a Glasgow Irishman – a real lad. He'd seen a wagon going along, it was the Germans bringing their rations up, so he climbed over the bank, bayoneted the driver and pinched their mail. He brought it back to the line and we had schnapps and in the mailbag was a box of cigars coming up for the German commander. Freyberg sent it back to our general.[46]
>
> Sergeant Richard Tobin, Hood Battalion, 189th Brigade, 63rd (Royal Naval) Division

Although they had been held up just short of Beaucourt, the despised matelots of the RND had achieved a notable breakthrough just north of the Ancre. The combination of the inspirational leadership of Colonel Bernard Freyberg and the hard-headed pragmatism of their despised commanding officer, Major General Cameron Shute had proved surprisingly effective.

On their right flank, on the other side of the river, the men of the 39th Division had also met with considerable success overrunning the old fortress village of St Pierre Divion above the Ancre and thereby duly conforming to the overall advance as planned. To their left the 51st Division under the command of Major General G. M. Harper, was facing the village of Beaumont Hamel, and its final objective was the Frankfort Trench, up on Redan Ridge, where it was to establish a link with its neighbours. Once again, in a strange case of *déjà vu* a mine was exploded in the original crater on Hawthorn Ridge at the Zero Hour of 0545. Some 30,000 lbs of ammonal high explosive had at a stroke despatched the flanking threat posed by the German crater garrison. This time it was not the prelude to disaster, as the Scots charged forward behind their creeping barrage and swiftly overran the German front line and after hard fighting captured Y Ravine and the mangled ruins of Beaumont Hamel.

To the left of the 51st Division things were not going so well. The 2nd Division was facing the Redan Ridge.

> The signal to go over was a mine going up. The morning was very foggy, a good job for us too, as Fritz didn't expect us. We collared some of them asleep and some without boots on, we got the first three lines

> easy, but had to fight mighty hard for the rest. The ground was awful, lots of our fellows got stuck in the mud and we had to leave them there to die.[47]
>
> Sergeant Sibley, 99th Company, Machine Gun Corps, 99th Brigade, 2nd Division

Despite the handicaps, the initial advance went well on the right where the 5th Brigade advanced tucked close in behind the creeping barrage. It undoubtedly caught the Germans on the hop for most of them were still sheltering in their dugouts when their front lines were overrun and the brigade soon attained its first objective, the Beaumont Trench. Unfortunately, on the left the 6th Brigade was stymied by the bristling power of the 'original' Quadrilateral Redoubt which, just as on 1 July, provided a deadly flanking fire. The creeping barrage moved remorselessly forward on its planned course, but the infantry were prevented from following close behind by a deadly combination of mud, uncut barbed wire and enfilading machine-gun fire raking through the stumbling ranks. Unsurprisingly the attack failed with heavy loss of life. The same fate was shared by the 3rd Division further to the north.

Finally, to cover the left flank of the V Corps, the 31st Division of the XIII Corps returned to its ill-fated stamping ground in front of John Copse. Its thankless task was to provide a defensive flank to cover the advance further to the south. Perversely the 13th and 12th East Yorkshires actually did rather well, capturing the German front line and establishing a strong post in the old mine crater. Yet the failure of the 3rd Division left them hopelessly isolated in an echo of many another Somme story. The German counter-attacks pounded away at their positions, while the German shells rained down on No Man's Land and cut them off from all support. There was no hope of maintaining the isolated salient and that night the Yorkshiremen ended the day just as their predecessors of the 31st Division had five months earlier – back in the British front line.

Overall, the situation as night fell on 13 November was mixed. Gough remained optimistic and decided to order the V Corps forward again on a front stretching between Beaucourt and the Ten Tree Alley Trench, which ran across Redan Ridge about 500 yards south of the village of Serre. For the moment Serre was to be forgotten. As usual the situation lay in the balance as the British reorganised for the next push and the German reserves moved forward to bolster their line. The 190th Brigade of the Royal Naval Division was ordered to attack Beaucourt at 0745. Much of the credit for its success seems to have rested on the shoulders of Lieutenant Colonel Bernard Freyberg who, once again, took command of the situation just as the attack seemed to be faltering.

> We'd lost a lot of men on the first day. I went in as platoon sergeant on the first morning and within the first quarter of an hour we had our company commander killed, two out of the three subalterns wounded, only one subaltern left, and I was the sort of second-in-command – and that happened in the first ten minutes. On the second day of that show they formed a composite battalion of the Hood Battalion and the Honorable Artillery Company, I suppose there might have been a couple of a hundred of us left altogether and Freyberg who was commanding the Hood Battalion was in charge when we went in and took Beaucourt on the second day. It was much to everybody's surprise because they never thought we would get as far as that. But we did. I think it was the most intense battle I was ever in, it was really grim. We were very thin on the ground and the Germans had brought up reinforcements. I think, luckily for us, the Germans brought up hadn't been on the Somme before and they didn't know the intensity of this warfare and they panicked. Otherwise we shouldn't have got through. When we got right the way through Beaucourt there were Germans with their hands up quite a distance further on, where we couldn't go because of our own curtain of shells. Freyberg was wounded just near me. He stood out in the open and we said, 'For God's sake get in, Sir!' But he was like that and he paid the price – he went down. We got beyond the village and there were no trenches, we went into shell holes as deep as we could get. But they gave us the most almighty pasting with really big stuff. I think they were 11-in howitzers, chiefly. It was a very grey day and you could see these things coming towards you before they hit. It is a most unnerving decision. They came in salvos of four. Of course, there were all the ordinary field guns, but I remember seeing these little black balls getting bigger and bigger until they came in the most almighty roar round you. They took their toll.[48]
>
> Sergeant Reginald Haine, 1st Battalion, Honorable Artillery Company, 190th Brigade, 63rd (Royal Naval) Division

The stretcher bearers were kept busy by the constant stream of casualties littered across the torn battlefield, in the trail of the advancing troops.

> Many stretcher bearers were at work in No Man's Land carrying wounded back to the shelter of a high bank, whence they could be evacuated to the Beaucourt Hamel road. There was a great scarcity of stretchers: the best available substitutes were ground sheets and trench ladders. Help was given by German prisoners and good clearance was being made in this part of the line. In the Hun front line I found Sergeant Haine in temporary command.[49]
>
> Medical Officer Captain R. S. Morshead, Royal Army Medical Corps attached to 1st Battalion, Honorable Artillery Company, 190th Brigade, 63rd (Royal Naval) Division

Beaucourt had finally fallen at 1030 p.m. The Germans seem to have attempted to mass for a counter-attack at Baillescourt Farm to the east, but they were soon dealt with by a concentrated artillery bombardment. Further north the 51st and 2nd Divisions had a hard fight on their hands in the attempt to establish themselves along the Redan Ridge. After hard fighting the Highlanders got forward into Munich Trench but a misplaced barrage crashed down to loosen their tentative grip. They retired to consolidate in what became known as New Munich Trench and the line reached by the 2nd Division largely conformed alongside their left flank.

Based on the initially optimistic reports from his divisional commanders, Gough was determined to continue the fight and had indeed issued orders for a resumption of the attack on 15 November. He seems to have been caught up in the kind of frenzy that afflicts gamblers unwilling to accept defeat; just one more throw of the dice might rescue the situation. Only after the direct intervention of Haig were the orders countermanded and the attack cancelled. Even Haig had now had enough and he despatched his Chief of Staff Lieutenant General Launcelot Kiggell as an emissary to ensure the attacks were suspended. But Gough had the bit between his teeth and he was determined to improve the tactical position for the winter months. After some further consultation Haig sanctioned one last push on the Somme front.

The last attack of the great battle went in on 18 November. The assault by the II Corps (19th ,18th, and 4th Canadian Divisions) and the V Corps (32nd and 37th Divisions) is a tragic tale. This was war in a man-made hell with the weather contributing everything it could to the overall misery. For the infantry involved, this attack represented the epitome of suffering. Even moving into the line was a trial beyond measure for the new divisions, faced as they were with wastelands awash with freezing water and cloying mud.

> It was snowing hard and freezing, and pitch dark. We were guided by the star shells from the firing line. It was impossible to follow the trench and too risky to get in it. I did get in it once and got stuck up to my waist in mud and ice-cold water. The water in the trench had a covering of ice about an inch thick, and snow on top of it. But as soon as your weight was on it – in you went! That was enough for me![50]
>
> Private C. Reuben Smith, 7th Battalion, East Kent Regiment, 55th Brigade, 18th Division

The mud on the Somme had become as much of an enemy as the Germans. It seemed uniquely deep, sticky and with a deadly suction capable of clinging to men who were already weakened by exhaustion or wounds.

> It was a horror quite apart, quite unlike anything else in this war! Imagine a man, wounded on patrol in front of our lines, or during an attack, struggling a few yards towards our people, overcome by the sucking ooze, sinking, sinking inch by inch, in full view of willing friends, not one of whom can do a thing to help him; sinking and sinking, until, although he calls and calls for help, he realises no help can come – and he begs his own people to end his horror with a bullet.[51]
>
> Captain Arthur Acland, 57th Brigade, 19th Division

This was an all too real situation. Men *did* slip slowly into the grim mire with no chance of escape.

> The mud was so bad, ploughing our way to the front line, we found two English soldiers up to their armpits in mud, one dead, the other facing him was stark mad. We gave him food and got him out as soon as we could, but he died. They had been stuck for 48 hours.[52]
>
> Lieutenant Edgar Lord, 15th Battalion, Lancashire Fusiliers, 96th Brigade, 32nd Division

The men moved forward in the dark for Zero Hour, which was set at 0610. From a distance the bombardment was an amazing kaleidoscope of beautiful colours. In the front-line trenches it was misery incarnate.

A day of days. We were up at 6 a.m. and were greatly surprised to find the ground covered with snow. Zero hour was 6.10 a.m. and to the second our artillery started. It was a wonderful sight: dawn just beginning to break through; the ground, the trenches, shell holes all dead white; a low white mist above the ground and with this the flashes and noise of the guns and in the distance the Boche star signals of red and white. It was the weirdest awe-inspiring sight that I have ever seen – words fail. The gun flashes were wonderful – sometimes battery fire – at others almost as quick as machine-gun fire. The flashes were of every hue: dull red, yellow, green-yellow, purple and white according to the nature of the explosive. Overhead was the dull swish and clanking of our heavy shells. No Hun shells came over in reply. The front involved as far as we could see to left and right and our little area is practically in the centre. The bombardment lasted twenty minutes only, but it was a terrific one. After that we could hear machine gun fire rattling like hell.[53]

Captain Arthur Hardwick, 59th Field Ambulance, 19th Division

The weather could not really have been worse. The snow that had fallen overnight was replaced in sequence by driving sleet and then pouring rain. This caused some confusion: with near nil visibility the troops simply could not see where they were going.

The barrage opens and simultaneously with the opening bars our lads go right away. Jerry was late with his barrage and our boys are the other side of it, but nothing can be seen of them as a very heavy mist is lying close to the ground. Worried looks are the general run of the first hour.[54]

Private Robert Cude, 7th Battalion, East Kent Regiment, 55th Brigade, 18th Division

The 55th Brigade were attacking the Desire Trench.

A runner came back breathless and excited saying we had taken the trench, but all was not over. The fight lasted all day. The Germans expecting an attack got out of their trenches and dug themselves in behind their trench, filling their trench with barbed wire. Some of our men fell into this trap in the dark, others lost their way and were surrounded and captured without a fight. The East Surreys on our left and the West Kents on our right were in the same predicament.[55]

Private C. Reuben Smith, 7th Battalion, East Kent Regiment, 55th Brigade, 18th Division

More troops were sent up and in the end Desire Trench was consolidated and a communications trench dug back to the former British front line. Colonel Alfred Irwin was keen to see how his men of the 8th East Surreys were faring in their lodgement taken that morning in Desire Trench. He moved forward just as he had in the attack made with such optimism by his men on 1 July so many thousands of lifetimes ago. This time his luck ran out.

> In the morning before it got light I went up to have a look round this new ground we'd taken. I went round with a company commander who was very pleased with what he'd done and his arrangements. I started off back to my battalion headquarters just as it was getting light. I hadn't gone more than a few yards before I was shot in the thigh. I fell into a shell hole full of water; it was freezing, full of water and ice. Every time I raised my head to try and put a bandage on my leg the sniper had another go at me. So I had to lie in the water and just wait for help, which did come in the form of Canadian stretcher bearers later in the morning. But my unfortunate orderly – I thought I was doing the best I could for him, I told him to go on when I was hit, but he was hit on the way back and died.[56]
>
> Lieutenant Colonel Alfred Irwin, 8th Battalion, East Surrey Regiment, 55th Brigade, 18th Division

In the circumstances, the II Corps troops did relatively well south of the Ancre, capturing Desire Trench, although falling short of the village of Grandcourt. North of the Ancre, the V Corps made some small advances and successfully consolidated the new line. At the end of it all the tactical situation had not materially altered but the cost had been high and the morale of the men began to suffer serious damage.

> The suffering is terrible and some of the men are about mad with the cold and the exposure. Snow in the morning followed by rain all day has made things pitiable. What I am seriously thinking now is that those boys lying stiff and cold all around Beaumont Hamel, insensible to it all, are perhaps lucky, and better off now than we are. This is what is called dying for your country, but it is actually selling your soul to a few profiteers for a shilling, and being massacred to satisfy their selfish purposes. And they call it WAR – and a legitimate thing at that.[57]
>
> Private Arthur Wrench, Headquarters, 154th Brigade, 51st Division

Behind the waves of attacking troops came the medical officers working as part of the teams of men clearing up the battlefield. They were searching everywhere and anywhere that a wounded man, whether British or German, might have sought shelter *in extremis*. Some of the sights they saw stretched them to the limit.

> On descending about forty steps one was in a large floored and timbered chamber, some 50 feet long; and at the further end a second set of steps led to a similar chamber, one side of each being lined with a double layer of bunks filled with dead and wounded Germans, the majority of whom had become casualties early on the morning of the 13th. The place was, of course, in utter darkness; and, when we flashed our lights on and the wounded saw our escort with rifles ready, there was an outbreak of, '*Kamerad!*' while a big bevy of rats squeaked and scuttled away from their feast on the dead bodies on the floor. The stench was indescribably abominable: for many of the cases were gas-gangrenous.[58]
>
> Captain David Rorie, 1/2nd Highland Field Ambulance, 51st (Highland) Division

In the end they found fourteen Germans still alive. The plight of such wounded men can hardly be imagined: in total darkness, without food or water, drifting in and out of consciousness and with no way of getting help. In such cases it must have been a blessed relief as they slowly slipped away into oblivion. After that it was only a matter of time before the seeds of their dissolution hatched forth into maggots. The last two months on the Somme had brought a dark Gothic horror to the battlefields.

> I have found a Hun aid post and dwell undisturbed beneath many tons of chalk. I regard this aid post as my very own as I was there first and had to clean it out. The chief amusement was the removal of a very dead Hun in a waterproof sheet. He was of a piebald hue and dropped maggots wherever he was carried. He would insist on sliding out of the sheet, and the scooping of him back was not only difficult, but at times impossible. It was not the whole of him at all when we got him outside.[59]
>
> Medical Officer Captain Charles McKerrow, 10th Battalion, Northumberland Fusiliers, 68th Brigade, 23rd Division

Many soldiers attained, through necessity, an impervious callousness to the horrors that they encountered. They seemed oblivious to the graveyard that surrounded them and in which they lived day by day. Hard pragmatism was the underlying principle; if they were to survive they must conquer the environment that threatened them.

> I had some German canned horse and bully beef for dinner which I heated up in a 'billy cooker'. We were drinking Fritz's coffee we found in some of their water bottles in No Man's Land about three to four weeks old. Eating your meals with dead Germans' boots staring you in the face out of the parapet. Also we are using the dead bodies of Fritz to step on in the trenches to get out of the mud – we don't take any more notice of a dead person now than we do of a rat.[60]
>
> Private Herbert Butt, 102nd Battalion, 11th Canadian Brigade, 4th Canadian Division

But even the most hard-bitten soldiers could feel revulsion or nausea at the dissolute state that some bodies had attained. It was impossible to conceive that the mess in front of them had once been a man just like them.

> On my preliminary investigation in the dim light I could see only his field boots. I had come without my torch. Subsequently, on looking closer, I found that his flesh was moving with maggots. More precisely, I noticed that portions of his uniform were heaving up and down at points where they touched the seething mass below. The smell was pretty awful. None of the men would touch him, although troops as a rule are not noticeably fastidious. The job was unanimously voted to me, because it's supposed, quite wrongly, that doctors don't mind. I went down the stairway with a length of telephone wire and lashed it round the poor fellow's feet. We hauled him up and dragged him away for some distance. The corpse left behind it a trail of wriggling, sightless maggots, which recalled the trail in a paper-chase. Having moulded a shell hole as a grave, we erected a board at the man's head, 'An unknown German Soldier' with date of burial.[61]
>
> Medical Officer Lieutenant Lawrence Gameson, 73rd Brigade, Royal Field Artillery, 15th Division

The heedless shells ripped up the ground paying no respect to the burial grounds where the previous victims of the fighting had been interred. Now they were roughly exhumed and splattered across the shell holes once more.

> Not a single cross is left standing over a German soldier's grave, but some of the bodies buried there are torn up again and lie scattered all over the place. It is horrible to see. Perhaps the Germans are not even human to violate the last resting place of their own men who have given their lives for their country, and it strikes me there is not much glory these days in dying for your country.[62]
>
> Private Arthur Wrench, Headquarters, 154th Brigade, 51st Division

IT WAS NOT, however, such horrors that persuaded Haig that it was necessary to close down the Somme offensive after the attack of 18 November 1916. Sheer military logic dictated that the cost of making further major efforts to try and radically improve the tactical position would be too high. It was simply impossible for the men to get forward in such extreme ground and weather conditions. This was not just wearing out the Germans; it was fast eroding the body and soul of the British Army.

A new set of plans had been drawn up under the general control of the French commander-in-chief, General Joseph Joffre at the Chantilly Conference of 15 November 1916. According to the new plans 1917 would be the new 'year of victory'. During the winter the pressure would be maintained on the Western Front, at least so far as weather permitted. The Allies would then launch twin British and French offensives north and south of the Somme. Rawlinson was very concerned to limit the degree of any winter fighting. He was firmly of the opinion that his divisions had reached the end of their tether.

> All the divisions allotted to the Fourth Army for the winter operations have taken part in the Battle of the Somme twice, most of them three or four times. They have had very heavy losses amounting in some cases from 7,000 to 10,000 men, and have suffered very severely in officers, NCOs and specialists. Experience proves that after severe periods of fighting in which divisions have had heavy losses, the time taken by a battalion to recover and regain its state of efficiency

depends almost entirely on what nucleus of trained officers and NCOs remains available to train and weld together the old and new elements. In every offensive action that is carried out an ever increasing toll is taken of these priceless instructors and if battalions are bled dry there is serious risk of lowering the standard of fighting efficiency to a point which may render doubtful the success of the operations in the coming spring campaign.[63]

Lieutenant General Sir Henry Rawlinson, Headquarters, Fourth Army

For the time being at least it was clear that the British offensive was over.

But what of the Germans? They had survived the great crisis at the end of September only by the skin of their teeth. They looked forward to a gloomy future as defeat seemed to be the only likely outcome to the war.

GHQ had to bear in mind that the enemy's great superiority in men and material would be even more painfully felt in 1917 than in 1916. They had to face the danger that 'Somme fighting' would soon break out at various points on our fronts, and that even our troops would not be able to withstand such attacks indefinitely, especially if the enemy gave us no time for rest and for the accumulation of material. Our position was uncommonly difficult and a way out hard to find. We could not contemplate an offensive ourselves, having to keep our reserves available for defence. There was no hope of a collapse of any of the Entente Powers. If the war lasted our defeat seemed inevitable. Economically we were in a highly unfavourable position for a war of exhaustion. At home our strength was badly shaken. Questions of the supply of foodstuffs caused great anxiety, and so, too, did questions of *morale*. We were not undermining the spirits of the enemy populations with starvation blockades and propaganda. The future looked dark.[64]

General Erich Ludendorff, German Headquarters

Haig and his Intelligence Officer Brigadier Sir John Charteris had not been wrong in detecting signs of deterioration in the German position, but they *had* underestimated the ability of a mighty nation state to withstand hardship and loss.

The Germans began to look elsewhere for a chance of long-term victory and, unhappily for them, looked to a return to unrestricted submarine warfare in an effort to 'starve' the British of the food and resources they needed as an island to survive. This ultimately led to the

United States joining the war and merely worsened the overall German situation. On the Western Front they adopted an essentially defensive stance, chastened by their experiences on the offensive at Verdun as well as the long horror of the Somme. New defensive techniques were slowly emerging to counter the ever-increasing sophistication of the British massed artillery. The success of using shell holes as machine-gun posts led inexorably to the idea of an elastic defence system, dominated by concrete pillbox strong points with interconnected fields of machine-gun fire dominating vast fields of barbed wire. Instead of always fighting to the last with reserve troops committed to counter-attacking, the front-line troops were henceforth permitted to retreat rather than be overrun. Counter-attack divisions were held further back, beyond the range of the British field artillery, ready to strike just as any British attack was running out of steam. Much of the fighting of 1917 would be a complex clash between the concept of 'bite and hold' and 'elastic' defence.

The great Somme offensive had ended, but the fighting could not simply be switched off and many of the men in the front line would not have known that 'The Battle' was over. Minor piecemeal operations continued to flare up as both sides squabbled over the exact final course of the trenches that wove their complex interlocked pattern across the desolate lunarscape of the Somme. The guns still roared out their message of hate and all that long miserable winter men would continue to die in a welter of frozen mud and blood.

AS THE DUST SETTLED on the human catastrophe there were sad discoveries that seemed to bring the battle full circle to the opening tragedy. The late advances towards Beaumont Hamel and Thiepval allowed those soldiers lucky enough to survive the intervening five months to search the original No Man's Land for traces of their old friends and companions who had been killed during the first failed attack on 1 July – it seemed a lifetime ago. So it was that Lieutenant Edgar Lord once again tried to find the body of his long-lost best friend.

> I decided to look at the Thiepval battlefield, thinking as a vain hope I might look for Ivan Doncaster. A miracle took me to the place where he lay. I might have been a mile away in any direction as I had not

> been on the ground before. We found him about 30 yards from the German wire along with many of his comrades. They must have gone steadily forward to their deaths amid a murderous hail of machine-gun bullets. What a sad task it was identifying his skeleton by his hair, shirt, breeches and lastly by his identity disc, which I removed to send to his people. With a volunteer or two, we fashioned a shell hole into a form of a grave and reverently laid him to rest, covering his body with earth and saying a prayer for his parents, who were even yet, possibly hoping he was a prisoner. I fashioned a cross from pieces of wood, inscribed his name and regiment, and took a photograph of his grave in front of the Boche wire. A skeleton hanging on the wire with a tattered shirt fluttering in the breeze made a very grisly background to the scene. There but for the grace of God was I![65]
>
> Lieutenant Edgar Lord, 15th Battalion, Lancashire Fusiliers, 96th Brigade, 32nd Division

Despite the sacrifice of Ivan Doncaster and so many of his men there would certainly be no breakthrough on the Somme in 1916. The Germans had held the British onslaught. The war *would* go on deep into 1917 at the very least. The Germans would have the winter months to rebuild their defences, dig new lines of trenches across the fields of France and Belgium, build new pillboxes, replenish stocks of munitions and train a whole new generation of young soldiers to take their place in the line of battle. For the British there was the grim prospect of doing it all over again almost from scratch. Although they could not know it, the new killing fields of Arras, Ypres and the dread Passchendaele Ridge beckoned them all. The Somme had raised the threshold of total war and presaged a new era of even greater horror on the Western Front.

CHAPTER FOURTEEN

Assessment

The sheer horror of the Somme has for a long time been part of British twentieth century mythology. The overall context of the Great War has long been forgotten and the teaching of the subject reduced to an adjunct of English literature that can be brutally summarised in just five words: 'the pity of it all'. Politicians are portrayed as Machiavellian, but simultaneously weak, generals are stupid, soldiers are brave helpless victims and war poets – war poets are the latter-day saints made flesh. A typical example of this crude sentimental approach is the treatment given to the first disastrous casualty figures from 1 July – the first day of the Battle of the Somme. Often the figure of 57,470, of which 19,240 were killed, is not enough and emotional vampires wilfully exaggerate this to a claim of 60,000 dead. The overall British casualties during the battle are, indeed, higher than any sane individual would like to comprehend at 419,654, of which some 131,000 were dead. To this should be added the 204,253 French casualties and the approximately 450,000 – 600,000 German casualties. Each and every one was a tragedy, especially if one believes that every life has a value that transcends mere numbers. Yet it is still commonplace to see journalists referring to the 'millions' of British dead. In fact, the whole British Empire lost 908,371 dead in the entire course of the Great War. It is asserted that the flower of British manhood had been slaughtered; indeed, that Britain had sacrificed her future virility on the Western Front. Communities are pictured absolutely denuded of men and the decline of the whole empire is put down to this 'blood' forfeit. This is simply nonsense: the casualties *were* dreadful, but hyperbolic magnification surely only diminishes their sacrifice in trying to pretend that it was somehow greater than it was.

The Somme was so awful not because of the venality or stupidity of individuals, but because the leaders of the great Western nations had set themselves to resolve long-standing problems through war, with the active or passive encouragement of much of their civilian populations. War demanded that these nations strain every sinew to defeat each other. War meant the mobilisation of all their men and resources: the very power of the European nation states meant that the numbers of armed men and the powers of destruction they wielded exceeded anything that had previously been dreamed of. As soldiers struck down their enemies, more appeared, springing forward from the schools and railheads; new weapons took an ever greater toll on flesh and blood. Killing a few thousand men barely dented the manpower resources of the modern industrial state; millions marched to the drum and millions would be killed, maimed and mentally crippled before one side or the other was so worn down they could no longer struggle on. Once such a global war had been declared then the future of a generation was handed to cold-hearted military professionals like Sir Douglas Haig, Erich von Falkenhayn and Joseph Joffre. The fighting was not futile unless the war was futile. The responsibility for all the manifold sacrifices lies not so much with the generals as with the enthusiasm with which the world embraced war in 1914.

The Battle of the Somme demonstrated that until an enemy nation state had been defeated or at least ground down, then mere geographical objectives mattered very little – the only objective was the long-term destruction of the German Army. Bapaume was a first-day objective on 1 July; when the battle finished on 18 November it may have been a little closer to hand, but it still lay behind three lines of German defence works. Yet the desire to avoid more 'Somme fighting' led the Germans voluntarily to withdraw to the new Hindenburg Line some 25 miles further back in the spring of 1917. This extended retreat was not a coincidence or some fanciful whim of the Germans – they did it to shorten their line and forestall the imminent renewal of British and French pressure on the Somme. They abandoned the tactical position imposed on them by the incremental advances of the British and French and retreated to one of their own choosing – while they still could. The Allies gained much ground, but the tactical advantage had passed once more to the Germans. The destroyed strip of ground they gained availed the Allies little when push came to shove once more in 1917.

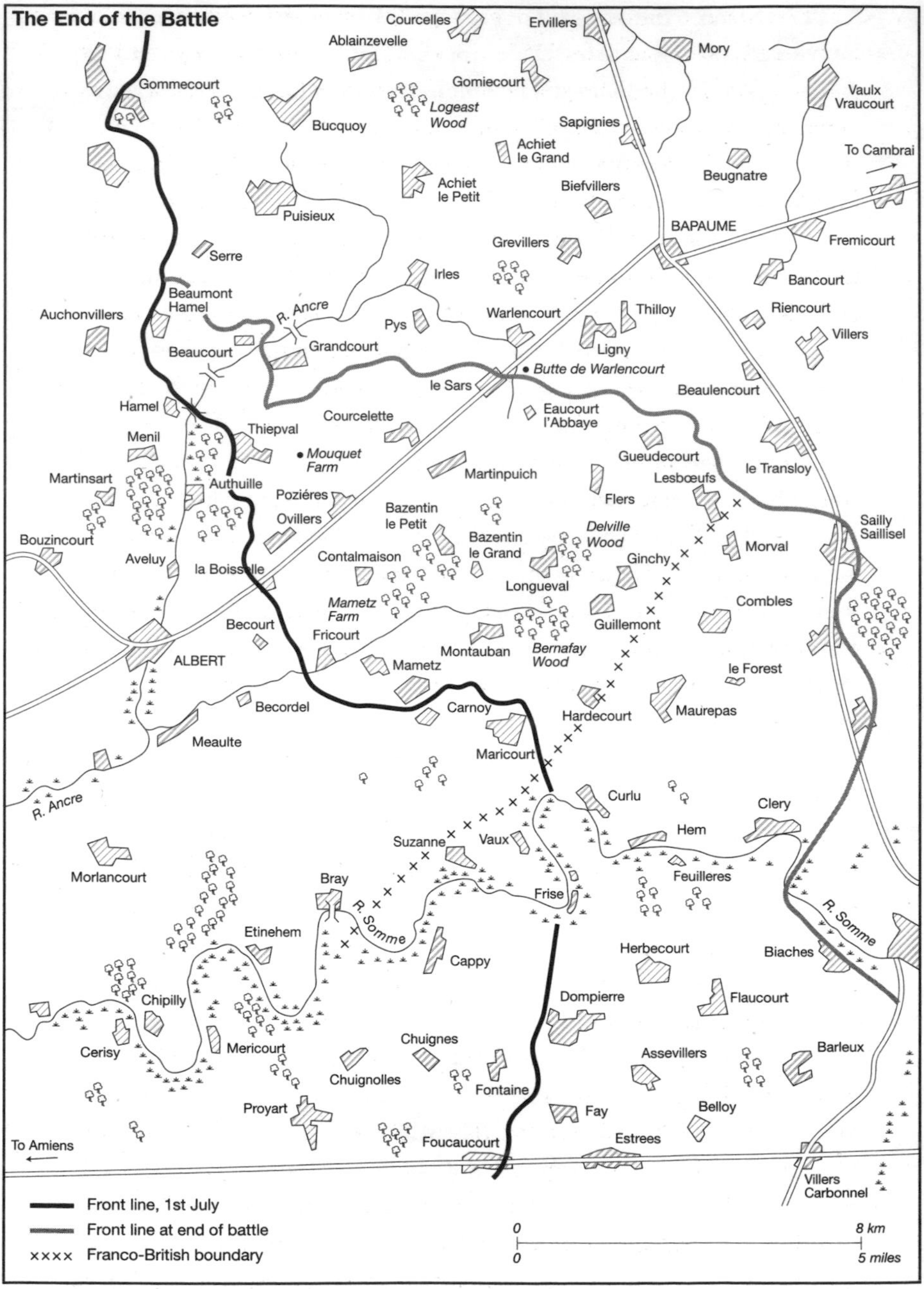
The End of the Battle
Courcelles
Ervillers
Ablainzevelle
Mory
Gommecourt
Gomiecourt
Vaulx
Vraucourt
Logeast
Wood
Bucquoy
Sapignies
Achiet
le Grand
To Cambrai
Beugnatre
Achiet
le Petit
Biefvillers
Puisieux
BAPAUME
Grevillers
Fremicourt
Serre
Irles
Bancourt
Beaumont
Hamel
Riencourt
Auchonvillers
R. Ancre
Pys
Warlencourt
Thilloy
Villers
Grandcourt
Ligny
Beaucourt
Butte de Warlencourt
le Sars
Beaulencourt
Hamel
Eaucourt
l'Abbaye
Courcelette
Menil
Thiepval
Mouquet
Farm
Gueudecourt
Martinsart
Martinpuich
le Transloy
Lesbœufs
Authuille
Flers
Poziéres
Bazentin
le Petit
Sailly
Saillisel
Ovillers
Delville
Wood
Bouzincourt
Bazentin
le Grand
Morval
Aveluy
Contalmaison
Ginchy
la Boisselle
Longueval
Combles
Mametz
Farm
Becourt
Guillemont
Fricourt
Montauban
Bernafay
Wood
ALBERT
le Forest
Mametz
Becordel
Carnoy
Hardecourt
Maurepas
Meaulte
Maricourt
R. Ancre
Curlu
Clery
Hem
Suzanne
Vaux
Morlancourt
Feuilleres
Bray
Frise
R. Somme
R. Somme
Etinehem
Cappy
Herbecourt
Biaches
Chipilly
Dompierre
Flaucourt
Cerisy
Mericourt
Chuignes
Assevillers
Barleux
Chuignolles
Fontaine
Proyart
Fay
Belloy
Estrees
To Amiens
Foucaucourt
Villers
Carbonnel
Front line, 1st July
Front line at end of battle
×××× Franco-British boundary
0
8 km
0
5 miles

The Somme shows why the hopes and plans of the 'Easterners' such as David Lloyd George and Winston Churchill, were an irrelevance to the main battle; they only diffused the Allies strength on sideshows that could not materially influence the main battles on the Western Front where the war *would* be decided. All the divisions despatched to Gallipoli, Salonika and Mesopotamia merely allowed the peripheral Turkish and Bulgarian allies of the Germans the opportunity to strike painful blows at the British and French, sucking in ever more of their precious troops, guns and munitions that would have been far better deployed on the Western Front. Defeat at Gallipoli probably did greater damage to the standing of the British Empire than any imaginary victory could ever have achieved. A defensive posture against Turkey and Bulgaria would have been far more conducive to a shortened war than any pipedreams of an easy 'back-door' route to Germany that, in the desire for an easy option, flagrantly ignored the tactical and strategical imperatives of Continental war. Where, indeed, would the German High Command have preferred to see the half a million men diverted to Mesopotamia? Fighting their way up the Tigris and Euphrates Rivers through a disease-infested swampy plain or providing another two army corps to be thrown into the decisive actions of the Western Front? The answer is obvious.

So in the end was General Sir Douglas Haig right? In fact, as we have seen, much of the responsibility for the Allied strategy adopted in 1916 was not his. The imperatives of Continental alliances meant that he was restricted by the broad framework dictated by the 'senior' partner in the *Entente Cordiale*. It was France and the still omnipotent General Joseph Joffre that determined the shape of the Allied strategy in 1916. That gainsaid, then yes – the broad thrust of Haig's strategy in 1916 was probably correct. War is a Pandora's Box, which once opened inevitably brings awful sacrifices. Haig's way was excruciatingly painful but it was the only realistic way at the time. During the Second World War the British evaded the brunt of the massive casualties rendered inevitable by modern Continental war; yet the butcher's bill still had to be paid – this time by the soldiers of the Soviet Union who died in their millions to slowly grind down the forces and will of the German Third Reich over four long years. On the occasions when British forces were involved in serious fighting in attacks against prepared positions they, too, suffered serious casualties. There was still no back door, no painless route map to success. In war someone always has to suffer.

Yet, surely Haig and his senior subordinates should have blushed in retrospect at the number of tactical mistakes that were made – and worse, endlessly repeated – during the course of the Battle of the Somme? There seemed to be no limit to the number of times that it had to be demonstrated to them that isolated attacks on a narrow front would not succeed without overpowering artillery to devastate everything in both that and the adjoining sectors. The British rarely seemed to realise that an attack to 'improve' a tactical position did not do so unless it succeeded. Too often there was no proper analysis of how many guns and shells needed to be fired to subdue a given frontage and depth of trench lines. And there seemed to be no limit to their optimism that the German Army and the entire German Empire stood ready to collapse if there was just one more push towards Bapaume.

There was still no clear realisation that the techniques of 'bite and hold' offered the best way forward at this stage of the war: attacking on a wide front, after a devastating short bombardment, using a creeping barrage to chaperone the infantry forward, but only seeking to advance up to 1,500 yards, before carefully consolidating behind a standing barrage wall of shells that could smash to pieces any attempted German counter-attack. This was the way to kill the maximum number of Germans with the minimum of Allied casualties. But it *was* slow. It demanded logistical preparations that would have daunted a Hercules, the deployment of thousands of guns, the expenditure of millions of shells, and of course it offered no hope of a breakthrough, no hope to an end to the war in 1916, perhaps not even in 1917. Although Rawlinson in particular clearly understood much of the intellectual arguments for 'bite and hold', the British were continually tempted by the chimera of short-cuts and temporary expedience, constantly attempting to cut corners to success and ending up losing their way time and time again. Well into 1917, Haig continued to order attacks that attempted to achieve penetration of all three German trench lines, which in watering down the strength to the artillery barrage on the front line predestined their failure.

The massed guns and fast developing artillery techniques were the *real* new weapons of war that emerged during the Battle of the Somme: the tremendous barrages creeping or standing; the gradual acceptance of the prime importance of counter-battery fire to neutralise or destroy the German guns; the use of the photographs and artillery observation aircraft of the Royal Flying Corps to reach behind the German lines and allow the guns to strike them where it would hurt most; the introduction of new ideas of sound and flash ranging to uncover the location of concealed German batteries. The vastly expanded Royal Artillery surely learnt its trade at the Battle of the Somme. The gunners quickened their gun drill and the artificers learnt how to keep their guns going in the most adverse of circumstances, experience that would stand them in good stead when under pressure later in the war. Their officers mastered the techniques and mathematics of accurate ranging, appreciated the value of meteorological corrections and learnt how to prepare the complex gun programmes that lay behind the deadly marvel that was the creeping barrage. It was only when the British Army learnt how to use their massed artillery to the maximum possible effect that they would sweep to victory against a severely worn down and weakened German Army in 1918. But first they had to learn to range their guns accurately without prior registration – predicted fire was still not possible in 1916. Of course, alongside the infantry, the artillery was just the most important element of the burgeoning 'all-arms battle' that encompassed aircraft, machine guns, mortars, gas shells and the as yet unfulfilled promise of tanks. The all-arms battle demanded a total mastery of logistics to gather the weapons of war, to weld them together as one, ready to strike at the same place at the same time and thereby maximise the effect on an enemy that had been worn down to the point where it can no longer respond sufficiently robustly to the challenge it faced. There was a learning curve and the British Army slowly ascended it, though occasional, heart-stopping 'big dipper' moments still occurred right to the very end of the war.

And what of the men? Let us first pay tribute to the courage and indomitable defence put up by the men of the German Army. From start to finish they fought as heroes: their artillery engaging in a never-ending duel with the British and French artillery; the infantry stoically enduring the horrendous artillery bombardments liable to crash down on them at all times of the day and night only to emerge time after time to man their machine guns and fight to the death, or launch a desperate counter-attack to retrieve some lost trench or copse. In truth, some *did* crack under the awful strain, or ran at the last moment as the glittering British bayonets approached them, and who indeed can blame them? There was even a moment near the end of September 1916 when it looked as though Haig might be right and the German Army *was* losing it collective will to resist. However, their infantry and artillery reserves arrived in time and collectively they fought on revitalised. Overall it was a supreme example of sustained courage in one of the greatest defensive battles ever fought in the history of warfare.

And the British? If this book has achieved anything, I hope it will be a renewed respect for the British soldier at war. *All of them.* Not just the gallant infantry, but the men of the Royal Artillery, the Royal Flying Corps, the Royal Engineers, the Army Service Corps, the Army Ordnance Corps – everyone and anyone that was sucked into the gaping maw of the Somme. Not just the usual soldier poets, the tragic young working-class heroes and the mounds of dead or wounded. Let us not forget other less popular stereotypes: the ordinary soldiers and gunners who did not see themselves as victims, the staff officers ground down by overwork and responsibility, the brigadier general risking his life to see what was happening to his men, a few arrant cowards intent only in dodging their fate, the sanctimonious padres and the 'blood and guts' old colonels. All of them had lives that they put at risk in the cause of their country and each in their own way did their best in that cause. Whether it was worthwhile or even necessary is a larger question that should trouble us all. Once a nation is committed to war then someone has to pay the levy in blood. Let one of those who had to endure the war have the last word as to whether it was worth it.

> I do not think we are any nearer the finish than a year or so ago, except for the fact that many hundreds of thousands more are dead on both sides. I am convinced that the end can only come that way and that at the end there will be nothing but an enormous barrage of enormous shells on both sides and that whichever side has the last few infantry to face it will win. That is if both sides don't get nerve shattered to death before and give in from pure exhaustion and hatred of it all.[1]
>
> Captain Philip Pilditch, C Battery, 235th Brigade, Royal Field Artillery, 47th Division

Acknowledgements

I would like to thank all the following people and institutions.

My lovely wife, Polly Napper who keeps me safely on the straight and narrow.

Promising author Keith Lowe who has been an absolute diamond throughout the difficult gestation of this book. In his day job as an editor he towers above any lesser mortals and brought a welcome sense of humour to what must have been a very difficult task. Thanks Keith!

All the designers and copy editors at Weidenfeld and Nicolson, particularly Jo Murray, Jo Saunders and Gwyn Lewis.

Nigel Steel, although he manifestly failed to get me to properly understand what a split infinitive is and how to avoid it. The best pal you could wish for over the last ten years.

All in the IWM Department of Documents. Special thanks to Rod Suddaby, still a demon fast bowler as he speeds into his mid-50s, and the proud custodian of an archive that never fails to astound me the more I use it. Also special thanks to the very wonderful Tony Richards, and the three students who helped me out when times were hard: Gary Speak, Colin McDonald and Mark Ashcroft.

All in the IWM Sound Archive (Margaret Brooks, Richard Hughes, Richard McDonough and John Stopford-Pickering). It is a pleasure to work with people who have been so quietly supportive over the past few years.

Peter Boyden and the strangely enigmatic figure of Simon Moody at the National Army Museum.

All in the IWM Photo Archive. Particular thanks to Rose Gerrard, Richard Bayford Glyn Biesty, Damon Cleary, Greg Smith and Gordon McLeod who collectively have the patience of a saint being threatened by some peculiarly unpleasant demise.

Bryn Hammond for the use of his long awaited (particularly by his supervisor) thesis *The Theory and Practice of British Tank – Other Arms Cooperation on the Western Front in the Great War*. A work of genius in the making and another true pal.

Chris McCarthy who is definitely a father figure to a whole generation of IWM historians. His book *The Somme: The Day by Day Account* is a classic.

Gary Sheffield and John Bourne who were kind enough to allow me early access to their much-anticipated book *Douglas Haig: War Diaries and Letters 1914-18* (Weidenfeld & Nicolson, forthcoming 2005) and thus saved me a great deal of time and trouble. I owe particular thanks to Gary Sheffield who as a historian combines the manly thrust of Hubert Gough, with the determination and graft of Douglas Haig.

The irrepressible Max Arthur who gave me a slim hope that one day my books too might sell.

John Terraine and Correlli Barnett, of course, who began it all as far as people of my generation are concerned.

Robin Prior and Trevor Wilson who have provided an easily accessible, cool analysis which encapsulates so much that others have been only dimly reaching for. Their book *Command on the Western Front* is a marvellous piece of sustained argument.

As always I hope this book makes the reader want to read more from all the fantastic sources I have accessed. This book is just the tip of a very large iceberg. The various archives hold thousand of collections and there are hundreds of great personal experience books that add to our picture of the Somme. I would earnestly thank all the copyright holders I have been able to contact and beg the forbearance of those I could not trace. Thanks to all of you.

The quotations from letters, diaries, personal accounts and oral history interviews used in this book have occasionally, where necessary, been lightly edited for overall readability. Punctuation and spellings have been largely standardised, material has occasionally been re-ordered and irrelevant material has been omitted, usually without any indication in the text. Nevertheless, changes in the actual words used in the original sources have been avoided wherever possible.

APPENDIX A

Life in the Trenches

Existence in the trenches of the Somme could be a short and brutish experience. Within the range of the roaring guns there was no safety in numbers, no genuine shelter from the storm, no real peace of mind. The stresses imposed would be unbearable to the modern mind – yet the vast majority of men endured everything that was thrown at them. Every time the men went forward into the front line they knew that there was a fair chance that they might never return. Whether they were holding the line or about to make an attack, they knew that their lives had reached a distinct crossroads. They hoped to survive unscathed, but they naturally feared death or the type of wound that would leave them crippled for life.

The approach of the infantry was usually made through the dark claustrophobia of the cramped communication and support trenches that criss-crossed the battlefield like a maze. On they plodded led by guides – usually they had no idea of where they were going or what they would be doing. When they got to the front line they found it a far cry from the neatly regimented trenches they had hitherto encountered in training. The carefully constructed parapet, revetting, firestep, duckboards, regular bays and parados were almost entirely absent. Here the trenches were often little more than crude muddy ditches, or shell holes chained together to make a rough line. Often they had been hewn out by desperate men who knew that they had to get under cover fast or die. Only if left undisturbed would the more sophisticated elements of trench warfare gradually be added. But the trenches were rarely left undisturbed for long.

German shell fire was the bane of the infantry's lives. If they survived for a few days, the men soon began to learn how to identify by sound the various types of shells. One common light shell fired by the 77-mm gun, equivalent to the British 18-pounder, was known as the 'whizz-bang' – which perfectly described what it did.

> 'Whizz-bangs' are not very jolly when fired exactly at you, as they were at the company headquarters; as Ethel says, 'It is not the bullet I mind, it is the bang!' So with the 'Whizz-Bangs' – when fired at you, the 'Whizz' part is almost absent, only lasts a fraction of a second and then there comes the sharp 'Bang'. It is quite startling, but is over so soon that it is really not so bad as the larger shells which one hears coming some time before. In their case the agony is prolonged.[1]
>
> Major Walter Vignoles, 10th Battalion, Lincolnshire Regiment, 101st Brigade, 34th Division

The most common large shells were the 5.9-ins which exploded with a large black cloud of smoke. They were nicknamed 'coal boxes' or 'Jack Johnsons' after a well-known pre-war American boxer.

Another menacing type of shell was fired by the German *minenwerfers*. These short range German trench mortars would be brought forward to pound the British front line whenever the situation was static enough to give them the chance.

> A form of Boche frightfulness called by us 'oil cans' from their resemblance to a small oil drum. These drums are about a foot in diameter and about 18 inches high and are filled with explosive containing very little shrapnel, the result is that they make a tremendous explosion with violent concussion, so that if they drop in the bay in which a man chances to be, they knock him very queer. The effect, however, is very local, and one can see them coming, so that the men very soon got in the way of watching for them and dodging them. As a matter of fact, most of them fall outside the trench and burst quite harmlessly. One night I was out and saw five 'oil cans' in the air together; the fuse makes a streak in the sky as it burns going through the air. None dropped very near me; the sergeants with me and I stood watching them to see which way they were going, before making a move, it is the only thing to do, and if a man keeps his head he can usually get away.[2]
>
> Major Walter Vignoles, 10th Battalion, Lincolnshire Regiment, 101st Brigade, 34th Division

Gas was a weapon that still had the power to cause panic amongst the men. The cloud attacks of 1915 were now largely replaced by artillery gas shells that landed with an insignificantly unthreatening 'plop' before releasing their contents into the atmosphere. Essentially the various forms of gas were designed to render victims incapable of functioning as soldiers. A small dose would cause breathing difficulties, uncontrollable crying but too much and it could kill or cause life-long chest problems. There was something primordial in the fear of not being able to breath in safety. There was also the very real lurking fear that the Germans could at any moment unleash new and ever more deadly forms of gas.

> Jerry started to shell with gas shells a village to our rear in the valley. He plastered this place and soon our eyes began to water copiously. We thought it was only tear gas, but as we began to splutter, cough and squirm, we found we had been too optimistic. I thought my heart would lose itself, as I was very sick, but as the shelling ceased, about an hour later I began to be more composed. We were all a little windy, as we had been told some time before that the Huns had invented a new gas which was fatal if the victim had any exercise within half an hour. This proved to be untrue, as we took an 8 mile march to the rear with no ill effects.[3]
>
> Lieutenant Edgar Lord, 15th Battalion, Lancashire Fusiliers, 96th Brigade, 32nd Division

By the middle of August 1916 a new gas mask had begun to make its appearance. It was not initially popular with the men for although it allowed them to function in gas and preserved their lives, they were awful to wear, combining discomfort with a strange futuristic appearance.

> An instrument of torture! A muzzle covered the face from below the eyes and fitted tightly under the chin. This was connected to a tin container, not unlike a regulation water bottle, lodged on the chest, by a reinforced, concertinaed rubber tube, from which a 'flipper' through which one exhaled protruded. A pair of large, metal-rimmed goggles was pulled over the eyes and required constant attention to keep it in place. After a while the padded interior of the muzzle became very soggy and the 'flipper' dripped saliva. However, though most unpleasant and uncomfortable, it proved efficient and saved us from the horrible effect of the gas.[4]
>
> Signaller Dudley Menaud-Lissenburg, 97th Battery, 147th Brigade, Royal Field Artillery, 29th Division

The British Army never properly mastered the art of digging reinforced dugouts to shelter their men while they were occupying the trenches – certainly not by 1916. The biggest and best dugouts in the front lines were reserved for the company headquarters where the company commander and his officers would be housed along with the senior NCOs and signallers – if there was room. The men usually had to make do with individual cubby holes scraped out of the side of the trench. In some sectors the men were able to occupy dugouts that had been captured from the Germans. These were magnificent efforts in comparison to the shallow scrapings of the British troops. They offered an illusion of security although the very fact they had been captured illustrated that there was nowhere actually safe.

> The old German trenches occupied by us on Pozières Ridge – between Pozières village and the farm – contained a number of commodious dugouts, 20 feet and more in depth, floored, and in some cases partitioned into several rooms. One, in particular, which was occupied by B Company headquarters, was lit by electricity, generated by a sort of bicycle peddled by a man. The only drawback was that the mouths of the dugouts faced the enemy line. More than once a German shell blew in an entrance, inflicting loss on the occupants below. On one occasion I was sheltering with others in the dugout when a shell exploded just above its mouth. Although none of us was hurt, we had visions of being trapped alive; but when the smoke cleared, we glimpsed daylight up the stairway, and were able to scratch a hole large enough to enable us to crawl out on our hands and knees.[5]
>
> Sergeant H. Preston, 9th Battalion (Queensland), 3rd Brigade, 1st Division, Australian Imperial Force

The underground bunkers had only recently been home to the evicted German tenants. A few had left their mark during their long occupation; a collection of possessions that revealed some inkling of their interests and personality. Not all the Germans were the uncultured boors of propaganda.

> I write this within 200 yards of our most advanced line, sitting in a German dugout, which has very lately been the headquarters of an artillery officer. He has left behind all his belongings and most of his books. The latter are really of an extraordinary variety. There are

books on optics and on philosophy, novels and poetry, Nietzsche and Balzac. I am sure there are several hundred volumes altogether. The fact that we are here seems to annoy the Hun intensely and we are under constant fire. As the roof is thick and the walls are strong, one can treat his exuberance with contempt. It must be very annoying for the one-time owner to watch his chimney smoking from afar, and to know that some barbarian is enjoying his coffee.[6]

Medical Officer Captain Charles McKerrow, 10th Battalion, Northumberland Fusiliers, 68th Brigade, 23rd Division

Such a refined dugout was certainly the exception. By their very nature most of the underground bunkers were dank, gloomy and unwelcoming places that offered very little in the way of home comforts.

Most men had to make do with the open trenches. Their uniforms soon became filthy, copiously bespattered with mud and nameless horrors. With no fresh water available for a proper wash and shave, here was a real life of grime.

When an occasional opportunity arose in the early dawn hours, I stripped, and my batman threw dirty water taken from shell holes in a canvas bucket all over me much to the amusement of nearby onlookers. Short periods of sleep were snatched in various locations, sometimes in shell holes, reminding me of Bruce Bairnsfather's famous cartoon, 'If you know of a better 'ole go to it'. One night I slept in the remains of a tomb belonging to the Waterlot family in Guillemont churchyard, and another in a recently captured German dugout. Removing blankets lying on the wire bunks, and casting them aside on the ground, I began to wonder if I was developing delusions. The blankets were moving in all directions, and on closer examination, I realised that this was caused by the infestation of millions of lice. My machine gunners also became infested, and whenever possible, removed their shirts to pick off any visible lice. On one occasion, I heard one say to another, 'There goes another Arsenal supporter!' as he threw it away. I gathered that the remark was made on account of its colour.[7]

Lieutenant Horace Paviere, 61st Company, Machine Gun Corps, 20th Division

In such dirty, cramped living conditions, lice were almost inevitable. They soon spread from man to man, till they became a near universal irritation.

When men first arrived with new drafts to the front they were often shocked at the sight of men openly delousing or 'chatting', as it was often called. These lice were not fleas, but a creeping parasite that was a light fawn colour and left irritating blotchy red bites. In the German dugouts an entirely different louse seemed to be endemic, which was smaller and red in colour. Various powders were commercially available but their efficacy was often in doubt and the men swore that the lice thrived on them. The best way to deal with them was to get the lice one by one in a ceaseless battle of attrition that mirrored the war itself.

> In the light of a few candles I made out half a dozen fellows with their shirts off. I soon found out it was a delousing session and they were cracking big body lice between their thumbnails. Lice lay in the seams of trousers and in the deep furrows of long woollen underpants. A lighted candle applied where they were thickest made them pop and splatter small blood spots onto one's face and hands. A delousing session could take a couple of hours. I felt downright sick and I left the dugout to go into the sunlight.[8]
>
> Private Thomas Jennings, 6th Battalion, Royal Berkshire Regiment, 53rd Brigade, 18th Division

Far worse than the lice were the rats. The men were acutely aware of the rats' predilection for feasting on the plentiful corpses lying out in No Man's Land, and the thought of being eaten alive or dead was enough to give most of them the horrors.

> I found out last night where a rat starts eating when he finds a corpse. I was just dozing off in my hammock when I felt a sharp pain in the knuckle of my middle finger, right hand. Evidently a rat had mistaken me for a dead man. Two nights ago, I found a similar cut on the knuckle of the same finger on the other hand. It is badly swollen now. Why the rats should start here I cannot imagine – unless it is that the bone is near the skin here and he uses his tooth against the bone![9]
>
> Lieutenant Leonard Pratt, 1/4th Battalion, Duke of Wellington's Regiment, 147th Brigade, 49th Division

From the lowly private to the highest regimental officer one enemy was common to them all – the mud – it soon began to dominate their lives. The Somme mud seemed to be a demonic elemental force intent on slowly sucking the life out of them.

> How we cursed that mud! We cursed it sleeping, we cursed it waking, we cursed it riding, we cursed it walking. We ate it and cursed; we drank it and cursed; we swallowed it and spat it; we snuffed it and wept it; it filled our nails and our ears; it caked and lined our clothing; we wallowed in it, we waded through it, we swam in it, and splashed it about – it stuck our helmets to our hair, it plastered our wounds, and there were men drowned in it. Oh, mud, thou daughter of the devil, thou offspring of evil, back to your infernal regions, and invade the lower circle of the inferno that you may make a fit abiding-place for the slacker and the pacifist.[10]
>
> Captain R. Hugh Knyvett, 15th (Queensland) Battalion, 4th Brigade, 4th Division, Australian Imperial Force

For the most part the officers suffered alongside their men, but at least their rank brought them sources of solace denied to the ordinary soldier.

> I found the battalion a huddled mass of soaked humanity. I was more tired than I liked to admit but I called a meeting of officers, explained the situation as best I could, and then lay down in the mud under a GS wagon and slept for an hour and a half. It was dark when Cyril Illingworth woke and told me it was time to move, and I must confess that I never felt more like, 'Shamefully throwing away my arms in the face of the enemy.' However, whisky and hot water made of me a hero again and I blessed the inventor of this life-giving liquor and wondered what the Germans drank instead.[11]
>
> Lieutenant Colonel Ronald Bodley, 10th Battalion, Rifle Brigade, 59th Brigade, 20th Division

The men had to make do with a rum ration. Contrary to popular mythology this was not administered to get the 'Tommies' roaring drunk before they went over the top. It was a tightly controlled ration meant primarily to help keep out the cold and generally invigorate the men.

Armies of men cannot exist on their own. The amount of supplies needed every day would have fed a teeming city and thousands of tons of food and water had to be got forward every night. Munitions, too, had to be brought up; the guns were voracious beasts in their ceaseless demands for shells. The logistical demands of creating and maintaining the infrastructure of war were simply phenomenal: the trenches alone sucked in incredible quantities of wood, sandbags, corrugated iron and barbed wire.

General Service wagons rumbled constantly through the night and their drivers from the Army Service Corps, Royal Engineers and Royal Artillery had an absolutely vital role. Although they were not 'at the sharp end' in the front line they, too, were risking their lives. The German artillery had registered the range of many of the main roads and junctions and at night they would open up randomly to wreak havoc on any convoy of wagons unlucky enough to be passing at the time. It was a strange game of chance that the drivers had no option but to play night after night. The only prize was survival and the knowledge that the men or the guns were being fed.

> That crossroad was shelled over and over again. A great hole appeared in the middle, perhaps 12 feet deep, and the pioneers would contrive to fill it up again, carrying stones or sandbags, and always ready to dodge away when German artillery would blast it away again. The strange thing was that there was nowhere to drive into, and we horsemen had to make a bolt, under fire, diving straight into a heavy crater filled with stinking water. Our horses were up to their bellies and even higher in mud and water. How we ever got them out was a mystery. If they had received shell fragments, we cut their traces and many received a bullet to end their suffering and agony.[12]
>
> Driver Rowland Luthor, C Battery, 92nd Brigade, Royal Field Artillery, 20th Division

The infantry held in reserve and support trenches alongside the main roads watched the nightly carnage with horror.

> Our trench ran parallel with the main road to Mametz in which direction all our transports came. I believe the 'Boche' knew every inch of the road. Daily and hourly we witnessed almost indescribable scenes on the roadside, our transports being hurled into the air like pieces of paper blown by the wind. The groans and cries of the wounded and dying pierced us through and through and made our blood run cold. I never slept a single moment in this position.[13]
>
> Private John Lawton, 1/5th Battalion, King's Liverpool Regiment, 165th Brigade, 55th Division

The teams of horses pulling the wagons couldn't take cover even if they had had the time or a comprehension of what was happening around them. They were a big target for the shrapnel and shell splinters to hit.

> Three men were wounded and seven horses hit. This morning at 12.30 to 1 a.m., I was coming back from a dressing station and I came through the transport lines. I had a flashlight and I turned it on some of the dear horses and patted them. I went on to the next. The light showed a great hole all stopped up with wadding. I thought, 'This is one of the wounded horses'. I went on and the next one had a hole in the head, the next in the legs and body, and so it went on. The flash-light showed up enough to tell me how terribly they had been wounded in taking food up to our men. Indeed, so bad were they that the transport officer said he might lose the lot. But all was silent. Only one was breathing a little heavily, that was all. I had just come from a dressing station. Our men suffer very bravely. But if you went into a dressing station after a battle blindfolded you would know at once from the occasional groans, expressions and movements, that man were there in pain. If you went through our transport lines blindfolded you would not have known that several of our horses were wounded, for they suffer in absolute silence.[14]
>
> Chaplain David Railton, 1/19th Battalion (St Pancras), London Regiment, 141st Brigade, 47th Division

The wagons could only get so far forward and they would drop off the supplies at dumps behind the front line. The food was divided up by the company sergeant majors and then carried up the last few hundred yards in sandbags slung over the shoulders of the ration parties sent back by the battalion in the front line. Given the problems in getting the food forward it was of necessity fairly basic fare. Tinned food was the staple with corned beef – the dreaded 'bully beef' of legend – predominating alongside the Machonachies meat and vegetable stew. Dry 'dog' biscuits, or if they were lucky bread, helped the men fill up along with bacon, cheese and jam. One staple of the diet was tea. The British Army had its own recipe for tea, which seemed to involve far too much of everything being stewed until it was unrecognisable by anyone with functioning taste buds.

> The tea, corrosively strong and sweet as a concentrated syrup, served in mugs with the enamel chipped off just where you put your lips. Contact with the naked tin can be avoided by drinking from the segment immediately above the handle. The state of the mugs can't

> be helped because they get such a bashing about, but there's no excuse for the ghastly brew.[15]
>
> Medical Officer Lieutenant Lawrence Gameson, 45th Field Ambulance, Royal Army Medical Corps, 15th Division

Yet most men loved it. Tea was for many a panacea for almost all ills. The potent combination of sugar and caffeine gave a temporary, but comforting 'high'.

What goes in must come out. Latrine discipline had to be maintained by the men at the front. If the men 'went' anywhere they pleased then the trenches would soon have been uninhabitable. Sanitation was hugely important and the presence of swarms of flies coupled with open latrines held a very real threat of dysentery. Rough latrines were dug in side trenches, mere holes in the ground occasionally boxed in or with a pole as a seat. They were liberally doused in quicklime to try and keep back the threat of disease.

Living conditions naturally improved further back from the line. Of course, the generals and their teams of staff officers did not share the privations and risks faced by the men in the front line. They needed to be at the centre of a communications hub that stretched forward to the battalions in the line and back to the High Command. The staff needed somewhere to work in reasonable safety, to draw up their detailed plans and from which they could disseminate their orders. They either occupied former German dugouts, or purpose built headquarters dug by the Royal Engineers.

For the British infantry all hopes were centred on the time when they would be relieved at the end of their tour of duty in the front line. Nobody could stand it for long under these conditions and five days was about the norm. The relief rarely went entirely smoothly as the new troops often had trouble finding their way to the right spot in the wasteland that surrounded them. Then the officers and NCOs had to ensure that the new garrison understood the local situation, the strength and weaknesses of the trenches, the locations of the trench stores and the linking points with neighbouring units. It was often a long, drawn-out process. The combination of fear, exhaustion, stress, extreme physical discomfort and illness was a potent brew. Officers, NCOs and men were all ground down and at the end of their physical and mental tether by the time their tour in the line came to an end.

> I collected the remnants of my section and began to struggle back through countless mud-holes. I was so weak that I kept falling down, and in the process getting muddier and muddier. Stretcher bearers came running up to help, imagining that I had been wounded. With hindsight, I now feel that I refused their offer ungraciously. The main contributory cause of the weakness was an acute attack of dysentery from which I had been suffering for some days and at that time I would rather have died than reported sick. No latrines were available, and I was forced to evacuate in numerous shell holes.[16]
>
> Lieutenant Horace Paviere, 61st Company, Machine Gun Corps, 20th Division

Next morning they would slowly begin to recover their natural vigour. However bad they may have felt, once they were removed from the source of the danger and privation the natural elastic resilience of youth served them well.

> It is queer by what stages one recovers from a whirl like that of the last few days, and they are invariably the same. During the worst rush one does not sleep, wash, or shave, and only eats haphazardly, a scrap here and there. The way these strains take me is that I can't speak quickly or loudly. My voice dwindles to a sort of whisper and the words follow the brain in a slow and halting way. Sometimes I can't think of even the simplest words in which to give an order. The first step to recovery is sleep. Then follows the first shave and a consequent feeling of increased morale and self-respect, then a wash and perhaps clean clothes, regular meals and the old order starts again.[17]
>
> Captain Philip Pilditch, C Battery, 235th Brigade, Royal Field Artillery, 47th Division

APPENDIX B

British Order of Battle The Somme 1916

Guards Division

1st Guards Brigade

2/Grenadier Guards, 2/Coldstream Guards, 3/Coldstream Guards, 1/Irish Guards

2nd Guards Brigade

3/Grenadier Guards. 1/Coldstream Guards, 1/Scots Guards, 2/Irish Guards

3rd Guards Brigade

1/Grenadier Guards, 4/Grenadier Guards, 2/Scots Guards, 1/Welch Guards

Pioneers:

4/Coldstream Guards

1st Division

1st Brigade

10/Glosters ,1/Black Watch, 8/Royal Berkshires, 1/Camerons

2nd Brigade

2/Royal Sussex, 1/Loyal North Lancashire, 1/Northamptons, 2/King's Royal Rifle Corps

3rd Brigade

1/South Wales Borderers, 1/Glosters, 2/Welch, 2/Royal Munster Fusiliers

Pioneers:

1/6th Welch

2nd Division

5th Brigade

17/Royal Fusiliers, 24/Royal Fusiliers, 2/Oxfordshire and Buckinghamshire Light Infantry, 2/Highland Light Infantry

6th Brigade

1/King's Regiment, 2/South Staffordshires, 13/Essex, 17/Middlesex

99th Brigade

22/Royal Fusiliers, 23/Royal Fusiliers, 1/Royal Berkshires, 1/King's Royal Rifle Corps

Pioneers:

10/Duke of Cornwall's Light Infantry

3rd Division

8th Brigade

2/Royal Scots, 8/East Yorkshires, 1/Royal Scots Fusiliers, 7/King's Shropshire Light Infantry

9th Brigade

1/Northumberland Fusiliers, 4/Royal Fusiliers, 13/King's Regiment, 12/West Yorkshires

76th Brigade

8/King's Own, 2/Suffolks, 10/Royal Welch, 1/Gordon Highlanders

Pioneers:

20/King's Royal Rifle Corps

4th Division

10th Brigade

1/Royal Warwicks, 2/Seaforths, 1/Royal Irish Fusiliers, 2/Royal Dublin Fusiliers

11th Brigade

1/Somerset Light Infantry, 1/East Lancashires, 1/Hampshires, 1/Rifle Brigade

12th Brigade

1/King's Own, 2/Lancashire Fusiliers, 2/Essex, 2/Duke of Wellington's Regiment

Pioneers:

21/West Yorkshire

5th Division

13th Brigade

14/Royal Warwicks, 15/Royal Warwicks, 2/King's Own Scottish Borderers, 1/Royal West Kents

15th Brigade

16/Royal Warwicks, 1/Norfolks, 1/Bedfords, 1/Cheshires

95th Brigade

1/Devons, 12/Glosters, 1/East Surreys, 1/Duke of Cornwall's Light Infantry

Pioneers:

1/6th Argyll and Sutherland Highlanders

6th Division

16th Brigade

1/Buffs (Royal East Kent), 8/Bedfords, 1/King's Shropshire Light Infantry, 2/York and Lancaster

18th Brigade

1/West Yorkshires, 11/Essex, 2/Durham Light Infantry, 14/Durham Light Infantry

71st Brigade

9/Norfolks, 9/Suffolks, 1/Leicesters, 2/Sherwood Foresters

Pioneers:

11/Leicester

7th Division

20th brigade

8/Devons, 9/Devons, 2/Borders, 2/Gordon Highlanders

22nd Brigade

2/Royal Warwicks, 2/Royal Irish, 1/Royal Welch Fusiliers, 20/Manchesters

91st Brigade

2/Queen's, 1/South Staffordshires, 21/Manchesters, 22/Manchesters

Pioneers:

24/Manchesters

8th Division

23rd Brigade

2/Devons, 2/West Yorkshires, 2/Middlesex, 2/Scots Rifles

24th Brigade[1]

1/Worcestershires, 1/Sherwood Foresters, 2/Northamptons, 2/East Lancashires

25th Brigade

2/Lincolns, 2/Royal Berkshires, 1/Royal Irish Rifles, 2/Rifle Brigade

Pioneers:

22/Durham Light Infantry

9th (Scottish) Division

26th Brigade

8/Black Watch, 7/Seaforths, 5/Camerons, 10/Argyll and Sutherland Highlanders

27th Brigade

11/Royal Scots, 12/Royal Scots, 6/King's Own Scottish Borderers, 9/Scottish Rifles

South African Brigade

1/ Cape Province, 2/Natal & O.F.S., 3/Transvaal and Rhodesia, 4/Scottish

Pioneers:

9/Seaforth

11th Division

32nd Brigade

9/West Yorkshires, 6/Green Howards, 8/Duke of Wellington's Regiment, 6/York and Lancaster

33rd Brigade

6/Lincolns, 6/Border Regiment, 7/South Staffordshires, 9/Sherwood Foresters

34th Brigade

8/Northumberland Fusiliers, 9/Lancashire Fusiliers, 5/Dorsets, 11/Manchesters

Pioneers:

6/East Yorkshires

12th Division – Major General A. B. Scott

35th Brigade

7/Norfolks, 7/Suffolks, 9/Essex, 5/Royal Berkshires

36th Brigade

8/Royal Fusiliers, 9/Royal Fusiliers, 7/Royal Sussex, 11/Middlesex

37th Brigade

6/Queen's, 6/Buffs (Royal East Kent), 7/East Surreys, 6/Royal West Kents

Pioneers:

5/Northamptons

14th (Light) Division

41st Brigade

7/King's Royal Rifle Corps, 8/King's Royal Rifle Corps, 7/Rifle Brigade, 8/Rifle Brigade

42nd Brigade

5/Oxfordshire and Buckinghamshire Light Infantry, 5/King's Shropshire Light Infantry, 9/King's Royal Rifle Corps, 9/Rifle Brigade

43rd Brigade

6/Somerset Light Infantry, 6/Duke of Cornwall's Light Infantry, 6/King's Own Yorkshire Light Infantry, 10/Durham Light Infantry

Pioneers:

11/King's

15th (Scottish) Division

44th Brigade

9/Black Watch, 8/Seaforth, 8th/10th Gordons, 7/Camerons

45th Brigade

13/Royal Scottish, 6th/7th Royal Scots Fusiliers, 6/Camerons, 11/Argyll and Sutherland Highlanders

46th Brigade
10/Scottish Rifle, 7th/8th King's Own Scottish Borderers, 10th/11th Highland Light Infantry, 12/Highland Light Infantry

Pioneers:
9/Gordons

16th (Irish) Division

47th Brigade
6/Royal Irish, 6/Connaught Rangers, 7/Leinster, 8/Royal Munster Fusiliers

48th Brigade
7/Royal Irish Rifles, 1/Royal Munster Fusiliers, 8/Royal Dublin Fusiliers, 9/Royal Dublin Fusiliers

49th Brigade
7/Royal Inniskilling Fusiliers, 8/Royal Inniskilling Fusiliers, 7/Royal Irish Fusiliers, 8/Royal Irish Fusiliers

Pioneers: 11/Hampshires

17th Division

50th Brigade
10/West Yorkshires, 7/East Yorkshires, 7/Green Howards, 6/Dorsets

51st Brigade
7/Lincolns, 7/Border Regiment, 8/South Staffordshires, 10/Sherwood Foresters

52nd Brigade
9/Northumberland Fusiliers, 10/Lancashire Fusiliers, 9/Duke of Wellington's Regiment, 12/Machesters

Pioneers:
7/York and Lancaster

18th (Eastern) Division

53rd Brigade
8/Norfolks, 8/Suffolks, 10/Essex, 6/Royal Berkshires

54th Brigade
11/Royal Fusiliers, 7/Bedfords, 6/Northamptons, 12/Middlesex

55th Brigade
7/Queen's, 7/Buffs (Royal East Kent), 8/East Surrey, 7/Royal West Kent

Pioneers:
8/Royal Sussex

19th (Western) Division

56th Brigade
7/King's Own, 7/East Lancashires, 7/South Lancashires, 7/L. N. Lancashires

57th Brigade

10/Royal Warwick, 8/Glosters, 10/Worcesters, 8/North Staffordshires

58th Brigade

9/Cheshires, 9/Royal Welch Fusiliers, 9/Welch, 6/Wiltshires

Pioneers:

5/South Wales Borderers

20th (Light) Division

59th Brigade

10/King's Royal Rifle Corps, 11/King's Royal Rifle Corps, 10/Rifle Brigade, 11/Rifle Brigade

60th Brigade

6/Oxford and Buckinghamshire Light Infantry, 6/King's Shropshire Light Infantry, 12/King's Royal Rifle Corps, 12/Rifle Brigade

61st Brigade

7/Somerset Light Infantry, 7/Duke of Cornwall's Light Infantry, 7/King's Own Yorkshire Light Infantry, 12/King's

Pioneers:

11/Durham Light Infantry

21st Division

62nd Brigade

12/Northumberland Fusiliers, 13/Northumberland Fusiliers, 1/Lincolns, 10/Green Howards

63rd Brigade[2]

8/Lincolns 8/Somerset Light Infantry, 4/Middlesex, 10/York and Lancaster

64th Brigade

1/East Yorkshires, 9/King's Own Yorkshire Light Infantry, 10/King's Own Yorkshire Light Infantry, 15/Durham Light Infantry

Pioneers:

14/Northumberland Fusiliers

23rd Divison

68th Brigade

10/Northumberland Fusiliers, 11/Northumberland Fusiliers, 12/Durham Light Infantry, 13/Durham Light Infantry

69th Brigade

11/West Yorkshires, 8/Green Howards, 9/Green Howards, 10/Duke of Wellington's Regiment.

70th Brigade[3]
11/Sherwood Foresters, 8/King's Own Yorkshire Light Infantry, 8/York and Lancaster, 9/York and Lancaster

Pioneers:
9/South Staffordshires

24th Division

17th Brigade
8/Buffs (Royal East Kent), 1/Royal Fusiliers, 12/Royal Fusiliers, 3/Rifle Brigade

72nd Brigade
8/Queen's, 9/East Surreys, 8/Royal West Kents, 1/North Staffordshires

73rd Brigade
9/Royal Sussex, 7/Northamptons, 13/Middlesex, 2/Leinsters

Pioneers:
12/Sherwood Foresters

25th Division

7th Brigade
10/Cheshires, 3/Worcesters, 8/Loyal North Lancashires, 1/Wiltshires

74th Brigade
11/Lancashire Fusiliers, 13/Cheshires, 9/Loyal North Lancashires, 2/Royal Irish Rifles

75th Brigade
11/Cheshires, 8/Border Regiment, 2/South Lancashires, 8/South Lancashires

Pioneers:
6/South Wales Borderers

29th Division

86th Brigade
2/Royal Fusiliers, 1/Lancashire Fusiliers, 16/Middlesex, 1/Royal Dublin Fusiliers

87th Brigade
2/South Wales Borderers, 1/King's Own Scottish Borderers, 1/Royal Inniskilling Fusiliers, 1/Border Regiment

88th Brigade
4/Worcestershires, 1/Essex, 2/Hampshires, Royal Newfoundland Regiment

Pioneers:
2/Monmouth

30th Division

21st Brigade
18/King's, 2/Green Howards, 2/Wiltshires, 19/Manchesters

89th Brigade
17/King's, 19/King's, 20/King's, 2/Bedfords

90th Brigade
2/Royal Scots Fusiliers, 16/Manchesters, 17/Manchesters, 18/Manchesters

Pioneers:
11/South Lancashires

31st Division

92nd Brigade
10/East Yorkshires, 11/East Yorkshires, 12/East Yorkshires, 13/East Yorkshires

93rd Brigade
15/West Yorkshires, 16/West Yorkshires, 18/West Yorkshires, 18/Durham Light Infantry

94th Brigade
11/East Lancashires, 12/York and Lancaster, 13/York and Lancaster, 14/York and Lancaster

Pioneers:
12/King's Own Yorkshire Light Infantry

32nd Division

14th Brigade
19/Lancashire Fusiliers[4], 1/Dorsetshires, 2/Manchesters, 15/Highland Light Infantry

96th Brigade
16/Northumberland Fusiliers, 15/Lancashire Fusiliers, 16/Lancashire Fusiliers, 2/Royal Inniskilling Fusiliers

97th Brigade
11/Border Regiment, 2/King's Own Yorkshire Light Infantry, 16/Highland Light Infantry, 17/Highland Light Infantry

Pioneers:
17/Northumberland Fusiliers[5]

33rd Division

19th Brigade
20th Royal Fusiliers, 2/Royal Welch Fusiliers, 1/Cameronians, 5/Scottish Rifles

98th Brigade
4/King's Regiment, 1/4th Suffolk, 1/Middlesex, 2/Argyll and Sutherland Highlanders

100th Brigade
1/Queen's Regiment, 2/Worcestershires, 16/King's Royal Rifle Corps, 1/9th Highland Light Infantry

Pioneers:
18/Middlesex Regiment

34th Division

101st Brigade
15/Royal Scots, 16/Royal Scots, 10/Lincolns, 11/Suffolks

102nd (Tyneside Scottish) Brigade[6]
20/Northumberland Fusiliers, 21/ Northumberland Fusiliers, 22/Northumberland Fusiliers, 23/ Northumberland Fusiliers

103rd (Tyneside Irish) Brigade[7]
24/ Northumberland Fusiliers, 25/ Northumberland Fusiliers, 26/ Northumberland Fusiliers, 27/ Northumberland Fusiliers

Pioneers:
18/ Northumberland Fusiliers[8]

35th (Bantam) Division

104th Brigade
17/Lancashire Fusiliers, 18/Lancashire Fusiliers, 20/Lancashire Fusiliers, 23/Manchester

105th Brigade
15/Cheshire, 16/Cheshire, 14/Glosters, 15/Sherwood Foresters

106th Brigade
17/Royal Scots, 17/West Yorkshires, 19/Durham Light Infantry, 18/Highland Light Infantry

Pioneers:
19/Northumberland Fusiliers

36th (Ulster) Division

107th Brigade
8/Royal Irish Rifles, 9/Royal Irish Rifles, 10/Royal Irish Rifles, 15/Royal Irish Rifles

108th Brigade
11/Royal Irish Rifles, 12/Royal Irish Rifles, 13/Royal Irish Rifles, 9/Royal Irish Fusiliers

109th Brigade
9/Royal Inniskilling Fusiliers, 10/ Royal Inniskilling Fusiliers, 11/ Royal Inniskilling Fusiliers, 14/Royal Irish Rifles

Pioneers:
16/Royal Irish Rifles

37th Divison

110th Brigade[9]
6/Leicesters, 7/Leicesters, 8/Leicesters, 9/Leicesters

111th Brigade[10]
10/Royal Fusiliers, 13/Royal Fusiliers, 13/King's Royal Rifle Corps, 13/Rifle Brigade

112th Brigade[11]
11/Royal Warwicks, 6/Bedfords, 8/East Lancashires, 10/Loyal North Lancashires

Pioneers:
9/North Staffordshires[12]

38th (Welsh) Division

113th Brigade
13/Royal Welch Fusiliers, 14/Royal Welch Fusiliers, 15/Royal Welch Fusiliers, 16/Royal Welch Fusiliers

114th Brigade
10/Welch, 13/Welch, 14/Welch, 15/Welch

115th Brigade
10/South Wales Borderers, 11/South Wales Borderers, 17/Royal Welch Fusiliers, 16/Welch

Pioneers:
19/Welch

39th Division

116th Brigade
11/Royal Sussex, 12/Royal Sussex, 13/Royal Sussex, 14/Hampshires

117th Brigade
16/Sherwood Foresters, 17/Sherwood Foresters, 17/King's Royal Rifle Corps, 16/Rifle Brigade

118th Brigade
1/6th Cheshires, 1/1st Cambridgeshires, 1/1st Hertfordshires, 4th/5th Black Watch

Pioneers:
13/Glosters

41st Division

112th Brigade
12/East Surreys, 15/Hampshires, 11/Royal West Kents, 18/King's Royal Rifle Corps

123rd Brigade
11/Queen's, 10/Royal West Kents, 23/Middlesex, 20/Durham Light Infantry

124th Brigade
10/Queen's, 26/Royal Fusiliers, 32/Royal Fusiliers, 21/King's Royal Rifle Corps

Pioneers:
19/Middlesex

46th (North Midland) Division (T.F.)

137th Brigade
1/5th South Staffordshires, 1/6th South Staffordshires, 1/5th North Staffordshires, 1/6th North Staffordshires

138th Brigade
1/4th Lincolns, 1/5th Lincolns, 1/4th Leicesters, 1/5th Leicesters

139th Brigade
1/5th Sherwood Foresters, 1/6th Sherwood Foresters, 1/7th Sherwood Foresters, 1/8th Sherwood Foresters

Pioneers:
1/Monmouths

47th (1/2nd London) Division (T.F.)

140th Brigade
1/6th Londons (City of London), 1/7th Londons (City of London), 1/8th Londons (Post Office Rifles), 1/15th Londons (Civil Service Rifles)

141st Brigade
1/17th Londons (Poplar and Stepney Rifles), 1/18th Londons (London Irish Rifles), 1/19th Londons (St Pancras), 1/20th Londons (Blackheath and Woolwich)

142nd Brigade
1/21st Londons (1st Surrey Rifles), 1/22nd Londons (The Queen's), 1/23rd Londons, 1/24th Londons (The Queen's)

Pioneers:
1/4th Royal Welch Fusiliers

48th Division (South Midland) Division (T.F.)

143rd Brigade
1/5th Royal Warwicks, 1/16th Royal Warwicks, 1/7th Royal Warwicks, 1/8th Royal Warwicks

144th Brigade
1/4th Glosters, 1/6th Glosters, 1/7th Worcestershires, 1/8th Worcestershires

145th Brigade
1/5th Glosters, 1/4th Oxfordshire and Buckinghamshire Light Infantry, 1/1st Buckinghamshires, 1/4th Royal Berkshires

Pioneers:
1/5th Sussex

49th (West Riding) Division (T.F.)

146th Brigade

1/5th West Yorkshires, 1/6th West Yorkshires, 1/7th West Yorkshires, 1/8th West Yorkshires

147th Brigade

1/4th Duke of Wellington's Regiment, 1/5th Duke of Wellington's Regiment, 1/6th Duke of Wellington's Regiment, 1/7th Duke of Wellington's Regiment

148th Brigade

1/4th King's Own Yorkshire Light Infantry, 1/5th King's Own Yorkshire Light Infantry, 1/4th York and Lancaster, 1/5th York and Lancaster

Pioneers

3/Monmouth (Replaced by 19/Lancashire Fusiliers 6th August)

50th (Northumberland) Division (T.F.)

149th Brigade

1/4th Northumberland Fusiliers, 1/5th Northumberland Fusiliers, 1/6th Northumberland Fusiliers, 1/7th Northumberland Fusiliers

150th Brigade

1/4th East Yorkshires, 1/4th Green Howards, 1/5th Green Howards, 1/5th Durham Light Infantry

151st Brigade

1/5th Border Regiment, 1/6th Durham Light Infantry, 1/8th Durham Light Infantry, 1/9th Durham Light Infantry

Pioneers:

1/7th Durham Light Infantry

51st (Highland) Division (T.F.)

152nd Brigade

1/5th Seaforths, 1/6th Seaforths, 1/6th Gordons, 1/8th Argyll and Sutherlands

153rd Brigade

1/6th Black Watch, 1/7th Black Watch, 1/5th Gordons, 1/7th Gordons

154th Brigade

1/9th Royal Scots, 1/4th Seaforths, 1/4th Gordons, 1/7th Argyll and Sutherlands

Pioneers:

1/8th Royal Scots

55th (West Lancashire) Division (T.F.)

164th Brigade

1/4th King's Own, 1/8th King's, 2/5th Lancashire Fusiliers, 1/4th Loyal North Lancashires

165th Brigade
1/5th King's, 1/6th King's, 1/7th King's, 1/9th King's

166th Brigade
1/5th King's Own, 1/10th King's, 1/5th South Lancashires, 1/5th Loyal North Lancashires

Pioneers:
1/4th South Lancashires

56th (1st London) Division (T.F.)

167th Brigade
1/1st London Royal Fusiliers, 1/3rd London Royal Fusiliers, 1/7th Middlesex, 1/8th Middlesex

168th Brigade
1/4th London Royal Fusiliers, 1/12th London Rangers, 1/13th London (Kensington), 1/14th London (London Scottish)

169th Brigade
1/2nd Royal Fusiliers, 1/5th London Rifle Brigade, 1/9th London Queen's Victoria's Rifles, 1/16th London Queen's Westminster Rifles

Pioneers
1/5th Cheshire

63rd (Royal Naval) Division

188th Brigade
Anson Battalion, Howe Battalion, 1/Royal Marine Battalion, 2/Royal Marine Battalion

189th Brigade
Hood Batttalion, Nelson Battalion, Hawke Battalion, Drake Battalion

190th Brigade
1/Honourable Artillery Company, 7/Royal Fusiliers, 4/Befords, 10/Royal Dublin Fusiliers

Pioneers:
14/Worcestershires

1st Australian Division

1(New South Wales) Brigade
1st Battalion, 2nd Battalion, 3rd Battalion, 4th Battalion

2nd (Victoria) Brigade
5th Battalion, 6th Battalion, 7th Battalion, 8th Battalion

3rd Brigade
9th (Queensland) Battalion, 10th (S. Australia) Battalion, 11th (W. Australia) Battalion, 12th (S. and W. Australia, Tas.) Battalion

Pioneers:
1st Australian Pioneer Battalion

2nd Australian Division

5th (New South Wales) Brigade

17th Battalion, 18th Battalion, 19th Battalion, 20th Battalion

6th (Victoria) Brigade

21st Battalion, 22nd Battalion, 23rd Battalion, 24th Battalion

7th Brigade

25th (Queensland) Battalion, 26th (Q'land, Tas.) Battalion, 27th (S. Australia) Battalion, 28th (W. Australia) Battalion

Pioneers:

2nd Australian Pioneer Battalion

4th Australian Division

4th Brigade

13th (New South Wales) Battalion, 14th (Victoria) Battalion, 15th (Q'land, Tas.) Battalion, 16th (S. and W. Australia) Battalion

12th Brigade

45th (New South Wales) Battalion, 46th (Victoria) Battalion, 47th (Q'land, Tas) Battalion, 48th (S. and W. Australia) Battalion

13th Brigade

49th (Queensland) Battalion, 50th (S. Australia Tas.) Battalion, 51st (W. Australia) Battalion, 52nd (S. and W. Australia, Tas.) Battalion

Pioneers:

4th Australian Pioneer Battalion

5th Australian Division

8th Brigade

29th (Victoria) Battalion, 30th (New South Wales) Battalion, 31st (Q'land, Vic) Battalion, 32nd (S. & W. Australian) Battalion

14th (New South Wales) Brigade

53rd Battalion, 54th Battalion, 55th Battalion, 56th Battalion

15th (Victoria) Brigade

57th Battalion, 58th Battalion, 59th Battalion, 60th Battalion

Pioneers:

5th Australian Pioneer Battalion

1st Canadian Division

1st Brigade

1st (Ontario) Battalion, 2nd (East Ontario) Battalion, 3rd (Toronto Regiment) Battalion, 4th Battlion

2nd Brigade
5th (Western Cavalry) Battalion, 7th Battalion (1st British Columbia), 8th Battalion (90th Rifles), 10th Battalion

3rd Brigade
13th Battalion (Royal Highlanders), 14th Battalion (R. Montreal Regt), 15th Battalion (48th Highlanders), 16th Battalion (Canadian Scottish)

Pioneers:
1st Canadian Pioneer Battalion

2nd Canadian Division

4th Brigade
18th (W. Ontario) Battalion, 19th (Central Ontario) Battalion, 20th (Central Ontario) Battalion, 21st (Eastern Ontario) Battalion

5th Brigade
22nd (Canadian Francais) Battalion, 24th Battalion (Victoria Rifles), 25th Battalion (Nova Scotia Rifles), 26th (New Brunswick) Battalion

6th Brigade
27th (City of Winnipeg) Battalion, 28th (North-West) Battalion, 29th (Vancouver) Battalion, 31st (Alberta) Battalion

Pioneers:
2nd Canadian Pioneers Battalion

3rd Canadian Division

7th Brigade
Princess Patricia's Canadian Light Infantry, Royal Canadian Regiment, 42 Battalion (Royal Highlanders), 49th (Edmonton) Battalion

8th Brigade
1st Canadian Mounted Regiment, 2nd Canadian Mounted Regiment, 4th Canadian Mounted Regiment, 5th Canadian Mounted Regiment

9th Brigade
43rd Battalion (Cameron Highlanders), 52nd (New Ontario) Battalion, 58th Battalion, 60th Battalion (Victoria Rifles)

Pioneers:
3rd Canadian Pioneer Battalion

4th Canadian Division

10th Brigade
44th Battalion, 46th (S. Saskatchewan) Battalion, 47th (British Columbia) Battalion, 50th (Calgary) Battalion

11th Brigade
54th (Kootenay) Battalion, 75th (Mississauga) Battalion, 87th Battalion (Canadian Grenadier Gds), 102nd Battalion

12th Brigade
38th (Ottawa) Battalion, 72nd Battalion (Seaforth Highlanders), 73rd Battalion (Royal Highlanders), 78th Battalion (Winnipeg Grenadiers)

Pioneers:
67th Canadian Pioneer Battalion

New Zealand Division

1st New Zealand Brigade
1/Auckland, 1/Canterbury, 1/Otago, 1/Wellington

2nd New Zealand Brigade
2/Auckland, 2/Canterbury, 2/Otago, 2/Wellington

3rd New Zealand Rifle Brigade
1/New Zealand Rifle Brigade, 2/New Zealand Rifle Brigade, 3/New Zealand Rifle Brigade, 4/New Zealand Rifle Brigade

Pioneers:
New Zealand Pioneer Battalion

1 With 23rd Division until 15th July, in exchange for 70th Brigade

2 Exchanged with 110th Brigade of 37th Division, 7 July

3 With 8th Division until 15th July in exchange for 24th Brigade

4 Replaced by 5th/6th Royal Scots, 29 July

5 Replaced by 12/L.N. Lancs., 19 October

6 Attached to 37th Division 7 July–21 August. Replaced by 111th Brigade

7 Attached to 37th Division 7 July–21 August. Replaced by 112th Brigade

8 Attached to 37th Division 7 July–21 August. Replaced by 9/North Staffordshire

9 Exchanged with 63rd Brigade, 21st Division, 7 July

10 Attached 7 July–21 August to 34th Division

11 Attached 7 July–21 August to 34th Division

12 Attached 7 July–21 August to 34th Division

APPENDIX C

German Order of Battle The Somme 1916

2nd Army – General von Below

3rd Guard Division

Guards Fusiliers, Lehr Regiment, Grenadier Regiment No. 9

4th Guard Division

5th Guards Foot, 5th Guards Grenadiers, Reserve Regiment No. 93

5th Division

Grenadier Regiments Nos. 8 and 12, Regiment No. 52

6th Division

Regiments Nos. 20, 24 and 64

7th Division

Regiments Nos. 26, 27[1] and 165

8th Division

Regiments Nos. 72, 93 and 153

12th Division

Regiments Nos. 23, 62 and 63

16th Division

Regiments Nos. 28, 29, 68 and 69

24th Division

Regiments Nos. 133, 139 and 179

26th Division

Grenadier Regiment No. 119, Regiments Nos. 121 and 125

27th Division

Regiments No. 120, Grenadier Regiment No. 123, Regiment No. 124 and 127

38th Division

Regiments Nos. 94, 95 and 96

40th Division

Regiments Nos. 104, 134 and 181

52nd Division

Regiments Nos. 66, 161 and 170

56th Division

Fusilier Regiment No. 35, Regiment Nos. 88 and 118

58th Division

Regiment Nos. 106 and 107, Reserve Regiment No. 120

111th Division

Fusilier Regiment No. 73, Regiments Nos. 76 and 164

117th Division

Regiment No. 157, Reserve Regiments Nos. 11 and 22

183rd Division

Regiments Nos. 183 and 184, Reserve Regiment No. 122

185th Division[2]

Regiments Nos. 185, 186 and 190

208th Division

Regiments Nos. 25 and 185, Reserve Regiment No. 65

222nd Division

Regiments Nos. 193 and 397, Reserve Regiment No. 81

223rd Division

Regiment Nos. 144 and 173, Ersatz Regiment No. 29

1st Guard Reserve Division

Guards Reserve Regiments Nos. 1 and 2, Reserve Regiment No. 64

2nd Guard Reserve Division

Reserve Regiments Nos. 15, 55, 77 and 91

7th Reserve Division

Reserve Regiments Nos. 36, 66 and 72

12 Reserve Division

Reserve Regiments Nos. 23, 38 and 51

17th Reserve Division

Regiments Nos. 162 and 163, Reserve Regiments Nos. 75[3] and 76

18th Reserve Division

Reserve Regiments Nos. 31, 84 and 86

19th Reserve Division

Reserve Regiments Nos. 73, 78, 79 and 92

23rd Reserve Division

Reserve Grenadier Regiment No. 101, Reserve Regiments Nos. 101 and 102, Regiment No. 392

24th Reserve Division

Reserve Regiments Nos. 101, 107 and 133

26th Reserve Division

Reserve Regiments Nos. 99, 119, 121, Regiment No. 180

28th Reserve Division

Reserve Regiments Nos. 109, 110 and 111

45th Reserve Division

Reserve Regiments Nos. 210, 211 and 212

50th Reserve Division

Reserve Regiments Nos. 229, 230 and 231

51st Reserve Division

Reserve Regiments Nos. 233, 234, 235 and 236

52nd Reserve Division

Reserve Regiments Nos. 238, 239 and 240

4th Ersatz Division

Regiments Nos. 359, 360, 361 and 362

5th Ersatz Division

Landwehr Regiments Nos. 73, 74, Reserve Ersatz Regiment No. 3

2nd Bavarian Division

Bavarian Regiments Nos. 12, 15 and 20

3rd Bavarian Division

Bavarian Regiments Nos. 17, 18 and 23

4th Bavarian Division

Bavarian Regiments Nos. 5 and 9, Bavarian Reserve Regiment No. 5

5th Bavarian Division

Bavarian Regiments Nos. 7, 14, 19 and 21

6th Bavarian Division

Bavarian Regiments Nos. 6, 10, 11 and 13

10th Bavarian Division

Bavarian Regiment No. 16, Bavarian Reserve Regiments Nos. 6 and 8

6th Bavarian Reserve Division

Bavarian Reserve Regiments Nos. 16, 17, 20 and 21

Bavarian Ersatz Division

Bavarian Reserve Regiments Nos. 14 and 15, Ersatz Regiment No. 28

89th Reserve Brigade

Reserve Regiments Nos. 209 and 213

Marine Brigade

Marine Regiments Nos. 1, 2 and 3

1 Replaced by Regiment No. 393 for second tour

2 Reorganised for second tour, composition being Regiments Nos. 65, 161 and Reserve Regiment No. 28

3 Left division before second tour

Notes to the Text

1 The Rocky Road

1 O. Von Bismarck, Letter, 9/7/1866

2 H. Rawlinson, quoted in R. Prior & T. Wilson, *Command on the Western Front* (Oxford: Blackwell, 1992), p. 25

3 Ibid., p. 78

4 D. Haig, *The Man I Knew* (London: Moray Press, 1936), p. viii

5 D. Haig, quoted in W. S. Churchill, *World Crisis, 1916–1918* (London: Thornton Butterworth), Part II, p. 445

6 J. Charteris, *At G.H.Q.* (London: Cassell & Co, 1931), p. 129

7 J. Charteris, *Field Marshal Earl Haig* (London: Cassell & Co, 1929), pp. 205–6

8 J. Charteris, *At G.H.Q.*, p. 164

9 D. Haig, diary entry 18/1/1916 quoted in G. Sheffield & J. Bourne (eds), *Douglas Haig: War Diaries and Letters 1914–18* (Weidenfeld & Nicolson, forthcoming)

10 J. Charteris, *At G.H.Q.*, p. 134

11 D. Haig, diary entry 1/1/1916, edited by R. Blake, *The Private Papers of Douglas Haig, 1914–1919* (London: Eyre & Spottiswoode, 1952), p. 122

12 J. Charteris, *At G.H.Q.*, p. 129

13 J. Joffre, quoted in J. E. Edmonds, *History of the Great War: Military Operations, France and Belgium, 1916* (Woking: Shearer Publications, 1986), pp. 26–7

14 D. Haig, diary entry 29/3/1916, edited by R. Blake, *The Private Papers of Douglas Haig, 1914–1919*, p. 137

15 D. Haig, diary entry 26/5/1916, quoted in G. Sheffield & J. Bourne (eds), *Douglas Haig: War Diaries and Letters 1914–18*

16 D. Haig, letter to Viscount Bertie of Thame 5/6/1916, quoted in G. Sheffield & J. Bourne (eds) *Douglas Haig: War Diaries and Letters 1914–18*

2 Armies and Weapons

1 IWM SOUND: H. Hayward, AC 9422

2 A. Dalby, quoted in L. Milner, *Leeds Pals: A History of the 15th (Service) Battalion, West Yorkshire Regiment, 1914–1918* (Barnsley: Leo Cooper, 1993), pp. 22 & 25

3 M. Fleming, ibid., pp. 23 & 25–6

4 Anon. Reporter, *Manchester Guardian* 22/3/1915, quoted in M. Stedman, *Salford Pals: 15th, 16th, 19th and 20th Battalions Lancashire Fusiliers* (Barnsley: Leo Cooper, 1993), p. 53

5 IWM DOCS: W. T. Colyer, Manuscript account, 'War Impressions', pp. 200–201

6 IWM SOUND: B. Farrer, AC 9552, Reel 13

7 IWM DOCS: W. T. Colyer, Manuscript account, 'War Impressions'

8 National Army Museum: F. A. M. Maxwell, Manuscript copies of letters, 23/6/1916

9 IWM DOCS: D. N. Menaud-Lissenburg, Typescript memoir, p. 175

10 IWM SOUND: G. Cole, AC 9535, Reel 6

11 IWM SOUND: M. S. Cleeve, AC 7310, Reel 2

12 IWM SOUND: L. G. Ounsworth, AC 332, Reel 4

13 IWM DOCS: A. F. D. Darlington, Typescript account

14 Ibid.

15 IWM DOCS: E. B. Lord, Typescript account, pp. 13–14

16 F. C. Stanley, *The History of the 89th Brigade, 1914–1918* (Liverpool: Daily Post, 1919), p. 119

17 Ibid., pp. 119–120

18 IWM DOCS: S. W. Appleyard, Transcript diary, pp. 56–7

19 IWM DOCS: W. T. Colyer, Manuscript account, 'War Impressions', pp. 200–201

20 IWM SOUND: P. Neame, AC 48, Reel 4

3 Moving On Up

1 IWM SOUND: R. Miller, AC 11961, Reel 4

2 IWM DOCS: A. L. Atkins, Typescript letter, p. 22

3 IWM DOCS: A. V. Conn, Typescript account

4 IWM DOCS: D. Starrett, Typescript account, pp. 48–9

5 IWM DOCS: A. V. Conn, Typescript account

6 D. Haig, diary entry 4/4/1916, quoted in G. Sheffield & J. Bourne (eds), *Douglas Haig: War Diaries and Letters 1914–18*

7 H. Rawlinson quoted in R. Prior & T. Wilson, *Command on the Western Front*, p. 149

8 D. Haig, diary entry 27/6/1916, quoted in G. Sheffield & J. Bourne (eds), *Douglas Haig: War Diaries and Letters 1914–18*

9 IWM DOCS: A. Home, Typescript diary, 22/6/1916

10 D. Haig, diary entry 17/6/1916, quoted in G. Sheffield & J. Bourne (eds), *Douglas Haig: War Diaries and Letters 1914–18*

11 IWM DOCS: B. S. Philpotts Collection: F. H. Aincham, Typescript account

12 IWM DOCS: W. H. Bloor, Typescript diary, 23/6/1916

13 J. E. Edmonds, *History of the Great War: Military Operations, France and Belgium, 1916*, p. 283

14 IWM DOCS: S. W. Appleyard, Transcript diary, p. 57

15 IWM DOCS: F. L. Cassel, Typescript account

16 IWM DOCS: R. Stockman, Typescript memoir

17 Ibid.

18 T. Snow, quoted in J. E. Edmonds, *History of the Great War: Military Operations, France and Belgium, 1916*, p. 460

19 IWM DOCS: W. T. Colyer, Manuscript account, 'War Impressions'

20 IWM DOCS: C. Carter, Typescript account, Pt 3, pp. 2–3

21 IWM SOUND: N. M. Dillon, AC 9752, Reel 7

22 IWM DOCS: D. N. Menaud-Lissenburg, Typescript memoir, pp. 168–9

23 IWM SOUND: M. S. Cleeve, AC 7310, Reel 2

24 Ibid., Reel 3

25 Ibid., Reel 2

26 IWM DOCS: D. N. Menaud-Lissenburg, Typescript memoir, pp. 180–1

27 IWM DOCS: C. C. May, Typescript diary, 16/6/1916

28 IWM SOUND: L. G. Ounsworth, AC 332, Reel 4

29 N. Fraser-Tytler, *Field Guns in France* (London: Hutchinson & Co, 1922), pp. 73–4

30 IWM DOCS: A. L. Atkins, Typescript letter, pp. 25–6

31 IWM DOCS: W. P. Nevill, Edited from manuscript letters, 16/6/1916, 18/6/1916 & 22/6/1916

32 IWM DOCS: D. N. Menaud-Lissenburg, Typescript memoir, p. 178

33 IWM DOCS: W. H. Bloor, Typescript diary, 24/6/1916

34 IWM DOCS: C. G. Lawson, Typescript letters, 24/6/1916

35 IWM DOCS: R. G. Ingle, Typescript diary, 24/6/1916

36 IWM DOCS: C. C. May, Typescript diary, 25/6/1916

37 IWM DOCS: W. H. Bloor, Typescript diary, 25/6/1916

38 IWM DOCS: D. N. Menaud-Lissenburg, Typescript memoir, pp. 168–9

39 IWM DOCS: W. H. Bloor, Typescript diary, 26/6/1916

40 Diary quoted in T. Chalmers, *History of the 15th Battalion, The Highland Light Infantry* (Glasgow: John McCallum & Co, 1934), p. 68

41 Ibid.

42 IWM DOCS: F. L. Cassel, Typescript account

43 Ibid.

44 Ibid.

45 Ibid.

46 IWM DOCS: H. C. Rees, 'A Personal Record of the War, 1915–1916–1917'

47 IWM DOCS: W. T. Colyer, Manuscript account, 'War Impressions'

48 Ibid.

49 IWM DOCS: R. G. Ingle, Typescript diary, 25/6/1916

50 IWM SOUND: R. Miller, AC 11961, Reel 4

51 IWM DOCS: C. C. May, Typescript diary, 28/6/1916

52 Ibid., 29/6/1916

53 IWM SOUND: H. Tansley, AC 13682, Reel 1 (Recorded for BBC Radio 4, *A Summer Day on the Somme*, broadcast 27/6/1976)

54 IWM DOCS: E. B. Lord, Typescript account, p. 16

55 IWM DOCS: A. L. Atkins, Typescript letter, p. 29

56 C. W. Wood, quoted in *The Robin Hoods: 1/7th, 2/7th and 3/7th Battalions, Sherwood Foresters* (Nottingham: J. & H. Bell Ltd, 1921), p. 201

57 D. Haig, diary entry 30/6/1916, quoted in G. Sheffield & J. Bourne (eds), *Douglas Haig: War Diaries and Letters 1914–18*

58 W. D. Allen quoted in O. Rutter, *The*

History of the Seventh (Service) The Royal Sussex Regiment (London: Times Publishing Company, 1934), p. 83

59 IWM DOCS: D. N. Menaud-Lissenburg, Typescript memoir, p. 182

60 IWM DOCS: W. T. Colyer, Manuscript account, 'War Impressions'

61 Ibid.

62 IWM SOUND: A. Irwin, AC 211

63 IWM DOCS: W. P. Nevill, Manuscript letter, 18/6/1916

64 J. Engall, 'A Farewell letter, 30/6/1916', *The New Chequers* (The Journal of the Friends of Lochnagar), No. 4, pp. 24–5

65 IWM DOCS: C. C. May, Typescript diary, 17/6/1916

66 IWM DOCS: E. C. Crosse, Typescript diary, 4/7/1916–5/7/1916

67 N. Hodgson, Poem: *Before Action*, 30/6/1916

68 IWM DOCS: E. C. Crosse, Typescript manuscript, 'The History of the Chaplains' Department in the War, 1914–1918', pp. 62–3

69 Diary quoted in T. Chalmers, *History of the 15th Battalion*, p. 69

4 1 July 1916

1 IWM DOCS: C. C. May, Typescript diary, 1/7/1916

2 H. Baumber, 'The Grimbsy Chums', *The New Chequers*, p. 9

3 IWM DOCS: W. T. Colyer, Manuscript account, 'War Impressions'

4 Ibid.

5 IWM SOUND: A. Irwin, AC 211

6 A. W. Andrews (edited by S. Richardson), *Orders are Orders: A Manchester Pal on the Somme* (Manchester: Neil Richardson, 1987), p. 48

7 IWM DOCS: W. A. Vignoles, Typescript manuscript, p. 81

8 F. Hawkings, *From Ypres to Cambrai: The 1914–1919 Diary of Infantryman Frank Hawkings* (Morley: Elmfield Press, 1974), p. 97

9 IWM DOCS: W. A. Vignoles, Typescript manuscript, pp. 79–82

10 IWM SOUND: B. Farrer, AC 9552, Reel 13

11 IWM SOUND: A. Hurst, AC 11582, Reel 7

12 A. W. Andrews (edited by S. Richardson), *Orders are Orders* , p. 48

13 National Army Museum: F. W. Jacobs, Typescript account, 'In the Third Hun Trenches'

14 IWM DOCS: S. W. Appleyard, Transcript diary, p. 59

15 IWM DOCS: H. Russell, Typescript manuscript, p. 6

16 IWM DOCS: A. Schuman, 'Memoirs', p. 4

17 F. Hawkings, *From Ypres to Cambrai*, pp. 97–8

18 National Army Museum: F. W. Jacobs, Typescript account, 'In the Third Hun Trenches'

19 D. G. C. Hawker, quoted in J. Q. Henriques, *The War History of the 1st Battalion Queen's Westminster Rifles, 1914–1918* (London: Medici Society, 1923), pp. 100–101

20 J. H. Foaden, quoted in F. Maurice, *The History of the London Rifle Brigade, 1859–1919* (London: Constable, 1921), p. 141

21 R. F. Ebbetts, Ibid., p. 143

22 D. G. C. Hawker, quoted in J. Q.

Henriques, *The War History of the 1st Battalion Queen's Westminster Rifles*, p. 101

23 Ibid., pp. 101–2

24 R. E. Petley, quoted in F. Maurice, *The History of the London Rifle Brigade*, p. 145

25 V. W. F. Dickins, quoted in C. A. Cuthbert Keeson, *The History and Records of Queen Victoria's Rifles, 1792–1922* (London: Constable, 1923), p. 162

26 IWM DOCS: S. W. Appleyard, Transcript diary, p. 59 60

27 IWM DOCS: S. A. Newman, Manuscript account

28 C. C. Dickens, quoted in O. F. Bailey & H. M. Hollier, *The Kensingtons: 13th London Regiment* (London: Regimental Old Comrades Association, 1935), p. 77

29 W. R. Smith, quoted in, *500 of the Best Cockney War Stories* (London: *London Evening News*), p. 49

30 IWM SOUND: P. Neame, AC 48, Reel 5

31 IWM DOCS: A. Schuman, 'Memoirs', p. 4

32 H. C. Sparks, quoted in J. H. Lindsay, *The London Scottish in the Great War* (London: Regimental Headquarters, 1925), p. 114

33 G. F. Telfer, quoted in C. A. Cuthbert Keeson, *The History and Records of Queen Victoria's Rifles*, p. 169

34 J. H. Foaden, quoted in F. Maurice, *The History of the London Rifle Brigade*, pp. 141–2

35 R. E. Petley, pp. 146–7

36 IWM DOCS: A. Schuman, 'Memoirs', pp. 4–5

37 National Army Museum: F. W. Jacobs, Typescript account, 'In the Third Hun Trenches'

38 S. J. M. Sampson, quoted in C. A. Cuthbert Keeson, *The History and Records of Queen Victoria's Rifles*, p. 166

39 IWM DOCS: H. C. Rees, 'A Personal Record of the War, 1915–1916 –1917'

40 IWM SOUND: A. V. Pearson, AC 13680, Reel 1 (Recorded for BBC Radio 4, *A Summer Day on the Somme*)

41 IWM SOUND: F. Raine, AC 9751, Reel 7

42 IWM SOUND: R. Glenn, AC 13082

43 IWM SOUND: D. E. Cattell, AC 13673, Reel 1 (Recorded for BBC Radio 4, *A Summer Day on the Somme*)

44 IWM SOUND: A. S. Durrant, AC 13675, Reel 1 (Recorded for BBC Radio 4, *A Summer Day on the Somme*)

45 IWM DOCS: H. C. Rees, 'A Personal Record of the War, 1915–1916 –1917'

46 IWM DOCS: W. T. Colyer, Manuscript account, 'War Impressions'

47 Ibid.

48 Ibid.

49 Ibid.

50 J. E. Edmonds, *History of the Great War, Military Operations, France and Belgium, 1916*, fn, p. 431

51 IWM DOCS: D. N. Menaud-Lissenburg, Typescript memoir, pp. 182–3

52 IWM SOUND: G. Ashurst, AC 9875, Reel 15 & 16

53 Ibid.

54 IWM DOCS: D. N. Menaud-Lissenburg, Typescript memoir, p. 183

55 IWM SOUND: G. Ashurst, AC 9875, Reel 15 & 16

56 National Army Museum: J. L. Stewart-Moore, Typescript account, p. 35

57 Lt. Col. A. Ricardo, quoted in C.

Fall, *The History of the 36th (Ulster) Division* (Belfast: McCaw, Stevenson & Orr Ltd, 1922), p. 52

58 IWM DOCS: D. Starrett, Typescript account, pp. 64–5

59 F. P. Crozier, *A Brass Hat in No Man's Land* (London: Jonathan Cape, 1930), pp. 104–5

60 IWM DOCS: D. Starrett, Typescript account, pp. 64–5

61 Ibid., pp. 65–6

62 IWM DOCS: W. J. Grant, Manuscript account, 'Diary of D Battery, 154th Brigade of 36th (Ulster Division) RFA in the Great War'

63 IWM DOCS: J. L. Jack, Typescript memoir, pp. 5–6

64 B. Meadows, quoted in J. W. Arthur & I. S. Munro, *The Seventeenth Highland Light Infantry* (Glasgow: David J. Clark, 1920), p. 45

65 IWM DOCS: J. L. Jack, Typescript memoir, pp. 5–6

66 B. Meadows, quoted in J. W. Arthur & I. S. Munro, *The Seventeenth Highland Light Infantry*, p. 45

67 Ibid., p. 46

68 Ibid., pp. 46~–7

69 IWM DOCS: F. L. Cassel, Typescript account

70 Ibid.

71 von Soden orders of 1/7/1916, quoted in J. E. Edmonds, *History of the Great War*, note, p. 423

72 F. P. Crozier, *A Brass Hat in No Man's Land*, pp. 109–110

73 IWM SOUND: H. Tansley, AC 13682, Reel 1 (Recorded for BBC Radio 4 *A Summer Day on the Somme)*

74 Ibid.

75 IWM SOUND: A. Hanbury-Sparrow, AC 4131, Reel 1

76 H. Baumber, 'The Grimbsy Chums', *The New Chequers*, No. 2, p. 9

77 J. Maw, *The New Chequers,* No. 9, p. 54

78 IWM SOUND: C. Lewis, AC 4162, Reel 1

79 H. Baumber, 'The Grimbsy Chums', *The New Chequers*, No. 2, p. 9

80 IWM SOUND: A. Dickinson, AC 13674, Reel 1 (Recorded for BBC Radio 4 *A Summer Day on the Somme)*

81 Ibid.

82 IWM DOCS: W. A. Vignoles, Typescript manuscript, pp. 77 & 84

83 J. H. Turnbull, *The New Chequers*, No. 1, p. 10

84 H. Baumber, 'The Grimbsy Chums', *The New Chequers*, No. 2, pp. 9–10

85 H. Beaumont, 'Memories of the Somme Offensive', *The New Chequers*, No. 9, pp. 46–7

86 IWM SOUND: C. Lewis, AC 4162, Reel 1

87 J. H. Turnbull, *The New Chequers*, No. 1, p. 11

88 Ibid.

89 D. H. James, 'My Recollections', *The New Chequers*, No. 5, pp. 25–6

90 A. E. Fitzgerald orders of 25/6/1916 quoted in J. E. Edmonds, *History of the Great War,* p. 350

91 R. Gee, 'In case I cannot write again', *The New Chequers*, No. 2, pp 20–21

92 Ibid.

93 IWM DOCS: E. C. Crosse, Typescript manuscript, 'The History of the Chaplains' Department in the War, 1914–1918', pp. 68, 70 & 71

94 IWM DOCS: E. C. Crosse,

Typescript diary, 1/7/1916

95 IWM DOCS: Y. R. N. Probert, Typescript diary, 1/7/1916

96 IWM DOCS: A. P. Burke, Typescript letter, p. 33

97 IWM: Y. R. N. Probert, Typescript diary, 1/7/1916

98 IWM DOCS: A. P. Burke, Typescript letter, p. 33

99 Ibid.

100 IWM DOCS: A. V. Conn, Typescript account

101 IWM DOCS: F. Henwood, Typescript account

102 IWM DOCS: R. Cude, Typescript diary, 1/7/1916

103 IWM DOCS: C. W. Alcock, Manuscript letter, 15/7/1916

104 IWM SOUND: A. Irwin, AC 211

105 IWM DOCS: A. E. A. Jacobs, Manuscript letter, 15/7/1916

106 IWM DOCS: L. L. Jeeves, Typescript article, 'In the Battle of the Somme', p. 27

107 Ibid.

108 IWM DOCS: R. Cude, Typescript diary, 1/7/1916

109 National Army Museum: F. A. M. Maxwell, Manuscript copy of letter, 2/7/1916

110 IWM DOCS: L. L. Jeeves, Typescript article, 'In the Battle of the Somme', p. 27

111 A. W. Andrews (edited by S. Richardson), *Orders are Orders: A Manchester Pal on the Somme* (Manchester: Neil Richardson, 1987), p.49

112 IWM SOUND: E. Bryan, AC 4042, Reel 1

113 A. W. Andrews (edited by S. Richardson), *Orders are Orders*, p. 49

114 Ibid., pp. 49–50

115 Ibid., p. 50

116 Lt. Col. Bedall, quoted in J. E. Edmonds, *History of the Great War*, fn, pp. 328–9

117 IWM SOUND: P. J. Kennedy, AC 13679, Reel 1 (Recorded for BBC Radio 4, *A Summer Day on the Somme)*

118 IWM DOCS: W. H. Bloor, Typescript diary, 1/7/1916

119 Ibid.

120 A. W. Andrews (edited by S. Richardson), *Orders are Orders*, pp. 50–1

121 IWM DOCS: W. H. Bloor, Typescript diary, 1/7/1916

122 IWM SOUND: P. J. Kennedy, AC 13679, Reel 1 (Recorded for BBC Radio 4, *A Summer Day on the Somme*)

123 Ibid.

124 Ibid.

125 IWM DOCS: H.Wyllie, Transcript diary, 31/5/1916

126 G. Lewis, *Wings Over the Somme*, p. 3

127 L. Hawker quoted by T. M. Hawker, *Hawker V.C.*, p. 18

128 W. O. Tudor-Hart, quoted in C. Cole, *RFC Communiques, 1915 1916* (London: Kimber, 1969), pp. 298–9

129 L. Hawker quoted in B. G. Gray & the DH2 Research Group, 'The Anatomy of an Aeroplane: The de Havilland DH2 Pusher Scout', Cross & Cockade, Vol. 21, No. 3, p. 16

130 M. Baring, '*Flying Corps Headquarters* (Edinburgh & London: William Blackwood & Sons, 1968), p. 155

131 D. Haig, diary entry 1/7/1916, quoted in G. Sheffield & J. Bourne (eds), *Douglas Haig: War Diaries and Letters 1914–18*

132 IWM SOUND: C. R. Quinnell, AC 554, Reel 16

133 IWM DOCS: E. H. E. Collen, Manuscript diary, 1/7/1916

134 IWM DOCS: S. T. Kemp, Typescript account, p. 47

135 IWM DOCS: T. D. Pratt, Manuscript account

136 IWM DOCS: E. B. Lord, Typescript account, p. 16

137 Ibid., pp. 16–17

138 Ibid., pp. 17–18

5 The Morning After

1 IWM SOUND: Ms Llewellyn, AC 4163, Reel 1

2 IWM DOCS: L. I. L. Ferguson, War diary, 5/7/1916

3 IWM SOUND: M. S. Cleeve, AC 7310, Reel 3 & 4

4 R. H. Lindsey-Renton, quoted in C. A. Cuthbert Keeson, *The History and Records of Queen Victoria's Rifles*, p. 165

5 IWM DOCS: S. T. Kemp, Typescript account, p. 47

6 IWM SOUND: S. Jordan, AC 10391, Reel 4

7 IWM DOCS: E. B. Lord, Typescript account, p. 18

8 Ibid., p. 19

9 IWM DOCS: E. C. Crosse, Typescript manuscript, 'The History of the Chaplains' Department in the War, 1914-1918', pp. 71–2

10 IWM DOCS: E. C. Crosse, Typescript diary, 4/7/1916–5/7/1916

11 IWM DOCS: E. C. Crosse, Typescript manuscript, op.cit., p. 73

12 IWM DOCS: E. B. Lord, Typescript account, p. 18

13 IWM DOCS: A. P. B. Irwin, Manuscript letter, 3/7/1916

14 IWM DOCS: A. E. A. Jacobs, Manuscript letter, 15/7/1916

15 IWM DOCS: C. G. Lawson, Typescript letter, 6/7/1916

16 IWM DOCS: F. H. Drinkwater, Typescript diary, 2/7/1916

6 Creeping Forward

1 H. Rawlinson, quoted in R. Prior & T. Wilson, *Command on the Western Front*, pp. 185–6

2 D. Haig, diary entry 3/7/1916, quoted in G. Sheffield & J. Bourne (eds), *Douglas Haig: War Diaries and Letters 1914–18*

3 IWM DOCS: B. S. Philpotts Collection: A. C. Sparkes, Typescript letter, 15/9/1916

4 National Army Museum: F. A. M. Maxwell, Manuscript copy of letter, 2/7/1916

5 D. H. James, 'My Recollections', *The New Chequers*, No. 5, p. 26

6 IWM DOCS: B. W. Downes, Typescript account, p. 17

7 IWM DOCS: W. H. Bloor, Typescript diary, 3/7/1916

8 IWM DOCS: S. T. Kemp, Typescript account, pp. 47–8

9 Ibid., p. 48

10 Ibid., pp. 48–9

11 Ibid., p. 49

12 IWM DOCS: W. A. Gates Collection, S. Stevenson-Jones, Edited from typescript letter, 13/7/1968 & Thiepval article

13 Ibid.

14 Ibid.

15 Ibid.

16 IWM DOCS: L. I. L. Ferguson, War diary, 7/7/1916

17 Ibid.

18 Ibid.

19 Ibid.

20 Ibid.

21 Ibid.

22 IWM SOUND: T. Bracey, AC 9419, Reel 10

23 IWM SOUND: C. R. Quinnell, AC 554, Reel 17

24 H. Sadler, quoted in O. Rutter, *The History of the Seventh (Service)*, p. 90

25 Ibid., p. 91

26 IWM SOUND: C. R. Quinnell, AC 554, Reel 17

27 IWM SOUND: A. Razzell, AC 11952, Reel 6

28 Ibid.

29 Ibid.

30 W. L. Osborn, quoted in O. Rutter, *The History of the Seventh (Service)*, pp. 86–7

31 J. R. Wilton, Ibid., pp. 89–90

32 W. L. Osborn, Ibid., p. 87

33 H. Sadler, Ibid., pp. 91–2

34 IWM DOCS: E. H. E. Collen, Manuscript diary, 7/7/1916

35 IWM SOUND: A. Razzell, AC 11952, Reel 6

36 Ibid.

37 IWM DOCS: R. D. Mountfield, Manuscript letter, 23/7/1916

38 Ibid.

39 Ibid.

40 Ibid.

41 H. C. O'Neill, *The Royal Fusiliers in the Great War*, (London: William Heinemann, 1922), p. 118

42 IWM DOCS: A. E. Perriman, Typescript account

43 IWM SOUND: V. G. Lansdown, AC 10147

44 IWM DOCS: A. E. Perriman, Typescript and manuscript accounts

45 IWM SOUND: V. G. Lansdown, AC 10147

46 IWM DOCS: A. E. Perriman, Typescript and manuscript accounts

47 Ibid.

48 D. Haig, diary entry 9/7/1916, quoted in G. Sheffield & J. Bourne (eds), *Douglas Haig: War Diaries and Letters 1914–18*

49 R. J. W. Carden, quoted in C. H. Dudley Ward, *Regimental Records of the Royal Welch Fusiliers* (London: Forster Groom & Co, 1928), Vol. III, p. 205

50 G. Jones, quoted in C. H. Dudley Ward, *Regimental Records of the Royal Welch Fusiliers*, p. 206

51 Ibid., p. 207

52 IWM SOUND: T. J. Price, AC 9492

53 IWM SOUND: G. Richards, AC 9929

54 G. Jones, quoted in C. H. Dudley Ward, *Regimental Records of the Royal Welch Fusiliers*, p. 210

55 IWM DOCS: C. K. McKerrow, Typescript diary, 19/7/1916

56 IWM DOCS: W. H. Bloor, Typescript diary, 11/7/1916

57 Ibid., 13/7/1916

58 R. Prior & T. Wilson, *Command on the Western Front*, p. 191

59 D. Haig, quoted in R. Prior & T.

Wilson, *Command on the Western Front*, p. 193

60 D. Haig, diary entry 12/7/1916, quoted in G. Sheffield & J. Bourne (eds), *Douglas Haig: War Diaries and Letters 1914–18*

61 D. Haig, diary entry 14/7/1916, ibid.

62 IWM DOCS: E. C. Crosse, Typescript diary, 14/7/1916

63 N. Fraser-Tytler, *Field Guns in France*, p. 89

64 IWM DOCS: B. W. Downes, Typescript manuscript

65 Ibid.

66 S. Carey, quoted in L. S. Uys, 'The South Africans at Delville Wood' *South African Military History Journal*, Vol. VII, No. 2

67 IWM DOCS: J. M. Cordy, Typescript memoir, p. 18

68 Ibid., pp. 18–19

69 IWM SOUND: L. G. Ounsworth, AC 332, Reel 5

70 IWM DOCS: F. J. G. Gambling, Typescript memoir, p. 8

71 Ibid.

72 N. Fraser-Tytler, *Field Guns in France*, p. 89

73 IWM SOUND: L. G. Ounsworth, AC 332, Reel 6

74 IWM DOCS: B. W. Downes, Typescript manuscript

75 National Army Museum: F. A. M. Maxwell, Manuscript copy of letter, 15/7/1916 & 16/7/1916

76 Ibid.

77 Ibid.

78 Ibid.

79 Ibid.

80 Ibid.

81 Ibid.

82 Ibid., 2/7/1916

83 IWM SOUND: L. G. Ounsworth, AC 332, Reel 6

84 IWM DOCS: R. Cude, Typescript diary, 14/7/1916

7 Stumbling to Disaster

1 H. Mallett, quoted in L. S. Uys, 'The South Africans at Delville Wood' *South African Military History Journal*, Vol. VII, No. 2

2 E. V. Vivian, ibid.

3 Medlicort, ibid.

4 O. H. de Burgh Thomas, ibid.

5 F. Marillier, ibid.

6 O. H. de Burgh Thomas, ibid.

7 F. Marillier, ibid.

8 Medlicort, ibid.

9 Medlicort, ibid.

10 V. Wepener, ibid.

11 E. F. Thackeray, ibid.

12 IWM DOCS: T. A. Jennings, Manuscript account, 'Hark! I Hear the Bugles Calling', pp. 14–16

13 Ibid., p. 16

14 Ibid., pp. 16–18

15 Ibid, pp. 18–19

16 IWM DOCS: H. G. Wood, Manuscript letter, 21/7/1916

17 IWM DOCS: F. J. Fields, Typescript account

18 Ibid.

19 Ibid.

20 A. W. Andrews (edited by S. Richardson), *Orders are Orders*, pp. 58–59

21 Ibid.

22 H. Preston, *Reveille*, Vol. 8, No. 12, p. 30

23 Ibid.

24 Ibid., p. 31

25 J. R. O. Harris, quoted in C. E. W. Bean, *The Australian Imperial Force in France, 1916* (Sydney: Angus & Robertson Ltd, 1938), p. 553

26 Ibid., p. 554

27 IWM SOUND: F. Brent, AC 4037, Reel 1

28 P. Kinchington, *Reveille*, Vol. 8, No. 12, p. 30

29 H. Preston, ibid, p. 31

30 Ibid.

31 T. Young, quoted in N. Browning, *The Blue & White Diamond: The History of the 28th Battalion, 1915–1919* (Bassendean, W.A.: Advance Press, 2002), p. 154

32 P. Blythe, Ibid., pp. 165–6

33 E. R. Norgard, ibid., p. 166

34 D. Haig, diary entry 29/7/1916, quoted in G. Sheffield & J. Bourne (eds), *Douglas Haig: War Diaries and Letters 1914–18*

35 IWM SOUND: A. Razzell, AC 11952, Reel 7

36 IWM SOUND: C. R. Quinnell, AC 554, Reel 17

37 Ibid.

38 IWM SOUND: A. Razzell, AC 11952, Reel 7

39 IWM SOUND: C. R. Quinnell, AC 554, Reel 17 & 18

40 C. I. Smith, *Reveille*, Vol. 5, No. 6, p. 31

41 Ibid.

42 Ibid.

43 Ibid.

44 Ibid.

45 Ibid.

46 Ibid., pp. 31–2

47 A. Jacka, quoted in E. J. Rule, *Jacka's Mob* (Melbourne: Military Melbourne, 1999), p. 30

48 C. I. Smith, *Reveille*, Vol. 5, No. 6, p. 32

49 Ibid.

50 E. J. Rule, *Jacka's Mob*, p. 29

51 A. Jacka, quoted in E. J. Rule, *Jacka's Mob*, p. 30

52 E. J. Rule, *Jacka's Mob*, p. 29

53 Ibid., p. 30

54 H. W. Murray, *Reveille*, Vol. 9, No. 4, p. 33

55 Ibid.

56 Ibid.

57 Ibid.

8 From Bad to Worse

1 IWM DOCS: H. Tudor, Typescript diary, 26/7/1916

2 F. C. Stanley, *The History of the 89th Brigade, 1914–1918*, pp. 154–5

3 W. L. S. Churchill, memorandum 1/8/1916, in M. Gilbert (ed), *Winston S. Churchill*, Companion Vol. III, Part 2 *May 1915–December 1916* (London: Heineman, 1972), p. 1537

4 D. Haig, note on letter from CIGS dated 2/8/1916, quoted in G. Sheffield & J. Bourne (eds), *Douglas Haig: War Diaries and Letters 1914–18*

5 D. Haig, diary entry 8/8/1916, ibid.

6 IWM DOCS: Fourth Army Papers, O.A.D. 91, p. 1

7 Ibid., p. 2

8 Ibid.

9 Ibid.

10 IWM DOCS: A. Russell, Typescript manuscript, pp. 60–1

11 Ibid., pp. 61–2

12 IWM DOCS: Fourth Army Papers, O.A.D. 123 p. 1

13 Ibid., p. 2

14 IWM DOCS: F. J. Fields, Typescript account

15 Ibid.

16 IWM DOCS: H. D. Paviere, Typescript account, p. 36–7

17 IWM DOCS: Y. R. N. Probert, Typescript diary, 10/9/1916

18 IWM DOCS: B. H. Whayman, Typescript account, p. 3

19 IWM SOUND: W. Grover, AC 10441, Reel 2

20 T. M. Kettle, quoted in L. Housman, *War Letters of Fallen Englishmen* (London: Victor Gollancz, 1930), p. 167

21 T. M. Kettle, 'Political Testament', Internet source

22 T. M. Kettle, quoted in L. Housman, *War Letters of Fallen Englishmen,* p. 167

23 T. M. Kettle (written 4/9/1916), quoted in R. Feilding, *War Letters to a Wife* (London: The Medici Society, 1929), p. 131

24 E. Dalton, quoted in T. Burke, 'In Memory of Tom Kettle', *Journal of the Royal Dublin Fusiliers Association*, Vol. 9, 9/2002, p. 4

25 Young, quoted in T. Denman, *Ireland's Unknown Soldiers: The 16th (Irish) Division in the Great War* (Dublin: Irish Academic Press, 1992), p. 98

26 IWM SOUND: F. W. S. Jourdain, AC 11214

27 R. Feilding, *War Letters to a Wife*, p. 116

28 IWM SOUND: F. W. S. Jourdain, AC 11214

29 R. Feilding, *War Letters to a Wife*, p. 114

30 Ibid., p. 119

31 IWM DOCS: J. H. Reynolds, Typescript memoir

32 IWM DOCS: P. H. Pilditch, Typescript memoir, p. 315

9 You are not Alone

1 IWM DOCS: A. V. Conn, Typescript account – edited from several versions of this incident

2 IWM SOUND: A. Razzell, AC 11952, Reel 7

3 Ibid.

4 N. D. Cliff, *To Hell and Back with the Guards* (Braunton, Devon: Merlin Books Ltd, 1988), p. 79

5 IWM DOCS: W. Kerr, Typescript memoir, p. 90

6 Ibid., p. 91

7 IWM SOUND: B. Farrer, AC 9552, Reel 14

8 IWM DOCS: R. Bulstrode, Typescript memoir, pp. 66–8

9 IWM DOCS: W. Kerr, Typescript memoir, p. 92

10 IWM DOCS: E. S. B. Hamilton, Typescript dairy, 6/8/1916

11 Ibid.

12 Ibid.

13 IWM DOCS: L. Gameson, Typescript, 10/8/1916

14 Ibid., 14/8/1916

15 Ibid., 15/8/1916–9/9/1916

16 Ibid.

17 Ibid., 13/8/1916

18 Ibid.

19 Ibid., 15/8/1916–9/9/1916

20 Ibid.

21 Ibid.

22 Ibid.

23 IWM SOUND: T. J. Price, AC 9492

24 IWM DOCS: H. Russell, Typescript manuscript, p. 6

25 N. D. Cliff, *To Hell and Back with the Guards*, p. 79

26 IWM DOCS: R. D. Mountfield, Manuscript letter, 23/7/1916

27 IWM SOUND: J. Dray, AC 27053, Reel 1

10 When Push Comes to Shove

1 IWM DOCS: Fourth Army Papers, O.A.D. 116, p. 1

2 D. Haig, diary entry 14/4/1916 quoted in G. Sheffield & J. Bourne (eds), *Douglas Haig: War Diaries and Letters 1914–18*

3 D. Haig, diary entry 26/8/1916, ibid.

4 J. Charteris, *At G.H.Q.*, p. 165

5 IWM DOCS: Fourth Army Papers, 28/8/1916, H. Rawlinson Initial Proposals for attack on 15/9/1916, pp. 3–4

6 D. Haig, diary entry 29/8/1916, quoted in G. Sheffield & J. Bourne (eds), *Douglas Haig: War Diaries and Letters 1914–18*

7 IWM DOCS: Fourth Army Papers, O.A.D. 131, pp. 1–2

8 Ibid., pp. 2–3

9 IWM DOCS: Fourth Army Papers, Conference, 10/9/1916

10 IWM DOCS: Fourth Army Papers, Instructions for the Employment of Tanks, 11/9/16

11 IWM DOCS: E. G. de Caux, Typescript memoir, p. 24

12 IWM DOCS: Albert Whitehurst, Typescript memoir

13 IWM DOCS: D. Railton, Typescript letter, 12/9/1916

14 IWM DOCS: E. G. de Caux, Typescript memoir, p. 24

15 IWM DOCS: Albert Whitehurst, Typescript memoir

16 IWM DOCS: G. V. Dennis, Typescript account, p. 74

17 IWM DOCS: H. Horne, Typescript diary, 15/9/1916

18 W. J. Gray, quoted in C. A. Cuthbert Keeson, *The History and Records of Queen Victoria's Rifles*, pp. 190–1

19 Ibid., pp. 191–2

20 Ibid., p. 192

21 IWM DOCS: G. V. Dennis, Typescript account, p. 75

22 IWM DOCS: H. Horne, Typescript diary, 15/9/1916

23 IWM: C. H. Morden, Typescript account, p. 2

24 National Army Museum: L. Cattermole, Typescript account, 'Attack on the Somme', p. 2

25 Ibid., p. 3

26 Ibid.

27 IWM DOCS: M. M. Hood, Typescript memoir

28 Weinert, quoted in T. Pidgeon, *The Tanks at Flers* (Cobham: Fairmile Books,

1995) Vol. I, p. 132

29 National Army Museum: L. Cattermole, Typescript account, 'Attack on the Somme', pp. 4–5

30 IWM SOUND: G. Cole, AC 9535, Reel 4

31 National Archives: CAB 45/135, H. Karslake letter, 28/1/1936

32 IWM DOCS: A. Whitehurst, Typescript memoir

33 M. J. Guiton, quoted in P. Davenport, *The History of the Prince of Wales' Own Civil Service Rifles* (London: Civil Service Rifles, 1921), p. 115

34 IWM DOCS: Albert Whitehurst, Typescript memoir

35 IWM DOCS: D. D. S. Cree, Typescript memoir

36 IWM DOCS: Albert Whitehurst, Typescript memoir

37 IWM DOCS: D. D. S. Cree, Typescript memoir

38 IWM DOCS: J. C McIntyre, Typescript memoir

39 D. D. S. Cree, Typescript memoir

40 IWM DOCS: E. J. D. Routh, Manuscript diary, 15/9/1916

41 IWM DOCS: D. D. S. Cree, Typescript memoir

42 IWM DOCS: Albert Whitehurst, Typescript memoir

43 IWM DOCS: D. D. S. Cree, Typescript memoir

44 Ibid.

45 Ibid.

46 IWM DOCS: R. E. Davy, Manuscript letter, 22/9/1916

47 IWM DOCS: E. G. de Caux, Typescript memoir, p. 26

48 IWM DOCS: E. Gore-Brown Collection: E. G. de Caux, Typescript letter, 30/9/1916

49 IWM DOCS: G. V. Dennis, Typescript account, p. 76

50 Ibid.

51 A. H. R. Reiffer, quoted in T. Pidgeon, *The Tanks at Flers,* Vol. I, p. 167

52 IWM SOUND: C. Lewis, AC 4162, Reel 1

53 IWM SOUND: V. Huffam, AC 4136 Reel 1

54 IWM SOUND: A. H. R. Reiffer, AC 4212

55 IWM SOUND: S. Hastie, AC 4126, Reel 1

56 IWM SOUND: A. H. R. Reiffer, AC 4212

57 IWM SOUND: S. Hastie, AC 4126, Reel 1

58 Ibid.

59 Braunhofer, quoted in T. Pidgeon, *The Tanks at Flers,* Vol. I, p. 172

60 A. Arnold, ibid., p. 173

61 IWM DOCS: G. V. Dennis, Typescript account, p. 77

62 The best analysis, which effectively clears Basil Henriques of these charges, is that carried out by Trevor Pidgeon's brilliant book, *Tanks at Flers*.

63 B. Henriques, *Indiscretions of a Warden* (London: Methuen & Co, 1937), pp. 118–9

64 B. Henriques, quoted in L. L. Loewe, *Basil Henriques* (London: Routledge & Kegan Paul, 1976), p. 44

65 B. Henriques, *Indiscretions of a Warden*, p. 119

66 W. T. Dawson, quoted in T. Pidgeon, *The Tanks at Flers,* Vol. I, p. 86

67 Bdr. Osborne, quoted by

B. Hammond in pending thesis, 'The Theory and Practice of British Tanks – other Arms Cooperation on the Western Front in the Great War'

68 B. Henriques, *Indiscretions of a Warden*, p. 119

69 Ibid., pp. 119–120

70 IWM SOUND: P. Neame, AC 48, Reel 11 & 13

71 IWM DOCS: T. G. Rogers, 'Letters', pp. 282–283

72 IWM DOCS: A. Home, Typescript diary, 15/9/1916

73 Ibid., 18/9/1916

11 Hammering On

1 IWM DOCS: A. Home, Typescript diary, 22/9/1916

2 Ibid., 18/9/1916

3 IWM SOUND: H. Calvert, AC 9955

4 IWM DOCS: A. Russell, Typescript manuscript, pp. 70–1

5 IWM SOUND: H. Calvert, AC 9955

6 IWM DOCS: A. Home, Typescript diary, 25/9/1916

7 H. Gough, *The Fifth Army* (London: Hodder & Stoughton, 1931), p. 148

8 IWM DOCS: A. Angus, Typescript memoir, p. 9

9 National Army Museum: F. Maxwell, Letter, 27/9/1916

10 IWM SOUND: R. G. Emmett, Typescript account in folder

11 G. E. Cornaby, quoted in anon author, *The 54th Infantry Brigade: Some Records of Battle and Laughter in France* (Aldershot: Gale & Polden, 1919), p. 53

12 IWM SOUND: R. G. Emmett, Typescript account in folder

13 G. E. Cornaby, op. cit.

14 IWM SOUND: R. G. Emmett, Typescript account in folder

15 IWM DOCS: S. T. Fuller, Manuscript diary, 26/9/1916

16 National Army Museum: F. Maxwell, Letter, 27/9/1916

17 Ibid.

18 IWM SOUND: R. G. Emmett, Typescript account in folder

19 National Army Museum: F. Maxwell, Letter, 27/9/1916

20 G. E. Cornaby, quoted in anon author, *The 54th Infantry Brigade*, pp. 55–6

21 IWM DOCS: T. A. Jennings, Manuscript memoir, 'Hark! I Hear the Bugles Calling', pp. 23–5

22 Ibid., pp. 26–7

23 Ibid., p. 27

24 IWM SOUND: T. E. Adlam, AC 35, Reel 3

25 Ibid.

26 Ibid.

27 Ibid., Reel 4

28 Ibid., Reel 3

29 Ibid.Reel 4

30 IWM DOCS: G. C. Pratt, Typescript account

31 Ibid.

32 Ibid.

33 Ibid.

34 Ibid.

35 Ibid.

36 Ibid.

37 Ibid.

38 IWM DOCS: A. Angus, Typescript memoir, pp. 9–10

39 IWM DOCS: G. C. Pratt, Typescript

account

40 Ibid.

41 Ibid.

42 Ibid.

43 Ibid.

44 Ibid.

45 Ibid.

46 Ibid.

47 IWM DOCS: J. Meo, Manuscript diary, 22/9/1916

48 Ibid., 24/9/1916

49 Ibid., 25/9/1916 & 30/9/1916

50 Ibid., 30/9/1916

51 Ibid.

52 Ibid., 1/10/1916

53 Ibid., 8/10/1916

54 IWM DOCS: W. H. Bloor, Typescript diary, 28/9/1916

55 Ibid., 30/9/1916

56 H. Sulzbach, *With the German Guns: 50 Months on the Western Front, 1914–1918* (London: Frederick Warne Ltd, 1981), p. 90

12 October Attrition

1 D. Haig, letter to George V 5/10/1916, quoted in G. Sheffield & J. Bourne (eds), *Douglas Haig: War Diaries and Letters 1914–18*

2 D. Haig, diary entry 5/10/1916, ibid.

3 J. Charteris, *At G.H.Q.*, pp. 170–1

4 J. Charteris, *At G.H.Q.*, p. 171

5 J. A. Chamier, quoted in H. A. Jones & W. Raleigh, *The War in the Air* (Oxford: Clarendon Press, 1922-1937), Vol. II, pp. 298–299

6 IWM DOCS: W. H. Bloor, Typescript diary, 1/10/1916

7 Ibid., 2/10/1916 & 3/10/1916

8 N. Fraser-Tytler, *Field Guns in France*, p. 108

9 IWM DOCS: W. H. Bloor, Typescript diary, 3/10/1916

10 Ibid.

11 Ibid., 5/10/1916

12 G. Lewis, *Wings Over the Somme*, p. 75 & 78

13 IWM DOCS: Albert Whitehurst, Typescript memoir

14 IWM DOCS: W. J. N. Howell, Typescript account

15 IWM DOCS: W. Harfleet, Typescript letter

16 IWM DOCS: W. J. N. Howell, Typescript account

17 IWM DOCS: W. Harfleet, Typescript letter

18 IWM DOCS: Albert Whitehurst, Typescript memoir

19 IWM DOCS: W. J. N. Howell, Typescript account

20 IWM DOCS: W. S. Reid, Typescript letter, 13/10/1970

21 IWM DOCS: Albert Whitehurst, Typescript memoir

22 D. Haig, diary entry 14/10/1916, quoted in G. Sheffield & J. Bourne (eds), *Douglas Haig: War Diaries and Letters 1914–18*

23 N. Fraser-Tytler, *Field Guns in France*, pp. 110–11

24 Ibid., pp. 111–12

25 A. C. Johnston, quoted in A. Crookenden, *The History of the Cheshire Regiment in the Great War*, (Chester: W. H. Evans & Sons, 1938) pp. 91–2

26 IWM DOCS: V. F. S. Hawkins

quoted in J. C. Latter, *The History of the Lancashire Fusiliers, 1914–1918*, (Aldershot: Gale & Polden Ltd, 1949), p. 167

27 IWM SOUND: R. C. Cooney, AC 494, Reel 3

28 IWM DOCS: J. T. Lawton, Typescript memoir, p. 9

29 IWM DOCS: K. W. Mealing, Typescript memoir, p. 17

30 Ibid., p. 18

31 Ibid., pp. 18–19

32 Ibid., p. 19

33 Ibid., pp. 20 & 24

34 Ibid.p. 21

35 Ibid., p. 22

36 Ibid., pp. 22–3

37 IWM DOCS: W. H. Bloor, Typescript diary, 15/10/1916

38 Ibid.

39 IWM Docs: H. C. Rees, 'A Personal Record of the War, 1915–1916–1917'

40 Ibid.

41 IWM DOCS: H. Tudor, Typescript diary, 16/10/1916

42 W. D. Croft, *Three Years with the 9th (Scottish) Division* (London: John Murray, 1919), pp. 84–5

43 T. A. K. Cubitt, quoted in F. Loraine Petre, *The History of the Norfolk Regiment* (Norwich: Jarrold & Sons, N.D.), pp. 259–60

44 IWM DOCS: A. G. P. Hardwick, Typescript diary, 19/10/1916

45 N. Fraser-Tytler, *Field Guns in France*, p. 119

46 IWM Docs: H. C. Rees, 'A Personal Record of the War, 1915–1916–1917'

47 Ibid.

48 Ibid.

49 National Army Museum: E. R. Buckell, Typescript account, 'The Somme', p. 6

50 N. Fraser-Tytler, *Field Guns in France*, pp. 124–5

51 IWM DOCS: L. Gameson, Typescript diary and notes, 26/10/1916

52 Ibid., 10/1916

53 Ibid.

54 IWM DOCS: C. S. Myers letter, 9/10/1916, in papers of L. Gameson, Typescript, 26/10/1916

55 IWM DOCS: L. Gameson, Typescript diary and notes, 15/10/1916

56 National Army Museum: E. R. Buckell, Typescript account, 'The Somme', p. 6

57 IWM DOCS: A. G. P. Hardwick, Typescript diary, 27/10/1916

58 IWM DOCS: A. E. Abrey, Manuscript letter, 30/10/1916

13 Last Shake on the Ancre

1 IWM DOCS: A. Home, Typescript diary, 15/11/1916

2 IWM DOCS: R. J. Blackadder, Typescript account, '151 Siege Battery, R.G.A.', p. 7

3 IWM DOCS: H. Tudor, Typescript diary, 4/11/1916

4 DLI Museum: H. Cruddace, Manuscript account

5 Ibid.

6 IWM DOCS: H. Tudor, Typescript diary, 4/11/1916

7 DLI Museum: H. Cruddace, Manuscript account

8 Ibid.

9 Durham Archives: R.B. Bradford, Report of 6/11/1916

10 Ibid.

11 Ibid.

12 R. B. Bradford, quoted in E. Wyrall, *The History of the Fiftieth Division* (London: Country Press Ltd, 1939), p. 178

13 R. B. Bradford, ibid., p. 179

14 Durham Archives: R.B. Bradford, Report of 6/11/1916

15 Ibid.

16 DLI Museum: H. Cruddace, Manuscript account

17 H. Green, quoted in A. L. Raines, *The Fifth Battalion The Durham Light Infantry* (Privately Published, 1931), p. 72

18 C. D. Marley, ibid.

19 H. Green, ibid.

20 ibid.

21 Durham Archives: R.B. Bradford, Report of 6/11/1916

22 Ibid.

23 IWM DOCS: A. Home, Typescript diary, 6/11/1916

24 D. Haig, diary entry 12/11/1916, quoted in G. Sheffield & J. Bourne (eds), *Douglas Haig: War Diaries and Letters 1914–18*

25 D. Jerrold, *Georgian Adventure* (London: Right Book Club, 1937), p. 162

26 Ibid., p. 175

27 R. V. C Bodley, *Indiscretions of a Young Man* (London: Harold Shaylor, 1931), pp. 56 & 85

28 D. Jerrold, *Georgian Adventure*, pp. 176–7

29 IWM SOUND: J. Murray, AC 8201, Reel 35

30 D. Jerrold, *Georgian Adventure*, pp. 178–9

31 Ibid., p. 180

32 A. P. Herbert poem, internet source

33 D. Jerrold, *Georgian Adventure*, p. 188

34 IWM SOUND: J. Murray, AC 8201, Reel 35

35 Ibid.

36 Ibid., Reel 36

37 Ibid., Reel 36

38 Ibid., Reel 36 & 37

39 D. Jerrold, *Georgian Adventure*, p. 192

40 Ibid.

41 IWM DOCS: S. C. Hawkins, Manuscript diary, 13/11/1916

42 D. Jerrold, *Georgian Adventure*, pp. 192–3

43 Ibid., p.193

44 IWM SOUND: J. Murray, AC 8201, Reel 36 & 37

45 Ibid.

46 IWM SOUND: R. Tobin, AC 4243, Reel 36

47 IWM DOCS: Sibley, Manuscript memoir, p. 12

48 IWM SOUND: R. L. Haine, AC 33, Reel 3

49 R. S. Morshead, quoted in G. Goold Walker, *The Honourable Artillery Company in the Great War, 1914–1919* (London: Seeley, Service & Co, 1930), p. 77

50 IWM DOCS: C. R. Smith, Manuscript account, p. 54

51 IWM DOCS: A. N. Acland, Typescript account, p. 43

52 IWM DOCS: E. B. Lord, Typescript account, p. 33

53 IWM DOCS: A. G. P. Hardwick, Typescript diary, 18/11/1916

54 IWM DOCS: R. Cude, Typescript diary, 18/11/1916

55 IWM DOCS: C. R. Smith, Manuscript account, p. 54

56 IWM SOUND: A. Irwin, AC 211

57 IWM DOCS: A. E. Wrench, Typescript diary, 18/11/1916

58 D. Rorie, *A Medico's Luck in the War* (Aberdeen: Milne & Hutchison, 1929), p. 113

59 IWM DOCS: C. K. McKerrow, Typescript diary, 4/10/1916

60 IWM DOCS: H. R. Butt, Typescript diary, 12/11/1916

61 IWM DOCS: L. Gameson, Typescript diary and notes, 4/10/1916

62 IWM DOCS: A. E. Wrench, Typescript diary, 16/11/1916

63 IWM DOCS: Fourth Army Papers, H. Rawlinson letter to D. Haig, 7/11/1916

64 E. Ludendorff, *My War Memories* (London: Hutchinson & Co, 1920), Vol. I, p. 307

65 IWM DOCS: E. B. Lord, Typescript account, pp. 30–1

14 Assessment

1 IWM DOCS: P. H. Pilditch, Typescript memoir, p. 331

Appendix A

1 IWM DOCS: W. A. Vignoles, Typescript manuscript, p. 52–3

2 Ibid., pp. 51–2 & 57

3 IWM DOCS: E. B. Lord, Typescript account, p. 21

4 IWM DOCS: D. N. Menaud-Lissenburg, Typescript memoir, p. 188

5 H. Preston, 'To Do or Die', *Reveille*, Vol. 9, No. 5, p. 6

6 IWM DOCS: C. K. McKerrow, Typescript diary, 18/7/1916

7 IWM DOCS: H. D. Paviere, Typescript account, pp. 40–1

8 IWM DOCS: T. A. Jennings, Manuscript account, 'Hark! I Hear the Bugles Calling', p. 10

9 IWM DOCS: L. W. Pratt, Typescript manuscript

10 R. Hugh Kynvett, *Over There with the Australians* (New York: Charles Scribners Sons, 1918), p. 215

11 R. V. C Bodley, *Indiscretions of a Young Man*, p. 89

12 IWM DOCS: R. M. Luthor, Typescript memoir, p. 26

13 IWM DOCS: J. T. Lawton, Typescript memoir, p. 9

14 IWM DOCS: D. Railton, Typescript letter, 1/10/1916

15 IWM DOCS: L. Gameson, Typescript diary and notes, p. 60

16 IWM DOCS: H. D. Paviere, Typescript account, p. 42

17 IWM DOCS: P. H. Pilditch, Typescript memoir, p. 328

Index

Maps in italics

All Orion/Phoenix titles are available at your local bookshop or from the following address:

Mail Order Department
Littlehampton Book Services
FREEPOST BR535
Worthing, West Sussex, BN13 3BR
telephone 01903 828503, *facsimile* 01903 828802
e-mail MailOrders@lbsltd.co.uk
(Please ensure that you include full postal address details)

Payment can be made either by credit/debit card (Visa, Mastercard, Access and Switch accepted) or by sending a £ Sterling cheque or postal order made payable to *Littlehampton Book Services*.

DO NOT SEND CASH OR CURRENCY.

Please add the following to cover postage and packing

UK and BFPO:
£1.50 for the first book, and 50p for each additional book to a maximum of £3.50

Overseas and Eire:
£2.50 for the first book plus £1.00 for the second book and 50p for each additional book ordered

---

BLOCK CAPITALS PLEASE

name of cardholder ....

address of cardholder ....

....

....

....

postcode ....

delivery address (if different from cardholder)

....

....

....

....

postcode ....

☐ I enclose my remittance for £..................

☐ please debit my Mastercard/Visa/Access/Switch (delete as appropriate)

card number ☐☐☐☐☐☐☐☐☐☐☐☐☐☐☐☐

expiry date ☐☐☐☐ Switch issue no. ☐☐

signature ....

prices and availability are subject to change without notice